Optimality Theory in Phonology

Optimality Theory in Phonology

A Reader | Edited by John J. McCarthy

Blackwell
Publishing

350 Main Street, Malden, MA 02148-5020, USA
108 Cowley Road, Oxford OX4 1JF, UK
550 Swanston Street, Carlton, Victoria 3053, Australia

First published 2004 by Blackwell Publishing Ltd

Library of Congress Cataloging-in-Publication Data

Optimality theory in phonology : a reader / edited by John J. McCarthy.
    p. cm.
Includes bibliographical references and index.
    ISBN 0-631-22688-5 (hard. : alk. paper) — ISBN 0-631-22689-3 (pbk. : alk. paper)
  1. Grammar, Comparative and general—Phonology. 2. Optimality theory (Linguistics) I. McCarthy, John J., 1953–
    P217.3.067 2003
    415—dc21

                                                          2003005153

A catalogue record for this title is available from the British Library.

Set in 10/12pt Sabon
by Graphicraft Limited, Hong Kong
Printed and bound in the United Kingdom
by T. J. International, Padstow, Cornwall

For further information on
Blackwell Publishing, visit our website:
http://www.blackwellpublishing.com

Contents

Preface   viii

Contributors' Addresses   x

Acknowledgments   xiii

Part I | The Basics   I

    1   Optimality Theory: Constraint Interaction in
        Generative Grammar   3
        Alan Prince and Paul Smolensky

    2   Generalized Alignment: Introduction and Theory   72
        John J. McCarthy and Alan Prince

    3   Faithfulness and Identity in Prosodic Morphology   77
        John J. McCarthy and Alan Prince

Part II | Formal Analysis   99

    4   Computing Optimal Forms in Optimality Theory:
        Basic Syllabification   101
        Bruce Tesar

    5   Learnability in Optimality Theory   118
        Bruce Tesar and Paul Smolensky

    6   Non-computable Functions in Optimality Theory   141
        Elliott Moreton

Part III | Prosody   165

    7   Generalized Alignment: Prosody   167
        John J. McCarthy and Alan Prince

    8   Ternary Rhythm and the *LAPSE Constraint   178
        Nine Elenbaas and René Kager

9   Quality-Sensitive Stress   191
    Michael Kenstowicz

10 Unbounded Stress and Factorial Typology   202
    Eric Baković

11 Head Dependence in Stress–Epenthesis Interaction   215
    John Alderete

12 Feet and Tonal Reduction at the Word and Phrase
    Level in Chinese   228
    Moira Yip

13 OCP Effects in Optimality Theory   246
    Scott Myers

Part IV | Segmental Phonology   269

14 Austronesian Nasal Substitution and Other
    NC̥ Effects   271
    Joe Pater

15 Phonetically Driven Phonology: The Role of
    Optimality Theory and Inductive Grounding   290
    Bruce Hayes

16 Positional Faithfulness   310
    Jill Beckman

17 Positional Faithfulness and Voicing Assimilation in
    Optimality Theory   343
    Linda Lombardi

18 Positional Asymmetries and Licensing   365
    Cheryl Zoll

19 Partial Class Behavior and Nasal Place Assimilation   379
    Jaye Padgett

20 Dissimilation as Local Conjunction   394
    John Alderete

21 Synchronic Chain Shifts in Optimality Theory   407
    Robert Kirchner

Part V | Interfaces   417

22 Transderivational Identity: Phonological Relations
    Between Words   419
    Laura Benua

23 Backness Switch in Russian   438
    Jerzy Rubach

24   Generalized Alignment: The Prosody–Morphology
     Interface   451
     John J. McCarthy and Alan Prince

25   The Prosodic Structure of Function Words   464
     Elisabeth Selkirk

26   The Emergence of the Unmarked   483
     John J. McCarthy and Alan Prince

27   Maximal Words and the Maori Passive   495
     Paul de Lacy

28   External Allomorphy as Emergence of the Unmarked   513
     Joan Mascaró

29   Derived Environment Effects in Optimality Theory   523
     Anna Łubowicz

30   Licensing and Underspecification in Optimality Theory 533
     Junko Itô, Armin Mester, and Jaye Padgett

31   The Implications of Lexical Exceptions for the Nature
     of Grammar   542
     Sharon Inkelas, Orhan Orgun, and Cheryl Zoll

32   The Phonological Lexicon   552
     Junko Itô and Armin Mester

33   Variation and Change in Optimality Theory   569
     Arto Anttila and Young-mee Yu Cho

References   581

Index of Languages and Language Families   591

Index of Constraints   594

Index of Topics   598

Preface

Optimality Theory (OT) has applications throughout the field of linguistics. But its first and greatest influence has been in phonology. This book is a compilation of readings on OT in phonology, starting with the original and most important one, Prince and Smolensky's *Optimality Theory: Constraint Interaction in Generative Grammar*. The readings cover a broad range of topics in phonology and related disciplines. Both previously published and never before published works are included.

The readings have been selected with a second-semester phonology course in mind, though they would also be suitable for a seminar or for independent reading. To enhance this work's usefulness as a textbook, I have included brief introductory notes at the beginning of each chapter to set the stage and point out connections with other chapters. Each chapter also concludes with a list of study and research questions. The questions appear in approximate order of difficulty: some are relatively easy reviews of the material; some are more challenging, requiring further thought and research; others are open-ended research topics and even notoriously unsolved problems, included here in the hope that they will elicit an answer. There is ample material for homework exercises, term papers, and dissertations in this book and in these study questions.

The decisions about what to include were extremely difficult, and many excellent works had to be omitted. When I was in doubt, considerations of length were decisive: articles that were already short or that could easily be made short were given priority. It is safe to say that no one else would make exactly these decisions, nor would I, I am sure, if I started all over again.

Almost without exception, the chapters of this book are excerpts from the original works. To cover a wide range of topics within limited space, I had to be severe in making cuts. If the original article had three sections, each describing a different example, two were cut. If there was interesting discussion that strayed from the main point, it was removed. Acknowledgments, digressive footnotes, appendices, and the like were excised automatically. Such minor omissions are not indicated in the text, though major ones are marked with "[. . .]", and the original numbering of sections, examples, and notes is retained, as are most of the cross-references. The excisions were all negotiated with the contributors, who gave their (sometimes reluctant) approval to the result. In some cases, authors went further, revising their chapters to smooth out the seams.

Each chapter includes the bibliography from the original work (minus any references that were cited only in the excised material). To these original bibliographies, two sigla have been added. The symbol ◄ marks references to works that are included in this reader. (The ◄ is mnemonic for "look at the table of contents in the front of the book.") The symbol ► marks references that are incomplete; it points to the bibliography at the back of the book, which includes better versions of those references plus all works cited in the Editor's Notes and Study and Research Questions. The notes and exercises also supplement the individual chapter bibliographies by pointing to more recent literature.

I would not have embarked on this project without instigation from Tami Kaplan and continuing support from her and from Sarah Coleman, both with Blackwell. I could not have completed it without the assistance of Maria Gouskova, whose care, common sense, and wisdom have been indispensable as the book came together. The index was largely the work of Michael Becker, Kathryn Flack, and Shigeto Kawahara, who did the job with remarkable care and swiftness. You readers and I owe a large debt to Margaret Aherne, copy-editor without peer, who not only turned a huge, messy manuscript into a handsome book, but also detected more than a few errors of substance in constraints, tableaux, and arguments. To all of these and to the authors, who have been generous with their time and help, I am very grateful.

John J. McCarthy
Amherst, Massachusetts
2003

Contributors' Addresses

John Alderete
Linguistics Program
406 Welsh Humanities Building
University of South Carolina
Columbia, SC 29208, USA

Arto Anttila
Department of Linguistics
New York University
719 Broadway, 5/F
New York, NY 10003, USA
arto.anttila@nyu.edu

Eric Baković
Linguistics Department
University of California, San Diego
9500 Gilman Drive, #0108
La Jolla, CA 92093, USA
bakovic@ling.ucsd.edu

Jill Beckman
Linguistics Department
570 English Philosophy Building
The University of Iowa
Iowa City, IA 52242, USA
jill-beckman@uiowa.edu

Laura Benua
40 Third Avenue
Nyack, NY 10960, USA
lbenua@hotmail.com

Paul de Lacy
Department of Linguistics
Faculty of Modern and Medieval Languages
University of Cambridge
Sidgwick Avenue
Cambridge CB3 9DA, England
pvd22@cam.ac.uk

Nine Elenbaas
Albert van Dalsumlaan 187
3584 HD Utrecht
The Netherlands
nine_elenbaas@hotmail.com

Bruce Hayes
Department of Linguistics
University of California
Los Angeles, CA 90095, USA
bhayes@humnet.ucla.edu

Sharon Inkelas
Department of Linguistics
1203 Dwinelle Hall
University of California
Berkeley, CA 94720, USA
inkelas@socrates.berkeley.edu

Junko Itô
Department of Linguistics
University of California, Santa Cruz
1156 High Street
Santa Cruz, CA 95064, USA
ito@ling.ucsc.edu

René Kager
Utrecht Institute of Linguistics OTS
Universiteit Utrecht
Trans 10
3512 JK Utrecht
The Netherlands
rene.kager@let.uu.nl

Michael Kenstowicz
Department of Linguistics & Philosophy,
  E39-245
MIT
Cambridge, MA 02139, USA
kenstow@mit.edu

Robert Kirchner
Department of Linguistics
4-32 Assiniboia Hall
University of Alberta
Edmonton, Alberta T6G 2E7, Canada
kirchner@ualberta.ca

Linda Lombardi
Linguistics Department
Marie Mount Hall 1401
University of Maryland
College Park, MD 20742, USA
linda_lombardi@umail.umd.edu

Anna Lubowicz
Department of Linguistics
3601 Watt Way
Grace Ford Salvatori Hall 301
University of Southern California
Los Angeles, CA 90089, USA

Joan Mascaró
Departament de Filologia Catalana
Universitat Autònoma de Barcelona
08193 Bellaterra, Spain
joan.mascaro@uab.es

John J. McCarthy
Department of Linguistics
University of Massachusetts
Amherst, MA 01003, USA
jmccarthy@linguist.umass.edu

Armin Mester
Department of Linguistics
University of California, Santa Cruz
1156 High Street
Santa Cruz, CA 95064, USA
mester@ling.ucsc.edu

Elliott Moreton
Department of Linguistics
CB #3155
Dey Hall 320
University of North Carolina
Chapel Hill, NC 27599, USA

Scott Myers
Department of Linguistics
University of Texas at Austin
Austin, TX 78712, USA
s.myers@mail.utexas.edu

Orhan Orgun
Linguistics Department
University of California, Davis
Davis, CA 95616, USA
ocorgun@ucdavis.edu

Jaye Padgett
Department of Linguistics
University of California, Santa Cruz
1156 High Street
Santa Cruz, CA 95064, USA
padgett@cats.ucsc.edu

Joe Pater
Department of Linguistics
University of Massachusetts
Amherst, MA 01003, USA
pater@linguist.umass.edu

Alan Prince
Department of Linguistics
18 Seminary Place
Rutgers University
New Brunswick, NJ 08903, USA
prince@ruccs.rutgers.edu

Jerzy Rubach
Fall
Linguistics Department
570 English Philosophy Building
The University of Iowa
Iowa City, IA 52242, USA
jerzy_rubach@uiowa.edu

Spring
Instytut Anglistyki
Uniwersytet Warszawski
ul. Nowy Swiat 4
00-497 Warszawa, Poland
rubach@mail.uw.edu.pl

Elisabeth Selkirk
Department of Linguistics
University of Massachusetts
Amherst, MA 01003, USA
selkirk@linguist.umass.edu

Paul Smolensky
Department of Cognitive Science
239A Krieger Hall
Johns Hopkins University
Baltimore, MD 21218, USA
smolensky@jhu.edu

Bruce Tesar
Department of Linguistics
18 Seminary Place
Rutgers University
New Brunswick, NJ 08903, USA
tesar@ruccs.rutgers.edu

Moira Yip
University College London
Department of Phonetics and Linguistics

Gower Street
London WC1E 6BT, England
moira@linguistics.ucl.ac.uk

Young-mee Yu Cho
Department of Asian Languages and Cultures
330 Scott Hall, College Avenue Campus
Rutgers University
New Brunswick, NJ 08901, USA
yucho@rci.rutgers.edu

Cheryl Zoll
Department of Linguistics & Philosophy,
   E-39-245
MIT
Cambridge, MA 02139, USA
czoll@mit.edu

Acknowledgments

The editor and publisher wish to thank the following for permission to use copyright material in this book:

1   Prince, Alan and Smolensky, Paul (1993) *Optimality Theory: Constraint Interaction in Generative Grammar*. New Brunswick, NJ: Rutgers University Center for Cognitive Science. Technical report RuCCS-TR-2. Reprinted by permission of Alan Prince and Paul Smolensky.

2   McCarthy, John J. and Prince, Alan (1993) Generalized alignment. In *Yearbook of Morphology*, ed. Geert Booij and Jaap van Marle, pp. 79–153. Dordrecht: Kluwer. © 1993 by Kluwer Academic Publishers. Reprinted with kind permission of Kluwer Academic Publishers.

3   McCarthy, John J. and Prince, Alan (1999) Faithfulness and identity in Prosodic Morphology. In *The Prosody–Morphology Interface*, ed. René Kager, Harry van der Hulst, and Wim Zonneveld, pp. 218–309. Cambridge: Cambridge University Press. © 1999 by Cambridge University Press.

4   Tesar, Bruce (1995) *Computing Optimal Forms in Optimality Theory: Basic Syllabification*. Report no. CU-CS-763-95. Boulder, CO: Department of Computer Science, University of Colorado. Reprinted by permission of Bruce Tesar.

5   Tesar, Bruce and Smolensky, Paul (1998) Learnability in Optimality Theory. *Linguistic Inquiry* 29: 229–68. © 1998 by the Massachusetts Institute of Technology.

6   Moreton, Elliott (1996/1999) Non-computable Functions in Optimality Theory. Unpublished manuscript. Amherst, MA: University of Massachusetts, Amherst. Reprinted by permission of Elliott Moreton.

7   McCarthy, John J. and Prince, Alan (1993) Generalized alignment. In *Yearbook of Morphology*, ed. Geert Booij and Jaap van Marle, pp. 79–153. Dordrecht: Kluwer. © 1993 by Kluwer Academic Publishers. Reprinted with kind permission of Kluwer Academic Publishers.

8 Elenbaas, Nine and Kager, René (1999) Ternary rhythm and the *LAPSE CON-STRAINT. *Phonology* 16: 273–330. © 1999 by Cambridge University Press.

9 Kenstowicz, Michael (1996) Quality-sensitive stress. *Rivista di Linguistica* 9: 157–87.

10 Baković, Eric (1998) Unbounded stress and factorial typology. In *RuLing Papers 1: Working Papers from Rutgers University*, ed. Ron Artstein and Madeline Holler, pp. 15–28. New Brunswick, NJ: Department of Linguistics, Rutgers University. Reprinted by permission of Eric Baković.

11 Alderete, John (1999) Faithfulness to prosodic heads. In *The Derivational Residue in Phonological Optimality Theory*, ed. Ben Hermans and Marc van Oostendorp, pp. 29-50. Amsterdam: John Benjamins. Reprinted with kind permission of John Benjamins Publishing Company, Amsterdam/Philadelphia. www.benjamins.com.

12 Yip, Moira (1999) Feet, tonal reduction and speech rate at the word and phrase level in Chinese. In *Phrasal Phonology*, ed. René Kager and Wim Zonneveld, pp. 171–94. Nijmegen: Nijmegen University Press. Reprinted by permission of Nijmegen University Press.

13 Myers, Scott (1997) OCP effects in Optimality Theory. *Natural Language and Linguistic Theory* 15: 847–92. © 1997 by Kluwer Academic Publishers. Reprinted with kind permission of Kluwer Academic Publishers.

14 Pater, Joe (1999) Austronesian nasal substitution and other NÇ effects. In *The Prosody–Morphology Interface*, ed. René Kager, Harry van der Hulst, and Wim Zonneveld, pp. 310–43. Cambridge: Cambridge University Press. © 1999 by Cambridge University Press.

15 Hayes, Bruce (1999) Phonetically driven phonology: the role of Optimality Theory and inductive grounding. In *Functionalism and Formalism in Linguistics*, vol. 1: *General Papers*, ed. Michael Darnell, Frederick J. Newmeyer, Michael Noonan, Edith Moravcsik, and Kathleen Wheatley, pp. 243–85. Amsterdam: John Benjamins. Reprinted with kind permission of John Benjamins Publishing Company, Amsterdam/Philadelphia. www.benjamins.com.

16 Beckman, Jill (1998) *Positional Faithfulness*. Doctoral dissertation. Amherst, MA: University of Massachusetts, Amherst. Published (1999) by Garland Publishing in Outstanding Dissertations in Linguistics Series. Reprinted by permission of Jill Beckman.

17 Lombardi, Linda (1999) Positional faithfulness and voicing assimilation in Optimality Theory. *Natural Language and Linguistic Theory* 17: 267–302. © 1999 by Kluwer Academic Publishers. Reprinted with kind permission of Kluwer Academic Publishers.

18 Zoll, Cheryl (1998) Positional asymmetries and licensing. Unpublished manuscript. Cambridge, MA: MIT. Reprinted by permission of Cheryl Zoll.

19 Padgett, Jaye (1995) Partial class behavior and nasal place assimilation. In *Proceedings of the 1995 Southwestern Workshop on Optimality Theory*

(SWOT), ed. Keiichiro Suzuki and Dirk Elzinga. Tucson, AZ: Department of Linguistics, University of Arizona. Reprinted by permission of Jaye Padgett.

20 Alderete, John (1997) Dissimilation as local conjunction. In *Proceedings of the North East Linguistic Society 27*, ed. Kiyomi Kusumoto, pp. 17–32. Amherst, MA: GLSA Publications. Reprinted by permission of John Alderete.

21 Kirchner, Robert (1996) Synchronic chain shifts in Optimality Theory. *Linguistic Inquiry* 27: 341–50. © 1996 by the Massachusetts Institute of Technology.

22 Benua, Laura (1997) *Transderivational Identity: Phonological Relations between Words*. Doctoral dissertation: University of Massachusetts, Amherst. Published (2000) by Garland Publishing in Outstanding Dissertations in Linguistics Series. Reprinted by permission of Laura Benua.

23 Rubach, Jerzy (2000) Backness switch in Russian. *Phonology* 17: 39–64. © 2000 by Cambridge University Press.

24 McCarthy, John J. and Prince, Alan (1993) Generalized alignment. In *Yearbook of Morphology*, ed. Geert Booij and Jaap van Marle, pp. 79–153. Dordrecht: Kluwer. © 1993 by Kluwer Academic Publishers. Reprinted with kind permission of Kluwer Academic Publishers.

25 Selkirk, Elisabeth (1996) The prosodic structure of function words. In *Signal to Syntax: Bootstrapping from Speech to Grammar in Early Acquisition*, ed. James L. Morgan and Katherine Demuth, pp. 187–214. Mahwah, NJ: Lawrence Erlbaum Associates.

26 McCarthy, John J. and Prince, Alan (1994) The emergence of the unmarked: Optimality in prosodic morphology. In *Proceedings of the North East Linguistic Society 24*, ed. Mercè Gonzàlez, pp. 333–79. Amherst, MA: GLSA Publications. Reprinted by permission of John McCarthy and Alan Prince.

27 de Lacy, Paul (2002) Maximal words and the Māori passive. Reproduced by permission of Paul de Lacy.

28 Mascaró, Joan (1996) External allomorphy as emergence of the unmarked. In *Current Trends in Phonology: Models and Methods*, ed. Jacques Durand and Bernard Laks, pp. 473–83. Salford, Manchester: European Studies Research Institute, University of Salford. Reprinted by permission of Joan Mascaró.

29 Łubowicz, Anna (2002) Derived environment effects in Optimality Theory. *Lingua* 112: 243–80. © 2002, with permission from Elsevier.

30 Itô, Junko, Mester, Armin, and Padgett, Jaye (1995) Licensing and underspecification in Optimality Theory. *Linguistic Inquiry* 26: 571–614. © 1995 by the Massachusetts Institute of Technology.

31 Inkelas, Sharon, Orgun, Orhan, and Zoll, Cheryl (1997) The implications of lexical exceptions for the nature of grammar. In *Derivations and Constraints in Phonology*, ed. Iggy Roca, pp. 393–418. Oxford: Oxford University Press. Reprinted by permission of Sharon Inkelas, Orhan Orgun, and Cheryl Zoll.

32   Itô, Junko and Mester, Armin (1999) The phonological lexicon. In *The Handbook of Japanese Linguistics,* ed. Natsuko Tsujimura, pp. 62–100. Oxford: Blackwell. Reprinted by permission of Blackwell Publishing.

33   Anttila, Arto and Cho, Young-mee Yu (1998) Variation and change in Optimality Theory. *Lingua* 104: 31–56. © 1998, with permission from Elsevier.

Every effort has been made to trace copyright holders and to obtain their permission for the use of copyright material. The editor and publisher apologize for any errors or omissions in the above list and would be grateful if notified of any corrections that should be incorporated in future reprints or subsequent editions of this book.

Part I
The Basics

Chapter 1 | Alan Prince and
Paul Smolensky

Optimality Theory: Constraint Interaction in Generative Grammar

Editor's Note

Optimality Theory first gained wide exposure from a course taught by Prince and Smolensky at the 1991 Summer Institute of the Linguistic Society of America. The earliest and still the most detailed exposition of the theory is their 1993 manuscript, an excerpt from which is here published for the first time. There has been much interest in this emerging theory; it has been the subject of a large and growing professional literature, an extensive electronic archive (http://roa.rutgers.edu), many courses and conference papers, and several textbooks. Although it was originally applied to phonology, the relevance of OT to topics in phonetics, morphology, syntax, sociolinguistics, psycholinguistics, and semantics has become increasingly apparent.

This chapter includes these excerpts: introductory material and motivation for the theory, including an analysis of Berber syllabification, drawn from sections 1 and 2 of Prince and Smolensky (P&S) (1993); an explanation of how constraints and constraint hierarchies evaluate candidates (section 5 of P&S 1993); the basic CV syllable theory with elaborations (section 6 and part of section 8 in P&S 1993); the theory of inventories and the lexicon (most of section 9 in P&S 1993). Readers may encounter sporadic references to other parts of P&S (1993): sections 3 and 4 on blocking and triggering (exemplified with Tongan stress, Tagalog infixation, Hindi stress, and Latin foot and word structure); section 7 on Lardil phonology; and section 10 on OT's relationships with functionalism, computation, Connectionism, Harmony Theory, and constraint-and-repair theories.

Readers approaching OT for the first time should begin with sections 1.2 and 2 of this chapter, followed by section 6, and then section 5. Readers can then go on to read the other parts of this chapter or other chapters in this book. Some natural pairings: the constraint Hɴᴜᴄ in section 2 of this chapter re-emerges in stress theory in chapter 9; the CV syllable theory in section 6 of this chapter is studied from the perspectives of parsing and learning in chapters 4 and 5, respectively; the idea of faithfulness constraints (section 6.2.1) is generalized in chapter 3; emergence of

Excerpt (with minor revisions by the authors) from:
Prince, Alan and Smolensky, Paul (1993) *Optimality Theory: Constraint Interaction in Generative Grammar*. New Brunswick, NJ: Rutgers University Center for Cognitive Science. Technical report RuCCS-TR-2. [Available on Rutgers Optimality Archive, ROA-537.]

the unmarked is discussed briefly at the end of section 6.1 in this chapter and is the subject of chapter 26; lexicon optimization, which is discussed in section 9.3 of this chapter, is the topic of chapter 32.

[. . .]

1.2   Optimality

The standard phonological rule aims to encode grammatical generalizations in this format:

(1) $A \rightarrow B / C{-}D$

The rule scans potential inputs for structures CAD and performs the change on them that is explicitly spelled out in the rule: the unit denoted by A takes on property B. For this format to be worth pursuing, there must be an interesting theory which defines the class of possible predicates CAD (Structural Descriptions) and another theory which defines the class of possible operations $A \rightarrow B$ (Structural Changes). If these theories are loose and uninformative, as indeed they have proved to be in reality, we must entertain one of two conclusions:

(i)   phonology itself simply doesn't have much content, is mostly 'periphery' rather than 'core', is just a technique for data-compression, with aspirations to depth subverted by the inevitable idiosyncrasies of history and lexicon; or
(ii)   the locus of explanatory action is elsewhere.

We suspect the latter.
  The explanatory burden can of course be distributed quite differently than in the re-write rule theory. Suppose that the input–output relation is governed by conditions on the well-formedness of the *output*, 'markedness constraints', and by conditions asking for the *exact preservation of the input* in the output along various dimensions, 'faithfulness constraints'. In this case, the inputs falling under the influence of a constraint need share no input-specifiable structure (CAD), nor need there be a single determinate transformation (A→B) that affects them. Rather, we generate (or admit) a set of candidate outputs, perhaps by very general conditions indeed, and then we assess the candidates, seeking the one that best satisfies the relevant constraints. Many possibilities are open to contemplation, but some well-defined measure of value excludes all but the best.[1] The process can be schematically represented like this [the function H-eval, 'Harmonic Evaluation', determines the relative Harmony of the candidates]:

(2)   Structure of Optimality-theoretic Grammar
     a.   Gen (In_k) $\rightarrow$ $\{\text{Out}_1, \text{Out}_2, \ldots\}$
     b.   H-eval $(\text{Out}_i, 1 \leq i \leq \infty)$ $\rightarrow$ Out_{real}

The grammar must define a pairing of underlying and surface forms, (input$_i$, output$_j$). Each input is associated with a candidate set of possible analyses by the function Gen (short for 'generator'), a fixed part of Universal Grammar. In the rich representational system employed below, an output form retains its input as a subrepresentation, so that departures from faithfulness may be detected by scrutiny of output forms alone. A 'candidate' is an input–output pair, here formally encoded in what is called 'Out$_i$' in (2).

Gen contains information about the representational primitives and their universally irrevocable relations: for example, that the node σ may dominate a node *Onset* or a node μ (implementing some theory of syllable structure), but never vice versa. Gen will also determine such matters as whether every segment must be syllabified – we assume not, below, following McCarthy 1979 and others – and whether every node of syllable structure must dominate segmental material – again, we will assume not, following Itô 1986, 1989.

The function H-eval determines the relative Harmony of the candidates, imposing an order on the entire set. An optimal output is at the top of the harmonic order on the candidate set; by definition, it best satisfies the constraint system. Though Gen has a role to play, the burden of explanation falls principally on the function H-eval, a construction built from well-formedness constraints, and the account of interlinguistic differences is entirely tied to the different ways the constraint-system H-eval can be put together, given UG.

H-eval must be constructible in a general way if the theory is to be worth pursuing. There are really two notions of generality involved here: general with respect to UG, and therefore cross-linguistically; and general with respect to the language at hand, and therefore across constructions, categories, descriptive generalizations, etc. These are logically independent, and success along either dimension of generality would count as an argument in favor of the optimality approach. But the strongest argument, the one that is most consonant with the work in the area, and the one that will be pursued here, broaches the distinction, seeking a formulation of H-eval that is built from maximally universal constraints which apply with maximal breadth over an entire language.

Optimality Theory, in common with much recent work, shifts the burden from the theory of operations (Gen) to the theory of well-formedness (H-eval). To the degree that the theory of well-formedness can be put generally, the theory will fulfill the basic goals of generative grammar. To the extent that operation-based theories cannot be so put, they must be rejected.

Among possible developments of the optimality idea, we need to distinguish some basic architectural variants. Perhaps nearest to the familiar derivational conceptions of grammar is what we might call 'harmonic serialism', by which Gen provides a set of candidate analyses for an input, which are harmonically evaluated; the optimal form is then fed back into Gen, which produces another set of analyses, which are then evaluated; and so on until no further improvement in representational Harmony is possible. Here Gen might mean: 'do any *one* thing: advance all candidates which differ in one respect from the input.' The Gen ⇆ H-eval loop would iterate until there was nothing left to be done or, better, until nothing that could be done would result in increased Harmony. A significant proposal of roughly this character is the *Theory of Constraints and Repair Strategies* of Paradis 1988a, 1988b, with a couple of caveats: the *constraints* involved are a set of parochial level-true phonotactic state-ments, rather than being universal and violable, as we insist; and the *repair strategies* are quite narrowly defined in terms of structural description and structural change rather than being of the 'do-unto-α' variety. A key aspect of Paradis's work is that it confronts the problem of well-definition of the notion 'repair': what to do when applying a repair strategy to satisfy one constraint results in violation of another constraint (at an intermediate level of derivation). Paradis refers to such situations as 'constraint conflicts' and although these are not conflicts in our sense of the term – they cannot be, since all of her constraints are surface- or level-true and therefore never disagree among themselves in the assessment of output well-formedness – her work is of unique importance in addressing and shedding light on fundamental complexities in the idea of wellformedness-driven rule-application. The 'persistent rule' theory of Myers 1991 can similarly be related to the notion of Harmony-governed serialism. The program for *Harmonic Phonology* in Goldsmith 1991, 1993 is even more strongly of this character; within its lexical levels, all rules are constrained to apply harmonically. Here again, however, the rules are conceived of as being pretty much of the familiar sort, *triggered* if they increase Harmony, and Harmony itself is to be defined in specifically phonotactic terms. A subtheory which is very much in the mold of harmonic serialism, using a general procedure to produce candidates, is the 'Move-x' theory of rhythmic adjustment (Prince 1983, Hayes 1991).[2]

A contrasting view would hold that the Input → Output map has no internal structure: all possible variants are produced by Gen in one step and evaluated in parallel. In the course of this paper, we will see instances of both kinds of analysis, though we will focus predominantly on developing the parallel idea, finding strong support for it, as do McCarthy & Prince 1993. Definitive adjudication between parallel and serial conceptions, not to mention hybrids of various kinds, is a challenge of considerable subtlety, as indeed the debate over the necessity of serial Move-α illustrates plentifully (e.g., Aoun 1986, Browning 1991, Chomsky 1981), and the matter can be sensibly addressed only after much well-founded analytical work and theoretical exploration.

Optimality Theory abandons two key presuppositions of earlier work. First, that it is possible for a grammar to narrowly and parochially specify the Structural Description and Structural Change of rules. In place of this is Gen, which generates for any given input a large space of candidate analyses by freely exercising the basic structural resources of the representational theory. The idea is that the desired output lies somewhere in this space, and the constraint system of the grammar is strong enough to find it. Second, Optimality Theory abandons the widely held view that constraints are language-particular statements of phonotactic truth. In its place is the assertion that constraints are essentially universal and of very general formula-tion, with great potential for disagreement over the well-formedness of analyses; an individual grammar consists of a ranking of these constraints, which resolves any conflict in favor of the higher-ranked constraint. The constraints provided by Universal Grammar are simple and general; interlinguistic differences arise from the permutations of constraint-ranking; typology is the study of the range of systems that re-ranking permits. Because they are ranked, constraints are regularly violated in the grammatical forms of a language. Violability has significant consequences not only for the mechanics of description, but also for the process of theory construction:

a new class of predicates becomes usable in the formal theory, with a concomitant shift in what we can think the actual generalizations are. We cannot expect the world to stay the same when we change our way of describing it.
[. . .]

2 Optimality in Grammar: Core Syllabification in Imdlawn Tashlhiyt Berber

Here we argue that certain grammatical processes can only be properly understood as selecting the *optimal output* from among a set of possibilities, where the notion *optimal* is defined in terms of the constraints bearing on the grammatical domain at issue.

2.1 The heart of Dell & Elmedlaoui

The Imdlawn Tashlhiyt dialect of Berber (ITB) has been the object of a series of remarkable studies by François Dell and Mohamed Elmedlaoui (Dell & Elmedlaoui 1985, 1988, 1989). Perhaps their most surprising empirical finding is that in this language any segment – consonant or vowel, obstruent or sonorant – can form the nucleus of a syllable. One regularly encounters syllables of the shape *tK, rB, xZ, wL*, for example. (Capitalization represents nucleus-hood of consonants.) Table 1 provides illustrative examples, with periods used to mark syllable edges.[3]

Table 1

Nucleus type	Example	Morphology	Reference
voiceless stop	.ra.tK.ti.	ra-t-kti	1985: 113
voiced stop	.bD.dL.	bddl	1988: 1
	.ma.ra.tGt.	ma=ra-t-g-t	1985: 113
voiceless fricative	.tF.tKt.	t-ftk-t	1985: 113
	.tX.zNt.	t-xzn-t	1985: 106
voiced fricative	.txZ.nakk^w.	t-xzn#nakk^w	1985: 113
nasal	.tzMt.	t-zmt	1985: 112
	.tM.zħ.	t-mzħ	1985: 112
liquid	.tR.gLt.	t-rgl-t	1985: 106
high vowel	.il.di.	i-ldi	1985: 106
	.rat.lult.	ra-t-lul-t	1985: 108
low vowel	.tR.ba.	t-rba	1985: 106

Dell and Elmedlaoui marshall a compelling range of evidence in support of the claimed patterns of syllabification. In addition to native speaker intuition, they adduce effects from segmental phonology (emphasis spread), intonation, versification practice, and prosodic morphology, all of which agree in respecting their syllabic analysis.

The domain of syllabification is the phonological phrase. All syllables must have onsets except when they occur in absolute phrase-initial position. There, syllables may begin with vowels, either with or without glottal striction (Dell & Elmedlaoui 1985: 127 fn. 20), evidently a matter of phonetic implementation. Since any segment at all can form the nucleus of a syllable, there is massive potential ambiguity in syllabification, and even when the onset requirement is satisfied, a number of distinct syllabifications will often be potentially available. But the actual syllabification of any given string is almost always unique. Dell & Elmedlaoui discovered that assignment of nuclear status is determined by the relative sonority of the elements in the string. Thus we find the following typical contrasts:

(3)   Sonority Effects on Nuclear Status
    a.   tzMt — *tZmt   '*m* beats *z* as a nucleus'
    b.   rat.lult — *ra.tL.wL.t '*u* beats *l* as a nucleus'

Orthography: we write *u* for the nuclear version, *w* for the marginal version of the high back vocoid, and similarly for *i* and *y*: as with every other margin/nucleus pair, we assume featural identity.

All the structures in (3), including the ill-formed ones, are locally well-formed, composed of licit substructures. In particular, there is nothing wrong with syllables *tZ*, *tL*, or *wL* nor with word-final sequences *mt* – but the more sonorous nucleus is chosen in each case. By examining the full range of such contrasts, Dell and Elmedlaoui establish the relevance of the following familiar kind of 8-point hierarchy:

(4)   Sonority Scale
    |Low V| > |High V| > |Liquid| > |Nasal| > |Voiced Fric.| > |Voiceless Fric.| > |Voiced Stop| > |Voiceless Stop|

We write $|\alpha|$ for the sonority or intrinsic prominence of α.

With the sonority scale in hand, Dell and Elmedlaoui then propose an iterative syllable-construction procedure that is designed to select the correct nuclei. Their algorithm can be stated in the following way, modified slightly from Dell & Elmedlaoui 1985: 111(15):

(5)   Dell–Elmedlaoui Algorithm for Core Syllabification (DEA)
    Build a core syllable ("CV") over each substring of the form XY, where
        X is any segment (except [*a*]), and
        Y is a matrix of features describing a step of the sonority scale.
    Start Y at the top of the sonority scale and replace it successively with the matrix of features appropriate to the next lower step of the scale.
    (Iterate from Left to Right for each fixing of the nuclear variable Y.)

Like all such procedures, the DEA is subject to the Free Element Condition (FEC: Prince 1985), which holds that rules establishing a level of prosodic structure apply only to elements that are not already supplied with the relevant structure. By the FEC, the positions analyzed by the terms X,Y must be free of syllabic affiliation. Effectively, this means that any element seized as an onset is no longer eligible to be a nucleus, and that a segment recruited to nucleate a syllable is not then available to serve as an onset.

There are other syllabification phenomena in ITB that require additional rules beyond the DEA; we will abstract away from these and focus on the sense of DEA itself.[4] We will also put aside some wrinkles in the DEA which are related to parenthesized expressions in (5) – the lack of a glide counterpart for /a/, the phrase-initial loosening of the onset requirement, and the claimed left-to-rightness of the procedure.[5]

The DEA is a rule, or rather a schema for rules, of exactly the classical type A → B / C—D. Each rule generated by the schema has a Structural Description specified in featural terms and a Structural Change ('construct a core syllable'). To see how it works, consider the following derivations:

(6)   DEA in Action

Steps of the DEA		/ratlult/ 'you will be born'
Seek [X][+low,–cns]	*& Build*	(ra)tlult
Seek [X][–low,–cns]	*& Build*	(ra)t(lu)lt
Seek [X][+cns,+son,–nas]		*–blocked by FEC–*
Seek [X][+cns,+son,+nas]		—
Seek [X][–son,+cnt,+voi]		—
Seek [X][–son,+cnt,–voi]		—
Seek [X][–son,–cnt,+voi]		—
Seek [X][–son,–cnt,–voi]	*& Build*	(ra)t(lu)(IT)[6]

(7)   DEA in Action

Steps of the DEA		/txznt/ 'you sg. stored'
Seek [X][+low,–cns]		—
Seek [X][–low,–cns]		—
Seek [X][+cns,+son,–nas]		—
Seek [X][+cns,+son,+nas]	*& Build*	tx(zN)t
Seek [X][–son,+cnt,+voi]		—
Seek [X][–son,+cnt,–voi]	*& Build*	(tX)(zN)t
Seek [X][–son,–cnt,+voi]		—
Seek [X][–son,–cnt,–voi]		—

(8)   DEA in Action

Steps of the DEA		/txznas/ 'she stored for him'
Seek [X][+low,–cns]	*& Build*	txz(**na**)s
Seek [X][–low,–cns]		—
Seek [X][+cns,+son,–nas]		—
Seek [X][+cns,+son,+nas]		*–blocked by FEC–*
Seek [X][–son,+cnt,+voi]	*& Build*	t(**xZ**)(na)s
Seek [X][–son,+cnt,–voi]		—
Seek [X][–son,–cnt,+voi]		—
Seek [X][–son,–cnt,–voi]		*–blocked by FEC–*

The DEA provides an elegant and straightforward account of the selection of syllable nuclei in the language. But it suffers from the formal arbitrariness characteristic of re-writing rules when they are put to the task of dealing locally with problems that fall under general principles, particularly principles of output shape. (By 'formal arbitrariness', we mean that a formal system rich enough to allow expression of the desired rule will also allow expression of many undesired variations of the rule, so that the rule itself appears to be an arbitrary random choice among the universe of possibilities.) The key to the success of the DEA is the way that the variable Y scans the input, starting at the top of the sonority scale and descending it step by step as the iterative process unfolds. We must ask, why start at the top? why *descend* the scale? why not use it in some more elaborate or context-dependent fashion? why apply the scale to the nucleus rather than the onset?[7]

The answers are to be found in the theory of syllable structure markedness, which is part of Universal Grammar. The more sonorous a segment is, the more satisfactory it is as a nucleus. Conversely, a nucleus is more satisfactory to the degree that it contains a more sonorous segment. It is clear that the DEA is designed to produce syllables with optimal nuclei; to ensure that the syllables it forms are the most *harmonic* that are available, to use the term introduced in §1. Dell and Elmedlaoui clearly understand the role of sonority in choosing between competing analyses of a given input string; they write:

> When a string . . . PQ . . . could conceivably be syllabified as . . . Pq . . . or as . . . pQ . . . (i.e. when either syllabification would involve only syllable types which, when taken individually, are possible in ITB), the only syllabification allowed by ITB is the one that takes as a syllabic peak the more sonorous of the two segments. (Dell & Elmedlaoui 1985: 109)

But if phonology is couched in re-writing rules, this insight cannot be cashed in as part of the function that assigns structural analyses. It remains formally inert.

Dell and Elmedlaoui refer to it as an 'empirical observation', emphasizing its extra-grammatical status.

The DEA itself makes no contact with any principles of well-formedness; it merely scans the input for certain specific configurations, and acts when it finds them. That it descends the sonority scale, for example, can have no formal explanation. But the insight behind the DEA can be made active if we re-conceive the process of syllabi-fication as one of choosing the optimal output from among the possible analyses rather than algorithmic structure-building. Let us first suppose, with Dell and Elmedlaoui, that the process of syllabification is serial, affecting one syllable at a time (thus, that it operates like Move-α or more exactly, Move-x of grid theory). At each stage of the process, let all possible single syllabic augmentations of the input be presented for evaluation. This set of candidates is evaluated by principles of syllable well-formedness and the most harmonic structure in the set is selected as the output. We can state the process informally as follows:

(9) Serial Harmonic Syllabification (informal)
     Form the optimal syllable in the domain.
     Iterate until nothing more can be done.

This approach depends directly on the principles of well-formedness which define the notion 'optimal'. No instructions are issued to the construction process to contemplate only one featurally specified niche of the sonority scale. Indeed, the Harmonic Syllabification algorithm has no access to any information at all about absolute sonority level or the specific featural composition of vowels, which are essential to the DEA; it needs to know whether segment α is *more* sonorous than segment β, not what their sonorities or features actually are. All possibilities are entertained simultaneously and the choice among them is made on grounds of general principle. That you start at the top of the scale, that you descend the scale rather than ascending it or touring it in some more interesting fashion, all this follows from the principles that define relative well-formedness of nucleus–segment pairings. The formal arbitrariness of the DEA syllable-constructing procedure disappears because the procedure itself ('make a syllable') has been stripped of intricacies.[8]

This is an instance of Harmony-increasing processing (Smolensky 1983, 1986; Goldsmith 1991, 1993). The general rubric is this:

(10) Harmonic Processing
      Go to the most harmonic available state.

We speak not of 'relative well-formedness' but rather of *relative Harmony*. Har-mony is a well-formedness scale along which a maximal Harmony structure is well-formed and all other structures are ill-formed.

We conclude that the Dell–Elmedlaoui results establish clearly that harmonic processing is a grammatical mechanism; and that optimality-based analysis gives results in complex cases. Let us now establish a formal platform that can support this finding.

2.2   Optimality Theory

What, then, is the *optimal* syllable that Harmonic Syllabification seeks? In the core process that we are focusing on, two constraints are at play, one ensuring onsets, the other evaluating nuclei. The onset constraint can be stated like this (Itô 1986, 1989):

(11)   The Onset Constraint (ONS)
       Syllables must have onsets (except phrase initially).

As promised, we are not going to explicate the parenthesized caveat, which is not really part of the basic constraint (McCarthy & Prince 1993: §4). The nuclear constraint looks like this:[9]

(12)   The Nuclear Harmony Constraint (HNUC)
       A higher sonority nucleus is more harmonic than one of lower sonority.
       i.e. If $|x| > |y|$ then Nuc/x > Nuc/y.

The formalizing restatement appended to the constraint uses some notation that will prove useful:

For 'x is more harmonic than y' we write x > y.
For 'the intrinsic prominence of x' we write $|x|$.
'A/x' means 'x belongs to category A, x is the constituent-structure child of A'.

The two kinds of order > and > are distinguished notationally to emphasize their conceptual distinctness. Segments of high sonority are not more harmonic than those of lower sonority. It is only when segments are contemplated in a structural context that the issue of well-formedness arises.

It is necessary to specify not only the relevant constraints, but also the set of candidates to be evaluated. To do this we need to spell out the function Gen that admits to candidacy a specific range of structurings or parses of the input. In the case at hand, we want something roughly like this:

(13)   Gen (*input*~i~)
       The set of (partial) syllabifications of *input*~i~ which differ from *input*~i~ in no more than one syllabic adjunction.

For any form *input*~i~ to undergo Serial Harmonic Syllabification, the candidate set Gen(*input*~i~) must be evaluated with respect to the constraints ONS and HNUC. There would be little to say if evaluation were simply a matter of choosing the candidate that satisfies both constraints. Crucially, and typically, this straightforward approach cannot work. Conflict between the constraints ONS and HNUC is unavoidable; there are candidate sets in which no candidate satisfies both constraints.

Consider, for example, the syllabification of the form /ħaul-tn/ 'make them (m.) plentiful' (Dell & Elmedlaoui 1985: 110). Both ONS and HNUC agree that the core syllable *ħa* should be formed: it has an onset as well as the best possible nucleus. Similarly, we must have a final syllable *tN*. But what of the rest of the string? We have two choices for the sequence /ul/: a superior nucleus lacking an onset, as in *ul*; or an onsetted syllable with an inferior nucleus, as in *wL*. This situation can be perspicuously displayed in tabular form:[10]

(14)   Constraint Inconsistency

Candidates /ħaul-tn/	Ons	Hnuc
~.wL.~		|l|
~.ul.~	*	|u|

The cells contain information about how each candidate fares on the relevant constraint. A blank cell indicates that the constraint is satisfied; a star indicates violation. (In the case of a scalar constraint like Hnuc we mention the contents of the evaluated element.) The first form succeeds on Ons, while the second form violates the constraint. The relative performance is exactly the opposite on Hnuc: because $|u| > |l|$, the second, onsetless form has the better nucleus. The actual output is, of course, *.ħa.wL.tN*. The onset requirement, in short, takes priority.

Such conflict is ubiquitous, and to deal with it, we propose that a relation of *domination*, or priority-ranking, can be specified to hold between constraints. When we say that one constraint *dominates* another, we mean that when they disagree on the relative status of a pair of candidates, the dominating constraint makes the decision. If the dominating constraint does not decide between the candidates – as when both satisfy or both violate the constraint equally – then the comparison is passed to the subordinate constraint. (In the case of a more extensive hierarchy, the same method of evaluation can be applied repeatedly.)

In the case at hand, it is clear that Ons must dominate Hnuc. The top priority is to provide syllables with onsets; the relative Harmony of nuclei is a subordinate concern whose force is felt only when the Ons issue is out of the way. We will write this relation as Ons ≫ Hnuc. Given such a hierarchy, an optimality calculation can be usefully presented in an augmented version of display (14) that we will call a *constraint tableau*:

(15)   Constraint Tableau for Partial Comparison of Candidates from /ħaultn/

Candidates	Ons	Hnuc
☞ ~.wL.~		|l|
~.ul.~	* !	|u|

Constraints are arrayed across the top of the tableau in domination order. As above, constraint violations are recorded with the mark *, and blankness indicates total success on the constraint. These are the theoretically important conventions; in addition, there is some clarificatory typography. The symbol ☞ draws the eye to the optimal candidate; the ! marks the *crucial* failure for each suboptimal candidate, the exact point where it loses out to other candidates. Cells that do not participate in the decision are shaded. In the case at hand, the contest is decided by the dominant constraint ONS; HNUC plays no role in the comparison of .*wL*. and .*ul*. HNUC is literally irrelevant to this particular evaluation, as a consequence of its dominated position – and to emphasize this, we shade its cells. Of course, HNUC is not irrelevant to the analysis of *every* input; but a precondition for relevance is that there be a set of candidates that tie on ONS, all passing it or all failing it to the same extent.

If we were to reverse the domination ranking of the two constraints, the predicted outcome would be changed: now .*ul*. would be superior to .*wL*. by virtue of its relative success on HNUC, and the ONS criterion would be submerged. Because of this, the ranking ONS ≫ HNUC is *crucial*; it must obtain in the grammar of Berber if the actual language is to be generated.

The notion of domination shows up from time to time in one form or another in the literature, sometimes informally, sometimes as a clause clarifying how a set of constraints is to be interpreted. For example, Dell and Elmedlaoui write, "The prohibition of hiatus . . . *overrides*" the nuclear sonority comparison (Dell & Elmedlaoui 1985: 109, emphasis added). For them, this is an extra-grammatical observation, with the real work done by the Structural Descriptions provided by the DEA and the ordering of application of the subrules. Obviously, though, the insight is clearly present. Our claim is that the notion of domination, or 'overriding', is the truly fundamental one. What deserves extra-grammatical status is the machinery for constructing elaborately specific Structural Descriptions and modes of rule application.

To see how Serial Harmonic Syllabification (9) proceeds, let us examine the first stage of syllabifying the input /txznt/ 'you sg. stored, pf.'. It is evident that the first syllable constructed must be .*zN*. – it has an onset, and has the highest sonority nucleus available, so no competing candidate can surpass or even equal it. A more discursive examination of possibilities might be valuable; the larger-scale comparisons are laid out in the constraint tableau below.

Here are (some of the) leading candidates in the first round of the process:

(16)   Constraint Tableau for Serial Syllabification of /txznt/ (partial, first step)

Candidates	ONS	HNUC	Comments
☞ tx(zN)t		n	optimal: onsetted, best available nucleus
txz(N)t	* !	n	no onset, HNUC irrelevant
t(xZ)nt		z !	$|z| < |n|$
(tX)znt		x !	$|x| < |n|$
txz(nT)		t !	$|t| < |n|$

Syllabic parsing is conceived here as a step-by-step serial process, just as in the DEA. A candidate set is generated, each produced by a single licit change from the input; the relative status of the candidates is evaluated, yielding an optimal candidate (the output of the first step); and that output will then be subject to a variety of further single changes, generating a new candidate set to be evaluated; and so on, until there are no bettering changes to be made: the final output has then been determined.

This step-by-step Harmony evaluation is not intrinsic to the method of evaluation, though, and, in the more general context, when we discard the restricted definition of Gen in (13), it proves necessary to extend the procedure so that it is capable of evaluating entire parsed strings, and not just single (new) units of analysis. To do this, we apply the same sort of reasoning used to define domination, but *within* the constraint categories. To proceed by example, consider the analysis of /txznt/ taking for candidates all syllabified strings. We present a sampling of the candidate space.

(17)   Parallel Analysis of Complete Syllabification of /txznt/

Candidates	Ons	Hnuc		Comments
☞ .tX.zNt.		n	x	optimal
.Tx.zNt.		n	t !	$|n| = |n|, |t| < |x|$
.tXz.nT.		x !	t	$|x| < |n|$, t irrelevant
.txZ.Nt.	* !	z	n	Hnuc irrelevant
.T.X.Z.N.T.	* ! * * * *	n z x t t		Hnuc irrelevant

In evaluating the candidates we have kept to the specific assumptions mentioned above: the onset requirement is suspended phrase-initially, and the nonnuclear status of peripheral obstruents is, as in the DEA itself, put aside.

In this tableau, all the relevant information for harmonic evaluation of the parse of the whole string is present. We start by examining the first column, corresponding to the dominant constraint Ons. Only the candidates which fare best on this constraint survive for further consideration. The first three candidates all have syllables with onsets; the last two do not (to varying degrees). Lack of onset in even a single non-initial syllable is immediately fatal, because of the competing candidates which satisfy Ons.

The remaining three parses are not distinguished by Ons, and so Hnuc, the next constraint down the hierarchy, becomes relevant. These three parses are compared by Hnuc as follows. The most sonorous nucleus of each parse is examined: these are the most harmonic nuclei according to Hnuc. For each of the first two candidates the most sonorous nucleus is *n*. For the last candidate, the most sonorous nucleus is *x*, and it drops out of the competition since *n* is more sonorous than *x*. We are left with the first two candidates, so far tied on all comparisons. The Hnuc evaluation continues now to the next-most-harmonic nuclei, where the competition is finally settled in favor of the first candidate .tX.zNt.

What we have done, in essence, is to replace the iterative procedure (act/evaluate, act/evaluate, ...) with a recursive scheme: collect the results of all possible actions, then sort recursively. Rather than producing and pruning a candidate set at each step of sequential processing, striving to select at each step the action which will take us eventually to the correct output, the whole set of possible parses is defined and harmonically evaluated. The correct output is the candidate whose complete structure best satisfies the constraint hierarchy. And 'best satisfies' can be recursively defined by descending the hierarchy, discarding all but the best possibilities according to each constraint before moving on to consider lower-ranked constraints.

The great majority of analyses presented here will use the parallel method of evaluation. A distinctive prediction of the parallel approach is that there can be significant interactions of the top-down variety between aspects of structure that are present in the final parse. In §4 and §7 [omitted here – Ed.] we will see a number of cases where this is borne out, so that parallelism is demonstrably crucial; further evidence is presented in McCarthy & Prince 1993. 'Harmonic serialism' is worthy of exploration as well, and many hybrid theories can and should be imagined; but we will have little more to say about it. (But see fn. 49 below on Berber syllabification. [omitted here – Ed.])

The notion of parallel analysis of complete parses in the discussion of constraint tableau (17) is the crucial technical idea on which many of our arguments will rest. It is a means for determining the relative harmonies of entire candidate parses from a set of conflicting constraints. This technique has some subtleties, and is subject to a number of variant developments, so it is worth setting out with some formal precision exactly what we have in mind. A certain level of complexity arises because there are two dimensions of structure to keep track of. On the one hand, each individual constraint typically applies to several substructures in any complete parse, generating a *set* of evaluations. (ONS, for example, examines every syllable, and there are often several of them to examine.) On the other hand, every grammar has multiple constraints, generating multiple sets of evaluations. Regulating the way these two dimensions of multiplicity interact is a key theoretical commitment.

Our proposal is that evaluation proceeds by constraint. In the case of the mini-grammar of ONS and HNUC, entire syllabifications are first compared via ONS alone, which examines each syllable for an onset; should this fail to decide the matter, the entire syllabifications are compared via HNUC alone, which examines each syllable's nucleus.

Another way to use the two constraints would be to examine each (completely parsed) candidate syllable-by-syllable, assessing each syllable on the basis of the syllabic mini-grammar. The fact that ONS dominates HNUC would then manifest itself in the Harmony assessment of each individual syllable. This is also the approach most closely tied to continuous Harmony evaluation during a step-by-step constructive derivation. Here again, we do not wish to dismiss this conception, which is surely worthy of development. Crucially, however, this is not how Harmony evaluation works in the present conception.

In order to characterize harmonic comparison of candidate parses with full generality and clarity, we need to specify two things: first, a means of comparing entire candidates on the basis of a single constraint; then, a means of combining the evaluation of these constraints. The result is a general definition of *Harmonic Ordering of Forms*; this is, in its formal essence, our theory of constraint interaction in generative grammar. It is the main topic of §5.

[. . .]

5   The Construction of Grammar in Optimality Theory

Phonological theory contains two parts: a theory of substantive universals of phonological well-formedness and a theory of formal universals of constraint interaction. These two components are respectively the topics of §5.1 and §5.2. Since much of this work concerns the first topic, the discussion here will be limited to a few brief remarks. In §5.3, we give Pāṇini's Theorem, a theorem about the priority of the specific which follows from the basic operation of Optimality Theory as set out in §5.2.

5.1   Construction of harmonic orderings from phonetic and structural scales

To define grammars from hierarchies of well-formedness constraints, we need two distinct constructions: one that takes given constraints and defines their interactions, the other that pertains to the constraints themselves. The first will be discussed at some length in §5.2; we now take up the second briefly.

Construction of constraints amounts in many ways to a theory of contextual markedness (Chomsky & Halle 1968: ch. 9, Kean 1974, Cairns & Feinstein 1982, Cairns 1988, Archangeli & Pulleyblank 1992). Linguistic phonetics gives a set of scales on phonetic dimensions; these are not well-formedness ratings, but simply the analyses of phonetic space that are primitive from the viewpoint of linguistic theory. (We use the term 'scale' in the loosest possible sense, to encompass everything from unary features to n-ary orderings.)

Issues of relative well-formedness, or markedness, arise principally when elements from the different dimensions are combined into interpretable representations. High sonority, for example, does not by itself entail high (or low) Harmony; but when a segment occurs in a structural position such as nucleus, onset, or coda, its intrinsic sonority in combination with the character of its position gives rise to markedness-evaluating constraints such as HNUC above. Similarly, tongue-height in vowels is neither harmonic nor disharmonic in isolation, but when the dimension of ATR (Advanced Tongue Root) is brought in, clear patterns of relative well-formedness or Harmony emerge, as has been emphasized in the work of Archangeli & Pulleyblank (1992). These *Harmony scales* are intimately tied to the repertory of constraints that grammars draw on. Inasmuch as there are principled harmonic concomitants of dimensional combination, we need ways of deriving Harmony scales from phonetic scales. Symbolically, we have

(94)   Harmony Scale from Interaction of Phonetic Scales
$$\{a > b \ldots\} \otimes \{x > y > \ldots\} = ax > \ldots$$

The goal of contextual markedness theory is to give content to the operator ⊗. Below in §8 we introduce a formal mechanism of *Prominence Alignment* which generates constraint rankings from paired phonetic scales, yielding a Harmony scale on their combination. In the syllable structure application of §8, the two phonetic scales which are aligned are segmental prominence (the sonority dimension) and syllable position prominence (Peak is a more prominent position than Margin). The result is a Harmony scale on associations of segments to syllable positions.

It is important to distinguish the three kinds of scales or hierarchies which figure in Optimality Theory. To minimize confusions, we have given each its own distinctive comparison symbol. Two of these figure in (94): elements are ordered on a phonetic scale by the relation '>', and on a Harmony scale according to '≻'. The third type of hierarchy in the theory is the domination hierarchy, along which constraints are ranked by the relation '≫'. These different types of scales are enumerated and exemplified in the following table:

(95)   Three Different Scales in Optimality Theory

Type of scale or hierarchy	Relates	Symbol	Example	Meaning
Phonetic scale	Points along elementary representational dimensions	>	$a > l$	a is more sonorous than l
Harmony scale	Well-formedness of structural configurations built from elementary dimensions	≻	$á ≻ í$	a nucleus filled by a is more harmonic than a nucleus filled by l
Domination hierarchy	Relative priority of well-formedness	≫	Ons ≫ Hnuc	the constraint Ons strictly dominates the constraint Hnuc

5.2   The theory of constraint interaction

In order to define harmonic comparison of candidates consisting of entire parses, we will proceed in two steps. First, we get clear about comparing entire candidates on the basis of a single constraint, using Ons and Hnuc from the Berber analysis in §2 as our examples. Then we show how to combine the evaluation of these constraints using a domination hierarchy.

5.2.1   Comparison of entire candidates by a single constraint

The first order of business is a precise definition of how a single constraint ranks entire parses. We start with the simpler case of a single binary constraint, and then generalize the definition to non-binary constraints.

5.2.1.1   ONS: *Binary constraints*

It is useful to think of ONS as examining a syllable to see if it has an onset; if it does not, we think of ONS as assessing a **mark** of violation, *ONS. ONS is an example of a *binary constraint*; a given syllable either satisfies or violates the constraint entirely. The marks ONS generates are all of the same type: *ONS. For the moment, all the marks under consideration are identical. Later, when we consider the interaction of multiple binary constraints, there will be different types of marks to distinguish; each binary constraint $\mathbb{C}$ generates marks of its own characteristic type, *$\mathbb{C}$. Furthermore, some constraints will be non-binary, and will generate marks of different types representing different degrees of violation of the constraint: the next constraint we examine, HNUC, will illustrate this.

When assessing the entire parse of a string, ONS examines each σ node in the parse and assesses one mark *ONS for each such node which lacks onset. Introducing a bit of useful notation, let A be a prosodic parse of an input string, and let $\text{ONS}(A) = (*\text{ONS}, *\text{ONS}, \dots)$ be a list containing one mark *ONS for each onsetless syllable in A. Thus for example $\text{ONS}(.tx\acute{z}.\acute{n}t.) = (*\text{ONS})$: the second, onsetless, syllable earns the parse *.txź.ńt.* its sole *ONS mark. (Here we use $\acute{z}$ to indicate that z is parsed as a nucleus.)

ONS provides a criterion for comparing the Harmony of two parses A and B; we determine which of A or B is more harmonic ('less marked') by comparing $\text{ONS}(A)$ and $\text{ONS}(B)$ to see which contains fewer *ONS marks. We can notate this as follows:

$$A >_{\text{ONS}}{}^{\text{parse}} B \text{ iff } \text{ONS}(A) >^{(*)} \text{ONS}(B)$$

where '$>_{\text{ONS}}{}^{\text{parse}}$' denotes comparison of entire parses and '$\text{ONS}(A) >^{(*)} \text{ONS}(B)$' means 'the list $\text{ONS}(A)$ contains fewer marks *ONS than the list $\text{ONS}(B)$'. (We will use the notation '$(*)$' as a mnemonic for 'list of marks'.) If the lists are the same length, then we write[11]

$$A \approx_{\text{ONS}}{}^{\text{parse}} B \text{ iff } \text{ONS}(A) \approx^{(*)} \text{ONS}(B).$$

It is extremely important to realize that what is crucial to $>^{(*)}$ is not numerical counting, but simply comparisons of more or less. This can be emphasized through a recursive definition of $>^{(*)}$, a definition which turns out to provide the basis for the entire Optimality Theory formalism for Harmony evaluation. The intuition behind this recursive definition is very simple.

Suppose we are given two lists of identical marks *$\mathbb{C}$; we need to determine which list is shorter, and we can't count. Here's what we do. First, we check to see if either list is empty. If both are, the conclusion is that neither list is shorter. If one list is empty and the other isn't, the empty one is shorter. If neither is empty, then we remove one mark *$\mathbb{C}$ from each list, and start all over. The process will eventually terminate with a correct conclusion about which list is the shorter – but with no information about the numerical lengths of the lists.

Formalizing this recursive definition is straightforward; it is also worthwhile, since the definition will be needed anyway to characterize the full means of evaluating the relative harmonies of two candidate parses.

We assume two simple operations for manipulating lists. The operation we'll call **FM** extracts the First Member (or ForeMost element) of a list; this is what we use to extract the First Mark *C from each list. The other operation **Rest** takes a list, throws away its First Member, and returns the rest of the list; we use this for the recursive step of 'starting over', asking which list is shorter after the first * has been thrown out of each.

Since we keep throwing out marks until none are left, it's also important to deal with the case of empty lists. We let ( ) denote an empty list, and we define FM so that when it operates on ( ), its value is ø, the null element.

Now let α and β be two lists of marks. We write $\alpha >^{(*)} \beta$ for 'α is more harmonic than β', which in the current context means 'α is *shorter* than β', since marks are anti-harmonic. To express the fact that an empty list of marks is more harmonic than a non-empty list, or equivalently that a null first element indicates a more harmonic list than does a non-null first element *C, we adopt the following relation between single marks:

(96)   Marks are Anti-harmonic
$$\text{ø} >^* \text{*C}$$

Remembering that $\approx$ denotes 'equally harmonic', we also note the obvious facts about identical single marks:

$$\text{ø} \approx^* \text{ø} \text{ and } \text{*C} \approx^* \text{*C}$$

Our recursive definition of $>^{(*)}$ can now be given as follows, where α and β denote two lists of identical marks:

(97)   Harmonic Ordering – Lists of Identical Marks
   $\alpha >^{(*)} \beta$ iff either:
      (i) $FM(\alpha) >^* FM(\beta)$
or
      (ii) $FM(\alpha) \approx^* FM(\beta)$ and $Rest(\alpha) >^{(*)} Rest(\beta)$

'$\beta <^{(*)} \alpha$' is equivalent to '$\alpha >^{(*)} \beta$'; '$\alpha \approx^{(*)} \beta$' is equivalent to 'neither $\alpha >^{(*)} \beta$ nor $\beta >^{(*)} \alpha$'. (In subsequent order definitions, we will omit the obvious counterparts of the final sentence defining $<^{(*)}$ and $\approx^{(*)}$ in terms of $>^{(*)}$.)

To repeat the basic idea of the definition one more time in English: α is shorter than β iff (if and only if) one of the following is true: (i) the first member of α is null and the first member of β is not (i.e., α is empty and β is not), or (ii) the list left over after removing the first member of α is shorter than the list left over after removing the first member of β.[12]

Now we can say precisely how ONS assesses the relative Harmony of two candidate parses, say .tx́.znt́. and .txź.ńt. ONS assesses the first as more harmonic than the second, because the second has an onsetless syllable and the first does not. We write this as follows:

.tx́.znt́. $>_{ONS}^{parse}$ .txź.ńt. because $ONS(.tx́.znt́.) = ( ) >^{(*)} (*ONS) = ONS(.txź.ńt.)$

where $>^{(*)}$ is defined in (97).

As another example:

*.tx́.znt́. ≈*ₒₙₛ*ᵖᵃʳˢᵉ .txź.nt́.* because Oɴs(.tx́.znt́.) = ( ) ≈*⁽*⁾* ( ) = Oɴs(.txź.nt́.)

In general, for any binary constraint ℂ, the harmonic ordering of entire parses which it determines, $>_{\mathbb{C}}^{parse}$, is defined as follows, where A and B are candidate parses:

(98) Harmonic Ordering of Forms – Entire Parses, Single Constraint ℂ
        A $>_{\mathbb{C}}^{parse}$ B iff ℂ(A) $>^{(*)}$ ℂ(B)

with $>^{(*)}$ as defined in (97).

It turns out that these definitions of $>^{(*)}$ (97) and $>_{\mathbb{C}}^{parse}$ (98), which we have developed for binary constraints (like Oɴs), apply equally to non-binary constraints (like Hɴᴜᴄ); in the general case, a constraint's definition includes a harmonic ordering of the various types of marks it generates. The importance of the definition justifies bringing it all together in self-contained form:

(99) Harmonic Ordering of Forms – Entire Parse, Single Constraint
        Let ℂ denote a constraint. Let A,B be two candidate parses, and let α,β be the
        lists of marks assigned them by ℂ:
        α ≡ ℂ(A),   β ≡ ℂ(B)
        ℂ by definition provides a Harmony order $>^{*}$ of the marks it generates. This
        order is extended to a Harmony order $>^{(*)}$ over lists of marks as follows:
        α $>^{(*)}$ β iff either:
                (i)   FM(α) $>^{*}$ FM(β)
            or
                (ii) FM(α) ≈* FM(β) and Rest(α) $>^{(*)}$ Rest(β)
        This order $>^{(*)}$ is in turn extended to a Harmony order over candidate parses
        (with respect to ℂ), $>_{\mathbb{C}}^{parse}$, as follows:
        A $>_{\mathbb{C}}^{parse}$ B iff ℂ(A) ≡ α $>^{(*)}$ β ≡ ℂ(B)

The case we have so far considered, when ℂ is binary, is the simplest precisely because the Harmony order over marks which gets the whole definition going, $>^{*}$, is so trivial:

ø $>^{*}$ *ℂ

'a mark absent is more harmonic than one present' (96). In the case we consider next, however, the ordering of the marks provided by ℂ, $>^{*}$, is more interesting.

5.2.1.2 *Hɴᴜᴄ: Non-binary constraints*
Turn now to Hɴᴜᴄ. When it examines a single syllable, Hɴᴜᴄ can usefully be thought of as generating a symbol designating the nucleus of that syllable; if the nucleus is *n*, then Hɴᴜᴄ generates *ń*. Hɴᴜᴄ arranges these nucleus symbols in a Harmony order, in which $\hat{x} >_{Hɴᴜᴄ} \hat{y}$ if and only if x is more sonorous than y:
|x| > |y|.

If A is an entire prosodic parse, Hnuc generates a list of all the nuclei in A. For reasons soon to be apparent, it will be convenient to think of Hnuc as generating a list of nuclei *sorted from most to least harmonic, according to Hnuc* – i.e., from most to least sonorous. So, for example, Hnuc(.txź.nt.) = (ń, ź).

When Hnuc evaluates the relative harmonies of two entire syllabifications A and B, it first compares the most harmonic nucleus of A with the most harmonic nucleus of B: if that of A is more sonorous, then A is the winner without further ado. Since the lists of nuclei Hnuc(A) and Hnuc(B) are assumed sorted from most to least harmonic, this process is simply to compare the First Member of Hnuc(A) with the First Member of Hnuc(B): if one is more harmonic than the other, according to Hnuc, the more harmonic nucleus wins the competition for its entire parse. If, on the other hand, the two First Members of Hnuc(A) and Hnuc(B) are equally harmonic according to Hnuc (i.e., equally sonorous), then we eject these two First Members from their respective lists and start over, comparing the Rest of the nuclei in exactly the same fashion.

This procedure is exactly the one formalized above in (99). We illustrate the formal definition by examining how Hnuc determines the relative harmonies of

$$A \equiv .t\acute{x}.z\acute{n}t. \quad \text{and} \quad B \equiv .\acute{i}x.z\acute{n}t.$$

First, $\mathbb{C} \equiv$ Hnuc assigns the following:

$$\alpha \equiv \mathbb{C}(A) = (\acute{n}, \acute{x}) \qquad \beta \equiv \mathbb{C}(B) = (\acute{n}, \acute{i})$$

To rank the parses A and B, i.e. to determine whether

$$A >_{\mathbb{C}}^{\text{parse}} B,$$

we must rank their list of marks according to $\mathbb{C}$, i.e. determine whether

$$\mathbb{C}(A) \equiv \alpha >^{(*)} \beta \equiv \mathbb{C}(B).$$

To do this, we examine the First Marks of each list, and determine whether

$$FM(\alpha) >^* FM(\beta).$$

As it happens,

$$FM(\alpha) \approx FM(\beta),$$

since both First Marks are $\acute{n}$, so we must discard the First Marks and examine the Rest, to determine whether

$$\alpha' \equiv \text{Rest}(\alpha) >^{(*)} \text{Rest}(\beta) \equiv \beta'.$$

Here,

$$\alpha' = (\acute{x}); \quad \beta' = (\acute{i}).$$

So again we consider First Marks, to determine whether

$FM(\alpha') >^* FM(\beta')$.

Indeed this is the case:

$FM(\alpha') = \acute{x} >^* \acute{t} = FM(\beta')$

since $|x| > |t|$. Thus we finally conclude that

$.t\acute{x}.z\acute{n}t. >_{\text{HNUC}}^{\text{parse}} .\acute{t}x.z\acute{n}t.$

HNUC assesses nuclei $\acute{x}$ from most to least harmonic, and that is how they are ordered in the lists HNUC generates for Harmony evaluation. HNUC is an unusual constraint in this regard; the other non-binary constraints we consider in this work will compare their *worst* marks first; the mark lists they generate are ordered from least- to most-harmonic. Both kinds of constraints are treated by the same definition (99). The issue of whether mark lists should be generated worst- or best-first will often not arise, for one of two reasons. First, if a constraint $\mathbb{C}$ is binary, the question is meaningless because all the marks it generates are identical: $*\mathbb{C}$. Alternatively, if a constraint applies only once to an entire parse, then it will generate only one mark per candidate, and the issue of ordering multiple marks does not even arise. (Several examples of such constraints, including edgemostness of main stress, or edgemostness of an infix, are discussed in §4 [omitted here – Ed.].) But for constraints like HNUC which are non-binary and which apply multiply in a candidate parse, part of the definition of the constraint must be whether it lists worst- or best-marks first.

5.2.2   Comparison of entire candidates by an entire constraint hierarchy

We have now defined how a single constraint evaluates the relative Harmonies of entire candidate parses (99). It remains to show how a collection of such constraints, arranged in a strict domination hierarchy $[\mathbb{C}_1 \gg \mathbb{C}_2 \gg \ldots]$, *together* perform such an evaluation: that is, how constraints interact.

Consider the part of the Berber constraint hierarchy we have so far developed: [ONS ≫ HNUC]. The entire hierarchy can be regarded as assigning to a complete parse such as *.txź.ńt.* the following list of lists of marks:

(100a)   [ONS ≫ HNUC](*.txź.ńt.*) = [ONS(*.txź.ńt.*), HNUC(*.txź.ńt.*)] = [(*ONS), (ń, ź)]

The First Member here is the list of marks assigned by the dominant constraint: (*ONS). Following are the lists produced by successive constraints down the domination hierarchy; in this case, there is just the one other list assigned by HNUC. As always, the nuclei are ordered from most- to least-harmonic by HNUC.

We use square brackets to delimit this list of lists, but this is only to aid the eye, and to suggest the connection with constraint hierarchies, which we also enclose in square brackets. Square and round brackets are formally equivalent here, in the sense that they are treated identically by the list-manipulating operations FM and Rest.

The general definition of the list of lists of marks assigned by a constraint hierarchy is simply:

(101)   Marks Assigned by an Entire Constraint Hierarchy
        The marks assigned to an entire parse A by a constraint hierarchy [C1 ≫
        C2 ≫ ...] is the following list of lists of marks:
        [C1 ≫ C2 ≫ ...](A) ≡ [C1(A), C2(A), ...]

Consider a second example, .tx̂.zn̂t.:

(100b)   [ONS ≫ HNUC](.tx̂.zn̂t.) = [ONS(.tx̂.zn̂t.), HNUC(.tx̂.zn̂t.)] = [( ), (n̂, x̂)]

Since there are no onsetless syllables in this parse, ONS(.tx̂.zn̂t.) = ( ), the empty list. A third example is:

(100c)   [ONS ≫ HNUC](.îx.zn̂t.) = [( ), (n̂, t̂)]

As always in Berber, the ONS constraint is lifted phrase-initially, so this parse incurs no marks *ONS.

Now we are ready to harmonically rank these three parses. Corresponding directly to the example tableau (17) of §2, repeated here:

(102)   Constraint Tableau for Three Parses of /txznt/

Candidates	ONS	HNUC
☞ .tx̂.zn̂t.		n̂ x̂
.îx.zn̂t.		n̂ t̂!
.txẑ.n̂t.	*!	n̂ ẑ

we have, from (100a–c):

(103)   Marks Assessed by the Constraint Hierarchy on Three Parses of /txznt/

A	[ONS ≫ HNUC] (A)
.tx̂.zn̂t.	[( ) , (n̂ x̂)]
.îx.zn̂t.	[( ) , (n̂ t̂)]
.txẑ.n̂t.	[(*ONS) , (n̂ ẑ)]

To see how to define the Harmony order $>_{[ONS \gg HNUC]}$ that the constraint hierarchy imposes on the candidate parses, let's first review how Harmony comparisons are performed with the tableau (102). We start by examining the marks in the first,

Ons, column. Only the candidates which fare best by these marks survive for further consideration. In this case, one candidate, *.txź.ńt.*, is ruled out because it has a mark *Ons while the other two do not. That is, this candidate is less harmonic than the other two with respect to the hierarchy [Ons ≫ Hnuc] because it is less harmonic than the other two with respect to the dominant individual constraint Ons. The remaining two parses *.tx̂.zńt.* and *.îx.zńt.* are equally harmonic with respect to Ons, and so to determine their relative Harmonies with respect to [Ons ≫ Hnuc] we must continue by comparing them with respect to the next constraint down the hierarchy, Hnuc. These two parses are compared by the individual constraint Hnuc in just the way we have already defined: the most harmonic nuclei are compared first, and since this fails to determine a winner, the next-most harmonic nuclei are compared, yielding the final determination that *.tx̂.zńt.* $>_{[\text{Ons} \gg \text{Hnuc}]}$ *.îx.zńt.*

For the case of [Ons ≫ Hnuc], the definition should now be clear:

(104)   Harmonic Ordering of Forms – Entire Parses by [Ons ≫ Hnuc]

$A >_{[\text{Ons} \gg \text{Hnuc}]} B$ iff either

    (i) $A >_{\text{Ons}} B$

or

    (ii) $A \approx_{\text{Ons}} B$ and $A >_{\text{Hnuc}} B$

For a general constraint hierarchy, we have the following recursive definition:

(105)   Harmonic Ordering of Forms – Entire Parse, Entire Constraint Hierarchy

$A >_{[\text{C1} \gg \text{C2} \gg \ldots]} B$ iff either

    (i) $A >_{\text{C1}} B$

or

    (ii) $A \approx_{\text{C1}} B$ and $A >_{[\text{C2} \gg \ldots]} B$

All the orderings in (104) and (105) are of complete parses, and we have therefore omitted the superscript ^parse. The Harmony order presupposed by this definition, $>_{\text{C1}}{}^{\text{parse}}$, the order on entire parses determined by the single constraint C1, is defined in (99).

It is worth showing that the definitions of whole-parse Harmony orderings by a single constraint $>_{\text{C}}$ (99) and by a constraint hierarchy $>_{[\text{C1} \gg \text{C2} \ldots]}$ (105) are essentially identical. To see this, we need only bring in FM and Rest explicitly, and insert them into (105); the result is the following:

(106)   Harmonic Ordering of Forms – Entire Parses, Entire Constraint Hierarchy (Opaque Version)

Let $\text{CH} \equiv [\text{C1} \gg \text{C2} \gg \ldots]$ be a constraint hierarchy and let A,B be two candidate parses. Let α,β be the two lists of lists of marks assigned to these parses by the hierarchy:

$\alpha \equiv \text{CH}(A), \quad \beta \equiv \text{CH}(B)$

It follows that:

$\text{FM}(\alpha) = \text{C1}(A), \quad \text{Rest}(\alpha) = [\text{C2} \gg \ldots](A);$

$\text{FM}(\beta) = \text{C1}(B), \quad \text{Rest}(\beta) = [\text{C2} \gg \ldots](B)$

The hierarchy $\mathbb{CH}$ determines a harmonic ordering over lists of lists of marks as follows:

$\alpha >^{[(*)]} \beta$ iff either

(i) $FM(\alpha) >^{(*)} FM(\beta)$ (i.e., $C1(A) >^{(*)} C1(B)$, i.e., $A >_{C1} B$)

or

(ii) $FM(\alpha) \approx^{(*)} FM(\beta)$ (i.e., $A \approx_{C1} B$)

and

$Rest(\alpha) >^{[(*)]} Rest(\beta)$

The harmonic ordering over candidate parses determined by $\mathbb{CH}$ is then defined by:

$A >_{\mathbb{CH}}{}^{parse} B$ iff $\mathbb{CH}(A) \equiv \alpha >^{[(*)]} \beta \equiv \mathbb{CH}(B)$

This definition of $>_{\mathbb{CH}}{}^{parse}$ is identical to the definition of $>_{\mathbb{C}}{}^{parse}$ (99) except for the inevitable substitutions: the single constraint $\mathbb{C}$ of (99) has been replaced with a constraint hierarchy $\mathbb{CH}$ in (106), and, accordingly, one additional level has been added to the collections of marks.

The conclusion, then, is that whole-parse Harmony ordering by constraint hierarchies is defined just like whole-parse Harmony ordering by individual constraints. To compare parses, we compare the marks assigned them by the constraint hierarchy. This we do by first examining the First Marks – those assigned by the dominant constraint. If this fails to decide the matter, we discard the First Marks, take the Rest of the marks (those assigned by the remaining constraints in the hierarchy) and start over with them.

Thus, there is really only one definition for harmonic ordering in Optimality Theory; we can take it to be (99). The case of binary marks (§5.2.1.1) is a simple special case, where 'less marked' reduces to 'fewer (identical) marks'; the case of constraint hierarchies (106) is a mechanical generalization gotten by making obvious substitutions.

5.2.3   Discussion

5.2.3.1   Non-locality of interaction

As mentioned at the end of §2, the way that constraints interact to determine the Harmony ordering of an entire parse is somewhat counter-intuitive. In the Berber hierarchy [ONS ≫ HNUC], for example, perhaps the most obvious way of ordering two parses is to compare the parses syllable-by-syllable, assessing each syllable independently first on whether it meets ONS, and then on how well it fares with HNUC. As it happens, this can be made to work for the special case of [ONS ≫ HNUC] if we evaluate syllables in the correct order: from most- to least-harmonic. This procedure can be shown to more-or-less determine the same optimal parses as the different harmonic ordering procedure we have defined above, but only because some very special conditions obtain: first, there are only two constraints, and second, the dominant one is never violated in optimal parses. [note omitted.] Failing such special conditions, however, harmonic ordering as defined above and as used in the remainder of this work gives results which, as far as we know, cannot be duplicated or even approximated using the more obvious scheme of syllable-by-syllable evaluation. Indeed, when we extend our analysis of Berber even one step beyond the simple pair of constraints ONS and HNUC (see §8), harmonic ordering clearly becomes required to get the correct results.

It is important to note also that harmonic ordering completely finesses a nasty conceptual problem which faces a syllable-by-syllable approach as soon as we expand our horizons even slightly. For in general we need to rank complex parses which contain much more structure than mere syllables. The 'syllable-by-syllable' approach is conceptually really a 'constituent-by-constituent' approach, and in the general case there are many kinds and levels of constituents in the parse. Harmonic ordering completely avoids the need to decide in the general case how to correctly break structures into parts for Harmony evaluation so that all the relevant constraints have the proper domains for their evaluation. In harmonic ordering, each constraint ℂ independently generates its own list of marks ℂ(A) for evaluating a parse A, considering whatever domains within A are appropriate to that constraint. In comparing A with parse B, the marks ℂ(A) are compared with the marks ℂ(B); implicitly, this amounts to comparing A and B with respect to the domain structure peculiar to ℂ. This comparison is decoupled from that based on other constraints which may have quite different domain structure.

The interaction of constraints in a constituent-by-constituent approach is in a sense limited to interactions within a constituent: for ultimately the comparison of competing parses rests on the assessment of the Harmony of individual constituents as evaluated by the set of constraints. Optimality Theory is not limited to constraint interactions which are local in this sense, as a number of the subsequent analyses will illustrate.

5.2.3.2   Strictness of domination
Our expository example [ONS ≫ HNUC] in Berber may fail to convey just how strong a theory of constraint interaction is embodied in harmonic ordering. In determining the correct – optimal – parse of an input, as the constraint hierarchy is descended, each constraint acts to disqualify remaining competitors with absolute independence from all other constraints. A parse found wanting on one constraint has absolutely no hope of redeeming itself by faring well on any or even all lower-ranking constraints. It is remarkable that such an extremely severe theory of constraint interaction has the descriptive power it turns out to possess.

Such strict domination of constraints is less striking in the Berber example we have considered than it will be in most subsequent examples. This is because the dominant constraint is never violated in the forms of the language; it is hardly surprising then that it has strict veto power over the lower constraint. In the general case, however, most of the constraints in the hierarchy will *not* be unviolated like ONS is in Berber. Nonetheless, *all* constraints in Optimality Theory, whether violated or not in the forms of the language, have the same strict veto power over lower constraints that ONS has in Berber.

5.2.3.3   Serial vs. Parallel Harmony Evaluation and Gen
Universal Grammar must also provide a function Gen that admits the candidates to be evaluated. In the discussion above we have entertained two different conceptions of Gen. The first, closer to standard generative theory, is based on serial or derivational processing; some general procedure (Do-α) is allowed to make a certain

single modification to the input, producing the candidate set of all possible out-comes of such modification. This is then evaluated; and the process continues with the output so determined. In this serial version of grammar, the theory of rules is narrowly circumscribed, but it is inaccurate to think of it as trivial. There are constraints inherent in the limitation to a single operation; and in the requirement that each individual operation in the sequence improve Harmony. (An example that springs to mind is the Move-x theory of rhythmic adjustments in Prince 1983; it is argued for precisely on the basis of entailments that follow from these two conditions, pp. 31–43.)

In the second, parallel-processing conception of Gen, all possible ultimate outputs are contemplated at once. Here the theory of operations is indeed rendered trivial; all that matters is what structures are admitted. Much of the analysis given in this work will be in the parallel mode, and some of the results will absolutely require it. But it is important to keep in mind that the serial/parallel distinction pertains to Gen and not to the issue of harmonic evaluation *per se*. It is an empirical question of no little interest how Gen is to be construed, and one to which the answer will become clear only as the characteristics of harmonic evaluation emerge in the con-text of detailed, full-scale, depth-plumbing, scholarly, and responsible analyses.

Many different theories of the structure of phonological outputs can be equally well accommodated in Gen, and the framework of Optimality Theory *per se* involves no commitment to any set of such assumptions. Of course, different structural assumptions can suggest or force different formal approaches to the way that Optim-ality theoretic constraints work. In this work, to implement faithfulness straight-forwardly, we entertain a non-obvious assumption about Gen which will be useful in implementing the parallel conception of the theory: we will assume, following the lead of McCarthy 1979 and Itô 1986, 1989, that every output for an input *In* – every member of Gen(*In*) – includes *In* as a substructure. In the theory of syllable structure developed in Part II, Gen(/txznt/) will be a set of possible syllabifica-tions of /txznt/ all of which contain the input string /txznt/, with each underlying segment either associated to syllable structure or left unassociated. We will interpret unassociated underlying segments as phonetically unrealized (*cf.* 'Stray Erasure'). On this conception, input segments are never 'deleted' in the sense of disappearing from the structural description; rather, they may simply be left free – unparsed. Our discussion of Berber in this section has focused on a fairly restricted subset of the full candidate set we will subsequently consider; we have considered only syllabifications in which underlying segments are in one-to-one correspondence with syllable positions. In following sections, we turn to languages which, unlike Berber, exhibit syllabifications manifesting deletion and/or epenthesis.

5.2.3.4   Binary vs. non-binary constraints

As might be suspected, it will turn out that the work done by a single non-binary constraint like HNUC can also be done by a *set* (indeed a sub-hierarchy) of binary constraints. This will prove fundamental for the construction of the Basic Segmental Syllable Theory in §8, and we postpone treatment of the issue until then. For now it suffices simply to remark that the division of constraints into those which are binary and those which are not, a division which we have adopted earlier in this section, is not in fact as theoretically fundamental as it may at this point appear.

5.3   Pāṇini's Theorem on Constraint-ranking

One consequence of the definition of harmonic ordering is that there are conditions under which the presence of a more general constraint in a superordinate position in a hierarchy will eliminate all opportunities for a more specialized constraint in a subordinate position to have any effects in the grammar. The theorem states, roughly, that if one constraint is more general than another in the sense that the set of inputs to which one constraint applies non-vacuously includes the other's non-vacuous input set, and if the two constraints *conflict* on inputs to which the more specific applies non-vacuously, then the more specific constraint must dominate the more general one in order for its effects to be visible in the grammar. (This is an oversimplified first cut at the true result; such claims must be stated carefully.) Intuitively, the idea is that if the more specific constraint were lower-ranked, then for any input to which it applies non-vacuously, its effects would be over-ruled by the higher-ranked constraint with which it conflicts. The utility of the result is that it allows the analyst to spot certain easy ranking arguments.

We call this Pāṇini's Theorem on Constraint-ranking, in honor of the first known investigator in the area; in §7.2.1 [omitted here – Ed.], we discuss some relations to the Elsewhere Condition of Anderson 1969 and Kiparsky 1973. In this section we introduce some concepts necessary to develop a result; the proof is relegated to the Appendix [omitted here – Ed.]. The result we state is undoubtedly but one of a family of related theorems which cover cases in which one constraint hides another.

Due to the complexities surrounding this issue, we will formally state and prove the result only in the case of constraints which are Boolean at the whole-parse level: constraints which assign a single mark to an entire parse when they are violated, and no mark when they are satisfied.

(107)   Dfn. Separation
A constraint $\mathbb{C}$ *separates* a set of structures if it is satisfied by some members of the set and violated by others.

(108)   Dfn. Non-vacuous Application
A constraint $\mathbb{C}$ *applies non-vacuously* to an input i if it separates Gen(i), the set of candidate parses of i admitted by Universal Grammar.

A constraint may sometimes apply vacuously to an input, in that every possible parse of i satisfies the constraint. For example, in §7 [omitted here – Ed.] we will introduce a constraint FREE-V which requires that stem-final vowels *not* be parsed into syllable structure. (E.g., FREE-V favors *yi.li.yil.⟨i⟩* over faithful *yi.li.yi.li* 'oyster sp.' in Lardil.) Clearly, this constraint is vacuously satisfied for a stem which is not vowel-final (e.g., *kentapal* 'dugong'); all the parses of such an input meet the constraint since none of them have a stem-final vowel which is parsed!

(109)   Dfn. Accepts
A constraint hierarchy $\mathbb{CH}$ *accepts* a parse P of an input i if P is an optimal parse of i.

When CH is the entire constraint hierarchy of a grammar, it is normally the case that only one parse P of an input i is optimal: the constraint set is sufficient to winnow the candidate set down to a single output. In this section we will need to consider, more generally, initial portions of the constraint hierarchy of a grammar, i.e., all the constraints from the highest-ranked down to some constraint which may not be the lowest-ranked. In these cases, CH will often consist of just a few constraints, insufficient to winnow the candidate set down to a single parse; in that case, CH will accept an entire set of parses, all equally harmonic, and all more harmonic than the competitors filtered out by CH.

(110)   Dfn. Active
        Let C be a constraint in a constraint hierarchy CH and let i be an input. C is *active on i in* CH if C separates the candidates in Gen(i) which are admitted by the portion of CH which dominates C.

In other words, the portion of CH which dominates C filters the set of candidate parses of i to some degree, and then C filters it further. When C is not active for an input i in CH, the result of parsing i is not at all affected by the presence of C in the hierarchy.

(111)   Pāṇinian Constraint Relation
        Let S and G be two constraints. S *stands to* G *as special to general in a Pāṇinian relation* if, for any input i to which S applies non-vacuously, any parse of i which satisfies S fails G.

For example, the constraint FREE-V stands to PARSE as special to general in a Pāṇinian relation: for any input to which FREE-V applies non-vacuously (that is, to any input with a stem-final vowel V), any parse which satisfies FREE-V (that is, which leaves V unparsed) must violate PARSE (in virtue of leaving V unparsed). For inputs to which the more specialized constraint FREE-V does *not* apply non-vacuously (C-final stems), the more general constraint PARSE need not conflict with the more specific one (for C-final stems, FREE-V is vacuously satisfied, but PARSE is violated in some parses and satisfied in others).
    Now we are finally set to state the theorem:

(112)   Pāṇini's Theorem on Constraint-ranking
        Let S and G stand as specific to general in a Pāṇinian constraint relation. Suppose these constraints are part of a constraint hierarchy CH, and that G is active in CH on some input i. If G≫S, then S is not active on i.

In §7 [omitted here – Ed.], we will use this theorem to conclude that in the grammar of Lardil, the more specific constraint FREE-V must dominate the more general constraint PARSE with which it conflicts, since otherwise FREE-V could not be active on an input like /yiliyili/.
[. . .]

6 Syllable Structure Typology I: The C/V Theory

6.1 The Jakobson typology

It is well known that every language admits consonant-initial syllables .CV~., and that some languages allow no others; that every language admits open syllables .~V. and that some admit only those. Jakobson puts it this way: "There are languages lacking syllables with initial vowels and/or syllables with final consonants, but there are no languages devoid of syllables with initial consonants or of syllables with final vowels" (Jakobson 1962: 526; Clements & Keyser 1983: 29).

As noted in the fundamental work of Clements & Keyser 1983, whence the quotation was cadged, these observations yield exactly four possible inventories. With the notation Σ^{XYZ} to denote the language whose syllables fit the pattern XYZ, the Jakobson typology can be laid out as follows, in terms of whether onsets and codas are obligatory, forbidden, or neither:

(113) CV Syllable Structure Typology

		Onsets	
		required	not required
Codas	forbidden	Σ^{CV}	$\Sigma^{(C)V}$
	allowed	$\Sigma^{CV(C)}$	$\Sigma^{(C)V(C)}$

There are two independent dimensions of choice: whether onsets are required (first column) or not (second column); whether codas are forbidden (row one) or allowed (row two).

The *Basic Syllable Structure Constraints*, which generate this typology, divide notionally into two groups. First, the structural or 'markedness' constraints – those that enforce the universally unmarked characteristics of the structures involved:

(114) ONS
A syllable must have an onset.

(115) −CODA
A syllable must *not* have a coda.

Second, those that constrain the relation between output structure and input:

(116) PARSE
Underlying segments must be parsed into syllable structure.

(117) FILL
Syllable positions must be filled with underlying segments.

PARSE and FILL are Faithfulness constraints: they declare that perfectly well-formed syllable structures are those in which input segments are in one-to-one correspondence with syllable positions.[13] Given an interpretive phonetic component that omits unparsed material and supplies segmental values for empty nodes, the ultimate force of PARSE is to forbid deletion; of FILL, to forbid insertion.

It is relatively straightforward to show that the Factorial Typology on the Basic Syllable Structure Constraints produces just the Jakobson Typology. Suppose Faithfulness dominates *both* structural constraints. Then the primacy of respecting the input will be able to force violations of both ONS and –CODA. The string /V/ will be parsed as an onsetless syllable, violating ONS; the string /CVC/ will be parsed as a closed syllable, violating –CODA: this gives the language $\Sigma^{(C)V(C)}$.

When a member of the Faithfulness family is dominated by one or the other or both of the structural constraints, a more aggressive parsing of the input will result. In those rankings where ONS dominates a Faithfulness constraint, every syllable must absolutely have an onset. Input /V/ cannot be given its faithful parse as an onsetless syllable; it can either remain completely unsyllabified, violating PARSE, or it can be parsed as .□V., where '□' refers to an empty structural position, violating FILL.

Those rankings in which –CODA dominates a Faithfulness constraint correspond to languages in which codas are forbidden. The imperative to avoid codas must be honored, even at the cost of expanding upon the input (*FILL) or leaving part of it outside of prosodic structure (*PARSE).

In the next section, we will explore these observations in detail. The resulting Factorial construal of the Jakobson Typology looks like this (with '$\mathcal{F}$' denoting the Faithfulness set and 'F_i' a member of it):

(118)   Factorial Jakobson Typology

		Onsets	
		ONS ≫ F_j	$\mathcal{F}$ ≫ ONS
Codas	–CODA ≫ F_i	Σ^{CV}	$\Sigma^{(C)V}$
	$\mathcal{F}$ ≫ –CODA	$\Sigma^{CV(C)}$	$\Sigma^{(C)V(C)}$

At this point, it is reasonable to ask whether there is any interesting difference between our claim that constraints like ONS and –CODA can be violated under domination and the more familiar claim that constraints can be *turned off* – simply omitted from consideration. The Factorial Jakobson Typology, as simple as it is, contains a clear case that highlights the distinction. Consider the language $\Sigma^{(C)V(C)}$. Since onsets are not required and codas are not forbidden, the Boolean temptation would be to hold that both ONS and –CODA are merely absent. Even in such a language, however, one can find certain circumstances in which the force of the supposedly nonexistent structural constraints is felt. The string CVCV, for example, would always be parsed .CV.CV. and never .CVC.V. Yet both parses consist of licit syllables; both are entirely faithful to the input. The difference is that .CV.CV.

satisfies ONS and –CODA while .CVC.V. violates both of them. We are forced to conclude that (at least) one of them is still active in the language, even though roundly violated in many circumstances. This is the basic prediction of ranking theory: when all else is equal, a subordinate constraint can emerge decisively. In the end, summary global statements about *inventory*, like Jakobson's, emerge through the cumulative effects of the actual parsing of individual items.

6.2 The Faithfulness interactions

Faithfulness involves more than one type of constraint. Ranking members of the Faithfulness family with respect to each other and with respect to the structural constraints ONS and –CODA yields a typology of the ways that languages can enforce (and fail to enforce) those constraints. We will consider only the Faithfulness constraints PARSE and FILL (the latter to be distinguished by sensitivity to Nucleus or Ons); these are the bare minimum required to obtain a contentful, usable theory, and we will accordingly abstract away from distinctions that they do not make, such as between deleting the first or second element of a cluster, or between forms involving metathesis, vocalization of consonants, de-vocalization of vowels, and so on, all of which involve further Faithfulness constraints, whose interactions with each other and with the markedness constraints will be entirely parallel to those discussed here.

6.2.1 Groundwork

To make clear the content of the Basic Syllable Structure Constraints ONS, –CODA, PARSE, and FILL, it is useful to lay out the Galilean arena in which they play. The inputs we will be considering are C/V sequences like CVVCC; that is, any and all strings of the language {C,V}*. The grammar must be able to contend with any input from this set: we do not assume an additional component of language-particular input-defining conditions; the universal constraints and their ranking must do all the work (see §9.3 for further discussion). The possible structures which may be assigned to an input are all those which parse it into syllables; more precisely, into zero or more syllables. There is no insertion or deletion of *segments* C, V.

What is a syllable? To avoid irrelevant distractions, we adopt the simple analysis that the syllable node σ must have a daughter *Nuc* and *may* have as leftmost and rightmost daughters the nodes *Ons* and *Cod*.[14] The nodes Ons, Nuc, and Cod, in turn, may each dominate C's and V's, or they may be empty. Each Ons, Nuc, or Cod node may dominate at most one terminal element C or V.

These assumptions delimit the set of candidate analyses. Here we list and name some of the more salient of the mentioned constraints. By our simplifying assumptions, they will stand at the top of the hierarchy and will be therefore unviolated in every system under discussion:

Syllable form:
(119) NUC
Syllables must have nuclei.

(120)   *COMPLEX
No more than one C or V may associate to any syllable position node.[15]

Definition of C and V, using M(argin) for Ons and Cod and P(eak) for Nuc:
(121)   *M/V
V may not associate to Margin nodes (Ons and Cod).

(122)   *P/C
C may not associate to Peak (Nuc) nodes.

The theory we examine is this:

(123)   Basic CV Syllable Theory
• Syllable structure is governed by the Basic Syllable Structure Constraints ONS, −CODA, NUC; *COMPLEX, *M/V, *P/C; PARSE, and FILL.
• Of these, ONS, −CODA, PARSE, and FILL may be relatively ranked in any domination order in a particular language, while the others are fixed in superordinate position.
• The Basic Syllable Structure Constraints, ranked in a language-particular hierarchy, will assign to each input its optimal structure, which is the output of the phonology.

The output of the phonology is subject to phonetic interpretation, about which we will here make two assumptions, following familiar proposals in the literature:

(124)   Underparsing Phonetically Realized as Deletion
An input segment unassociated to a syllable position ('underparsing') is not phonetically realized.

This amounts to 'Stray Erasure' (McCarthy 1979, Steriade 1982, Itô 1986, 1989). Epenthesis is handled in the inverse fashion:

(125)   Overparsing Phonetically Realized as Epenthesis
A syllable position node unassociated to an input segment ('overparsing') is phonetically realized through some process of filling in default featural values.

This is the treatment of epenthesis established in such works as Selkirk 1981, LaPointe & Feinstein 1982, Broselow 1982, Archangeli 1984, Kaye & Lowenstamm 1984, Piggott & Singh 1985, and Itô 1986, 1989.

The terms 'underparsing' and 'overparsing' are convenient for referring to parses that violate Faithfulness. If an input segment is not parsed in a given structure (not associated to any syllable position nodes), we will often describe this as 'underparsing' rather than 'deletion' to emphasize the character of our assumptions. For the same reason, if a structure contains an empty syllable structure node (one not associated to an input segment), we will usually speak of 'overparsing' the input rather than 'epenthesis'.

Suppose the phonology assigns to the input /CVVCC/ the following bisyllabic structure, which we write in three equivalent notations:

(126)   Transcription of Syllabic Constituency Relations, from /CVVCC/
   a.

   b.   [$_\sigma$ [$_{Ons}$ C] [$_{Nuc}$ V]] [$_\sigma$ [$_{Ons}$] [$_{Nuc}$ V] [$_{Cod}$ C]] C

   c.   .CV́.□V́C.⟨C⟩

Phonetic interpretation ignores the final C and supplies featural structure for a consonant to fill the onset of the second syllable.

   The dot notation (126c) is the most concise and readable; we will use it throughout. The interpretation is as follows:

(127)   Notation
   a.   .X.   'the string X *is a* syllable'
   b.   ⟨x⟩   'the element x has no parent node; is free (unparsed)'
   c.   □   'a node *Ons, Nuc,* or *Cod* is empty'
   d.   x́   'the element x is a Nuc'

In the CV theory, we will drop the redundant nucleus-marking accent on V́. Observe that this is a 'notation' in the most inert and de-ontologized sense of the term: a set of typographical conventions used to refer to well-defined formal objects. The objects of linguistic theory – syllables here – are not to be confused with the literal characters that depict them. Linguistic operations and assessments apply to structure, not to typography.

   We will say a syllable 'has an onset' if, like both syllables in the example (126), it has an Ons node, whether or not that node is associated to an underlying C; similarly with nuclei and codas.

   The technical content of the Basic Syllable Structure Constraints (114–15) above can now be specified. The constraint ONS (114) requires that a syllable node σ have as its leftmost child an Ons node; the presence of the Ons node satisfies ONS whether empty or filled. The constraint –CODA (115) requires that syllable nodes have no Cod child; the presence of a Cod node violates –CODA whether or not that node is filled. Equivalently, any syllable which does not contain an onset in this sense earns its structure a mark of violation *ONS; a syllable which does contain a coda earns the mark *–CODA.

   The PARSE constraint is met by structures in which all underlying segments are associated to syllable positions; *each* unassociated or free segment earns a mark *PARSE. This is the penalty for deletion. FILL provides the penalty for epenthesis: each unfilled syllable position node earns a mark *FILL, penalizing insertion. Together, PARSE and FILL urge that the assigned syllable structure be faithful to the input string, in the sense of a one-to-one correspondence between syllable positions and segments. This is Faithfulness in the basic theory.

6.2.2   Basic CV syllable theory

We now pursue the consequences of our assumptions. One important aspect of the Jakobson Typology (113) follows immediately:

(128)   THM. Universally Optimal Syllables
No language may prohibit the syllable .CV. Thus, no language prohibits onsets or requires codas.

To see this, consider the input /CV/. The obvious analysis .CV. (i.e., [$_\sigma$ [$_{Ons}$ C] [$_{Nuc}$ V]]) is *universally optimal* in that it violates *none* of the universal constraints of the Basic CV Syllable Theory (123). No alternative analysis, therefore, can be more harmonic. At worst, another analysis can be equally good, but inspection of the alternatives quickly rules out this possibility.

   For example, the analysis .CV☐. violates –CODA and FILL. The analysis .C☐.V. violates ONS in the second syllable and FILL in the first. And so on, through the infinite set of possible analyses – [.⟨C⟩V.], [.C☐.⟨V⟩.], [.☐.C ☐.☐V.], etc. *ad inf*. No matter what the ranking of constraints is, a form that violates even one of them can never be better than a form, like .CV., with no violations at all.

   Because every language has /CV/ input, according to our assumption that every language has the same set of possible inputs, it follows that .CV. can never be prohibited under the Basic Theory.

6.2.2.1   *Onsets*

Our major goal is to explicate the interaction of the structural constraints ONS and –CODA with Faithfulness. We begin with onsets, studying the interaction of ONS with PARSE and FILL, ignoring –CODA for the moment. The simplest interesting input is /V/. All analyses will contain violations; there are three possible one-mark analyses:

(129)   /V/ →

   (1)   .V.   i.e., [$_\sigma$ [$_{Nuc}$ V]]
   (2)   ⟨V⟩   i.e., no syllable structure
   (3)   .☐V.   i.e., [$_\sigma$ [$_{Ons}$] [$_{Nuc}$ V]]

Each of these alternatives violates exactly one of the Basic Syllable Structure Constraints (114–17).

(130)   Best Analyses of /V/

Analysis	Interpretation	Violation	Remarks
.V.	σ lacks Ons	*ONS	satisfies FILL, PARSE
⟨V⟩	null parse	*PARSE	satisfies ONS, FILL
.☐V.	Ons is empty	*FILL	satisfies ONS, PARSE

Every language must evaluate all three analyses. Since the three candidates violate one constraint each, any comparison between them will involve weighing the importance of different violations. The optimal analysis for a given language is determined precisely by whichever of the constraints ONS, PARSE, and FILL is *lowest* in the constraint hierarchy of that language. The lowest constraint incurs the least important violation.

Suppose .V. is the optimal parse of /V/. We have the following tableau:

(131)   Onset Not Required

/V/	FILL	PARSE	ONS
☞ .V.			*
⟨V⟩		* !	
.□V.	* !		

The relative ranking of FILL and PARSE has no effect on the outcome. The violations of PARSE and FILL are fatal because the alternative candidate .V. satisfies both constraints.

Of interest here is the fact that the analysis .V. involves an onsetless syllable. When this analysis is optimal, then the language at hand, by this very fact, does not absolutely require onsets. The other two inferior analyses do succeed in satisfying ONS: ⟨V⟩ achieves this vacuously, creating no syllable at all; .□V. creates an onsetful syllable by positing an empty Ons node, leading to epenthesis. So if .V. is best, it is because ONS is the lowest of the three constraints, and we conclude that the language does not require onsets. We already know from the previous section, Thm. (128), that onsets can never be forbidden. This means the following condition holds:

(132)   If PARSE, FILL ≫ ONS, then onsets are not required.

(The comma'd grouping indicates that PARSE and FILL each dominate ONS, but that there is no implication about their own relative ranking.)

On the other hand, if ONS is not the lowest ranking constraint – if either PARSE or FILL is lowest – then the structure assigned to /V/ will be consistent with the language requiring onsets. The following two tableaux lay this out:

(133)   Enforcement by Overparsing (Epenthesis)

/V/	ONS	PARSE	FILL
.V.	* !		
⟨V⟩		* !	
☞ .□V.			*

(134)   Enforcement by Underparsing (Deletion)

/V/	FILL	ONS	PARSE
.V.		* !	
☞ ⟨V⟩			*
.□V.	* !		

These lucubrations lead to the converse of (132):

(135)   If ONS dominates either PARSE or FILL, then onsets are required.

   There is an important difference in status between the two ONS-related implications. To prove that something is *optional*, in the sense of 'not forbidden' or 'not required' in the inventory, one need merely exhibit one case in which it is observed and one in which it isn't. To prove that something is *required*, one must show that everything in the universe observes it. Thus, formal proof of (135) requires considering not just one trial input, as we have done, but the whole (infinite) class of strings on {C,V}* which we are taking to define the universal set of possible inputs for the Basic Theory. We postpone this exercise until the appendix [omitted here – Ed.]; in §8 we will develop general techniques which will enable us to extend the above analysis to arbitrary strings, showing that what is true of /V/ and /CV/ is true of all inputs.
   The results of this discussion can be summarized as follows:

(136)   Onset Theorem
        Onsets are not required in a language if ONS is dominated by both PARSE and FILL.
        Otherwise, onsets are required.

In the latter case, ONS is enforced by underparsing (phonetic deletion) if PARSE is the lowest-ranking of the three constraints; and by overparsing (phonetic epenthesis) if FILL is lowest.
   If FILL is to be articulated into a family of node-specific constraints, then the version of FILL that is relevant here is FILL^{Ons}. With this in mind, the onset finding may be recorded as follows:

Lowest constraint	Onsets are . . .	Enforced by . . .
ONS	Not required	N/A
PARSE	Required	V 'Deletion'
FILL^{Ons}	Required	C 'Epenthesis'

6.2.2.2   Codas
The analysis of onsets has a direct parallel for codas. We consider the input /CVC/ this time; the initial CV provides an onset and nucleus to meet the ONS and NUC

constraints, thereby avoiding any extraneous constraint violations. The final C induces the conflict between –CODA, which prohibits the Cod node, and Faithfulness, which has the effect of requiring just such a node. As in the corresponding onset situation (130), the parses which violate only one of the Basic Syllable Structure Constraints are three in number:

(137)   Best Analyses of /CVC/

Analysis	Interpretation	Violation	Remarks
.CVC.	σ has Cod	*–CODA	satisfies FILL, PARSE
.CV⟨C⟩.	No parse of 2nd C	*PARSE	satisfies –CODA, FILL
.CV.C口̇.	2nd Nuc is empty	*FILL	satisfies –CODA, PARSE

The optimal analysis of /CVC/ in a given language depends on which of the three constraints is lowest in the domination hierarchy. If .CVC. wins, then the language must allow codas; –CODA ranks lowest and violation can be compelled. If .CVC. loses, the optimal analysis must involve open (codaless) syllables; in this case –CODA is enforced through empty nuclear structure (phonetic V-epenthesis) if FILL is lowest, and through non-parsing (phonetic deletion of C) if PARSE is the lowest, most violable constraint. In either case, the result is that open syllables are *required*. This is a claim about the optimal parse of every string in the language, and not just about /CVC/, and formal proof is necessary; see the appendix.

The conclusion, parallel to (136), is this:

(138)   Coda Theorem
Codas are allowed in a language if –CODA is dominated by both PARSE and FILL^{Nuc}.
Otherwise, codas are forbidden.

In the latter case, –CODA is enforced by underparsing (phonetic deletion) if PARSE is the lowest-ranking of the three constraints; and by overparsing (epenthesis) if FILL^{Nuc} is the lowest.

The result can be tabulated like this:

Lowest constraint	Codas are . . .	Enforced by . . .
–CODA	Allowed	N/A
PARSE	Forbidden	C 'Deletion'
FILL^{Nuc}	Forbidden	V 'Epenthesis'

Motivation for distinguishing the constraints FILL^{Ons} and FILL^{Nuc} is now available. Consider the languages Σ^{CV} in which only CV syllables are allowed. Here ONS and –CODA each dominate a member of the Faithfulness group. Enforcement of the dominant constraints will be required. Suppose there is only one FILL constraint, holding over all kinds of nodes. If FILL is the lowest-ranked of the three constraints, we have the following situation:

(139)   Triumph of Epenthesis

Input	Optimal analysis	Phonetic
/V/	.□V.	.CV.
/CVC/	.CV.C□̇.	.CV.CV̇.

The single uniform FILL constraint yokes together the methods of enforcing the onset requirement ('C-epenthesis') and the coda prohibition ('V-epenthesis'). There is no reason to believe that languages Σ^{CV} are obligated to behave in this way; nothing that we know of in the linguistic literature suggests that the appearance of epenthetic onsets requires the appearance of epenthetic nuclei in other circumstances. This infelicitous yoking is avoided by the natural assumption that FILL takes individual node-classes as an argument, yielding $FILL^{Nuc}$ and $FILL^{Ons}$ as the actual constraints. In this way, the priority assigned to filling Ons nodes may be different from that for filling Nuc nodes.[16]

   It is important to note that onset and coda distributions are completely independent in this theory. Any ranking of the onset-governing constraints {ONS, $FILL^{Ons}$, PARSE} may coexist with any ranking of coda-governing constraints {–CODA, $FILL^{Nuc}$, PARSE}, because they have only one constraint, PARSE, in common. The universal factorial typology allows all nine combinations of the three onset patterns given in (136) and the three coda patterns in (138). The full typology of interactions is portrayed in the table below. We use subscripted *del* and *ep* to indicate the phonetic consequences of enforcement; when both are involved, the onset-relevant mode comes first.

(140)   Extended CV Syllable Structure Typology

			Onsets		
			required		not required
			ONS, $FILL^{Ons}$ $\gg$ PARSE	ONS, PARSE $\gg$ $FILL^{Ons}$	PARSE, $FILL^{Ons}$ $\gg$ ONS
Codas	forbidden	–CODA, $FILL^{Nuc}$ $\gg$ PARSE	$\Sigma^{CV}_{del,del}$	$\Sigma^{CV}_{ep,del}$	$\Sigma^{(C)V}_{del}$
		–CODA, PARSE $\gg$ $FILL^{Nuc}$	$\Sigma^{CV}_{del,ep}$	$\Sigma^{CV}_{ep,ep}$	$\Sigma^{(C)V}_{ep}$
	allowed	PARSE, $FILL^{Nuc}$ $\gg$ –CODA	$\Sigma^{CV(C)}_{del}$	$\Sigma^{CV(C)}_{ep}$	$\Sigma^{(C)V(C)}$

If we decline to distinguish between the Faithfulness constraints, this simplifies to the Jakobson Typology of (118).

6.2.3   The theory of epenthesis sites

The chief goal of syllabification-driven theories of epenthesis is to provide a principled account of the location of epenthetic elements (Selkirk 1981, Broselow 1982, LaPointe and Feinstein 1982, Itô 1986, 1989). Theories based on manipulation of the segmental string are capable of little more than summary stipulation on this point (e.g., Levin 1985: 331; see Itô 1986: 159, 1989 for discussion). The theory developed here entails tight restrictions on the distribution of empty nodes in optimal syllabic parses, and therefore meets this goal. We confine attention to the premises of the Basic CV Syllable Structure Theory, which serves as the foundation for investigation of the theory of epenthesis, which ultimately involves segmental and prosodic factors as well.

There are a few fundamental observations to make, from which a full positive characterization of syllabically motivated epenthesis emerges straightaway:

(141)   Prop. 1. $*[\ ]_{Cod}$
   Coda nodes are never empty in any optimal parse.

Structures with unfilled Cod can never be optimal; there is always something better. To see this, take a candidate with an unfilled Cod and simply remove that one node. This gives another candidate which has one less violation of –Coda and one less violation of Fill. Since removing the node has no other effects on the evaluation, the second candidate must be superior to the first. (To show that something is *non-optimal*, we need merely find something better: we don't have to display the best.)

We know from the earlier discussion that Ons and Nuc must be optimally unfilled in certain parses under certain grammars. So the remaining task is to determine the conditions under which these nodes must be posited and left empty.

(142)   Prop. 2. $*.(\square)\acute{\square}.$
   A whole syllable is never empty in any optimal parse.

The same style of argument applies. Consider a parse that has an entirely empty syllable. Remove that syllable. The alternative candidate thereby generated is superior to the original because it has (at least) one less Fill^{Nuc} violation and no new marks. The empty syllable parse can always be bested and is therefore never optimal.

Of course, in the larger scheme of things, whole syllables can be epenthesized, the canonical examples being Lardil and Axininca Campa (Hale 1973, Klokeid 1976, Itô 1986, Wilkinson 1988, Kirchner 1992a; Payne 1981, Payne et al. 1982, Spring 1990, Black 1991, McCarthy & Prince 1993). In all such cases, it is the impact of additional constraints that forces whole-syllable epenthesis. In particular, when the prosody/morphology interface constraints like Lx≈Pr ["every lexical word corresponds to a prosodic word" – Ed.] are taken into account, prosodic minimality requirements can force syllabic epenthesis, as we will see for Lardil in §7 [omitted here – Ed.].

(143)   Prop. 3. *.(□)□̂C.
　　　No syllable can have *Cod* as its only filled position.

Any analysis containing such a syllable is bested by the alternative in which the content of this one syllable (namely 'C') is parsed instead as .C□̂.. This alternative incurs only the single mark *FILL^{Nuc}, but the closed-syllable parse .(□)□̂C. shares this mark and violates –CODA as well. (In addition, the closed-syllable parse must also violate either ONS or FILL^{Ons}.)

　　Such epentheses are not unknown: think of Spanish /slavo/ → *eslavo* and Arabic /ħmarar/ → *ʔiħmarar*. We must argue, as indeed must all syllable theorists, that other constraints are involved (for Arabic, see McCarthy & Prince 1990).

(144)   Prop. 4. *[ ][ ]
　　　Adjacent empty nodes cannot occur in an optimal parse.

Propositions 1, 2, and 3 entail that [ ][ ] cannot occur inside a syllable. This leaves only the intersyllabic environment .C □̂.□V~. This bisyllabic string incurs two marks, *FILL^{Nuc} and *FILL^{Ons}. Consider the alternative parse in which the substring /CV/ is analyzed as tautosyllabic .CV~. This eliminates both marks and incurs no others. It follows that two adjacent epentheses are impossible.

　　We now pull these results together into an omnibus characterization of where empty nodes can be found in optimal parses.

(145)   FILL Violation THM. Location of Possible Epenthesis Sites
　　　Under the Basic Syllable Structure Constraints, epenthesis is limited to the following environments:
　　　a.　Onset, when Nucleus is filled:
　　　　　.□V.
　　　　　.□VC.
　　　b.　Nucleus, when Onset is filled:
　　　　　.C □̂.
　　　　　.C □̂C.
　　　Furthermore, two adjacent epentheses are impossible, even across syllable boundaries.

The last clause rules out, for example, *.C □̂.□V. We note that the Fill Violation Theorem will carry through in the more complex theory developed below in §8, in which the primitive C/V distinction is replaced by a graded sonority-dependent scale. [. . .]

8　Universal Syllable Theory II: Ordinal Construction of C/V and Onset/Coda Licensing Asymmetry

[Limitations of space do not permit inclusion of all of §8 of Prince and Smolensky (1993). But because the results in §8 are important and far-reaching, I have included the introduction to §8, which summarizes those results. – Ed.]

Syllabification must reconcile two conflicting sources of constraint: from the bottom up, each segment's inherent featural suitability for syllable peak or margin; and from top down, the requirements that syllables have certain structures and not others. The core conflict can be addressed in its most naked form through the idealization provided by CV theory. Input C's need to be parsed as margins; input V's need to be parsed as peaks. Syllables need to be structured as Onset-Peak-Coda; ideally, with an onset present and a coda absent. In the Basic Theory, only one input segment is allowed per syllable position. Problematic inputs like /CCVV/ are ones which bring the bottom-up and top-down pressures into conflict. These conflicts are resolved differently in different languages, the possible resolutions forming the typology explored in §6.

The CV theory gives some articulation to the top-down pressures: syllable shapes deviate from the Onset-Peak ideal in the face of bottom-up pressure to parse the input. By contrast, the bottom-up is construed relatively rigidly: C and V either go into their determined positions, or they remain unparsed. In real syllabification, of course, a richer set of possibilities exists. A segment ideally parsed as a peak may actually be parsed as a margin, or vice versa, in response to top-down constraints on syllable shape. One of the most striking examples of the role of optimality principles in syllabification, Tashlhiyt Berber (§2), exploits this possibility with maximal thoroughness. Berber syllabification on the one hand and CV syllabification on the other constitute extremes in the flexibility with which input segments may be parsed into different syllable positions in response to top-down pressure. In between the extremes lies the majority of languages, in which some segments can appear only as margins (like C in the CV theory), other segments only as peaks (like V), and the remaining segments, while ideally parsed into just one of the structural positions, can under sufficient top-down pressure be parsed into others.

In this section we will seek to unify the treatments of the two extremes of syllabification, Berber and the CV theory. Like the CV theory, the theory developed here will deal with an abstract inventory of input segments, but instead of just two abstract segments, each committed to a structural position, the inventory will consist of abstract elements distinguished solely by the property of *sonority*, taken to define a strict order on the set of elements. For mnemonic value we denote these elements $a, i, \ldots, d, t$; but it should be remembered that all dimensions other than sonority are idealized away. In the CV theory, the universally superordinate constraints *M/V and *P/C prohibit parsing V as a margin or C as a peak. In the more realistic theory we now turn to, the corresponding constraints are not universally superordinate: the constraints against parsing any segment α as a margin (*M/α) or as a peak (*P/α) may vary cross-linguistically in their rankings. What Universal Grammar requires is only that more sonorous segments make more harmonic peaks and less harmonic margins.

From these simple assumptions there will emerge a universal typology of inventories of possible onsets, peaks, and codas. The inventories will turn out to be describable in terms of derived parameters π_{Ons}, π_{Nuc}, and π_{Cod}, each with values ranging over the sonority order. The margin inventories are the sets of segments *less* sonorous than the corresponding parameter values π_{Ons} or π_{Cod}, and the peak inventory is the set of segments *more* sonorous than the value of π_{Nuc}, Languages in which $\pi_{Ons} > \pi_{Nuc}$ are therefore languages with ambidextrous segments, which can be parsed as either onset or nucleus. The following diagram pictures the situation; the double line marks the zone of overlap.

(185)   Languages with Ambidextrous Segments

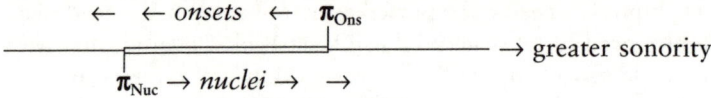

$$\leftarrow \quad \leftarrow onsets \quad \leftarrow \quad \pi_{Ons}$$

$$\text{——————————————————————} \rightarrow \text{greater sonority}$$

$$\pi_{Nuc} \rightarrow nuclei \rightarrow \quad \rightarrow$$

The theory entails a universal licensing asymmetry between onsets and codas: codas can contain only a subset, possibly strict, of the segments appearing in onsets. This fundamental licensing asymmetry will be shown to follow from the asymmetry between Onset and Coda in the Basic Syllable Structure Constraints. From the fact that Onsets should be present and Codas absent, it will follow in the theory that Coda is a weaker licenser.[17] To our knowledge, no other approach has been able to connect the structural propensities of syllables with the licensing properties of syllabic positions, much less to derive one from the other. This is surely a significant result, one that indicates that the theory is on the right track in a fundamental way. The exact nature of the obtained licensing asymmetry has some empirical imperfections which can be traced to the oversimplified analysis of codas in the internal structure of the syllable, and we suggest possible refinements.

The present section constitutes a larger-scale exploration of our general line of attack on the problem of universal typology. Universal Grammar provides a fixed set of constraints, which individual languages rank differently in domination hierarchies; UG also provides certain universal conditions on these hierarchies, which all languages must respect. The results obtained here involve a further development of the basic idea: *parametrization by ranking*. The parameters π_{Ons}, π_{Nuc}, and π_{Cod} are epiphenomenal, in that they do not appear at all in Universal Grammar, or indeed, in particular grammars: they are not, for example, mentioned in any constraint. These parameters are not explicitly set by individual languages. Rather, individual languages simply rank the universal constraints, and it is a *consequence* of this ranking that the (derived, descriptive) parameters have the values they do in that language. The procedures for reading off these parameter values from a language's constraint domination hierarchy are not, in fact, entirely obvious.

The analysis developed here introduces or elaborates several general concepts of the theory:

(186)   Push/Pull Parsing
The parsing problem is analyzed in terms of the direct conflict between two sets of constraints:
  a.   *ASSOCIATE* constraints
       PARSE, FILL, ONS, and the like, which penalize parses in which input segments or structural nodes *lack* structural associations to a parent or child;
  b.   *DON'T-ASSOCIATE* constraints
       *M/V, *P/C, and −CODA and their like, which penalize parses which *contain* structural associations of various kinds.

(187) Universal Constraint Sub-Hierarchies
The DON'T-ASSOCIATE constraints *M/V, *P/C, superordinate in the CV theory, are replaced by an articulated set of anti-association constraints *M/a, *M/i, ..., *M/d, *M/t; *P/a, *P/i, ..., *P/d, *P/t which penalize associations between Margin or Peak nodes on the one hand and particular input segments on the other. Universal Grammar requires that the domination hierarchy of each language rank these constraints *M/α, *P/α relative to one another in conformity with the following universal domination conditions:

*M/a ≫ *M/i ≫ ... ≫ *M/d ≫ *M/t   (Margin Hierarchy)
*P/t ≫ *P/d ≫ ... ≫ *P/i ≫ *P/a   (Peak Hierarchy)

The Margin Hierarchy states that it's less harmonic to parse *a* as a margin than to parse *i* as margin, less harmonic to parse *i* as a margin than *r*, and so on down the sonority ordering. The Peak hierarchy states that it's less harmonic to parse *t* as a peak than *d*, and so on up the sonority order.

(188) Associational Harmony
The universal Margin and Peak Hierarchies ensure the following universal ordering of the Harmony of possible associations:

M/t > M/d > ... > M/i > M/a
P/a > P/i > ... > P/d > P/t

These represent the basic assumption that the less sonorous an element is, the more harmonic it is as a margin; the more sonorous, the more harmonic it is as a Peak.

(189) Prominence Alignment
These universal rankings of constraints (187) and orderings of associational Harmonies (188) exemplify a general operation, Prominence Alignment, in which scales of prominence along two phonological dimensions are harmonically aligned. In this case, the first scale concerns prominence of structural positions within the syllable:

Peak > Margin

while the second concerns inherent prominence of the segments as registered by sonority:

a > i > ... > d > t

(190) Encapsulation
It is possible to greatly reduce the number of constraints in the theory by encapsulating sets of associational constraints *M/α, *P/α into defined constraints which explicitly refer to *ranges* of sonority. This corresponds to using a coarse-grained sonority scale, obtained by collapsing distinctions. This must be done on a language-specific basis, however, in a way sensitive to the language's total constraint hierarchy: which sets of associational constraints can be successfully encapsulated into composite constraints depends on how the language inserts other constraints such as PARSE, FILL, ONS, and so on, into the Margin and Peak Hierarchies, and how these two Hierarchies are interdigitated in the language. Encapsulation opens the way to developing a substantive theory of the sonority classes operative in syllable structure phenomena.

Along with these conceptual developments, this section introduces a collection of useful techniques for reasoning about constraint domination hierarchies in complex arenas such as that defined by the segmental syllable theory. A few of these techniques are:

(191)   Harmonic Bounding for Inventory Analysis
In order to show that a particular kind of structure φ is not part of a universal or language-particular inventory, we consider any possible parse containing φ and show constructively that there is some competing parse (of the same input) which is more harmonic; thus no structure containing φ can ever be optimal, as it is always bounded above by at least one more-harmonic competitor. (This form of argument is used to establish the distribution of epenthesis sites in §6.2.3.)

(192)   Cancellation/Domination Lemma
In order to show that one parse B is more harmonic than a competitor A which does not incur an identical set of marks, it suffices to show that every mark incurred by B is either (i) cancelled by an identical mark incurred by A, or (ii) dominated by a higher-ranking mark incurred by A. That is, for every constraint violated by the more harmonic form B, the losing competitor A either (i) matches the violation exactly, or (ii) violates a constraint ranked higher.

(193)   The Method of Universal Constraint Tableaux
A generalization of the method of language-specific constraint tableaux is developed; it yields a systematic means for using the Cancellation/Domination Lemma to determine which parse is optimal, not in a specific language with a given constraint hierarchy, but in a typological class of languages whose hierarchies meet certain domination conditions but are otherwise unspecified.

[...]

9   Inventory Theory and the Lexicon

All grammatical constraints are violable, in principle. A constraint such as ONS, 'syllables have onsets', in and of itself and prior to its interaction with other constraints, does not assert that syllables lacking onsets are impossible, but rather that they are simply less harmonic than competitors possessing onsets. Its function is to sort a candidate set by measuring adherence to (equivalently: divergence from) a formal criterion. Constraints therefore define relative rather than absolute conditions of ill-formedness, and it may not be immediately obvious how the theory can account for the absolute impossibility of certain structures, either within a given language or universally. Yet in the course of the preceding analyses we have seen many examples of how Optimality Theory explains language-particular and universal limits to the possible. In this section, we identify the general explanatory strategy that these examples instantiate, and briefly illustrate how this strategy can be applied to explaining segmental inventories. We then consider implications for the lexicon, proposing a general induction principle which entails that the structure of the constraints in a language's grammar is strongly reflected in the content of its lexicon. This principle, Lexicon Optimization, asserts that when a learner must choose among candidate underlying forms which are equivalent in that they all produce the same phonetic output and in that they all subserve the morphophonemic relations of the language equally well, the underlying form chosen is the one whose output parse is most harmonic.

9.1   Language-particular inventories

We begin by examining a simple argument which illustrates the central challenge of accounting for absolute ill-formedness in a theory of relative well-formedness:

> For Optimality Theory, syllables without onsets are not absolutely ill-formed, but only relatively. The syllable .VC. (for example) is *more* ill-formed than the syllable .CV., but .VC. is not *absolutely* ill-formed. How can Optimality Theory bar .VC. from any language's syllable inventory?

> What Optimality Theory would need in order to outlaw such syllables is some additional mechanism, like a *threshold* on ill-formedness, so that when the graded ill-formedness of syllables passes this threshold, the degree of ill-formedness becomes absolutely unacceptable.

The fallacy buried in this argument has two facets: a failure to distinguish the inputs from the outputs of the grammar, coupled with an inappropriate model of grammar in which the ill-formed are those *inputs* which are rejected by the grammar. In Optimality Theory, the job of the grammar is not to accept or reject *inputs*, but rather to assign the best possible structure to every input. The place to look for a definition of ill-formedness is in the set of *outputs* of the grammar. These outputs are, by definition, well-formed; so what is ill-formed – absolutely ill-formed – is any structure which is never found among the outputs of the grammar. To say that .VC. syllables are not part of the inventory of a given language is not to say that the grammar rejects /VC/ and the like as input, but rather that no *output* of the grammar ever contains .VC. syllables.

We record this observation in the following remark:

(277)   Absolute Ill-formedness
         A structure φ is (absolutely) ill-formed with respect to a given grammar iff there is no input which when given to the grammar leads to an output that contains φ.

Note further that in a demonstration that .VC. syllables are ill-formed according to a given grammar, the input /VC/ has no *a priori* distinguished status. We need to consider every possible input in order to see whether its output parse contains a syllable .VC. Of course, /VC/ is a promising place to start the search for an input which would lead to such a parse, but, before concluding that .VC. syllables are barred by the grammar, we must consider all other inputs as well. Perhaps the optimal parse of /C/ will turn out to be .□C., providing the elusive .VC. syllable. It may well be possible to show that if *any* input leads to .VC. syllables, then /VC/ will – but in the end such an argument needs to be made.

If indeed .VC. syllables are ill-formed according to a given grammar, then the input /VC/ must receive a parse other than the perfectly faithful one: .VC. At least one of the Faithfulness constraints PARSE and FILL must be violated in the optimal parse. We can therefore generally distinguish two paths that the grammar can follow in order to parse such problematic inputs: violation of PARSE, or violation of FILL. The former we have called 'underparsing' the input, and in some other accounts would correspond to a 'deletion repair strategy'; the latter, overparsing, corresponds to an 'epenthesis repair strategy' (cf. §1.2). (In §10.3 [omitted here – Ed.] we explicitly compare Optimality Theory to some repair theories.) These two means by which a grammar may deal with problematic inputs were explicitly explored in the Basic CV Syllable Structure Theory of §6. There we found that .VC. syllables were barred by either

(i)   requiring onsets: ranking either PARSE or FILL^{Ons} lower than ONS; or
(ii) forbidding codas: ranking either PARSE or FILL^{Nuc} lower than −CODA.

One particularly aggressive instantiation of the underparsing strategy occurs when the optimal structure assigned by a grammar to an input is the *null* structure: no structure at all. This input is then grammatically completely unrealizable, as discussed in §4.3.1 [omitted here – Ed.] . There is some subtlety to be reckoned with here, which turns on what kinds of structure are asserted to be absent in the null output. In one sense, the *null* means 'lacking in realized phonological content', with maximal violation of PARSE, a possibility that can hardly be avoided in the candidate set if underparsing is admitted at all. In another sense, the null form will fail to provide the morphological structure required for syntactic and semantic interpretation, violating M-PARSE [a constraint that requires the structural realization of input morphological properties – Ed.]. To achieve full explicitness, the second move requires further development of the morphological apparatus; the first requires analogous care in formulating the phonetic interpretation function, which will be undefined in the face of completely unparsed phonological material. In this discussion, we will gloss over such matters, focusing on the broader architectural issues.

It would be a conceptual misstep to characterize this as *rejection of the input* and to appeal to such rejection as the basis of a theory of absolute ill-formedness. For example, it would be wrong to assert that a given grammar prohibits .VC. syllables because the input /VC/ is assigned the null structure; this is a good hint that the grammar may bar .VC. syllables, but what needs to be demonstrated is that *no* input leads to such syllables. In addition, a grammar which assigns some non-null structure to /VC/, for example .□V.⟨C⟩, might nonetheless prohibit .VC. syllables.

Subject to these caveats, it is clear that assigning null structure to an input is one means a grammar may use to prevent certain structures from appearing in the output. The Null Parse is a possible candidate which must always be considered and which may well be optimal for certain particularly problematic inputs. We have already seen two types of examples where null structures can be optimal. The first example emerged in the analysis of Latin minimal word phenomenon in §4.3.1, where, given a certain interpretation of the data, under the pressure of FTBIN ["feet are binary at some level of analysis, mora (μ) or syllable (σ)" – Ed.] and Lx≈PR, the optimal parse of the monomoraic input is null (but see Mester 1992: 19–23). The second was in the CV Syllable Structure Theory of §6, where it was shown that the structure assigned to /V/ is null in any language requiring onsets and enforcing ONS by underparsing: that is, where PARSE is the least significant violation, with {ONS, FILL^{Ons}} ≫ PARSE.

9.1.1   Harmonic Bounding and nucleus, syllable, and word inventories

Absolute ill-formedness, explicated in (277), is an emergent property of the interactions in a grammar. Showing that a structure φ is ill-formed in a given language requires examination of the system. One useful strategy of proof is to proceed as follows. First we let A denote an arbitrary candidate parse which contains the (undesirable) structure φ. Then we show how to modify *any such analysis* A to produce a particular (better) competing candidate parse B of the same input, where B does not contain φ and where B is provably more harmonic than A. This is sufficient to establish that no structure containing φ can ever be optimal. The structure φ can never occur in any output of the grammar, and is thus absolutely ill-formed. We can call this method of proof "Harmonic Bounding" – it establishes that every parse containing the structure φ is bettered by, bounded above by, one that lacks φ.

The strategy of Harmonic Bounding was implicitly involved, for example, in the analysis of the minimal word phenomenon (§4.3.1). In this case, the impossible structure is $\varphi = [\mu]_{PrWd}$. We examined the most important type of input, a monomoraic one like /re/, and showed that the analysis containing φ, A = [[ré]$_F$]$_{PrWd}$, is less harmonic than a competitor B = ⟨re⟩, the Null Parse, which lacks φ. The method of constructing B from A is simply to replace structure with no structure.

To complete the demonstration that the Latin constraint hierarchy allows no monomoraic words in the output, we must consider every input that could give rise to a monomoraic word. We need to examine inputs with less than one mora, showing that they do not get overparsed as a single empty mora: [[□$_\mu$]$_F$]$_{PrWd}$. We also must consider inputs of more than one mora, showing that these do not get underparsed, with only one mora being parsed into the PrWd: [[μ]$_F$]$_{PrWd}$⟨μ . . .⟩. Both of these are also harmonically bounded by the Null Parse of the relevant inputs. On top of whatever violation marks are earned by complete structuring of monomoraic input – marks that are already sufficient to establish the superiority of the Null Parse – these moraic over- and underparses incur *FILL and *PARSE marks as well, and it is even clearer that a monomoraic parse cannot be optimal.

Similarly, in the analysis of Lardil in §7 [omitted here – Ed.], we provided the core of the explanation for why no words in its inventory can be monomoraic. The result is the same as in Latin, but enforcement of Lx≈PR and FTBIN for monomoraic inputs is now by overparsing rather than by underparsing, due to differences in the constraint ranking. The structure we wish to exclude is again $\varphi = [\mu]_{PrWd}$, and, as in Latin, we examined monomoraic inputs such as /maʈ/ to see if their parses contained φ. In all such cases, the optimal parses are bisyllabic competitors B, the second mora of which is unfilled. We also examined vowel-final bimoraic inputs like /wiʈe/ because, for longer inputs, a final vowel is optimally unparsed, a pattern which would lead to monomoraicity if universally applied. However, both moras in bimoraic inputs must be parsed, so again we fail to produce a monomoraic output. Inputs with three or more moras leave a final vowel unparsed, but parse all the others (184). Thus, there are no inputs, long or short, which produce monomoraic outputs.

It is worth emphasizing that, even though the lack of monomoraic words in the Latin and Lardil inventories is a result of the high ranking of Lx≈Pr and FtBin in the domination hierarchy, it would be distinctly incorrect to summarize the Optimality Theory explanation as follows: "Lx≈Pr and FtBin are superordinate therefore unviolated, so any monomoraic input is thereby rendered absolutely ill-formed." An accurate summary is: "Lx≈Pr and FtBin dominate a Faithfulness constraint (Parse in Latin; Fill in Lardil), so for any input at all – including segmentally monomoraic strings as a special case – monomoraic parses are always less harmonic than available alternative analyses (Null Parse for Latin, bisyllable for Lardil); therefore outputs are never monomoraic."

Successful use of the Harmonic Bounding argument does not require having the optimal candidate in hand; to establish $*\varphi$ in the absolute sense, it is sufficient to show that there is always a B-without-φ that is better than any A-with-φ. Whether any such B is optimal is another question entirely. This can be seen clearly in the kind of argument pursued repeatedly above in the development of the Basic Segmental Syllable Theory in §8. For example, as part of the process of deriving the typology of segmental inventories licensed by various syllable positions, we showed that the inventory of possible nuclei could not include a segment α in any language in which $*P/\alpha \gg \{Fill^{Nuc}, *M/\alpha\}$).[18] These are languages in which it is

(i)   more important to keep α out of the Nucleus (P = 'peak') than to fill the Nucleus, and
(ii)   more important to keep α out of the Nucleus than to keep it out of the syllable margins.

The φ we want to see eliminated is the substructure Nuc/α, in which the segment α is dominated by the node Nucleus. Let A denote an arbitrary parse containing Nuc/$\alpha = \acute{\alpha}$, so that a segment α appearing in the input string is parsed as a nucleus: A = ~$\acute{\alpha}$~. The bounding competitor B is identical to A except that the structure in question, Nuc/α, has been replaced by the string in which α is an onset sandwiched between two empty nuclei: B = ~$\hat{\square}$.$\alpha\hat{\square}$~. In terms of the slash-for-domination notation, the crucial replacement pattern relating A to B can be shown as

A = . . . Nuc/α . . .   B = . . . Nuc/$\square$. Ons/α Nuc/$\square$. . . .

We have then the following argument:

(278) Harmonic Bounding Argument, showing α is an impossible nucleus
    a. Assumed constraint ranking
        $*P/\alpha \gg \{\text{FILL}^{\text{Nuc}}, *M/\alpha\}$
    b. Structures
        i.   φ = ά   (segment α qua nucleus)
        ii. A = ~ ά ~   (any parse taking α to be a nucleus)
        iii. B = ~ ☐.α☐ ~   (analysis A modified in a specific way to make α
                                      nonnuclear)
    c. Argument: show that B bests A.

It should be clear that B is always more harmonic than A in the given languages. The mark $*P/\alpha$ incurred by nucleizing α in A is worse than both the marks $*M/\alpha$ (for marginalizing α) and $*\text{FILL}^{\text{Nuc}}$ (for positing empty nuclei) that are incurred by B. Hence, in such a grammar the optimal parse can never include φ = Nuc/α, no matter what the input. The conclusion is that α is not in the inventory of possible nuclei for these languages. However, we cannot conclude that every occurrence of α is in onset position, as in the bounding analysis B, or indeed, without further argument, that *any* occurrence of α is in onset position. There may be other analyses that are even more harmonic than B in specific cases; but we are assured that α will never be a nucleus in any of these.

    The Harmonic Bounding strategy is implicitly involved in a number of results derived above. Samek-Lodovici (1992) makes independent use of the same method of proof (taking B to be a kind of Null Parse) to establish the validity of his Optimality theoretic analysis of morphological gemination processes.

9.1.2 Segmental inventories

Having illustrated the way prosodic inventories are delimited, from the structural level of the syllable position (e.g., Nuc) up through the syllable itself to the word, we can readily show how the technique extends downward to the level of the segment. Now we take as inputs not strings of already formed segments, but rather strings of feature sets. These must be optimally parsed into segments by the grammar, just as (and at the same time as) these segments must be parsed into higher levels of phonological structure. The segmental inventory of a language is the set of segments found among the optimal *output parses* for all possible inputs.

    We now illustrate this idea by analyzing one particular facet of the segmental inventory of Yidinʸ (Kirchner 1992b). Our scope will be limited: the interested reader should examine the more comprehensive analysis of the Yidinʸ inventory developed in Kirchner's work, which adopts the general Optimality Theory approach to inventories, but pursues different analytic strategies from the ones explored here.

    The consonant inventory of Yidinʸ looks like this:

Labial	Coronal	Retroflex coronal	Palatalized coronal	Velar
b	d		dʸ	9
m	n		nʸ	ŋ
	l			
	r	ɽ		

Here [r] is a "trilled apical rhotic" and [ɻ] an "apical postalveolar (retroflex) rhotic continuant," according to Dixon (1977: 32).

Complex articulations are found only at coronal place of articulation; this is the generalization we wish to derive. The complexities include palatalization in [dʸ, nʸ] and the retroflexion in [ɻ]. We propose to analyze the normal and palatalized coronals as follows, along lines developed in Clements 1976, 1991 and Hume 1992:

(279)   Representation of Coronals
      a. Normal   b. Palatalized
           PLACE   PLACE

           C-Pl   C-Pl   V-Pl

           Cor   Cor   Cor

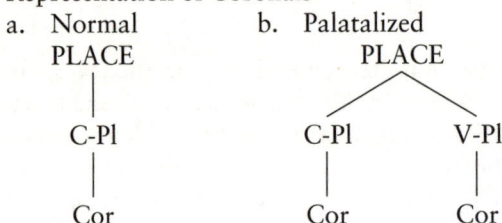

In line with the findings of Gnanadesikan 1992 and Goodman 1993, we hold that retroflexion is dorsalization rather than coronalization (as it is in Kirchner 1992b). To focus the discussion, we will deal only with the coronalized coronals. As a compact representation of these structures, we will use bracketing to denote the structure of the Place node, according to the following scheme:

(280)   Bracketing Notation for Place Geometry
      a. [α]   'feature α occupies C-Place, there is no V-Place' node
      b. [α β] 'feature α occupies C-Place and feature β occupies V-Place'

With this notation, structure (279a) is denoted by [Cor] and structure (279b) is denoted by [Cor Cor].

In this representational system, the palatalized coronals are literally *complex*, with two places of articulation, while the other, unmarked coronals are literally simple. The generalization is now clear: of all the possible structurally complex places, only one is admitted into the Yidinʸ lexicon: the one in which the primary and secondary places are both Cor – generally held to be the unmarked place of articulation (Avery & Rice 1989, and see especially the papers in Paradis & Prunet 1991, reviewed in McCarthy & Taub 1992).

Informally speaking, two generalizations are involved:

(281)   Coronal Unmarkedness (Observation)
      "Don't have a place of articulation other than Coronal."

(282)   Noncomplexity (Observation)
      "Don't have structurally complex places of articulation."

Our goal is to analyze the interaction between coronal unmarkedness and complexity markedness. This is of particular interest because it exemplifies a common pattern of interaction: each constraint is individually violable, but no form is admitted which violates both of them at once. There are consonants with single Lab or Vel specifications, violating coronal unmarkedness, and there are consonants with two place specifications, violating noncomplexity. But no consonant with any noncoronal place feature has a complex specification. We dub this generalization pattern *banning the worst of the worst*.

The worst-of-the-worst interaction is absent in the Basic CV Syllable Structure Theory. The two dimensions of well-formedness there – Onset well-formedness (more harmonic when present) and Coda well-formedness (more harmonic when absent) – operate independently. Requiring Onset, prohibiting Coda will generate the entire Jakobson Typology; the *worst-of-the-worst languages do not appear. Such a language would allow onsets to be absent, and codas to be present, but not in the same syllable; its inventory would include CV, V, CVC but exclude VC. This inventory is not possible according to the Basic CV Syllable Structure Theory, and we know of no reason to believe that this is anything but a desirable result.

The techniques already developed enable a direct account of the interaction between coronality and structural complexity. We assume that the input to the grammar is a string of root nodes each with a set of (unassociated) features. The output is an optimal parse in which these features are associated to root nodes (with the root nodes associated to syllable-position nodes, and so on up the prosodic hierarchy). To minimize distractions, let's assume a universally superordinate constraint requiring root nodes to have a child PL (Place) node. (This parallels the assumption made in §6 that the syllable node always has a child Nuc, due to universal superordinance of the relevant constraint Nuc.) For the present analysis of consonant inventories, we similarly assume a universally superordinate constraint, or restriction on Gen, to the effect that in consonants the presence of V-Place entails the presence of C-Place. (This head/dependent type of relationship is conveniently encoded in the bracketing notation of (280), because the configuration [α] is always interpreted as 'α is C-Pl'.)

Our focus will be on which of the place features in an input feature set gets associated to the PL node. As always, unparsed input material is phonetically unrealized; underparsing is therefore a principal means of barring certain feature combinations from the inventory. If certain infelicitous combinations of features should appear in an input feature set, the grammar may simply leave some of them unparsed; the feature combinations which surface phonetically define a segmental inventory from which certain ill-formed feature combinations have been absolutely banned.

In Yidin^y, the feature set {Cor, Cor} gets completely parsed. Both Cor features are associated to the PL node in the optimal parse, and the segment surfaces as d^y or n^y, depending on which other features are in the set. On the other hand, the set {Lab, Lab} does *not* get completely parsed: the inventory does not include complex labials. In contrast, the unit set {Lab} does get completely parsed; the language has simple labials.

To minimize notation we will deal only with Cor and Lab; any other noncoronal place features receive the same analysis for present purposes as Lab.

Coronal unmarkedness can be formally stated as the following universal Harmony scale:

(283)   Coronal Unmarkedness: Harmony Scale
        PL/Cor > PL/Lab

The notation 'PL/Cor' refers to a structural configuration in which PL dominates Cor, understood to be through some intermediate node – either C-Pl or V-Pl. The simplest theory, which we develop here, treats the two intermediate nodes alike for purposes of Harmony evaluation.

Following the same analytic strategy as for Universal Syllable Position/Segmental Sonority Prominence Alignment of §8, we convert this Harmony scale to a domination ranking of constraints on associations:

(284)   Coronal Unmarkedness: Domination Hierarchy
         *PL/Lab ≫ *PL/Cor

Following the general 'Push/Pull' approach to grammatical parsing summarized in §8, the idea here is that all associations are banned, some more than others. The constraint hierarchy (284) literally says that it is a more serious violation to parse labial than to parse coronal. Coronal unmarkedness in general means that to specify PL as coronal is the least offensive violation. The constraint *PL/Lab is violated whenever Lab is associated to a PL node; this constraint universally dominates the corresponding constraint *PL/Cor because Lab is a less well-formed place than Cor. In addition to these two associational constraints we have the usual Faithfulness constraints Parse and Fill. They are parametrized by the structural elements they pertain to; in the present context, they take the form:

(285)   Parse^{Feat}
         An input feature must be parsed into a root node.

(286)   Fill^{PL}
         A PL node must not be empty (unassociated to any features).

Just as with the segmental syllable theory, we have a set of deeply conflicting universal constraints: association constraints (*PL/Lab, *PL/Cor), which favor no associations, and Faithfulness constraints which favor associations (Parse^{Feat} from the bottom up, Fill^{PL} from the top down). This conflict is resolved differently in different languages by virtue of different domination hierarchies. The four constraints can be ranked in 4! = 24 ways overall; Universal Grammar, in the guise of Coronal Unmarkedness (283), rules out the half of these in which *PL/Lab is ranked below *PL/Cor, leaving 12 possible orderings, of which 8 are distinct. These induce a typology of segment inventories which includes, as we will shortly see, the Yidin^y case.

In languages with a wider variety of complex segments than Yidin^y, we need to distinguish an input which will be parsed as [Cor Vel] – a velarized coronal like [t^y] – from an input which will be parsed as [Vel Cor] – a palatalized velar like [k^y]. (Both these segments occur, for example, in Irish and Russian.) For this purpose we assume that the feature set in the first input is {Cor, Vel'} and in the second, {Cor', Vel}; the notation f' means that the feature f is designated in the feature set as secondary, one which is most harmonically parsed in the secondary place position. That is, we have the constraint:

(287) * [f′

f′ is not parsed as the primary place of articulation (not associated to C-Pl).

Since f and f′ designate the same place of articulation, parsing either of them incurs the same mark *PL/f; there are no separate marks *PL/f′ because *PL/f refers only to the place of articulation f.

Now we are ready to analyze the interaction between coronal unmarkedness and complexity in Yidin^y. The analysis is laid out for inspection in table (288).

(288) Segmental Inventory

Input POA's	Candidates	FILL^{PL}	*PL/Lab	PARSE^{Feat}	*PL/Cor	*[f′
Coronalized coronal {PL, Cor, Cor′}	a. ☞ [Cor Cor′]				**	
	b. [Cor′ Cor]				**	*!
	c. [Cor] ⟨Cor′⟩			*!	*	
	d. [Cor′] ⟨Cor⟩			*!	*	*
	e. [] ⟨Cor, Cor′⟩	*!		**		
Labialized labial {PL, Lab, Lab′}	f. [Lab Lab′]		**!			
	g. ☞ [Lab] ⟨Lab′⟩		*	*		
	h. [] ⟨Lab, Lab′⟩	*!		**		
Coronalized labial {PL, Lab, Cor′}	i. [Lab Cor′]		*!		*	
	j. [Lab] ⟨Cor′⟩		*!	*		
	k. ☞ [Cor′] ⟨Lab⟩			*	*	*
	l. [] ⟨Lab, Cor′⟩	*!		**		
Labialized coronal {PL, Cor, Lab′}	m. [Cor Lab′]		*!		*	
	n. ☞ [Cor] ⟨Lab′⟩			*	*	
	o. [Lab′] ⟨Cor⟩		*!	*		*
	p. [] ⟨Cor, Lab′⟩	*!		**		
Simple coronal {PL, Cor}	q. ☞ [Cor]				*	
	r. [] ⟨Cor⟩	*!		*		
Simple labial {PL, Lab}	s. ☞ [Lab]		*			
	t. [] ⟨Lab⟩	*!		*		

The size of the table gives a misleading impression of intricacy. The idea behind this analysis is quite simple. Association must be forced, since the anti-association constraints *PL/α militate against it. The location of PARSE amid the anti-association constraints marks a kind of cut-off point: those *PL/α below PARSE are overruled and association of their α is compelled; those above PARSE, by contrast, are under no bottom-up pressure to associate. Only the top-down pressure of FILL will compel association – but since violations must be minimal, only minimal association can be forced. Glancing across the top of the tableau, one can see that all Cor's will be forced into association by PARSE, but Lab-association, driven only by FILL, will be minimal.

Here we give the details of the argument just outlined. Since *PL/Lab ≫ PARSE^{Feat}, it is more harmonic to leave Lab features unparsed (incurring *PARSE^{Feat}) than to associate them to PL (incurring *PL/Lab). Thus, *ceteris paribus*, Lab features remain unparsed.

The only reason that Lab nodes are ever parsed at all is to satisfy FILL^{PL}, which dominates *PL/Lab. FILL is exactly the *ceteris* that is not *paribus*. If the only features available in the set are Lab features, then failing to parse all of them would leave PL unfilled, earning a worse mark *FILL^{PL} than is incurred by parsing one of the Lab nodes.

On the other hand, only *one* Lab feature need be parsed to satisfy FILL^{PL}. When two are available, as in (f–h), parsing both would only increase the degree of violation of *PL/Lab. Since violations are minimal, the least necessary concession is made to FILL^{PL}. If two Labs are available in the set, one of them satisfies its intrinsic tendency to remain unparsed, while the other sacrifices this for the higher goal of ensuring that PL is not completely empty.

The situation is reversed for Cor, however; it is more harmonic to parse these features than to leave them unparsed, because PARSE^{Feat} ≫ *PL/Cor.

As we see from the tableau, the Yidin^y inventory includes simple labials, as in rows (g,s), simple coronals, as in rows (k,n,q), and complex coronals as in row (a) but no other complex Places.[19] The grammar foils the attempt to create a complex labial from the input {PL,Lab,Lab′} in rows (f–h) by underparsing this set: a simple labial is output, as in (g), with one of the Lab features unparsed. The input {PL,Lab,Cor′} in rows (i–l) also fails to generate a complex segment, because the grammar parses only the Cor feature, outputting a simple coronal, row (k). The same output results from the input {PL,Cor,Lab′} of rows (m–p). This then is an instance of what we called 'Stampean Occultation' in §4.3.1 [not included here – Ed.]; potential complex places involving Lab cannot surface, because the grammar always interprets them as something else, behind which they are effectively hidden. In the simplest case, the learner would never bother to posit them (see §9.3 for discussion).

9.2   Universal inventories

In addition to language-particular inventories, any theory must make possible an account of universal inventories. We have already seen a number of examples of universal inventory construction, and the preceding analysis of segmental inventories provides yet another, which we will now explore. The general issue of universal inventories has two aspects which we will exemplify; the following statements are intended to fix the terms of the discourse.

(289)   Absolute Universal Inventory Characterizations
    a.   *Absence.* A structure φ is absent from the universal inventory if, for every possible grammar and every possible input, the optimal output parse of that input for that grammar lacks φ.
    b.   *Presence.* A structure φ is universally present in language inventories if, for any possible grammar, there is some input whose optimal parse in that grammar contains φ.

(290)   Relative Universal Inventory Characterizations
    An *implicational universal* of the form 'ψ in an inventory implies φ in the inventory' holds if, for every possible grammar in which there is some input whose optimal parse includes ψ, there is an input whose optimal parse in that same grammar includes φ.

The phrase 'possible grammar' refers to the well-formedness constraints provided by Universal Phonology, interacting via a particular domination hierarchy consistent with the domination conditions imposed by Universal Phonology.

9.2.1   Segmental inventories

The segmental inventory of Yidin^y, barring only the worst-of-the-worst (complex, with at least one noncoronal Place), is but one of the inventories in the universal typology generated by the 12 possible domination hierarchies which can be constructed from the four constraints *PL/Cor, *PL/Lab, Fill^{PL}, Parse^{Feat}, consistent with the universal domination condition (283) that yields Coronal Unmarkedness. This typology includes, for example, inventories which exclude all segments with complex places, and inventories which exclude all labials. The basic sense of the typology emerges from a couple of fundamental results, which correspond directly to the informal observations of Noncomplexity (282) and Coronal Unmarkedness (281), taken as implicational universals:

(291)   Complex ⇒ Simple
    $[\pi \; \psi] \Rightarrow [\pi], [\psi]$
    If the segment inventory of a language includes a complex segment with primary place π and secondary place ψ, it has a simple segment with place π and a simple segment with place ψ.

(292)   Lab ⇒ Cor
    $[\ldots \text{Lab} \ldots] \Rightarrow [\ldots \text{Cor} \ldots]$
    If the segment inventory of a language admits labials, it admits coronals.

    a.   Harmonic Completeness w.r.t. Simple Segments [Lab] ⇒ [Cor]
        If a language has simple labials, then it has simple coronals.

    b.   Harmonic Completeness w.r.t. Primary Place [Lab ψ'] $\Rightarrow$ [Cor ψ']
        If a language has a complex segment with primary place Lab and secondary place ψ, then it has a complex segment with primary place Cor and secondary place ψ.

    c.   Harmonic Completeness w.r.t. Secondary Place [π Lab$'$] $\Rightarrow$ [π Cor$'$]
        If a language has a complex segment with secondary place Lab and primary place π, then it has a complex segment with secondary place Cor and primary place π.

Recall that we are using 'Lab' to denote any noncoronal place of articulation. All noncoronals satisfy these implicational universals, because like Lab they all satisfy the Coronal Unmarkedness constraint domination condition (284). Both 'Lab' and 'Cor' should be taken here as no more than concrete place-holders for 'more marked entity' and 'less marked entity'.

Harmonic completeness means that when a language admits forms that are marked along some dimension, it will also admit all the forms that are less marked along that dimension. More specifically, if some structure is admitted into a language's inventory, and if a subpart of that structure is swapped for something more harmonic, then the result is also admitted into that language's inventory. The implications Complex $\Rightarrow$ Simple and Lab $\Rightarrow$ Cor ensure harmonic completeness in exactly this sense.

These results entail that *only* harmonically complete languages are admitted by the constraint system, no matter what rankings are imposed. In other words, harmonic completeness in POA is a necessary condition for the admissibility of a language under the constraint system at hand. This result is not as strong as we would like: it leaves open the possibility that there are nevertheless some harmonically complete languages that the system does not admit. For example, if the factorial typology turned out to generate only those languages where the distinctions among the coronals were *exactly the same* as those among the labials, the theorems Complex $\Rightarrow$ Simple and Lab $\Rightarrow$ Cor would still hold true, for such languages are harmonically complete. (In fact, we know by construction that this is not the case: the Yidin^y hierarchy allows secondary articulations among the coronals but nowhere else.) What we want, then, is that harmonic completeness be also a sufficient condition for admissibility, so that *all* harmonically complete languages are admitted. Let us single out and name this important property:

(293)   Strong Harmonic Completeness (SHARC) Property
       If a typology admits *all and only* the harmonically complete languages, then we say that it has Strong Harmonic Completeness (SHARC).

If a typology has the SHARC, then it manifests what has been referred to in the literature as 'licensing asymmetry'. For place of articulation, in the circumscribed realm we have been examining, this comes out as follows:

(294)   POA Licensing Asymmetry
       In any language, if the primary place Lab licenses a given secondary place, then so does Cor; but there are languages in which the secondary places licensed by Cor are a strict superset of those licensed by Lab.

In the common metaphor, Cor is a 'stronger' licenser of secondary places than Lab. With the SHARC, there is the broader guarantee that every asymmetric system is possible. We know that the system of constraints examined here has the POA licensing asymmetry property, because harmonic completeness is a necessary property of admitted languages, and because we have produced at least one (Yidin^y) where the secondary articulations among the coronals are a strict superset of those permitted with labials. The factorial typology of the constraint system presented here does not in fact have the SHARC, as the reader may determine, but is a step in that direction.

It is worth noting that the SHARC is undoubtedly not true of POA systems in languages, and therefore not true of the entire UG set of constraints pertaining to POA. Indeed, it is unlikely that harmonic completeness is even a necessary condition on POA systems, as John McCarthy has reminded us. With respect to labialization, for instance, many systems have k^w or g^w with no sign of t^w or d^w. With respect to Simple $\Rightarrow$ Complex, one recalls that Irish has velarized labials and palatalized labials, but no plain labials. McCarthy points to the parallel case of Abaza, which has pharyngealized voiceless uvulars but not plain ones. We do not see this as cause for dismay, however. Virtually any theory which aims to derive implicational universals must include subcomponents which, in isolation, predict the necessity of harmonic completeness and even its sufficiency as well. The constraints discussed here are a very proper subset of those relevant to POA. In particular, the key domination hierarchy is concerned only with context-free comparison of single features, and contains no information about effects of combination (labial+velar, round+back, ATR+high, etc.), which greatly alter the ultimate predictions of the system (Chomsky & Halle 1968: ch. 9, Cairns 1969, Kean 1974, Stevens & Keyser 1989, Archangeli & Pulleyblank 1992). Optimality Theory, by its very nature, does not demand that individual constraints or constraint groups must be *true* in any simple a-systematic sense. What this means is that an established subsystem or module can be enriched by the introduction of new constraints, without necessarily revising the original impoverished module at all. (We have already seen this in the transition from the basic syllable structure theory to the analysis of Lardil.) This fact should increase one's Galilean confidence that finding a subtheory with the right properties is a significant advance.

The POA subtheory examined here derives the relative diversity of coronals in inventory from the single fact of their unmarkedness. These two characteristics are so commonly cited together that it can easily be forgotten that underspecification theory cannot relate them. This important point comes from McCarthy & Taub 1992:

> Equally important as evidence for the unmarked nature of coronals is the fact that they are extremely common in phonemic inventories, where they occur with great richness of contrast. . . . [The] phonetic diversity of coronals is represented phonologically by setting up a variety of distinctive features that are dependent on the feature coronal. . . .
>
> As explanations for different aspects of coronal unmarkedness, underspecification and dependent features are distinct or even mutually incompatible. By the logic of dependency, a segment that is specified for a dependent feature . . . must also be specified for the corresponding head feature . . . For example, even if the English plain alveolars

t, d, l, r and *n* are underspecified for [coronal] the dentals $\theta/\eth$ and palato-alveolars *č/ǰ/š/ž* must be fully specified to support the dependent features [distributed] and [anterior]. As a consequence, the dentals and palato-alveolars should not participate in the syndrome of properties attributed to coronal underspecification, and conversely, the plain alveolars should not function as a natural class with the other coronals until application of the [coronal] default rule.

It seems clear that the only way out is to abandon underspecification in favor of markedness theory (cf. Mohanan 1991). This is an ill-advised maneuver if it means embracing nothing more substantial than an elusive hope. The present theory shows that solid formal sense can be made of the notion of markedness, and, more significantly, that results about subtleties of inventory structure – permitted featural combinations – can be deduced from hypotheses about the relative markedness of individual atomic features. The coronal diversity result parallels the result in §8 that onsets are stronger licensers of segments than codas. In the syllable structure case, it is the structural markedness of the Cod node relative to the Ons node which impairs its ability to license segments. Here, licensing is diminished by the markedness of Lab as a place relative to Cor. Formally, the relationship of licenser to licensed is quite different in the two cases, but in both cases the markedness of the licenser governs its ability to license. We have, then, a very general mode of subtheory construction within Optimality Theory which allows us to argue from the markedness of atomic components to limitations on the structure of systems.

We now turn to the demonstrations of (291) and (292), with the goal of identifying a general technique for establishing such implicational universals.[20]

The argument establishing (291) runs as follows:

(295)   Proof of Complex $\Rightarrow$ Simple
   For the case of the secondary place, i.e., proof that if a language has [π ψ′] it has [ψ]:
   a.   By definition of admission into the inventory, the output [π ψ′] must appear in an optimal parse of some input; the only possible such input is {PL,π,ψ′}.
   b.   This means that [π ψ′] (incurring two marks *PL/π, *PL/ψ) must be more harmonic than all competing parses of the input {PL,π,ψ′}, including [π]⟨ψ′⟩ (incurring the marks *PL/π, *PARSE^Feat).
   c.   This entails that PARSE^Feat must dominate *PL/ψ.
   d.   This in turn implies that with the input {PL,ψ}, the parse [ψ] (incurring *PL/ψ) is more harmonic than its only competitor, [ ]⟨ψ⟩ (incurring *PARSE^Feat [as well as *FILL^PL]), hence [ψ] is the optimal parse.
   e.   Which means that the simple segment [ψ] is admitted into the segmental inventory.

Broadly put, the argument runs like this. Association must be compelled, over the resistance of the anti-association constraints. Either PARSE or FILL can be responsible. The existence of [π ψ′] in an optimal output guarantees that association of ψ is in fact compelled by the grammar and indeed compelled by PARSE, since FILL would be satisfied by merely parsing π. Therefore, the association [ψ] must also occur, driven by PARSE. A similar but slightly more complex argument also establishes that [π] must be admitted.

The parallel argument establishing (292) is just a little more complicated:

(296)   Proof of Lab ⇒ Cor
        For the case of simple segments, (292a):
        a.   If a grammar admits simple labials, then the feature Lab in some input feature set must get associated to PL: [Lab] must appear in the optimal parse of this input.
        b.   In order for this to happen, the association [Lab incurring *PL/Lab, must be more harmonic than leaving Lab unparsed (incurring *PARSE^Feat, and also possibly *FILL^PL if there are no other features in the set to fill PL).
        c.   This means the language's domination hierarchy must meet certain conditions: either
                (i)   PARSE^Feat ≫ *PL/Lab
             or
                (ii) FILL^PL ≫ *PL/Lab.
        d.   These conditions (i–ii) on the ranking of *PL/Lab entail that the same conditions must hold when *PL/Lab is replaced by the universally lower-ranked constraint *PL/Cor: since *PL/Lab ≫ *PL/Cor, by Coronal Unmarkedness (283), if (i), then:
                (i′) PARSE^Feat ≫ *PL/Lab ≫ *PL/Cor;
             if (ii), then:
                (ii′) FILL^PL ≫ *PL/Lab ≫ *PL/Cor.
        e.   This in turn entails that parsing Cor must be better than leaving it unparsed: the input {PL,Cor} must be parsed as [Cor] (incurring *PL/Cor), since the alternative [ ] ⟨Cor⟩ would incur both *FILL^PL and *PARSE^Feat, at least one of which must be a worse mark than *PL/Cor by d.
        f.   This means that coronals are admitted into the inventory.

Again, the argument can be put in rough-and-ready form. Association must be compelled, either bottom-up (by PARSE) or top-down (by FILL). The appearance of [Lab – primary labial place – in an optimal output of the grammar guarantees that labial association has in fact been compelled one way or the other. Either a dominant PARSE or a dominant FILL forces violation of *PL/Lab 'don't have a labial place'. The universal condition that labial association is worse than coronal association immediately entails that the less drastic, lower-ranked offense of coronal association is also compelled, by transitivity of domination.

These two proofs (295, 296) illustrate a general strategy:

(297)   General Strategy for Establishing Implicational Universals ψ ⇒ φ
        a.   If a configuration ψ is in the inventory of a grammar G, then there must be some input I_ψ such that ψ appears in the corresponding output, which, being the optimal parse, must be more harmonic than all competitors.

b. Consideration of some competitors shows that this can only happen if the constraint hierarchy defining the grammar G meets certain domination conditions.

c. These conditions entail – typically by dint of universal domination conditions – that an output parse containing φ (for some input I_φ) is also optimal.

9.2.2   Syllabic inventories

The general strategy (297) was deployed in §8 for deriving a number of implicational universals as part of developing the Basic Segmental Syllable Theory. One example is the Harmonic Completeness of the inventories of Possible Onsets and Nuclei (216), which states that if τ is in the onset inventory, then so is any segment less sonorous than τ, and if α is in the nucleus inventory, then so is any segment more sonorous than α. A second example is (255), which asserts that if τ is in the inventory of possible codas, then τ is also in the inventory of possible onsets. The fact that the converse is *not* an implicational universal is the content of the Onset/Coda Licensing Asymmetry (259).

So far, our illustrations of universal inventory characterizations have been of the implicational or relative type (290). Examples of the absolute type (289) may be found in the Basic CV Syllable Structure Theory. A positive example is the result (128) that every syllable inventory contains CV, the universally optimal syllable. A negative example is the result (145) which states that, in syllabic theory (which does not include constraints like Lx≈Pr), two adjacent empty syllable positions (phonetically realized as two adjacent epenthetic segments) are universally impossible: the universal word inventory, under the Basic Theory, includes no words with two adjacent epenthetic segments.

9.3   Optimality in the lexicon

The preceding discussions have been independent of the issue of what inputs are made available for parsing in the actual lexicon of a language. Under the thesis that might be dubbed *Richness of the Base*, which holds that *all* inputs are possible in all languages, distributional and inventory regularities follow from the way the universal input set is mapped onto an output set by the grammar, a language-particular ranking of the constraints. This stance makes maximal use of theoretical resources already required, avoiding the loss of generalization entailed by adding further language-particular apparatus devoted to input selection. (In this we pursue ideas implicit in Stampe 1969, 1973/79, and deal with Kisseberth's grammar/lexicon 'duplication problem' by having no duplication.) We now venture beyond the Richness of the Base to take up, briefly, the issue of the lexicon, showing how the specific principles of Optimality Theory naturally project the structure of a language's grammar into its lexicon.

Consider first the task of the abstract learner of grammars. Under exposure to phonetically interpreted grammatical outputs, the underlying inputs must be inferred. Among the difficulties is one of particular interest to us: the many-to-one nature of the grammatical input-to-output mapping, arising from the violability of Faithfulness. To take the example of the Yidin^y segmental inventory illustrated above in the tableau (288), two different inputs surface as a simple labial: the input {PL,Lab} which earns the faithful parse [Lab], and the input {PL,Lab,Lab′} which is parsed [Lab]⟨Lab′⟩. These outputs are phonetically identical: which underlying form is the learner to infer is part of the underlying segmental inventory? Assuming that there is no morphophonemic evidence bearing on the choice, the obvious answer – posit the first of these, the faithfully parsable contender – is a consequence of the obvious principle:

(298)   Lexicon Optimization[21]
         Suppose that several different inputs $I_1, I_2, \ldots, I_n$ when parsed by a grammar G lead to corresponding outputs $O_1, O_2, \ldots, O_n$, all of which are realized as the same phonetic form Φ – these inputs are all *phonetically equivalent* with respect to G. Now one of these outputs must be the most harmonic, by virtue of incurring the least significant violation marks: suppose this optimal one is labelled O_k. Then the learner should choose, as the underlying form for Φ, the input I_k.

This is the first time that parses of *different inputs* have been compared as to their relative Harmony. In all previous discussions, we have been concerned with determining the output that a given input gives rise to; to this task, only the relative Harmony of competing parses of the same input is relevant. Now it is crucial that the theory is equally capable of determining which of a set of parses is most harmonic, even when the inputs parsed are all different.

   Morphophonemic relations can support the positing of input–output disparities, overriding the Lexicon Optimization principle and thereby introducing further complexities into lexical analysis. But for now let us bring out some of its attractive consequences. First, it clearly works as desired for the Yidin^y consonant inventory. Lexicon Optimization entails that the analysis of the Yidin^y constraint hierarchy (288) simultaneously accomplishes two goals: it produces the right *outputs* to provide the Yidin^y inventory, and it leads the learner to choose (what we hypothesize to be) the right *inputs* for the underlying forms. The items in the Yidin^y lexicon will not be filled with detritus like feature sets {PL,Cor,Lab′} or {PL,Lab,Lab′}. Since the former surfaces just like {PL,Cor} and the latter just like {PL,Lab}, and since the parses associated with these simpler inputs avoid the marks *PARSE^{Feat} incurred by their more complex counterparts, the needlessly complex inputs will never be chosen for underlying forms by the Yidin^y learner.[22]

   Lexicon Optimization also has the same kind of result – presumed correct under usual views of lexical contents – for many of the other examples we have discussed. In the Basic CV Syllable Structure Theory, for example, Lexicon Optimization entails that the constraints on surface syllable structure will be echoed in the lexicon as well. In the typological language family $\Sigma^{CV}_{del,del}$, for example, the syllable inventory consists solely of CV. For any input string of Cs and Vs, the output will consist entirely of CV syllables; mandatory onsets and forbidden codas are enforced by underparsing (phonetic nonrealization). Some inputs that surface as [CV] are given here:

(299)   Sources of CV in $\Sigma^{CV}_{del,del}$
    a.   /CVV/ $\rightarrow$ .CV.$\langle$V$\rangle$
    b.   /CCVV/ $\rightarrow$ $\langle$C$\rangle$.CV.$\langle$V$\rangle$
    c.   /CCCVVV/ $\rightarrow$ $\langle$C$\rangle\langle$C$\rangle$.CV.$\langle$V$\rangle\langle$V$\rangle$

The list can be extended indefinitely. Clearly, of this infinite set of phonetically equivalent inputs, /CV/ is the one whose parse is most harmonic (having no marks at all); so *ceteris paribus* the $\Sigma^{CV}_{del,del}$ learner will not fill the lexicon with supererogatory garbage like /CCCVVV/ but will rather choose /CV/. Ignoring morphological combination (which functions forcefully as *ceteris imparibus*) for the moment, we see that CV-language learners will never insert into the lexicon any underlying forms that violate the (surface) syllable structure constraints of their language; that is, they will always choose lexical forms that can receive faithful parses given their language's syllable inventory.

Morphological analysis obviously enlivens what would otherwise be a most boringly optimal language, with no deep/surface disparities at all. [See ch. 5, §2, of Tesar & Smolensky 2000 for some recent discussion. – Ed.]

[...]

While properly reformulating Lexicon Optimization from a form-by-form optimization to a global lexicon optimization is a difficult problem, one that has remained open throughout the history of generative phonology, a significant step towards bringing the Minimal Lexical Information principle under the scope of Lexicon Optimization as formulated in (298) is suggested by a slight reformulation, the Minimal Redundancy principle: to the maximal extent possible, information should be excluded from the lexicon which is predictable from grammatical constraints. Such considerations figure prominently, e.g., in discussions of underspecification (e.g., Kiparsky's Free Ride). An example of the consequences of this principle, if taken to the limit, is this: in a language in which t is the epenthetic consonant, a t interior to a stem which happens to fall in an environment where it would be inserted by epenthesis if absent in underlying form should for this very reason *be* absent in the underlying form of that stem. A rather striking example of this can be provided by the CV Theory. Consider a $\Sigma^{(C)V}_{ep}$ language (onsets are optional and codas are forbidden, enforced by overparsing – 'epenthesis'). The Minimal Lexical Redundancy principle would entail that a stem that surfaces as .CV.CV.CV. must be represented underlyingly as /CCC/, since this is overparsed as .C$\square$.C$\square$.C$\square$., which is phonetically identical to .CV.CV.CV.: it is redundant to put the V's in the lexicon of such a language. Given the constraints considered thus far, Lexicon Optimization as stated in (298) selects /CVCVCV/ and not /CCC/ in this case; again, avoiding deep/surface disparities whenever possible. But this is at odds with the principle that the lexicon should not contain information which can be predicted from the grammar.

The approach to parsing we have developed suggests an interesting direction for pursuing this issue. As stated in (186), the Push/Pull Parsing approach views parsing as a struggle between constraints which *prohibit* structure and constraints which *require* structure. As noted in §3.1 [omitted here – Ed.], the most general form of the structure-prohibiting constraint is *STRUC which penalizes any and all structure. There is a specialization of it which would be invisible during parsing but which can play an important role in learning:

(303) *SPEC
     Underlying material must be absent.

Each underlying feature in an input constitutes a violation of this constraint.[23] But these violations cannot influence parsing since the underlying form is fixed by the input, and no choice of alternative output parses can affect these violations of *SPEC. But Lexicon Optimization is an inverse of parsing: it involves a fixed phonetic *output*, and varying underlying *inputs*; thus, among phonetically equivalent inputs, *SPEC favors those with fewest featural and segmental specifications.

Now an interesting change occurs if *SPEC outranks Faithfulness: Lexicon Optimization (298) selects /CCC/ over /CVCVCV/ in the CV theory example – since minimizing Faithfulness violations (and thereby deep/surface disparities) is now less important than minimizing underlying material. If, on the other hand, Faithfulness dominates *SPEC, we are back to /CVCVCV/ as the optimal underlying form.

Clearly a great deal of work needs to be done in seriously pursuing this idea. Still, it is remarkable how the addition of *SPEC to the constraint hierarchy can allow Lexicon Optimization – in its original straightforward formulation (298) – to capture an important aspect of the Minimal Lexical Information and Minimal Redundancy principles. It remains to be seen whether a constraint like *SPEC can supplant other possible constraints aimed specifically at limiting allomorphy, demanding (for example) a 1:1 relation between a grammatical category and its morphemic exponent. It is important to note that the addition of *SPEC makes no change whatever to any of the analyses we have considered previously. This raises the intriguing question of whether there are other constraints which are invisible to parsing – the operation of the grammar – but which play indispensable roles in grammar acquisition.

[...]

Notes

1 This kind of reasoning is familiar at the level of grammar selection in the form of the Evaluation Metric (Chomsky 1951, 1965). On this view, the resources of Universal Grammar (UG) define many grammars that generate the same language; the members of that set are evaluated, and the optimal grammar is the real one.

2 An interesting variant is what we might call 'anharmonic serialism', in which Gen produces the candidate set by a nondeterministic sequence of constrained procedures ('do one thing; do another one') which are themselves not subject to harmonic evaluation. The candidate set is derived by running through every possible sequence of such actions; harmonic evaluation looks at this candidate set. To a large extent,

classical Move-α theories (Chomsky 1981) work like this.

3 Glosses are *ratkti* 'she will remember'; *bddl* 'exchange!'; *maratgt* 'what will happen to you?'; *tftkt* 'you suffered a strain'; *txznt* 'you stored'; *txznakk^w* 'she even stockpiled'; *tzmt* 'it (f.) is stifling'; *tmzħ* 'she jested'; *trglt* 'you locked'; *ildi* 'he pulled'; *ratlult* 'you will be born'; *trba* 'she carried-on-her-back'; where 'you' = second person singular and the English past translates the perfect.

4 Not the least of these is that syllables can have codas; the DEA serves essentially to locate syllable nuclei, which requires that onsets be taken into consideration. But it is not difficult to imagine plausible extensions which lead to adjunction of

codas. More subtle, perhaps, are these phenomena:

a. obstruents are always nonsyllabic in the envs. #— and —#.
b. sonorant C's are optionally nonsyllabic —# under certain conditions.
c. the 1st element of a tautomorphemic geminate is never an onset.

In addition, the DEA does not completely resolve sequences /~aa~/, which according to other sources, surface as ~aya~ (Guerssel 1986). The appropriate approach to epenthetic structure within OT involves the constraint FILL, which makes its appearance below in §3.1 [omitted here – Ed.] and receives full discussion in §6.

5   We deal with the fact that [a] cannot occupy syllable margins in §8. The commonly encountered relaxation of the onset requirement in initial position is resolved in McCarthy & Prince 1993 in terms of constraint interaction, preserving the generality of ONS. Dell & Elmedlaoui are themselves somewhat ambivalent about the need for directionality (Dell & Elmedlaoui 1985: 108); they suggest that "the requirement [of directionality] is not concerned with left to right ordering *per se*, but rather with favoring applications of [the DEA] that maximize the sonority differences between [onset and nucleus]" (Dell & Elmedlaoui 1985: 127 fn. 22). In addition, they note that directionality falsely predicts *.i.tBd.rin. from /i=t-!bdri-n/ 'for the cockroaches', whereas the only licit syllabification is .it.bD.rin. The reason for this syllabification is not understood. A directionless theory leaves such cases open for further principles to decide.

6   We show the form predicted by the DEA. The form is actually pronounced rat.lult. because obstruents cannot be nuclear next to phrase boundaries, as mentioned in n.4.

7   These are exactly the sort of questions that were fruitfully asked, for example, of the classic Transformational Grammar (TG) rule of Passive that moved subject and object, inserted auxiliaries, and formed a PP: why does the post-verbal NP move up not down? why does the subject NP move at all? why is by+NP a PP located in a PP position? and so on.

8   Further development of this idea could eliminate complications at the level of the general theory; in particular, the appearance of obeying the Free Element Condition during serial building of structure could be seen to follow from the fact that disobeying it inevitably decrements the Harmony of the representation.

9   It is also possible to conceive of the operative constraint in a kind of 'contrapositive' manner. Because all underlying segments of ITB are parsed, a segment is a nucleus iff it is not a member of the syllable margin. Consequently, negative constraints identifying the badness of syllable margins can have the same effect as positive constraints identifying the goodness of nuclei. We investigate this approach in §8.

10 Properly speaking, if we limit our attention to the core syllable stage of the procedure, we should be comparing core .u. with core .wL. But the comparison remains valid even after coda consonants are adjoined and we wish to emphasize that the two cited analyses of /ħaul-tn/ differ only in treatment of the sequence /ul/.

11 In §5.1 we define several formally distinct orders in terms of one another. At the risk of overburdening the notation, in this section only, we use superscripts like [parse] and [*] to keep all these orders distinct. We prefer to resist the temptation to sweep conceptual subtleties under the rug by using extremely concise notation in which many formally distinct relations are denoted by the same symbol. It is important to remember, however, that the symbols '>' and '≈' – no matter what their subscripts and superscripts – always mean 'more harmonic' and 'equally harmonic'. We need to compare the Harmonies of many different kinds of elements, and for clarity while setting up the fundamental definitions of the theory, we distinguish these different Harmony comparison operators. Once the definitions are grasped, however, there is no risk of confusion in dropping superscripts and subscripts; this we will do elsewhere. The superscripts and subscripts can always be inferred from context – once the whole system is understood.

12 A simple example of how this definition (97) works is the following demonstration that

$(*C) >^{(*)} (*C, *C)$.

Define α and β as follows (we use '$\equiv$' for 'is defined to be'):

$\alpha \equiv (*C)$ $\beta \equiv (*C, *C)$.

Then

$\alpha >^{(*)} \beta$ because
(97.ii) $FM(\alpha) = *C \approx^\circ *C = FM(\beta)$ and
$Rest(\alpha) = (\,) >^{(*)} (*C) = Rest(\beta)$;

where the last line, $(\,) > (*C)$, is in turn demonstrated by letting

$\alpha' \equiv (\,)$ $\beta' \equiv (*C)$

and noting that

$\alpha' >^{(*)} \beta'$ because
(97.i) $FM(\alpha') = \emptyset >^\circ *C = FM(\beta')$

by (96).

13 Both FILL and PARSE are representative of families of constraints that govern the proper treatment of child nodes and mother nodes, given the representational assumptions made here. As the basic syllable theory develops, FILL will be articulated into a pair of constraints (see §6.2.2.2):

FILL^{Nuc}: Nucleus positions must be filled with underlying segments.
FILL^{Mar}: Margin positions (Ons and Cod) must be filled with underlying segments.

Since unfilled codas are never optimal under syllable theory alone, shown below in §6.2.3 (141), FILL^{Mar} will often be replaced by FILL^{Ons} for perspicuity.

14 For versions of the structural constraints within the perhaps more plausible moraic theory of syllable structure see Kirchner 1992b,c, Hung 1992, Samek-Lodovici 1992, 1993, Zoll 1992, 1993, McCarthy & Prince 1993.

15 On *complex* margins, see Bell 1971, a valuable typological study. Clements 1990 develops a promising quantitative theory of cross-linguistic margin-cluster generalizations in what can be seen as harmonic terms. The constraint *COMPLEX is intended as no more than a cover term for the interacting factors that determine the structure of syllable margins. For a demonstration of how a conceptually similar *complex* vs. *simple* distinction derives from constraint interaction, see §9.1–2 below.

16 It would also be possible to break this yoke by having two separate PARSE constraints, one that applies to C and another to V. Basic syllable structure constraints that presuppose a C/V distinction, however, would not support the further development of the theory in §8, where the segment classes are derived from constraint interactions.

17 The demonstration will require some work, however; perhaps this is not surprising, given the simplicity of the assumptions.

18 Here, *M/α and *P/α are the constraints against parsing α as a Margin (Onset, Coda) and as a Peak (Nucleus), respectively; this is the contrapositive of the Possible Peak Condition (231).

19 In the tableau, a label like 'Labialized Labial' for the input {PL,Lab,Lab} is keyed to what *would result* from a faithful parse. The actual grammar underparses this input, and the output is a simple labial. Such labels are intended to aid the reader in identifying the input collocation and do not describe the output.

20 Another related technique, used in §8 and to an extended degree in Legendre, Raymond, & Smolensky 1993, can be effectively used here as well; the results are more general but the technique is a bit more abstract. This other technique, which might be called the Technique of Necessary and Sufficient Conditions, goes as follows:

Step 1: Determine necessary and sufficient conditions on the ranking of constraints in a hierarchy in order that each of the relevant structures be admitted into the inventory by that constraint ranking.
Step 2: Examine the logical entailments that hold between these conditions. These are arguments of the form: in order to admit structure φ it is necessary that the constraints be ranked in such-and-such a way, and this entails that the constraint ranking meets the sufficient conditions to admit structure ψ.

To carry out Step 1, to determine the necessary and sufficient conditions for a structure φ to be admitted, one takes a general parse containing φ and compares it to all alternative parses of the same input, and asks, how do the constraints have to be ranked to ensure that φ is more harmonic than all the competitors? And this in turn is done by applying the Cancellation-Domination Lemma (§8.2.6 [omitted here, but see (192) – Ed.]): for each mark m incurred by φ, and for each competitor C, if m is not cancelled by an identical mark incurred by C then it must be dominated by at least one mark of C.

In the present context, this technique gives the following results (Step 1):

(α) In order that [χ] be admitted into a inventory it is necessary and sufficient that:
either PARSE^{feat} or FILL^{PL} ≫ *PL/χ

(β) In order that [π ψ] be admitted into an inventory it is necessary and sufficient that:
a. PARSE^{feat} ≫ *PL/ψ, and
b. either PARSE^{feat} or *[f′ ≫ *PL/π, and
c. either PARSE^{feat} or *FILL^{PL} ≫ *PL/π

From here, Step 2 is fairly straightforward. The result Complex ⇒ Simple (291) for the secondary place ψ follows immediately, since (β.a) ⇒ (α) for χ = ψ. The result Complex ⇒ Simple for the primary place π follows similarly since (β.c) ⇒ (α) for χ = π.

For the Harmonic Completeness results (292), we use the Coronal Unmarkedness domination condition (284): *PL/Lab ≫ *PL/Cor. This means that whenever any of the domination conditions in (α) or (β) hold of the feature Lab, it must also hold of the feature Cor; for in that case, each asserts that some constraint must dominate *PL/Lab, which means the same constraint must also dominate *PL/Cor since *PL/Lab ≫ *PL/Cor. Spelling this observation out in all the cases a–c of (292) proves the result Lab ⇒ Cor.

21 The term 'lexicon' here is really overly restrictive, since this is actually a principle for inducing underlying forms in general, not just those of lexical entries. For example, it can apply in syntax as well. The rules of the syntactic base might well generate structures such as [[[[[he]$_{\text{NP}}$]$_{\text{NP}}$]$_{\text{NP}}$]$_{\text{NP}}$]$_{\text{NP}}$ as well as simple [he]$_{\text{NP}}$. But, as we shall see, the principle (298) will imply that the simpler alternative will be selected as the underlying form.

22 The Yidin^{y} system follows the pattern called 'Stampean Occultation' in §4.3.1 [omitted here – Ed.]. The principle of Lexicon Optimization thus makes explicit the content of the Occultation idea.

23 The constraint is thus identical to the featural measure of lexical complexity in Chomsky & Halle 1968: 381.

References

Anderson, Stephen R. 1969. *West Scandinavian Vowel Systems and the Ordering of Phonological Rules*. Doctoral dissertation. MIT, Cambridge, MA.

Aoun, Joseph. 1986. *Generalized Binding: The Syntax and Logical Form of Wh-interrogatives*. Studies in Generative Grammar 26. Dordrecht: Foris.

Archangeli, Diana. 1984. *Underspecification in Yawelmani Phonology and Morphology*. Doctoral dissertation. MIT, Cambridge, MA. [New York: Garland Press, 1988.]

Archangeli, Diana and Douglas Pulleyblank. 1992. Grounded phonology. MS. University of Arizona and University of British Columbia. ▶

Avery, P. and Keren Rice. 1989. Segment structure and coronal underspecification. *Phonology* 6, 179–200.

Bell, Alan. 1971. Some patterns of occurrence and formation of syllable structures. In *Working Papers on Language Universals*, no. 6, 23–137. Language Universals Project, Stanford University.

Black, H. Andrew. 1991. The optimal iambic foot and reduplication in Axininca Campa. *Phonology at Santa Cruz* 2, 1–18.

Broselow, Ellen. 1982. On the interaction of stress and epenthesis. *Glossa* 16, 115–32.

Browning, M. A. 1991. Bounding conditions on representation. *Linguistic Inquiry* 22, 541–62.

Cairns, Charles. 1969. Markedness, neutralization and universal redundancy rules. *Language* 45, 863–85.

Cairns, Charles. 1988. Phonotactics, markedness, and lexical representation. *Phonology* 5, 209–36.

Cairns, Charles and Mark Feinstein. 1982. Markedness and the theory of syllable structure. *Linguistic Inquiry* 13, 193–226.

Chomsky, Noam. 1951. *Morphophonemics of Modern Hebrew*. Master's thesis. University of Pennsylvania, Philadelphia.

Chomsky, Noam. 1965. *Aspects of the Theory of Syntax*. Cambridge, MA: MIT Press.

Chomsky, Noam. 1981. *Lectures on Government and Binding*. Dordrecht: Foris.

Chomsky, Noam and Morris Halle. 1968. *The Sound Pattern of English*. New York: Harper and Row.

Clements, G. N. 1976. Palatalization: linking or assimilation? In *Proceedings of the Twelfth Regional Meeting of the Chicago Linguistic Society*, ed. S. S. Mufwene, C. A. Walker, and S. B. Steever, 96–109. Chicago: Chicago Linguistic Society.

Clements, G. N. 1990. The role of the sonority cycle in core syllabification. In *Papers in Laboratory Phonology I*, ed. John Kingston and Mary Beckman, 283–333. Cambridge: Cambridge University Press.

Clements, G. N. 1991. Place of articulation in vowels and consonants: a unified theory. In *L'Architecture et la géométrie des représentations phonologiques*, ed. B. Laks and A. Rialland. Paris: CNRS-Editions.

Clements, G. N. and S. J. Keyser. 1983. *CV Phonology*. Cambridge, MA: MIT Press.

Dell, François and Mohamed Elmedlaoui. 1985. Syllabic consonants and syllabification in Imdlawn Tashlhiyt Berber. *Journal of African Languages and Linguistics* 7, 105–30.

Dell, François and Mohamed Elmedlaoui. 1988. Syllabic consonants in Berber: some new evidence. *Journal of African Languages and Linguistics* 10, 1–17.

Dell, François and Mohamed Elmedlaoui. 1989. Quantitative transfer in the nonconcatenative morphology of Imdlawn Tashlhiyt Berber. *Journal of Afroasiatic Languages* 3, 89–125.

Dixon, R. M. W. 1977. *A Grammar of Yidinʸ*. Cambridge: Cambridge University Press.

Gnanadesikan, Amalia. 1992. The feature geometry of coronal subplaces. MS. University of Massachusetts, Amherst. ▶

Goldsmith, John. 1991. Phonology as an intelligent system. In *Bridges between Psychology and Linguistics: A Swarthmore Festschrift for Lila Gleitman*, ed. Donna Jo Napoli and Judy Kegl, 247–67. Hillsdale, NJ: Lawrence Erlbaum Associates.

Goldsmith, John. 1993. Harmonic phonology. In *The Last Phonological Rule*, ed. John Goldsmith, 21–60. Chicago: University of Chicago Press.

Goodman, Beverley. 1993. *The Integration of Hierarchical Features into a Phonological System*. Doctoral dissertation. Cornell University, Ithaca.

Guerssel, M. 1986. Glides in Berber and syllabicity. *Linguistic Inquiry* 17, 1–12.

Hale, Kenneth. 1973. Deep-surface canonical disparities in relation to analysis and change: an Australian example. *Current Trends in Linguistics* 11, 401–58.

Hayes, Bruce. 1991. *Metrical Stress Theory: Principles and Case Studies*. Samizdat. Los Angeles. ▶

Hume, Elizabeth V. 1992. *Front Vowels, Coronal Consonants, and Their Interaction in Nonlinear Phonology*. Doctoral dissertation. Cornell University, Ithaca.

Hung, Henrietta. 1992. Relativized suffixation in Choctaw: a constraint-based analysis of the verb grade system. MS. Brandeis University, Waltham.

Itô, Junko. 1986. *Syllable Theory in Prosodic Phonology*. Doctoral dissertation. University of Massachusetts, Amherst.

Itô, Junko. 1989. A prosodic theory of epenthesis. *Natural Language and Linguistic Theory* 7, 217–60.

Jakobson, Roman. 1962. *Selected Writings 1: Phonological Studies*. The Hague: Mouton.

Kaye, Jonathan and Jean Lowenstamm. 1984. De la syllabicité. In *Forme sonore du langage*, ed. F. Dell, D. Hirst, and J.-R. Vergnaud. Paris: Hermann.

Kean, Mary-Louise. 1974. *The Theory of Markedness in Generative Grammar*. Doctoral dissertation. MIT, Cambridge, MA.

Kiparsky, Paul. 1973. 'Elsewhere' in phonology. In *A Festschrift for Morris Halle*, ed. S. Anderson and P. Kiparsky, 93–106. New York: Holt, Rinehart, and Winston.

Kirchner, Robert. 1992a. Lardil truncation and augmentation: a morphological account. MS. University of Maryland, College Park.

Kirchner, Robert. 1992b. *Harmonic Phonology within One Language: An Analysis of Yidin*^y. MA thesis. University of Maryland, College Park.

Kirchner, Robert. 1992c. Yidin^y prosody in Harmony Theoretic Phonology. MS. University of California, Los Angeles.

Klokeid, Terry Jack. 1976. *Topics in Lardil Grammar*. Doctoral dissertation. MIT, Cambridge, MA.

LaPointe, Steven and Mark Feinstein. 1982. The role of vowel deletion and epenthesis in the assignment of syllable structure. In *The Structure of Phonological Representations. Part II*, ed. H. van der Hulst and N. Smith, 69–120. Dordrecht: Foris.

Legendre, Géraldine, William Raymond, and Paul Smolensky. 1993. Analytic typology of case marking and grammatical voice. In *Proceedings of the Berkeley Linguistics Society*, 19. ▶

Levin [Blevins], Juliette. 1985. *A Metrical Theory of Syllabicity*. Doctoral dissertation. MIT, Cambridge, MA.

McCarthy, John. 1979. *Formal Problems in Semitic Phonology and Morphology*. Doctoral dissertation. MIT, Cambridge, MA.

McCarthy, John and Alan Prince. 1990. Prosodic Morphology and Templatic Morphology. In *Perspectives on Arabic Linguistics: Papers from the Second Symposium*, ed. M. Eid and J. McCarthy, 1–54. Amsterdam: John Benjamins.

McCarthy, John and Alan Prince. 1993. *Prosodic Morphology I: Constraint Interaction and Satisfaction*. MS. University of Massachusetts, Amherst, and Rutgers University, New Brunswick, NJ. ROA-482.

McCarthy, John and Alison Taub. 1992. Review of Carole Paradis and Jean-François Prunet, *The Special Status of Coronals*. *Phonology* 9, 363–70.

Mester, Ralf-Armin. 1992. The quantitative trochee in Latin. SRC-92-06, Syntax Research Center, University of California, Santa Cruz. To appear in *Natural Language and Linguistic Theory*. ▶

Mohanan, K. P. 1991. On the bases of radical underspecification. *Natural Language and Linguistic Theory* 9(2), 285–325.

Myers, Scott. 1991. Persistent rules. *Linguistic Inquiry* 22, 315–44.

Paradis, Carole. 1988a. On constraints and repair strategies. *Linguistic Review* 6, 71–97.

Paradis, Carole. 1988b. Towards a theory of constraint violations. *McGill Working Papers in Linguistics* 5, 1–44.

Paradis, Carole and Jean-François Prunet, eds. 1991. *The Special Status of Coronals: Internal and External Evidence. Phonetics and Phonology*, vol. 2. New York: Academic Press.

Payne, David. 1981. *The Phonology and Morphology of Axininca Campa*. Arlington, TX: Summer Institute of Linguistics.

Payne, David, Judith Payne, and Jorge Sánchez S. 1982. *Morfología, fonología y fonética del Asheninca del Apurucayali (Campa–Arawak preandino)*. Yarinacocha, Peru: Ministry of Education. Summer Institute of Linguistics.

Piggott, Glyne and Raj Singh. 1985. The phonology of epenthetic segments. *Canadian Journal of Linguistics* 30, 415–53.

Prince, Alan. 1983. Relating to the grid. *Linguistic Inquiry* 14, 19–100.

Prince, Alan. 1985. Improving tree theory. In *Proceedings of the Eleventh Annual Meeting of the Berkeley Linguistics Society*, ed. Mary Niepokuj, Mary VanClay, Vassiliki Nikiforidou, and Deborah Jeder, 471–90. Berkeley: University of California, Berkeley.

Samek-Lodovici, Vieri. 1992. Universal constraints and morphological gemination: a crosslinguistic study. MS. Brandeis University. ROA-149.

Samek-Lodovici, Vieri. 1993. A unified analysis of crosslinguistic morphological gemination. In *Proceedings of CONSOLE-1*, ed. P. Ackema and M. Schoorlemmer. The Hague: Holland Academic Graphics.

Selkirk, Elisabeth. 1981. Epenthesis and degenerate syllables in Cairene Arabic. In *Theoretical Issues in the Grammar of the Semitic Languages*, ed. H. Borer and J. Aoun. Cambridge, MA: MIT.

Smolensky, Paul. 1983. Schema selection and stochastic inference in modular environments. In *Proceedings of the National Conference on Artificial Intelligence*, 378–82. Menlo Park, CA: American Association for Artificial Intelligence.

Smolensky, Paul. 1986. Information processing in dynamical systems: foundations of

Harmony Theory. In *Parallel Distributed Processing: Explorations in the Microstructure of Cognition*, vol. 1: *Foundations*, ed. D. E. Rumelhart, J. L. McClelland, and the PDP Research Group, ch. 6, 194–281. Cambridge, MA: MIT Press/Bradford Books.

Spring, Cari. 1990. *Implications of Axininca Campa for Prosodic Morphology and Reduplication*. Doctoral dissertation. University of Arizona, Tucson.

Stampe, David. 1969. The acquisition of phonetic representation. In *Papers from the Fifth Regional Meeting of the Chicago Linguistic Society*, eds. Robert I. Binnick et al., 433–44. Chicago: Chicago Linguistic Society.

Stampe, David. 1973/79. *A Dissertation in Natural Phonology*. Doctoral dissertation. University of Chicago. [New York: Garland.]

Steriade, Donca. 1982. *Greek Prosodies and the Nature of Syllabification*. Doctoral dissertation. MIT, Cambridge, MA.

Stevens, Kenneth and S. J. Keyser. 1989. Primary features and their enhancement in consonants. *Language* 65, 81–106.

Tesar, Bruce and Paul Smolensky. 2000. *Learnability in Optimality Theory*. Cambridge, MA: MIT Press.

Wilkinson, Karina. 1988. Prosodic structure and Lardil phonology. *Linguistic Inquiry* 19, 325–34.

Zoll, Cheryl. 1992. When syllables collide: a theory of alternating quantity. MS. Brandeis University.

Zoll, Cheryl. 1993. Ghost segments and optimality. In *Proceedings of the West Coast Conference on Formal Linguistics 12*, ed. Erin Duncan et al., 183–99. Stanford, CA: Stanford Linguistics Association.

Study and Research Questions

1 Redefine HNUC ((12) in §2) so that it assigns *'s (cf. §5.2.1.2). Show that your redefined constraint works by substituting it in tableaux (16) and (17) of the same section. (More ambitious question: Prove that, in *all* cases, your definition gives exactly the same results as the one in the text.)

2 If the ranking of ONS and HNUC were reversed in Berber, how would syllabification change? Provide tableaux for some relevant examples.

3 Pick a tableau from anywhere in this book. The tableau should have at least three ranked constraints and at least three candidates. Show how the rule (105) in section 5 applies recursively to find the optimal candidate.

4 Show how HNUC can be replaced in the analysis of Berber by the universal constraint sub-hierarchies in (187) of §8. (You may find it helpful to look at chapter 9 first.)

5 Redo the Basic CV Syllable Theory (§6.2) using the MAX and DEP constraints of chapter 3. Show that the same results are obtained. (Some issues to contend with: overparsing and underparsing of segments in the redone theory; dealing with the motivation for the FILL-ONS/FILL-NUC distinction.)

6 Within the Basic CV Syllable Theory, a /CVCV/ sequence must be parsed as [CV.CV]. Other constraints that go beyond the Basic CV Theory could, however, force the parsing [CVC.V] under certain conditions. Think of some linguistically plausible constraints that might do this. (Suggestion: stress is a good place to look.)

7 Any language that allows CC coda clusters also allows simple C codas. Show how this implicational universal can be explained using the logic of Harmonic Bounding (§9.1.1).

8 Section 5.2.3.1 mentions a "nasty conceptual problem" that interferes with efforts to construct a local, constituent-by-constituent version of Eval. Describe that problem and some possible solutions to it. (Suggestion: think about foot theory as an example – see Part III.)

Chapter 2 | John J. McCarthy and
Alan Prince

Generalized Alignment: Introduction and Theory

Editor's Note

Alignment constraints are one of the many contributions Prince and Smolensky have made to OT. In their earliest work, they introduced alignment as a way of addressing a problem in the phonology of Lardil. Minimal word requirements demand that CVC roots be augmented by epenthesis: /maɾ/ → [maɽa] 'hand'. Minimal violation of faithfulness would predict *[maɾa], however, so why is [ɽ] epenthesized as well? They propose that CON includes a constraint requiring that root and syllable end in the same place – the first alignment constraint.

Other excerpts from "Generalized alignment" are reprinted as chapters 7 and 24. In the three excerpts, alignment is generalized to include other relationships between constituents, such as the relation between metrical feet and the word that hosts them. The current chapter presents the basic motivation for alignment constraints and the schema with which they are constructed. (For the notion "constraint schema" and further references, see McCarthy 2002: 17–18, 43.)

1   Introduction

Overt or covert reference to the **edges** of constituents is a commonplace throughout phonology and morphology. Some examples include:

- In English, Garawa, Indonesian and a number of other languages, the normal right-to-left alternation of stress is interrupted word-initially:

    (1)   Initial Secondary Stress in English
          (Tàta)ma(góuche)   *Ta(tàma)(góuche)
          (Lùxa)pa(líla)   *Lu(xàpa)(líla)

Excerpt from:

McCarthy, John J. and Prince, Alan (1993) Generalized alignment. In *Yearbook of Morphology*, ed. Geert Booij and Jaap van Marle, pp. 79–153. Dordrecht: Kluwer. [Available on Rutgers Optimality Archive, ROA-7.]

As the foot-brackets ( ) indicate, the favored outcome is one in which the edge of the Prosodic Word coincides with the edge of a foot (cf. Liberman and Prince 1977: 276).

- In Tagalog, the affix -um- falls as near as possible to the left edge of the stem, so long as it obeys the phonological requirement that its final consonant m not be syllabified as a coda:

(2)　-um- Infixation in Tagalog

u.ma.ral		'teach'
su.mu.lat	*um.su.lat	'write'
gru.mad.wet	*um.grad.wet	'graduate'

- In Ulwa, the affix -ka- 'his' falls immediately after the head foot of the word:

(3)　-ka- Infixation in Ulwa

(bás)ka	'hair'
(siwá)kanak	'root'

This affix is a suffix on the head foot, rather than on the word as a whole.

That is, the affix lies at the right edge of that foot.

These examples only hint at the generality of the phenomenon to be explored here, which extends to include all the various ways that constituents may be enjoined to share an edge in prosody and morphology.

Data like these have been given widely disparate treatments in the literature: directionality of foot-parsing, syllabic or segmental extrametricality, and prosodic circumscription. Examination of a wider range of cases would reveal additional mechanisms claimed to depend crucially on the special status of constituent-edges: prosodic and morphological subcategorization, prosodic templates, and the cycle. These different ways in which constituent-edges figure in phonology and morphology would seem to make any effort at unification hopeless.

Here we propose that the diverse ways in which constituent-edges figure in morphological and phonological processes can be subsumed under a single family of well-formedness constraints, called *Generalized alignment*:

(4)　Generalized Alignment
　　　Align(Cat1, Edge1, Cat2, Edge2) $=_{\text{def}}$
　　　　$\forall$ Cat1 $\exists$ Cat2 such that Edge1 of Cat1 and Edge2 of Cat2 coincide.

　　　Where
　　　Cat1, Cat2 $\in$ PCat $\cup$ GCat
　　　Edge1, Edge2 $\in$ {Right, Left}

PCat and GCat consist, respectively, of the sets of prosodic and grammatical (morphological or syntactic) categories provided by linguistic theory. Thus, a GA requirement demands that a designated edge of each prosodic or morphological constituent of type Cat1 coincide with a designated edge of some other prosodic or morphological constituent Cat2. (We return below at the end of Section 2 to issues of formalization.)

For the examples cited above, for instance, the particular parametrization of GA is as follows:

(5)   Generalized Alignment, Applied to (1)–(3)

    a.   English Stress
        Align(PrWd, L, Ft, L)
        This requirement is satisfied in [*(Tàta)ma(góuche)*], since the left edge of the Prosodic Word coincides with the left edge of a foot. (See Section 3 [= chapter 7 below] for the interaction of this type of constraint with others in the stress system.)

    b.   Tagalog *-um-*
        Align([*um*]$_{Af}$, L, Stem, L)
        This requirement is satisfied in |*umaral*, since the left edge of the affix *-um-* lies at the left edge of a stem. It is *minimally violated* (in a sense made precise below, Section 4) in |*sumulat* or |*grumadwet*.

    c.   Ulwa *-ka-*
        Align([*ka*]$_{Af}$, L, Ft′, R)
        This requirement is satisfied in (*siwá*)|-*ka-nak*, from /siwanak+ka/, since the left edge of the affix |*ka* coincides with the right edge of the head foot, Ft′.

By virtue of statements like these, GA is able to express perhaps the full range of reference to edges in grammar. Taken together with X′-like restrictions on immediate domination and interpreted within the appropriate theory of constraint satisfaction, GA provides a mechanism for completely specifying a class of formal languages that, when substantive parameters are set, ought to be all-but-coextensive with possible human languages. [. . .]

In conception, GA is most directly connected with the edge-based theory of the syntax–phonology interface (Chen 1987, Clements 1978: 35, Hale and Selkirk 1987, Selkirk 1986, Selkirk and Tateishi 1988, Selkirk and Shen 1990). In this theory, the phonological representation of a sentence is constructed by rules that map the edges of syntactic constituents, such as the maximal projection of a lexical category, onto the corresponding edges of phonological constituents, such as the Phonological Word or Phonological Phrase. Cohn (1989) and Inkelas (1989) extend this model from syntactic to morphological constituents; for example, Cohn proposes a rule mapping the edge of the root onto the edge of a Phonological Word. In terms of the functional notation introduced in (4), the edge-based theory of sentence phonology reduces to Align(GCat, Edge1, PCat, Edge1), a mapping from the edges of grammatical categories onto the same edges of prosodic categories. Through GA, we extend this approach fully, so that opposite as well as corresponding edges can be aligned, and so that Align(PCat, GCat), Align(PCat, PCat), and Align(GCat, GCat) are also licit expressions. Furthermore, we extend it to all GCat's, morphological as well as syntactic, and to all PCat's, including the word-internal prosodic categories syllable and foot, and even features and subsegmental nodes.

One crucial aspect of the enterprise, without which this degree of abstraction would be impossible, is the idea that GA is embedded in a theory of constraints on the well-formedness of phonological and morphological representations, rather than a theory of rules or procedures for constructing representations. (This is a further respect in which GA is different from the edge-based theory of the syntax–phonology interface.[1]) Indeed, GA would fail utterly if it were cast in terms of operations rather than constraints. In standard accounts, the operations subsumed by GA are extraordinarily diverse; consider how different the procedures are for building phonological structure from syntactic structure, for parsing words into feet, for prefixing an affix to a root, and for circumscribing the initial foot and suffixing to it. **As procedures,** these phenomena have nothing in common. The generality of Alignment is possible only in a system where it is imposed by constraints that evaluate the well-formedness of representations, without regard to the source of those representations.

A second crucial aspect of the enterprise, devolving from the first, is the idea that constraints on representation can be violated minimally, under specific conditions that compel violation. The case of Tagalog above is one example in which an Alignment constraint is minimally violated. For phonological reasons, the *m* of the affix *-um-* must not be syllabified as a coda. This phonological requirement takes precedence over Align([*um*]$_{Af}$, L, Stem, L), forcing mis-alignment of the affix-edge and stem-edge. But the departure from perfect Alignment is minimal, in the sense that the affix lies as near as possible to the designated edge, as can be seen by comparison of the actual forms with even more poorly aligned **sulumat* or **gradwumet*. Without the recourse of minimal violation, one would be forced to conclude that an analysis of Tagalog in terms of the constraint Align([*um*]$_{Af}$, L, Stem, L) is simply wrong, since this constraint is obviously unchallenged only in the occasional vowel-initial root like *aral*. GA, then, has a chance for success only if it is recognized that representational constraints need not be categorically true facts of a language.[2] [. . .]

Notes

1   Selkirk (1993) proposes an Optimality-Theoretic development of the edge-based theory of the syntax-phonology interface.
2   The English constraint Align(PrWd, L, Ft, L) is also violated under various conditions, principally when main-stress falls on the peninitial syllable and the initial syllable is light, hence unfootable: *A(mán)da, po(líce), A(méri)ca*. See Section 3 [= chapter 7 below] for discussion of related cases.

References

Chen, Y. 1987. "The Syntax of Xiamen Tone Sandhi". *Phonology Yearbook* 4, 109–150.

Clements, G. N. 1978. "Tone and Syntax in Ewe". In D. J. Napoli (ed.), *Elements of Tone, Stress, and Intonation*. Georgetown: Georgetown University Press, 21–99.

Cohn, A. 1989. "Stress in Indonesian and Bracketing Paradoxes". *Natural Language and Linguistic Theory* 7, 167–216.

Hale, K. and E. Selkirk 1987. "Government and Tonal Phrasing in Papago". *Phonology Yearbook* 4, 151–183.

Inkelas, S. 1989. *Prosodic Constituency in the Lexicon.* Ph.D. Dissertation, Stanford University.

Liberman, M. and A. Prince 1977. "On Stress and Linguistic Rhythm". *Linguistic Inquiry* 8, 249–336.

Selkirk, E. 1986. "On Derived Domains in Sentence Phonology". *Phonology Yearbook* 3, 371–405.

Selkirk, E. 1993. "The Prosodic Structure of Functional Elements: Affixes, Clitics, and Words". Handout of talk presented at Signal to Syntax Conference, Brown University. ◄

Selkirk, E. and K. Tateishi 1988. "Syntax and Phonological Phrasing in Japanese". In C. Georgopoulos and R. Ishihara (eds.), *Studies in Honour of S.-Y. Kuroda.* Amsterdam: Reidel.

Selkirk, E. and T. Shen 1990. "Prosodic Domains in Shanghai Chinese". In S. Inkelas and D. Zec (eds.), *The Phonology-Syntax Connection.* Chicago: University of Chicago Press, 313–337.

Study and Research Questions

1   In the alignment schema (4), Cat1 is universally quantified ($\forall$) and Cat2 is existentially quantified ($\exists$). Explain in your own words what the significance of this is. You might want to refer to the examples in (5) in your explanation. Also try reversing Cat1 and Cat2 in (5) and describe what happens.

2   Various phenomena are sensitive to edges of constituents. How are these phenomena, such as those in (1–3), analyzed in other phonological theories?

3   Think of some other phenomena that refer to constituent edges. Can all be analyzed using alignment constraints? (Reduction or deletion of word-final segments is a good place to look.)

Chapter 3 | John J. McCarthy and Alan Prince

Faithfulness and Identity in Prosodic Morphology

Editor's Note

It is no exaggeration to say that without faithfulness constraints there would be no OT. Without faithfulness, there would be nothing to oppose markedness constraints, and all lexical distinctions would be neutralized to some least-marked form like [ʔiʔi] or Chomsky's (1995) [ba]. Prince and Smolensky's original insight that forms the basis of the theory of faithfulness is this: output forms can only be evaluated in relation to some input. Faithfulness constraints require identity between input and output; exactly how they do that is the topic of this chapter.

In the earliest work on OT (e.g., section 6.2.1 in chapter 1), faithfulness constraints were formulated using a representational theory adopted from autosegmental and metrical phonology. Segmental deletion and insertion processes were understood as syllabic under- and overparsing, respectively. The faithfulness constraints PARSE and FILL militated against under- and overparsed configurations. In fact, though notionally distinct from markedness constraints, PARSE and FILL had the form of markedness constraints.

The current chapter presents an approach to faithfulness that is rooted in the analysis of reduplication. The faithfulness/reduplication connection might at first seem unexpected, but there are actually many similarities. The chapter also includes a list of faithfulness constraints intended to encompass diverse phonological processes, such as coalescence, breaking, and metathesis. For further references about correspondence theory, see McCarthy (2002: 43).

1 Introduction

[. . .] Reduplication is a matter of identity: the reduplicant copies the base. Perfect identity cannot always be attained, though; templatic requirements commonly obscure it. Base–copy parallelism is most striking when carried to an extreme – when otherwise well-behaved phonological processes are disrupted by the demands

Excerpt from:
McCarthy, John J. and Prince, Alan (1999) Faithfulness and identity in Prosodic Morphology. In *The Prosody–Morphology Interface*, ed. René Kager, Harry van der Hulst, and Wim Zonneveld, pp. 218–309. Cambridge: Cambridge University Press. [Available on Rutgers Optimality Archive, ROA-216.]

of reduplicative identity. It may happen that parallel phonological developments occur in both the base and the copy, even though the regular triggering conditions are found only in one or the other. This is "overapplication."[3] Similarly, regular phonological effects may fail to appear in the base or in the copy, when the relevant environment is found in just one of them. This is "underapplication." Either way, a phonologically expected asymmetry between the base and the copy is avoided, and identity between the base and the copy is maintained. Phonological processes of all types, at all levels, have been observed to show such behavior.

Identity figures much more widely in phonology proper, though perhaps less obviously. According to Optimality Theory, *faithfulness* constraints demand that the output be as close as possible to the input, along all the dimensions upon which structures may vary (Prince and Smolensky 1993). Derivation is determined to a large degree by the interaction between faithfulness constraints, demanding identity, and constraints on output structural configurations, which may favor modification of the input, contravening faithfulness. Input–output faithfulness and base–reduplicant identity, we argue, are effectively the same thing, controlled by exactly the same set of formal considerations, played out over different pairs of compared structures. The interplay between them leads to a number of significant results concerning the direction of reduplicative copying (sections 4.2 and 4.3), the connection between Generalized Template Theory and Correspondence Theory (section 4.3), the typology of reduplication/phonology interactions (section 5), and underapplication (section 6). The conclusion (section 7) summarizes the results and offers some prospects for future work. [Only sections 2 and 3 (excerpts) are reprinted here – Ed.]

2   Correspondence Theory

2.1   The role and character of correspondence

To comprehend phonological processes within Optimality Theory, we require a model of constraints on faithfulness of the output to the input (expanding on Prince and Smolensky 1991, 1993). To provide a basis for the study of over- and underapplication, we need to develop a model of constraints on identity between the base and the reduplicant (expanding on McCarthy and Prince 1993a). These twin goals turn out to be closely related, since they are united in Correspondence Theory, thereby eliminating the need for special, distinct theories of input–output faithfulness and base–reduplicant identity.

The motivation for a unified theory of faithfulness and identity is particularly clear when we consider the range of parallels between them:

Completeness of mapping

In the domain of base–reduplicant identity, completeness is total reduplication and incompleteness is partial reduplication, normally satisfying some templatic requirement on the canonical shape of the reduplicant.

In the domain of input–output faithfulness, incompleteness is phonological deletion.

Dependence on input/base

In the domain of base–reduplicant identity, the phonological material of the reduplicant normally is just that of the base. This dependence on the base is violated in systems with fixed default segments in the reduplicant: e.g., Yoruba, with fixed default *i*, as in /mu/ → *mí–mu* (Akinlabi 1984, McCarthy and Prince 1986, Pulleyblank 1988).

The parallel in the input–output domain is epenthesis, with default segments inserted under syllabic or other conditions.

Contiguity of mapping

In the domain of base–reduplicant identity, the copy is usually a *contiguous* substring of the base. For instance, in Balangao prefixing reduplication (Shetler 1976, McCarthy and Prince 1994a), contiguity protects reduplicant-medial coda consonants, though not reduplicant-final ones: . . . *tagta–tagtag*,* . . . *tata–tagtag*. Violation of the contiguity property is met with conspicuously in Sanskrit reduplication: *du–druv*.

Contiguity effects are also known in the input–output domain, though they are less well studied than other constraints on epenthesis or deletion. In Axininca Campa and Lardil, epenthetic augmentation is external to the root (McCarthy and Prince 1993a and references cited there): /tʰo/ → *tʰota*, **tʰato*; /ɾil/ → *ɾilta*, **ɾatil*, **ɾital*. Likewise, in Chukchee (Kenstowicz 1994, Spencer 1993), morpheme-edge epenthesis is preferred to morpheme-internal epenthesis: /miml-qaca-n/ → *mimləqacan*, **miməlqacan*. And in Diyari (Austin 1981, McCarthy and Prince 1994a), a prohibition on all syllable codas leads to deletion of word-final consonants, but not of word-medial ones, with the effect that all words are vowel-final; this provides an exact parallel to the Balangao reduplicant.

Linearity of mapping

Reduplication normally preserves the linear order of elements. But in Rotuman (Churchward 1940 [1978]), there is metathetic reduplication of disyllabic roots: /RED–pure/ → *puer–pure*.

Similarly, the input–output map typically respects linear order, but metathesis is a possibility. In the phonology of Rotuman, for example, a metathesis similar to the reduplicative phenomenon is observed in a morphological category called the incomplete phase (McCarthy 1995): *pure* → *puer*.

Anchoring of edges

The reduplicant normally contains an element from at least one edge of the base, typically the left edge in prefixed reduplicants and the right edge in suffixed reduplicants.

Edge-anchoring has been observed and studied even more extensively in the input–output domain, where it has been identified with the class of constraints on the *alignment* of edges of morphological and prosodic constituents (Prince and Smolensky 1991, 1993; McCarthy and Prince 1993a, b).

Featural identity

Copied segments in the base and the reduplicant are normally identical to one another, but may differ featurally for phonological reasons. For instance, nasal place-assimilation in Tübatulabal leads to imperfect featural identity of copied segments, as in *zam–banin* (Voegelin 1935, Alderete *et al.* 1996).

The same sort of identity, or phonologically motivated non-identity, of segments in input and output is the very crux of phonological alternation.

This range of parallels is remarkable, and demands explanation. Linguistic theory must relate the constraints on the matching of reduplicant and base (the copying constraints) to the constraints on the matching of phonological output and input (the faithfulness constraints). We propose to accomplish this by generalizing the notion of *correspondence*. Correspondence was introduced into OT as a base–reduplicant relation (McCarthy and Prince 1993a); here, we extend it to the input–output domain, and other linguistic relationships besides. The parallels observed above are accounted for if Universal Grammar (UG) defines *types* of constraints on correspondence, with distinct realizations of the constraint types for each domain in which correspondence plays a role.

Correspondence itself is a relation between two structures, such as base and reduplicant (B-R) or input and output (I-O). To simplify the discussion, we focus on correspondence between strings.[4]

(1) Correspondence

Given two strings S_1 and S_2, *correspondence* is a relation $\Re$ from the elements of S_1 to those of S_2. Elements $\alpha \in S_1$ and $\beta \in S_2$ are referred to as *correspondents* of one another when $\alpha \Re \beta$.

Here we will assume that the structural elements α and β are just (tokens of) segments, but it is a straightforward matter to generalize the approach to other units of phonological representation. For instance, correspondence of moras, syllables, feet, heads of feet, as well as tones, and even distinctive features or feature-class nodes, may be appropriate to support the analysis of quantitative transfer, compensatory lengthening, and floating features.[5]

Correspondence need not be limited to the B-R and I-O relations. For example, the same notions extend directly to relations between two stems, as in root-and-pattern, circumscriptional, or truncating morphology (Benua 1995, McCarthy and Prince 1994b, McCarthy 1995), and they can be connected with the types of cyclic or transderivational relationships within paradigms explored by Benua (1995, 1997) and Burzio (1994a, b).

In a correspondence-sensitive grammar, candidate reduplicants or outputs are subject to evaluation together with the correspondent base or input. Each candidate pair (S_1, S_2) comes from Gen[erator] equipped with a correspondence relation between S_1 and S_2. There is a correspondence relation for each (B, R) candidate pair. There is also a correspondence relation for each (I, O) candidate pair. Indeed, one can simply think of Gen as supplying correspondence relations between S_1 and all possible structures over some alphabet.[6] Eval[uator] then considers each candidate pair with its associated correspondence relations, assessing the completeness of correspondence in S_1 or S_2, the featural identity of correspondent elements in S_1 and S_2, and so on.

A hypothetical illustration will make these ideas more concrete. In (2a), we provide some (B, R) correspondences, and in (2b) we do the same for (I, O) correspondence. The comments on the right describe any interesting imperfections of correspondence. Correspondent segments are indicated here by subscripted indices, a nicety that we will usually eschew in the discussion later.

(2) Hypothetical illustrations

    a. Some B-R Correspondents

Input = /RED–badupi/

$b_1\,a_2\,d_3\,u_4\,p_5\,i_6$–$b_1\,a_2\,d_3\,u_4\,p_5\,i_6$
Total reduplication – perfect B-R correspondence.

$b_1\,a_2\,d_3$–$b_1\,a_2\,d_3\,u_4\,p_5\,i_6$
Partial reduplication – *upi* in B has no correspondents in R.

$b_1\,a_2\,t_3$–$b_1\,a_2\,d_3\,u_4\,p_5\,i_6$
The *t* in R has a non-identical correspondent in B, for phonological reasons (final devoicing).

$ʔ\,a_2\,d_3$–$b\,a_2\,d_3\,u_4\,p_5\,i_6$
The *ʔ* is *not* in correspondence with the base-initial *b*. This is a type of fixed-segment reduplication (cf. Tübatulabal in Alderete *et al.* 1996).

$ʔ_1\,a_2\,d_3$–$b_1\,a_2\,d_3\,u_4\,p_5\,i_6$
The *ʔ* in R has a non-identical correspondent in B. This and the preceding candidate are formally distinct, since Eval considers candidates with their correspondence relations.

    b. Some I-O Correspondents

Input = /$p_1\,a_2\,u_3\,k_4\,t_5\,a_6$/ A fully faithful

$p_1\,a_2\,u_3\,k_4\,t_5\,a_6$
analysis – perfect I-O correspondence.

$p_1\,a_2\,ʔ\,u_3\,k_4\,t_5\,a_6$
Hiatus prohibited by high-ranking ONSET, so epenthetic *ʔ* in O has no correspondent in I.

$p_1\,u_3\,k_4\,t_5\,a_6$
Hiatus prohibited, leading to V-deletion. The segment a_2 in I has no correspondent in O.

$p_1\,a_2\,u_3\,t_4\,t_5\,a_6$
The k_4 in I has a non-identical correspondent in O, for phonological reasons (assimilation).

b l u r k
No element of O stands in correspondence with any element in I. Typically fatal.

The variety of candidates shown emphasizes some of the richness of the Gen-supplied set. It falls to Eval, and the language-particular constraint hierarchy, to determine what is optimal, what is not, and what can never be optimal under any ranking of the constraints in UG.

2.2   Some constraints on correspondent elements

Constraints must assess correspondence and identity of correspondent elements. There are separate (and therefore separately rankable) constraints for each correspondence relation (input/output, base/reduplicant, etc.). The following are three of the constraint families that will play a leading role in our discussion; all relate the string S_1 (base, input, etc.) to the string S_2 (reduplicant, output, etc.).

(3)   The Max constraint family
    General Schema
       Every segment of S_1 has a correspondent in S_2.
    Domain-specific instantiations
      Max-BR
         Every segment of the base has a correspondent in the reduplicant.
           (Reduplication is total.)
      Max-IO
         Every segment of the input has a correspondent in the output.
           (No phonological deletion.)

(4)   The Dep constraint family
    General schema
       Every segment of S_2 has a correspondent in S_1.
         (S_2 is "dependent on" S_1.)
    Domain-specific instantiations
      Dep-BR
         Every segment of the reduplicant has a correspondent in the base.
           (Prohibits fixed default segmentism in the reduplicant.)
      Dep-IO
         Every segment of the output has a correspondent in the input.
           (Prohibits phonological epenthesis.)

(5)   The Ident(F) constraint family
    General schema
      Ident(F)
         Let α be a segment in S_1 and β be any correspondent of α in S_2.
         If α is [γF], then β is [γF].
           (Correspondent segments are identical in feature F.)
    Domain-specific instantiations
      Ident-BR(F)
         Reduplicant correspondents of a base [γF] segment are also [γF].
      Ident-IO(F)
         Output correspondents of an input [γF] segment are also [γF].

Some constraints on other aspects of the correspondence relation are listed in the appendix. Note further that each reduplicative affix has its own correspondence relation, so that in a language with several reduplicative affixes there can be several distinct, separately rankable constraints of the Max-BR type, etc. This means that different reduplicative morphemes within a language can fare differently with respect to constraints on correspondence – for example, one can be total reduplication, obeying Max-BR, and one can be partial, violating Max-BR. It also means that reduplicative morphemes can differ in how they interact with the phonology, in one and the same language, as Urbanczyk (1996, 1999) argues. It must be, then, that correspondence constraints are tied not only to specific dimensions (B-R, I-O), but also, in some cases at least, to specific morphemes or morpheme classes. Thus, the full schema for a faithfulness constraint may include such specifics as these: the element preserved, the dimension of derivation along which the two structures are related, the *direction* of inclusion along that dimension (as in the contrast between Max and Dep), and the morphological domain (stem, affix, or even specific morpheme) to which the constraint is relevant.

Now some comments on the specific constraints. Max-IO is a reformulation of the constraint Parse in Prince and Smolensky (1991, 1993) and other OT work, which liberates it from its connection with syllabification and phonetic interpretation. In addition, the Max family subsumes the reduplication-specific Max in McCarthy and Prince (1993a). Depending on which correspondence relation they regulate, the various Max constraints will (*inter alia*) prohibit phonological deletion, demand completeness of reduplicative copying, or require complete mapping in root-and-pattern morphology.

The Dep constraints approximate the function of Fill in Prince and Smolensky (1991, 1993) and other OT work. They encompass the anti-epenthesis effects of Fill without demanding that epenthetic segments be literally unfilled nodes, whose contents are to be specified by an auxiliary, partly language-specific component of phonetic interpretation. They also extend to reduplication and other relations.

The Ident constraints require that correspondent segments be featurally identical to one another. Unless dominated, the full array of these constraints will require complete featural identity between correspondent segments. Crucial domination of one or more Ident constraints leads to featural disparity and phonological alternation.

Various extensions of Ident have emerged from continuing research. One, proposed by Pater (1999), differentiates Ident(+F) and Ident(−F) versions for the same feature; the typological consequences of this move for the present theory are taken up in section 5.4 below. Another, adopted by Urbanczyk (1996), posits identity of moraic analysis of correspondent segments. Extensions of Ident to other aspects of prosodic structure are treated in Benua (1995) and McCarthy (1995). Another important development, pursued by Alderete (1996), Beckman (1997), and Selkirk (1995), is differentiation of Ident and other correspondence constraints by position: onset versus coda, stressed versus unstressed, root versus affix.[7] The first-named, more prominent position typically receives more faithful treatment, as evidenced by phenomena of position-sensitive neutralization. Finally, in the light of work in feature geometry (Clements 1985b, Padgett 1995a, etc.), it is plausible that constraints of the Ident family will quantify over classes of features.

The IDENT constraint family is constructed here on the assumption that seg-ments alone stand in correspondence, so identity of features is always demanded indirectly, through the segments bearing those features. As we noted above, it is a reasonably straightforward matter, though, to extend the correspondence relation to features as well as segments. Then the constraint IDENT(F) would be replaced by the MAX(F)/DEP(F) pair, plus an apparatus of additional constraints to ensure faithfulness of features to their original segmental associations. Featural cor-respondence is arguably necessary to deal with some floating feature phenomena (Zoll 1996) and with entailments between segmental and featural deletion (Lombardi 1995).

In section 2.1 we listed many parallels between B-R Identity and I-O Faithfulness. These parallels now have an explanation: they follow from the fact that both B-R and I-O are related by correspondence and that identical constraint types apply to each (and to other domains of correspondence as well).

There is an important further parallel to be drawn, which the generality of correspondence affords us. The correspondence constraints proposed above and in the appendix are strongly reminiscent of some principles and rules of auto-segmental association. For example, MAX, DEP, and LINEARITY recall the clauses of Goldsmith's (1976) Well-Formedness Condition: every tone-bearing element is associated with some tone; every tone is associated with some tone-bearing ele-ment; association lines do not cross. Likewise, CONTIGUITY and ANCHORING can be analogized to the requirement of directional one-to-one linking and the Initial Tone Association Rule in Clements and Ford (1979). These parallels are explained if we generalize correspondence still further, to include not only identity relations (like I-O and B-R) but also the relation of autosegmental association. The phe-nomena comprehended by the theory of autosegmental association are therefore a special case of correspondence.[8]

These parallels, and the consequent reduction of autosegmental association to correspondence, recapture one of the original ideas of Prosodic Morphology, one which was lost in the solely reduplicative correspondence theory of McCarthy and Prince (1993a): that template satisfaction is a special case of autosegmental associ-ation, involving associating floating melodemes to a templatic skeleton (McCarthy 1979, Marantz 1982, Clements 1985a, Mester 1986, McCarthy and Prince 1986, etc.). We now see that exactly the same relation – correspondence – and the same constraints – MAX, DEP, etc. – are at work in both domains, just as they are in faithfulness.

2.3   Correspondence theory and the PARSE/FILL Model

Most work within OT since Prince and Smolensky (1991, 1993) assumes that the phonological output is governed by a requirement that no input element may be literally removed. To-be-deleted elements are present in the output, but marked in some way. (This property is dubbed "Containment" in McCarthy and Prince 1993a;[9] ideas like it have played a role throughout much of modern syntactic theory, e.g., Postal 1970, Perlmutter (ed.) 1983, and Chomsky 1975.) Under this assump-tion, phonologically deleted segments are present in the output, but unparsed syllabically, making use of the notion of *Stray Erasure* in Steriade (1982). The I-O Faithfulness constraint PARSE regulates this mode of deletion, by prohibiting unsyllabified segments.

Because they reduce the prohibition on deletion to an easily stated structural constraint, these moves provide a direct and convenient way to handle a variety of basic cases. But this is by no means the only possible approach to faithfulness in OT (cf. Prince and Smolensky 1993: 25, note 12; Yip 1993; Myers 1993; and Kirchner 1993 for some other alternatives). Indeed, there are very significant differences in formal architecture between the serial operational theory from which Stray Erasure originated and OT's parallel, evaluative-comparative approach to well-formedness. The shared goal of both theories is to derive the properties of deletion patterns from independent principles of syllabification. Under standard deterministic Markovian serialism, there is no clear way to combine rules of literal deletion with operational rules of syllabification so as to get this result. So the burden must be placed entirely on the rules of syllabification, with deletion postponed to sweep up afterwards. OT's architecture admits this as a possible line of attack on the problem, but since all manners of alteration of the input are considered in parallel, there is no intrinsic need to limit Gen to an output representation without deletions, so long as the relation between input and output is kept track of – for example, by correspondence relations. An immediate (and desirable)[10] consequence of the correspondence/full-deletion approach is that deleted elements simply cannot play a role in determining the performance of output structures on constraints defined strictly on output representations. There is then no need to restrict these constraints to seeing only *parsed elements*, as for example Myers (1993) demonstrates to be true of the OCP [Obligatory Contour Principle: see chapter 13 – Ed.]; the point applies with equal force to a class of alignment constraints, as shown by Beckman (1995). Along the same lines, B-R correspondence sees only what is manifest in B, a fact that leads directly to strong predictions about overapplication in the reduplicative theory.

Much OT work since Prince and Smolensky (1991) assumes as well that no segment can be literally *added* to the output. Phonological epenthesis is seen as the result of providing prosodic structure with no segment to fill it, the phonetic identity of the epenthetic segment being determined by extra-systemic rules of (phonetic) interpretation, exactly as in Selkirk (1981), Lowenstamm and Kaye (1985), and Itô (1986, 1989). The constraint FILL militates against these unfilled prosodic nodes. Here again, a faithfulness issue is given a simple structural interpretation that allows for easy formulation and direct assault on the basic generalizations about the relation between epenthesis and syllabifiability. But, just as with deletion, the architectural shift opens new perspectives. Under OT, it is no longer formally necessary to segregate the cause of epenthesis (principles of syllabification) from the fact itself. Under correspondence, the presence of epenthetic elements is regulated by the DEP constraint family, and they appear in optimal forms with whatever kind and degree of featural specification the phonological constraints demand of them. An immediate, desirable consequence is that the choice of epenthetic material comes under *grammatical* control: independently required constraints on featural markedness select the least offensive material to satisfy (or better satisfy) the driving syllabic constraints. (See Prince and Smolensky 1993, ch. 9, Smolensky 1993, McCarthy 1993, and McCarthy and Prince 1994a for relevant discussion of featural markedness in epenthetic segments.) In addition, the actual featural value of epenthetic segments can figure in phonological generalizations (Spring 1994, Davis 1995), as is known to be the case in many situations (for example, Yawelmani Yokuts harmony, discussed in Kuroda 1967 and Archangeli 1985). This contrasts sharply with the FILL theory, in which the feature composition of epenthetic segments is determined post-phonologically, by a further process of phonetic implementation. This "phonetics" nevertheless deals in the very same materials as phonology, and is subject to interlinguistic variation of a sort that is more than reminiscent of standard constraint-permutation effects. Correspondence makes immediate sense of these observations, which appear to be in principle beyond the reach of FILL-based theories.

This discussion has brought forth a significant depth of empirical motivation behind the proposal to implement faithfulness via correspondence of representations. A primary motive is to capture the parallels between B-R Identity and I-O Faithfulness. This is reinforced by the observation that mapping between autosegmental tiers is regulated by the same formal principles of proper correspondence, allowing us to recapture the formal generality of earlier, autosegmental-associative theories of template satisfaction. By contrast, a Containment or PARSE/FILL approach to inter-tier association is hardly conceivable.[11] Correspondence also allows us to explain why certain constraints, such as Myers's tonal OCP, are totally insensitive to the presence of deletion sites, and why epenthetic elements show an unmarked feature composition, which can nevertheless play a role in phonological patterns such as vowel harmony. To these, we can add the ability to handle phenomena such as diphthongization and coalescence through the use of one-to-many and many-to-one relations. It is certainly possible, bemused by appearances, to exaggerate the differences between the PARSE/FILL approach and correspondence – both being implementations of the far more fundamental faithfulness idea, without which there is no OT – but it seems quite clear at this point that correspondence is the more promising line to pursue.

3   Approaches to Reduplication/Phonology Interaction

3.1   Reduplication/phonology interaction in Correspondence Theory

The full theory of reduplication involves correspondence between underlying stem and surface base, between surface base and surface reduplicant, and between underlying stem and surface reduplicant. The following diagram portrays this system of relations:

(6)   Full Model

Input   /Af$_{RED}$ + Stem/
        I-R Faithfulness   I-B Faithfulness
Output   R ⇌ B
            B-R Identity

In keeping with our practice so far, we will continue to employ a purely terminological distinction between identity and faithfulness, but we do this solely to emphasize the distinct dimensions along which these perfectly homologous notions are realized.

The relation between stem and reduplicant – *I-R Faithfulness* in the diagram – turns out to play a subsidiary role in the theory, essentially because of a universal metacondition on ranking, discussed in McCarthy and Prince (1995: section 6), which ensures that faithfulness constraints on the stem domain always dominate those on the affixal domains. From this, it follows that I-R Faithfulness appears in a subordinate position in every ranking, dominated by I-B Faithfulness, significantly limiting its effects. In many rankings, its presence will be completely or almost completely hidden; it therefore becomes convenient to study a simplified model, a proper sub-theory, in which I-R Faithfulness is not considered. Let us call this the "Basic Model," which directly follows McCarthy and Prince (1993a).

(7)   Basic Model

Input $/Af_{RED} + Stem/$

$\big\updownarrow$ *I-O Faithfulness*

Output $R \rightleftharpoons B$

B-R Identity

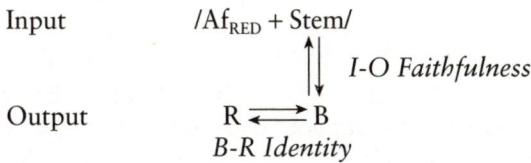

The Basic Model will be the major focus below; for extension to the Full Model, see McCarthy and Prince (1995: section 6).

The identity-preserving interactions between phonology and reduplication were named overapplication and underapplication in the pioneering work of Wilbur (1973a, b, c). Although these terms emerge from a particular conception of rules and rule application which is no longer viable, they can be given a more neutral characterization, in terms of relations rather than processes, and we will use them throughout in a strictly descriptive sense. A phonological mapping will be said to overapply when it introduces, in reduplicative circumstances, a disparity between the output and the lexical stem[12] that is not expected on purely phonological grounds. To put it even more neutrally, we can say that, in a situation where there is a two-way opposition between a marked element of limited distribution and an unmarked default element, overapplication is the appearance of the marked element outside of its normal distributional domain. A typical example is given in (8).

(8)   Overapplication in Madurese nasal harmony (Stevens 1968, 1985; Mester 1986: 197–200)

Stem	Simple	Reduplicated	Expected	Gloss
/neat/	nẽỹãt	ỹãt-nẽỹãt	*yat-nẽỹãt	"intentions"

A nasal span runs rightward from nasal consonants (column two). In the reduplicated form (column three), nasal spreading in the base is replicated in the reduplicant, even though the triggering nasal consonant is not copied. If reduplication were thought of as copying the underlying form of the base, the expected result would be the one in column four; it is from this perspective that nasal harmony is thought to overapply to force nasalized ỹ and ã in the reduplicant. Regardless of the mechanism involved, the effect is to introduce an unexpected disparity between the presumed lexical stem and the output – the presence of the nasalized ã. In terms of the surface repertory, we can say that the marked member of the ã/a opposition is found outside its canonical, post-nasal position.

Similarly, a phonological process will be said to underapply when there is a *lack* of expected disparity between the input stem and the output. In the most straightforward case, this amounts to the unmarked member of an opposition putting in an appearance where the marked member is expected. Akan reduplication provides a typical example: palatalization fails to apply in the reduplicant when it is not phonologically motivated in the base:

(9)   Underapplication in Akan (Christaller 1875, Schachter and Fromkin 1968, Welmers 1946)

	Stem	Reduplicated	Expected	Gloss
a.	kaʔ	kɪ-kaʔ	*tɕɪ-kaʔ	"bite"
b.	hawʔ	hɪ-hawʔ	*ɕɪ-hawʔ	"trouble"

Though Akan typically disallows velars and other back consonants before front vowels, the offending sequence is found in reduplicated forms like kɪ-kaʔ. In Wilbur's terms, the velar palatalization process *underapplies* in the reduplicant. More neutrally, we can observe that the general phonological pattern of the language leads us to expect a disparity between the underlying stem (with k) and the reduplicant (where we ought to see tɕ), and we do not find it. Put in markedness terms, the unmarked member of k/tɕ appears here not in its default environment, but in a position where, it seems, the marked member is required. The effect is to make the actual reduplicant more closely resemble the stem.

The third relevant descriptive category is that of *normal application*, whereby both base and reduplicant are entirely well-behaved phonologically, being treated as completely independent entities. Tagalog flapping provides an instance: there is an allophonic alternation between *d* and *r* in Tagalog, with the flap found intervocalically, much as in English. Reduplication makes no inroads on this generalization:

(10)   Normal application in Tagalog (Carrier 1979: 149f.)

	Stem	Reduplicated	Over	Under	Gloss
a.	datiŋ	d-um-ā-ɾatiŋ	*ɾ-um-ā-ɾatiŋ	*d-um-ā-datiŋ	"arrive"
b.	diŋat	ka-ka-ɾiŋat-diŋat	*ka-ɾiŋat-ɾiŋat	*ka-diŋat-diŋat	"suddenly"

As with underapplication and overapplication, it must be emphasized that the expression "normal application" is a term of art, describing a certain state of affairs, and there is no implication that normal application is particularly usual or more commonly encountered than its rivals, or even universally available. Indeed, the typology we develop below (section 5) includes circumstances where the theory does not always admit normal application as an option (see also McCarthy and Prince 1995: section 3.2).

Since the earliest work on this subject (e.g., Wilbur 1973a), it has been recognized that over- and underapplication support reduplicant–base identity. Suppose the cited phonological processes in Madurese and Akan had applied *normally*, yielding the results in the columns labeled "Expected": they would then increase disparity between base and reduplicant. If reduplication, by its very nature, involves identity between base and reduplicant, then any special interaction with phonology that serves to support reduplicant–base identity is functioning in aid of the reduplicative pattern itself. This is the insight we will explore, by examining the range of inter- actions between the competing and often irreconcilable demands of faithful corres- pondence between different representations.

Working within the Basic Model, (7), we will sketch the overall lie of the land. The constraints demanding B-R Identity are evaluated in parallel with the con- straints on phonological sequences and on I-O Faithfulness that are responsible for relations like Madurese V ~ Ṽ and Akan k ~ $t\varsigma$. With B-R Identity constraints dominant, we need only take seriously those candidates in which base and reduplicant actually match. With the relevant phonological constraints dominant as well, overapplication can result. Consider the Madurese case, which offers the following comparison of potential outputs:

(11)   Overapplication of nasal harmony in Madurese (from /neat/)

		Candidate	Chief Flaw	Remarks	Type
a.	☞	ỹãt-nẽỹãt	*I-O Faithfulness: nasal V in stem	Forced violation	Over
b.	*	yat-nẽyat	*Phonological constraint against NV$_{Oral}$	Fatal	Under
c.	*	yat-nẽỹãt	*B-R Identity	Fatal	Normal

The sequence NV$_{Oral}$ is disallowed in the language, where N = any nasal segment, including nasalized vowels and glides. The doubly nasalized form, (11a), is optimal, because it achieves perfect identity of base and reduplicant while still avoiding the forbidden sequence. The cost is the introduction of extra marked segments – nasal vocoids – into the representation; indeed, into an environment where they are not tolerated elsewhere in the language. Such considerations lead to a ranking require- ment on this kind of overapplication, which characterizes the interplay among constraints on B-R Identity and markedness relative to some structural condition, "Phono-Constraint" (Phono-Con).

(12)   An overapplication ranking pattern
       B-R Identity, Phono-Constraint $\gg$ Markedness

This ranking asserts that reduplicative identity and some phonological requirement (like the prohibition on NV$_{Oral}$) both take precedence over another phonological requirement, here the markedness constraint against nasality in vocoids. (This accords with the observation that in case of a simple marked versus unmarked contrast, classic overapplication involves the otherwise unexpected appearance of a marked element.) The primacy of base–reduplicant identity leads here to overapplication, examined in section 4. The responsible rankings, including (12) and others that involve conflict between B-R Identity and I-O Faithfulness, are examined and refined in the factorial typology of section 5.

Strikingly, classic underapplication does not emerge in this theory as a separate descriptive category that can be freely imposed *via* B-R Identity constraints. The reason is not far to seek. B-R Identity is equally respected in both underapplication and overapplication; by itself, therefore, B-R Identity cannot decide between them. Compare forms (11a) and (11b): ỹăt-nẽỹăt, versus *yat-nẽyat. Base and reduplicant are entirely identical in both candidates. Any decision between them must be made on other grounds.

To get phonology happening at all, the relation Phono-Constraint ≫ I-O Faithfulness must be maintained. In Madurese, this is what yields nasal spread in the language at large. With Phono-Constraint as the final arbiter, overapplication must result, because the underapplicational candidate fails to satisfy it. There is simply no way that the force of Phono-Constraint can be blunted by B-R Identity.

Normal application or reversion of the reduplicant to a less marked repertory, however, remains an option, when B-R Identity is crucially subordinated. In this case, reduplicative identity cannot compel the extension of phonology from base to reduplicant, or vice versa. Base and reduplicant therefore enjoy an independence measured by the number and kind of B-R Identity constraints that are crucially subordinated.

The theory, then, basically distinguishes two conditions: one in which B-R Identity is respected (to some degree, along certain dimensions), yielding overapplication; and one in which B-R Identity is set aside, yielding normal application or reversion to the unmarked in the reduplicant. The choice between under- and overapplicational candidates must be made on grounds other than B-R Identity. In the Madurese case just reviewed, the overapplicational candidate is chosen because it alone satisfies the phonological constraint banning NV_{Oral} while maintaining the required level of identity. How, then, does classic underapplication come about? It can only be that another independent constraint excludes the naively expected result, and that we are really looking at overapplication involving that other constraint.

The underapplication of palatalization in Akan provides an example. The independent constraint here is the OCP, which can be independently observed in the language to prevent palatalization when a coronal-coronal sequence would result (see McCarthy and Prince 1995: section 5 for the details). Indeed, one might expect the OCP to figure commonly in such interactions, since reduplication often produces nearby replications of features; and this is exactly what the OCP can rule out, through high rank. In such cases, the reduplicative situation will reflect a more general restriction on the language – though it may be one that is not particularly salient to the casual observer. Here and in McCarthy and Prince (1995: section 5) we argue that all proposed cases of underapplication are of this type, leading to a schema along these lines (where C stands for, for example, the relevant subcase of the OCP that is visibly active in Akan).

(13)   A skeletal ranking for underapplication as overapplication
       B-R Identity, C ≫ Phono-Constraint ≫ I-O Faithfulness

This ranking results in underapplication, because the mapping due to the subhierarchy Phono-Constraint ≫ I-O Faithfulness is blocked in certain circumstances by C, and reduplication happens to provide one of those circumstances. B-R Identity demands that base and reduplicant mirror each other quite closely, and the only way to attain this while satisfying C is to avoid the mapping triggered by Phono-Constraint. Thus, the full phonology – the mapping involving C – is *overapplied*. This line of argument is pursued in section 6.

A further significant property of Correspondence Theory emerges from the parallelism of constraint evaluation. The base and the reduplicant are evaluated symmetrically and simultaneously with respect to the language's constraint hierarchy. The base does not have serial priority over the reduplicant, and reduplication is not, in fact, the copying or replication of a previously fixed base. Instead, both base and reduplicant can give way, as it were, to achieve the best possible satisfaction of the entire constraint set. The result is that, under certain circumstances, when B-R Identity crucially dominates I-O Faithfulness, the base will be predicted to copy the reduplicant. Overapplicational cases of this type can be found in McCarthy and Prince (1995: section 3.6 to section 3.8, section 5.3). (Lushootseed may be yet another overapplicational case; see Urbanczyk 1996). Such analyses offer very strong evidence for Correspondence Theory as articulated here, and with it, for the claims of parallelist OT, particularly as contrasted with serialist theories of grammatical derivation.

For the theory of reduplicative phonology, the principal interest of the architecture proposed here is this: the phenomena called overapplication and underapplication follow in Correspondence Theory from the very constraints on reduplicant–base identity that permit reduplication to happen in the first place. The constraints responsible for the ordinary copying of a base also govern the copying of phonologically derived properties. Effectively, there is no difference between copying and over- or underapplication, and therefore such phonological interactions, along with normal application, turn out to be a fully expected concomitant of reduplicative structure, obtainable through the permutation of ranked universal constraints, as expected in OT. [...]

Appendix

A set of constraints on the correspondence relation

This appendix provides a tentative list of constraints on correspondent elements. Affinities with other constraint types are noted when appropriate. All constraints refer to pairs of representations (S_1, S_2), standing to each other as (I, O), (B, R), etc. The constraints also refer to a relation $\mathfrak{R}$, the correspondence relation defined for the representations being compared. Thus, each constraint is actually a constraint family, with instantiations for I-O, B-R, I-R, Tone to Tone-Bearer, and so on.

The formalization is far from complete, and aims principally to clarify. As in section 2, we imagine that a structure S_i is encoded as a set of elements, so that we can talk about $\Re$ on (S_1, S_2) in the usual way as a subset, any subset, of $S_1 \times S_2$. We use the following standard jargon: for a relation $\Re \subset A \times B$, $x \in$ Domain $(\Re)$ iff $x \in A$ and $\exists y \in B$ such that $x\Re y$; and $y \in$ Range$(\Re)$ iff $y \in B$ and $\exists x \in A$ such that $x\Re y$.

(A.1)   MAX
    Every element of S_1 has a correspondent in S_2.
      Domain$(\Re) = S_1$

(A.2)   DEP
    Every element of S_2 has a correspondent in S_1.
      Range$(\Re) = S_2$.

MAX (= (3)) and DEP are analogous respectively to PARSE-segment and FILL in Prince and Smolensky (1991, 1993). Both MAX and DEP should be further differentiated by the type of segment involved, vowel versus consonant. The argument for differentiation of FILL can be found in Prince & Smolensky (1993), and it carries over to FILL's analogue DEP. In the case of MAX, the argument can be constructed on the basis of languages like Arabic or Rotuman (McCarthy 1995), with extensive vocalic syncope and no consonant deletion.

(A.3)   IDENT(F)
    Correspondent segments have identical values for the feature F.
      If $x\Re y$ and x is $[\gamma F]$, then y is $[\gamma F]$.

IDENT (= (5)) replaces the PARSE-feature and FILL-feature-node apparatus of Containment-type OT. See Pater (1999) and section 5.4 above for further developments. As stated, IDENT presupposes that only segments stand in correspondence, so all aspects of featural identity must be communicated through correspondent segments. Ultimately, the correspondence relation will be extended to features, to accommodate "floating" feature analyses, like those in Archangeli and Pulleyblank (1994) or Akinlabi (1996). (Also see Lombardi 1995, Zoll 1996.)

(A.4)   Contiguity
    a.   I-CONTIG ("No Skipping")
        The portion of S_1 standing in correspondence forms a contiguous string.
        Domain$(\Re)$ is a single contiguous string in S_1.
    b.   O-CONTIG ("No Intrusion")
        The portion of S_2 standing in correspondence forms a contiguous string.
        Range$(\Re)$ is a single contiguous string in S_2.

These constraints characterize two types of contiguity (see also Kenstowicz 1994). The constraint I-CONTIG rules out deletion of elements *internal* to the input string. Thus, the map $xyz \rightarrow xz$ violates I-CONTIG, because the Range of $\Re$ is {x, z}, and xz is not a contiguous string in the input. But the map $xyz \rightarrow xy$ does not violate

I-Contig, because *xy* is a contiguous string in the input. The constraint O-Contig rules out internal epenthesis: the map *xz* → *xyz* violates O-contig, but *xz* → *xzy* does not. The definition assumes that we are dealing with strings. When the structure S_k is more complex than a string, we need to define a way of plucking out a designated substructure that is a string, in order to apply the definitions to the structure.

(A.5)   {Right, Left}-Anchor(S_1, S_2)
Any element at the designated periphery of S_1 has a correspondent at the designated periphery of S_2.
    Let *Edge*(X, {L, R}) = the element standing at the *Edge* = L, R of X. Right-Anchor. If x = Edge(S_1, R) and y = Edge(S_2, R) then xℜy. Left-Anchor. Likewise, *mutatis mutandis*.

In prefixing reduplication, L-Anchor ≫ R-Anchor, and vice versa for suffixing reduplication. It is clear that Anchoring should subsume Generalized Alignment; as formulated, it captures the effects of Align(MCat, E_1, PCat, E_2) for E_1 = E_2 in McCarthy and Prince (1993b). It can be straightforwardly extended to (PCat, PCat) alignment if correspondence is assumed to be a reflexive relation. For example, in *bí.ta*, the left edge of the foot and the head syllable align because *b* and its correspondent (which is, reflexively, *b*) are initial in both.

(A.6)   Linearity ("No Metathesis")
S_1 is consistent with the precedence structure of S_2, and vice versa.
    Let x, y ∈ S_1 and x′, y′ ∈ S_2.
    If xℜx′ and yℜy′, then
        x < y iff ¬ (y′ < x′).

(A.7)   Uniformity ("No Coalescence")
No element of S_2 has multiple correspondents in S_1.
    For x, y ∈ S_1 and z ∈ S_2, if xℜz and yℜz, then x = y.

(A.8)   Integrity ("No Breaking")
No element of S_1 has multiple correspondents in S_2.
    For x ∈ S_1 and w, z ∈ S, if xℜw and xℜz, then w = z.

Linearity excludes metathesis. Uniformity and Integrity rule out two types of multiple correspondence – coalescence, where two elements of S_1 are fused in S_2, and diphthongization or phonological copying, where one element of S_1 is split or cloned in S_2. On the prohibition against metathesis, see Hume (1995, 1996) and McCarthy (1995). On coalescence, see Gnanadesikan (1995), Lamontagne and Rice (1995), McCarthy (1995), and Pater (1999).

Notes

[. . .]

3   The terms "overapplication" and "under-application" are due to Wilbur (1973a, b, c). See section 3.1 below.

4   We will simplify the discussion in a further respect: we will speak of $\mathfrak{R}$ relating string to string, though relations are properly defined on "sets." A string can always be regarded as a set of ordered pairs of its members with positional indices, and similar constructions can be put together for structures more complex than strings. Ultimately, $\mathfrak{R}$ can be defined over such sets.

Correspondence is treated as a relation rather than a function to allow for one-to-many relationships, as in diphthongization, for example, or coalescence. On these phenomena, see among others Cairns (1976), de Haas (1988), Hayes (1990), and, using correspondence, Gnanadesikan (1995), Lamontagne and Rice (1995), McCarthy (1995), and Pater (1999).

5   For formal development relevant to the full complexity of phonological structures, see Pierrehumbert and Beckman (1988), Kornai (1991), and van Oostendorp (1993). On quantitative transfer, see Levin (1983), Clements (1985a), Mester (1986: 239 note), McCarthy and Prince (1988), and Steriade (1988). On floating features, see among others Archangeli and Pulleyblank (1994), Akinlabi (1996), and Zoll (1996).

6   This way of characterizing Gen under correspondence was suggested to us at the Utrecht workshop by Sharon Inkelas and Orhan Orgun.

7   On differentiation of root versus affix faithfulness, see McCarthy and Prince (1995: section 6.2).

8   Stated as correspondence relations, the components of the Well-Formedness Condition and other autosegmental principles form a set of rankable, hence violable, constraints, leading to significant empirical differences from standard conceptions of autosegmental phonology. See Myers (1993) for an incisive discussion of tonal association under (pre-Correspondence) OT.

9   "Containment" is offered here as a term of art; hence, free association from the ordinary language homophone is unlikely to provide a reliable guide to its meaning.

10 Usually desirable. There are cases, going under the rubric of "opacity" (Kiparsky 1973), where deleted elements do influence the outcome.

11 A Containment or PARSE/FILL approach to B-R Identity is conceivable, but flawed empirically. See the discussion in McCarthy and Prince (1995: section 2.3).

12 In this discussion, we assume that underlying forms are represented in the familiar fashion with predictable allophonic information absent, so that "disparity" is disparity from this structure. Whether such predictable information appears in underlying forms is independent of the assumptions of OT, as noted below (section 4.1, discussion of (48)). The formulation of over- and underapplication in terms of marked/unmarked elements and defaults circumvents this ambiguity.

References

Akinlabi, Akinbiyi. 1984. Tonal underspecification and Yoruba tone, Ph.D. dissertation, University of Ibadan, Nigeria.
—— 1996. Featural affixation, *Journal of Linguistics* 32: 239–90.
Alderete, John. 1996. Faithfulness to prosodic heads, to appear in B. Hermans and M. van Oostendorp (eds.) [ROA-94, http://ruccs.rutgers.edu/roa.html] ◀

Alderete, John, Jill Beckman, Laura Benua, Amalia Gnanadesikan, John McCarthy, and Suzanne Urbanczyk. 1996. Reduplication and segmental markedness, ms. University of Massachusetts, Amherst, MA. [ROA-226, http://ruccs.rutgers.edu/roa.html] ▶
Archangeli, Diana. 1985. Yokuts harmony: evidence for coplanar representation in nonlinear phonology, *Linguistic Inquiry* 16: 335–72.

—— 1988. Aspects of underspecification theory, *Phonology* 5: 183–208.

Archangeli, Diana, and Douglas Pulleyblank. 1994. *Grounded Phonology*, Cambridge, MA: MIT Press.

Austin, Peter. 1981. *A Grammar of Diyari, South Australia*, Cambridge University Press.

Beckman, Jill. 1995. Shona height harmony: markedness and positional identity, in Beckman *et al.* (eds.), 1995, 53–75.

—— 1997. Positional faithfulness, Ph.D. dissertation, University of Massachusetts, Amherst, MA. ◄

Beckman, Jill, Laura Walsh Dickey, and Suzanne Urbanczyk (eds.). 1995. *University of Massachusetts Occasional Papers in Linguistics* 18: *Papers in Optimality Theory*, Amherst, MA: Graduate Linguistic Student Association.

Benua, Laura. 1995. Identity effects in morphological truncation, in Beckman *et al.* (eds.), 1995, 77–136. [ROA-74, http://ruccs.rutgers.edu/roa.html]

—— 1997. Transderivational identity: phonological relations between words, Ph.D. dissertation, University of Massachusetts, Amherst, MA. ◄

Burzio, Luigi. 1994a. *Principles of English Stress*, Cambridge University Press.

—— 1994b. Anti-allomorphy, handout of talk presented at "Going Romance 1994," Utrecht.

Cairns, Charles E. 1976. Universal properties of umlaut and vowel coalescence rules: implications for Rotuman phonology, in A. Juilland (ed.), *Linguistic Studies Offered to Joseph Greenberg*, 3 vols. (Phonology), Saratoga, CA: Anma Libri, II, 271–83.

Carrier, Jill. 1979. The interaction of phonological and morphological rules in Tagalog: a study in the relationship between rule components in grammar, Ph.D. dissertation, Massachusetts Institute of Technology, Cambridge, MA.

Chomsky, Noam. 1975. *Reflections on Language*, New York, NY: Pantheon.

Christaller, Rev. J. G. 1875 [1964]. *A Grammar of the Asante and Fante Language, called Tshi [Chee, Twi]: based on the Akuapem Dialect with Reference to the other (Akan and Fante) Dialects*, Basel: Basel Evangelical Missionary Society. [Reproduced Farnborough, Hants., England: Gregg Press.]

Churchward, C. Maxwell. 1940. *Rotuman Grammar and Dictionary*, Sydney: Australasian Medical Publishing Co. [Reprinted 1978. New York, NY: AMS Press.]

Clements, G. N. 1985a. The problem of transfer in nonlinear morphology, *Cornell Working Papers in Linguistics* 7: 38–73.

—— 1985b. The geometry of phonological features, *Phonology* 2: 225–52.

Clements, G. N. and K. Ford. 1979. Kikuyu tone shift and its synchronic consequences, *Linguistic Inquiry* 10: 179–210.

Davis, Stuart. 1995. Emphasis spread in Arabic and grounded phonology. *Linguistic Inquiry* 26: 465–98.

Gnanadesikan, Amalia. 1995. Markedness and faithfulness constraints in child phonology, ms. University of Massachusetts, Amherst. [ROA-67, http://ruccs.rutgers.edu/roa.html] ►

Goldsmith, John. 1976. Autosegmental phonology, Ph.D. dissertation, Massachusetts Institute of Technology, Cambridge, MA.

Haas, Willem G. de. 1988. A formal theory of vowel coalescence, Ph.D. dissertation, Catholic University of Nijmegen.

Hayes, Bruce. 1990. Diphthongization and coindexing, *Phonology* 7: 31–71.

Hermans, Ben, and Mark van Oostendorp (eds.). To appear. *The Derivational Residue in Phonology*, Amsterdam: John Benjamins. ►

Hume, Elizabeth. 1995. Metathesis effects. Paper presented at the Montréal-Ottawa-Toronto Phonology Workshop, February 1995.

—— 1996. A non-linearity based account of metathesis in Leti, ms. Ohio State University, Columbus, OH. ►

Itô, Junko. 1986. Syllable theory in prosodic phonology, Ph.D. dissertation, University of Massachusetts, Amherst, MA.

—— 1989. A prosodic theory of epenthesis, *Natural Language and Linguistic Theory* 7: 217–60.

Kenstowicz, Michael. 1994. Syllabification in Chukchee: a constraints-based analysis, in A. Davison, N. Maier, G. Silva, and W. S. Yan (eds.), *Proceedings of the Formal Linguistics Society of Mid-America* 4, Iowa City, IA: Department of Linguistics, University of Iowa, 160–81.

Kiparsky, Paul. 1973. Phonological representations, in O. Fujimura (ed.), *Three Dimensions of Linguistic Theory*, Tokyo: Taikusha, 1–136.

—— 1986. The phonology of reduplication, ms. Stanford University, CA.

Kirchner, Robert. 1993. Turkish vowel disharmony in Optimality Theory. Talk presented
at Rutgers Optimality Workshop I, Rutgers
University, New Brunswick, NJ. ▶

Kornai, András. 1991. Formal phonology, Ph.D.
dissertation, Stanford University, CA.

Kuroda, S.-Y. 1967. *Yawelmani Phonology*,
Cambridge, MA: MIT Press.

Lamontagne, Greg, and Keren Rice. 1995. A
correspondence account of coalescence, in
Beckman *et al.* (eds.), 211–24.

Levin, Juliette. 1983. Reduplication and prosodic structure, ms. Massachusetts Institute
of Technology, Cambridge, MA.

Lombardi, Linda. 1995. Why Place and Voice
are different: constraint interactions and feature faithfulness in Optimality Theory, ms.
University of Maryland, College Park. [ROA-
105, http://ruccs.rutgers.edu/roa.html] ▶

Lowenstamm, Jean, and Jonathan Kaye. 1985.
Compensatory lengthening in Tiberian Hebrew, in L. Wetzels and E. Sezer (eds.), *Studies in Compensatory Lengthening*, Dordrecht:
Foris.

Marantz, Alec. 1982. Re reduplication, *Linguistic Inquiry* 13: 435–82.

McCarthy, John J. 1979. Formal problems in
Semitic phonology and morphology, Ph.D.
dissertation, Massachusetts Institute of Technology, Cambridge, MA.

—— 1993. The parallel advantage: containment,
consistency, and alignment. Talk presented at
Rutgers Optimality Workshop I, Rutgers University, New Brunswick, NJ.

—— 1995. Extensions of faithfulness: Rotuman
revisited, ms. University of Massachusetts,
Amherst, MA. To appear in *Natural Language and Linguistic Theory*. (ROA-110,
http://ruccs.rutgers.edu/roa.html] ▶

McCarthy, John J., and Alan S. Prince. 1986.
Prosodic Morphology, ms. University of
Massachusetts, Amherst, MA and Brandeis
University, Waltham, MA. ▶

—— 1988. Quantitative transfer in reduplicative
and templatic morphology, in Linguistic
Society of Korea (ed.), *Linguistics in the Morning Calm* vol. 2, Seoul: Hanshin Publishing
Company, 3–35.

—— 1993a. Prosodic Morphology I: constraint interaction and satisfaction, ms.
University of Massachusetts, Amherst, MA
and Rutgers University, New Brunswick, NJ,
RuCCS-TR-3. ▶

—— 1993b. Generalized alignment, in G. E.
Booij and J. van Marle (eds.), *Yearbook of
Morphology 1993*, Dordrecht: Kluwer, 79–
153. ◀

—— 1994a. The emergence of the unmarked:
Optimality in Prosodic Morphology, in M.
Gonzàlez (ed.), *Proceedings of the North East
Linguistic Society* 24, Amherst, MA: Gradu-
ate Linguistic Student Association, University
of Massachusetts, 333–79. ◀

—— 1994b. Prosodic Morphology: an overview,
papers presented at the Workshop on Prosodic Morphology, University of Utrecht, June
1994. ▶

—— 1995. Faithfulness and reduplicative
identity, in Beckman *et al.* (eds.), 249–384.
[ROA-60, http://ruccs.rutgers.edu/roa.html]

Mester, R. Armin. 1986. Studies in tier structure, Ph.D. dissertation, University of Massachusetts, Amherst, MA.

Myers, Scott. 1993. OCP effects in Optimality
Theory, ms. University of Texas, Austin.

Oostendorp, Marc van. 1993. Phonological lines
in bracketed grids and autosegmental representations, ms. University of Tilburg.

Padgett, Jaye. 1995a. Feature classes, in Beckman *et al.* (eds.), 1995, 385–420.

—— 1995b. Review of John Goldsmith (ed.),
(1993) in *Phonology* 12: 147–55.

Pater, Joe. 1999. Austronesian nasal substitution
and other *NC̥ effects. ◀

Perlmutter, David (ed.). 1983. *Studies in Relational Grammar*, vol. 1, University of Chicago
Press.

Pierrehumbert, Janet, and Mary Beckman. 1988.
Japanese Tone Structure, Cambridge, MA:
MIT Press.

Postal, Paul. 1970. On coreferential complement
subject deletion, *Linguistic Inquiry* 1: 439–
500.

Prince, Alan S., and Paul Smolensky. 1991.
Notes on Connectionism and Harmony
Theory in linguistics, Technical report
CU-CS-533-91, Department of Computer
Science, University of Colorado, Boulder,
CO.

—— 1993. Optimality Theory: constraint interaction in generative grammar, ms. Rutgers
University, New Brunswick, NJ, and University of Colorado, Boulder, CO. ◀

Pulleyblank, Douglas. 1988. Vocalic underspecification in Yoruba, *Linguistic Inquiry* 19:
233–70.

Schachter, Paul, and Victoria Fromkin. 1968. *A Phonology of Akan: Akuapem, Asante, and Fante, UCLA Working Papers in Phonetics 9.*

Selkirk, Elisabeth. 1981. Epenthesis and degenerate syllables in Cairene Arabic, in H. Borer and J. Aoun (eds.), *Theoretical Issues in the Grammar of the Semitic Languages*, Cambridge, MA: Department of Linguistics and Philosophy, Massachusetts Institute of Technology.

—— 1995. Surface restrictions in the distribution of lexical contrasts: the role for root faithfulness. Handout for *Linguistics 751*, University of Massachusetts, Amherst.

Shetler, Joanne. 1976. *Notes on Balangao Grammar*, Huntington Beach, CA: Summer Institute of Linguistics.

Smolensky, Paul. 1993. Harmony, markedness, and phonological activity. Paper presented at Rutgers Optimality Workshop I, Rutgers University, New Brunswick, NJ. ▶

Spencer, Andrew. 1993. The optimal way to syllabify Chukchee. Paper presented at Rutgers Optimality Workshop I, Rutgers University, New Brunswick, NJ.

Spring, Cari. 1994. The Axininca future reflexive, ms. California State University, San Marcos, CA. [Presented at 23rd Western Conference on Linguistics, 1993.]

Steriade, Donca. 1982. Greek prosodies and the nature of syllabification, Ph.D. dissertation, Massachusetts Institute of Technology, Cambridge, MA.

—— 1988. Reduplication and syllable transfer in Sanskrit and elsewhere, *Phonology 5*: 73–155.

Stevens, Alan M. 1968. *Madurese Phonology and Morphology*, American Oriental Series 52, New Haven, CT: American Oriental Society.

—— 1985. Reduplication in Madurese, in *Proceedings of the Second Eastern States Conference on Linguistics*, Columbus, OH: Linguistics Department, Ohio State University, 232–42.

Urbanczyk, Suzanne. 1996. Patterns of reduplication in Lushootseed, Ph.D. dissertation, University of Massachusetts, Amherst, MA.

—— 1999. Double reduplications in parallel. ▶

Voegelin, C. F. 1935. Tübatulabal grammar, *University of California Publications in American Archaeology and Ethnology 34*: 55–190.

Welmers, William. 1946. *A Descriptive Grammar of Fanti, Language* dissertation 39, *Language* vol. 22, no. 3 Supplement.

Wilbur, Ronnie. 1973a. The phonology of reduplication, Ph.D. dissertation, University of Illinois, Urbana-Champaign, IL.

—— 1973b. Reduplication and rule ordering, in *Papers from the Ninth Regional Meeting of the Chicago Linguistic Society*, Chicago, IL: Chicago Linguistic Society, 679–87.

—— 1973c. The Identity Constraint: an explanation of the irregular behavior of some exceptional reduplicated forms, *Studies in the Linguistic Sciences 3*: 143–54.

Yip, Moira. 1993. Cantonese loanword phonology and Optimality Theory, *Journal of East Asian Linguistics 2*: 261–91.

Zoll, Cheryl. 1996. Parsing below the segment in a constraint-based framework, Ph.D. dissertation, University of California, Berkeley, CA. [ROA-143, http://ruccs.rutgers.edu/roa.html]

Study and Research Questions

1 Using the ranking schemata in (13) and positing *ad hoc* markedness constraints as needed, construct tableaux for the examples in (8–10).

2 Various examples in §2.1 are used to illustrate different faithfulness effects. Use the constraints given in the chapter's appendix to construct tableaux for these examples. (You may need to invent some *ad hoc* markedness constraints.)

3 Section 2.3 sketches an argument, based on epenthesis, for correspondence over PARSE/FILL. Supply the details of this argument with appropriate examples (which may be artificial), constraints, and tableaux.

4 Enforcing featural faithfulness is the job of IDENT(F) constraints, though the chapter mentions the possibility of replacing them with MAX(F) and DEP(F) constraints. How do IDENT(F) and

Max(F)/Dep(F) differ in what they presuppose about features? What kinds of phenomena might be used to argue for one or the other?

5   In (1), correspondence is defined as a relation on strings. But the surrounding text and notes raise the possibility of generalizing correspondence to other phonological structures. Posit some correspondence-based faithfulness constraints for phonology *above* the segment. What issues arise?

Part II
Formal Analysis

Computing Optimal Forms in Optimality Theory: Basic Syllabification

Editor's Note

On first exposure to Optimality Theory, many people see the size of the candidate set as a problem. As GEN is commonly understood, there is no limit on the number of candidates that can be derived from a single input. (This follows primarily from the assumption that epenthesis can apply one, two, or more times in a candidate.) The worry is that EVAL will never finish sorting the infinite candidate set, so no outputs will ever be generated.

This concern, though certainly natural, is misconceived in two ways. First, it neglects the well-known distinction between competence and performance. OT is a theory of competence, and as such it's obliged to be well-defined but not necessarily easy to compute. Second, a theory of performance associated with OT need not proceed by the Sisyphean strategy of sorting an infinite set. As this chapter shows, there are much more clever ways to compute the optimal form. (For further references on computational modeling and formal analysis of OT, see McCarthy 2002: 216–20, 233.)

1 The Parsing Problem in Optimality Theory

In Optimality Theory (Prince & Smolensky 1993), grammaticality is defined in terms of optimization. For any given linguistic input, the grammatical parse, or structural description, of that input is selected from a set of candidate parses for that input. The grammatical parse is optimal in that it does the best job of satisfying a ranked set of universal constraints. The formal definition of the theory includes a function, called GEN, which maps an input to a set (possibly infinite) of candidate parses. Each candidate parse by definition contains the input. Each of these candidates may be evaluated in terms of the number of times it violates each universal

Originally circulated as:
Tesar, Bruce (1995) *Computing Optimal Forms in Optimality Theory: Basic Syllabification.* Report no. CU-CS-763-95. Boulder, CO: Department of Computer Science, University of Colorado. [Available on Rutgers Optimality Archive, ROA-52.]

constraint. The ranking of the universal constraints is strict: one violation of a given constraint is strictly worse than any number of violations of a lower-ranked constraint.

A grammar specifies a function: the grammar itself does not specify an algorithm, it simply assigns a grammatical structural description to each input. However, one can ask the computational question of whether efficient algorithms exist to compute the description assigned to a linguistic input. This is the parsing problem that I consider here. Although the term "parsing" is more commonly associated with models of language comprehension, I am treating it as the more general issue of assigning structure to input, an issue relevant to both comprehension and production. In fact, the treatment of the Basic CV Syllable Theory discussed in this paper is more easily thought of as relating to production: the input is an underlying form, and the structural description includes the surface form. In Optimality Theory, the parsing problem is easily understood as an optimization problem: search the space of candidate structural descriptions for the one that optimally satisfies the ranked constraints.

The general spirit of Optimality Theory is to generate a large and general space of candidate structural descriptions for an input, leaving much of the work to the constraints to determine grammaticality. This makes the parsing problem non-trivial; GEN is often envisioned as generating an infinite number of candidate structural descriptions for an input, in which case simple exhaustive search is not even tenable. Even if GEN were finite, the number of candidates would still grow exponentially in the length of the input.

Although Optimality Theory is easily understood mathematically in terms of the generation and evaluation of all candidates in parallel, it is unnecessary, and in fact counterproductive, to consider the computation of optimal forms in those terms. The algorithm presented in this paper uses a technique known as Dynamic Programming. Intuitively, the algorithm operates by gradually constructing a few candidate parses as it works through the input. When the end of the input is reached, only a few complete parses have been constructed, one of which is guaranteed to be optimal. As an illustration, the Basic CV Syllable Theory is discussed and a complete parser is described for that theory.

1.1   Preliminary: An intuitive illustration of Dynamic Programming

Due to the nature of the problem under consideration, the analysis presented in this paper will at times involve considerable formal complexity. With that in mind, the fundamental idea underlying the analysis, Dynamic Programming, is here introduced via an intuitive analogy. Suppose that there are two towns, X and Y. In between these towns is a river, which must be crossed in order to travel from X to Y. There are three bridges across the river: A, B, and C. Suppose that we wish to find the shortest – the optimal – route from X to Y.

We know that any path between X and Y must cross one of the three bridges. There are many different ways to get from town X to each of the three bridges, and many different ways to get from each of the bridges to town Y. However, we can simplify our problem by first only considering the best way to get from X to A, the best way from X to B, and the best way from X to C. Having found each of these "sub-routes", we could make a small table for future reference: it would have three entries, each giving the route and the distance of the route to one of the bridges. Next, we could consider the best way to get to Y from each of the three bridges. Once we determine the shortest route from bridge A to town Y, we can easily calculate the shortest route from X to Y which crosses bridge A, by adding the distance of the shortest route from A to Y with the table entry giving the distance from X to A. In the same fashion, we can calculate the shortest route from X to Y crossing B, by combining the shortest route from B to Y and using the already calculated shortest route from X to B. The same can be done for bridge C. At this point, we need only choose the shortest of three routes: the shortest route of those for each of the three bridges.

Notice that there are many possible routes between X and Y: just considering bridge A, every possible route from X to A may be combined with every possible route from A to Y. In fact, the problem is best understood in that fashion, as the problem of searching the space of all possible routes between X and Y to find the shortest one. But while the problem is most easily stated and understood in those terms, it is not most easily solved in those terms. The above illustration gives the essence of Dynamic Programming: break a large problem, like traveling from X to Y, into smaller sub-problems, like traveling from X to A, and traveling from A to Y.

The value of this way of thinking is perhaps even more apparent if we change the problem so that there are two rivers between X and Y: the second river having three bridges, D, E, and F. In this case, we would first put into our table the shortest route from X to the bridges A, B, and C. Next, for bridge D, we would consider the shortest route from each of the bridges A, B, and C. We would then make another table entry giving the shortest route from town X to bridge D: this will be the shortest of three routes, the shortest route from X to D via bridge A, via bridge B, and via bridge C. Next, similar table entries would be written down for bridges E and F. Finally, we could calculate the shortest route from town X to town Y by considering the shortest route via bridge D, via E, and via F. Again, at the end, we need only compare three complete routes between X and Y.

The algorithm presented in this paper will use Dynamic Programming to compute optimal forms. Each segment of the input is something like a river in the above illustration. There are a limited number of ways to deal with an input segment, and the best way to do each can be recorded in a table. Once all of the input segments have been considered in order, only a very few entire parses of the input need be compared in order to determine the optimal one.

2   The Basic CV Syllable Theory

The Basic CV Syllable Theory is described in §6 of Prince & Smolensky 1993. An input to the grammar is a sequence of segments categorized as consonants and vowels, that is, a member of $\{C,V\}^+$. The structural descriptions generated by GEN are strings of syllables with the following restrictions: nuclei are mandatory, onsets and codas are optional, and positions are assumed to contain at most one input segment. The order of the input segments must be preserved, and each input segment must either be placed in a syllabic position or marked as unparsed in the structure. Further, a C may only be parsed as an onset or a coda, while V may only be parsed as a nucleus. Notice that this is a statement of the universal set of structural descriptions to be considered, and not the inventory for any particular language. For a given input, GEN generates all possible syllable structures that contain the input, and meet the restrictions just given.[1]

Officially, the universal constraints of the Basic CV Syllable Theory are:

(1)   ONS – syllables must have onsets
       NOCODA – syllables must not have codas
       PARSE – input segments must be parsed (into syllabic positions)
       FILL^{Nuc} – a nucleus position must be filled (with a V)
       FILL^{Ons} – an onset position must be filled (with a C)

These constraints are violable and may be ranked differently by different languages.

The problem of computing the optimal structural description is non-trivial because GEN is allowed to underparse and overparse. *Underparsing* refers to any segment of the input which is not assigned (parsed) to a specific syllabic position within a structural description. *Overparsing* refers to any syllabic position contained in the structural description which does not have an input segment parsed into it. Because overparsing may in principle occur an unbounded number of times, the space of candidate structural descriptions for any given input is infinite.

Prince and Smolensky implicitly describe the space of possible structural descriptions. Immediately below, I give a formal description of this space. This description is used when constructing the parser. By showing how to construct a parser for this particular description, it should be fairly clear how similar parsers would be constructed for other theories with similar formal descriptions.

For computational purposes, we will regard a structural description of an input as a string of *syllabic positions*, referred to as a *position structure*, which are matched with the input segments. The positions are represented by the symbols {o,n,d}, for onset, nucleus, and coda, respectively ("C" is reserved for consonant). In a given structural description, each position may be filled with at most one input segment, and each input segment may be parsed into at most one position. Any input segment not parsed into a syllabic position is so marked in the structural description. For a given position structure, each allowable way of matching the input with the structure counts as a candidate structural description. An allowable matching is one in which the order of the input segments is preserved, and in which V segments are only parsed into n positions, while C segments are only parsed into o and d positions.

Figure 1 shows some examples of candidate parses for the input /VC/:

Figure 1

```
n - d     n - d - o - n     o - n - n
|   |     |   |       |           |
V   C     V       C         V   C
```

The lower case letters are syllable positions. Syllable positions with vertical bars under them are filled by the input segments immediately under the vertical bars. Any syllable position without a vertical bar underneath is unfilled in that parse (to be filled by epenthesis at the phonetic stage). An input segment (V or C) which is not underneath a vertical bar is not parsed into any position, and will not be apparent in the surface form.

Here are a couple of parses that are not generated by GEN:

Figure 2

```
o - n      n - o
|   |      |   |
V   C      V   C
```

The first is not generated because GEN forbids parsing a V in an onset position, and forbids parsing a C in a nucleus position. The second is not generated because the position grammar of GEN will not generate an onset position without a following nucleus position.

I will use the following *position grammar* to describe the set of allowable position structures:

(2) $S \Rightarrow e \mid oO \mid nN$
      $O \Rightarrow nN$
      $N \Rightarrow e \mid dD \mid oO \mid nN$
      $D \Rightarrow e \mid oO \mid nN$

The terminals in the position grammar are the syllabic positions and the empty string (e). The non-terminals {S, O, N, D} may be thought of as corresponding to states in the derivation of a position structure. S is the starting state. O signifies that the last position generated was an onset (o), N that a nucleus (n) was just generated, and D a coda (d).

(3) $S \Rightarrow nN \Rightarrow ndD \Rightarrow ndoO \Rightarrow ndonN \Rightarrow ndon$

Those non-terminals which may evaluate to e correspond to possible finishing states. O is not a finishing state, because a syllable with an onset must also have a nucleus. This position grammar guarantees that each syllable has a nucleus, that onsets precede nuclei, that codas follow nuclei, and that there is at most one of each type of position per syllable.

It should here be emphasized that the position grammar just discussed is a descriptive formalism useful in understanding GEN; it is NOT a computational mechanism. The actual computational mechanism understandable in terms of the position grammar is the set of operations contained in the Operations Set, described below.

3   Parsing the CV Theory

The challenge is to efficiently choose the optimal structural description from an infinite set of candidates. The solution is to avoid dealing with whole structural descriptions, and instead build up the optimal one piece by piece. The basic technique used to do this is Dynamic Programming (see, e.g., Corman, Leiserson, & Rivest 1990). The algorithm presented here is related to chart parsing (see, e.g., Kay 1980), an algorithm used in natural language parsing that employs Dynamic Programming. Dynamic Programming has also been used for optimization in sequence comparison (see, e.g., Sankoff & Kruskal 1983) and Hidden Markov models (see, e.g., Rabiner 1989). The algorithm presented here combines the use of Dynamic Programming for language structure processing with Dynamic Programming for optimization, resulting in optimization-based language processing.

The algorithm proceeds by creating a table, called the Dynamic Programming Table, and filling in the cells of the table. Once all of the cells have been filled, the optimal form is quite easily determined. Section 3.1 describes the table and explains how it contributes to computing the optimal form. Section 3.2 describes the operations used to fill the cells of the table, both how they relate to the table and how they relate to the Basic CV Syllable Theory.

3.1   The Dynamic Programming Table

Table 1 shows the DP Table for the input /VC/, with the constraint ranking ONS $\gg$ NOCODA $\gg$ FILL^{Nuc} $\gg$ PARSE $\gg$ FILL^{Ons}.

Each cell in this table contains a structure. Each column of this table stands for a segment of the input except the first column, BOI, which corresponds to the "beginning of the input". Notice that each cell in the column headed i_1 contains a V; further, every structure in the column headed i_2 contains both a V and a C, in the correct order. The label on each row is a non-terminal of the position grammar, and corresponds to a type of syllable position. Notice that for each structure in the N row, the last-generated position in the structure is a nucleus. The O row contains structures ending in an onset, while the D row contains structures ending in a coda. The S row only contains structures in which no positions at all have been generated (i.e., all of the input segments seen are unparsed). Thus, each cell contains a structure which contains all of the input segments up through the one heading the column of the cell, and with a last generated syllable position corresponding to the row of the cell. The cell in row D and in column i_2, $[D,i_2]$, contains a structure which includes the input segments i_1 and i_2, and the last syllable position in the structure is a coda.

Table 1   Dynamic Programming Table for /VC/

	BOI	$i_1 = V$	$i_2 = C$
S		⟨V⟩	⟨VC⟩
O	.□	.□V.□	.□V.C
N	.□◌́	.□V	.□V.⟨C⟩
D	.□◌́□.	.□V□.	.□VC.

Optimal Parse: .□V.⟨C⟩   This parse is represented in cell $[N,i_2]$.

The value of the table is that each cell does not contain just any structure meeting the requirements just described; each cell contains the best structure meeting those requirements. Each cell contains a structure representing the best way of parsing the input up through the segment for that column ending in the row-appropriate position. The last column (the column for the last input segment) includes the complete parses to be considered. The optimal parse is easily chosen from among this set of possibilities.

In general, a given input string I is parsed by constructing a DP Table. The table has one column for each segment of the input, plus a first column, BOI. The BOI column is present because positions may be generated at the beginning, before any of the input has been examined (this would correspond to epenthesis at the beginning of the utterance). Each cell corresponds to a *partial description*, which is a structural description of part of the input. The table cell $[N,i_2]$ corresponds to the optimal way of parsing up through the second segment of the input, with a nucleus being the last structural position in the partial description. Each cell also contains the constraint violation marks assessed to the partial description, and representing the Harmony of that description (these marks are not depicted in table 1).

The parsing algorithm proceeds by filling in the columns of the table one at a time, left to right. After the best way of parsing the input through segment i_{j-1} ending in each non-terminal has been calculated (the entries of column i_{j-1}), those values are then used to determine the best way (for each possible final position) of parsing the input through segment i_j (the entries of column i_j). Once all the values for the last column are determined, the Harmony values in the table cells of the last column in rows corresponding to possible finishing states are compared (this is explained in greater detail below). The cell (among those being compared) containing the highest Harmony value thus also contains the optimal parse of the input.

3.2   The Operations Set

Operations are used to fill cells in the DP Table. An operation works by taking the partial description in a previously filled cell, adding an element of structure to it, and putting the new description in the new cell. A cell entry is determined by considering all of the operations that might fill the cell, and selecting the one with the highest resulting Harmony to actually fill the cell. This is the essence of Dynamic Programming: because the partial descriptions in later cells contain the partial descriptions listed in earlier cells, the earlier cell entries may be used directly, rather than explicitly recalculating all of the possibilities for later cells.

Each operation is based upon one of three primitive actions. The three primitive actions are:

(4)   (a)   parsing a segment of input into a new syllabic position;
       (b)   underparsing an input segment;
       (c)   overparsing a new syllabic position.

Primitive actions (a) and (c) involve generating positions, so they must be coordinated with productions in the position grammar of GEN; (b) does not involve position generation. On the other hand, actions (a) and (b) consume input, while (c) does not. Operations are versions of the primitive actions coordinated with the specifics of the model (*Gen* and the universal constraints). An operation may be specified by four things: the new cell (being filled), the previous cell containing the description being added to, the structure added to the partial description, and the constraint violation marks incurred by the operation. A candidate structural description of an input may thus be viewed as resulting from a sequence of operations. It should be emphasized that an operation does not transform one entire structural description into another, but merely adds to a partial description.

As an example, consider the actions that might fill cell $[O,i_2]$ of the DP Table. Recall that the structure in this cell must contain input segments i_1, and i_2, and the last syllabic position in the structure must be an onset. One possibility is the underparsing action: take the structure from the cell immediately to the left in the same row, $[O,i_1]$, and add to it the input segment i_2 marked as underparsed. We don't need to consider any other ways of filling this cell with i_2 underparsed, because we have already guaranteed that $[O,i_1]$ contains the best way of parsing through i_1 ending in an onset. The resulting Harmony of the operation will be the Harmony listed in $[O,i_1]$, with the mark {*PARSE} added to it (indicating the constraint violated by underparsing). If i_2 is a consonant, then another possibility is to parse i_2 into a newly generated onset position. This requires having a structure from the previous column to which an onset position may be legally appended. The position grammar (2) shows that an onset position may be generated directly from the non-terminals S, N, and D; this corresponds to the intuitive notions that an onset must be at the beginning of a syllable, and may be the first position of a description (generated from S), may immediately follow a nucleus position (generated from N), or may immediately follow a coda position (generated from D). An onset position may not immediately follow another onset position, because then the first onset belongs to a syllable with no nucleus. Fortunately, we have already determined that the cells $[S,i_1]$, $[N,i_1]$, and $[D,i_1]$ contain the optimal partial descriptions for the allowed three cases. Finally, the cell $[O,i_2]$ may be filled by an overparsing operation that would take a structure which already contains i_2 and append an unfilled onset position.

The set of possible operations is called the Operations Set, and is organized to indicate what operations may fill each type of cell (the cells are here typed by row). Table 2 shows the operations for filling cells in row O (the rest of the Operations Set for the CV Syllable Theory appear in the appendix). Each row in the table corresponds to an operation. The new cell column shows the type of cell to be filled by the operation. The condition column contains any additional conditions that must be met in order for the operation to apply (in this case, the restriction of V to nuclei, etc.). The previous cell column indicates the relative position of the cell containing the partial description being added to by the operation. The structure column indicates the additional structure added by the operation. The violations column shows the constraint violation marks incurred by the added structure. The final two columns are informational: the production column lists the position grammar production used by the operation if one is used, and the operation type column indicates the type of operation. The term i_j in each operation is a variable, meant to match whatever segment heads the column of the cell currently being filled; there is not a separate operation in the Operations Set for each column (input segment).

Table 2   The Operations Set operations for filling an O row cell

New cell	Condition	Previous cell	Struc	Violations	Information Production	Operation type
$[O,i_j]$		$[O,i_{j-1}]$	$\langle i_j \rangle$	{*PARSE}		Underparsing
$[O,i_j]$	IF $i_j = C$	$[S,i_{j-1}]$	o/i_j	{ }	$S \Rightarrow oO$	Parsing
$[O,i_j]$	IF $i_j = C$	$[N,i_{j-1}]$	o/i_j	{ }	$N \Rightarrow oO$	Parsing
$[O,i_j]$	IF $i_j = C$	$[D,i_{j-1}]$	o/i_j	{ }	$D \Rightarrow oO$	Parsing
$[O,i_j]$		$[S,i_j]$	$o/\square$	{*FILL^{Ons}}	$S \Rightarrow oO$	Overparsing
$[O,i_j]$		$[N,i_j]$	$o/\square$	{*FILL^{Ons}}	$N \Rightarrow oO$	Overparsing
$[O,i_j]$		$[D,i_j]$	$o/\square$	{*FILL^{Ons}}	$D \Rightarrow oO$	Overparsing

The Operations Set relates to the DP Table as follows. The Operations Set gives all of the possible operations that may fill a given cell in the Dynamic Programming Table. Each of the possible operations "competes" to fill in the cell. The product of each operation is a partial structure consisting of (a) the partial structure contained in the operation's previous cell with the operation's additional structure appended to it, and (b) the Harmony of the new partial structure, which consists of the list of marks in the operation's previous cell with the marks incurred by the operation added to it. The operation producing the most harmonic partial description (that is, the one whose resulting list of marks is least offensive with respect to the constraint ranking of the grammar) actually gets to fill the cell. Told from the point of view of the algorithm, examine each of the operations which can fill the current cell, select the one which produces the most harmonic partial structure, and place that operation's partial structure and list of marks into the current cell.

The cell [S,BOI] is the starting cell: no input has yet been examined, and no positions have been generated. So, [S,BOI] has a Harmony value of no constraint violations in it. The other cells in the BOI column may be filled from there by overparsing operations. The cells in the BOI column may only be filled by overparsing operations, as there are no input segments for other operations to work with.

One crucial aspect has not yet been explained about the application of these operations. The parsing and underparsing operations have a previous state cell from the previous column in the DP Table, i_{j-1}. However, the overparsing operations refer to other cells in the same column of the DP Table as the cell being filled. How, in general, can these cells be filled, if the value for each cell in the column depends upon the values in the other cells of the column? The answer involves some intricate details of the algorithm, and is given in the next section.

Notice that, in the Operations Table, the Parsing operations contain IF conditions. These are used to enforce constraints of the CV theory that consonants (C)

may only fill onsets and codas, and vowels (V) only nuclei. These restrictions are assumed to be part of GEN, and so are included here as IF conditions.

3.3   Limiting structure: position grammar cycles

The overparsing operations consume no input, and so they map between cells within a single column. In principle, an unbounded number of such operations could apply, and in fact structures with arbitrary numbers of unfilled positions are output by GEN (as formally defined). However, the algorithm need only explicitly consider a finite number of overparsing operations within a column. The position grammar has four non-terminals. Therefore, at most three overparsing operations can take place consecutively without the repeating of a non-terminal. A set of consecutive overparsings that both begins and ends with the same non-terminal can be considered a *cycle*. An example of a cycle of overparsings is an entire epenthesized syllable. The FILL constraints serve to penalize overparsings by penalizing any structural positions unfilled by input segments. One effect of these constraints is that cycles of overparsing operations are effectively banned (that is, no optimal structure will contain a cycle).

This fact is not specific to the Basic Syllable Theory. For any theory within Optimality Theory, the constraints must ban cycles of overparsings in order for the optimal value to be well-defined. If the constraints make a description containing such a cycle more harmonic than a description differing only by the removal of that cycle, then there is no optimal value, because one could always increase the Harmony by adding more such cycles of overparsings. If such cycles have no Harmony consequences, then there will be an infinite number of optimal descriptions, as any optimal description can have more cycles of overparsings added to create a description with equal Harmony. Thus, for optimization with respect to the constraints to be well-defined and reasonable, the constraints must strictly penalize overparsing cycles. The number of non-terminals in the position grammar bounds the number of consecutive overparsings that may occur without having a cycle.

Operations are properly applied to the Dynamic Programming Table by first filling in all cells of a column considering only underparsing and parsing operations (which only use values from the previous column). Next, a pass is then made through the column cells, considering the overparsing operations: if the resulting Harmony of an overparsing operation into a cell from another cell in the same column is higher than the Harmony already listed in the cell, replace the Harmony in the cell with that resulting from the considered overparsing operation. If at least one cell's entry was replaced by an overparsing operation, then another pass is made through the column. This is repeated until a pass is made in which no overparsing operations replace any cell values. Because the constraints guarantee that cycles are not optimal, and there are four non-terminals, the maximum number of productive passes through the column is three.

The ban on overparsing cycles is the crucial observation that allows the algorithm to complete the search in a finite amount of time; although the space of structural descriptions to be searched is infinite, there is a provably correct (input-dependent) bound on the space of descriptions that actually need to be considered.

3.4   Selecting the optimal parse

Once the entire table has been completed, the optimal parse may be selected. In the position grammar, certain non-terminals may evaluate to the empty string. This means that they can be the last non-terminal in a derivation, and therefore that the syllable position to which each corresponds is a valid end of syllable position. Therefore, the cells in the final column, in rows corresponding to these non-terminals, contain valid complete parses of the input. For the Basic Syllable Theory, the non-terminals are N and D, signifying that a syllable may end in a nucleus or a coda, and S, for the null parse. These three entries are compared, and the entry with the highest Harmony is selected as the optimal parse of the input.

3.5   Outline of the parsing algorithm

Note: OP(i_j) stands for the result (structure and marks) of applying operation OP for column i_j.

Set [S,BOI] to no structure and no violation marks

Fill each other cell in column BOI with the best overparsing operation that currently applies
Repeat until no cell entries change
  For each row X in BOI
    For each overparsing operation OP for X
      If Harmony(OP(BOI)) > Harmony([X,BOI]), set [X,BOI] to OP(BOI)

For each column i_j, proceeding from left to right
  For each row X
    Fill [X,i_j] with the result of the underparsing operation for X
    For each parsing operation OP for X
      If Harmony (OP(i_j)) > Harmony([X,i_j]), set [X,i_j] to OP(i_j)
  Repeat until no cell entries change
    For each row X
      For each overparsing operation OP for X
        If Harmony (OP(i_j)) > Harmony([X,i_j]), set [X,i_j] to OP(i_j)

Select from the final column the most Harmonic of the entries in rows S, N, and D

4   A Sample Parse

Table 3 shows the completed Dynamic Programming Table for the input /VC/, with the constraint ranking ONS ≫ NOCODA ≫ FILL^{Nuc} ≫ PARSE ≫ FILL^{Ons}.

Table 3   The completed Dynamic Programming Table for /VC/

	BOI	$i_1 = V$	$i_2 = C$
S	START	under from:[S,BOI] *Parse ⟨V⟩	under from:[S,i_1] *Parse *Parse ⟨VC⟩
O	over from:[S,BOI] *Fill^{Ons} .□	over from:[N,i_1] *Fill^{Ons} *Fill^{Ons} .□V.□	parse from:[N,i_1] *Fill^{Ons} .□V.C
N	over from:[O,BOI] *Fill^{Ons} *Fill^{Nuc} .□□́	parse from:[O,BOI] *Fill^{Ons} .□V	under from:[N,i_1] *Fill^{Ons} *Parse .□V.⟨C⟩
D	over from:[N,BOI] *Fill^{Ons} *Fill^{Nuc} *NoCoda .□□́□.	over from:[N,i_1] *Fill^{Ons} *NoCoda .□V□.	parse from:[N,i_1] *Fill^{Ons} *NoCoda .□VC.

Optimal Parse: .□V.⟨C⟩   This parse is represented in cell [N,i_2].

The top line of each cell contains on the left an indication of the type of operation that filled the cell, and on the right (after the "from:" label) the row and column designation of the previous cell (the already filled cell whose structure was added onto by the operation to fill the current cell). The abbreviations indicate the kind of operation that filled the cell: "over" for overparsing, "under" for underparsing, and "parse" for parsing. The constraint violation marks assessed to the partial description are given on the middle line of each cell, and the bottom of each cell shows the partial description represented by that cell. The cell containing the optimal parse is indicated manually, and the cells which constitute the steps in the construction of the optimal parse are double-lined.

Parsing begins by filling the cells of the first column (see table 4). The first cell, [S,BOI], is automatically filled with no structure, which incurs no constraint violations. Next, the cell [O,BOI] is filled. For this, the Operations Set is consulted. The Operations Set lists seven operations that can fill a cell in the O row (see table 2). However, the underparsing and parsing operations do not apply here because they make reference to entries in an earlier column, which does not exist here. Of the three overparsing operations, two require entries in cells not yet filled: [N,BOI] and [D,BOI]. The remaining operation uses the entry in [S,BOI] as the previous cell and adds an unfilled onset position. This structure is placed in the cell, along with the incurred mark listed in the operation. Next, the cell [N,BOI] is filled. Of the nine operations listed for a cell in the nucleus row, two may be considered here. The first is for previous cell [S,BOI], and results in violations of Ons and Fill^{Nuc}. The second is for previous cell [O,BOI], and results in violations of Fill^{Ons} and Fill^{Nuc}. Because Ons ≫ Fill^{Ons}, the result of the first operation has lower Harmony than the result of the second; thus, the second operation gets to fill the cell. The cell [D,BOI] is filled similarly. That completes the first pass through the column for the

Table 4   The DP Table with the underparsing and parsing operations completed for column i_1

	BOI		$i_1 = V$		$i_2 = C$
S	START		under *PARSE ⟨V⟩	[S,BOI]	
O	over *FILL^Ons .□	[S,BOI]	under *FILL^Ons *PARSE .□⟨V⟩	[O,BOI]	
N	over *FILL^Ons *FILL^Nuc .□□́	[O,BOI]	parse *FILL^Ons .□V	[O,BOI]	
D	over *FILL^Ons *FILL^Nuc *NoCoda .□□́□.	[N,BOI]	under *FILL^Ons *FILL^Nuc *NoCoda *PARSE .□□́□.⟨V⟩	[N,BOI]	

overparsing operations. Next, a second pass is performed; now, for each cell, all of the overparsing operations may be considered, because each cell in the column contains an entry. However, no further overparsing operations change any of the cell entries, because none improve the Harmony of the entry, so the filling of the first column is complete.

Now, column i_1 must be filled. The cells are first filled via the underparsing and parsing operations. We will focus in detail on how cell $[O,i_1]$ gets filled. First, the one underparsing operation fills the cell; this results in a structure which has an unfilled onset position, and in which the first input segment, $i_1 = V$, is left unparsed. Next, the three parsing operations are considered. But none apply, because the input segment is a V, and an onset position may only have a C parsed into it. The underparsing and parsing operations for the rest of the column are now performed. The results of the steps up to this point are shown in table 4.

Finally, we consider the overparsing operations. For $[O,i_1]$, there are three overparsing operations, each of which appends an unfilled onset, and incurs the mark *FILL^Ons. The first adds an unfilled onset to the structure in its previous cell, $[S,i_1]$, resulting in a partial structure with marks *PARSE and *FILL^Ons. The second has previous cell $[N,i_1]$, and results in marks *FILL^Ons and *FILL^Ons. The third has previous cell $[D,i_1]$, and results in the marks *FILL^Ons, *FILL^Nuc, *NoCoda, *PARSE, and *FILL^Ons. Of the three, the second overparsing operation has the highest resulting Harmony: the highest-ranked constraint violated by the second operation is *FILL^Ons, while each of the other two violates a higher-ranked constraint. Importantly, it also has higher Harmony than the entry already in cell $[O,i_1]$, because FILL^Nuc ≫ FILL^Ons. Therefore, the result of this overparsing operation replaces the earlier entry in the cell. Overparsing also replaces the entry in $[D,i_1]$. On the next pass through the column, no cell entries are replaced by further overparsing operations, so the column is complete.

Once all of the columns have been completed, the optimal parse may be selected. The final candidates are the structures in the cells in the final column, and in rows S, N, and D. Only these rows are considered because they correspond to the non-terminals that may evaluate to the empty string e in the position grammar (the possible final non-terminals). The optimal parse is in cell $[N,i_2]$, as shown in table 3.

5   Discussion

5.1   Computational complexity

Each column in the DP Table is processed in constant time for any fixed grammar: the number of cells in each column is the number of non-terminals in the position grammar, and the number of passes through the column is bounded from above by the number of non-terminals. There is one column for each input segment (plus the BOI column). Therefore, the algorithm is linear in the size of the input.

5.2   Ties

One possibility not shown in the above example is for two different operations to tie for optimality when attempting to fill a cell. To illustrate, there are two ways to derive an essentially identical partial description: first insert and then delete, or first delete and then insert. In this case, the tie might be seen as a kind of anomaly, having no significance to the ultimate phonetic realization. However, if more than one truly different partial description for the same cell incurred identical marks, including all of them in the cell permits all of the optimal descriptions to be recovered from the table, if that cell should happen to figure in the set of descriptions ultimately found to be optimal.

5.3   Creating parsers

For any given grammar with a regular position structure grammar, the Operations Set may be constructed as follows. First, for any cell $[X,i_j]$ where X is a non-terminal (x is the corresponding syllabic position unless X is S), one allowable operation is to underparse the input segment. So, include the underparsing operation that takes the structure in $[X,i_{j-1}]$ and adds an underparsed i_j to it. For each position grammar production with the non-terminal X on the right-hand side, two operations are possible: the generated position x has the next input segment parsed into it, or it is left unfilled. So, for each production $Y \Rightarrow xX$ generating X, create two operations: a parsing operation which takes the structure in $[Y,i_{j-1}]$ and appends a position x with i_j parsed into it, and an overparsing operation which takes the structure in $[Y,i_j]$ and appends an unfilled position x. Add to each operation any conditions which restrict its application (such as the restriction of vowels to nucleus positions in the Basic Syllable Theory). Finally, each operation must be supplied with marks indicating the constraint violations incurred by its application.

5.4   Regular and context-free position grammars

The fact that the position grammar used in the formal description of the Basic CV Syllable Theory is a regular grammar is very significant to guaranteeing the linear time efficiency of the parsing algorithm. However, the approach underlying the algorithm presented here may be extended to Optimality Theoretic grammars with context-free position grammars. The complexity will more likely be cubic in the general case. This and other issues concerning parsing in Optimality Theory with both regular and context-free position grammars, which cannot be discussed here for reasons of space, are discussed in Tesar (1994),[2] and more extensively in Tesar (1995).

5.5   Locality

A property of the Basic CV Syllable Theory important to the success of the algorithm is the "locality" of the constraints. Each constraint may be evaluated on the basis of at most one input segment and two consecutive syllable positions. What really matters here is that the constraint violations incurred by an operation can be determined solely on the basis of the operation itself. The information used by the constraints in the Basic Syllable Theory include the piece of structure added and the very end of the partial description being added on to (the last syllabic position generated). These restrictions on constraints are sufficient conditions for the kind of algorithm given in this paper. Ongoing work which cannot be discussed here investigates what actual restrictions on constraints are necessary.

An example of a constraint that would not be local in the context of the Basic Syllable Theory is a constraint which requires that the number of syllables be at least two, as when a word must contain a foot, and a foot must be binary at the level of syllables. That constraints referring to feet are not easily computed using the formal description given in this paper should not be surprising, as there is no explicit representation of feet in the structures. To properly handle such theories, a more complex set of position structures will probably be required, perhaps a context-free space of structures in which foot nodes may dominate one or more syllable nodes, and so forth. In that case, the binary foot constraint would be local in the sense relevant to context-free position structures in Optimality Theory: the constraint could be evaluated solely on the basis of a foot node and the syllable nodes immediately dominated by it.

Notes

1   Strictly speaking, Prince and Smolensky describe these restrictions by fixing the constraints Nuc, *COMPLEX, *M/V, and *P/C at the top of the hierarchy. This insures that they are unviolated in optimal forms, so I here treat them as part of GEN.

2   Many of the ideas presented here were earlier circulated as Tesar 1994. T. Mark Ellison has independently developed some work (Ellison 1994) on computing optimal forms in Optimality Theory that is similar in principle to part of this paper, although

expressed in a different set of formalisms. Among the additional ideas provided in this paper are independent characterizations of the formal description of the grammar, the input, and the parser, as well as a method for creating a parser from a description of the grammar which can parse any linguistic input.

Appendix: The rest of the operations set

Table 5

New cell	Condition	Previous cell	Struc	Violations	Information Production	Operation type
$[S,i_j]$		$[S,i_{j-1}]$	$\langle i_j \rangle$	$\{*\text{PARSE}\}$		Underparsing
$[N,i_j]$		$[N,i_{j-1}]$	$\langle i_j \rangle$	$\{*\text{PARSE}\}$		Underparsing
$[N,i_j]$	IF $i_j = V$	$[S,i_{j-1}]$	n/i_j	$\{*\text{ONS}\}$	$S \Rightarrow nN$	Parsing
$[N,i_j]$	IF $i_j = V$	$[O,i_{j-1}]$	n/i_j	$\{\}$	$O \Rightarrow nN$	Parsing
$[N,i_j]$	IF $i_j = V$	$[N,i_{j-1}]$	n/i_j	$\{*\text{ONS}\}$	$N \Rightarrow nN$	Parsing
$[N,i_j]$	IF $i_j = V$	$[D,i_{j-1}]$	n/i_j	$\{*\text{ONS}\}$	$D \Rightarrow nN$	Parsing
$[N,i_j]$		$[S,i_j]$	$n/\square$	$\{*\text{ONS} *\text{FILL}^{Nuc}\}$	$S \Rightarrow nN$	Overparsing
$[N,i_j]$		$[O,i_j]$	$n/\square$	$\{*\text{FILL}^{Nuc}\}$	$O \Rightarrow nN$	Overparsing
$[N,i_j]$		$[N,i_j]$	$n/\square$	$\{*\text{ONS} *\text{FILL}^{Nuc}\}$	$N \Rightarrow nN$	Overparsing
$[N,i_j]$		$[D,i_j]$	$n/\square$	$\{*\text{ONS} *\text{FILL}^{Nuc}\}$	$D \Rightarrow nN$	Overparsing
$[D,i_j]$		$[D,i_{j-1}]$	$\langle i_j \rangle$	$\{*\text{PARSE}\}$		Underparsing
$[D,i_j]$	IF $i_j = C$	$[N,i_{j-1}]$	d/i_j	$\{*\text{NOCODA}\}$	$N \Rightarrow dD$	Parsing
$[D,i_j]$		$[N,i_j]$	$d/\square$	$\{*\text{NOCODA}\}$	$N \Rightarrow dD$	Overparsing

References

Corman, Thomas, Charles Leiserson, and Ronald Rivest. 1990. *Introduction to Algorithms.* Cambridge, MA: MIT Press.

Ellison, T. Mark. 1994. Phonological Derivation in Optimality Theory. *Proceedings of the Fifteenth International Conference on Computational Linguistics,* pp. 1007–13.

Jakobson, Roman. 1962. *Selected Writings 1: Phonological Studies.* The Hague: Mouton.

Kay, Martin. 1980. *Algorithmic Schemata and Data Structures in Syntactic Processing.* CSL-80-12, October 1980.

Prince, Alan and Paul Smolensky. 1993. *Optimality Theory: Constraint Interaction in Generative Grammar.* Technical Report CU-CS-696-93, Department of Computer Science, University of Colorado at Boulder, and Technical Report TR-2, Rutgers Center for Cognitive Science, Rutgers University, New Brunswick, NJ. March. ◄

Rabiner, L. R. 1989. A Tutorial on Hidden Markov Models and Selected Applications in Speech Recognition. *Proc IEEE* 77(2): 257–86.

Sankoff, David and Joseph Kruskal. 1983. *Time Warps, String Edits, and Macromolecules: The Theory and Practice of Sequence Comparison.* Reading, MA: Addison-Wesley.

Tesar, Bruce. 1994. *Parsing in Optimality Theory: A Dynamic Programming Approach.* Technical Report CU-CS-714-94, April 1994. Department of Computer Science, University of Colorado, Boulder.

Tesar, Bruce. 1995. Computational Optimality Theory. Ph.D. dissertation. University of Colorado, Boulder.

Study and Research Questions

1 Why is the parsing model described in this chapter not affected by the infinite size of the candidate set?

2 How does this parsing model use EVAL and the constraint hierarchy? If you are familiar with other parsing models, you might ask to what extent they too integrate parsing with a theory of grammar.

3 The model described here uses the PARSE/FILL approach to faithfulness. How would you go about applying the same basic ideas using the correspondence approach described in chapter 2?

Chapter 5 | Bruce Tesar and
Paul Smolensky

Learnability in Optimality Theory

Editor's Note

Although the ostensive goal of linguistic theory is to explain language learning, theoretical discussions often proceed with little attention to the learning problem. This is particularly true in phonology. Explicit discussion of how learners acquire traditional rules, rule orderings, and underlying representations is virtually non-existent.

From the outset, though, research in OT has been coupled with an explicit model of learning, beginning with the one described in this chapter. (In its earliest instantiation, this chapter was first circulated a few months after Prince and Smolensky 1993.) The basic architecture of OT is well adapted to the learnability enterprise: the learner's task is limited to acquiring a constraint ranking and a lexicon. This chapter proposes an algorithm for learning constraint ranking; for some ideas from the same authors about learning a lexicon of underlying representations, see chapter 5 of Tesar and Smolensky (2000). For a brief summary of this chapter and references to other literature on learnability and acquisition, see McCarthy (2002: 202–16, 230–2).

How exactly does a theory of grammar bear on questions of learnability? Restrictions on what counts as a possible human language can restrict the learner's search space. But this is a coarse observation: alone it says nothing about how data may be brought to bear on the problem, and further, the number of possible languages predicted by most linguistic theories is extremely large.[1] It would clearly be a desirable result if the nature of the restrictions imposed by a theory of grammar could contribute further to language learnability.

The central claim of this article is that the character of the restrictions imposed by Optimality Theory (Prince and Smolensky 1991, 1993) have demonstrable and significant consequences for central questions of learnability. Optimality Theory explains linguistic phenomena through the complex interaction of violable constraints. The main results of this article demonstrate that those constraint interactions are

Excerpt from:
Tesar, Bruce and Smolensky, Paul (1998) Learnability in Optimality Theory. *Linguistic Inquiry* 29: 229–68. [Available on Rutgers Optimality Archive, ROA-155 and 156.]

nevertheless restricted in a way that permits the correct grammar to be inferred from grammatical structural descriptions. These results are theorems, based on a formal analysis of the Optimality Theory framework; proofs of the theorems are contained in an appendix [omitted here – Ed.]. The results have two important properties. First, they derive from central principles of the Optimality Theory framework. Second, they are nevertheless independent of the details of any substantive analysis of particular phenomena. The results apply equally to phonology, syntax, and any other domain admitting an analysis in terms of Optimality Theory. Thus, these theorems provide a learnability measure of the restrictiveness inherent in Optimality Theory's account of crosslinguistic variation per se: constraint reranking.

The structure of the article is as follows. Section 1 formulates the learning problem we investigate. Section 2 addresses this problem by developing the principle of Constraint Demotion, which is incorporated into an error-driven learning procedure in section 3. Section 4 takes up some issues and open questions raised by Constraint Demotion, and section 5 presents conclusions [4 and 5 omitted here – Ed.]. An appendix contains the formal definitions, theorems, and proofs.

1   Learnability and Optimality Theory

Optimality Theory (henceforth, OT) defines grammaticality by optimization over violable constraints. The defining reference is Prince and Smolensky 1993 (henceforth, P&S). Section 1.1 provides the necessary OT background, and section 1.2 outlines the approach to language learnability proposed here, including a decomposition of the overall problem; the results of this article solve the subproblem involving direct modification of the grammar.

1.1   Optimality Theory

In this section we present the basics of OT as a series of general principles, each exemplified within the Basic CV Syllable Theory of P&S (which draws upon ideas from McCarthy 1979, Selkirk 1981, Steriade 1982, Clements and Keyser 1983, Itô 1989).

1.1.1   Constraints and their violation

The first principle is not unique to Optimality Theory; it is a principle of generative grammar having particular significance for the present discussion.

(1)   *Grammars specify functions*
      A grammar is a specification of a function that assigns to each *input* a structural description or *output*. (A grammar per se does not provide an algorithm for computing this function, e.g., by sequential derivation.)

In Basic CV Syllable Theory (henceforth, CVT), an input is a string of Cs and Vs (e.g., /VCVC/). An output is a parse of the string into syllables, denoted as follows:

(2) a. .V.CVC.   = [$_\sigma$ V] [$_\sigma$ CVC]   onsetless open syllable + closed syllable
     b. ⟨V⟩.CV.⟨C⟩   = V [$_\sigma$ CV] C   single onsetted open syllable
     c. ⟨V⟩.CV.CÚ.   = V [$_\sigma$ CV] [$_\sigma$ CÚ]   two onsetted open syllables
     d. .□V.CV.⟨C⟩   = [$_\sigma$ □ V] [$_\sigma$ CV] C   two onsetted open syllables

(These four forms will be referred to frequently in the article and will be consistently labeled *a–d*.)

Output *a* is an onsetless open syllable followed by a closed syllable; periods denote the boundaries of syllables (σ). Output *b* contains only one, open, syllable. The initial V and final C of the input are not parsed into syllable structure, as notated by the angle brackets ⟨ ⟩. These segments exemplify *underparsing* and are not phonetically realized, so *b* is "pronounced" simply as .CV. Thus, CV is the *overt form* contained in *b*. Parse *c* consists of a pair of open syllables, in which the nucleus of the second syllable is not filled by an input segment. This empty nucleus is notated Ú and exemplifies *overparsing*. The phonetic interpretation of this empty nucleus is an epenthetic vowel. Thus, *c* has CVCV as its overt form. As in *b*, the initial V of the input is unparsed in *c*. Parse *d* is also a pair of open syllables (phonetically, CVCV), but this time it is the onset of the first syllable that is unfilled (notated □; phonetically, an epenthetic consonant), whereas the final C is unparsed.

(3) *Gen*

     Universal Grammar (UG) provides a function Gen that, given any input *I*, generates Gen(*I*), the set of candidate structural descriptions for *I*.

The input *I* is an identified substructure contained within each of its candidate outputs in Gen(*I*). The domain of Gen implicitly defines the space of possible inputs.

In CVT, for any input *I*, the candidate outputs in Gen(*I*) consist in all possible parsings of the string into syllables, including the possible over- and underparsing structures exemplified above in *b–d*. All syllables are assumed to contain a nucleus position, with optional preceding onset and following coda positions. CVT adopts the simplifying assumption (true of many languages) that the syllable positions onset and coda may each contain at most one C, and the nucleus position may contain at most one V. The four candidates of /VCVC/ in (2) are only illustrative of the full set Gen(/VCVC/). Since the possibilities of overparsing are unlimited, Gen(/VCVC/) in fact contains an infinite number of candidates.

The next principle identifies the formal character of substantive grammatical principles.

(4) *Con*

     UG provides a set Con of universal well-formedness constraints.

The constraints in Con evaluate the candidate outputs for a given input in parallel (i.e., simultaneously). Given a candidate output, each constraint assesses a multiset of *marks*, where each mark corresponds to one violation of the constraint. The collection of all marks assessed to a candidate parse p is denoted *marks(p)*. A mark assessed by a constraint $\mathbb{C}$ is denoted *$\mathbb{C}$. A parse a is more marked than a parse b with respect to $\mathbb{C}$ iff $\mathbb{C}$ assesses more marks to a than to b. (The theory recognizes the notions "more marked" and "less marked" but not absolute numerical levels of markedness.)

The CVT constraints are given in (5).

(5) *Basic CV Syllable Theory constraints*
    ONSET   Syllables have onsets.
    NoCODA Syllables do not have codas.
    PARSE   Underlying (input) material is parsed into syllable structure.
    FILL^{Nuc} Nucleus positions are filled with underlying material.
    FILL^{Ons} Onset positions (when present) are filled with underlying material.

These constraints can be illustrated with the candidate outputs *a–d*. The marks incurred by these candidates are summarized in tableau (6).

(6) *Constraint tableau for* L_1

Candidates	ONSET	NoCODA	FILL^{Nuc}	PARSE	FILL^{Ons}
/VCVC/→ ☞ *d* .□V.CV.⟨C⟩				*	*
b ⟨V⟩.CV.⟨C⟩				* *	
c ⟨V⟩.CV.C□́.			*	*	
a .V.CVC.	*	*			

This is an OT *constraint tableau* (L_1 is defined in section 1.1.2). The competing candidates are shown in the left column. The other columns are for the universal constraints, each indicated by the label at the top of the column. Constraint violations are indicated with *, one for each violation.

Candidate a = .V.CVC. violates ONSET in its first syllable and NoCODA in its second; the remaining constraints are satisfied. The single mark that ONSET assesses .V.CVC. is denoted *ONSET. This candidate is a *faithful* parse: it involves neither under- nor overparsing and therefore satisfies the *faithfulness* constraints PARSE and FILL.[2] By contrast, b = ⟨V⟩.CV.⟨C⟩ violates PARSE, and more than once. This tableau will be further explained below.

1.1.2 Optimality and harmonic ordering

The central notion of optimality now makes its appearance. The idea is that by examining the marks assigned by the universal constraints to all the candidate outputs for a given input, we can find the least marked, or optimal, one; the only well-formed parse assigned by the grammar to the input is the optimal one (or optimal ones, if several parses should tie for optimality). The relevant notion of "least marked" is not the simplistic one of just counting numbers of violations. Rather, in a given language, different constraints have different strengths or priorities: they are not all equal in force. When a choice must be made between satisfying one constraint or another, the stronger must take priority. The result is that the weaker will be violated in a well-formed structural description.

(7)   *Constraint ranking*
      A grammar *ranks* the universal constraints in a *dominance hierarchy*.

When one constraint C_1 dominates another constraint C_2 in the hierarchy, the relation is denoted $C_1 \gg C_2$. The ranking defining a grammar is total: the hierarchy determines the relative dominance of every pair of constraints, as illustrated in (8).

(8) $C_1 \gg C_2 \gg \ldots \gg C_n$

A constraint ranking is translated into an ordering of structural descriptions via the principle of harmonic ordering, given in (9).

(9)   *Harmonic ordering*
      A grammar's constraint ranking induces a *harmonic ordering* $<$ of all structural descriptions. Two structures a and b are compared by identifying the highest-ranked constraint C with respect to which a and b are not equally marked: the candidate that is less marked with respect to C is the *more harmonic*, or the one with *higher Harmony* (with respect to the given ranking).

$a < b$ denotes that a is less harmonic than b. The harmonic ordering $<$ determines the relative Harmony of every pair of candidates. For a given input, the most harmonic of the candidate outputs provided by Gen is the *optimal* candidate: it is the one assigned to the input by the grammar. Only this optimal candidate is well formed; all less harmonic candidates are ill formed.[3]

A formulation of harmonic ordering that will prove quite useful for learning involves *Mark Cancellation*. Consider a pair of competing candidates a and b, with corresponding lists of violation marks *marks*(a) and *marks*(b). Mark Cancellation is a process applied to a pair of lists of marks, and it cancels violation marks in common to the two lists. Thus, if a constraint C assesses one or more marks *C to both *marks*(a) and *marks*(b), an instance of *C is removed from each list, and the process is repeated until *at most one* of the lists still contains a mark *C. (Note that if a and b are equally marked with respect to C, the two lists contain equally many marks *C, and all occurrences of *C are eventually removed.) The resulting lists of *uncanceled marks* are denoted *marks'*(a) and *marks'*(b). If a mark *C remains in the uncanceled mark list of a, then a is more marked with respect to C. If the highest-ranked constraint assessing an uncanceled mark has a mark in *marks'*(a), then $a < b$: this is the definition of harmonic ordering $<$ in terms of mark cancellation. Mark cancellation is indicated with diagonal shading in tableau (10): one mark *PARSE cancels between the first two candidates of (6), d and b, and one uncanceled mark *PARSE remains in *marks'*(b).

(10) *Mark Cancellation*

Candidates	Onset	NoCoda	Fill^{Nuc}	Parse	Fill^{Ons}
d .□V.CV.⟨C⟩				*	*
b ⟨V⟩.CV.⟨C⟩				* *	

Defining grammaticality via harmonic ordering has an important consequence.

(11) *Minimal violation*
The grammatical candidate minimally violates the constraints, relative to the constraint ranking.

The constraints of UG are *violable*: they are potentially violated in well-formed structures. Such violation is *minimal*, however, in the sense that the grammatical parse p of an input I will best satisfy a constraint $\mathbb{C}$, unless all candidates that fare better than p on $\mathbb{C}$ also fare worse than p on some constraint that is higher-ranked than $\mathbb{C}$.

Harmonic ordering can be illustrated with CVT by reexamining tableau (6) under the assumption that the universal constraints are ranked by a particular grammar, L_1, with the ranking given in (12).

(12) *Constraint hierarchy for* L_1
Onset ≫ NoCoda ≫ Fill^{Nuc} ≫ Parse ≫ Fill^{Ons}

The constraints (and their columns) are ordered in (6) from left to right, reflecting the hierarchy in (12). The candidates in this tableau have been listed in harmonic order, from highest to lowest Harmony; the optimal candidate is marked manually.[4] Starting at the bottom of the tableau, $a < c$ can be verified as follows. The first step is to cancel common marks; here, there are none. The next step is to determine which candidate has the worst uncanceled mark, that is, most violates the most highly ranked constraint: it is a, which violates Onset. Therefore, a is the less harmonic. In determining that $c < b$, first the common mark *Parse is canceled; c then earns the worse mark of the two, *Fill^{Nuc}. In determining that $b < d$, one *Parse mark is canceled, leaving *marks'*(b) = {*Parse} and *marks'*(d) = {*Fill^{Ons}}. The worse of these two marks is the uncanceled *Parse incurred by b.

L_1 is a language in which all syllables have the overt form .CV.: onsets are required, codas are forbidden. In case of problematic inputs such as /VCVC/ where a faithful parse into CV syllables is not possible, this language uses overparsing to provide missing onsets, and underparsing to avoid codas (it is the language denoted $\Sigma^{CV}_{ep,del}$ in P&S: sec. 6.2.2.2).[5]

Exchanging the two Fill constraints in L_1 gives the grammar L_2.

(13) *Constraint hierarchy for* L_2
Onset ≫ NoCoda ≫ Fill^{Ons} ≫ Parse ≫ Fill^{Nuc}

Now the tableau corresponding to (6) becomes (14); the columns have been reordered to reflect the constraint reranking, and the candidates have been reordered to reflect the new harmonic ordering.

(14)   *Constraint tableau for* L_2

Candidates	ONSET	NOCODA	FILL^{Ons}	PARSE	FILL^{Nuc}
/VCVC/→ ☞ *c* ⟨V⟩.CV.CÓ.				*	*
b ⟨V⟩.CV.⟨C⟩				* *	
d .□V.CV.⟨C⟩			*	*	
a .V.CVC.	*	*			

Like the syllables in L_1, all syllables in L_2 are CV; /VCVC/ gets syllabified differently, however. In L_2 underparsing is used to avoid onsetless syllables, and overparsing to avoid codas (L_2 is the language $\Sigma^{CV}_{del,ep}$ in P&S).

The relation between L_1 and L_2 illustrates a principle of OT central to learnability concerns.

(15)   *Typology by reranking*
Systematic crosslinguistic variation is due entirely to variation in language-specific rankings of the universal constraints in Con.[6] Analysis of the optimal forms arising from all possible rankings of Con gives the typology of possible human languages. UG may impose restrictions on the possible rankings of Con.

Analysis of all rankings of the CVT constraints reveals a typology of basic CV syllable structures that explains Jakobson's typological generalizations (Jakobson 1962, Clements and Keyser 1983); see P&S: sec. 6. In this typology, licit syllables may have required or optional onsets and, independently, forbidden or optional codas.

One further principle of OT will figure in our analysis of learnability: richness of the base. This principle states that the set of possible inputs is universal; grammatical inventories are determined by the outputs a grammar assigns to all possible inputs. Discussion of this principle will be postponed until its point of relevance, section 4.3 [omitted here – Ed.].

1.2   Decomposing the learning problem

The results presented in this article address a particular subproblem of the overall enterprise of language learnability. That subproblem, and the corresponding results, are best understood in the context of an overall approach to language learnability.

This section briefly outlines that approach. The nature of and motivation for the approach are further discussed in section 4.2 [omitted here].

To begin, three types of linguistic entities must be distinguished:

(16) *Three types of linguistic entities*
    a. *Full structural descriptions*: the candidate outputs of Gen, including overt structure and input.
    b. *Overt structure*: the part of a description directly accessible to the learner.
    c. *The grammar*: determines which structural descriptions are grammatical.

In terms of CVT, full structural descriptions are exemplified by the descriptions listed in (2). Overt structure is the part of a structural description that actually is realized phonetically. For example, in $b = \langle V \rangle . CV . \langle C \rangle$, the overt structure is CV; the unparsed segments $\langle V \rangle$ and $\langle C \rangle$ are not included, nor are the syllable boundaries. Unparsed segments are present in the full structural description, but not the overt structure. The part of the grammar to be learned is the ranking of the constraints, as exemplified in (12).

It is important to keep in mind that the grammar evaluates full structural descriptions; it does not evaluate overt structure in isolation. This is, of course, hardly novel to OT; it is fundamental to linguistic theory in general. The general challenge of language acquisition, under any linguistic theory, is that of inferring the correct grammar from overt data, despite the gap between the two arising from the hidden elements of structural descriptions, absent from overt data.

It is also important to distinguish three processes, each of which plays an important role in the approach to language acquisition proposed here:

(17) *Three processes*
    a. *Production-directed parsing*: mapping an underlying form (input) to its optimal description – given a grammar.
    b. *Robust interpretive parsing*: mapping an overt structure to its full structural description, complete with all hidden structure – given a grammar.
    c. *Learning the grammar*: determining a grammar from full grammatical descriptions.

Production-directed parsing is the computation of that structural description, among those candidates produced by Gen containing a given input, which is optimal with respect to a given ranking. Production-directed parsing takes a part of a structural description, the underlying form, and fills in the rest of the structure. Robust interpretive parsing also takes a part of a structural description and fills in the rest, but it starts with a different part, the overt structure. Robust interpretive parsing is closer to what many readers probably associate with the word *parsing*. *Robustness* refers to the fact that an overt structure not generated by the grammar currently held by the learner is not simply rejected: rather, it is assigned the most harmonic structure possible. The learner can, of course, tell that this interpretive parse is not grammatical by her current grammar (by comparing it to the structural description that her grammar assigns, via production-directed parsing, to the underlying form of the interpretive parse); in fact, the learner will exploit that observation during

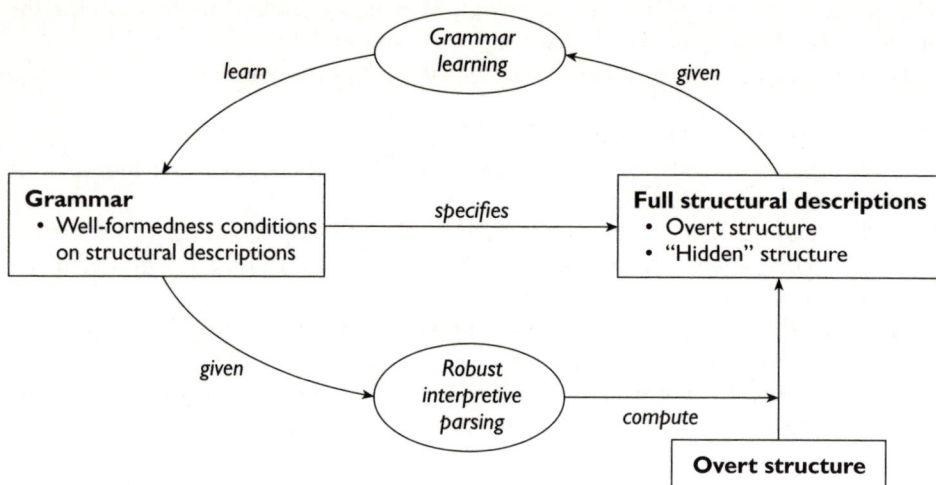

Figure 1   Decomposition of the learning problem

learning. For instance, recall that L_1 has only open syllables in optimal descriptions. When presented with the overt form *VCV*, robust interpretive parsing in L_1 will assign it the description .V.CV., because that is the best description consistent with the overt form (better than, for example, .VC.V.). When presented with the input /VCV/, production-directed parsing in L_1 will assign the description .□V.CV. Both production-directed parsing and robust interpretive parsing make use of the same harmonic ordering of structural descriptions induced by the constraint ranking. They differ in the part of the structure they start from: production-directed parsing starts with an underlying form and chooses among candidates with the same underlying form; robust interpretive parsing starts with an overt structure and chooses among candidates with the same overt structure.

These entities and processes are all intimately connected, as schematically shown in figure 1. Any linguistic theory must ultimately be able to support procedures that are tractable performance approximations to both parsing and learning. Ideally, a grammatical theory should provide sufficient structure so that procedures for both parsing and grammar learning can be strongly shaped by grammatical principles.

In the approach to learning developed here, full structural descriptions do not just bear a logical relationship between overt structures and grammars: they also play an active role in the learning process. We propose that a language learner uses a grammar to interpret overt forms by imposing on those overt forms the best structural descriptions, as determined by his current ranking. The learner then makes use of those descriptions in learning.

Specifically, we propose that a learner starts with an initial ranking of the constraints. As overt forms are observed, the learner uses the currently hypothesized ranking to assign structural descriptions to those forms. These hypothesized full structures are treated by the grammar-learning subsystem as the target parses to be assigned by the correct grammar: they are used to change the hypothesized ranking, yielding a new grammar. The new ranking is then used to assign new full descriptions to overt forms. This process continues, back and forth, until the correct ranking is converged upon. At that point, the ranking will assign the correct structural descriptions to each of the overt structures, and the overt structures will indicate that the ranking is correct and should not be changed.

The process of computing optimal structural descriptions for underlying forms (production-directed parsing) has already been addressed elsewhere. Algorithms that are provably correct for significant classes of OT grammars have been developed, based upon dynamic programming (Tesar 1994, 1995a,b, 1998). For positive initial results in applying similar techniques to robust interpretive parsing, see Tesar 1999.

At this point, we put aside the larger learning algorithm, for the present article is devoted to the subproblem in figure 1 labeled *grammar learning*: inferring constraint rankings from full structural descriptions. The next two sections develop an algorithm for performing such inference. This algorithm has a property important for the success of the overall learning approach: when supplied with the correct structural descriptions for a language, it is guaranteed to find the correct ranking. Furthermore, the number of structural descriptions required by the algorithm is quite modest, especially when compared with the number of distinct rankings.

2   Constraint Demotion

OT is inherently comparative; the grammaticality of a structural description is determined not in isolation, but with respect to competing candidates. Therefore, the learner is not informed about the correct ranking by positive data in isolation; the role of the competing candidates must be addressed. This fact is not a liability, but an advantage: a comparative theory gives comparative structure to be exploited. Each piece of positive evidence, a grammatical structural description, brings with it a body of *implicit negative evidence* in the form of the competing descriptions. Given access to Gen and the underlying form (contained in the given structural description), the learner has access to these competitors. Any competing candidate, along with the grammatical structure, determines a *data pair* related to the correct ranking: the correct ranking must make the grammatical structure more harmonic than the ungrammatical competitor. Call the observed grammatical structure the *winner*, and any competing structure a *loser*. The challenge faced by the learner is then, given a suitable set of such *loser/winner pairs*, to find a ranking such that each winner is more harmonic than its corresponding loser. Constraint Demotion solves this challenge, by demoting the constraints violated by the winner down in the hierarchy so that they are dominated by the constraints violated by the loser. The main principle is presented more precisely in this section, and an algorithm for learning constraint rankings from grammatical structural descriptions is presented in section 3.

2.1   The basic idea

In the CV language L_1, the winner for input /VCVC/ is .□V.CV.⟨C⟩. Tableau (6) gives the marks incurred by the winner (labeled d) and by three competing losers.

These may be used to form three loser/winner pairs, as shown in (18). A *mark-data pair* is the paired lists of constraint violation marks for a loser/winner pair.

(18)   *Mark-data pairs* (L_1)

loser < winner		marks(loser)	marks(winner)
$a < d$	.V.CVC. < .□V.CV.⟨C⟩	*ONSET *NOCODA	*PARSE *FILL^{Ons}
$b < d$	⟨V⟩.CV.⟨C⟩ < .□V.CV.⟨C⟩	*PARSE *PARSE	*PARSE *FILL^{Ons}
$c < d$	⟨V⟩.CV.CÓ. < .□V.CV.⟨C⟩	*PARSE *FILL^{Nuc}	*PARSE *FILL^{Ons}

To make contact with more familiar OT constraint tableaux, the information in (18) will also be displayed in the format of (19).

(19)   *Initial data*

loser/winner pairs	not yet ranked				
	FILL^{Nuc}	FILL^{Ons}	PARSE	ONSET	NOCODA
d ✓ .□V.CV.⟨C⟩		⊛	⊛		
a .V.CVC.				*	*
d ✓ .□V.CV.⟨C⟩		⊛	⊛		
b ⟨V⟩.CV.⟨C⟩			*	*	
d ✓ .□V.CV.⟨C⟩		⊛	⊛		
c ⟨V⟩.CV.CÓ.	*		*		

At this point, the constraints are unranked; the dashed vertical lines separating constraints in (19) convey that no relative ranking of adjacent constraints is intended. The winner is indicated with a ✓; ☞ will denote the structure that is optimal according to the current grammar, which may not be the same as the winner (the structure that is grammatical in the target language). The constraint violations of the winner, *marks(winner)*, are distinguished by the symbol ⊛. Diagonal shading denotes mark cancellation, as in tableau (10).

Now, in order that each loser be less harmonic than the winner, the marks incurred by the former, *marks(loser)*, must collectively be worse than *marks(winner)*. According to (9), what this means more precisely is that the loser must incur the worst uncanceled mark, compared with the winner. This requires that uncanceled marks be identified, so the first step is to cancel the common marks in (18), as shown in (20). The canceled marks have been ~~struck out~~. Note that the cancellation operation that transforms *marks* to *marks′* is defined only on *pairs* of sets of marks; for example, *PARSE is canceled in the pairs $b < d$ and $c < d$, but not in the pair

$a < d$. Note also that cancellation of marks is done token by token: in the row $b < d$, one but not the other mark *PARSE in *marks(b)* is canceled.

(20)   *Mark-data pairs after cancellation* (L_1)

	loser/winner pairs	marks'(loser)	marks'(winner)
$a < d$	.V.CVC. < .□V.CV.⟨C⟩	*ONSET *NOCODA	*PARSE *FILL^{Ons}
$b < d$	⟨V⟩.CV.⟨C⟩ < .□V.CV.⟨C⟩	~~*PARSE~~ *PARSE	~~*PARSE~~ *FILL^{Ons}
$c < d$	⟨V⟩.CV.C□́. < .□V.CV.⟨C⟩	~~*PARSE~~ *FILL^{Nuc}	~~*PARSE~~ *FILL^{Ons}

The table (20) of mark-data after cancellation is the data on which Constraint Demotion operates. Another representation in tableau form is given in (19), where common marks in each loser/winner pair of rows are indicated as "canceled" by diagonal shading. This tableau also reveals what successful learning must accomplish: the ranking of the constraints must be adjusted so that, for each pair, all of the uncanceled winner marks ⊛ are dominated by at least one loser mark *. Given the standard tableau convention of positioning the highest-ranked constraints to the left, the columns containing uncanceled ⊛ marks need to be moved far enough to the right (down in the hierarchy) so that, for each pair, there is a column (constraint) containing an uncanceled * (loser mark) that is further to the left (more dominant in the hierarchy) than all of the columns containing uncanceled ⊛ (winner marks).

The algorithm to accomplish this is based upon the principle in (21).

(21)   *Constraint Demotion*
For any constraint $\mathbb{C}$ assessing an uncanceled winner mark, if $\mathbb{C}$ is not dominated by a constraint assessing an uncanceled loser mark, demote $\mathbb{C}$ to immediately below the highest-ranked constraint assessing an uncanceled loser mark.

Constraint Demotion works by demoting the constraints with uncanceled winner marks down far enough in the hierarchy so that they are dominated by an uncanceled loser mark, ensuring that each winner is more harmonic than its competing losers.

Notice that it is not necessary for *all* uncanceled loser marks to dominate all uncanceled winner marks; one will suffice. However, given more than one uncanceled loser mark, it is often not immediately apparent which one needs to dominate the uncanceled winner marks.[7] The pair $a < d$ above is such a case; it is not clear whether PARSE and FILL^{Ons} should be dominated by ONSET or by NOCODA (or both). This is the challenge successfully overcome by Constraint Demotion.

2.2   Stratified domination hierarchies

OT grammars are defined by rankings in which the domination relation between any two constraints is specified. The learning algorithm, however, works with a larger space of hypotheses, the space of *stratified hierarchies*. A stratified domination hierarchy has the following form:

(22)   *Stratified domination hierarchy*
$$\{C_1, C_2, \ldots, C_3\} \gg \{C_4, C_5, \ldots, C_6\} \gg \ldots \gg \{C_7, C_8, \ldots, C_9\}$$

The constraints $C_1, C_2, \ldots, C_3$ constitute the first stratum in the hierarchy: they are not ranked with respect to one another, but they each dominate all the remaining constraints. Similarly, the constraints $C_4, C_5, \ldots, C_6$ constitute the second stratum: they are not ranked with respect to one another, but they each dominate all the constraints in the lower strata. In tableaux, strata will be separated from each other by solid vertical lines, and constraints within the same stratum will be separated by dashed lines, with no relative ranking implied.

The original notion of constraint ranking, in which a domination relation is specified for every pair of candidates, can now be seen as a special case of the stratified hierarchy, where each stratum contains exactly one constraint. That special case will be labeled here a *total ranking*. Henceforth, *"hierarchy" will mean stratified hierarchy*; when appropriate, hierarchies will be explicitly qualified as "totally ranked."

The definition of harmonic ordering (9) needs to be elaborated slightly for stratified hierarchies. When C_1 and C_2 are in the same stratum, two marks $*C_1$ and $*C_2$ are equally weighted in the computation of Harmony. In effect, all constraints in a single stratum are collapsed, and treated as though they were a single constraint, for the purposes of determining the relative Harmony of candidates. Minimal violation with respect to a stratum is determined by the candidate incurring the smallest sum of violations assessed by all constraints in the stratum. The tableau in (23) gives a simple illustration.

(23)   *Harmonic ordering with a stratified hierarchy:* $C_1 \gg \{C_2, C_3\} \gg C_4$

	C_1	C_2	C_3	C_4
p_1	*!		*	
p_2			*	*!
☞ p_3		*		
p_4			* *!	

Here, all candidates are compared with the optimal one, p_3. In this illustration, parses p_2 and p_3 violate different constraints that are in the same stratum of the hierarchy. Therefore, these marks cannot decide between the candidates, and it is left to the lower-ranked constraint to decide in favor of p_3. Notice that candidate p_4 is still eliminated by the middle stratum because it incurs more than the minimal number of marks from constraints in the middle stratum. (The symbol *! indicates a mark fatal in comparison with the optimal parse.)

With respect to the comparison of candidates, marks assessed by different constraints in the same stratum can be thought of as "canceling," because they do not decide between the candidates. It is crucial, though, that the marks not be canceled for the purposes of learning. The term *Mark Cancellation*, as used in the rest of this article, should be understood to refer only to the cancellation of marks assessed by the same constraint to competing candidates, independent of the constraint hierarchy.

2.3   An example: Basic CV Syllable Theory

Constraint Demotion (abbreviated CD) will now be illustrated using CVT; specifically, with the target language L_1 of (6) and (12), which constructs only CV syllables by epenthesizing onsets and deleting potential codas as needed. The initial stratified hierarchy $\mathcal{H}_0$ consists of a single stratum containing all the constraints.

(24) $\mathcal{H} = \mathcal{H}_0 = \{\text{FILL}^{\text{Nuc}}, \text{FILL}^{\text{Ons}}, \text{PARSE}, \text{ONSET}, \text{NOCODA}\}$

Suppose that the first loser/winner pair is $b < d$ of (18). Mark Cancellation is applied to the corresponding pair of mark lists, resulting in the mark-data pair shown in (25).

(25)   *Mark-data pair, step 1* (L_1)

	loser < winner	marks'(loser)	marks'(winner)
$b < d$ ⦙	$\langle V \rangle.CV.\langle C \rangle < .\square V.CV.\langle C \rangle$	~~*PARSE~~ *PARSE	~~*PARSE~~ *FILL^{Ons}

Now CD can be applied. The highest-ranked (in $\mathcal{H}$) uncanceled loser mark – the only one – is *PARSE. The *marks'(winner)* are checked to see if they are dominated by *PARSE. The only winner mark is *FILL^{Ons}, which is *not* so dominated. CD therefore calls for demoting FILL^{Ons} to the stratum immediately below PARSE. Since no such stratum currently exists, it is created. The resulting hierarchy is (26).

(26) $\mathcal{H} = \{\text{FILL}^{\text{Nuc}}, \text{PARSE}, \text{ONSET}, \text{NOCODA}\} \gg \{\text{FILL}^{\text{Ons}}\}$

This demotion is shown in tableau form in (27). The uncanceled winner mark ⊛ is demoted to a (new) stratum immediately below the stratum containing the highest uncanceled loser mark *, which now becomes a fatal violation *! rendering irrelevant the dominated violation ⊛ (which is therefore greyed out).

(27)   *First demotion*

loser/winner pair	FILL^{Nuc} ⦙	FILL^{Ons} ⦙	PARSE ⦙	ONSET ⦙	NOCODA	FILL^{Ons}
d ☞✓ $.\square V.CV.\langle C \rangle$		⊛	⊛			⊛
b $\langle V \rangle.CV.\langle C \rangle$			* *!			

Now another loser/winner pair is selected. Suppose this is $a < d$ of (18), as shown in (28).

(28)   *Mark-data pair for CD, step 2 (L_1)*

loser < winner	marks′(loser)	marks′(winner)
$a < d$ ⋮ .V.CVC. < .□V.CV.⟨C⟩	*ONSET *NOCODA	*PARSE *FILL^{Ons}

There are no common marks to cancel. CD calls for finding the highest-ranked of the *marks′(loser)*. Since ONSET and NOCODA are both top-ranked, either will do; choose, say, ONSET. Next, each constraint with a mark in *marks′(winner)* is checked to see if it is dominated by ONSET. FILL^{Ons} is so dominated. PARSE is not however, so it is demoted to the stratum immediately below that of ONSET.

(29) $\mathcal{H} = \{\text{FILL}^{Nuc}, \text{ONSET}, \text{NOCODA}\} \gg \{\text{FILL}^{Ons}, \text{PARSE}\}$

In tableau form, this demotion is shown in (30). (Both the ONSET and NOCODA violations are marked as fatal, *!, because both are highest-ranking violations of the loser; they belong to the same stratum.)

(30)   *Second demotion*

loser/winner pair	FILL^{Nuc}	PARSE	ONSET	NOCODA	FILL^{Ons}	PARSE
d ☞✓ .□V.CV.⟨C⟩		⊛			⊛	⊛
a V.CVC.			*!	*!		

Suppose now that the next loser/winner pair is $c < d$.

(31)   *Mark-data pair for CD, step 3 (L_1)*

loser < winner	marks′(loser)	marks′(winner)
$c < d$ ⋮ ⟨V⟩.CV.C□. < .□V.CV.⟨C⟩	~~*PARSE~~ *FILL^{Nuc}	~~*PARSE~~ *FILL^{Ons}

Since the uncanceled loser mark, *FILL^{Nuc}, already dominates the uncanceled winner mark, *FILL^{Ons}, no demotion results, and $\mathcal{H}$ is unchanged. This is an example of an *uninformative* pair, given its location in the sequence of training pairs; no demotions result.

Suppose the next loser/winner pair results from a new input, /VC/, with a new optimal parse, .□V.⟨C⟩, as shown in (32).

(32)   *Mark-data pair for CD, step 4* (L₁)

loser < winner	marks'(loser)	marks'(winner)
⟨VC⟩ < .□V.⟨C⟩	~~*Parse~~ *Parse	~~*Parse~~ *Fill^{Ons}

Since the winner mark *Fill^{Ons} is not dominated by the loser mark *Parse, it must be demoted to the stratum immediately below Parse, resulting in the hierarchy in (33).

(33) $\mathcal{H}$ = {Fill^{Nuc}, Onset, NoCoda} ≫ {Parse} ≫ {Fill^{Ons}}

This demotion is shown in tableau (34).

(34)   *Third demotion*

loser/winner pair	Fill^{Nuc}	Onset	NoCoda	Fill^{Ons}	Parse	Fill^{Ons}
☞✓ .□V.⟨C⟩				⊛	⊛	⊛
⟨VC⟩					* *!	

As it happens, this stratified hierarchy generates precisely L_1, using the interpretation of stratified hierarchies described above.[8] For any further loser/winner pairs that could be considered, the loser is guaranteed to have at least one uncanceled mark assessed by a constraint dominating all the constraints assessing uncanceled marks to the winner. Thus, no further data will be informative: L_1 has been learned.

2.4   Why not constraint promotion?

CD is defined entirely in terms of *demotion*; all movement of constraints is downward in the hierarchy. One could reasonably ask if this is an arbitrary choice; couldn't the learner just as easily *promote* constraints toward the correct hierarchy? The answer is no, and understanding why reveals the logic behind CD.

Consider the tableau shown in (35), where d is the winner, and a the loser. The ranking depicted in the tableau makes the loser, a, more harmonic than the winner, d, so the learner needs to change the hierarchy to achieve the desired result, $a < d$.

(35)   *The disjunction problem*

loser/winner pair	Fill^{Ons}	Onset	Fill^{Nuc}	NoCoda	Parse
d ✓ .□V.CV.⟨C⟩	⊛				⊛
a V.CVC.		*		*	

There are no marks in common, so no marks are canceled. For the winner to be more harmonic than the loser, at least one of the loser's marks must dominate all of the winner's marks. This relation is expressed in (36).

(36)   (ONSET or NOCODA) $\gg$ (FILL^{Ons} and PARSE)

Demotion moves the constraints corresponding to the winner's marks. They are contained in a conjunction (**and**); thus, once the highest-ranked loser mark is identified, *all* of the winner marks need to be dominated by it, so all constraints with winner marks are demoted if not already so dominated. A hypothetical *promotion* operation would move the constraints corresponding to the *loser's* marks up in the hierarchy. But notice that the loser's marks are contained in a *disjunction* (**or**). It isn't clear which of the loser's violations should be promoted – perhaps all of them, or perhaps just one. Other data might require one of the constraints violated by the loser to be dominated by one of the constraints violated by the winner. This loser/winner pair gives no basis for choosing.

Disjunctions are notoriously problematic in general computational learning theory. CD solves the problem of disentangling the disjunctions by demoting the constraints violated by the winner. There is no choice to be made among them; all must be dominated. The choice between the constraints violated by the loser is made by picking the one highest-ranked in the current hierarchy (in (35), that is ONSET). Thus, if other data have already determined that ONSET $\gg$ NOCODA, that relationship is preserved. The constraints violated by the winner are demoted only as far as necessary.

2.5   The initial hierarchy

The illustration of CD given in section 2.3 started with initial hierarchy $\mathcal{H}_0$, given in (24), having all the constraints in one stratum. Using that as an initial hierarchy is convenient for demonstrating some formal properties. By starting with all constraints at the top, CD can be understood to demote constraints down toward their correct position. Because CD demotes constraints only as far as necessary, a constraint never gets demoted below its target position and will not be demoted further once reaching its target position. The formal analysis in appendix sections A.1 to A.3 assumes $\mathcal{H}_0$ as the initial hierarchy and proves the following result:

(37)   *Theorem: Correctness of CD*
        Starting with all constraints in Con ranked in the top stratum, and applying CD to informative positive evidence as long as such exists, the process converges on a stratified hierarchy such that all totally ranked refinements of that hierarchy correctly account for the learning data.

However, using $\mathcal{H}_0$ as the initial hierarchy is not required by CD. In fact, convergence is obtained no matter what initial hierarchy is used; this is proven in section A.4. Because the data observed must all be consistent with some total ranking, there is at least one constraint never assessing an uncanceled winner mark: the constraint top-ranked in the total ranking. There may be more than one such constraint (there are three for L_1); there will always be at least one. These constraints will never be demoted for any loser/winner pair, because only constraints assessing uncanceled winner marks for some loser/winner pair get demoted. Therefore, these constraints will stay put, no matter where they are in the initial hierarchy. If $\mathcal{H}_0$ is used, these constraints start at the top and stay there. For other initial hierarchies, these constraints stay put, and the other constraints eventually get demoted below them. This may leave some "empty strata" at the top, but that is of no consequence; all that matters is the relative position of the strata containing constraints.

This is not all there is to be said about the initial hierarchy; the issue is discussed further in section 4.3 [omitted here – Ed.].

3   Selecting Competing Descriptions: Error-Driven Constraint Demotion

Having developed the basic principle of CD, we now show how it can be incorporated into a procedure for learning a grammar from correct structural descriptions.

3.1   Parsing identifies informative competitors

CD operates on loser/winner pairs, deducing consequences for the grammar from the fact that the winner must be more harmonic than the loser. The winner is a positive example provided externally to the grammar learner: a parse of some input (e.g., an underlying lexical form in phonology; a predicate/argument structure in syntax), a parse taken to be optimal according to the target grammar. The loser is an alternative parse of the same input, which must be suboptimal with respect to the target grammar (unless it happens to have exactly the same marks as the winner). Presumably, such a loser must be generated by the grammar learner. Whether the loser/winner pair is informative depends both on the winner and on the loser.

An antagonistic learning environment can of course always deny the learner necessary informative examples, making learning the target grammar impossible. We consider this uninteresting and assume that as long as there remain potentially informative positive examples, these are not maliciously withheld from the learner (but see section 4.3 [omitted] for a discussion of the possibility of languages underdetermined by positive evidence). This still leaves a challenging problem, however. Having received a potentially informative positive example, a winner, the learner needs to find a corresponding loser that forms an informative loser/winner pair. In principle, if the winner is a parse of an input I, then any of the competing parses in Gen(I) can be chosen as the loser; typically, there are an infinity of choices, not all of which will lead to an informative loser/winner pair. What is needed is a procedure for choosing a loser that is guaranteed to be informative, as long as any such competitor exists.

The idea (Tesar 1998) is simple. Consider a learner in the midst of learning, with current constraint hierarchy $\mathcal{H}$. A positive example p is received: the target parse of an input I. It is natural for the learner to compute her own parse p' for I, optimal with respect to her current hierarchy $\mathcal{H}$. If the learner's parse p' is different from the target parse p, learning should be possible; otherwise, it isn't. This is because if the target parse p equals the learner's parse p', then p is already optimal according to $\mathcal{H}$; no demotion occurs, and no learning is possible. On the other hand, if the target parse p is *not* the learner's parse p', then p is suboptimal according to $\mathcal{H}$, and the hierarchy needs to be modified so that p becomes optimal. In order for a loser to be informative when paired with the winner p, the Harmony of the loser (according to the current $\mathcal{H}$) must be greater than the Harmony of p; only then will demotion occur to render p more harmonic than the loser. The obvious choice for this loser is p'; it is of maximum Harmony according to $\mathcal{H}$, and if any competitor to the winner has higher Harmony according to $\mathcal{H}$, then p' must. The type of parsing responsible for computing p' is production-directed parsing, as defined in (17): given an input I and a stratified hierarchy $\mathcal{H}$, compute the optimal parse(s) of I. This is the problem solved in a number of general cases in Tesar 1995a, as discussed in section 1.2.

If the optimal parse given the current $\mathcal{H}$, the loser, should happen to equal the correct parse, the winner, the execution of CD will produce no change in $\mathcal{H}$; no learning can occur. In fact, CD need be executed only when there is a mismatch between the correct parse and the optimal parse assigned by the current ranking. This is an *error-driven* learning algorithm (Wexler and Culicover 1980). Each observed parse is compared with a computed parse of the input. If the two parses match, no error occurs, and so no learning takes place. If the two parses differ, the error is attributed to the current hypothesized ranking, and so CD is used to adjust the hypothesized ranking. The resulting algorithm is called *Error-Driven Constraint Demotion* (EDCD).

(38)   *Error-Driven Constraint Demotion* (EDCD)
    Given: a hierarchy $\mathcal{H}$ and a set *PositiveData* of grammatical structural descriptions.
    For each description *winner* in PositiveData:
        Set *loser* to be the optimal description assigned by $\mathcal{H}$ to I, the underlying form of *winner*.
        If *loser* is identical to *winner*, keep $\mathcal{H}$;
        Else:
        • apply Mark Cancellation, getting $(marks'(loser), marks'(winner))$;
        • apply CD to $(marks'(loser), marks'(winner))$ and $\mathcal{H}$;
        • adopt the new hierarchy resulting from demotion as the current hierarchy.

This algorithm demonstrates that using the familiar strategy of error-driven learning does not require inviolable constraints or independently evaluable parameters. Because OT is defined by means of optimization, errors are defined with respect to the relative Harmony of several entire structural descriptions, rather than particular diagnostic criteria applied to an isolated parse. CD accomplishes learning precisely on the basis of the comparison of entire structural descriptions.[9]

Further discussion and exemplification of EDCD can be found in Tesar 1998, and in Tesar and Smolensky 1996.[10]

3.2   Data Complexity: the amount of data required to learn the grammar

The data complexity of a learning algorithm is the amount of data that needs to be supplied to the algorithm in order to ensure that it learns the correct grammar. For EDCD, an opportunity for progress toward the correct grammar is presented every time an error occurs (a mismatch between a positive datum and the corresponding parse that is optimal with respect to the current hypothesized grammar). Any such error results in a demotion, and the convergence results ensure that each demotion brings the hypothesized grammar ever closer to the correct grammar. Therefore, it is convenient to measure data complexity in terms of the maximum number of errors that could occur before the correct grammar is reached.

With EDCD, an error can result in the demotion of one or several constraints, each being demoted down one or more strata. The minimum amount of progress resulting from a single error is the demotion of one constraint down one stratum. The worst-case data complexity thus amounts to the maximum distance between a possible starting hierarchy and a possible target hierarchy to be learned, where the distance between the two hierarchies is measured in terms of one-stratum demotions of constraints. The maximum possible distance between two stratified hierarchies is $N(N - 1)$, where N is the number of constraints in the grammar; this then is the maximum number of errors made prior to learning the correct hierarchy. This result is proved in the appendix as (74).

(39)   *Theorem: Computational complexity of CD*
      Starting with an arbitrary initial hierarchy, the number of informative loser/
      winner pairs required for learning is at most $N(N - 1)$, where N = number of
      constraints in Con.

The significance of this result is perhaps best illustrated by comparing it with the number of possible grammars. Given that any target grammar is consistent with at least one total ranking of the constraints, the number of possible grammars is the number of possible total rankings, $N!$. This number grows very quickly as a function of the number of constraints N, and if the amount of data required for learning scaled with the number of possible total rankings, it would be cause for concern indeed. Fortunately, the data complexity just given for EDCD is quite reasonable in its scaling. In fact, it does not take many universal constraints to give a drastic difference between the data complexity of EDCD and the number of total rankings. When $N = 10$, the EDCD data complexity is 90, and the number of total rankings is over 3.6 million. With 20 constraints, the EDCD data complexity is 380, and the number of total rankings is over 2 billion billion (2.43×10^{18}). This reveals the restrictiveness of the structure imposed by OT on the space of grammars: a learner can efficiently home in on any target grammar, managing an explosively sized grammar space with quite modest data requirements by fully exploiting the inherent structure provided by strict domination.

The power provided by strict domination for learning can be further underscored by considering that CD uses as its working hypothesis space not the space of total rankings, but the space of all stratified hierarchies, which is much larger and

contains all total rankings as a subset. The disparity between the size of the working hypothesis space and the actual data requirements is that much greater.
[. . .]

Notes

1   Even a Universal Grammar with only 20 binary parameters admits over a million grammars.

2   The PARSE and FILL constraints defined here constitute the parse/fill model of faithfulness in OT. The parse/fill model is used in P&S and in much of the OT literature. More recently, an alternative conception of faithfulness has been proposed, the correspondence model (McCarthy and Prince 1995). The distinctions between the two are irrelevant to the learnability work described here; the same results hold for OT grammars adopting the correspondence model of faithfulness.

3   If two candidates are assessed exactly the same set of marks by the constraints, then they are equally harmonic (regardless of the constraint ranking). If they tie as the most harmonic candidates for an input, then the two outputs are both optimal, with the interpretation of free alternation. $a \sim b$ denotes that a and b have equal Harmony. In practice, it is rather rare to have more than one optimal output for an input, so for convenience we will refer to each input as having only one optimal output.

4   Determining that this candidate is optimal requires demonstrating that it is more harmonic than *any* of the infinitely many competing candidates: see P&S: sec. 7.3 for one technique.

5   As discussed in P&S in detail, the relevant rankings that yield L_1 are {ONSET, PARSE} $\gg$ FILL^{Ons} (onsets epenthesized) and {NOCODA, FILL^{Nuc}} $\gg$ PARSE (codas avoided by deletion). There are many total rankings of the constraints that meet these requirements and therefore give rise to the same language L_1; (12) is just one of them.

6   Some analyses have been proposed, using the OT framework, that posit language-specific constraints in addition to universal ones. However, the learning account presented here presumes the standard OT

approach to typology: the constraints are all universal, and it is their ranking that is language-specific.

7   This problem is closely related to (but not identical to) the Credit Problem as defined by Dresher (1996). Dresher characterizes the problem as that of relating overt forms and grammars directly: given an overt form, it is not clear which grammar settings are responsible for it. The approach to learning advocated here decomposes the problem into two: the problem of determining which full structural description holds of an overt form, and the problem of which grammar settings (here, dominating constraints) are responsible for a given *structural description*. Constraint Demotion solves the latter. Use of the term *Credit Problem* to refer to the general problem (not specific to language) of identifying the element of a computational system that is responsible for a given behavioral property dates back at least to Minsky 1961.

8   Note that (33) satisfies the ranking requirements for L_1 given in note 5.

9   There is a choice to be made in exactly how to apply this approach to a set of observed, optimal structural descriptions, resulting in two variations. Because applying CD to a single mark-data pair does not ensure that the observed parse (the winner) is yet optimal with respect to all candidates (not just the loser), the learner could reparse the input according to the new constraint ranking. If the resulting parse is different from the winner, the new parse may be used to create a new mark-data pair, to which CD is applied. This process could be repeated until the learner's hierarchy selects the winner as the optimal description. This allows the learner to extract more information out of a single winner, at the cost of greater processing dedicated to each winner. The decision here is whether or not to repeatedly apply parsing and CD to a single winner.

10 For a simple example of learning L_1 using EDCD, suppose, as in the text, that the initial hierarchy has all constraints in a single stratum and the first learning datum is .□V.CV.⟨C⟩. This is the winner; the loser is a parse of the input contained in this datum, /VCVC/, which is optimal according to the learner's current hierarchy. With all constraints equally ranked, there are many optimal structures, including all of a–d in tableau (6); suppose the learner happens to pick ⟨V⟩.CV.⟨C⟩. This then is the loser in the first loser/winner pair, so in this case EDCD performs exactly the same demotion as in (27). The new hierarchy has FILL^{Ons} demoted to the second stratum.

There are now three optimal parses of /VCVC/: the correct one, .□V.CVC., and .□V.CV.C□. Suppose the learner picks the latter parse as the next loser, to compare with the correct parse, the winner. The resulting demotion is the same as in (30): PARSE is demoted below FILL^{Nuc}. Suppose the learner now receives, as in the text, another learning datum .□V.⟨C⟩. The input contained in this datum, /VC/, has two optimal parses given the current hierarchy: the correct one and the null parse ⟨VC⟩. If the learner selects the latter as the loser, the resulting demotion is exactly (34), and L_1 is learned.

References

Clements, George N., and Samuel Jay Keyser. 1983. *CV Phonology.* Cambridge, Mass.: MIT Press.

Dresher, B. Elan. 1996. Charting the learning path: Cues to parameter setting. MS, University of Toronto. [Revised version to appear in *Linguistic Inquiry*.] ▶

Itô, Junko. 1989. A prosodic theory of epenthesis. *Natural Language & Linguistic Theory* 7: 217–60.

Jakobson, Roman. 1962. *Selected Writings 1: Phonological Studies.* The Hague: Mouton.

McCarthy, John. 1979. *Formal Problems in Semitic Phonology and Morphology.* Doctoral dissertation, MIT, Cambridge, Mass.

McCarthy, John, and Alan Prince. 1995. Faithfulness and reduplicative identity. In *University of Massachusetts Occasional Papers 18: Papers in Optimality Theory*, 249–384. GLSA, University of Massachusetts, Amherst. Rutgers Optimality Archive ROA-60, http://ruccs.rutgers.edu/roa.html. ◀

Minsky, Marvin. 1961. Steps toward artificial intelligence. *Proceedings of the Institute of Radio Engineers* 49: 8–30.

Prince, Alan, and Paul Smolensky. 1991. *Notes on Connectionism and Harmony Theory in Linguistics.* Technical report CU-CS-533-91. Department of Computer Science, University of Colorado, Boulder.

Prince, Alan, and Paul Smolensky. 1993. *Optimality Theory: Constraint Interaction in Generative Grammar.* MS, Rutgers University,

New Brunswick, N.J., and University of Colorado, Boulder. Technical report RuCCS TR–2, Rutgers Center for Cognitive Science. ◀

Selkirk, Elisabeth. 1981. Epenthesis and degenerate syllables in Cairene Arabic. In *MIT Working Papers in Linguistics 3: Theoretical Issues in the Grammar of Semitic Languages.* MITWPL, Department of Linguistics and Philosophy, MIT, Cambridge, Mass.

Steriade, Donca. 1982. *Greek Prosodies and the Nature of Syllabification.* Doctoral dissertation, MIT, Cambridge, Mass.

Tesar, Bruce. 1994. *Parsing in Optimality Theory: A Dynamic Programming Approach.* Technical report CU-CS-714-94, Department of Computer Science, University of Colorado, Boulder.

Tesar, Bruce. 1995a. *Computational Optimality Theory.* Doctoral dissertation, Department of Computer Science, University of Colorado, Boulder. Rutgers Optimality Archive ROA-90, http://ruccs.rutgers.edu/roa.html.

Tesar, Bruce. 1995b. *Computing Optimal Forms in Optimality Theory: Basic Syllabification.* Technical report CU-CS-763-95, Department of Computer Science, University of Colorado, Boulder. Rutgers Optimality Archive ROA-52, http://ruccs.rutgers.edu/roa.html. ◀

Tesar, Bruce. 1998. Error-driven learning in Optimality Theory via the efficient computation of optimal forms. In *Is the Best Good Enough? Papers from the Workshop on Optimality in Syntax*, ed. Pilar Barbosa, Danny Fox, Paul Hagstrom, Martha Jo McGinnis, and David Pesetsky. Cambridge, Mass.: MIT Press and MITWPL. ▶

Tesar, Bruce. 1999. Robust interpretive parsing with alignment constraints. ▶

Tesar, Bruce, and Paul Smolensky. 1996. *Learnability in Optimality Theory* (long version). Technical report JHU-CogSci-96-4, Department of Cognitive Science, The Johns Hopkins University, Baltimore, Md. Rutgers Optimality Archive ROA-156, http://ruccs.rutgers.edu/roa.html. ▶

Wexler, Kenneth, and Peter Culicover. 1980. *Formal Principles of Language Acquisition.* Cambridge, Mass.: MIT Press.

Study and Research Questions

1   Redo the example in §2.3 using the Error-Driven Constraint Demotion algorithm in (38).

2   In §2.4, it is argued that constraint promotion is problematic because of the difficulty of disentangling disjunctions. Find a real-life example like (35) elsewhere in this book and show how Constraint Demotion deals with it and why constraint promotion cannot.

3   In (16), a distinction is made between the structural description of a candidate and the candidate's overt form. Constraint Demotion operates on candidate structural descriptions, though learners can only observe overt forms. In various papers, Tesar (1997a, 1997b, 1998a, 1998b, 1998c) has addressed the issue of learning from overt forms only. Read one of these papers, then explain and comment on Tesar's proposals.

Chapter 6 | Elliott Moreton

Non-computable Functions in Optimality Theory

Editor's Note

An OT grammar as defined in chapter 1 is a ranking of markedness constraints and faithfulness constraints – and nothing else. Therefore, as this chapter shows, the only reason to violate a faithfulness constraint is if violation leads to improvement in markedness. This result, which is derived from the most basic premises of the theory, has significant empirical consequences, such as the impossibility of circular chain-shifts. The discussion intersects with an important issue in phonology of the early 1970s, polarity-switching rules. (For non-technical overview of this chapter, see McCarthy 2002: 101–3.)

1 Introduction

"Phonological theory", say Prince and Smolensky (1993, hereinafter P&S, p. 67), "contains two parts: a theory of substantive universals of phonological well-formedness, and a theory of formal universals of constraint interaction." The theory they espouse, Optimality Theory (hereinafter OT), claims to provide an exhaustive statement of how constraints interact, leaving the grammarian with just two tasks: to discover what the universal constraints are, and how they are ranked in particular languages.

In this view, languages differ only in how they rank the universal constraint set. Predictions about what will turn up in natural languages follow from P&S's "factorial typology" – one looks at the empirical consequences of all possible rankings of the universal constraint set. This naturally involves knowing what the constraints actually are.

Excerpt (with revisions by the author) from:
Moreton, Elliott (1996) Non-computable Functions in Optimality Theory. Unpublished manuscript. Amherst, MA: University of Massachusetts, Amherst. [Available on Rutgers Optimality Archive, ROA-364.]
   This excerpt, published here for the first time, is based on a 1999 revision, with further emendations by the author to aid continuity.

There is another way to go about it, which this paper will illustrate. If we have reason to believe that every constraint (or at least every constraint relevant to a particular question) has such-and-such a property, it may follow that the constraint hierarchy as a whole is incapable of computing certain mappings from underlying to surface forms. A local property of each individual constraint can entail a global property of the whole grammar, thus allowing us to make predictions without exact knowledge of the constraints.

In particular, it will be shown that an OT phonological grammar which has only markedness and faithfulness constraints is incapable of producing certain kinds of exchange-rule, metathesis, and augmentation effects. This extends and explains an observation originally due to Anderson & Browne (1973) to the effect that exchange-rule effects are always morphologically triggered.

The paper is organized as follows: section 2 translates OT and our auxiliary hypotheses into formal terms so that we can prove theorems about them. The actual proofs are done in section 3. Section 4 draws real-world conclusions and tests them against the empirical data. Section 5 is a concluding discussion.

2   Formal Properties of Optimality Theory

The following sections formalize classical OT, to make rigorous the notions of (2.1) *computability by a grammar*, (2.2) *constraint-hierarchy grammar*, and (2.3) *classical OT*.

2.1   Phonological grammars

Phonological theories normally involve at least three levels of linguistic representation:

- The *underlying (phonological) representation*, assembled directly from information stored in the lexicon. This forms the *input to* the phonological component of the grammar. Underlying representations will be written between slashes: /kentapal/.
- The *surface (phonological) representation*, which is the *output of* the phonological component and input to the phonetic component, here written between square brackets: [kentapal].
- The *phonetic representation*, which is what the speaker actually does with their mouth, written here between double quotes: "kentapal".

Optimality Theory is a theory of constraint interaction, not of representations. We want our deductions about OT to hold even if the theory of representations changes. Hence, we have to treat input and output forms as unanalyzable atoms. Hence, the term *grammar* will refer to a function G from a countable set **A** ("inputs") to subsets of another countable set **B** ("outputs"). A grammar G such that the inputs and outputs are precisely the underlying and surface phonological representations, respectively, of a natural language, and such that G performs the same mapping as a speaker's phonological competence, will be called a *natural grammar*.

In natural grammars, these subsets of **B** usually contain only one element: free phonological (as distinguished from phonetic) variation is less common, and will be ignored here. In order to simplify exposition, we shall incorrectly assume that all natural grammars have the property of *exactness*:

(2)   *Defn* Let **A** and **B** be two countable sets, and suppose G: **A** → 2^B is such that $\forall$ a $\in$ **A**, $|G(a)| = 1$. Then G is said to be *exact*.

Confining our interest to the class of exact grammars, we are now able to formulate the question, "what does a grammar do?"

(3)   *Defn* Suppose **A** and **B** are countable sets, and G: **A** → 2^B is an exact grammar. We say that G *computes* the function f: **A** → **B** if $\forall$ a $\in$ **A**, $G(a) = \{f(a)\}$.

The question now becomes: for a given class of exact grammars from **A** → 2^B, what functions can be computed by a member of that class?

2.2   Constraint-hierarchy grammars and Optimality Theory

Let **A**, **B** be countable sets.

(4)   *Defn* A *constraint over* **A** × **B** is any function C: **A** × **B** → $\mathbb{N}$ such that the domain of C is all of **A** × **B**. If a $\in$ **A**, b $\in$ **B**, we write C/a/[b] (rather than the more usual C(a,b) – as a reminder of which argument corresponds to the underlying representation, and which to the surface representation). Then a is called the *input* to C, and b is called the *candidate*. The value of C/a/[b] is called the *score* awarded by C to the candidate b for the input a.[1]

(5)   *Defn* A *constraint hierarchy over* **A** × **B** is an ordered n-tuple **C** = $(C_1, \ldots, C_n)$, where each C_i is a constraint over **A** × **B**.[2]

(6)   *Defn* A *score vector (of length n)* is an ordered n-tuple v = $(r_1, \ldots, r_n)$, where $r_i \in \mathbb{N}$.

(7)   *Defn* Let v = $(r_1, \ldots, r_n)$, v' = $(r'_1, \ldots, r'_n)$ be score vectors. We say v < v' iff $\exists$ k such that
       (i) $\forall$ i < k: $r_i = r'_i$ (vacuously true if k = 1)
       (ii) $r_k < r'_k$
       If it is not true that v < v', we say v $\geq$ v'. If v < v' or v = v', we say v $\leq$ v'. The < relation is clearly transitive, antisymmetric, and irreflexive, so it is a total ordering.
(8)   *Lemma* Let V be a nonempty set of score vectors of length n. Then V contains a unique minimal element; i.e., $\exists$ v' $\in$ V such that $\forall$ v $\in$ V, we have $v^* \leq v$.[3]

Proof By induction on n. The proposition is obviously true for score vectors of length 1. Suppose it is true for those of length $n - 1$. Let $V' = \{(v_1, \ldots, v_{n-1}) | (v_1, \ldots, v_n) \in V\}$, i.e., V' is the set of vectors obtained by truncating those in V to the length $n - 1$. Then by the inductive hypothesis, V' has a unique least element v'^*. Let $L = \{(v_1, \ldots, v_n) \in V | (v_1, \ldots, v_{n-1}) = v'^*\}$. Of all elements of L, one – call it v^* – will have the smallest value of v_n, and hence will be minimal in L. Suppose $w = (w_1, \ldots, w_n)$ is any element of V. Then $(v_1, \ldots, v_{n-1}) \leq (w_1, \ldots, w_{n-1})$, by construction of L. If the inequality is strict, then $v^* < w$. If it is not strict, then $(w_1, \ldots, w_{n-1}) = v'^*$, so $w \in L$, and $v^* \leq w$, by construction of v^*. Hence v^* is minimal in V. If v^* and w^* are both minimal in V, then both are in L, so $v_1^* = w_1^*, \ldots, v_{n-1}^* = w_{n-1}^*$. Furthermore, $v_n = w_n$, so $v^* = w^*$. Hence v^* is unique.

(9)   *Defn* Let $C = (C_1, \ldots, C_n)$ be a constraint hierarchy over $A \times B$, $a \in A$, $b \in B$. We define $C/a/[b]$ to be the score vector $(C_1/a/[b], \ldots, C_n/a/[b])$, and say that $C/a/[b]$ is the *score* awarded by C to the candidate b relative to the input a.

(10)   *Defn* Let G be a 3-tuple $(A \times B, Gen, C)$ such that
(i) $A \times B$ is a countable set;
(ii) $Gen: A \rightarrow 2^B$ is such that $\forall a \in A$, $Gen(a) \neq \emptyset$;
(iii)   C is a constraint hierarchy over $A \times B$.
For any $a \in A$ we define
$G(a) = \{b_0 \in B | C/a/[b_0] \leq C/a/[b]$ for all $b \in Gen(a)\}$
Then G is said to be a *constraint-hierarchy grammar*. The element a is called the *input*, the set $Gen(a)$ is the *candidate set*, and the set $G(a)$ is the *output*.

(11)   *Lemma* If $G = (A \times B, Gen, C)$ is a constraint-hierarchy grammar, then $\forall a \in A$, $G(a) \neq \emptyset$.
Proof By (ii) of (10) above, $Gen(a) \neq \emptyset$. Hence we can apply Lemma (8) to the set $V = \{C/a/[b] | b \in Gen(a)\}$. This set contains a minimal element v^*, and $G(a)$ is simply the (obviously nonempty) subset of S whose elements receive a score of v^* relative to a. QED.

Constraint-hierarchy grammars are, as a class, uninteresting:

(12)   *Lemma* Let A, B be any countable sets, and let $f: A \rightarrow B$ be any function defined on all of A. Then there exists a constraint-hierarchy grammar $G = (A \times B, Gen, C)$ that computes f.
Proof There are at least two equally trivial ways to construct such a grammar.
(i)   (Trivial Gen) For any $a \in A$, let $Gen(a) = A$. Let $C = (C_1)$, where for any $a \in A$, $b \in B$, C_1 is given by
$C_1/a/[b] = 0$ iff $b = f(a)$
$C_1/a/[b] = 1$ otherwise.
Then obviously $\forall a \in A$, $G(a) = \{f(a)\}$.
(ii)   (Trivial C) For any $a \in A$, let $Gen(a) = \{f(a)\}$. Let $C = (C_1)$, where C_1 is the trivial constraint such that for any $a \in A$, $b \in B$, $C_1/a/[b] = 0$. Then obviously $\forall a \in A$, $G(a) = \{f(a)\}$.

The claim that every natural-language grammar can be computed by some constraint-hierarchy grammar is therefore an empty one. We already know it to be true, since it rules nothing out. Definition (10) provides a framework or notational device, rather than a theory of language. If we want falsifiable predictions, we will have to constrain Gen( ) and **C** to prevent the tricks used in (12 i) and (12 ii). The next section of this paper investigates a widely used model which does so constrain them, and which consequently cannot compute certain functions.

2.3   The "classical OT" model

The model we are going to look at is a variant of the standard version of Optimality Theory, as presented in, e.g., Prince & Smolensky (1993), which we will call "classical OT". It makes two assumptions which disallow the tricks used in (12).

One is that for any input /a/, [a] ∈ Gen(/a/); that is, the candidate set always contains a *fully faithful candidate*. This forestalls (12 ii), the trivial-**C** trick.

The other is that there are only two types of constraint: *faithfulness* constraints, which favor candidates that are like the input over those that differ from it, and *markedness* constraints, which favor candidates that have (lack) some configuration over those that lack (have) it. Intuitively, markedness constraints represent the tendency of a grammar to prefer certain surface forms over others, while faithfulness constraints represent the tendency to keep the output like the input. This disposes of (12 i), the trivial-Gen( ) trick, since the single constraint needed to make the trick work will not necessarily belong to either of these categories.

The first of these assumptions is standard (see, e.g., P&S p. 80); the second, while implicit in much OT work (e.g., Kirchner 1996), has not to my knowledge been explicitly and seriously proposed – and with good reason, as we shall see.

It will be necessary to add one more hypothesis, *homogeneity*, which asserts that input and output representations are made out of the same structural elements. This is not a standard OT assumption, nor are we proposing it as an axiom about natural language. Rather, it will be used in the theoretical argument to prove a theorem, and in the empirical argument to single out the class of real-world processes to which we expect the theorem to apply.

In the following subsections (2.3.1–2.3.5), we formalize the classical OT assumptions and briefly discuss their interpretation. The next section, section 3, will explore the computational power of classical OT grammars, and show how its hypotheses restrict the class of computable functions.

2.3.1   Gen( ) and the fully faithful candidate

This is an uncontroversial assumption, whose formalization is repeated here in (13):

(13)   *Defn* If for some constraint-hierarchy grammar (**A** × **B**, Gen, **C**) we have
∀ a ∈ **A**, [a] ∈ Gen(/a/), then Gen( ) is said to be *inclusive*.

Classical OT grammars have inclusive Gen( ) functions; P&S (p. 80) even propose a version in which Gen(/a/) = **A** for all a ∈ **A**.

Inclusivity implies that $A \subseteq B$. This will be taken up again when homogeneity is discussed in section 2.3.4.

2.3.2   Markedness constraints

A markedness constraint is one that ignores the input and looks only at the candidate:

(14)   *Defn* If C is a constraint over $A \times B$ such that $\forall$ a, a' $\in A$, C[a] = C[a'], then C is a *markedness constraint*.[4]

Markedness constraints are therefore those that penalize ill-formed surface structures. Since the input is irrelevant to a markedness constraint, we can omit the first argument and write simply "C[b]".
[...]

2.3.3   Faithfulness constraints

A faithfulness constraint is one which always gives a perfect score to the fully faithful candidate.

(19)   *Defn* If C is a constraint over $A \times B$ such that $\forall$ a $\in A$, C/a/[a] = 0, then C is a *faithfulness constraint*.

[...]

2.3.4   Homogeneity of inputs and outputs

We have saved the most unintuitive assumption for last. It will be both convenient and crucial to assume further that $A = B$, that is, that the grammar is *homogeneous*. Convenient, because it allows us to state and prove theorems about constraint interaction much more simply; crucial, because (as we shall see later) it is precisely the homogeneous part of natural grammars that is well-behaved with respect to the theorems we shall derive.

(23)   A grammar G: $A \rightarrow 2^B$ is said to be *homogeneous* if $A = B$.

Once we start talking about formal grammars that mimic natural grammars, A will become the set of possible underlying representations, and B the set of possible surface representations. A real linguistic theory defines A and B by enumerating the formal elements used to build these representations (nodes, association lines, etc.) and the rules for putting them together. To claim that $A = B$ is to claim that, in the grammars of present interest, underlying and surface phonological representations are made of the same components, assembled in the same way.

Homogeneity is not a credible condition on OT grammars of natural languages. Right from the very start, OT grammar fragments have assumed the input to contain structures never found in outputs, and vice versa.

It is, for example, a common assumption that the input to the "phonological" component of the grammar is heavily annotated with nonphonological information

– phonologically empty morphemes (e.g., McCarthy & Prince 1995), morphological constituency (e.g., Beckman 1998), Level 1 vs. Level 2 affix class (e.g., Benua 1997), part of speech and case (e.g., P&S's Lardil), syntactic constituency (Truckenbrodt 1996), and much more. None of these annotations can be changed by Gen( ), no output is ever unfaithful to them, and none are in the candidate output set.

There are also structures commonly supposed to be present in the output but not the input. Phonological phrase boundaries, for instance, seem to be determined entirely by the interaction of constraints (Truckenbrodt 1996). After all, where would the phrasing in the input come from? Not the lexicon, surely. And not the syntax alone either, since phrasing exhibits highly un-syntactic properties like rate- and length-sensitivity (Shih 1986, Du 1988). Moreover, if a phrase boundary some-how made it into the input, Truckenbrodt's constraints would in effect erase it and overwrite it; the output would be faithful only by coincidence.

But most "phonological" representations *are* in fact present in both input and output: distinctive features, low-level prosodic constituency such as syllables or prosodic words, association lines. These are the elements that turn up in the lex-icon, and that can be changed by Gen( ). Homogeneous grammars can deal with much of the core business of phonology – assimilation, dissimilation, segmental inventories, phonotactics, syllable structure, phonologically conditioned allophony, anything resulting from the influence of sounds on other sounds.

In a natural grammar, those representational elements that are found in both inputs and outputs we may call *homogeneous elements*.[5] Those constraints which refer only to homogeneous elements in both arguments we may call *homogeneous constraints*. Any natural grammar will have nonhomogeneous elements and nonhomogeneous constraints, but it will also have homogeneous elements and homogeneous constraints. This paper will argue that, if we confine our attention to phonological processes involving only homogeneous elements, we will need only conservative constraints to implement them. We will accordingly so confine our attention for the rest of the theoretical discussion (up to the end of section 3).

2.3.5 Summary: classical OT

The model of OT with which we are concerned here is thus the one satisfying the following postulate:

(24) *Defn* Let $G = (S \times S, \text{Gen}, C)$ be a homogeneous constraint-hierarchy gram-mar. If every C_i is either a markedness constraint or a faithfulness constraint, we say that C is *conservative*. If, in addition, Gen( ) is inclusive and G is exact, then we say that G is a *classical OT grammar*.

3 Computable Functions in Classical OT Grammars

We are now in a position to show that classical OT is a constraining theory; there are functions it cannot compute, and hence phonological phenomena it predicts to be nonexistent. Our argument can be stated informally as follows.

The requirement in (24) of a conservative C and inclusive Gen( ) means that if the output is not identical to the input, it must be less marked than the input. To see why, notice that the inclusive-Gen( ) requirement means that the candidate set always contains the input, which scores perfectly on all faithfulness constraints. Since the output can't do better on the faithfulness constraints, it must do better on the markedness constraints.

If, therefore, a classical OT grammar sends underlying /A/ to surface [B], then [B] must be less marked than the fully faithful candidate [A]. It follows that the grammar cannot also send underlying /B/ to surface [A], since this would entail that [A] is less marked than the fully faithful candidate [B], and hence that [A] is less marked than itself.

We will show more generally that a classical OT grammar cannot compute *circular chain shifts* – any function that sends /A1/ → [A2], /A2/ → [A3], . . . , /An/ → [A1] – or *infinite chain shifts* – any function that sends /A1/ → [A2], /A2/ → [A3], . . . Furthermore, this is an if-and-only-if theorem: any function that does *not* give rise to a circular or infinite chain shift *can* be computed by a classical OT grammar.

These statements are formalized and proven in section 3.1 as the *characterization theorem* for classical OT grammars, defining precisely what functions classical OT can and cannot compute.

3.1   The characterization theorem

We begin by establishing that the output of a classical OT grammar is either the input, or something less marked than the input.

(25)   *Defn* Let C be a conservative constraint hierarchy. Define C^M and C^F to be the constraint hierarchies consisting respectively of the markedness constraints $(C^M_1, \ldots, C^M_p)$ and the faithfulness constraints $(C^F_1, \ldots, C^F_q)$ of C, such that the dominance relations in C^M and C^F are the same as those in C.

(26)   *Lemma* Let G = (S × S, Gen, C) be a classical OT grammar, and suppose a, b ∈ S are such that a ≠ b and G(a) = {b}. Then $C^M[a] > C^M[b]$.
   Proof By definition of the function G( ), we have C/a/[a] > C/a/[b]. By definition of faithfulness, though, we have $C^F/a/[a] = (0, 0, \ldots, 0) \le C^F/a/[b]$. If it were also true that $C^M[a] \le C^M[b]$, then it would follow that C/a/[a] ≤ C/a/[b], contradicting our hypothesis. Hence $C^M[a] > C^M[b]$. QED.

This sharply restricts the set of computable functions:

(27)   *Defn* Let f:S → S be any function. Let $f^n(a)$ represent f(f(. . . (a) . . .)), with f iterated n times. Let $f^0(a) = a$. Suppose that for any a ∈ S, there is a smallest number π(a) such that $f^{\pi(a)}(a) = f^{\pi(a)+1}(a)$. Then we say that f is *eventually idempotent*, and that π(a) is the *potential* of a under f.

(28) *Thm* (characterization theorem for classical OT grammars) Let f:S → S be any function. Then f is computable by a classical OT grammar if and only if f is eventually idempotent.

Proof (⇒) Suppose f is computable by a classical OT grammar C = (S × S, Gen, C). Let a be any element of S, and consider the sequence A = ({a}, G(a), G^2(a), G^3(a), ...), where again G^k(a) represents G iterated k times on a. (Each G^i(a) is guaranteed to exist by the homogeneity of G.) For convenience's sake let us write A = ({a^0}, {a^1}, (a^2), ...). Let M = {C^M(a^0), C^M(a^1), ...). This is a set of score vectors, so by Lemma (8) it has a minimal element C^M(a^K) for some K. Then C^M(a^K) ≤ C^M(a^{K+1}). By Lemma (26), this means a^K = a^{K+1}. But a^k = f^k(a), so f^K(a) = f^{K+1}(a), making f eventually idempotent. QED.

(⇐) Suppose f is eventually idempotent. We will construct a classical OT grammar G = (S × S, Gen, C) that computes f. Let C = (C_1, C_2), where for any a, b ∈ S,

C_1/a/[b] = 0 iff b ∈ {a, f(a)}
C_1/a/[b] = 1 otherwise
C_2[b] = π(b)

where π(b) is the potential of b under f, a number which is guaranteed to exist since f is eventually idempotent. Then G is a classical OT grammar, since C_1 is a faithfulness constraint and C_2 is a markedness constraint. For any input a ∈ S, the candidates will receive the following score vectors:

Candidate	Score Vector
a	(0, π(a))
f(a)	(0, π(f(a)))
others	(1, unknown)

The set containing the candidate with the smallest score vector is G(a). Clearly, if f(a) = a, then G(a) = a = {f(a)}. If f(a) ≠ a, then π(f(a)) = π(a) − 1, so (0, π(f(a))) < (0, π(a)), and again G(a) = {f(a)}. QED.

(29) *Corollary* Suppose G = (S, C) is an OT grammar. Then there exists a classical OT grammar[6] G′ = (S × S, Gen, C′) such that G′ computes the same function as G, and C′= (C_1' C_2').

Proof Done already in the proof of (28).

So everything that can be done in classical OT can be done with just one faithfulness constraint and one markedness constraint! This does not mean that classical OT is in any sense trivial. Quantifier order is important here. What Corollary (29) says is that *for any* eventually idempotent function, *there exists* a two-constraint classical OT grammar that computes it. What OT claims is that *there exists* a set of constraints such that *for any* phonological system found in nature, the constraints can be ranked to give a classical OT grammar that computes it.

Two constraints that would handle, say, Berber, could not be reranked to yield any other language, nor are they likely to be at all linguistically insightful or psychologically real. Any list of hypothetical constraints that might plausibly be *the* universal constraints will be much more interesting than that.

3.2   Phonological processes incompatible with classical OT

Classical OT can compute all and only eventually idempotent functions; hence, a natural grammar that was not eventually idempotent would be a clear counter-example. What makes a function f:S $\rightarrow$ S fail to be eventually idempotent? [...]

An eventually idempotent function f will look like figure (31). Elements having equal potential under f are shown at the same height from the bottom of the diagram; the right-hand column shows what that potential is.

(31)   *Eventually idempotent function*

Potential

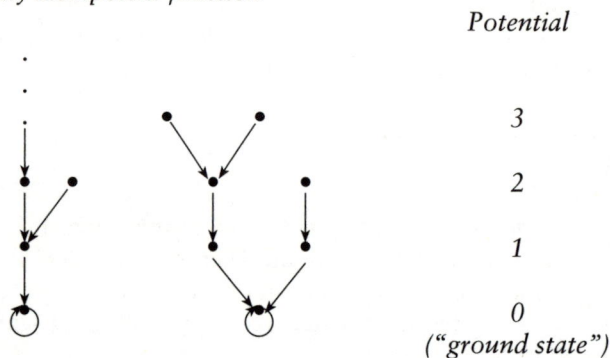

("ground state")

[...]
In general, the configurations that are ruled out are the following ones, in which the arrows indicate the action of G, and in which [a_i'] is phonologically identical to /a_i/.

(36)   *Infinite chain shift*

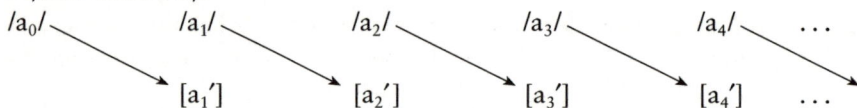

(37)   *Circular chain shift*

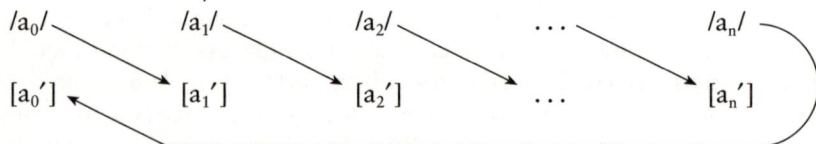

Caveat: An *apparent* circular chain shift could arise from phonetic neutralization of a phonological contrast, e.g., if /a/$\rightarrow$[b'] and /b/$\rightarrow$[a'], where [a] and [a'], [b] and [b'] have different phonological representations but are the same phonetically (for example, the analysis of Taiwanese tone sandhi in Yip 1980). Theorem (28) does not exclude such a process. The difficulties in applying a phonetic-neutralization analysis are discussed below, in section 4.5.3.

The hypotheses of Theorem (28) can be relaxed to rule out patterns (36) and (37) even when $[a_{i'}]$ is phonologically different from $/a_i/$, as long as $[a_{i'}]$ is more faithful to $/a_i/$ than $[a_{i+1'}]$ is. Suppose, for example, that G produces the map $/u:/\rightarrow[o]$, and $/o:/$ $\rightarrow[u]$. Then $[u]$ is more faithful to $/u:/$ than $[o]$ is. It follows from Lemma (26) that when $/u:/$ is the input, $[o]$ beats $[u]$ on markedness, so $[o]$ is less marked in G than $[u]$. The same argument shows that $[u]$ is less marked in G than $[o]$, a contradiction. So no G can produce that map. Formally, and more generally:

(38) *Thm* (rotation theorem) Let S be a countable set, and let $N:S \rightarrow 2^S$ be exact. Suppose A and A′ are nonempty subsets of S, and suppose there exist functions f, g: A $\rightarrow$ A′ such that
  (i)   f and g are bijections from A to A′
  (ii) $\forall$ a$\in$ A, $f(a) \neq g(a)$
  (iii) $\forall$ a$\in$ A, $f(a) = N(a)$
  (iv) $\forall$ a$\in$ A, $C^F/a/[g(a)] \leq C^F/a/[f(a)]$
Then there does not exist any classical OT grammar $G = (S \times S, Gen, C)$ such that $G(a) = N(a)$ for all a $\in$ S.
Proof By contradiction. Suppose such a G exists; then C is conservative. By (i), $h = f \circ g^{-1}$ is a bijection from A′ to A′. Choose any $a_0' \in$ A′, and let $a_i' = h^i(a_0')$. Let $a_i = g^{-1}(a_i')$. Then $f(a_i) = g(a_{i+1}) = a_{i+1}'$.
By (ii), we have $h(a_i') \neq a_i'$, so $a_i' \neq a_{i+1}'$. Therefore, by (iii), $C/a_i/[a_i'] > C/a_i/[a_{i+1}']$ (since $[a_{i+1}'] = G(a_i)$, the victorious candidate when $/a_i/$ is the input).
By (iv), $C^F/a_i/[a_i'] \leq C^F/a_i/[a_{i+i}']$. Hence, by Lemma (26), $C^M[a_i'] > C^M[a_{i+1}']$. Since i can become arbitrarily large, the set $\{C^M[a_i'] \mid i = 0, 1, 2, \dots\}$ has no least element. But Lemma (8) tells us that it *must* have a least element. $\rightarrow\leftarrow$
Ergo, no such G can exist. QED.

(The "only if" half of the characterization theorem follows from this as a corollary by setting A = B = S and letting g be the identity function.)

Theorem (38) is representationally neutral – i.e., independent of any theory of phonological representations. The $/a_i/$ could be a string of phonemes, or a string of feature matrices, or a sophisticated autosegmental tier structure parsed into a prosodic tree – it doesn't matter. As long as Gen( ) and C satisfy the hypotheses of conservativity, (36) and (37) are not possible phonological processes.

4 Empirical Test of Classical OT

What we have up to this point is a mathematical theorem which can be informally summarized as follows:

(39) Suppose you have written an OT grammar which has the following properties:
  (i)   The inputs and candidates are made from the same kit of representational elements ("homogeneity").
  (ii) There is always a fully faithful candidate ("inclusivity").

(iii)   Every constraint is either a markedness constraint or a faithfulness constraint ("conservativity").

Then that grammar cannot compute circular or infinite chain shifts.[7]

In order to translate this into a testable prediction about natural languages, we have to confront the problem, already discussed in §2.3.4, that natural languages are far from homogeneous. Our solution is to use parsimony and assume that if a really existing phonological process *can* be described homogeneously, then it *must* be. Take for example a familiar phenomenon like coda-nasal place assimilation in Japanese (Itô 1986). Since the entire process takes place without reference to nonhomogeneous features like part of speech, we assume that in any plausible natural grammar of Japanese, none of the constraints active in this process make reference to nonhomogeneous elements. We can then excise that part of the grammar responsible for the process and apply the theorem to it in isolation.

Hypothesis (39 ii), inclusivity, is a theory-internal assumption which is taken to be true whenever (39 i) is true; its validity will not be questioned here.

Hypothesis (39 iii), conservativity, is a claim about natural languages, as discussed in §2.3. It is what is being tested. If this hypothesis is correct, then the only way for the forbidden chain shifts to arise is for Hypothesis (39 i), homogeneity, to be violated. The empirical test of conservativity is therefore:

(40)   Suppose a process is found in a natural language which creates a circular or infinite [chain shift]. Then the process can only be expressed with reference to nonhomogeneous representational elements.

In order to falsify this claim, we must seek something very specific: a process that satisfies the hypotheses of Theorem (38), but violates its conclusion. This process must relate *homogeneous* sets of *underlying* and *surface* representations, which means

- An SPE-style rule (Chomsky & Halle 1968) relating two *intermediate* levels of representation in a suspicious fashion (e.g., the famous SPE vowel-shift rule) is not relevant, since OT does not recognize any intermediate levels.
- A process which relies upon some representational feature found only in inputs or only in candidate outputs is not relevant, since Theorem (38) requires homogeneity. Processes triggered by, e.g., morphology or by phrase-level phonology therefore do not count.

The violation must occur synchronically and productively, so that we know it is occurring in the grammar rather than being a lexicalized historical relic.

We can imagine at least five different processes that could cause forbidden chain shifts. In order of increasing plausibility, they are:

- *Unconditional augmentation.* Regardless of how long the input is, the output is longer.
- *Symmetrical metathesis.* Underlying /ab/ surfaces as [ba], while underlying /ba/ becomes [ab].

- *Alternations with zero*. The language deletes and epenthesizes the same segment in the same environment, so that /abc/ → [ac], while /ac/ → [abc].
- *Segmental exchange rules*. These rules invert the value of a feature specification, changing, e.g., voiced to voiceless and vice versa.
- *Rules of paradigmatic replacement*. The language arbitrarily substitutes one segment or autosegment for another, turning /a/ into [b] and /b/ into [a].

In other words, it never happens that the hypotheses of Theorem (38) are fulfilled and its conclusions violated. For homogeneous processes, therefore, it seems that only markedness and faithfulness constraints are necessary.

This extends and generalizes an empirical observation about segmental exchange rules due to Anderson and Browne (1973). We state it in OT terms as follows:

(42)   *Conservativity of phonology*
       If a constraint refers only to homogeneous representational elements – those occurring both in inputs and in candidate outputs – then it is either a markedness constraint or a faithfulness constraint, in the sense of Definitions (14) and (19).

4.1   Unconditional augmentation

A natural grammar with a phonological requirement that the output be longer than the input would create an infinite chain shift, violating Theorem (28): /ba/ → [baba], /baba/ → [bababa], etc. This simply doesn't happen, ever (John McCarthy, p.c. 1995). Augmentation is always to meet some static target condition – word minimality, say, or a syllable-weight requirement – that fixes a floor beneath which the input is not allowed to fall. These facts are eminently consistent with the conservativity of phonology.

4.2   Symmetrical metathesis

A metathesis rule that simply switched two segments around irrespective of their original order, such as that shown in (43), would exhibit circular chain shift.

(43) $V_1V_2 \rightarrow V_2V_1$

We would see effects like

(44)   /boa/ → [bao]
       /bao/ → [boa]

       [A process reversing the order of a nasal and a glottal stop regardless of original order has been reported for the Yuman language Kiliwa (Mixco 1971: Rule 16). However, it turns out that one half of the rule only applies to forms of the verb 'to be' (M. Mixco, p.c. 1996).]

[. . .]

There are only two possibilities: either the metathetic surface forms [of Kiliwa] are out-and-out lexicalized (and hence are not derived by the phonology at all), or else the metathesis is triggered specifically by the morpheme 'to do', and hence, relying on a nonhomogeneous representational element, does not fall in the scope of the theorem.

4.3   Alternations with zero

A language which epenthesized and deleted the same segment in the same environment would generate a circular chain shift, as shown hypothetically in (51):

(51)   a. $\emptyset \rightarrow e / \_\#$
           $e \rightarrow \emptyset / \_\#$

       b.   /bile/ → [bil]
            /bil/ → [bile]

There are languages which epenthesize and delete the same segment, but invariably in disjoint environments – Eastern Massachusetts English (McCarthy 1993), Sawai (Whisler 1992), Mohawk (Postal 1979, Hopkins 1987), Bedouin Hijazi Arabic (Al-Mozainy 1981), Korean (Ahn 1991). In no case[8] does the insertion and deletion of the same segment give rise to a chain shift forbidden by classical OT, again lending support to the contention that phonology is conservative.

4.4   Segmental exchange rules

A forbidden chain shift could also be created by a segmental exchange rule, also known as a polarity rule, flip-flop rule, or alpha-switching rule. Such a rule inverts distinctive-feature values in such a way as to change Segment A into Segment B, and vice versa, creating the circular chain shift shown in the hypothetical example below:

(52)   [α voice] → [−α voice] / _\#
       /bad/ → [bat]
       /bat/ → [bad]

The term "polarity" was coined early in the twentieth century by the Africanist Carl Meinhof, who thought it a common organizing principle not only of phonology but of morphology as well (Meinhof 1912). The debate over the existence or nonexistence of phonological exchange rules dates from the publication of Chomsky and Halle's *The Sound Pattern of English* in 1968, in which they are used to account for the synchronic reflex of the Great English Vowel Shift. For discussion of the theoretical implications within rule-based phonology, see, e.g., Chomsky (1967),

Chomsky & Halle (1968), McCawley (1974), Anderson & Browne (1973), Anderson (1974).

Chomsky and Halle's English data is not relevant here. The chain shift relation they propose in their Vowel Shift Rule holds only between intermediate levels of representation; the rotated vowels undergo diphthongization and other mutations which destroy the triggering environment of the polarity rules (Chomsky & Halle 1968, p. 188). The same is true of their rules of Rounding Adjustment (ibid., p. 217) and Backness Readjustment (ibid., p. 209) (which in any case applies only "in certain irregular forms" such as *mouse~mice, break~broke*), and of Bever's (1967, pp. 85ff.) Menomini vowel-glide coalescence rule. The debate, however, sent many linguists off on a hunt for examples from other languages: Menomini (Bever 1967, Chomsky & Halle 1968), Czech (Wolfe 1970, Anderson & Browne 1973), Old Prussian (Wolfe 1970, Anderson & Browne 1973), Tiberian Hebrew (Malone 1972), Icelandic (Anderson 1972), Luo (Gregersen 1972, Anderson & Browne 1973), Dinka (Anderson & Browne 1973), and Flemish Brussels Dutch (Zonneveld 1976).

In their comprehensive review of the subject, Anderson & Browne (1973) conclude that "the class of segmental exchange rules is limited to the domain of morpholexical processes"; i.e., the triggering environment for the exchange refers at least in part to morphology; McCawley (cited in Zonneveld 1976) writes that "the more plausible examples that I know of of exchange rules . . . share an important characteristic: their environment is not phonological but morphological." A striking example is the use of voicing inversion in the inflectional morphology of the Luo noun (Gregersen 1972, Okoth-Okombo 1982).

Zonneveld (1976) presents data which is supposed to reflect a phonologically conditioned exchange rule in the Dutch dialect spoken in Flemish Brussels in the early 1930s (van Loey 1933, Mazereel 1931). Rules of Precluster Shortening (53) and Auxiliary Verb Reduction (54) result in a regular and productive alternation of /V:/ with [V].

(53)   /V/ → [−long] / __$C_1 C_2$.[9]

(54)   /V/ → [−long] / [__, −stress, Aux]

For most vowels, that is the extent of the alternation. However, the back vowels exhibit a change of vowel quality as well: [u:]~[o], [o:]~[u]. Zonneveld's data (taken from van Loey 1933 and Mazereel 1931) is here cited in full:

(55)   [u:] ~ [o]

[mu:kə]	'to make'	[gəmokt]	'made'
		[moksəl]	'manufacture'
[sxu:mə]	'be ashamed'	[sxomtə]	'ashamed'
[vlu:mink]	'Fleming'	[vloms]	'Flemish'

(56)   [o:] ~ [u]

[vo:t]	'foot'	[vutsʃə]	'foot [diminutive]'
[ro:pə]	'to call'	[rupt]	'[s/he] calls'
[mo:tə]	'must [stressed]'	[mut]	'must [unstressed]'

We seem to have here a perfect configuration for the rotation theorem (38). For any phonotactically permissible X and Y, we expect [XuY] to be more faithful to /Xu:Y/ than [XoY] is, and we expect [XoY] to be more faithful to /Xo:Y/ than [XuY] is.

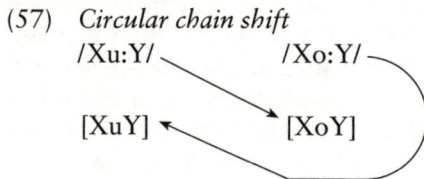

(57) *Circular chain shift*

$$/Xu{:}Y/ \quad\quad /Xo{:}Y/$$

$$[XuY] \quad\quad [XoY]$$

The hypotheses of Theorem (38) are satisfied, hence, Flemish Brussels Dutch cannot be modelled by a classical OT grammar. Since the conditioning environment is purely phonological (the change of vowel quality is triggered by shortening), we conclude that phonology is not necessarily conservative.

Or do we? The forms given in (55–56) do not come from contemporary inform-ants; they were culled from a 1931 book (Mazereel) and a 1933 paper (van Loey); the latter simply repeats some of the former's data without adding anything new. The three linguists' descriptions of the same data are shown below.

(58) *Flemish Brussels Dutch vowel shortening: back vowels*

Mazereel (1931)	*Van Loey (1933)*	*Zonneveld (1976)*
[o:] ~ [u, ɔ]	[o:] ~ [u]	[o:] ~ [u]
[u:] ~ [u, ɔ]	[u:] ~ [ɔ]	[u:] ~ [o]

In (59), we have the entirety of Mazereel's data on shortening,[10] from which van Loey's and Zonneveld's is drawn.

(59) *Shortening in Flemish Brussels Dutch (Mazereel 1931)*

(a) [u:] ~ [ɔ]

[mu:kə], [mɔkə]	'to make'	[gəmɔkt]	'made'
		[mɔksəl]	'manufacture'
[stru:t], [strɔ:t]	'street'	[strɔtsʲə]	'street [diminutive]'
[ru:p]	'turnip'	[rɔpkə]	'turnip [diminutive]'
[du:pə]	'baptize'	[dɔpsəl]	'baptism'
[sχu:mə]	'be ashamed'	[sχɔmtə]	'ashamed'
[vlu:minʲkʲ]	'Fleming'	[vlɔms]	'Flemish'

(b) [o:] ~ [u]

[vo:t]	'foot'	[vutsʲə]	'foot [diminutive]'
[mo:tə]	'must [stressed]'	[mutə]	'must [unstressed]'
[do:n]	'to do [stressed]'	[dun]	'to do [unstressed]'
[ro:pə]	'to call'	[rupt]	'[s/he] calls'

There is clearly disagreement about what the vowel alternation really is. Where Zonneveld has [o:]~[u] and [u:]~[o], Mazereel has [o:]~[u] and [u:]~[ɔ]. Zonneveld's [o] is "the usual" mid back vowel, and [o:] presumably that times two; his [u] is "the usual" high back vowel, and [u:] twice that. Mazereel's [ɔ] is tense mid back rounded;[11] there is no [ɔ:]. It is clearly distinct from his [o], which is a lax mid back rounded vowel[12] whose long counterpart has the same quality: [o:]. His [u] is tense high back rounded;[13] "[d]e [u:]", he says, "is de lange [u]" (Mazereel 1931, p. 16). Lest there should be any doubt that [o] and [ɔ] are phonetically different, van Loey (1933, p. 314) illustrates the difference for his Dutch-speaking readers with a minimal pair showing their phonemic difference in Modern Dutch: [bɔm] 'bomb' versus [bom] 'tree'.

Thus, while the [o:] ~ [u] half of the alternation is confirmed, the original sources contradict the claim that [u:] alternates with [o]. If anything, it alternates with [ɔ]. And worse news is still to come. A linguist who has done field work on the dialect has this to say:

> [I]t is the case that long /o:/ becomes /u/ in vowel shortening contexts, but it is not the case that /u:/ becomes /O/ (open o) in the Brussels dialect. This is because /u:/ does not exist in the Brussels dialect; what Mazereel, and other people as well represent as /u:/ is not [u:], but a mid back hyperrounded vowel, most likely with retracted tongue root as well. . . . [I]t clearly is not an [u:]. (W. de Reuse, electronic p.c. 1995; quoted by permission)

The actual alternation, then, is between [o:] and [u] on the one hand, and two completely different vowels on the other – quite a long way removed from circular chain shift.[14]

Anderson and Browne's generalization therefore stands: if an exchange rule creates a circular chain shift, then it is conditioned at least in part by something other than just the phonological representation – or, in OT terms, the constraints that cause it to happen are sensitive to something beyond just phonology. This again is consistent with our claim that phonology is conservative.

4.5   Paradigm replacement: tone sandhi in Taiwanese

One final possibility must be considered. There exists a well-known, well-documented, and dramatic instance of circular chain shift which does not fit into any of the aforementioned categories: the tone-sandhi alternations of Taiwanese. In addition to other alternations, in certain environments an underlying high level tone [55] becomes mid level [33], a mid level tone becomes low falling [31], a low falling tone becomes high falling [53], and a high falling tone becomes high level, producing a circular chain shift of length four. A similar circle of length two is found on checked syllables, which end in one of /p, t, k, ʔ/: high falling [54] exchanges with mid falling [32]. [. . .] This is shown schematically in (61) below. Tones in the phrase-final environment ("E1") change as shown by the arrows in the elsewhere environment ("E2").

(61)   *Taiwanese E1–E2 tone sandhi circles*

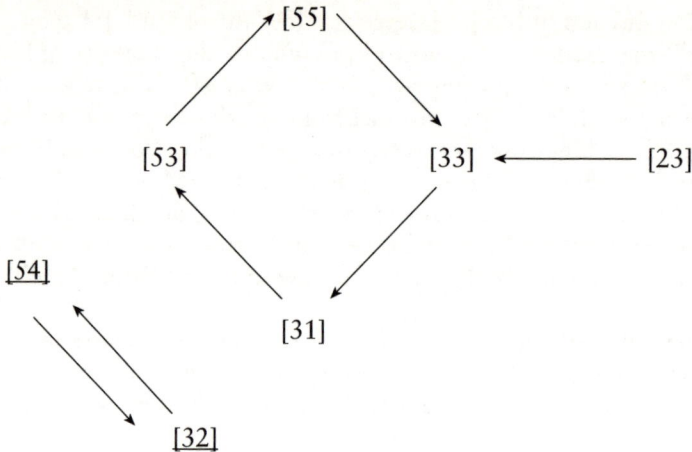

This pattern seems to be a spectacular violation (in fact, *two* spectacular violations) of the conclusion to Theorem (28).

> *[The length-two circle, which occurs in "checked" syllables only, is phonetically dubious, but the length-four circle in the free syllables is well-supported by speaker judgments and instrumental measurements (Cheng 1968; Chang 1988; Lin 1988, pp. 47–53; Du 1988, pp. 110–15).]*

[...]

4.5.3   The arbitrary nature of Taiwanese tone sandhi

The alternations are phonetically arbitrary – a high level tone is lowered, then made to fall, then raised, then levelled again – and are not linked in any phonologically intelligible way to the triggering environment (phrase-internal versus phrase-final). Every attempt to make sense out of them has failed.

   Early feature-matrix theories of tone exploited coincidental properties of a certain featural representation to express the tone-sandhi rule as an exchange rule (Wang 1967) or a set of disjunctively ordered rules (Cheng 1968, 1973; Woo 1969). The rules were arbitrary and were motivated only by the need to represent the observed sandhi facts.

   Rule-based autosegmental approaches required both unmotivated rules and phonetic neutralization of a phonological contrast, so that, e.g., [33] → [31] → [53] → [55] → [33'], where [33] and [33'] have different phonological representations but sound exactly the same (Du 1988; see also Yip 1980, Wright 1983). In OT this stratagem is technically possible, but not linguistically plausible. (1) In a phonetically grounded phonology it is implausible that [33] is more marked than [33'], as Lemma (26) would require. (2) Richness of the Base predicts a nonexistent class of morphemes with underlying /33'/ and thus different sandhi behavior from /33/.

   It looks as if the Taiwanese general tone-sandhi alternation is, synchronically speaking, completely arbitrary and idiosyncratic, not derivable from simple, logical, plausibly innate constraints, even if they are allowed to be nonconservative. It is not the kind of phenomenon OT was intended to explain, but a case of out-and-out paradigm replacement peculiar to Taiwanese.

5   Conclusions

In this paper we have developed and illustrated a novel means of getting predictions out of OT with only the vaguest idea of what the constraints actually are. A local property of the individual constraints can lead to a global property of every grammar that uses those constraints, which manifests itself in the data as a language universal.

Moreover, the particular local property we chose to illustrate this method (conservativity) led to a predicted language universal (the lack of circular and infinite chain shifts) which was in fact borne out by the data. The universal was remarkable enough to have attracted attention before; the OT framework provides a very natural explanation of it in terms of the basic concepts of markedness and faithfulness, which do not exist in serial-derivational theories. The motto of classical OT, embodied in its postulate of conservativity, is "if it ain't broke, don't fix it" – the phonology only changes things to make them "better", with "better" being defined as a condition on surface representations. This is why circular chain shifts are impossible within that framework – there is no way for A to be "better" than B and B to simultaneously be "better" than A. We have shown that this is the *entire* empirical content of classical OT, in the absence of information about the individual constraints.

So far, so good. But as usual, in trying to settle one problem we have stirred up two or more previously quiescent others. To prove this I will touch upon two of the most disturbing here, and suggest at least the outlines of a campaign against them.

One is the puzzling importance of representational homogeneity. In order to prove the characterization theorem, we had to be able to feed the grammar with its own output, so we insisted that input and output representations be built in the same way. And it turned out that real-world processes sensitive only to homogeneous representational elements behaved as predicted, while those sensitive to non-homogeneous elements sometimes misbehaved.

This is not what one would expect at first glance. There is a natural way to integrate nonhomogeneous constraints into the system of markedness and faithfulness. Morphological and syntactic information is only present in inputs; we expect it to figure in faithfulness constraints but not markedness constraints, producing effects like those of "positional faithfulness" discussed in Beckman (1998) – faithfulness to root-initial syllables, differential faithfulness to roots and affixes, etc. Phrase-level phonological information is only present in outputs; we expect it to figure in markedness constraints but not faithfulness constraints, producing effects like phrase-final lengthening. Hence we expect no circular chain shifts at all. Yet the grammar seems to allow, for no immediately obvious reason, nonhomogeneous constraints a latitude forbidden to homogeneous ones.

Our second problem is the idiosyncratic nature of the circular chain shifts. When they do arise, they have a language-particular look about them, in either the triggering environment or the alternation itself. It is very difficult to believe that anything like the phenomena of Kiliwa 'do' or Taiwanese tone sandhi (see section 4.5.3) could be attributed to the interaction of innate constraints – the very bedrock of the OT outlook.

The two problems may be linked. It may be that innateness and conservativity go hand-in-hand, and that the correct generalization is rather that constraints involving solely innate representational elements are themselves innate and conservative. If a language has an alternation that cannot be computed by these constraints, the learner can detect this by the failure of the learning algorithm to converge; the deficiency would then be suppleted by adding an undominated *ad hoc* constraint which simply insisted that a particular lexical item, in a particular environment, must surface in a particular way – making of each nonconservativity a lexical exception. Some such mechanism is necessary in any case to deal with processes (such as Germanic ablaut, the dramatic vowel-coalescence phenomena of Yup'ik (Reed et al. 1977), or the mutations caused by Kwakiutl glottalizing suffixes (Boas 1947, Bach n.d.)) which are triggered by specific lexical items and have phonologically unwieldy effects that are probably most economically described as paradigm replacements.

If innateness and conservativity are a package deal, we would expect that constraints referring to presumably innate morphological or syntactic categories (such as N versus V, or content-word versus function-word, or root versus affix) would be conservative, while those referring to presumably language-particular ones (such as first versus second conjugation, or specific lexical items) would not be. Thus unfaithfulness to the underlying segmentism might be compelled by a particular affix, but not by the mere fact of being a root.

These questions are still wide open, though. We must be content for the nonce with having identified them.

Notes

1   Intuitively, a constraint is a measure of how bad a given input–candidate pair is in a particular respect. Here we are allowing the badness score to be no smaller than zero, and to be arbitrarily large. We have to justify both of these assumptions.

In constructing a grammar to describe competence in a particular language, one might find it convenient, and linguistically insightful, to hypothesize a constraint C which gives negative scores. If there is a number n which is the smallest score that C ever awards, then C is just a notational variant of an orthodox constraint C′, where C′/a/[b] = C/a/[b] – n. Replacing C with C′ does not change the output of any constraint-hierarchy grammar containing C. If allowing negative scores is to have any detectable effect, we must allow arbitrarily large negative scores. But then we are no longer guaranteed that Lemma (8) [below] will hold; it is possible to construct sets of score vectors with no smallest element. The "detectable effect" is to make G possibly uncomputable. Hence, we can get along without negative-valued constraints.

To forbid constraints which give arbitrarily large positive scores would certainly simplify the definition of the ≤-relation on score vectors, since then, as P&S (p. 200) point out, there would be a simple order-preserving isomorphism between score vectors and the natural numbers. However, any such constraint-hierarchy grammar would just be a special case of the class of grammars described here, so the only effect on our arguments in this paper would be to make the proof of Lemma (8) trivial.

2   I'm ignoring the possibility that there might be infinitely many constraints, because it complicates matters and is not linguistically plausible.

3   This lemma is essential for the success of P&S's H-Eval; without it there is no guarantee that the algorithm will terminate.

4   The constraint C is of course really a two-place function; however, C/a/is a one-place function obtained by saturating the first argument of C.

5   The stock of available representational elements is here assumed to be universal; so is the status of each one as homogeneous or nonhomogeneous. A homogeneous element is homogeneous in all languages – Richness of the Base (P&S) makes it available in the input, and Gen( ) makes it available in the output. If that element never surfaces in a given language, we assume that some constraints conspire to stifle it.

6   Not a unique one, though. In the construction of C'_2, we can replace "1" with "2" or "1776" or whatever we please, as long as it doesn't equal 0.

7   An ordinary finite linear chain shift can be computed without any difficulties by a classical OT grammar, as pointed out by Kirchner (1996), who uses conservative constraints to implement chain shifts of lengths two and three in various languages.

8   A possible counterexample from Georgian is described by Fähnrich (1987): [v] is "usually" deleted before [o] and [u] (p. 25). Vowel hiatus, however, is "sometimes" resolved by epenthesis, "chiefly" of [v] and [b] (p. 27). Our immediate doubts about the regularity of this phenomenon are only deepened when he later informs us that verbs whose stems end in [-ev] exhibit many "peculiarities" in the passive conjugation, among them that they lose the [v] before the suffix [-od] (p. 82). If the deletion rule were regular, this would not be "peculiar".

9   There are some constraints on the consonants: C_2 must be an obstruent, and C_2 has to be a plosive if C_1 is a liquid (Zonneveld 1976).

10 Mazereel (1931), pp. 26–7, 44–5.

11 "De [ɔ] is geronde wijde middelachterklinker (mid back wide round)" (Mazereel 1931, p. 15; English gloss in original).

12 "De [o] is een korte nauwe geronde middelachterklinker (mid back narrow round)" (Mazereel 1931, p. 15).

13 "De [u] is de geronde bovenachterklinker (high back wide round)" (Mazereel 1931, p. 16).

14 It might not even be the business of the phonology at all. Van Loey cites these forms because he is trying to prove that certain vowels were present in an earlier stage of the Brussels Dutch dialect; part of his evidence for this is that they are still present as "shortened sounds" in various contemporary words, among them those of (59). His discussion suggests (though not conclusively) that they were isolated lexical relics: "Een bewijs dat het Brussels eenmaal de klanken a) /ɔ:/, /u:/, /ɔʲ/; b) /i:/, /u:/, /y:/; c) /e:/, /o:/, /ø:/; d) /ɔw/ heft gekend, is niet alleen het feit, dat ze (of sommige daarvan) rondom Brussel nog gehoord worden . . . , maar ook dat ze nog anwezig zijn als verkorte klanken in [24 examples]" (p. 312) ["A proof that Brussels Flemish once had the sounds a) . . . b) . . . c) . . . is not only that they (or some of them) are still heard around Brussels, but also that they are still present as shortened sounds in [24 examples]"].

Bibliography

Ahn, Sang-Cheol. 1991. Vowel deletion and epenthesis: the vowel [ï]. *Studies in the Linguistic Sciences* 21 (2): 1–18.

Al-Mozainy, H. Q. 1981. *Vowel Alternations in a Bedouin Hijazi Arabic Dialect: Abstractness and Stress*. Dissertation, University of Texas, Austin.

Anderson, Stephen R. 1972. Icelandic u-umlaut and breaking in a generative grammar. In S. Anderson and P. Kiparsky (eds.), *A Festschrift for Morris Halle*. New York: Holt, Rinehart, and Winston.

——. 1974. *The Organization of Phonology*. New York: Academic Press.

——, and W. Browne. 1973. On keeping exchange rules in Czech. *Papers in Linguistics* VI, 4: 445–82.

Bach, Emmon. (no date). Building words in Haisla. MS, University of Massachusetts, Amherst.

Beckman, Jill N. 1998. *Positional Faithfulness*. Ph.D. dissertation, University of Massachusetts, Amherst.

Benua, Laura. 1997, *Transderivational Identity: Phonological Relations between Words*. Ph.D. dissertation, University of Massachusetts, Amherst. ◄

Bever, Thomas. 1967. *Leonard Bloomfield and the Phonology of the Menomini language*. Dissertation, MIT.

Boas, Franz. 1947. Kwakiutl grammar. *Transactions of the American Philosophical Society*, New Series, 37 (1): 203–376.

Chang, Yueh-Chin. 1988. Sandhi tonal des syntagmes dissyllabiques du min-nan parlé à Taiwan. *Cahiers linguistique asie-orientale* 17 (2): 193–234.

Cheng, Richard L. 1968. Tone sandhi in Taiwanese. *Linguistics* 41: 19–42.

——. 1973. Some notes on tone sandhi in Taiwanese. *Linguistics* 100: 5–25.

Chomsky, Noam. 1967. Some general properties of phonological rules. *Language* 43: 102–28.

——, and Morris Halle. 1968. *The Sound Pattern of English*. Cambridge, MA: MIT Press.

Du, Tsai-Chwun. 1988. *Tone and Stress in Taiwanese*. Dissertation, University of Illinois/Urbana-Champaign.

Fähnrich, Heinz. 1987. *Kurze Grammatik der georgischen Sprache*. Leipzig: Verlag Enzykopädie.

Gregersen, Edgar. 1972. Consonant polarity in Nilotic. Paper presented to the 3rd annual conference on African linguistics, Indiana University.

Hopkins, Alice W. 1987. Vowel dominance in Mohawk. *IJAL* 53 (4): 445–59.

Itô, Junko. 1986. *Syllable Theory in Prosodic Phonology*. Ph.D. dissertation, University of Massachusetts, Amherst.

Kirchner, Robert. 1996. Synchronic chain shifts in Optimality Theory. *Linguistic Inquiry* 27: 341–50. ◄

Lin, Hwei-Bing. 1988. *Contextual Stability of Taiwanese Tones*. Dissertation, University of Connecticut.

Malone, Joseph L. 1972. A Hebrew flip-flop rule and its historical origins. *Lingua* 30: 423–48.

Mazereel, G. 1931. *Klank en Vormleer van het Brusselsch Dialect*. Leuven: De Vlaamsche Drukkerij.

Meinhof, Carl. 1912. *Die Sprachen der Hamiten*. Hamburg: L. Friedrichsen & Co.

McCarthy, John J. 1993. A case of surface constraint violation. *Canadian Journal of Linguistics* 38 (2): 169–96.

——, and Alan Prince. 1995. Faithfulness and reduplicative identity. In Jill Beckman et al. (eds.), *Papers in Optimality Theory. UMOP 18*. ◄

McCawley, James D. 1974. Review of *The Sound Pattern of English*. *IJAL* 40: 50–88.

Mixco, Mauricio. 1971. *Kiliwa Grammar*. Dissertation, University of California (Berkeley).

Okoth-Okombo, Duncan. 1982. *Dholuo Morphophonemics in a Generative Framework*. Berlin: Dietrich Reimer Verlag.

Postal, Paul M. 1979. *Some Syntactic Rules in Mohawk*. New York: Garland.

Prince, Alan and Paul Smolensky. 1993. *Optimality Theory: Constraint Interaction in Generative Grammar*. MS, Rutgers University, New Brunswick, NJ, and University of Colorado, Boulder. ◄

Reed, Irene, et multi alii. 1977. *Yup'ik Eskimo Grammar*. University of Alaska.

Shih, Chi-Lin. 1986. *The Prosodic Domain of Tone Sandhi in Chinese*. Dissertation, University of California, San Diego.

Truckenbrodt, Hubert. 1996. *Phonological Phrases: Their Relation to Syntax, Focus, and Prominence*. Dissertation, MIT.

van Loey, A. 1933. Historiese langevokalverschuivingen in het Brusselse dialekt. *Bulletin van de koninklijke commissie voor toponymie en dialectologie* 7: 308–28.

Wang, William S.-Y. 1967. Phonological features of tone. *IJAL* 33 (2): 93–105.

Whisler, R. 1992. Phonology of Sawai. In D. A. Burquest and W. D. Laidig (eds.), *Phonological Studies in Four Languages of Maluku*. SIL and University of Texas/Arlington Publications in Linguistics # 108.

Wolfe, Patricia M. 1970. Some theoretical questions on the historical English Vowel Shift. *Papers in Linguistics* 3: 221–35.

Woo, Nancy. 1969. *Prosody and Phonology*. Dissertation, MIT.

Wright, Martha S. 1983. *A Metrical Approach to Tone Sandhi in Chinese Dialects*. Dissertation, University of Massachusetts, Amherst.

Yip, Moira. 1980. *The Tonal Phonology of Chinese*. Dissertation, MIT.

Zonneveld, W. 1976. An exchange rule in Flemish Brussels Dutch. *Linguistic Analysis* 2 (2): 109–14.

Study and Research Questions

1   Study the definitions in (14) and (19) of "markedness constraint" and "faithfulness constraint". Restate these definitions informally. Then look through this book and select several markedness and faithfulness constraints. Show whether they do or do not meet these definitions.

2   Re-read §2.3.4. In this section, Moreton writes: "Homogeneity is not a credible condition on OT grammars of natural languages." Evaluate his evidence for this assertion and work out what it would take to make this condition credible.

3   If morphology allows rotations and phonology doesn't, what does this mean about the organization of the grammar?

4   In the text below (52), there are many references to work on polarity rules in different languages. Look up one of these references and evaluate the case for the polarity-switching rule and whether it is morphological or phonological.

5   Provide a line-by-line exegesis of the Rotation Theorem (38) and its proof.

Part III

Prosody

Chapter 7 | John J. McCarthy and Alan Prince

Generalized Alignment: Prosody

Editor's Note

The metrical theory of stress was originally formulated using a combination of rules and inviolable well-formedness constraints (see, e.g., Halle and Vergnaud 1987; Hammond 1984; Hayes 1980, 1995; Kager 1989; Liberman and Prince 1977; Prince 1983, 1990). Inviolable well-formedness constraints governed most aspects of metrical form, such as foot size, tree form, and labeling. The principal function of rules in metrical phonology was to place feet at or near word edges, to parse words into feet directionally, and to mark certain feet as bearers of main stress.

This chapter shows how alignment constraints, with their ability to refer to constituent edges, can supplant rules of foot-parsing and main-stress assignment. A crucial part of the story is the status of alignment constraints as ranked and violable, so edges exert an attractive force even on misaligned feet. See chapter 2 for the basic theory of alignment and chapter 24 for another application. Kager (1999: 117–24) provides a useful and accessible overview of alignment.

[...]
The alignment of the edges of prosodic constituents provides the first example of generalized alignment (GA) that we will examine in depth. By demonstrating the role of Alignment constraints in prosody proper, it complements the cases of morphological and morphophonological Alignment discussed in subsequent sections. Thus, this evidence contributes to demonstrating the true generality of GA.

To simplify the exposition by limiting the profusion of candidates under consideration, we will assume that certain constraints are undominated and therefore (because Gen always happens to provide candidates that satisfy them) unviolated in the languages under discussion. These constraints, which are treated by Prince and Smolensky (1993: Section 4) and McCarthy and Prince (1993: Section A.2), include the following:

Excerpt from:
McCarthy, John J. and Prince, Alan (1993) Generalized alignment. In *Yearbook of Morphology*, ed. Geert Booij and Jaap van Marle, pp. 79–153. Dordrecht: Kluwer. [Available on Rutgers Optimality Archive, ROA-7.]

(17)   Ft-Bin (Prince 1980, McCarthy and Prince 1986, 1991, 1993)
Feet must be binary under syllabic or moraic analysis.

Since our empirical focus will be limited to a rhythmically narrow range of systems, we note that the following holds of all admitted feet:

(18)   Foot-Form (Trochaic)
$Ft \rightarrow \sigma_s \sigma_w$

This foot-type is familiar as the syllabic trochee, a quantity-insensitive foot, which makes no distinctions of syllable weight.[6] (For recent discussion see Hayes 1991, Kager 1992a, 1992b, 1992c.) Another constraint assumed to hold quite generally is Parse-Syll:

(19)   Parse-Syll
All σ must be parsed by feet.

Parse-Syll is a familiar aspect of stress theory (e.g., Liberman and Prince 1977: 266, 294; Prince 1980: 535; Halle and Vergnaud 1987; Hayes 1987), corresponding broadly to the requirement that foot-parsing be "exhaustive" in rule-based metrical phonology.

We assume the dominance of Ft-Bin over Parse-Syll, so that exhaustive footing cannot be achieved through the use of unit feet. This dominance relation is quite normal, and if universal, would entail that Ft-Bin should be incorporated into Gen. (For relevant discussion, see e.g., McCarthy and Prince 1986, 1990; Hayes 1991, Kager 1993.) We will also assume that the size and syllabic composition of the Prosodic Word (PrWd) is fixed for any given input form by superordinate principles of syllabification on the one hand and interface on the other, so it cannot vary among candidates derived from that form. In particular, we exclude from considerations candidates with epenthetic syllables and those with multiple PrWd's dividing up a single morphological word. For discussion of the syllabification principles, see Prince and Smolensky (1993: section 6); of the interface, see McCarthy and Prince (1993: section 4).

Given these strictures, the foot-parsing imposed on an even-parity input /σσσσσσ/ is uniquely determined: [(σσ)(σσ)(σσ)], where '[. . .]' indicates PrWd constituency and '(. . .)' indicates foot constituency. All syllables are parsed into feet, and all feet are binary: since all constraints are met, nothing can be more harmonic. For an odd-parity input of sufficient length, however, various possibilities are attested among the world's languages:

(20)   Trochaic Stress Patterns, Schematically
a.   L→R Pattern: Wankumara (McDonald and Wurm 1979: 5, Hayes 1991)
[(όσ)(όσ)(όσ)σ]

b.   R→L Pattern: Warao (Osborn 1966: 114–15, Hayes 1980, 1991)
[σ(όσ)(όσ)(όσ)]

    c. 'Initial Dactyl' – Initial Trochee + R→L: Garawa (Furby 1974, Hayes 1980, 1991)

      [(óσ)σ(óσ)(óσ)]

    d. L→R + Final Trochee: Polish (Rubach and Booij 1985)

      [(óσ)(óσ)σ(óσ)]

Observe that PARSE-SYLL is violated, albeit minimally, in all these forms. The dominance of FT-BIN ensures this, as the following tableau illustrates:

(21) Necessity of PARSE-SYLL Violation in Odd-Length Strings

Candidates	FT-BIN	PARSE-SYLL
☞ (σσ)σ		*
☞ σ(σσ)		*
(σσ)(σ)	* !	
(σ)(σσ)	* !	

The nonuniqueness of optimality highlights the fact that other principles must be at play to decide among the minimal violators.

The verbal descriptions of the various attested patterns of forced nonparsing are based on the classification in standard rule-based treatments (Prince 1976, 1983, Hayes 1980, 1991). In rule-based metrical theory, the L→R pattern (20a) and the R→L pattern (20b) are seen as evidence for a directional sweep of foot-parsing, first pairing-up the leftmost (or rightmost) couple of syllables, then moving on to do the same to the remaining chunk of the word.[7]

This input-driven iterative foot-parse is impossible in OT, with its commitment to evaluating candidate output forms. It also runs afoul of the facts in (20c, d), in which pure directional iteration is compromised by a single trochee lying at the opposite end of the PrWd. (In rule-based metrical phonology, (20c, d) are accounted for by first laying down a single foot at one end, then iterating from the other.) Instead of iteration, GA supplies a set of output constraints that precisely control this interlinguistic variation.

We begin with the so-called 'initial dactyl' stress pattern (20c), which illustrates all of the essential elements of this application of GA. Stress in Garawa respects the following generalization:

(22) Stress in Garawa, Descriptively (Furby 1974, Hayes 1980, 1991)
    – main stress falls on the initial syllable;
    – secondary stress falls on the penult;
    – tertiary stress falls on every other syllable preceding the penult (but not on the peninitial)

Attested PrWd's of Garawa are generously long, so the pattern is particularly easy to see, as the following foot-parsings show:

(23)   Foot-Parsing in Garawa

[(óσ)]	yámi	'eye'
[(óσ)σ]	púnja.*la*	'white'
[(óσ)(óσ)]	wátjim.pàŋu	'armpit'
[(óσ)σ(óσ)]	káma.*la*.r̃inji	'wrist'
[(óσ)(óσ)(óσ)]	yáka.lâka.làmpa	'loose'
[(óσ)σ(óσ)(óσ)]	ŋánki.*r̃i*.kîrim.pàyi	'fought with boomerangs'
[(óσ)(óσ)(óσ)(óσ)]	ŋámpa.lâŋin.mûkun.jìna	'at our many'
[(óσ)σ(óσ)(óσ)(óσ)]	nár̃i.*ŋin*.mûkkun.jîna.mìr̃a	'at your own many'
[(óσ)(óσ)(óσ)(óσ)(óσ)]	nímpa.lâŋin.mûku.nânji.mìr̃a	'from your own two'

Since the goal here is to account for the foot-parsing only, the degrees of stress will be ignored.

One observation is immediately apparent from (23): the first two syllables of the PrWd are footed together, whatever the disposition of the rest of the word. This is a typical Alignment effect, obtaining between the two prosodic categories foot and PrWd:[8]

(24)   ALIGN-PRWD (Garawa)
        Align(PrWd, L, Ft, L)

That is, the left edge of each PrWd must match the left edge of some foot. This is a matter of empirical, not logical, necessity, as shown by the comparison of competing candidate parses for a trisyllabic or other odd-parity input (cf. (21)):

(25)   Application of ALIGN-PRWD

	Align
☞ [(σσ)σ]	✓
[σ(σσ)]	*

In the first candidate, the left edge of PrWd does indeed coincide with the left edge of a foot, satisfying Align(PrWd, L, Ft, L). In the second candidate, though, the left PrWd-edge coincides with the left edge of a syllable, but not of a foot. Hence, the first candidate is optimal. The same logic holds trivially for disyllables and can be extended readily to polysyllables of indefinite length.

In the terms of Prince and Smolensky (1991a,b, 1992, 1993), such relations are established by a constraint EDGEMOST, defined by them as follows:

(26)   EDGEMOST(φ;E;D)
        The item φ is situated at edge E of domain D. (Prince and Smolensky 1993: 35)

It should be clear that this is rendered by the GA scheme ALIGN(φ,E,D,E), where φ is a daughter of D. In the case at hand, we have EDGEMOST(F;L;PrWd) as the correlate of ALIGN(PrWd, L, Ft, L). GA is more general in two respects: it does not restrict the hierarchical relation of Cat1 and Cat2; and it does not require sameness of the shared edge. Thus, GA subsumes EDGEMOST.

There is also an Alignment effect at the *right* edge of Garawa PrWd's. This is apparent from the odd-parity forms in (23) containing five or more syllables. Five syllable words, for example, are parsed (σσ)σ(σσ), with right Alignment, rather than *(σσ)(σσ)σ. This phenomenon also requires a constraint enforcing Alignment of foot and PrWd:

(27)   ALIGN-FT (Garawa)
         Align(Ft, R, PrWd, R)
            "Every foot stands in final position in the PrWd."

ALIGN-FT differs from ALIGN-PRWD in two respects. One is obvious: the edges, left or right, that must be aligned. The other much less so: the order of constituent arguments is reversed, Align(PrWd, Ft) at the left edge, Align(Ft, PrWd) at the right edge. This move is crucial, as we will show shortly, since it permits Alignment, within OT, to supplant both the non-iterative and the iterative operations of standard rule-based metrical phonology.

ALIGN-PRWD and ALIGN-FT are in conflict in trisyllables. In OT, constraint conflicts lead to constraint violations, and from the resolution of the conflict the ranking relation between the conflicting constraints can be determined. The following tableau presents an argument for ranking these two constraints:

(28)   ALIGN-PRWD ≫ ALIGN-FT, from /σσσ/

Candidates		ALIGN-PRWD	ALIGN-FT
a. ☞	[(σ́σ)σ]		*
b.	[σ(σ́σ)]	* !	

The candidate (28b) violates ALIGN-PRWD, since the PrWd and the first foot do not commence together. It is, however, properly aligned on the right edge. In contrast, the candidate (28a) is well-aligned on the left and ill-aligned on the right. Thus, ALIGN-PRWD and ALIGN-FT are in conflict. Since (28a) is the actual output form, the conflict is resolved in favor of ALIGN-PRWD and at the expense of ALIGN-FT, proving that ALIGN-PRWD ≫ ALIGN-FT.

The optimal placement of a single foot in trisyllables is not the only circumstance when ALIGN-FT is violated. According to the definition of GA, Align(Cat1, ..., Cat2, ...) quantifies *universally* over the edges of tokens of Cat1 and *existentially* over the edge of some Cat2. *Every* Cat1 must share an edge with *some* Cat2. The two Alignment constraints of Garawa, then, have the following sense when spelled out:

(29)   Alignment in Garawa
         a.   ALIGN-PRWD: Align(PrWd, L, Ft, L)
                 Any [_PrWd is aligned with a (_Ft.

b.   ALIGN-FT: Align(Ft, R, PrWd, R)
Any $)_{Ft}$ is aligned with a $]_{PrWd}$.

ALIGN-PRWD is satisfied by any PrWd that begins crisply on a foot-edge – in fact, all the PrWd's of the language begin so, because, as was just shown, ALIGN-PRWD is undominated. But ALIGN-FT is violated by every foot that is not final in PrWd, so violations of it occur not only in trisyllables, but in all words of (23) containing more than one foot.

It might seem that a constraint that is violated so freely is of little use, but this is far from the truth. Pursuing an observation made to us by Robert Kirchner about EDGEMOST, we can see that ALIGN-FT is not a coarse sieve straining out non-final feet, but rather, through the Optimality-Theoretic imperative to violate constraints *minimally*, a fine mesh that subsumes the effects of directional iteration in rule-based theories. Prince and Smolensky propose that violation of EDGEMOST is gradient, with degree of violation measured by the distance of φ from the designated edge. The examples discussed by Prince and Smolensky typically involve applying EDGEMOST to a unique element, like a single affix or the prosodic head of a word, but Kirchner notes that if EDGEMOST applies to every foot, then it will minimize the distance of each foot from a designated edge – exactly as in directional iteration of foot-building. GA leads directly to this result. Because ALIGN-FT quantifies universally over tokens of foot, all instances of foot in some PrWd must be evaluated for the goodness of their alignment with the PrWd's right edge. The pattern with minimal violation is optimal, where the minimally violating pattern is the one in which no right foot-edge could lie any closer to the right PrWd-edge.

Given our assumptions about preconditions on the candidates to be considered (PARSE-SYLL, FT-BIN, and so on), the following list includes all of the admissible parses of a heptasyllable:

(30)   Heptasyllabic Parses
  a.   [(όσ)(όσ)(όσ)σ]
  b.   [(όσ)(όσ)σ(όσ)σ]
  c.   ☞[(όσ)σ(όσ)(όσ)]
  d.   [σ(όσ)(όσ)(όσ)]

The actual Garawa pattern is marked as optimal. Of these candidates, (30d) can be dismissed immediately, since it violates ALIGN-PRWD, an undominated constraint, as was shown above in (28). The remaining candidates differ in the disposition of non-initial feet in a way that can be derived from ALIGN-FT. The table (31) categorizes each individual foot of the candidate forms for degree of violation of ALIGN-FT.

(31)   Comparison of Heptasyllabic Parses by ALIGN-FT

		Ft-1	Ft-2	Ft-3
a.	[(όσ)₁ (όσ)₂ (όσ)₃ σ]	σσσσσ	σσσ !	σ !
b.	[(όσ)₁ (όσ)₂ σ (όσ)₃]	σσσσσ	σσσ !	Ø
c. ☞	[(όσ)₁ σ (όσ)₂ (όσ)₃]	σσσσσ	σσ	Ø

Violation of ALIGN-FT is gradient, not Boolean, so each foot is judged by the distance of its right edge from the right edge of the PrWd. Degree of violation is indicated graphically by the string of syllables separating the right edge of the foot under consideration from the right edge of the PrWd. The optimal candidate is the one whose constituent feet violate ALIGN-FT the least. Comparison of the rightmost foot is sufficient to eliminate the candidate (31a), whose last foot is non-final. Comparison of the penultimate foot eliminates all candidates except (31c), which is the actual output. In sum, ALIGN-FT quantifies over all the feet in a word, evaluating each for its fitness. Observe that it is not necessary to distinguish the violations by the foot that is responsible for them, as in table (31); aggregating the entire set of them gives the same results. The foot-by-foot breakdown is shown for purposes of clarity only.

Consideration of a wider field of candidates than in (31) does not change the outcome. As was already noted, the form (30d) violates dominant ALIGN-PRWD. Otherwise it would be superior in terms of ALIGN-FT even to the actual output (31c), showing that ALIGN-PRWD and ALIGN-FT conflict crucially in any odd-parity word, not just in trisyllables like (28). Less complete parsings, such as [(όσ)σσσ(όσ)], would also be superior on grounds of ALIGN-FT to the actual output form, but these would contravene the assumption that PARSE-SYLL is satisfied maximally in all legitimate candidates, subject only to dominant FT-BIN. Finally, it is logically possible to satisfy both constraints fully with complex PrWd parses like [[(όσ)][(όσ)][(όσ)]] or [[[(όσ)](όσ)](όσ)], imposing a multiple-PrWd structure on a single stem, but this too contravenes one of the initial assumptions introduced at the outset of the discussion.

We have shown, then, that Align(Ft, PrWd) subsumes the properties of directional iteration of foot assignment in rule-based metrical phonology. Quantifying over all instances of *foot* in a PrWd and evaluating each gradiently for alignment yields a system in which each foot lies as close as possible to the designated PrWd-edge. In contrast, Align(PrWd, Ft) quantifies universally over PrWd's, requiring only that there be *some* foot which is left-aligned, not that *all* feet be left-aligned. If Align(X, Y) held of every Y as well as every X, then all distinction would be lost between ALIGN-PRWD and ALIGN-FT, and whichever was dominant would completely overrule the other, rendering the subordinate constraint inactive in the grammar. In the case of Garawa, there would be no way to express the difference in status between right-edge and left-edge footing. This result illustrates the need for a crucial asymmetry in the definition of GA: universal quantification over the first constituent argument, existential quantification over the second.

A fundamental claim of OT is that languages differ principally in the ranking they impose on constraints. Permuting the ranking of these two senses of Align, combined with different parameters of the left or right edge, generates exactly the trochaic typology in (20):

(32)   Trochaic Stress Patterns, Analyzed
      a.   L→R Pattern: [(όσ)(όσ)(όσ)σ]
           Align(Ft, L, PrWd, L) ≫ Align(PrWd, R, Ft, R)

      b.   R→L Pattern: [σ(όσ)(όσ)(όσ)]
           Align(Ft, R, PrWd, R) ≫ Align(PrWd, L, Ft, L)

c.   'Initial Dactyl' – Trochee + R→L: [(όσ)σ(όσ)(όσ)]
     Align(PrWd, L, Ft, L) ≫ Align(Ft, R, PrWd, R)

d.   L→R + Final Trochee: [(όσ)(όσ)σ(όσ)]
     Align(PrWd, R, Ft, R) ≫ Align(Ft, L, PrWd, L)

Patterns (32c) and (32d) are left/right mirror images of one another, the former exemplified by Garawa, which we have seen, and the latter by Polish.

In the patterns in (32a,b), the constraint Align(Ft, PrWd) is dominant. This constraint evaluates all feet, requiring that they lie as close as possible to the PrWd edge. In contrast, Align(PrWd, Ft) looks at only a single foot, which should also lie near the PrWd edge. Since Align(Ft, PrWd) applies to all feet, while Align(PrWd, Ft) applies to just one, the ranking Align(Ft, PrWd) ≫ Align(PrWd, Ft) renders the lower-ranking constraint invisible – it can have no observable effect on the well-formedness of representations, so the pure L→R or R→L pattern is obtained.

(33)   Align(Ft, R, PrWd, R) ≫ Align(PrWd, L, Ft, L) in Warao (20b)

Candidates	Align(Ft, PrWd)	Align(PrWd, Ft)
a. ☞ [σ(όσ)(όσ)]	Ft-1: σσ -------------------- Ft-2: Ø	*
b. [(όσ)σ(όσ)]	Ft-1: σσσ ! -------------------- Ft-2: Ø	

The initial foot of (33b) is inferior, on grounds of ALIGN-FT, to the initial foot of (33a). Since the ALIGN-FT constraint is dominant, this inferiority is fatal, and so the lower-ranking ALIGN-PRWD constraint can have no effect.[9]

The typology can be extended further by permuting the ranking of Alignment with respect to the constraint PARSE-SYLL (19), which demands maximal parsing of syllables into feet, as in all the candidates examined thus far. If Align(Ft, R, PrWd, R) ≫ PARSE-SYLL, then the optimal candidate is [σσσσσ(όσ)], with a single foot lying at the right edge:

(34)   Align(Ft, R, PrWd, R) ≫ PARSE-SYLL, Applied to /σσσσ/

Candidates	Align(Ft, PrWd)	PARSE-SYLL
a. ☞ [σσ(όσ)]		*
b. [(όσ)(όσ)]	* !	

The penultimate foot of (34b) violates Align(Ft, R, PrWd, R). The degree of violation doesn't matter, since the other candidate (34a) is perfectly aligned, simply by virtue of positing only a single foot.[10] Thus, the pattern of 'non-iterative' foot-parsing can be obtained from a low ranking of PARSE-SYLL.

In principle, the typology should also be extensible by considering different arrangements of the edge (left or right) parameters than those considered in (32), but in practice no new stress patterns are obtained. For example, the grammar Align(PrWd, L, Ft, L) ≫ Align(Ft, L, PrWd, L), with two separate Alignment requirements imposed on the same edge, yields the same result as (32a). And constraints like Align(PrWd, L, Ft, R) or Align(Ft, R, PrWd, L) have no sensible interpretation, since alignment of different edges is impossible between a pair of constituents of which one contains the other in a hierarchy.[11] (Alignment of different edges is, however, essential to characterizing other phenomena discussed below in Section 4 and Section 6 [omitted here – Ed.].)

To complete the discussion of elementary stress-pattern theory, we observe that one foot must typically be picked out as the strongest, the head of the PrWd, Ft′. (A further distinction between secondary and tertiary stress, as in Garawa, is often not represented phonologically in contemporary discussions.) This task is commonly assigned to the *End Rule*, or in the work of Prince and Smolensky, the constraint EDGEMOST which generalizes the End Rule. As noted above, GA includes EDGEMOST, and here again we call on Alignment:

(35) ALIGN-HEAD
      Align(PrWd, Edge, H(PrWd), Edge)

In Garawa, we have Edge = L, and the constraint does not interact with the two Alignment constraints discussed above, which unambiguously fix the foot pattern by themselves. English, if we assume the characterization in section 1 above [omitted], shows the same broad pattern of footing as Garawa, guaranteed by ALIGN-PRWD ≫ ALIGN-FT, but in English ALIGN-HEAD, with Edge = R, must dominate ALIGN-PRWD:[12]

(36) English-type System

Candidates	ALIGN-HEAD	ALIGN-PRWD
☞ [Ma(níla)]		*
[(Máni)la]	* !	

The head-alignment constraint has obvious cognates in both morphology and syntax, presumably to be expressed in the same way. Observe that the order of arguments in the constraint Align(Cat, Edge, H(Cat), Edge) guarantees that for every Cat there is a corresponding H(Cat), in accord with the requirement that categories be headed. If we reverse the order, the constraint is vacuously satisfied in headless constituents. [...]

Notes

[...]

6 The constraints determining the headedness of feet can also be expressed in terms of GA. Trochaicity is Align(Ft, L, H(Ft), L), where H(Ft) = 'head of foot' = strongest syllable-daughter of F. See (35–36) for discussion.

7 In contrast, there seems to be little or no evidence of directionality in iambic foot-parsing. McCarthy and Prince (1993: section A.2) show that specification of directionality in iambic foot-parsing is superfluous, given avoidance of final stress, NONFINALITY. In the current context, this result must mean that the Alignment constraints enforcing directionality of foot-parsing are always low-ranking relative to NONFINALITY.

8 For broadly similar approaches to phenomena of this sort, see Burzio (1992a, b), Idsardi (1992). An exact parallel is found in Itô and Mester (1992).

9 This masking of the more specific constraint when dominated by a more general one is an instance of Pāṇini's Theorem on Constraint Ranking (Prince and Smolensky 1993: section 5.3).

10 In cases like (34), where a viable candidate does not violate the gradient constraint at all, we do not bother to show the degree of violation for remaining candidates.

11 The one situation where this could arise would be with recursion of PrWd. A constraint like Align(PrWd, L, Ft, R) – the initial edge of the PrWd must align with the final edge of a foot – is met by the subordinate PrWd in a structure like [(σσ) [(σσ)(. . .)]]. However, the topmost PrWd violates the constraint, and on the assumption that there is always a single PrWd analysis [(σσ)(σσ(. . .)], it may well be that success on the subordinated PrWd is not relevant to harmonic evaluation. Suppose that comparative evaluation of PrWd status proceeds on a 'worst-first' basis – match worst, then next worst, etc. Then both forms tie on the topmost PrWd, which fails the constraint; what's left in each passes the constraint, vacuously if there is no PrWd, so that the decision must be passed to other constraints. Among the others will be *STRUC, which penalizes all structure (Prince and Smolensky 1993: section 3), so that the single-PrWd analysis will always win.

12 We have chosen an example where nonfinality effects ('extrametricality') are irrelevant. For recent discussion of this phenomenon, and its interaction with edgemostness, aka alignment, see Prince and Smolensky (1993), Hung (1993).

References

Burzio, L. 1992a. "Metrical Consistency". Abstract of paper presented at DIMACS Workshop, Princeton University.

Burzio, L. 1992b. *Principles of English Stress*. MS, Johns Hopkins University. ▶

Furby, C. 1974. "Garawa Phonology". *Papers in Australian Linguistics* 7, 1–11.

Halle, M. and J. R. Vergnaud 1987. *An Essay on Stress*. Cambridge, MA: MIT Press.

Hayes, B. 1980. *A Metrical Theory of Stress Rules*. Ph.D. dissertation, MIT, Cambridge, MA.

Hayes, B. 1987. "A Revised Parametric Metrical Theory". In J. McDonough and B. Plunkett (eds.), *Proceedings of NELS 17*, Graduate Linguistic Student Association, University of Massachusetts, Amherst.

Hayes, B. 1991. *Metrical Stress Theory: Principles and Case Studies*. MS, UCLA. ▶

Hung, H. (1993). *The Rhythmic and Prosodic Organization of Edge Constituents*. Ph.D. dissertation, Brandeis University. ▶

Idsardi, W. 1992. *The Computation of Prosody*. Ph.D. dissertation, MIT.

Itô, J. and R. A. Mester 1992. *Weak Layering and Word Binarity*. MS, University of California, Santa Cruz.

Kager, R. 1992a. "Are There Any Truly Quantity-Insensitive Systems?" Paper presented at BLS. ▶

Kager, R. 1992b. "Shapes of the Generalized Trochee". Paper presented at WCCFL XI. ▶

Kager, R. 1992c. "Alternatives to the Iambic-Trochaic Law". *Natural Language and Linguistic Theory* (to appear). ▶

Kager, R. 1993. "Consequences of Catalexis". To appear in Proceedings of HILP-1.

Liberman, M. and A. Prince 1977. "On Stress and Linguistic Rhythm". *Linguistic Inquiry* 8, 249–336.

McCarthy, J. and A. Prince 1986. *Prosodic Morphology*. MS, University of Massachusetts and Brandeis University. ▶

McCarthy, J. and A. Prince 1990. "Foot and Word in Prosodic Morphology: The Arabic Broken Plurals". *Natural Language and Linguistic Theory* 8, 209–82.

McCarthy, J. and A. Prince 1991. "Prosodic Minimality". Lecture presented at University of Illinois Conference *The Organization of Phonology*.

McCarthy, J. and A. Prince 1993. *Prosodic Morphology I: Constraint Interaction and Satisfaction*. MS, University of Massachusetts, Amherst, and Rutgers University. ▶

McDonald, M. and S. Wurm 1979. *Basic Materials in Waŋkumara (Galali): Grammar, Sentences and Vocabulary*. Pacific Linguistics, Series B, no. 65, Australian National University, Canberra.

Osborn, H. 1966. "Warao I: Phonology and Morphophonemics". *International Journal of American Linguistics* 32, 108–23.

Prince, A. 1976. *'Applying' Stress*. MS, University of Massachusetts, Amherst.

Prince, A. 1980. "A Metrical Theory for Estonian Quantity". *Linguistic Inquiry* 11, 511–62.

Prince, A. 1983. "Relating to the Grid". *Linguistic Inquiry* 14, 19–100.

Prince, A. and P. Smolensky 1991a. "Optimality". Paper given at Arizona Phonology Conference.

Prince, A. and P. Smolensky 1991b. "Notes on Connectionism and Harmony Theory in Linguistics". In Technical Report CU-CS-533-91, Department of Computer Science, University of Colorado, Boulder, Colorado.

Prince, A. and P. Smolensky 1992. "Optimality: Constraint Interaction in Generative Grammar". Paper read at 12th West Coast Conference on Formal Linguistics, Los Angeles.

Prince, A. and P. Smolensky 1993. *Optimality Theory: Constraint Interaction in Generative Grammar*. MS, Rutgers University, New Brunswick, and University of Colorado, Boulder. ◀

Rubach, J. and G. Booij 1985. "A Grid Theory of Stress in Polish". *Lingua* 66, 281–319.

Study and Research Questions

1 Construct tableaux for all of the examples cited in (20) and (32). Your tableaux should deal with both six- and seven-syllable words, and they should include at least the five constraints ALIGN(Ft, L, PrWd, L), ALIGN(Ft, R, PrWd, R), ALIGN(PrWd, L, Ft, L), ALIGN(PrWd, R, Ft, R), and PARSE-SYLL.

2 The chapter sketches the factorial typology of the basic alignment constraints and PARSE-SYLL, but it does not delve deeply into the typological consequences of adding ALIGN-HEAD to the system. Work through the factorial typology with ALIGN-HEAD included. Comment on the existence, or at least the plausibility, of the patterns that emerge.

3 The alignment constraints in this chapter reckon extent of violation in terms of the number of syllables intervening between foot and word edges. It does not go without saying that syllables are what is counted, and alternatives are logically possible. What are some alternatives, and what are their potential empirical consequences?

4 It has been observed that iambic stress systems are (almost?) always left-to-right and never right-to-left: (σσ́)(σσ́)(σσ́)σ vs. *σ(σσ́)(σσ́)(σσ́). What does the theory proposed in this chapter have to say about this observation? (More ambitious question: modify the theory to explain this observation or provide a new theory.)

Chapter 8 | Nine Elenbaas and René Kager

Ternary Rhythm and the *LAPSE Constraint

Editor's Note

This chapter discusses an important challenge to the alignment-based theory of foot-parsing in chapter 7: languages with ternary stress alternation. In a ternary alternation, two unstressed syllables lie between any pair of stressed syllables, such as Cayuvava [ikitàparerépeha]. The key insight of this chapter is that ternary rhythm is a result of a constraint on stress lapses rather than a constraint on foot-parsing. The result is a theory that joins two threads of metrical phonology: conditions on constituency (as in Hayes 1980) and conditions on prominence (as in Prince 1983).

[...]

1.1 Binary Rhythm in Rule-based Theory

Many languages display a perfect rhythmic alternation of stressed and unstressed syllables. Universally, alternation is DIRECTIONAL, that is, oriented with respect to either the end or the beginning of the word. Pintupi (2a), for example, has rightward binary rhythm: the initial syllable and every following alternate non-final syllable are stressed (Hansen & Hansen 1969). A leftward pattern occurs in Warao (2b), where stress falls on the penult and on every alternating syllable preceding it (Osborn 1966).

(2) a. [(σ́σ)(σ̀σ)(σ̀σ)(σ̀σ)σ] yúmaɹìŋkamàratʲùɹaka 'because of mother-in-law'

     b. [σ(σ̀σ)(σ̀σ)(σ̀σ)(σ́σ)] enàhoròahàkutái 'the one who caused him to eat'

Excerpt from:
Elenbaas, Nine and Kager, René (1999) Ternary rhythm and the lapse constraint. *Phonology* 16: 273–330.

Rule-based metrical theory (Hayes 1980, 1995, Halle & Vergnaud 1987) models binary rhythm on the basis of three parametric choices. First, selection of the FOOT from the universal inventory. Pintupi and Warao both select head-initial feet (TROCHEES). Secondly, specification of whether foot construction is iterative or non-iterative. Both Pintupi and Warao have ITERATIVE patterns, parsing the maximal number of syllables into well-formed feet. In Hayes (1995), feet must be binary in order to be well-formed, so that one syllable remains unparsed in words with an odd number of syllables. The edge at which this occurs (the right edge in Pintupi, the left edge in Warao) is controlled by a third parameter, governing the DIRECTION of foot construction. Here Pintupi differs from Warao: footing is rightward (starting at the left edge) in Pintupi, leftward (starting at the right edge) in Warao. In sum, a rule-based theory of binary rhythm uses three parameters: foot type, iterativity and directionality.

1.2   Binary rhythm in constraint-based theory

Rule-based theory is challenged by OT (Prince & Smolensky 1993, McCarthy & Prince 1993a, b), a constraint-based theory abandoning serial derivations and rewrite rules. Instead, it defines phonological patterns in terms of harmony (or relative well-formedness of the output), as evaluated by constraints. Grammars are defined as language-particular rankings of a set of universal constraints. Constraints are violable, but violation must be minimal, and occurs only in order to avoid violation of higher-ranking constraints. The optimal candidate is selected from a (potentially infinite) set of output candidates, by strictly hierarchically ranked constraints. Selection involves recursive evaluation, starting at the top-marked constraints and proceeding by lower-ranked ones, until only one candidate remains.

In the domain of metrical phonology, OT has had to meet the challenge of defining a non-derivational counterpart of the rule-based notion of DIRECTIONAL foot construction. McCarthy & Prince (1993b) show that this is indeed possible, elaborating an idea which they attribute to Robert Kirchner. Their theory uses three constraints, involving binary foot size (FTBIN), exhaustive parsing of syllables by feet (PARSE-σ) and the vicinity of feet with respect to an edge of the Prosodic Word (ALL-FT-X). We will exemplify this theory on the basis of Pintupi. Recall that Pintupi foot parsing tilts towards the *left* edge of the PrWd. In the examples below this is apparent from forms that have an odd number of syllables (3a, c, e, f):

(3) a. [(όσ)σ]   tʲútaya   'many'
     b. [(όσ)(όσ)]   málawàna   'through (from) behind'
     c. [(όσ)(όσ)σ]   púliŋkàlatʲu   'we (sat) on the hill'
     d. [(όσ)(όσ)(όσ)]   tʲámulìmpatʲùŋku   'our relation'
     e. [(όσ)(όσ)(όσ)σ]   tʲílirìŋulàmpatʲu   'the fire for our benefit
                                                                   flared up'

     f. [(όσ)(όσ)(όσ)(όσ)σ] yúmaʈiŋkamàratʲùʈaka 'because of mother-in-law'

Deriving this foot distribution involves two notions typical of OT: CONSTRAINT INTERACTION and MINIMAL VIOLATION. The set of interacting constraints (Prince & Smolensky 1993, McCarthy & Prince 1993b) is stated as (4):

(4) a. FtBin
      Feet must be binary under syllabic or moraic analysis.
   b. Parse-σ
      All syllables must be parsed by feet.
   c. All-Ft-L
      Align (Ft-L, PrWd-L)
         'The left edge of every foot coincides with the left edge of some PrWd.'

These constraints are potentially in conflict, and therefore must be ranked. First, the maximal parsing by binary feet is achieved by the ranking FtBin ≫ Parse-σ. When foot binarity is a top priority, a word with an odd number of syllables cannot be parsed exhaustively, since that would create non-binary feet. But even though Parse-σ is necessarily violated, its violation must be minimal. Therefore all parsings are rejected that contain more than a single unparsed syllable, the minimal violation. The ranking FtBin ≫ Parse-σ enforces a maximal parse of PrWd into binary feet – roughly an alternating pattern.

Orientation towards the left edge is implemented by All-Ft-L (4c), a constraint stating the (surprisingly strong) requirement that every foot stand in the initial position of the PrWd. If All-Ft-L were undominated (that is, if it were surface-true), no candidates with multiple feet would ever be selected. That is, for every candidate with multiple feet, a better one is always available that has a single initial foot. However, All-Ft-L cannot be undominated in Pintupi, precisely because the language displays rhythmic alternation, and hence enforces multiple feet per word. Instead All-Ft-L exerts its influence in a more subtle way, by an interaction with Parse-σ. When dominated by Parse-σ, the role of All-Ft-L becomes restricted to selecting the candidate that minimally violates it. This is the one in which all feet are *as close as possible* to the designated PrWd edge, measured by numbers of syllables. We now have all evidence that is necessary for a complete ranking of all three constraints:

(5) *Ranking for binary rhythm in Pintupi*
     FtBin ≫ Parse-σ ≫ All-Ft-L

Tableau (6) displays this interaction. In the column below All-Ft-L, each violation mark denotes a distance of one syllable between some foot and the left PrWd edge (while spaces separate the violations of individual feet).

(6)

/puliŋkalatʲu/	FtBin	Parse-σ	All-Ft-L
☞ a. (pú.[iŋ).(kà.la).tʲu		*	**
b. (pú.[iŋ).ka.(là.tʲu)		*	***!
c. pu.([íŋ.ka).(là.tʲu)		*	* **!*
d. (pú.[iŋ).ka.la.tʲu		**!*	
e. (pú.[iŋ.ka.la.tʲu)	*!		
f. (pú.[iŋ).(kà.la).(tʲù)	*!		** ****

The ranking FtBin ≫ Parse-σ is justified by rejection of candidates (6e, f), both of which are exhaustively parsed (fully satisfying Parse-σ), but fatally violate FtBin by having feet that either exceed (6e) or fail to achieve (6f) binarity. Next, the ranking Parse-σ ≫ All-Ft-L is apparent from the rejection of candidate (6d), which has only one foot, at the left edge. It thus satisfies All-Ft-L, requiring every foot to be strictly initial in PrWd. Yet it fatally violates Parse-σ by its three unparsed syllables, since other candidates (6a–c) have fewer unparsed syllables. At this point, any remaining candidates (6a–c) have two binary feet differing only in their positions. All-Ft-L, the next constraint down, selects as optimal the candidate with all feet as close as possible to the left edge. This is (6a), which incurs two violations, whereas the others (6b, c) have three and four violations, respectively.

In sum, languages with binary alternation share the constraint ranking (7), where 'X' is an edge (L or R) specified in the foot-alignment constraint:

(7) *Binary rhythm*
     FtBin ≫ Parse-σ ≫ All-Ft-X

Let us now turn to ternary rhythm, and the extensions of ranking (7) which ternarity involves.

2 Cayuvava

Among ternary stress languages, Cayuvava (spoken in Bolivia) takes a special position in the sense that its ternarity is pure: all stresses are spaced exactly three syllables apart. The pattern, documented by Key (1961, 1967), can be stated as follows. Disyllabic words are stressed on the penult. In longer words stress falls on the antepenult and on every third syllable preceding it. Below we present the binary foot parsing predicted by the analysis of Hayes (1995):[1]

(8) a. [(σ́σ)]   dápa   'canoe' (K143)
     b. [(σ́σ)σ]   tómoho   'small water container' (K143)
     c. [σ(σ́σ)σ]   aríporo   'he already turned around' (K143)
     d. [σσ(σ́σ)σ]   aripírito   'already planted' (K144)
     e. [(σ̀σ)σ(σ́σ)σ]   àrihihíbee   'I have already put the top on' (K146)
     f. [σ(σ̀σ)σ(σ́σ)σ]   maràhahaéiki   'their blankets' (K150)
     g. [σσ(σ̀σ)σ(σ́σ)σ]   ikitàparerépeha 'the water is clean' (K149)

This ternary pattern was analysed in a rule-based framework by Levin (1985, 1988), Halle & Vergnaud (1987), Dresher & Lahiri (1991) and Hayes (1995). OT analyses were proposed by Kager (1994), Ishii (1996) and Elenbaas (1999). Before discussing the OT analyses, we briefly examine the rule-based analysis of Hayes (1995).

The central idea underlying Hayes' analysis is that ternary alternation can be analysed by binary feet in combination with a 'special' parsing mode. The final syllable is extrametrical, and the remaining syllables are footed while keeping a minimal distance between them:

(9)   a.   Final syllables are extrametrical (except in disyllabic words).
      b.   Assign trochees from right to left, under Weak Local Parsing.

WEAK LOCAL PARSING (WLP) is a parsing mode in which feet are not constructed back-to-back (cf. STRONG LOCAL PARSING), but are separated by one unparsed syllable. A syllable is skipped each time after a foot has been assigned. With binary feet, WLP yields inter-stress intervals of two syllables. This automatically accounts for the double upbeat observed in words of five or eight (i.e. $3n + 2$) syllables, where the initial syllable remains unfooted even though there would have been room to form a binary foot. In (10), syllables skipped by WLP are underlined. A binary foot cannot be built over the first two syllables since the syllable [ki] is skipped (10b). Nor can a monosyllabic foot be built on the initial syllable [i], as this would violate the (universal) requirement of foot binarity (10c).[2]

(10)   a.   i.<u>ki</u>.(tà.pa).<u>re</u>.(ré.pe).ha
       b.   *(ì.ki).(tà.pa).<u>re</u>.(ré.pe).ha   *because of WLP*
       c.   *(ì).<u>ki</u>.(tà.pa).<u>re</u>.(ré.pe).ha   *because of ban on degenerate feet*

This analysis will serve as a background for the discussion of two OT analyses of Cayuvava's strict ternarity. The first, which will eventually be rejected, is based on a direct counterpart of WLP, a foot-repulsion constraint *FTFT (Kager 1994). The second analysis uses a grid-based anti-lapse constraint (*LAPSE; Selkirk 1984, Elenbaas 1999). Unlike *FTFT, *LAPSE is not a constraint specifically designed to account for strict ternarity. Its scope is wider, generalising to bounded systems, including basically binary rhythmic systems with occasional ternarity, as we will show in §4 [omitted here – Ed.]. In §2.3 [omitted] we discuss an alternative analysis by Ishii (1996), which, like ours, avoids *FTFT, but instead uses a parsing-based anti-lapse constraint (PARSE-2; Kager 1994).

2.1   A foot-repulsion constraint: *FTFT

An early OT analysis of Cayuvava (Kager 1994) assumed a counterpart of Hayesian WLP in the constraint *FTFT:

(11)   *FTFT
       Feet must not be adjacent.

At first sight, this foot-repulsion constraint is highly appropriate for Cayuvava-style ternarity. Intuitively, skipping a single syllable becomes a matter of constraint inter-action: feet must not be adjacent, but otherwise parsing must be 'maximally dense', and oriented toward the *right* edge. Incorporating extrametricality in the form of NON-FINALITY (NON-FIN; Prince & Smolensky 1993), we arrive at the following ranking:[3]

(12)   *FTFT, NON-FIN ≫ PARSE-σ ≫ ALL-FT-R

The following tableau illustrates this analysis:

(13)

/ikitaparerepeha/	*FtFt	Non-Fin	Parse-σ	All-Ft-R
☞ a. i.ki.(tà.pa).re.(ré.pe).ha			* * * *	* * * *
b. i.(kì.ta).pa.re.(ré.pe).ha			* * * *	* * * * * !*
c. i.(kì.ta).pa.(ré.ɾe).pe.ha			* * * *	* * * * * !* *
d. i.ki.ta.pa.re.(ré.pe).ha			* * * * * !*	*
e. (ì.ki).(tà.pa).re.(ré.pe).ha	*!		* *	* * * * * * * * * *
f. (ì.ki).ta.(pà.re).re.(pé.ha)		*!	* *	* * * * * * * * *
g. (ì.ki).(tà.pa).(rè.re).(pé.ha)	*!**	*!		* * * * * * * * * * *

Undominated *FtFt and Non-Fin keep feet at a distance from each other and from the right edge, respectively. Among the candidates satisfying these requirements (13a–d), Parse-σ maximises the number of feet, ruling out a single-foot parsing (13d). (For words of eight syllables, the maximum number of feet is two; any parsings with more feet violate an undominated constraint, see (13e–g).) Finally, what favours (13a) over (13b, c) is All-Ft-R, pulling feet as far as possible to the right edge. Paradoxically, the *leftward* ternarity is due to a foot-alignment constraint referring to the *right* edge.

Note that this analysis is an exact OT analogue of the rule-based analysis of Hayes (1995). Each derivational mechanism (parameter setting) has a counterpart in the form of a ranked constraint:

(14) *Rule-based analysis*   *OT analysis*
     Extrametricality   Non-Fin   (≫ Parse-σ, All-Ft-R)
     Parsing mode (WLP)   *FtFt   (≫ Parse-σ)
     Iterativity   Parse-σ   (≫ All-Ft-R)
     Directionality   All-Ft-R   (≫ All-Ft-L)

The foot-repulsion constraint *FtFt, although it straightforwardly captures the Cayuvava pattern, will nevertheless be rejected. As explained earlier, we aim at accounting for ternarity without ternarity-specific tools. Examples of ternarity-specific tools are: ternary feet (Halle & Vergnaud 1987, Levin 1988, Dresher & Lahiri 1991, Hewitt 1992, Rice 1992); binary feet in combination with a special parsing mode (Weak Local Parsing (Hayes 1995) or Relativised Extrametricality (Hammond 1990)); or, in the OT framework, any constraint whose only motivation is to capture strictly ternary patterns, such as the foot-repulsion constraint *FtFt.

This paper will present various types of evidence (from analysis of particular languages as well as typological) in favour of *Lapse, an anti-lapse constraint that is not ternarity-specific, in the sense that it broadly enforces bounded rhythm, either binary or ternary. Immediately below, we will represent an analysis of Cayuvava based on *LAPSE, incorporating the insight from Ishii (1996) that ternarity arises from the interaction of foot alignment (ALL-FT-X) with an anti-lapse constraint. However, instead of the parsing-based anti-lapse constraint PARSE-2 employed by Ishii, we will use *LAPSE, which has a purely rhythmic, grid-based format.

2.2   A rhythmic anti-lapse constraint: *LAPSE

We conceive of ternarity as a basically RHYTHMIC phenomenon, which involves an organisation of strong and weak beats in ternary intervals. Following Liberman (1975), Liberman & Prince (1977), Prince (1983), Selkirk (1984) and many others, we assume that linguistic rhythm is represented as a hierarchical organisation of elements on the GRID. In bounded stress systems, strong beats are spaced one or two syllables apart, with an overall periodical tendency toward even spacing, either binary or ternary. Inter-stress distances are restricted both by upper and lower bounds. When inter-stress distance is too short, i.e. when two strong beats are adjacent, a rhythmic CLASH arises. When two strong beats are too far apart, there is a rhythmic LAPSE. Clashes and lapses are disfavoured in bounded stress systems.

Selkirk (1984: 52) proposes a Principle of Rhythmic Alternation, with an Anti-clash Provision and an Anti-lapse Provision.

(15)   *The Principle of Rhythmic Alternation*
    a.   *Anti-clash Provision*
        Every strong position on a metrical level n should be followed by at least one weak position on that level.

    b.   *Anti-lapse Provision*
        Any weak position on a metrical level n may be preceded by at most one weak position on that level.

Here we will focus on the Anti-lapse Provision (15b), which disallows a sequence of three or more weak beats, for example:

(16)   *   x   x   level 1
       x x x x x x x   level 0

Note that the Anti-lapse Provision broadly defines the rhythmic margins of bounded systems, accommodating both binary and ternary styles of alternation. Selkirk (1984: 109) suggests that Universal Grammar (UG) allows individual languages the option of a more stringent anti-lapse filter, banning any sequences of weak beats (including two weak beat sequences, which we might dub 'short lapses'). This option would be selected by languages enforcing strict metrical binarity, while ternary languages (which Selkirk does not actually discuss) would lack it.

We slightly adapt the statement of the Anti-lapse Provision as a constraint *LAPSE (Elenbaas 1999):

(17)   *Lapse
    Every weak beat must be adjacent to a strong beat or the word edge.

This statement, although empirically non-distinct from the Anti-lapse Provision in evaluating output patterns, has the virtue of capturing the local nature of lapse avoidance. Evaluation of rhythmic well-formedness by *Lapse involves no counting, not even up to two, as (implicit in 'at most') in the Anti-lapse Provision. All that *Lapse does is to check the linear adjacency of a weak beat with respect to rhythmic landmarks: either a strong beat or an edge.[4] In this view, strong beats and edges become the LICENSORS of weak beats. As is well known, stressed syllables and word edges function as licensors in a range of phenomena in both segmental and metrical phonology (McCarthy & Prince 1993b, Steriade 1995, Beckman 1997, Zoll 1997).

    Naturally, the logical disjunction in the statement of (17) invites the question of whether *Lapse is actually two constraints, rather than one. We hesitate to adopt this interpretation, as it is difficult to establish both branches in their own right by independent evidence. Under the first branch, 'every weak beat must be adjacent to a strong beat'. This is a cross-linguistically common restriction, satisfied by the strictly binary patterns attested in Warao (2b) and many other languages, as well as by the ternary pattern of Chugach Alutiiq (§3). However, under the second branch, 'every weak beat must be adjacent to the word edge'. Assuming binarity of feet, this amounts to a ternary word template of a 'single-stress-plus-adjacent-weak-beats'. We know of no languages that unambiguously instantiate this size restriction (see Kager 1995 for discussion of word and root maxima defined in terms of feet).

    (18) gives evaluations by *Lapse of sequences of weak beats of different lengths, situated in different positions in the domain (initially, finally and medially), with the violating weak beat appearing in bold.

(18)   *Evaluations by* *Lapse

	two weak beats	marks	three weak beats	marks
Initial	x	✓	x	*
	[x x x ...		[x x x x ...	
Final	x	✓	x	*
	... x x x]		... x x x x]	
Medial	x x	✓	x x	*
	... x x x x ...		... x x x x x x ...	

*Lapse is violated by any sequence of three (or more) weak beats. This may seem tantamount to a ternarity-specific constraint, apparently undermining our central claim that systematic ternarity needs no ternarity-specific tools. However, *Lapse is motivated independently in the analysis of Sentani and Finnish, both bounded stress languages in which local ternary patterns appear due to various interacting constraints. Here *Lapse will function to impose an upper limit on inter-stress intervals, instead of enforcing iterative ternary rhythm.

    The relation between *Lapse and ternarity is fairly indirect. *Lapse broadly determines a minimum of rhythmic organisation on the grid, leaving room for both binarity and ternarity, the choice between which is made by other constraints. The general idea is that ternarity is a state in which lapses are avoided, while the number of feet is *minimised*. (In contrast, the number of feet is *maximised* under binarity, due to PARSE-σ.) Accordingly, *LAPSE must be undominated in ternary systems. But how can we achieve the minimisation of foot number?

We now turn to Ishii's (1996) idea that ternarity arises by the interaction of foot alignment and an anti-lapse constraint. Ishii's key observation (anticipated by Kager 1994: §3) is that ALL-FT-X reduces the number of feet to the bare minimum still allowed by the anti-lapse constraint. (We disregard the fact that Ishii's anti-lapse constraint is crucially different from ours; we return to this issue in §2.3 [omitted here – Ed.].) The result is ternarity.

How does ALL-FT-X achieve this 'underparsing' goal? Any foot that is not strictly edge-adjacent violates the alignment constraint. Hence, the more feet, the more violations will arise for ALL-FT-X. Consider the following trochaic parsings of a six-syllable string:

(19) a.   x   x   x   b.   x   x
          x x x x x x   x   x x x   x x
          (σ σ)(σ σ)(σ σ)   (σ σ) σ (σ σ) σ
          ALL-FT-L: ** ****   ALL-FT-L: ***

Both satisfy *LAPSE, but parsing (19a) achieves this by having three feet, while parsing (19b) is more economical, having two feet only. The maximally dense parsing violates ALL-FT-L to a larger extent (incurring six marks) than the less dense parsing (which incurs three marks). This is at the expense of exhaustive parsing, motivating the partial ranking ALL-FT-X ≫ PARSE-σ.[5]

This is the core mechanism: ternarity, understood as an underparsing effect, is due to the following constraint interaction:

(20) *Ranking for ternarity*
      *LAPSE ≫ ALL-FT-X ≫ PARSE-σ

Let us now see how this works in the analysis of Cayuvava. We first consider words of length $3n$ syllables. The tableau in (21) shows the effect of *LAPSE for a six-syllable word.

(21)

/arihihibee/		*LAPSE	ALL-FT-L	PARSE-σ
a.	(á.ri).hi.hi.be.e	*!**		****
b.	a.ri.(hí.hi).be.e	*!	**	****
c.	(à.ri).(hí.hi).be.e	*!	**	**
☞ d.	(à.ri).hi.(hí.be).e		***	**
e.	(à.ri).hi.hi.(bé.e)	*!	****	**
f.	a.(rì.hi).hi.(bé.e)		* ***!*	**
g.	(à.ri).(hì.hi).(bé.e)		** **!**	

Observe the underparsing effect caused by ALL-FT-L: since its degree of violation is directly proportional to the sum of violations for individual feet, this constraint exerts pressure to minimise the number of feet. Foot number cannot drop below the bare minimum guaranteed by *Lapse, however. The net result of the ranking *Lapse ≫ All-Ft-X is a ternary pattern.

Let us discuss some individual candidates to support this conclusion. First, any single-foot candidates (21a, b) violate *Lapse. Even a two-foot parse offers no guarantee for satisfying *Lapse. For example, (21c, e) violate *Lapse due to their dis-rhythmic patterning of beats. Among the three candidates that satisfy *Lapse, the maximally dense three-foot parse (21g) is excluded by ALL-FT-L. When comparing two-foot parsings (21d) and (21f), a second major role of ALL-FT-L becomes apparent – regulating directionality of footing. ALL-FT-L pulls feet maximally to the left edge of the word, selecting the ternary form (21d).

The ranking arguments on the basis of six-syllable forms are spelled out below (where '>' should be read as 'is more harmonic than'):

(22) *Ranking arguments*
     a.   *Lapse ≫ All-Ft-L   (à.ri).hi.(hí.be).e > (á.ri).hi.hi.be.e
     b.   All-Ft-L ≫ Parse-σ   (à.ri).hi.(hí.be).e > (à.ri).(hì.hi).(bé.e)

The pattern of words with $3n + 1$ syllables is predicted equally straightforwardly. For a seven-syllable word, the minimal number of feet that is necessary to satisfy *Lapse is two. (Generally, the number of feet required for a word of $3n + 1$ syllables equals n.) Foot number is kept at a bare minimum by ALL-FT-L, penalising overparsing (see the three-foot candidate (23g)).

(23)

/marahahaeiki/	*Lapse	All-Ft-L	Parse-σ
a. (má.ra).ha.ha.e.i.ki	*!***		*****
b. ma.ra.(há.ha).e.i.ki	*!*	**	*****
☞ c. ma.(rà.ha).ha.(é.i).ki		* ****	***
d. ma.ra.(hà.ha).(é.i).ki		** ****!	***
e. ma.ra.(hà.ha).e.(í.ki)		** ****!*	***
f. (mà.ra).ha.(há.e).i.ki	*!	***	***
g. (mà.ra).(hà.ha).(é.i).ki		** ****!	*

The upshot of the examples seen thus far is this: beats are pulled as far to the left edge as is allowed by the anti-lapse constraint, resulting in a pattern where beats fall on every third syllable counting from the end.

The question then arises of what happens in the case of words with $3n + 2$ syllables, where there is enough room to accommodate an initial foot. This initial foot actually seems to come for free, as it does not cause extra violations of ALL-FT-L, as compared to the strictly ternary-rhythmic candidate:

(24) *Incorrect prediction due to* All-Ft-L ≫ Parse-σ
      (ì.ki).(tà.pa).re.(ré.pe).ha > i.ki.(tà.pa).re.(ré.pe).ha

Since there is a tie on All-Ft-L for these candidates, we predict the three-foot parsing to be optimal, due to a minimal violation of Parse-σ.

In fact, a minor modification of the hierarchy produces the double underparsing in words of length $3n + 2$ syllables. Con contains an (independently motivated) foot-alignment constraint militating against the initial foot. This constraint, All-Ft-R, evaluates the position of all feet with respect to the right edge: the more feet, the more violations. Clearly an initial foot causes extra violations of All-Ft-R. This constraint seals the fate of the lefthand candidate in (24) at the expense of violation of Parse-σ. All it takes to achieve the initial underparsing effect is to insert All-Ft-R between All-Ft-L and Parse-σ in the ranking hierarchy.

(25) *Final ranking for Cayuvava*
      *Lapse ≫ All-Ft-L ≫ All-Ft-R ≫ Parse-σ

This analysis is illustrated by the tableau in (26), which should now be self-explanatory:

(26)

/ikitaparerepeha/	*Lapse	All-Ft-L	All-Ft-R	Parse-σ
a. i.(kì.ta).pa.(ré.re).pe.ha	*!	* * * *	* * * * * *	* * * *
☞ b. i.ki.(tà.pa).re.(ré.pe).ha		* * * * * *	* * * *	* * * *
c. (ì.ki).(tà.pa).re.(ré.pe).ha		* * * * * *	* * * * *!* * * * *	* *
d. (ì.ki).ta.(pà.re).re.(pé.ha)		* * * * * * * *!*	* * * * * * * * *	* *
e. (ì.ki).(tà.pa).(rè.re).(pé.ha)		* * * * * * *!* * * *	* * * * * * * * * *	

The critical comparison is between candidates (26b) and (26c), which are identical in parsing except for the extra foot on the initial two syllables in (26c). Yet an initial foot does not incur extra violations of All-Ft-L, resulting in a tie between both candidates on All-Ft-L. There is an even lower-ranked constraint, however, for which the initial foot in (26c) incurs severe violations as compared to (26b). This is All-Ft-R, selecting (26b) as the optimal candidate.

We now add the additional ranking arguments:

(27) *Ranking arguments*
      a.   All-Ft-L ≫ All-Ft-R
           (àri.).hi.(hí.be).e   > a.(rì.hi).hi.(bé.e)
           ma.(rà.ha).ha.(é.i).ki   > ma.ra.(hà.ha).e.(í.ki)

      b.   All-Ft-R ≫ Parse-σ
           i.ki.(tà.pa).re.(ré.pe).ha   > (ì.ki).(tà.pa).re.(ré.pe).ha

Active involvement of both ALL-FT-L and ALL-FT-R in the selection of the optimal candidate is a result typical of OT. These constraints make directly conflicting requirements, but still the domination of one by the other is not tantamount to the inactivity of the dominated constraint. Rather subtly, the dominated constraint (ALL-FT-R) is active precisely in the context where the dominating constraint (ALL-FT-L) is unable to force a decision. Activity of a dominated constraint illustrates a crucial difference between OT and parametric theory: constraints are not 'switched off', but will become active whenever there is a chance.

[...]

Notes

1 Cayuvava lacks a distinction in syllable weight. Adjacent vowels are syllabified as two syllables, rather than as a single diphthongal syllable. Key (1961: 143) reports alternations between vowels and glides ([i] ~ [j], [u] ~ [w]) which reflect a process of gliding. The stress representations are calculated on a pre-phonetic representation that does not include the effects of gliding. For example, the word *iarau* 'the night' (Key 1961: 144) has two phonetic variants [járau] ~ [iárau]. Finally, Key gives no examples of monosyllabic content words. We tentatively interpret this as evidence for a disyllabic word minimum. Page references in (8) are to Key (1961).

2 An improvement over this analysis is due to Hammond (1990), who argues that Weak Local Parsing and extrametricality are functionally related: both produce parses in which binary feet are followed by a single unparsed syllable, either at the right edge of

a word, or at the right edge of a foot. This is 'relativised extrametricality', that is relativised to a domain (foot or PrWd).

3 Essentially this is Kager's analysis, with his *PARSE-2 constraint replaced by PARSE-σ. We will shortly return to *PARSE-2.

4 With undominated FTBIN, the following formulation of *LAPSE becomes empirically equivalent to (17): 'an unparsed syllable must be adjacent to a strong beat or the word edge'. The hybrid nature of this constraint, referring to both parsing and the grid, does not falsify our claim that the anti-lapse constraint is crucially grid-based. This is because even in this hybrid constraint, there is reference to the grid (*viz.* a strong beat). A purely parsing-based anti-lapse constraint will be shown in §2.3 [omitted here – Ed.] not to be viable.

5 The observation that ALL-FT-X prefers ternary over binary parsings is due to Kager (1994: 13).

References

Beckman, Jill (1997). Positional faithfulness, positional neutralisation and Shona vowel harmony. *Phonology* 14, 1–46.

Dresher, B. Elan and Aditi Lahiri (1991). The Germanic foot: metrical coherence in Old English. *LI* 22, 251–86.

Elenbaas, Nine (1999). *A Unified Account of Binary and Ternary Stress: Considerations from Sentani and Finnish*. PhD dissertation, Utrecht University.

Goldsmith, John (ed.) (1995). *The Handbook of Phonological Theory*. Cambridge, Mass. & Oxford: Blackwell.

Halle, Morris and Jean-Roger Vergnaud (1987). *An Essay on Stress*. Cambridge, Mass.: MIT Press.

Hammond, Michael (1990). *Deriving Ternarity*. MS, University of Arizona, Tucson.

Hansen, K. and L. Hansen (1969). Pintupi phonology. *Oceanic Linguistics* 8, 153–70.

Hayes, Bruce (1980). *A Metrical Theory of Stress Rules*. PhD dissertation, MIT. Distributed 1981, Indiana University Linguistics Club.

Hayes, Bruce (1995). *Metrical Stress Theory: Principles and Case Studies*. Chicago: University of Chicago Press.

Hewitt, Mark (1992). *Vertical Maximization and Metrical Theory*. PhD dissertation, Brandeis University.

Ishii, Toru (1996). An optimality theoretic approach to ternary stress systems. In B. Agbayani and N. Harada (eds.) *Proceedings of the South Western Optimality Theory Workshop (SWOT II)*. *UCI Working Papers in Linguistics* 2, 95–111.

Kager, René (1994). *Ternary Rhythm in Alignment Theory*. MS, Utrecht University. Available as ROA-35 from the Rutgers Optimality Archive.

Kager, René (1995). On foot templates and root templates. In M. den Dikken and K. Hengeveld (eds.) *Linguistics in the Netherlands 1995*. Amsterdam: Benjamins, 125–38.

Key, Harold (1961). Phonotactics of Cayuvava. *IJAL* 27, 143–50.

Key, Harold (1967). *Morphology of Cayuvava*. The Hague: Mouton.

Levin, Juliette (1985). *Evidence for Ternary Feet and Implications for a Metrical Theory of Stress Rules*. MS, University of Texas at Austin.

Levin, Juliette (1988). Generating ternary feet. *Texas Linguistic Forum* 29, 97–113.

Liberman, Mark (1975). *The Intonational System of English*. PhD dissertation, MIT.

Liberman, Mark and Alan Prince (1977). On stress and linguistic rhythm. *LI* 8, 249–336.

McCarthy, John and Alan Prince (1993a). *Prosodic Morphology I: Constraint Interaction and Satisfaction*. MS, University of Massachusetts, Amherst & Rutgers University. ▶

McCarthy, John and Alan Prince (1993b). Generalized alignment. *Yearbook of Morphology 1993*, 79–153. ◀

Osborn, Henry A. (1966). Warao I: phonology and morphophonemics. *IJAL* 32, 108–23.

Prince, Alan (1983). Relating to the grid. *LI* 14, 19–100.

Prince, Alan and Paul Smolensky (1993). *Optimality Theory: Constraint Interaction in Generative Grammar*. MS, Rutgers University & University of Colorado, Boulder. ◀

Rice, Curtis (1992). *Binarity and Ternarity in Metrical Theory: Parametric Extensions*. PhD dissertation, University of Texas at Austin.

Selkirk, Elisabeth (1984). *Phonology and Syntax: The Relation between Sound and Structure*. Cambridge, Mass.: MIT Press.

Steriade, Donca (1995). Underspecification and markedness. In Goldsmith (1995), 114–74.

Zoll, Cheryl (1997). Conflicting directionality. *Phonology* 14, 263–86.

Study and Research Questions

1 In Cayuvava, ALL-FT-R is ranked below its "opposite" ALL-FT-L, yet ALL-FT-R is sometimes decisive. How is that possible? (More ambitious question: Give a general characterization of the conditions under which the lower-ranking of ALL-FT-L and ALL-FT-R is decisive.)

2 Construct a factorial typology of the constraints in (25). Show how the different rankings dispose of the words in (8).

3 In the original article, Elenbaas and Kager discuss and reject an alternative analysis based on the idea that there is a constraint PARSE-2 defined as follows: "Of every two stress units one must be parsed into a foot" (Ishii 1996; Kager 1994). Apply this proposal to Cayuvava and note any problems that arise.

4 Kager has gone on to extend the *LAPSE approach from ternary to binary alternations like those discussed in chapter 7. Work through Kager (2001) (it is a handout) and discuss its implications for alignment theory.

Chapter 9 | Michael Kenstowicz

Quality-Sensitive Stress

Editor's Note

In the early development of metrical theory, it was thought that the effect of segmental or syllabic structure on stress could be reduced to a binary (or perhaps ternary) distinction of syllable weight (e.g., Hayes 1980; McCarthy 1979). This chapter addresses languages where traditional notions of syllable weight are not helpful because the locus of stress is affected by vowel quality.

Prince and Smolensky's analysis of Berber in section 2 of chapter 1 shows how a linguistic hierarchy like sonority can join with some position, such as the syllable nucleus, to form marked-ness constraints expressing the most and least harmonic fillers for that position. In this chapter, the same basic idea is at work in accounting for the attraction of stress to lower and/or more peripheral vowels. Some familiarity with the basic Ft/PrWd alignment constraints of chapter 7 is assumed.

1   Introduction

[. . .]
Our primary goal in this paper is to document cases in which vowel quality plays a role in determining the location of stress. Specifically, we show that in several diverse languages stress seeks out the most optimal vowel as determined by the hierarchies in (2).

(2)   a.   a, ä > e, o > i, u
      b.   a, ä, e, o, i, u > ə

That is, lower vowels are more optimal stress-bearing units than higher vowels (2a) and peripheral vowels are more optimal than central vowels (2b). Secondly, we argue that with its key idea of ranked and violable constraints, Optimality Theory

Excerpt from:
Kenstowicz, Michael (1996) Quality-sensitive stress. *Rivista di Linguistica* 9: 157–87. [Available on Rutgers Optimality Archive, ROA-33.]

(Prince & Smolensky 1993) provides a particularly perspicuous way to express this preference hierarchy.

In order to extend the OT model to the systems we consider here, several proposals are made. First, the PEAK-PROMINENCE constraint Prince & Smolensky (1993) develop for quantitative distinctions in Hindi stress is extended to the vocalic distinctions in (2). Second, comparable to the Prince & Smolensky (1993) analysis of Berber syllabification, the PEAK-PROMINENCE constraint is broken down into a set of micro constraints for each level in the hierarchy. It is demonstrated how these constraints can be interleaved with constraints that orient prominence with respect to the edges of the word. We also show that evaluation in terms of the prominence hierarchy must proceed in a "worst-to-best" fashion rather than "best-to-worst". Finally, in order to express the two opposing edge orientations in languages such as Mari (Cheremis), it is suggested that the scale in (2b) also optimizes the trough (nonpeak) portions of metrical constituents [omitted here – Ed.]. This parallels the margin constraints in the Prince & Smolensky (1993) analysis of Berber syllabification.

2   Preliminaries

[. . .]

In the more familiar languages studied in the metrical literature, the head of the metrical constituent is consistently found at its left or right edge in virtue of the constraints in (7).

(7)   HEAD-RIGHT: Align (Ft,R,ó,R): The right edge of the foot coincides with a stressed syllable
HEAD-LEFT: Align (Ft,L,ó,L): The left edge of the foot coincides with a stressed syllable.

In the languages we study here, stress seeks out the most prominent vowel in terms of the prominence hierarchies lower > higher and peripheral > central. Consequently, a constraint orienting stress in terms of this hierarchy (dubbed PEAK-PROMINENCE after Prince & Smolensky 1993) must dominate HEAD-R/L. We claim that the prominence hierarchy formally parallels the more familiar sonority hierarchy in syllabification. Just as more sonorous phonemes make better syllable peaks (nuclei) and less sonorous phonemes make better syllable margins (i.e. onsets and codas) so lower/peripheral vowels make better peaks in the stress wave while higher/centralized vowels make better troughs. Prince & Smolensky (1993: 127–67) formalize this phenomenon as the "alignment" of two separate prominence scales in Universal Grammar (UG): in the case of syllables, the Sonority Scale for phonemes a > e, o > i, u > ə > .... > p, t, k and the Peak > Margin (a.k.a. Nucleus > Onset, Coda) for syllables. A one-to-one alignment of the two scales generates the harmonic relations of (8) that grade phonemes for their suitability as syllable peaks and margins.

(8)   PEAK$_{\text{SYLL}}$ a > e, o > i, u > ..... > p, t, k
MARGIN$_{\text{SYLL}}$ p, t, k > ..... > i, u > e, o > a

Prince & Smolensky derive the scales in (8) by deploying the alignment as the series of micro constraints in (9) that evaluate candidate syllable peaks and margins from "worst to best". Under worst-to-best evaluation, candidates that are least optimal are eliminated before more optimal ones are assessed.

(9) PEAK PROMINENCE
   *P/p, t, k ≫ .... ≫ *P/i, u ≫ *P/e, o ≫ *P/a

   MARGIN PROMINENCE
   *M/a ≫ *M/e, o ≫ *M/i, u ≫ .... ≫ *M/p, t, k

Casting the role of sonority in this way has two effects: first, each step in the scale is a separate constraint that can be evaluated in a binary yes/no fashion. More importantly, other constraints can be interleaved inside the sonority hierarchy.

In this paper, we demonstrate the existence of languages whose metrical stress is defined through the alignment of the prominence scales lower > higher and peripheral > central of (2) with the Peak > Trough scale for metrical feet. The result is the grading of vocalic nuclei as optimal peaks and troughs of the stress "wave" (10a). These hierarchies are derived from the constraint rankings in (10b) whose order is fixed by UG and cannot be reversed by individual grammars.

(10) a. PEAK$_{FOOT}$ a, ä > e, o > i, u
                           a, ä, e, o, i, u > ə
         TROUGH$_{FOOT}$ i, u > e, o > a, ä
                           ə > i, u, e, o, a, ä

      b. *P/i, u ≫ *P/e, o ≫ *P/a, ä
          *P/ə ≫ *P/i, u, e, o, a, ä
          *T/a, ä ≫ *T/e, o ≫ *T/i, u
          *T/a, ä, e, o, i, u ≫ *T/ə

3   Bounded Quality-Sensitive Systems

In this section, we examine languages in which the word stress is located on the most prominent vowel in a disyllabic window at the right or the left edge of the prosodic word. These systems thus have a FT-BIN ≫ ALIGN-FT-L/R ≫ PARSE-σ[syllable] ranking schema that confines the peak of the prosodic word to this narrow window. The PEAK-PROMINENCE hierarchy rises above HEAD-R/L in the constraint hierarchy to situate the stress over the most prominent vowel inside the window. In the case of syllables with equivalent prominence, lower-ranked HEAD-R or HEAD-L then resolves the ties.

3.1   Kobon

The Kobon language of Papua New Guinea (Davies 1981) discriminates among its vowels in a particularly granulated way for purposes of stress placement.[2] The phonemic inventory of Kobon is composed of the familiar vowel triangle distinguishing low, mid, and high vowels supplemented with a pair of unrounded central vowels. Also, the low vowel [a] combines with a following high vowel [i] or [u] to form diphthongs.

(11)   i   ɨ   u
           e   ə   o
               a

Unaffixed word's stress is restricted to one of the final two syllables, seeking out the most prominent nucleus in this disyllabic window. The data in (12) illustrate this point. We depart from Davies' transcriptions by utilizing schwa for the mid central unrounded vowel.

(12)   a > e   hagápe   'blood' [226]
                       gáɫe#gáɫe   'to cry, of pig' [225]
         a > o   alágo   'snake species' [226]
                       kɨdolmáN   'arrow type' [226]
         a > i   ki.á   'tree species' [220]
         a > i   háu.i   'vine species' [221]
         a > u   ái.ud   'story' [221]
         a > ɨ   áñɨm#áñɨm   'to lightening' [225]
         a > ə   wái.əN   'cassowary' [221]
                       ái.ən   'witch' [221]
         o > u   mó.u   'thus' [220]
         o > i   si.óg   'bird species' [221]
         o > ɨ   gɨró#gɨró   'to "talk" – of mother pig to piglet' [225]
         i > ə   gaɫínəN   'bird species' [226]
                       wí.ər   'mango tree' [221]
         u > ə   ɫú.əɫ   'horizontal house timbers' [221]
         u > ɨ   mú.ɨs   'edible fungus species' [221]
         ə > ɨ   gɨsə́#gɨsɔ́   'to tap' [225]

When both vowels in the foot have equivalent prominence (13), stress lands on the penult, suggesting that HEAD-LEFT dominates HEAD-RIGHT.[3]

(13)   u ≈ u   dúbu#dúbu 'to make noise by footsteps' [225]
         i ≈ u   jínup#jínup 'to make squeaking noise, bird, rat' [225]
         ɨ ≈ ɨ   kɨjigɨl 'tattoo' [226]

While Davies' statement of the stress generalizations is tentative, it seems clear that for the data we do have, the postulated prominence hierarchy in (14a) is playing a decisive role.[4] This suggests that the Kobon vowel system is first sorted in terms of peripheral vs. central (14b) and then in terms of height (14c). We consider a vowel "central" if it is bounded on either side of the vowel triangle by another vowel: thus, schwa is bounded by [e] and [o], and [ɨ] is bounded by [i] and [u].

(14) a. *P/ɨ ≫ *P/ə ≫ *P/i, u ≫ *P/e, o ≫ *P/a ≫ HEAD-L ≫ HEAD-R
      b. a, e, o, i, u > ə, ɨ
      c. a > e, o > i, u > ə > ɨ

In Kobon, the entire PEAK-PROMINENCE constraint rises above the constraint that orients stress laterally in the foot as a left-headed trochee. Let us examine a few tableaux to show how the analysis works. A form such as *gaɨ́inəN* shows that the search for a more prominent vowel is confined to a disyllabic window at the right edge of the word. This follows if FT-BIN and ALIGN-FT-RIGHT dominate the PEAK-PROMINENCE package of constraints.

(15)

/gaɨinəN/	FT-BIN	AL-FT	*P/ɨ	*P/ə	*P/i, u	*P/e, o	*P/a	HEAD-L
a. (óσ)σ		σ#!					*	
b. (óσσ)	* !						*	
c. ☞ σ(óσ)					*			
d. σ(σó)				* !				*

In (16), the first two cases show where PEAK PROMINENCE seeks out the most prominent vowel before HEAD-L gets a chance to stress the penult. Thus in *si.óg* the *P/i, u constraint eliminates the (óσ) candidate before *P/e, o assesses its violation against (σó). The latter is the only candidate left and so is declared the output even though it violates the lower-ranking HEAD-LEFT constraint. The latter comes into play when the various PEAK-PROMINENCE constraints fail to make a decision, as in such forms as *jínup* where the vowels have equivalent inherent prominence. Here each candidate is assessed a violation by *P/i, u and so the decision is passed on to HEAD-LEFT which resolves the tie in favor of penultimate stress.

(16)

/mo.u/	*P/ɨ	*P/ə	*P/i, u	*P/e, o	*P/a	HEAD-L
a. ☞ (óσ)				*		
b. (σó)			*!			*

/si.og/	*P/ɨ	*P/ə	*P/i, u	*P/e, o	*P/a	HEAD-L
a. (óσ)			*!			
b. ☞ (σó)				*		*

/jinup/	*P/ɨ	*P/ə	*P/i, u	*P/e, o	*P/a	HEAD-L
a. ☞ (óσ)			*			
b. (σó)			*			*!

3.2   Chukchee

Like Kobon, the Paleo-Siberian language Chukchee exhibits a quality-based gradation among its vowels in their willingness to bear stress. The Chukchee hierarchy
distinguishes nonhigh vowels from high vowels and schwa from the rest and thus
discriminates its vowels in terms of both peripherality and height. Our data come
from the chapter on stress in Skorik's grammar (1961: 67–71) and from Krause
(1979).

We first survey the generalizations governing stress as set out by Skorik, putting
schwa to the side. A basic limitation is that stress is bound to the base – it never
appears on an inflectional suffix (17).

(17)   a. *pójg-a* 'spear' erg. [67], *wə́kw-a* 'stone' erg. [67], *íw-ək* 'to say' [68],
       winrét-ak 'help' Infin, *winrét-ərkən* 3sg., *winrét-ərkənitək* 2pl. [68]

       b. *jará-Nə* 'house' [68], *weló-lgən* 'ear' [68], *ekwét-ək* 'to send' [68],
       wiríN-ək 'to defend' [68], *reqoká-lgən* 'sand' [68], *migcirét-ək* 'to work'
       [68]

The location of stress within the base is governed by the following factors. When
the final syllable of the base is not the final syllable of the word (i.e. when one or
more syllabic suffixes follow), then stress is located on the final syllable of the base.
However, when there is no suffix (e.g., one of the allomorphs of the absolutive
sg.) or the suffix lacks a vowel, then stress is retracted from the final syllable of the
base (18).

(18)   *abs.sg.*   *abs.pl.*
       tití-Nə   'needle'   títi-t [69]
       qorá-Nə   'reindeer'   qóra-t
       melotá-lgən   'rabbit'   milúte-t[5]
       rícit   'belt'   ricít-ti
       wárat   'people'   warát-te
       játjol   'fox'   jatjól-te
       jéjwel   'orphan'   jejwél-ti

The plural suffix /-ti/ apocopates its vowel unless the base ends in a coronal to
produce an apparent shift of stress from left to right (e.g., *rícit, ricít-ti*) or from right
to left (e.g. *qorá-Nə, qóra-t*) in singular–plural pairs.

The data introduced so far indicate that certain constraints are active in Chukchee.
First, there is an undominated alignment constraint optimizing candidates in which
the right edge of the base coincides with the right edge of a binary foot: ALIGN-
BASE-RT, FT-BIN ≫ PARSE-σ. This constituent is right-headed (iambic) but an overriding constraint of NONFINALITY (Hung 1994) blocks candidates with stress on the
word-final syllable to choose outputs with a retracted (trochaic) stress: NONFINALITY
≫ HEAD-R.

(19)

/milute+t/	ALIGN-BASE-RT	NONFIN	HEAD-R
a. ☞ σ(σ́σ)			*
b. σ(σσ́)		*!	
c. (σ́σ)σ	*!		*

/ricit+ti/	ALIGN-BASE-RT	NONFIN	HEAD-R
a. σ(σ́σ)	*!		*
b. (σ́σ)σ			*!
c. ☞ (σσ́)σ			

Evidence for a prominence distinction among the vowels comes from cases (20a) in which the stress unexpectedly retracts from the final syllable of the base. They contrast with the examples in (20b) and indicate that stress will seek out a more prominent nonhigh vowel in the penultimate syllable of the base. In the nouns of (20), the absolutive sg. is marked by a reduplicative suffix that many disyllabic CVCV nouns take to protect themselves from apocope (Krause 1979).

(20) a. wéni-wen   'bell'   [68]
          céri-cer   'dirt'
          kéli-kel   'paper'
      b. nuté-nut   'land'
          piNé-piN   'snowfall'
          jilʔé-jil   'squirrel'

These data indicate that the *P/i, u portion of the PEAK-PROMINENCE constraint dominates HEAD-R. Due to the regular rule of vowel harmony whereby [i and [u] become [e] and [o] in words with [o] and [a] (Kenstowicz 1979), the stress prominence of the nonhigh vowels [o] and [a] with respect to the high vowels [i] and [u] unfortunately cannot be assessed. The tableaux in (21) show the role of PEAK PROMIN-ENCE in forcing violations of HEAD-RIGHT.

(21)

/keli+kel/	*P/i, u	HEAD-R
a. ☞ (σ́σ)σ		*
b. (σσ́)σ	*!	

/nute+nut/	*P/i, u	HEAD-R
a. (σ́σ)σ	*!	*
b. ☞ (σσ́)σ		

However, attraction of stress to the more prominent mid vowel is always over-ridden by NONFINALITY, as seen in the plurals *núte-t* and *píNe-t* (Krause 1979: 122). These forms indicate that NONFINALITY dominates *P/i, u.

(22)

/nute+t/	NONFINALITY	*P/i, u
a. ☞ (óσ)		*
b. (σó)	*!	

In (23), we summarize the constraint rankings of interest that have been introduced so far.

(23)   NONFINALITY ≫ *P/i, u ≫ HEAD-R ≫ HEAD-L

Let us now turn to the behavior of schwa. According to Skorik (1961: 70), if the final syllable of the base has a schwa nucleus then stress is retracted to the preceding vowel (24a) unless the preceding vowel is also schwa, in which case stress remains on the final syllable of the base (24b).

(24)   a.   pátgərg-ən   'hole' [70]
            pipíqəlg-ən   'mouse'
            tátləN-ək   'to answer'
            rócgəp-ək   'to enervate'
       b.   məcákw-ən   'shirt'
            təlwálq-ən   'fire site'
            rəkgát-ək   'to get stuck'
            rəmát-ək   'to wash up'

This behavior follows if the peripheral > central wing of the PEAK-PROMINENCE constraint (2b) splits off the schwa from the remaining vowels to make it the weak-est in the hierarchy: *P/ə ≫ *P/i, u, e, o, a. Stress will retract from the final syllable of the base to a preceding stronger vowel (25a); but when the preceding syllable is also schwa (25b), then the two candidates tie on PEAK-PROMINENCE and the lower-ranked HEAD-R constraint decides in favor of stress on the final syllable of the base.

(25)   a.

/pipiqəlg+ən/	*P/ə	*P/i, u	HEAD-R
☞σ(óσ)σ		*	*
σ(σó)σ	*!		

       b.

/rəmət+ək/	*P/ə	*P/i, u	HEAD-R
(óσ)σ	*		*!
☞(σó)σ	*		

There is, however, one respect in which the Chukchee schwa behaves differently from the other vowels in the prominence hierarchy. As shown by the forms in (26), when the penult is a schwa, the final syllable is stressed provided it is a stronger vowel. But when both the final and the penult are schwa, then the stress lands on the penult – as predicted by NONFINALITY ≫ HEAD-R.

(26) a.   ətlá   'mother' [K. 123]
           lǝlé-t   'eyes'
           ʔǝló   'day'
           ǝnré   'a little, somewhat'
           Pǝnín   'your'   [D. 43]
           Pǝnún   'middle'

      b.   ə́tlǝq   'tundra' [K. 124]
           kə́tPǝt   'sable'
           ə́ttǝm   'bone'
           cə́mNǝ   'old bull'

Thus, in a form such as lǝlé-t 'eyes' PEAK-PROMINENCE wins out over NONFINALITY while in núte-t 'land pl.' NONFINALITY wins out over PEAK-PROMINENCE. This contrast motivates breaking the PEAK-PROMINENCE constraint into the subhierarchies of (2a) and (2b). NONFINALITY splits the hierarchy between *P/ǝ and *P/i, u.

(27)   *P/ǝ ≫ NONFINALITY ≫ *P/i, u

The tableaux in (28) show the effect of ranking NONFINALITY below *P/ǝ. In ətlá (28a), *P/ǝ rejects the candidate with stress on the schwa, allowing the one with final stress to win. In ə́tlǝq (28b) the initially and finally stressed candidates tie at *P/ǝ, allowing the lower ranked NONFINALITY to decide in favor of retracted stress. Finally, in núte+t (28c) both candidates tie on *P/ǝ, in virtue of lacking a schwa. Once again, lower ranked NONFINALITY eliminates final stress in favor of retracted stress.

(28) a.

/ətla/	*P/ǝ	NONFIN
(ó̱σ)	* !	
☞(σǒ)		*

b.

/ətlǝq/	*P/ǝ	NONFIN
☞(óσ)	*	
(σó)	*	* !

c.

/nute+t/	*P/ǝ	NONFIN
☞(óσ)		
(σó)		* !

[...]

The diagram in (34) reviews the crucial rankings in our analysis; HEAD-RIGHT ≫ *P/e, o is motivated by *jatjól-te* (18).

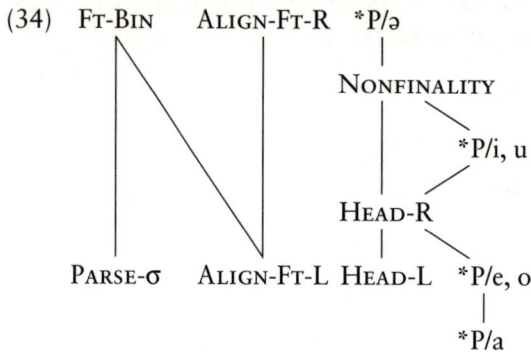

(34)   FT-BIN   ALIGN-FT-R   *P/ə
                              |
                         NONFINALITY
                              |
                            *P/i, u
                              |
                          HEAD-R
                              |
PARSE-σ   ALIGN-FT-L   HEAD-L   *P/e, o
                              |
                            *P/a

Let us summarize the crucial points of the discussion. First, Chukchee stress draws a three-way distinction in prominence among its vowels in their capacity to bear stress. This is captured by ranking the *P/i, u and *P/ə links of the PEAK-PROMINENCE constraint above HEAD-R. Second, the schwa behaves differently from the other vowels with respect to NONFINALITY. This is explained by ranking *P/ə above NONFINALITY. Thus, both the vowel height (2a) and the peripheral > central (2b) wings of the PEAK-PROMINENCE constraint are active in Chukchee.
[...]

Notes

[...]

2 Thanks to Stuart Davis for bringing these data to our attention.

3 We have found two exceptions in the cited data: *ru.ə́* 'day after tomorrow' [221] has stress on a weaker centralized vowel instead of the peripheral [u] while *kau.'ái* 'tree species' [221] has final stress instead of the expected penultimate stress.

4 Davies (1981: 226) remarks "the rules for positioning stress in two syllable words have yet to be determined. Relative vowel strength is almost certainly a conditioning factor since stress is almost always placed on the syllable which is strongest according to the following hierarchy: a/au/ai>o/e/u/i>ö/ɨ".

5 This form is stressed as *mílute-t*; we assume this is a printing error since it occurs in the list of examples Skorik uses to illustrate the generalization that when the suffix lacks a vowel then stress appears on the penult instead of the final syllable of the base.

References

Clyne, Paul (1979), *The Elements: A Parasession on Linguistic Units and Levels*. Chicago, Chicago Linguistics Society.

Davies, J. (1981), *Kobon*. Lingua Descriptive Series, vol. 3. Amsterdam, North Holland.

Hung, H. (1994), *The Rhythmic and Prosodic Organization of Edge Constituents*. Ph.D. dissertation, Brandeis University. ▶

Kenstowicz, M. (1979), "Chukchee vowel harmony and epenthesis", in Clyne (1979: 402–12).

Krause, S. (1979), *Topics in Chukchee Phonology and Morphology*. Ph.D. dissertation, University of Illinois.

Prince, A. and P. Smolensky (1993), *Optimality Theory: Constraint Interaction in Generative Grammar*. MS, Rutgers University. ◀

Skorik, P. Ja. (1961), *Grammatika čukotskogo Jazyka*. Moscow.

Study and Research Questions

1   According to (14), the vowel quality that most strongly attracts stress is [a]. Yet both Kobon and Chukchee have some words with unstressed [a]s. How is this possible?

2   In this excerpt, only languages with "bounded" quality-sensitive stress are discussed. That is, stress is limited to a window of syllables near the edge of the word or root. How is the bounding effect obtained in the analysis? Through ranking permutation, is it possible to get unbounded quality-sensitive stress, where there is no windowing effect? (The original article goes on to examine some cases of this type, and chapter 10 deals with the general problem of unbounded stress.)

3   Kenstowicz writes that, for stress purposes, "the Kobon vowel system is first sorted in terms of peripheral vs. central (14b) and then in terms of height (14c)". Explain how the evidence supports this generalization and how it is expressed in the analysis. Could there be a language that is like Kobon but with the opposite priority: vowels are first sorted in terms of height and then in terms of peripheral vs. central? What would the data and the analysis look like?

Chapter 10 | Eric Baković

Unbounded Stress and Factorial Typology

Editor's Note

Metrical phonology has from the outset recognized a distinction between languages with bounded and unbounded stress. Bounded stress, also called alternating or rhythmic, is based on binary feet and some kind of directional parse or equivalent (see chapter 7). Unbounded stress lacks rhythmic or alternating characteristics; stress is, instead, attracted to heavy syllables regardless of how far they are from the word edge or other stresses. There is also a default case to consider: where does stress go in words with no heavy syllables? For example, according to some authorities (Wright 1896), stress in Classical Arabic falls on the rightmost heavy syllable or, if no syllable is heavy, the initial syllable.

Unbounded stress has been analyzed in many different ways. An important difference among analyses is the role and type of metrical feet posited: unbounded feet, no feet at all, or binary feet. This chapter argues for an analysis in terms of binary feet, drawing on some ideas in Prince (1985).

1 Introduction

The stress systems of the world's languages can be roughly divided into two categories: bounded (or alternating) and unbounded (or nonalternating). In some unbounded stress systems, main stress consistently falls on a syllable at or near an edge (left or right), regardless of syllable weight.[1] In other unbounded stress systems, main stress falls on the leftmost or rightmost heavy syllable, and in the absence of heavy syllables, on the leftmost or rightmost syllable. Each of the four combinations of leftmost and rightmost in this statement corresponds to attested languages (see Hayes 1995: 296ff); the two cases in which the sides are the same are called *default to same side*, and the two cases in which the sides are different are called *default to opposite side*.

Excerpt (with revisions by the author) from:
Baković, Eric (1998) Unbounded stress and factorial typology. In *RuLing Papers 1: Working Papers from Rutgers University*, ed. Ron Artstein and Madeline Holler, pp. 15–28. New Brunswick, NJ: Department of Linguistics, Rutgers University. [Available on Rutgers Optimality Archive, ROA-244.]

Lists of languages fitting each of these gross typological characterizations are given in (1). These lists are based on those of Hayes 1995: 296–7, with additional languages (in particular, those in (1a)) from Walker 2000.

(1)   Unbounded stress systems: gross typological instantiations

    a.   *Consistently edgemost*
        Leftmost: Tinrin, Yeletnye
        Rightmost: Uzbek, Yavapai, Yawelmani

    b.   *Default to same side (DTS)*
        Leftmost heavy, else leftmost: Amele, Au, Indo-European accent, Khalkha Mongolian, Lhasa Tibetan, Lushootseed, Mordwin, Murik, Yana
        Rightmost heavy, else rightmost: Aguacatec, Golin, Kelkar's Hindi, Klamath, Sindhi, Western Cheremis

    c.   *Default to opposite side (DTO)*
        Leftmost heavy, else rightmost: Komi Yaz'va, Kwakw'ala
        Rightmost heavy, else leftmost: Chuvash, Classical Arabic, Eastern Cheremis, Huasteco, Kuuku-Yaʔu, Selkup

It is generally agreed that it is incumbent upon any adequate theory of unbounded stress systems to predict that in the general case, light-syllable forms are consistently stressed on an edgemost syllable, and that forms with heavy syllables are stressed in one of three ways: on the same edge as light-syllable forms (consistently edgemost systems), on the heavy syllable closest to that edge (default to same side or DTS systems), or on the heavy syllable furthest from that edge (default to opposite side or DTO systems). The ensuing sections of this paper examine in detail the necessary rankings and interactions among well-established metrical constraints that do in fact generate this gross typology of unbounded stress systems in addition to that of bounded stress systems.

The table in (2) shows the pairs of purely classificatory and largely oversimplified forms employed for the purposes of this paper. 'σ' denotes a light syllable, 'η' a heavy syllable, and main stressed syllables are marked with an acute accent. The left edge is arbitrarily chosen as the default; each of these systems is understood to have a mirror-image counterpart with the default on the right. These idealized forms encompass all that is relevant to the points made in this paper, barring any obscuring interactions with morphological or even other phonological factors (recall, for example, the abstractions made explicit in note 1).

(2)   Table of classificatory forms

	Edgemost	*DTS*	*DTO*
Light-syllable form	σ́σσσσσ	σ́σσσσσ	σ́σσσσσ
Form with heavy syllables	σ́σηση σ	σσή ση σ	σσησή σ

The paper is organized as follows. In section 2, I review noniterative foot construction, a representational assumption made about the stress pattern of light-syllable forms in unbounded stress systems, and what has become the standard Optimality Theory (OT) analysis of it. Forms with heavy syllables, which force semi-iterative foot construction in these quantity-sensitive stress systems, are considered and analyzed in section 3. Constraints responsible for main stress placement are tossed into the mix in section 4, accounting for the distinction between DTS and DTO systems. A couple of residual issues are addressed in section 5, and section 6 concludes the paper.

2   (Non)iterativity

In forms consisting of light syllables, unbounded stress systems differ from bounded ones in that there is only one stress, at or near an edge (3a). Bounded stress systems, on the other hand, have multiple stresses in an alternating pattern (3b), with the most prominent or main stress being at or near an edge and the others being less prominent or secondary (indicated by a grave accent).

(3)   a.   σ́ σ σ σ σ σ
       b.   σ́ σ σ̀ σ σ̀ σ

This difference between the two types of system was once taken to be evidence for a formal distinction between "unbounded" and "bounded" feet, respectively (whence the classificatory labels given to the systems themselves; see Prince 1976). The structural analyses thus given to the forms in (3) were as in (4), where parentheses indicate foot boundaries.

(4)   a.   (σ́ σ σ σ σ σ)
       b.   (σ́ σ) (σ̀ σ) (σ̀ σ)

Instead of admitting both bounded and unbounded feet into the typology of foot types, Prince (1985) argues that iteratively constructed bounded feet in forms like (3b)/(4b) could simply be noniteratively constructed to account for the single stress in forms like (3a). The structural analysis given to the form in (3a) under this view is thus as in (5a) instead of as in (4a).

(5)   a.   (σ́ σ) σ σ σ σ
       b.   (σ́ σ) (σ̀ σ) (σ̀ σ)

The gross typological distinction between bounded and unbounded stress can be captured by the interaction among the Generalized Alignment constraints ALLFT-L and ALLFT-R (McCarthy & Prince 1993b) and the metrification constraint PARSE-σ (Prince & Smolensky 1993). These three constraints are defined in (6). (Here and throughout, a Prosodic Word – the domain of footing – is referred to as a PrWd.)

(6) a. ALLFT-L – Align (Ft, L, PrWd, L)
The left edge of every foot is aligned with the left edge of a PrWd.

b. ALLFT-R – Align (Ft, R, PrWd, R)
The right edge of every foot is aligned with the right edge of a PrWd.

c. PARSE-σ – Parse Syllable
Syllables are footed.

A violation of one of the alignment constraints is assessed for each syllable that separates the designated edge of a foot from the designated edge of the PrWd. A violation of PARSE-σ is assessed for each unfooted syllable. When PARSE-σ is dominant, its demand to foot all syllables overrides any desire on the part of the alignment constraints to have all feet aligned with the left or right edge of the PrWd, as shown in T1.[2] (I ignore until section 4 the distinction between main and secondary stress in the set of output candidates, and hence do not indicate stress on them at all until then.)

T1 Iterative Footing: PARSE-σ ≫ {ALLFT-L, ALLFT-R}

Input: σ σ σ σ σ σ	PARSE-σ	ALLFT-L	ALLFT-R
a. (σ σ) σ σ σ σ	*!***		****
b. ☞ (σ σ) (σ σ) (σ σ)		******	******
c. σ σ σ σ (σ σ)	*!***	****	

When either ALLFT-L or ALLFT-R dominates PARSE-σ, the situation is reversed: only an edgemost pair of syllables is footed, at the expense of exhaustive metrification (cf. Halle & Vergnaud 1987, Halle 1989, 1990). The higher-ranked member of the pair ALLFT-L and ALLFT-R determines the edge at which the foot is placed, as shown in T2.

T2 Noniterative Footing: ALLFT-L ≫ {PARSE-σ, ALLFT-R}

Input: σ σ σ σ σ σ	ALLFT-L	PARSE-σ	ALLFT-R
a. ☞ (σ σ) σ σ σ σ		****	****
b. (σ σ) (σ σ) (σ σ)	*!*****		******
c. σ σ σ σ (σ σ)	*!***	****	

Making ALLFT-L dominant as in T2 results in default main stress at the left edge. The opposite ranking of ALLFT-L and ALLFT-R results in default main stress at the right edge. I henceforth consistently rank ALLFT-L above ALLFT-R in order to confine our attention to the left edge-oriented cases, with the understanding that anything I say about ALLFT-L and ALLFT-R must be said of ALLFT-R and ALLFT-L, respectively, when speaking about the mirror-image, right edge-oriented cases. (The same understanding will hold for the pair of head foot alignment constraints to be introduced in section 4.)

The ranking of AllFt-L above Parse-σ is thus a necessary component of the analysis of (left edge-oriented) unbounded stress systems, as these are analyzed in (5a) following Prince (1985). The relative ranking of Parse-σ and AllFt-R becomes important when syllable quantity is taken into consideration, a topic to which we now turn.

3   Quantity (In)sensitivity

The Weight-to-Stress Principle (WSP; Prince 1980, 1990) demands that all heavy syllables be prominent in foot structure and on the grid; i.e., that they be (stressed) foot heads. The WSP potentially conflicts with both alignment constraints because it wants even nonperipheral heavy syllables to be foot heads. Thus, when ranked below AllFt-L in the ranking established in T2, the WSP will be forced to be violated by any non-leftmost heavy syllables, as shown in T3. This yields a consistently edgemost main stress system.[3]

T3   Quantity Insensitive Footing: AllFt-L ≫ {WSP, Parse-σ, AllFt-R}

Input: σ σ η σ η σ	AllFt-L	WSP	Parse-σ	AllFt-R
a. ☞ (σ σ) η σ η σ		**	****	****
b. (σ σ) (η) σ (η) σ	*!******		**	********
c. σ σ (η) σ (η) σ	*!******		****	****

When ranked above AllFt-L, the quantity-sensitive nature of the WSP forces heavy syllables to be footed regardless of their position in the form, causing some left misalignment. If in addition Parse-σ is ranked above AllFt-R an initial foot will also be present in the optimal form, better satisfying Parse-σ as shown in T4. On the other hand, if AllFt-R dominates Parse-σ the initial foot is absent (though not if the initial syllable were heavy), better satisfying AllFt-R as shown in T5.

T4   Quantity Sensitive Footing I: WSP ≫ AllFt-L ≫ Parse-σ ≫ AllFt-R

Input: σ σ η σ η σ	WSP	AllFt-L	Parse-σ	AllFt-R
a. (σ σ) η σ η σ	*!*		****	****
b. ☞ (σ σ) (η) σ (η) σ		******	**	********
c. σ σ (η) σ (η) σ		******	***!*	****

T5   Quantity Sensitive Footing II: WSP ≫ AllFt-L ≫ AllFt-R ≫ Parse-σ

Input: σ σ η σ η σ	WSP	AllFt-L	AllFt-R	Parse-σ
a. (σ σ) η σ η σ	*!*		****	****
b. (σ σ) (η) σ (η) σ		******	*****!***	**
c. ☞ σ σ (η) σ (η) σ		******	****	****

In light-syllable forms, as we already know from T2, AllFt-L emerges from beneath the now-irrelevant WSP, and is satisfied at some expense to lower-ranked Parse-σ and AllFt-R.

A necessary but entirely uncontroversial assumption being made here is that the ranking of AllFt-R above Parse-σ as in T5 cannot force the absence of the initial and only foot in light-syllable forms in T2; that is, the conflicting demands of both alignment constraints cannot vacuously secure their mutual satisfaction by simply not having any feet to align. The alignment constraints themselves do not enforce the presence of any feet; rather, culminativity (Hayes 1995) is guaranteed by universally top-ranked Lx≈Pr (Prince & Smolensky 1993, McCarthy & Prince 1993a, b), which demands that every lexical word be a PrWd, together with a headedness requirement demanding that a PrWd be headed by a foot.[4]

Under the ranking in T5, then, an initial foot is absent in forms with heavy syllables and present otherwise. This is because AllFt-R decides between candidates (b) and (c), which fare equally on higher-ranked AllFt-L – the only relevant candidates due to the overarching demands of the even higher-ranked WSP. More generally, given a pair of intuitively "opposite" constraints H and L, the higher-ranked member of the pair H does not necessarily render the lower-ranked member L inactive. L is potentially active if an even higher-ranked constraint C winnows a particular candidate set down to include only candidates that fare equally on H but not equally on L. In the case under discussion, 'H' is AllFt-L, 'L' is AllFt-R, and the 'even higher-ranked constraint C' is the WSP, which is only relevant in forms with heavy syllables – thus accounting for the observed complementary distribution of initial feet ("absent in forms with heavy syllables and present otherwise").

The same result is demonstrated by Samek-Lodovici (1998) with similarly opposite (though nongradiently evaluated) focus-alignment constraints in syntax, which under a ranking configuration entirely parallel to the one in T5 results in the "mixed-focus" system of Kanakuru, with leftward and rightward focus being in complementary distribution. Nelson (1998) shows the activity of the same ranking schema in the formation of nicknames in French, accounting for the complementary distribution of left-anchored and right-anchored hypocoristic forms observed in that language. However, not all pairs of intuitively opposite constraints exhibit this ranking effect, as I demonstrate in the following section.

4   Main Stress

Whether the total ranking of the constraints considered so far is as in T4 or as in T5, the result in light-syllable forms is the same, as in T2: only one foot, on the left edge, and hence initial main stress. This is because ALLFT-L is the highest-ranked constraint relevant to the evaluation of light-syllable forms, and this constraint prefers the monopodal candidate. The higher-ranked WSP is only relevant in the evaluation of forms with heavy syllables, forcing the presence of multiple feet as in T4 and T5. Only one of these multiple feet may bear main stress, however, and this variable is the topic of the present section.

I begin with the uncontroversial assumption that the head of a PrWd is a foot, and that this head foot is the one that bears main stress. The constraints responsible for the placement of the head of a PrWd are the alignment constraints in (7) (McCarthy & Prince 1994; cf. the End Rule of Prince 1983).

(7)   a.   HDFT-L – Align (PrWd, L, Hd(PrWd), L)
          The left edge of every PrWd is aligned with the left edge of its head.
      b.   HDFT-R – Align (PrWd, R, Hd(PrWd), R)
          The right edge of every PrWd is aligned with the right edge of its head.

Like the foot-alignment constraints in (6), the head-alignment constraints in (7) are assumed to be gradiently violable: a violation is assessed for each syllable that separates the designated edge of the head foot from the designated edge of the PrWd. Note also that these constraints, again like those in (6), are intuitively "opposites" of each other. However, unlike those in (6), the constraints in (7) target a unique element: *the head foot* of the PrWd as opposed to *all feet* in the PrWd. There is no opportunity for the higher-ranked of the constraints in (7) to pass a decision among output candidates to the lower-ranked one, because every violation of one of these constraints translates into a nonviolation of the other; any set of candidates that tie on one of the constraints (i.e., violate or satisfy it equally) necessarily tie on the other. No matter what the rest of the constraint hierarchy dictates, the lower-ranked of the constraints in (7) is guaranteed to be inactive; that is, it is guaranteed never to be able to make a decision between any two competing output candidates.

This is a corollary of Prince's (1997) *Total Deactivation Property*, noted by Grimshaw (2001) with respect to a pair of morphosyntactic clitic-alignment constraints. The uniqueness of the target and the gradient violability of the alignment constraints in (7) and of those considered by Grimshaw entails a one-to-one correspondence between violations of one constraint and nonviolations of the other, so that their combined violations always total the same number (as long as the members of the candidate set are of equal length).

Having established this, consider first the ranking in T4, under which forms both with and without heavy syllables receive at least an initial foot because PARSE-σ outranks ALLFT-R. Now recall that in light-syllable forms, this ranking predicts initial stress as in T2. (In order to maintain this prediction ALLFT-L must at least dominate conflicting HDFT-R, a ranking argument I leave for the reader to verify.) The further ranking of HDFT-L above HDFT-R, no matter where they are otherwise ranked with respect to other constraints, predicts a system with consistently initial main stress and secondary stress on all noninitial heavy syllables. This is shown in T6.[5]

T6   Consistently Edgemost Main Stress:
{WSP ≫ AllFt-L ≫ Parse-σ ≫ AllFt-R}, {HdFt-L ≫ HdFt-R}

Input: σ σ η σ η σ	AllFt-L	Parse-σ	AllFt-R	HdFt-L	HdFt-R
a. wsp! (ó σ) η σ η σ		****	****		****
b. ce ☞ (ó σ) (ὴ) σ (ὴ) σ	******	**	********		****
b. dto1 (ò σ) (ή) σ (ή) σ	******	**	********	*!***	*
c. dto2 σ σ (ὴ) σ (ή) σ	******	***!*	****	*!***	*
c. dts σ σ (ή) σ (ὴ) σ	******	***!*	****	*!*	***

Now consider the opposite ranking of these constraints – that is, HdFt-R dominates HdFt-L. In the uninteresting case where HdFt-R also dominates AllFt-L, every form (regardless of the light vs. heavy syllable distinction) has a word-final main-stress foot. (Again, I leave it to the reader to verify this.) The case of interest, in which AllFt-L dominates HdFt-R, predicts main stress on the initial foot in light-syllable forms as shown above in T2, and on the last heavy syllable in forms with heavy syllables as shown below in T7. In other words, this is a default-to-opposite-side (DTO) system.

T7   DTO Main Stress 1:
WSP ≫ AllFt-L ≫ {{Parse-σ ≫ AllFt-R}, {HdFt-R ≫ HdFt-L}}

Input: σ σ η σ η σ	AllFt-L	Parse-σ	AllFt-R	HdFt-R	HdFt-L
a. wsp! (ó σ) η σ η σ		****	****	****	
b. ce (ó σ) (ὴ) σ (ὴ) σ	******	**	********	**!**	
b. dto1 ☞ (ò σ) (ή) σ (ή) σ	******	**	********	*	****
c. dto2 σ σ (ὴ) σ (ή) σ	******	***!*	****	*	****
c. dts σ σ (ή) σ (ὴ) σ	******	***!*	****	**!*	**

Consider now the reverse ranking of AllFt-R and Parse-σ. As shown in T5 and discussed at length above, this ranking can force the absence of an initial foot. This thus yields another default-to-opposite-side system, but one with no initial foot in forms with (only noninitial) heavy syllables, as shown in T8. (The empirical significance of the two predicted DTO main stress systems in T7 and T8 is discussed in section 5 below.)

T8   DTO Main Stress 2:
WSP ≫ ALLFT-L ≫ {{ALLFT-R ≫ PARSE-σ}, {HDFT-R ≫ HDFT-L}}

Input: σ σ η σ η σ	ALLFT-L	ALLFT-R	PARSE-σ	HDFT-R	HDFT-L
a. WSP! (ó σ) η σ η σ		****	****	****	
b. CE (ó σ) (ή) σ (ή) σ	******	******!***	**	**!**	
b. DTO1 (ò σ) (ή) σ (ή) σ	******	******!***	**	*	****
c. DTO2 ☞ σ σ (ή) σ (ή) σ	******	****	****	*	****
c. DTS σ σ (ή) σ (ή) σ	******	****	****	**!*	**

The ranking of HDFT-R above HDFT-L demands main stress placement on the *rightmost available foot*, where "rightmost available" is defined by the part of the constraint hierarchy dominating these constraints. In light-syllable forms, where the highest-ranked WSP isn't at issue, the next-highest-ranked constraint ALLFT-L makes the decisive choice in only allowing a single, left-aligned foot. In forms with one or more (noninitial) heavy syllables, the WSP forces minimal violation of ALLFT-L by forcing the heavy syllable(s) to be footed. The rightmost available foot in light-syllable forms is thus the initial and only one, and so the leftmost syllable receives default main stress, as shown in T2. In forms with heavy syllables, on the other hand, the rightmost available foot is the rightmost of the WSP-footed heavy syllables, and this rightmost heavy syllable receives main stress, as shown in T7 and T8.

Consider again the T8 ranking in which ALLFT-R dominates PARSE-σ. If HDFT-L dominates HDFT-R but is in turn dominated by ALLFT-R, the result is a system with stress on the leftmost available foot: the initial foot in light-syllable forms, as in T2, and the first heavy syllable in forms with heavy syllables – a default-to-same-side (DTS) system, as in T9.

T9   DTS Main Stress:
WSP ≫ ALLFT-L ≫ ALLFT-R ≫ {PARSE-σ, {HDFT-L ≫ HDFT-R}}

Input: σ σ η σ η σ	ALLFT-L	ALLFT-R	PARSE-σ	HDFT-L	HDFT-R
a. WSP! (ó σ) η σ η σ		****	****		****
b. CE (ó σ) (ή) σ (ή) σ	******	******!***	**		****
b. DTO1 (ò σ) (ή) σ (ή) σ	******	******!***	**	****	*
c. DTO2 σ σ (ή) σ (ή) σ	******	****	****	***!*	*
c. DTS ☞ σ σ (ή) σ (ή) σ	******	****	****	**	***

The ranking of HDFT-L above HDFT-R says to put main stress on the leftmost available foot, where "leftmost available" is again defined by the higher-ranked portion of the hierarchy. Part of this higher-ranked portion includes ALLFT-R, which by virtue of its rank above PARSE-σ chooses candidates without an initial foot. If HDFT-L were to dominate HDFT-R and ALLFT-R, we would get the uninteresting case of consistently edgemost stress, just as in T6: the leftmost available foot would indeed be leftmost, satisfying both ALLFT-L and HDFT-L. But because HDFT-L is dominated by ALLFT-R, initial feet in forms with heavy syllables are dispreferred (unless the initial syllable itself is heavy, of course). The leftmost available foot is thus the one on the leftmost heavy syllable, and in the absence of heavy syllables, on the leftmost syllable.

Note the transparent relation between the elements of the description of DTS and DTO unbounded stress systems and the ranking statements that account for them here. Whether the default in light-syllable forms is to the same or opposite side relative to forms with heavy syllables essentially depends on the relative ranking between the members of both pairs of alignment constraints. If the edges referred to by the higher-ranked of each pair match, then it's the same side; if they don't, then it's the opposite side. (This theoretically satisfying result is retained from Prince 1985.)

5 Residual Issues

On the face of it, the foregoing analyses make a strong and apparently falsified prediction: that all heavy syllables will be footed (see T7, T8, T9) and hence presumably (secondarily) stressed. However, there do exist unbounded stress systems with no (reported) secondary stresses. This is unproblematic in the case of consistently edgemost stress systems, where the WSP can simply be subordinated (see T3). But high rank of the WSP is absolutely essential to the above analyses of DTS and DTO systems – there need to be multiple feet for ALLFT-R to emerge in the case of DTS and for HDFT-R to emerge in the case of DTO. The immediate prediction is that these other feet should be stressed.

At worst, this prediction is simply a sub-case of the more general opacity effect caused by exhaustivity and conflation (Halle & Vergnaud 1987: 50ff, Halle 1989, 1990). Halle (& Vergnaud) identify a number of cases in which exhaustive parsing of forms is necessary to locate main stress, even in the absence of secondary stress. (In serial terms, foot construction applies exhaustively, the head foot is located and stressed, and conflation rules remove all non-head feet.) The cases at hand, as analyzed here and in Prince 1985, are ones in which *semi*-exhaustive parsing of forms *with heavy syllables* is necessary to locate main stress, even in the apparent absence of secondary stress.

In the present nonserial context, the necessary claim to make is that stress is partially independent of foot structure. Suppose that stress only surfaces on foot heads, but that foot heads needn't be stressed. The WSP would have to be rephrased accordingly, requiring only that heavy syllables be foot heads, and an independent battery of constraints would be required in order to determine whether foot heads are stressed (i.e., prominent on the grid) or not. (For a recent elaboration of this general idea, see Hyde 2001.) In short, whatever mechanism is necessary for the cases identified by Halle–Vergnaud should extend trivially to the cases under discussion here.

Another, independent prediction made in the case of T7 is the presence of an initial secondary stress foot in some DTO cases (compare T8). Cases like T7 are attested: according to Hayes 1995: 296 and Walker 2000: 50, Kuuku-Yaʔu would be an example of such a system; other examples of DTO systems seem to be of the T8 variety (though this must of course be verified case by case; see Gordon 2000). A fact worth noting here is that the distinction between the DTO systems in T7 and T8 is not complemented by a similar distinction between two DTS systems; i.e., between a system with an initial secondary stress foot (unattested) and one without such a foot (as in T9). This consequence is once again preserved from Prince 1985: because main stress in DTS systems is without exception on the leftmost possible syllable (still limiting our attention to cases in which the left edge is the default), a form with an initial secondary stress foot incurs additional and unnecessary violations of ALLFT-R.

6   Conclusion

Aside from the very general differences noted between bounded and unbounded stress systems in this paper, there are other particularities of each that need to be addressed in a complete unified theory of stress systems.[6] What I hope to have shown in this paper is that the gross characteristics of unbounded stress systems can be accounted for with different rankings of a set of constraints that are independently motivated in the analysis of (on the surface quite different) bounded stress systems. A desirable consequence of this result is that it may be the case that nothing new needs to be added to the basic theory of bounded stress in OT to account for unbounded stress systems: the differences among all stress systems are accounted for by different rankings of the same set of constraints. This has obviously desirable consequences for learnability, as demonstrated by Tesar (1999, 2000) with respect to the grammars defined by the factorially many possible different rankings of the same basic set of constraints considered here.

Notes

1   The distinction between "at" and "near" an edge is a nontrivial one that I nevertheless put aside here, as it involves the partially independent variables of extrametricality and rhythmic foot type (trochaic vs. iambic). I henceforth use the terms "left(most)," "right(most)," and "edge(most)" with this caveat in mind. (See Prince & Smolensky 1993, Hayes 1995, Hung 1994, Walker 2000, and references therein on extrametricality.)

The variable interpretations of "syllable weight" and "stress" are also glossed over here, as they also involve independent considerations. (See Gordon 1999, Hayes 1995: §7, de Lacy 1997, Morén 1999, and references therein on the problem of syllable weight.)

2   Minimal violation of the higher-ranked member of the pair ALLFT-L and ALLFT-R when PARSE-σ is dominant derives directionality effects in odd-parity strings in bounded

stress systems, an observation attributed by McCarthy & Prince (1993b) to Robert Kirchner.

3 Initial or peninitial, depending on rhythmic foot type (see note 1). See Hyman 1977 and Walker 2000 on the general rarity of peninitial stress and, more interestingly, the unattestedness of default-to-peninitial.

4 This headedness requirement is consistent with both the Weak Layering Hypothesis of Itô & Mester 1992 and the Strict Layering Hypothesis of Selkirk 1984, though the violability of Parse-σ is only consistent with the former. In more recent work, Selkirk (1995) argues for the violability of more general, category-independent versions of Parse-σ and the headedness requirement.

5 The first (a) candidate in this and in all subsequent tableaux fatally violates the top-ranked WSP. Due to page-width limitations, the WSP is simply left out of all tableaux and the first candidate is entirely shaded to indicate its early departure from the candidate set.

6 In the case of unbounded stress systems, many of these particularities have been recently discussed and analyzed by Walker (2000) and by Gordon (2000).

References

Gordon, Matthew. 1999. *Syllable Weight: Phonetics, Phonology, and Typology*. Doctoral dissertation, University of California, Los Angeles.

Gordon, Matthew. 2000. "Re-examining Default-to-Opposite Stress." *BLS* 26, 101–12.

Grimshaw, Jane. 2001. "Optimal Clitic Positions and the Lexicon in Romance Clitic Systems." In Géraldine Legendre, Jane Grimshaw, and Sten Vikner (eds.), *Optimality-Theoretic Syntax*, 205–40. MIT Press, Cambridge, MA.

Halle, Morris. 1989. "On Stress Placement and Metrical Structure." *CLS* 25, 157–73.

Halle, Morris. 1990. "Respecting Metrical Structure." *NLLT* 8, 149–76.

Halle, Morris, and Jean-Roger Vergnaud. 1987. *An Essay on Stress*. MIT Press, Cambridge, MA.

Hayes, Bruce. 1995. *Metrical Stress Theory: Principles and Case Studies*. University of Chicago Press, Chicago.

Hung, Henrietta. 1994. *The Rhythmic and Prosodic Organization of Edge Constituents*. Doctoral dissertation, Brandeis University. (ROA-24, Rutgers Optimality Archive, http://roa.rutgers.edu/.)

Hyde, Brett. 2001. *Metrical and Prosodic Structure in Optimality Theory*. Doctoral dissertation, Rutgers University. (ROA-476, Rutgers Optimality Archive, http://roa.rutgers.edu/.)

Hyman, Larry. 1977. "On the Nature of Linguistic Stress." In L. Hyman (ed.), *Studies in Stress and Accent (Southern California Occasional Papers in Linguistics* 4), 37–82.

Itô, Junko and Armin Mester. 1992. "Weak Layering and Word Binarity." Unpublished MS, University of California, Santa Cruz.

de Lacy, Paul. 1997. *Prosodic Categorisation*. MA thesis, University of Auckland, New Zealand. (ROA-236, Rutgers Optimality Archive, http://roa.rutgers.edu/.)

McCarthy, John and Alan Prince. 1993a. *Prosodic Morphology: Constraint Interaction and Satisfaction*. RuCCS Technical Report TR-3, Rutgers University, Piscataway, NJ. (ROA-482, Rutgers Optimality Archive, http://roa.rutgers.edu/.)

McCarthy, John and Alan Prince. 1993b. "Generalized Alignment." *Yearbook of Morphology* 1993, 79–153. (ROA-7, Rutgers Optimality Archive, http://roa.rutgers.edu/.) ◄

McCarthy, John and Alan Prince. 1994. "The Emergence of the Unmarked: Optimality in Prosodic Morphology." *NELS* 24, 333–79. (ROA-13, Rutgers Optimality Archive, http://roa.rutgers.edu/.) ◄

Morén, Bruce. 1999. *Distinctiveness, Coercion and Sonority: A Unified Theory of Weight*. Doctoral dissertation, University of Maryland, College Park.

Nelson, Nicole. 1998. "Mixed Alignment in French Hypocoristic Formation." In Ron Artstein and Madeline Holler (eds.), *RuLing Papers 1: Working Papers from Rutgers University*, 185–99. Department of Linguistics, Rutgers University, New Brunswick, NJ.

Prince, Alan. 1976. "Applying Stress." Unpublished MS, University of Massachusetts, Amherst.

Prince, Alan. 1980. "A Metrical Theory for Estonian Quantity." *Linguistic Inquiry* 11, 511–62.

Prince, Alan. 1983. "Relating to the Grid." *Linguistic Inquiry* 14, 19–100.

Prince, Alan. 1985. "Improving Tree Theory." *BLS* 11, 471–90.

Prince, Alan. 1990. "Quantitative Consequences of Rhythmic Organization." *CLS* 26-II, 355–98.

Prince, Alan. 1997. "Stringency and Anti-Paninian Hierarchies." Handout and Lecture from the 1997 LSA Linguistic Institute, Cornell University.

Prince, Alan and Paul Smolensky. 1993. *Optimality Theory: Constraint Interaction in Generative Grammar*. RuCCS Technical Report TR-2, Rutgers University, Piscataway, NJ. ◀

Samek-Lodovici, Vieri. 1998. "Opposite Constraints: Left and Right Focus-Alignment in Kanakuru." *Lingua* 104, 111–30.

Selkirk, Elisabeth. 1984. *Phonology and Syntax: The Relation Between Sound and Structure*. MIT Press, Cambridge, MA.

Selkirk, Elisabeth. 1995. "The Prosodic Structure of Function Words." *University of Massachusetts Occasional Papers* 18, 439–69. ◀

Tesar, Bruce. 1999. "Robust Interpretive Parsing in Metrical Stress Theory." *WCCFL* 17, 625–39.

Tesar, Bruce. 2000. "Using Inconsistency Detection to Overcome Structural Ambiguity in Language Learning." RuCCS Technical Report TR-58, Rutgers University, Piscataway, NJ. (ROA-426, Rutgers Optimality Archive, http://roa.rutgers.edu/.)

Walker, Rachel. 2000. "Mongolian Stress, Licensing, and Factorial Typology." ROA-172, Rutgers Optimality Archive, http://roa.rutgers.edu/.

Study and Research Questions

1   In chapter 8, it was shown that ALLFT-R can still be active even when ranked below its "opposite" ALLFT-L. In his discussion of tableau T5, Baković makes a similar point, but also goes on to note the possibility of total deactivation when the constraints in (7) are considered. Discuss the similarities and differences among these three cases. Formulate some general conditions under which alignment constraints on opposite edges can and cannot deactivate one another.

2   Quality-sensitive stress systems may be unbounded. What is the effect on the typology in this chapter of replacing WSP with the quality-sensitive constraint hierarchy in chapter 9?

3   This chapter does not explore the interdependent effects of extrametricality and trochaic/iambic foot type in unbounded stress systems (see note 1). Extend the analysis to include these effects. For concreteness, assume that there are two constraints enforcing extrametricality: NON-FIN(ó) "no stressed syllable is final in a prosodic word" and NON-FIN(Ft) "no foot is final in a prosodic word".

Chapter 11 | John Alderete

Head Dependence in Stress–Epenthesis Interaction

Editor's Note

This chapter shows that one of OT's most novel contributions, faithfulness constraints, can lead to a new understanding of a very familiar problem. Epenthetic vowels are not always "there" for stress purposes, an observation that has been analyzed with rule ordering and with special phonological representations for epenthetic vowels. Faithfulness constraints give access to the input, however, leading to the possibility that the distribution of stress is directly sensitive to a vowel's epenthetic status. The proposal made here involves a positional faithfulness constraint, for which readers should also consult chapters 12, 16, 17, and 18.

1 Introduction

What is the nature of the interaction between stress and epenthesis? Do epenthetic syllables count in word stress, or not? This paper will study these questions from various angles and discuss the theoretical issues they raise.

In *SPE*-style phonology (Chomsky & Halle 1968), stress–epenthesis interaction depends on rule ordering. If vowel insertion is ordered before stress assignment, epenthetic vowels will be counted and stressed according to the regular pattern; conversely, if stress precedes epenthesis, then the inserted vowels will be inactive in stress. While the Rule Ordering theory can account for virtually any pattern of stress–epenthesis interaction, this theory fails to offer an explanation of the phenomena. The behavior of epenthetic vowels in stress is described by stipulating the required rule ordering, leaving us to wonder why the state of affairs could not be different.

There are also empirical problems with the Rule Ordering theory. Epenthetic syllables do not always behave in a uniform way in relation to stress. They can be

Excerpt (with revisions by the author) from:
Alderete, John (1999) Faithfulness to prosodic heads. In *The Derivational Residue in Phonological Optimality Theory*, ed. Ben Hermans and Marc van Oostendorp, pp. 29–50. Amsterdam: John Benjamins. [Available on Rutgers Optimality Archive, ROA-433.]

ignored in some environments, and yet incorporated into the stress pattern in others. Stress–epenthesis interaction in the Papuan language Yimas is like this, and as we will see in detail below, such patterns point to a real flaw in the Rule Ordering approach.

In Yimas, the main stress regularly falls on the initial syllable of a word (1a). Epenthesis into this position, however, creates exceptions to regular initial stress, pushing stress forward a syllable (1b).

(1)   Yimas (Foley 1991)

a.	wáŋkaŋ		'bird'
	kúlanaŋ		'walk'
	wúratàkay		'turtle'
	mámantàkarman		'land crab'
b.	/pkam/	→ pɨkám	'skin of back'
	/tmi/	→ tɨmí	'say'
	/kcakk/	→ kɨcákɨk	'cut'
	/nmpanmara/	→ nɨmpánmara	'stomach'

There is a further complication on this pattern, which is that if the vowels of both the first and second syllable are derived by epenthesis, main stress defaults to the initial syllable (2). (See Foley 1991: 44ff. for motivation of an epenthetic analysis in words with strings of consonants such as these.)

(2)	/tkt/	→ tɨkɨt	'chair'
	/klwa/	→ kɨlɨwa	'flower'
	/krmknawt/	→ krɨmkɨnawt	'wasp'
	/tmpnawkwan/	→ tɨmpɨnàwkwan	'sago palm'

In sum, epenthetic vowels are generally invisible to stress (1b), but in a phonologically defined context, epenthetic vowels are stressed according to the regular pattern (2).

The Rule Ordering theory needs to say that Yimas has two rules of epenthesis. One process of *i*-insertion must apply before the assignment of initial stress in order to account for the fact that an epenthetic syllable is stressed when followed by another epenthetic syllable. A second rule of *i*-insertion, on the other hand, must follow stress assignment because of the fact that epenthesis, as the elsewhere case, creates exceptions to regular initial stress. The problems with the Rule Ordering theory, therefore, run deeper than simply failing to explain stress–epenthesis inter-action. In cases like Yimas, the rule-ordering approach leads to loss of generaliza-tion in the analysis of the epenthesis process itself. Concretely, the epenthesis process yields a uniform structural change and it is motivated as a means of syllabifying consonant clusters according to the phonotactics of the language. But the analysis of Yimas in terms of ordered rules misses these generalizations by positing two rules of epenthesis. The observations regarding the output of epenthesis, and that epenthesis is syllabically motivated, are stated more than once in the grammar.

In this paper, I propose to account for stress–epenthesis as constraint interaction within Optimality Theory (Prince & Smolensky 1993 (= P&S), McCarthy & Prince 1993a). The idea developed below is that Universal Grammar has a well-formedness constraint, HEAD-DEPENDENCE (HEAD-DEP henceforth), that bans the stressing (and footing) of epenthetic segments. When HEAD-DEP dominates a set of constraints responsible for 'regular stress', the result is that epenthetic vowels are invisible in stress. However, if HEAD-DEP is low ranking, a different pattern of stress–epenthesis interaction is predicted, i.e., metrical activity of epenthesis. The constraint inter-action theory developed here also provides a clear line of analysis for the more complicated cases exemplified above with Yimas. For such cases, the precise details of the system can be directly characterized by interleaving HEAD-DEP with the set of constraints deriving the regular pattern.

2   Head Dependence in Stress–Epenthesis Interaction

In Dakota (Mississippi Valley Siouan), stress regularly falls on the second syllable from the beginning of the word (3a). But syllabically conditioned epenthesis into the second syllable (3b) creates exceptions to canonical second syllable stress (see Kennedy 1994 and Sietsema 1988 on a syllable-based analysis of epenthesis in Dakota).

(3)   Dakota (Shaw 1976, 1985)

a.	čʰikté	'I kill you'
	mayákte	'you kill me'
	wičháyakte	'you kill them'
	owíčhayakte	'you kill them there'
b.	/ček/ → čék<u>a</u>	'stagger'
	/khuš/ → khúš<u>a</u>	'lazy'
	/čap/ → čáp<u>a</u>	'trot'
	cf. /kte/ → kté	's/he, it kills'

More generally, it seems that in Dakota the stress system avoids stressing vowels that are not present underlyingly. As a first approximation of the constraint HEAD-DEP, we can say that noncanonical stress in Dakota is due to the following prin-ciple: the stressed vowel must have a lexical counterpart in the input. Applying this constraint to the examples below, stress may be assigned to the canonically stressed syllable, i.e., the syllable to which stress is assigned by the regular pattern, if it contains a lexical vowel (4a). But if the second syllable contains an epenthetic vowel, stress falls elsewhere in the word because of the requirement that stressed vowels have lexical counterparts (4b).

(4)   Stress–Epenthesis Interaction in Dakota

a.   /čʰ i k t e/   b.   /č e k/   INPUT
          ↑   ↑
     [čʰ i k t é]   [č é k <u>a</u>]   OUTPUT

This notion of input-dependence makes it possible to construct a clear parallel in the domain of segmental processes sensitive to stress. Stronger faithfulness requirements on stressed vowels are also essential to the characterization of a common form of vowel reduction. Consider the case of Russian, one of a wide range of similar languages (see Beckman 1998 and Flemming 1993 for comprehensive surveys). In tonic positions, Russian licenses six full vowels, i.e., /i ɨ e a o u/, but in unstressed positions, only the three peripheral vowels surface.[1] This observation holds of lexical forms and is supported by morphophonemic alternations. For example, the stem-internal mid vowel surfaces under stress in the nominative form *stól*, yet in forms where stress is moved off the stem vowel, underlying /o/ lowers to *a*, e.g., *stal-óf*. This process of vowel reduction, referred to as 'A-Kanje', is exemplified with the nominal and verbal paradigms below.

(5) Russian A-Kanje (Jones and Ward 1969, Zubritskaya 1995)

a.	Nom. sg.	stól	slóv-o
	Gen.	stal-á	slóv-a
	Dat.	stal-ú	slóv-u
	Nom. pl.	stal-ý	slav-á
	Gen.	stal-óf	slóf
	Dat.	stal-ám	slav-ám
		'table'	'word'

b.	glaž-ú	važ-ú	1 per. sg.
	glóž-iš	vóz-iš	2 per.
	glóž-it	vóz-it	3 per.
	glóž-im	vóz-im	1 per. pl.
	glóž-it'i	vóz-it'i	2 per.
	glóž-ut	vóz-ət	3 per.
	'gnaw'	'carry'	

The fact that the stressed vowel resists the general pattern of reduction suggests a position-sensitive requirement on a par with the one employed above for Dakota. Mid vowels lower generally because of a context-free ban on mid vowels (discussed below). But this lowering process does not apply if the vowel occurs in an accented position. In such cases, mid vowels remain faithful to their input specification because of the high-ranking identity requirement for stressed vowels.

Characterizing vowel reduction in Russian as such paves the way for relating this observation to the metrical inactivity of epenthesis in Dakota. Both cases involve a constraint on the relation between the stressed vowel and its input counterpart, as restated directly below.

(6) a. Stressed vowels must have counterparts in the input.
     b. Stressed vowels must be identical to their input counterparts.

Furthermore, the above constraints have the effect of suppressing general phonological patterns. The requirement in (6a) causes noncanonical initial stress in Dakota, and the requirement in (6b) characterizes the fact that stressed vowels fail to undergo vowel reduction. These parallels are striking and call for an analysis that relates the two phenomena.

Both of the requirements given in (6) assert stronger requirements for stressed vowels, and in doing so, they require reference to 'counterparts' in related structures. This notion of a counterpart is fundamental to the correspondence theory of faithfulness proposed in McCarthy & Prince 1995. The constraints given below involve faithfulness with special reference to metrically prominent positions, i.e., prosodic heads like syllable heads of metrical feet or the main stress foot of a prosodic word.

(7)   HEAD-DEPENDENCE (Alderete 1995)
      Every segment contained in a prosodic head in S_2 has a correspondent in S_1.
      If β is contained in a prosodic head in S_2, then $\beta \in$ Range($\Re$).

(8)   HEAD-IDENTITY[F] (McCarthy 1995, Alderete 1995, Zubritskaya 1995, Beckman 1998).
      Correspondent segments contained in a prosodic head must be identical for F.
      If β is contained in a prosodic head in S_2, and $\alpha\Re\beta$, then α and β agree in the feature F.

HEAD-DEP is a refinement of the anti-epenthesis constraint DEPENDENCE, and HEAD-IDENT(ITY)[F] employs the same modification for the class of featural faithfulness constraints IDENT[F]. The consistent modification to these constraints is therefore the specification of a prosodic target, and with this modification, and nothing more, the two classes of phenomena are explained.[2]

The effect of HEAD-DEP is that prosodic heads are input-dependent. That is, only segments with input correspondents may occur in metrically strong positions. Because epenthetic vowels are introduced in the mapping from the input to the output, they have no input correspondents, and so parsing them internal to the prosodic head of a word will constitute a violation of HEAD-DEP. This notion of Head Dependence will be applied to the case of Dakota below, accounting for the basic fact that epenthetic vowels are never stressed. HEAD-DEP also explains the common fact that epenthetic vowels are not *counted* in the assignment of stress. This type of effect follows from the assumption that the material of the main stress foot is input-dependent, and so, with HEAD-DEP high-ranking, epenthetic vowels may also be prohibited from weak positions in the head foot of a word (see Alderete 1995 and Broselow 2001 for several examples of this kind).

Similarly, HEAD-IDENT[F] explains resistance to vowel reduction in stressed positions. Vowel reduction is part of a larger distributional pattern whereby a wider range of contrasts are licensed in strong positions than those allowed in metrically weak positions. With HEAD-IDENT[F] high-ranking in the grammar, this distributional asymmetry is explained. Returning to the example of Russian A-Kanje, /o/ lowers to *a* generally, but this regular pattern of vowel reduction is suppressed in the accented syllable, e.g., /stol-of/ → *stalóf*.

Sketching the basic components of the analysis, I assume a theory, developed originally in Beckman 1995 for vowel harmony, that phonological processes can be motivated as a means of minimizing structural markedness. Specifically, reduction of a mid vowel can be seen as a way of avoiding a violation of the featural markedness constraint *MID, a context-free constraint which yields a '*' for every mid vowel in a form. However, mid vowels fail to undergo vowel reduction in stressed syllables because of high-ranking HEAD-IDENT[F]: faithfulness to the vowel features of stressed vowels is ensured by this position-sensitive constraint. This is illustrated in the following OT tableau.

(9)   Head Identity in Russian A-Kanje: /stol-of/ → *stalóf*

Input: stol-of	HEAD-IDENT[F]	*MID	IDENT[F]
a. stolóf		**!	
b. staláf	*!		**
c. ☞ stalóf		*	*

The first candidate is fully faithful to the input, but it is ruled out by *MID because it has more violations of this constraint than its competitors, and *MID dominates the context-free faithfulness constraint IDENT[F]. The candidate in (9b) obeys *MID completely by lowering both mid vowels, but in doing so, this form is unfaithful to the featural specification of the stressed vowel, and this results in a fatal violation of top-ranked HEAD-IDENT[F]. The optimal form (9c), therefore, is the one which is both faithful to the features of the stressed vowel, and minimally violates the featural markedness constraint *MID by lowering all vowels elsewhere in the word.

Back to stress–epenthesis interaction. Recall that epenthesis is inactive in Dakota stress: surface stress is realized on the peninitial syllable, yet epenthesis into the second syllable correlates with initial stress. Noncanonical stress is characterized by ranking HEAD-DEP above a constraint responsible for deriving regular stress.

Following Shaw 1985 and Hayes 1995, second syllable stress is derived by forming an iambic foot that is properly aligned with the left edge of the word. Iambic structure is ensured by the rhythm type constraint, RHTYPE = I (P&S), and this iamb must be binary by high-ranking Foot Binarity (McCarthy & Prince 1986, Hayes 1995). The fact that stress prominences are not found after the second syllable suggests that foot construction is noniterative (Shaw 1985). Following McCarthy & Prince 1993b, nonrepeating stress is derived by a high-ranking alignment constraint, ALIGN-L (F, PrWd), which prohibits iterative footing by requiring that the left edge of all feet coincide with the left edge of some prosodic word.

These constraints on the location and form of feet enter into conflict with Head Dependence when epenthesis inserts a vowel in a regularly stressed position. The stress foot constraints posit the head syllable of the word peninitially, but stressing an epenthetic vowel in this position leads to a violation of HEAD-DEP. If HEAD-DEP is top-ranked, therefore, noncanonical stress will be the result, as illustrated in tableau (10).

(10)   Metrical Inactivity of Epenthesis in Dakota: /ček/ → *čéka̱*

Input: ček	HEAD-DEP	RHTYPE = I
{če ká̱}	á!	
☞ {čé ka̱}		*

In the candidates above, epenthetic *a* has no input correspondent; epenthetic vowels do not stand in correspondence with underlying vowels by definition. Therefore, parsing *a* internal to the syllable head of an iambic foot, as in the first candidate, fatally violates HEAD-DEP. The optimal candidate is thus the form that satisfies the input-dependence constraint by reversing the rhythm type of the stress foot.

An approach to stress–epenthesis interaction that employs the notion of Head Dependence differs fundamentally from the Rule Ordering theory in the way that phonological activity of epenthesis is characterized. In the derivational model, the behavior of epenthesis in stress is a matter of serial derivation: metrically active epenthesis is early in the derivation, while invisibility of epenthesis in the stress system is indicative of a later rule. The parallelist theory proposed here does not allow intermediate stages in the derivation, and so phonological activity of epenthesis cannot be characterized in this way. Rather, activity of epenthesis in stress is simply a matter of constraint ranking, a fundamental property of Optimality Theory. If Head Dependence is high-ranking relative to a set of constraints responsible for deriving regular stress, i.e., 'C_{Stress}', then epenthesis is metrically inactive (11a), as is the case in Dakota. On the other hand, if HEAD-DEP is low-ranking in the constraint system, then epenthetic vowels will be active in the system (11b). This type of stress–epenthesis interaction is exemplified by Swahili, where epenthetic vowels receive canonical penultimate stress (Broselow 1982).

(11)   a.   HEAD-DEP ≫ C_{Stress}: metrical inactivity of epenthesis
        b. C_{Stress} ≫ HEAD-DEP: metrical activity of epenthesis

The point here is that the constraint interaction theory characterizes the behavior of epenthesis with the position of Head Dependence in the constraint system. All patterns of stress–epenthesis interaction are thus predictable on the basis of ranking of HEAD-DEP relative to the constraints governing stress. The next section explores a logical consequence of this theory, namely that some languages may show the combined effect of these rankings, producing partial metrical activity of epenthesis.

3   Nonuniformity in Stress–Epenthesis Interaction

The interaction between stress and epenthesis is not always a uniform and across-the-board phenomenon. Epenthetic vowels may be stressed in a specific context, and yet consistently inactive elsewhere in the stress system. For example in Spanish, epenthesis into initial *sC* clusters is ignored by the stress system (Harris 1970, McCarthy 1980), and yet the same process, applied as a way of resolving triconsonantal clusters, is active in stress (Harris 1977, Alderete 1995). A second example of partial metrical activity of epenthesis is found in the Iroquoian language Mohawk. In this language, syllabically motivated epenthesis generally breaks up obstruent + resonant clusters, but the sensitivity of epenthetic vowels to the basic accent pattern is mixed: epenthesis into biconsonantal clusters is inactive in the system, yet epenthetic vowels that surface in a closed syllable are stressed according to the regular pattern (Michelson 1988, Piggott 1995). Similar cases of partial metrical activity of epenthesis are observed in the Malayo-Polynesian language

Lenakel (Lynch 1978) and in Arabic dialect phonology (see especially Farwaneh 1995). In this section, the complicated interactions between stress and epenthesis in Yimas will be studied and its implications for the role of derivationalism in phonology will be discussed.

Words in Yimas are regularly stressed on the initial syllable (1a), but epenthesis into initial clusters causes two complications for the regular pattern (1b), cf. (2). First, if only the initial syllable contains an epenthetic vowel, stress is shifted to the second syllable, e.g., *pɨkám*. This observation shows that the system avoids stressing epenthetic vowels. However, epenthetic vowels may be stressed in a particular context. When both the first and second syllables contain epenthetic vowels, stress defaults to the canonical position, i.e., the initial syllable, as in *krímkɨnawt*. Any theory of stress–epenthesis interaction needs to account for the mixed behavior of epenthetic vowels in cases like this.

Let us begin the analytical work by considering how partial metrical activity of epenthesis is derived within a derivational model. The basic premise of the Rule Ordering theory is that activity in stress is derived by the presence of some structure at the derivational instant at which stress is assigned. In Yimas, this entails a characterization of epenthesis as a pair of rules along the following lines. One rule of epenthesis, Epenthesis$_1$, applies before the assignment of initial stress, operating essentially in the context of triconsonantal clusters that cannot be incorporated into well-formed syllables. An independent rule of vowel insertion, Epenthesis$_2$, which is also motivated in contexts of unsyllabified consonants, must follow stress assignment. This is illustrated for two crucial forms in the following derivation.

(12)   Partial Metrical Activity in a Derivational Model

Underlying representations	/pkam/	/krmknawt/
Epenthesis$_1$	DNA	krɨmknawt
Initial stress	pkám	krímknawt
Epenthesis$_2$	pɨkám	krímkɨnawt
Surface representations	[pɨkám]	[krímkɨnawt]

The problem with the derivational approach can be summed up as follows: stress–epenthesis interaction as rule ordering requires the bifurcation of a unitary process of epenthesis. The epenthesis process itself yields a single structural change and is conditioned in essentially the same phonological environments, motivated as a means of syllabifying consonant clusters according to the phonotactics of the language (Foley 1991: 48). Therefore, the Rule Ordering approach to stress–epenthesis interaction leads to loss of generalization because the observations that characterize the epenthesis process are stated more than once.

Stress–epenthesis interaction in Yimas shows that a unitary process has divergent effects in the stress system: the behavior of epenthetic vowels in the pattern of primary stress is nonuniform. Patterns of nonuniformity of this kind are well-studied phenomena within Optimality Theory, and I will argue that nonuniformity in stress–epenthesis interaction receives a natural interpretation in parallelist OT.

Starting with the regular stress pattern itself, initial stress with alternating secondary stress on subsequent syllables diagnoses Yimas as a trochaic language. Therefore, RHTYPE = T is high ranking, relative to the analogous rhythm type constraint requiring iambic rhythm. Further, Foot Binarity is enforced at the level of the syllable, which, together with high-ranking RHTYPE = T, yields a syllabic trochee. The alignment constraint, ALIGN-L (F, PrWd), ensures left-to-right foot construction; iterative footing is accounted for by ranking the syllable-to-foot parsing constraint, PARSE-SYLL, above ALIGN-L, which asserts that all prosodic feet coincide with the left edge (following McCarthy & Prince 1993b). In sum, RHTYPE = T and Foot Binarity give the syllabic trochee, and the alignment constraint, interacting with the syllable parsing constraint, conspire to yield left-to-right iterative foot construction.

With this component of the constraint system fleshed out, we can now move to the constraint rankings that account for noncanonical second syllable stress. Recall that this stress pattern correlates with initial epenthesis. Since the constraints deriving the canonical pattern posit the syllabic head of the main stress foot on the initial syllable, epenthesis into this position puts the stress constraints in conflict with Head Dependence. So, parsing the first two syllables as a syllabic trochee, as in the first candidate given below, violates HEAD-DEP for the head syllable. By ranking HEAD-DEP above the alignment constraint, therefore, the right result is obtained.

(13)   Metrical Inactivity of Epenthesis: /kcakk/ → kɨcákɨk

Input: kcakk	HEAD-DEP	ALIGN-L
{kɨca} kɨk	ɨ!	
☞ kɨ {cákɨk}		σ

Because the epenthetic vowel ɨ has no input correspondent, parsing it as the head syllable of the word incurs a violation of the top-ranked HEAD-DEP. Therefore, the optimal form is the one that violates ALIGN-L as a means of satisfying HEAD-DEP. Furthermore, in disyllabic forms such as pɨkám, HEAD-DEP compels a rhythm type reversal, by domination of RHTYPE = T. Thus, consistent with the approach taken to metrical inactivity of epenthesis in section 2, failure to stress an epenthetic vowel is derived by ranking Head Dependence above stress-related constraints.

In one context, however, epenthetic vowels are recruited in stress assignment, indicating that Head Dependence is itself dominated in the system. As mentioned above, epenthesis into both the first and the second syllable correlates with regular initial stress, e.g., krímkɨnawt. While the system shows a general avoidance for stressing epenthetic vowels, it would seem that this imperative cannot compel post-peninitial stress because of a hard constraint enforcing a two syllable stress window. With the assumed trochaic foot structure, the stress window amounts to a general ban on two adjacent unfooted syllables, as defended by the researchers listed in (14).

(14) PARSE-SYLL-2 (Kager 1994, Alderete 1995, cf. Green & Kenstowicz 1995)
      In adjacent syllables, avoid more than one unfooted syllable.

Failure to foot both the first and the second syllable constitutes a violation of PARSE-SYLL-2, and since laying down metrical structure has the effect of assigning stress, the complex syllable parsing constraint will suffice as our stress window constraint.

  As for stressed epenthetic vowels, all that is required is to rank the stress window constraint above Head Dependence, as illustrated in the following tableau.

(15) Metrical Activity of Epenthesis: /krmknawt/ → krímkɨnawt

Input: krmknawt	PARSE-SYLL-2	HEAD-DEP	ALIGN-L
a. krɨm {kɨ.nawt}		ɨ	σ!
b. krɨm.kɨ {náwt}	*!		σσ
c. ☞ {krím.kɨ} nawt		ɨ	

Among the candidates provided above, (15b) is not acceptable because by pushing main stress beyond the second syllable, the first two syllables are left unfooted, resulting in a fatal violation of top-ranked PARSE-SYLL-2. This leaves the two alternatives, (15a) and (15c), which tie on HEAD-DEP because both forms posit a syllabic head over a nonlexical vowel. The decision therefore falls to the low-ranking ALIGN-L, which chooses in favor of (15c) because it is perfect with respect to left-edge alignment.

  To review the basic components of the analysis, partial metrical activity of epenthesis is accounted for by interleaving HEAD-DEP between two sets of stress-related constraints.

(16) Stress–Epenthesis Interaction in Yimas
      PARSE-SYLL-2 ≫ HEAD-DEP ≫ ALIGN-L, RHTYPE = T

The constraint rankings in which Head Dependence is in a dominating position yield the noncanonical pattern: in these rankings, HEAD-DEP compels violation of the stress constraints responsible for deriving regular initial stress. A different ranking in the system involves the domination of Head Dependence by the stress window constraint, with the effect that epenthetic vowels are recruited in the assignment of stress just in forms that begin with two epenthetic syllables. In conclusion, the theory of stress–epenthesis interaction proposed here meets the challenge of deriving partial metrical activity of epenthesis.

4   Conclusion

In this paper, a theory of stress–epenthesis interaction was developed that relies crucially on the notion of correspondence between inputs and related outputs and the

OT assumptions that constraints are ranked and violable. The properties inherent to this theory were shown to have a set of advantages, which I will now summarize.

First, these properties permit a nonderivational treatment of stress–epenthesis interaction. Correspondence between related strings is essential in the formal characterization of HEAD-DEP, and by reranking this constraint in relation to the constraints governing stress, the observed patterns of stress–epenthesis interaction are explained without the use of serial derivation. The theory is therefore consistent with recent research that outlines the strengths, both empirical and theoretical, of parallelist OT.

The second advantage of the approach taken here has to do with the analysis of nonuniformity. The principles of constraint ranking and domination were used effectively in the analysis of Yimas, which exemplified the rather common pattern of partial metrical activity of epenthesis. The mixed behavior of epenthesis in this case was handled straightforwardly by ranking HEAD-DEP both above and below the constraints deriving regular stress. The important point is that the OT approach contrasts sharply with the rule-based theory, which was shown to lead to loss of generalization in the characterization of the epenthesis process itself.

The theory developed here also has a theoretical advantage over plausible alternatives in that it paves the way for relating patterns of stress–epenthesis interaction to other phenomena, namely segmental processes like metrically conditioned vowel reduction. In the analysis of Dakota, noncanonical stress is the result of ranking HEAD-DEP above a constraint that derives a regular pattern of stress. Resistance to vowel reduction in stressed syllables is derived in a parallel fashion by employing the related constraint HEAD-IDENT[F]. In both cases, a head-sensitive faithfulness constraint is given high rank in the constraint hierarchy, with the effect of suppressing regular phonological patterns. The theory of faithfulness to prosodic heads therefore covers considerable empirical ground with very limited resources.

Notes

1   Russian vowel reduction is more complicated than this, requiring a distinction between three different domains (i.e., the tonic syllable, the pretonic syllable, and the complement set of syllables), as mid vowels reduce to a peripheral vowel in the pretonic position, but to a schwa elsewhere (Jones and Ward 1969). See Alderete 1995 for discussion of the theoretical implications of this three-way pattern of vowel reduction.

2   It is highly likely that faithfulness constraints defined for prosodic heads have a functional basis in psycholinguistic theories of lexical access. The prosodic faithfulness constraints employed here ensure preservation of the lexical specification for stressed units. Roughly speaking, both of these constraints protect lexical information from being destroyed in metrically strong positions by regular processes of the language. This accords nicely with psycholinguistic evidence that strong syllables play an important role in segmentation for lexical access (see Cutler & Norris 1988 for crucial experimental results, and Beckman 1998 for a comprehensive review).

References

Alderete, John. 1995. Faithfulness to Prosodic Heads. MS, University of Massachusetts, Amherst. ◀

Beckman, Jill. 1995. Shona Height Harmony: Markedness and Positional Identity. In J. Beckman et al., 1995, pp. 53–75.

Beckman, Jill. 1998. *Positional Faithfulness*. Doctoral dissertation, University of Massachusetts, Amherst. ◀

Beckman, Jill, Laura Walsh-Dickey, and Suzanne Urbanczyk, eds. 1995. University of Massachusetts Occasional Papers in Linguistics 18: *Papers in Optimality Theory*. Amherst, MA: Graduate Linguistic Student Association.

Broselow, Ellen. 1982. On the Interaction of Stress and Epenthesis. *Glossa* 16: 115–32.

Broselow, Ellen. 2001. Stress–Epenthesis Interactions. MS, State University of New York, Stony Brook. ROA-446.

Chomsky, Noam and Morris Halle. 1968. *The Sound Pattern of English*. Cambridge, MA: MIT Press.

Cutler, Anne and Dennis Norris. 1988. The Role of Strong Syllables in Segmentation for Lexical Access. *Journal of Experimental Psychology: Human Perception and Performance* 14: 113–21.

Farwaneh, Samira. 1995. *Directional Effects in Arabic Dialect Syllable Structure*. Doctoral dissertation, University of Utah.

Flemming, Edward. 1993. *The Role of Metrical Structure in Segmental Rules*. MA thesis, University of California, Los Angeles.

Foley, W. A. 1991. *The Yimas Language of New Guinea*. Stanford: Stanford University Press.

Green, Thomas and Michael Kenstowicz. 1995. The Lapse Constraint. *FLSM* 6.

Harris, James. 1970. A Note of Spanish Plural Formation. *Language* 46: 928–30.

Harris, James. 1977. Remarks on Diphthongization in Spanish. *Lingua* 41: 261–305.

Hayes, Bruce. 1995. *Metrical Stress Theory: Principles and Case Studies*. Chicago: University of Chicago Press.

Jones, Daniel and Dennis Ward. 1969. *The Phonetics of Russian*. Cambridge: Cambridge University Press.

Kager, René. 1994. Alignment and Ternary Stress. MS, Utrecht University.

Lynch, John D. 1978. *A Grammar of Lenakel*. Pacific Linguistics B55, Australian National University, Canberra.

Kennedy, Chris. 1994. Morphological Alignment and Head Projection. In J. Merchant et al., eds., *Phonology at Santa Cruz* 3: 47–64.

McCarthy, John. 1980. The Role of the Evaluation Metric in the Acquisition of Phonology. In C. L. Baker and John McCarthy, eds., *The Logical Problem of Language Acquisition*, pp. 218–56. Cambridge, MA: MIT Press.

McCarthy, John. 1995. Extensions of Faithfulness: Rotuman Revisited. MS, University of Massachusetts, Amherst. ▶

McCarthy, John and Alan Prince. 1986. Prosodic Morphology. MS, University of Massachusetts and Brandeis University. [Reprinted as Report No. RuCCS-TR-32, New Brunswick: Rutgers Center for Cognitive Science.] ▶

McCarthy, John and Alan Prince. 1993a. *Prosodic Morphology I: Constraint Interaction and Satisfaction*. Report No. RuCCS-TR-3, New Brunswick, NJ: Rutgers Center for Cognitive Science. ▶

McCarthy, John and Alan Prince. 1993b. Generalized Alignment. In G. Booij and J. van Marle, eds., *Yearbook of Morphology* 1993, pp. 79–153. Dordrecht: Kluwer. ◀

McCarthy, John and Alan Prince. 1995. Faithfulness and Reduplicative Identity. In J. Beckman et al., 1995, pp. 249–384. ◀

Michelson, Karen. 1988. *A Comparative Study of Lake Iroquoian Accent*. Dordrecht: Kluwer.

Piggott, G. L. 1995. Epenthesis and Syllable Weight. *Natural Language and Linguistic Theory* 13: 283–326.

Prince, Alan and Paul Smolensky. 1993. *Optimality Theory: Constraint Interaction in Generative Grammar*. Report No. RuCCS-TR-2, New Brunswick: Rutgers Center for Cognitive Science. ◀

Shaw, Patricia. 1976. *Theoretical Issues in Dakota Phonology and Morphology*. Doctoral dissertation, University of Toronto.

Shaw, Patricia. 1985. Modularism and Substantive Constraints in Dakota Lexical Phonology. *Phonology Yearbook* 2: 173–202.

Sietsema, Brian. 1988. Reduplication in Dakota. *CLS* 24: 337–52.

Zubritskaya, Katya. 1995. *The Categorial and Variable Phonology of Russian*. Doctoral dissertation, University of Pennsylvania.

Study and Research Questions

1   Consult some of the original references for the other cases of partial metrical activity of epenthesis reported at the beginning of §3. Try to apply the same basic analytic strategy as in Yimas (i.e., where HEAD-DEP is crucially dominated yet still active). Discuss any problems that arise.

2   Explore the interaction of HEAD-DEP with one or more of the stress constraints posited in chapters 7 through 10. If HEAD-DEP is ranked high enough, how could epenthesis affect stress placement in any of the languages discussed in these chapters?

3   Use the constraint demotion algorithm of chapter 5 to "learn" one of the systems analyzed in this paper, such as Dakota. As in chapter 5, you should assume that the learner has already deduced the input (from paradigmatic alternations, for example) and is solely concerned with ranking the constraints correctly.

Chapter 12 | Moira Yip

Feet and Tonal Reduction at the Word and Phrase Level in Chinese

Editor's Note

The processes of tone sandhi in the various Chinese languages are one of the classic problems of phonology and one of the more productive areas of phonological research. In this chapter, tone sandhi is analyzed as a reduction process using the theory of positional faithfulness (also see chapters 11, 16, 17, and 18). With the right understanding of foot structure in these languages and using the tools provided by positional faithfulness, many sandhi processes are remarkably straight-forward to analyze.

1 Introduction

The term "foot" has been used for two distinct types of structure in Chinese. In one type, only the head syllable retains its tone, whereas in the other, all syllables retain some vestige of their lexical tone. Diagnostics for such feet include sandhi domains (Shih 1986) and clash effects (Duanmu 1995). They are produced by morphosyntax–prosody alignment, and by rhythmic forces, such as Binarity. They are found inside words, inside compounds, and in many cases across words within a phrase. Indeed, compounds and phrases are not always readily distinguishable in Chinese. Throughout this paper I have tried to use data from words, compounds, and phrases, and I will comment on any significant differences.

The groups of syllables called feet in this paper are consistently the first prosodic grouping above the level of the syllable, hence the term "foot". Unlike in many other language families, prominence is not consistently realized as length, duration, or higher pitch, so identification of the head is sometimes difficult. The primary diagnostic here will be that if one and only one syllable surfaces with its citation tone unchanged, while the others either lose or change their tone, the intact syllable will be taken to be the head.

Excerpt (with revisions by the author) from:

Yip, Moira (1999) Feet, tonal reduction and speech rate at the word and phrase level in Chinese. In *Phrasal Phonology*, ed. René Kager and Wim Zonneveld, pp. 171–94. Nijmegen: Nijmegen University Press. [Available on Rutgers Optimality Archive, ROA-159.]

1.1   Feet in which only the head syllable bears its lexical tone

The first major foot-type is one in which non-head syllables are toneless, and their surface pitch is either spread from the head syllable, acquired from a phrasal boundary tone, or inserted by default. Using o for such syllables, such feet can be denoted as (Too..) or (..ooT). Such feet may be built on underlyingly toneless syllables, which may never be heads, or on syllables that lose their tone as a consequence of their position in the foot. Shanghai has a (Tooo..) pattern. The complex tone of the first syllable is realized over the first two syllables; other syllables get a default [l] tone. Here I use Selkirk and Shen's (1990) tone notation; actually, the inventory can be simplified to just /lh, hl/.

(1)   *Citation*   *Surface*

    a.   taw ʔiq pe ʻzo   mh mh hl lh   (m h l) (lh)   ʻpour a cup of tea'
           pour one cup tea

    b.   fi siaN   poqtsiN   hl mh mh hl   (h l) (m h)   ʻfly towards Beijing' (lit)
           fly towards Beijing

The syntax partially determines the structure of these units, as shown by Selkirk and Shen, but Duanmu (1995) has shown that these feet are preferentially binary, and show rhythmic clash avoidance effects.

    Wenzhou (Zhengzhang 1964) is in the relevant respects an example of the mirror-image type, (..oooT). Only the tone of the final syllable matters; all else is neutralized (p. 136: D4). (With certain final tones, the penult also matters; see §3.2.1 for details.) In the examples below, both strings end in a 45 toned syllable, preceded by a variety of other tones [Chinese tones are described with a 5-step scale, where 1 is lowest – Ed.]. The output strings have identical patterns controlled only by the final tone. The origins of the exact surface pattern will not concern us here. Using pinyin:

(2)   san chang liang duan   44 31 34 45   (2 4 43 34)   ʻ3 long 2 short'
       tong hang tong zou   31 31 31 45   (2 4 43 34)   ʻtogether walk
                                                   together walk'

    In this section we have seen examples of feet where non-heads are toneless. Here and throughout I abstract away from the surface pitch of these toneless syllables, although I touch on the case of spreading from the head in a later section. I restrict my analysis to explaining why the *underlying* tones of non-head syllables are lost.

1.2   Feet in which all syllables carry a lexical tone or its contextual allotone

The second type of foot is also usually but not always binary. Each syllable retains its lexical tone, or an allotone of that tone. Using T for a head syllable bearing a lexical, citation tone, and t for a non-head still bearing an underlying tone or its surface allotone, such feet can be denoted as (Ttt...) or (..ttT). Evidence for grouping these syllables into one prosodic unit comes from the use of that unit as the domain of tone sandhi rules.

1.2.1   Mandarin: (Ttt..)

The existence of feet in Mandarin is motivated primarily by their function as a domain for the well-known third-tone sandhi rule, which turns the first of two low 21(4) "third" tones into a high rising 35 "second" tone. Shih 1986 argues that the domain of this rule is a prosodic unit, the foot. The headedness of these feet is in dispute; traditionally they have been assumed to be right-headed, but Duanmu (1994, 1996) argues that they are left-headed. In support of this view, one might note Shih's (1989) claim that focussed elements induce a foot boundary to their left, with the consequence that they themselves head a left-headed foot. These feet are preferentially binary, but the syntax also exerts an influence. Monosyllabic feet are avoided, so strays are grouped into a ternary foot. For full details, see Shih 1986, 1989.

(3) a. wu wu wu wu   21 21 21 214   (35 21) (35 214)   '5555'

    b. shui leng hao   21 21 214   (35 35 214)   'It's better if the
       water cool good   water is cool'

    c. gei gou shui   21 21 214   (35 35 214)   'Give water to dog'
       give water dog

Within these feet, each syllable has a full lexical tone or its allotone.

1.2.2   Xiamen: (..ttT)

The mirror-image case can be found in Xiamen (also known as Taiwanese or Amoy). Xiamen has a set of tone sandhi processes known as the Min tone circle, by which each citation/pre-pausal/phrase-final tone changes to an allotone in non-final position. Citation tones are to the left of the arrows, non-final allotones to the right.

(4)   24 ⟶ 22 ⟶ 21 ⟶ 53 ⟶ 44

Chen 1987 shows that these changes take place in tonal domains which are largely defined by alignment with the syntax. For example, the subject and predicate normally form two separate domains, as in (5a), whereas the VP may form a single domain, as in (5b–c).

(5) a. teng jin sio   44 44 44   (44)(22 44)   'The soup is very hot'
    b. tsu san tng   53 44 21   (44 22 21)   'cook three meals'
    c. song-tsin t'en liong 21 22 44 24   (53 21 22 24)   'have no conscience'
       lose-out conscience

The syntactic conditioning, and the variable size, may make these seem more like phonological phrases than feet, but Hsu 1992 shows that there is a strong binary influence on these domains (at least in idioms), as expected if we are dealing with feet. Consider the following examples of four-syllabled idioms from Hsu (Chen's tone values); in (6b), the syntax alone would lead us to expect two domains, with breaks between NP and VP only. Instead, we find three domains, in obedience to a preference for maximally binary feet.

(6) a. [Ying-hiong]$_{NP}$ $_{VP}$[kiu bi] 44 24 21 53 (22 24)(53 53) 'A hero saves
                                                                          a beauty'
     b. [Tsai]$_{NP}$ $_{VP}$[ko pat tao]   24 55 21 53 (24)(55)(53 53) 'exceedingly
         Talent high eight peck   talented'

Note that one language may have more than one "foot" type. Chaoyang and Xiamen, for example, have both (..ttT) and (Too..) "feet". In such cases, the toneless syllables are underlyingly toneless.

The following questions arise. (i) Are both the (To) and (Tt) units feet, and if so why are the tones lost in the former but not in the latter? (ii) Are both the binary and the n-ary units really feet, or should this term be reserved for the rhythmic binary units of Shih 1986, 1989, Duanmu 1995? If feet are strictly binary, what do we call the larger units? The remainder of this paper addresses each of these issues in turn. Section 2 outlines a proposal for the typology of tone loss in non-head positions in which a positionally biased MAX constraint, HEADMAX(T), enforces tonal retention in heads. In non-heads tone loss is found when tonal markedness constraints out-rank the more general MAX(T) constraint that requires retention of all input tones. Section 3 then extends this to cases of partial tone loss. First, tonal markedness must distinguish between more marked tones, which survive only in heads, and less marked tones, which survive everywhere. Second, HEADMAX constraints must distinguish between head syllables and head feet. Section 4 briefly summarizes the results of these two sections. Section 5 [not reprinted here – Ed.] looks at possible n-ary feet in Nantong fast speech, and compares two very different approaches. A purely phonological account makes use of different grammars at different speeds, and requires n-ary feet. A phonology–phonetics interface account holds the grammar constant, with feet always binary, and a higher-level n-ary super-foot.

2 Tone Loss in Non-head Positions: Tone Loss = Vowel Reduction

The parallels between tone loss and vowel reduction are obvious. (Note that tone loss is not comparable to vowel *loss*, because only the latter removes an entire syllable.) Among the similarities are (i) both are found in non-head position; (ii) both are found in head-final systems (Muskogean and Algonquian: Hayes 1995, Wenzhou initial syllable tone); (iii) both are found in head-initial systems (Maithili, Icelandic, English: Hayes 1995, Shanghai tone); (iv) both come in two variants:

total elimination of contrasts to schwa (English), or tonelessness (Shanghai), or a reduction in the number of contrasts (e.g., Italian, Russian, Catalan; Taiwan or Wenzhou medial syllable tones (see below)); (v) both may go together: Mandarin toneless syllables also show vowels that are somewhat centralized and loss of post-nuclear material (Lin and Yan 1988). Tone loss is not limited to Chinese: see Noyer 1991 on Huave, Bickmore 1995 on Bantu. Also see Sietsema 1988, and many papers in Inkelas and Zec 1990, on the attraction of tones to head positions. These parallels suggest that we take a close look at treatments of vowel reduction as a starting point for our investigations.

2.1   Previous approaches to non-head change versus head-faithfulness

Dresher and van der Hulst (1995) point out that heads typically allow more phono-logical complexity, such as featural specification, than non-heads. They coin the term "head-dependent asymmetries" for this phenomenon. In OT, such asymmetries have been discussed by Alderete 1995 and Beckman 1995, 1996, building on ideas from Selkirk 1994. Alderete formulates faithfulness constraints that are specific to head positions. If these outrank markedness constraints, and markedness in turn outranks the more general faithfulness constraints that apply to non-heads as well, then marked segments/features will survive in head position only. He begins by noting that heads cannot contain epenthetic material, and formulates a constraint of the DEP family specific to head position.

(7)   HEAD(PCat)-DEP
      Every segment contained in a prosodic head PCat in S_2 has a correspondent in S_1. If PCat is a prosodic head in S_2, and PCat contains β, then β ∈ Range (ℜ).

Here, PCat = syllable. This will block epenthesis into heads and thus block stressing epenthetic vowels. An extension to DEP's partner, MAX, would block deletion from heads, and thus block loss of material such as codas or post-nuclear glides from stressed syllables.

The above constraints refer to entire segments and block their insertion/deletion in heads. Alderete continues by noting that the mere presence of a correspondent is not enough: heads must also be featurally identical, whereas non-heads may undergo neutralization. He thus proposes the following:

(8)   HEAD(PCat)-IDENT(F)
      Correspondent segments in prosodic heads PCat agree in value for feature [F]. If PCat is a prosodic head, PCat contains β, and αℜβ, then α and β agree in the value of F.

To explain retention of contrasts in heads, but their loss elsewhere, this constraint dominates featural markedness constraints. For example, if mid vowels are raised/lowered in non-heads only, HEAD-IDENT ≫ *MID ≫ IDENT.

This comes close to offering an explanation for tone reduction. Suppose HEAD-IDENT(T) $\gg$ *T $\gg$ IDENT(T). Consider the following tableau, using *T for the entire family of tonal markedness constraints, and indices for underlying associations (cf. McCarthy and Prince 1995).

(9)

σ́$_1$ σ$_2$ σ$_3$ t$_1$ t$_2$ t$_3$	HEAD-IDENT(T)	*T	IDENT(T)
σ́$_1$ σ$_2$ σ$_3$ t$_1$ t$_2$ t$_3$		***!	
☞ σ́$_1$ σ$_2$ σ$_3$ t$_1$		*	**
σ́$_1$ σ$_2$ σ$_3$	*!		***

However, this works perfectly if and only if the head syllable bears all and only its underlying tone, and the non-head syllables have no tone of any kind, at the surface.[1] Unfortunately, neither of these statements is reliably true for tone, because tone is a movable feature, and cannot be relied on to stay put on its underlying host. As a result a HEAD-IDENT account fails for tone, or other movable elements (cf. Zoll 1996, Akinlabi 1994). The following tableau illustrates how this approach fails for a case like Shanghai, where the head syllable has two underlying tones, and the second of these moves onto the second syllable in the output.

(10)

σ́$_1$ σ$_2$ σ$_3$ t$_1$ t$_1$ t$_2$ t$_3$	HEAD-IDENT(T)	*T	IDENT(T)
a. σ́$_1$ σ$_2$ σ$_3$ t$_1$ t$_1$	*	**	***!
● b. σ́$_1$ σ$_2$ σ$_3$ t$_1$ t$_2$	*	**	**

No matter what the ranking, the grammar will prefer candidate (b), with one tone of each syllable preserved, over candidate (a), in which both preserved tones originate in the head syllable and are redistributed in the output. Yet (b) is never the actual surface outcome, (a) is.

Let us recap the basic patterns to be explained. As I have already emphasized, tones do not necessarily stay in place. The following four facts must be explained: (i) If a syllable is a head, its underlying tone(s) must be preserved. (ii) If a syllable is a non-head, in many dialects its tone is lost. (iii) However, the "head" tones may not all surface on the head syllable (flop, spreading). (iv) Further, non-head syllables may have surface tones, from the head, or from phrasal sources, or by default. It is clear that *survival* of the tone is at stake here, suggesting an extension of MAX to features, not just segments. If features can only be referred to in terms of whether their host segments are featurally identical, their mobility becomes an intractable problem. Alderete's constraints regulate faithfulness strictly with reference to *output position*. But tonal preservation/loss depends on *input position*, in that tones that belong to the output head *in the input* are preserved, and tones that belong to output non-heads *in the input* are lost. In a derivational approach this is achieved by ordering tone loss before rules that readjust tone associations, such as flop, spreading, or default insertion, but a non-derivational grammar with a commitment to a single output level such as Optimality Theory (OT) cannot do this.

I will develop an alternative within OT in which tonal preservation is caused by extending the MAX family of constraints to features (cf. Myers 1993, Myers and Carleton 1996, McCarthy and Prince 1995), and allowing them to be relativized to head position.

2.2   The proposal

For tone retention in heads, we can use a constraint from the MAX-IO family (McCarthy and Prince 1995) [see chapter 3 – Ed.].

(11)   HEADMAX(F)
Every feature in S_1 associated in S_1 with a segment whose correspondent is contained in a prosodic head in S_2 has a correspondent in S_2.

The surface association of this tone will be governed by familiar constraints on tone associations, such as a preference for one-to-one association, a preference for syllables to bear tones, NO-FLOP (McCarthy 1995), and NO-SPREAD (McCarthy 1995). I will have nothing to say about these here.[2] For consistency, the general faithfulness constraint that enforces tonal retention will also be formulated as one of the MAX family, instead of one of the IDENT family. If these constraints are ranked HEADMAX(T) $\gg$ *T $\gg$ MAX(T), we will correctly deal with cases of tone loss in non-heads, and preservation of head tones. The following tableau shows how the new proposal works for the problem case where "head" tones show up on non-head syllables.

(12)

$\acute{\sigma}_1 \quad \sigma_2 \, \sigma_3$ $t_1 \; t_1 \; t_2 \; t_3$	HEADMAX(T)	*T	MAX(T)
☞a. $\acute{\sigma}_1 \, \sigma_2 \, \sigma_3$ $t_1 \; t_1$		**	**
b. $\acute{\sigma}_1 \, \sigma_2 \, \sigma_3$ $t_1 \; t_2$	*!	**	**

Two details remain to be explained. Recall that in actuality the syllables shown as toneless above may receive a default low tone, as in Shanghai. The grammar as given above will penalize insertion of a low tone, since this L violates *T. Suppose the grammar includes a constraint requiring syllables to bear tones, which I will refer to as *NOTONE. If we break *T up into *H and *L, and rank *NOTONE between *H and *L, then we can explain why only low tones survive/ are inserted on non-head syllables: *H ≫ *NOTONE ≫ *L. In the remainder of the paper I will abstract away from this issue, and show candidates with toneless syllables.

Secondly, we need one addition to this grammar in order to characterize the fact that underlyingly toneless syllables may never be heads. I call this the Stress-to-Tone Principle, "Heads must bear tone", by analogy with the Stress-to-Weight Principle, and the Weight-to-Stress Principle (WSP) of Prince 1990. Candidates which violate this will not be considered here.

2.3   Applying the proposal

Let us see how this proposal derives the major foot types discussed in section 1. For (Tt) or (tT) feet, we need only assume that MAX(T) outranks the tonal markedness constraint *T. The ranking of HEADMAX(T) is irrelevant: any ranking will give the same output.

(13)

/tt/	MAX(T)	*T
☞ a. Tt		**
b. To	*!	*

For (To) or (oT) feet, as we have already seen, HEADMAX(T) ≫ *T ≫ MAX(T). This is the case for which the proposal was developed, and the following tableau illustrates its workings. (Note: O stands for a stressed but toneless syllable.)

(14)

/tt/	HEADMAX(T)	*T	MAX(T)
☞ a. To		*	*
b. Tt		**!	
c. Oo	*!		**
d. Ot	*!	*	*

A third grammar is logically possible given these three constraints under review here. Suppose *T ≫ HEADMAX(T), MAX(T). Such a grammar would have no surface tones at all, so the net effect would be to produce a language that lacked tones, without any necessary commitment to toneless inputs. There are no other surface patterns produced by these three constraints.

Lastly, consider languages with both (tT) and (To) feet, such as Taiwanese. Inputs with fully-toned syllables surface as [tT], showing that the ranking is HEADMAX(T), MAX(T) ≫ *T. ALIGN-R(Head, Ft) captures the right-headed nature of the language. However, /to/ inputs surface as left-headed [To], so the Stress-to-Tone principle dominates right-headedness. Lastly, tone is not *inserted* in order to allow right-headed feet, so HEADDEP(T) ≫ ALIGN-R(Head, Ft).

Up to this point, I have only discussed languages in which tones are retained in their entirety, or in which they are completely lost, but many languages show a sort of partial tone reduction. I will distinguish two types. In the first, all non-head syllables show loss of some but not all tones. In the second, non-head syllables do not behave as a single class, with those in some positions (typically closer to the head) showing less neutralization than others. In the next two sections I deal with these in turn.

3   Partial Tonal Reduction: Tonal Markedness, Head Syllables, and Head Feet

3.1   Partial tonal reduction: Type I

In some languages hybrid feet exist, where the non-head syllables have tones that are partially neutralized and/or reduced, but not eliminated entirely. Recall that in Taiwanese tones have two allotones, one in final position, one in non-final position. Non-finally, there is in fact limited neutralization, so that /24/, /44/ merge into [22].

$(15) = (4)$ 24 ⟶ 22 ⟶ 21 ⟶ 53 ⟶ 44

All non-final (i.e., non-head) syllables undergo this change.

The approach I take here is very similar to Alderete's, in that it divides the featural markedness constraints into two groups, singling out one feature as more marked than the others. Consider the 24 tone, which only appears in peak position. We must divide *T into two parts, one referring to rising tones only: *RISING, vs *T, and assume the ranking HEADMAX(T) ≫ *RISING ≫ MAX(T) ≫ *T.

(16)   (Heads are underlined)

/24 24/	HEADMAX(T)	*RISING
☞ a. 22 <u>24</u>		*
b. 24 <u>24</u>		**!
c. 24 <u>22</u>	*!	*
d. 22 <u>22</u>	*!	

In later sections we will again need to distinguish between more and less marked tones.[3]

3.2   Partial tone reduction: Type 2

In this second and more interesting type, syllables closer to the head undergo partial neutralization, while syllables further away lose their tones entirely. Such words can be denoted as [o...o(tT)] or [(Tt)o...o]. Wenzhou and Suzhou are examples of these respectively.

3.2.1   Wenzhou: [o...o(tT)] (Zhengzhang 1964)

In unchecked syllables, Wenzhou has the tonal inventory: 44, 31, 45, 34, 42, 22. In compounds and some phrases, the general pattern is that the final syllable tone determines the contour of the overall span, in non-obvious ways whose details will not concern us here. For certain final tones, such as /45/, all preceding tones are neutralized, as shown in (2) in section 1.1. However, the tone of the penult has some influence in the case of a subset of final tones, although all preceding tones are still completely neutralized. It is this latter pattern that is the subject of this section. I will focus here only on whether or not an underlying tone has any influence on the output pattern, and not on the details of how particular input tones result in specific output tones.

The data below shows various strings ending in a /44/ tone. If the penult is from the type of tone known as Ping, a historical category that is not an obvious natural class synchronically, then we get the pattern shown in (17a). If the penult is from the other historical category, known as Ze, then we get the pattern in (17b). Examples are given in pinyin.[4]

(17)   Strings ending in /44/
   a.   Penult is "Ping", /44/ or /31/: Surface pattern [34 43 22 33]
         31 44 44 44   you zhi gong si   'oil factory'   (p. 134, A4)
         31 44 31 44   min zhi min gao   'people's property'

   b.   Penult is "Ze", /45, 22, 42, or 34/: Surface pattern [2 4 42 33]
         31 44 45 44   chang sheng   'long sound,   (p. 135, B4)
                       duan sheng   short sound'
         44 22 22 44   xiang xia di fang 'rural area'

Crucially, Faithfulness must distinguish the final (head) syllable from the penult, and each from all other syllables. To do this, I will borrow an idea proposed by Alderete 1995 for gradations of vowel reduction in Russian. He suggests that retention of some contrasts in the last two syllables is actually retention in the last binary foot. Suppose then that Wenzhou also has binary feet; in longer strings there is in fact an alternating pitch pattern that shows some indications of binary rhythm, but for the data under discussion we need only assume a single binary foot at the right edge, and this will be optimal in a grammar in which ALL-FT-R and FT-BIN are undominated.

We must now add to positional faithfulness in the head *syllable* (the notion used in our previous analyses) the idea of positional faithfulness in the head *foot*. The two constraints are given below:

(18)   HEADSYLL-MAX(F) (formerly HEAD-MAX(F))
       Every feature in S_1 associated in S_1 with a segment whose correspondent is contained in a head syllable in S_2 has a correspondent in S_2.

(19)   HEADFOOT-MAX(F)
       Every feature in S_1 associated in S_1 with a segment whose correspondent is contained in a head foot in S_2 has a correspondent in S_2.

It seems plausible that head syllables always require greater faithfulness than non-head syllables that are merely enclosed in head feet, so I hypothesize that in UG, HEADPCat$_a$-MAX(T) $\gg$ HEADPCat$_b$-MAX(T) iff PCat$_a$ < PCat$_b$.

Finally, we must allow tonal markedness to distinguish between the full range of "contour" distinctions (kept in the head syllable only) from the residual Ping/Ze distinction (kept on last two syllables only). We can achieve this by the use of two tonal markedness constraints, *CONTOUR and *T, which interrupt the faithfulness constraints at two different points, giving the ranking HEADSYLL-MAX(T) $\gg$ *CONTOUR $\gg$ HEADFOOT-MAX(T) $\gg$ *T $\gg$ MAX(T). The following tableau illustrates the workings of this mini-grammar. Note that candidates such as (e), in which the head (final) syllable has lost any tonal specifications, will be immediately ruled out by the top-ranked HEADSYLL-MAX(T), which outranks all markedness constraints including *Contour. The table uses C as a cover term for "contour" features, and PZ as a cover term for the Ping/Ze distinction. Every specification, whether C or PZ, incurs a * under *T. Obviously, the actual distinctive features responsible remain to be understood.[5]

(20)

	HeadSyll-Max(T)	*Contour	HeadFoot-Max(T)	*T

☞a.   PZ PZ
       | |
   σ σ (σ   σ)
           |
           C
		*	. *	* * *

b.   PZ PZ PZ
      | | |
   σ σ (σ   σ)
           |
           C
		*	*	* * * *!

c.   PZ
         |
   σ σ (σ   σ)
           |
           C
		*	* *!	* *

d.   PZ PZ
      | |
   σ σ (σ   σ)
         | |
         C C
		* *!		* * * *

e.   PZ PZ
      | |
   σ σ (σ   σ)
	*!		* *	* *

This interest of this approach is that it limits tone retention to a foot-sized window. The next language differs in that the foot in question is n-ary, not binary.[6]

3.2.2   Suzhou: [(Tt…t)o]

Suzhou differs from Wenzhou in two respects. It is left-headed not right-headed, and the foot within which some tones are retained is n-ary, not binary. The Suzhou generalizations, followed by data for syllables with no glottalization in the rhyme are given below; data are from Ye 1979; other sources report somewhat different facts.

(21) a. Initial syllables retain their own tone, and determine the tone of entire span.
      b. Final syllables lose their own tone, and their tone depends entirely on the preceding tone.
      c. Medial syllables retain their register, but lose their contour (in the sense of Yip 1980, Bao 1990): /44, 412, 55/ become 44; /13, 31/ become 33. True of any number of medial syllables.
      d. Voicing distinctions in onsets are preserved under tonal change.

(22)

	Underlying tones	Surface tones	Example	Gloss	Translation
a.	52 52 44	52 44 21	tã həu tɕI	hit fire	cigarette lighter
	52 412 23	52 44 21	siæ ts'ɛ lɛ	machine	small vegetable basket
b.	52 13 44	52 33 21	tsæ ñi kæ	date paste cake	jujube
	52 31 13	52 33 21	sia zɨ dɛ	write character	writing desk
c.	52 52 44 52	52 44 44 21	sɨ ts'æ ko tsɨ	desk	water fry melon seeds
	52 23 <u>33</u> 23	52 33 33 21	si ñin bə dɣ		dead man nose
	52 23 44 31	52 33 44 21	siæ zæ kɑ ɦã		little Cao's home lane
d.	13 52 31	13 44 21	ɦuã tɛ bin	jaundice illness	jaundice
	13 412 44	13 44 21	ɦIɣ pæ ho	oil quick-fry shrimp	quick-fried shrimp
e.	13 13 13	13 33 21	nø mən dʑiæ		south gate bridge
	13 31 31	13 33 21	ɦoŋ miɪ k'oŋ		red face
f.	13 412 <u>33</u> 21	13 44 <u>33</u> 21	zən tɕ'i ɦuə ɦiɪ		very vigorous people's commune
	13 13 44 31	13 33 44 21	zen min koŋ zo		
	13 13 31 31	13 33 33 21	loŋ dʑiæ dɑ dɛ		Longqiao group

The crucial difference from Wenzhou is that all medial syllables retain some contrast in Suzhou, so pursuing the same line as in Wenzhou we may postulate a left-headed non-final unbounded foot in Suzhou: [(σ̲ . . . . σ) σ]. The initial syllable is the head, all medial syllables are contained in the head foot, but the final syllable is not. This foot structure can be attributed to the ranking ALIGN-L(Foot, PrWd), FT-BIN-MIN ≫ FT-BIN-MAX, *ALIGN-R(Foot, PrWd).[7] Given this move, and decomposing *T into *CONTOUR and *T, the Wenzhou hierarchy now also deals with

Suzhou. I use R as a cover term for register, and C as a cover term for contour. All candidates are left-headed.

(23)

	HeadSyll-Max(T)	*Contour	HeadFoot-Max(T)	*T	Max(T)
☞a. R R $\quad$ │ │ $\quad$(σ σ) σ $\qquad$│ $\qquad$C		*	*	***	***
b. R R $\quad$ │ │ $\quad$(σ σ) σ	*!		**	**	****
c. R R $\quad$ │ │ $\quad$(σ σ) σ $\qquad$│ │ $\qquad$C C		**!		****	**
d. R $\quad$│ $\quad$(σ σ) σ $\qquad$│ $\qquad$C		*	**!	**	****
e. R R R $\quad$ │ │ │ $\quad$(σ σ) σ $\qquad$│ $\qquad$C		*	*	****!	**

Finally, let us see how the further refinements made necessary by the Wenzhou and Suzhou data play out when we return to the simpler languages discussed earlier. Reviewing the previous cases, we see that if the UG ranking HeadSyll-Max(T) ≫ HeadFoot-Max(T) ≫ Max(T) is interrupted at various points by the tonal markedness constraints, which may themselves be fragmented into two (or more?) blocks, we readily derive the range of languages discussed so far:

(24) • All non-head syllables lose all tones (Shanghai):
      HeadSyll-Max(T) ≫ *T ≫ HeadFoot-Max(T) ≫ Max(T)
     • All syllables (heads and non-heads) keep all tones (Mandarin):
      HeadSyll-Max(T) ≫ HeadFoot-Max(T) ≫ Max(T) ≫ *T

- Certain tones (e.g., Xiamen rising tone) lost everywhere except in head syllable; other tones kept on all syllables:
  HEADSYLL-MAX(T) ≫ *RISING ≫ HEADFOOT-MAX(T) ≫ MAX(T) ≫ *T
- Certain tones (e.g., Wenzhou contours) lost everywhere except in head syllable; other tones kept on syllables contained in head foot; other syllables lose all tones:
  HEADSYLL-MAX(T) ≫ *CONTOUR ≫ HEADFOOT-MAX(T) ≫ *T ≫ MAX(T)

We also predict a language type I have not yet encountered. Suppose HEADSYLL-MAX(T), HEADFOOT-MAX(T) ≫ *T ≫ MAX(T). Then all syllables in the head foot (binary or n-ary) will keep all tones, and all other syllables will lose all tones. I take it to be a weakness of this approach that such languages are not to my knowledge attested.

4   Conclusion to Sections 2 and 3

Sections 2 and 3 have provided us with several arguments for not limiting feet to the (T...o) type. First, languages such as Mandarin and Taiwanese clearly have (T..t) prosodic units, which I have called feet. It is true that one could construct an alternative account in which each tone-bearing syllable was its own foot, and the larger units are renamed prosodic word, phonological phrase, or some such. This, it seems to me, is largely a matter of terminology: cross-linguistically, we would then have grammars in which tones are lost in this larger prosodic unit, and grammars in which they are not, and the account offered here could be carried over renamed but otherwise unchanged. Second, if we consider each tone-bearing syllable to be its own foot in such languages, FT-BIN, which would of course prefer a (Tt) foot to two (T)(t) ones, must be outranked by an additional constraint banning tones in non-heads, a sort of Tone-to-Stress principle. The account offered here is superior in that it has no need of such a constraint. Thirdly, the Wenzhou and Suzhou analyses make crucial use of the idea that tones can be retained within feet, but not outside feet. Hence (T..t) feet are at the core of these analyses. Finally, while these sections have concentrated on the question of how and why tones are lost in some feet, and not in others, the data also bear on the question of whether feet are always binary, and it appears that they are not. I have made crucial use of n-ary feet in my analysis of Suzhou, for example.[8]

The core of the analysis offered here is very close in spirit to accounts of vowel reduction by Alderete and Beckman. The particular contribution of the tonal facts is twofold. First, the mobility of tone requires that faithfulness be handled through MAX, not IDENT. The analysis thus offers support for extending MAX to features, and for allowing positional MAX constraints, thus completing the array of positional faithfulness constraints. Second, the tonal facts show complex interactions between head syllable and head foot faithfulness, and foot size. In particular, n-ary feet as well as binary feet are needed to explain the full range of facts. See Yip (1999, 2002) for a closer look at n-ary feet in the Nantong dialect.

[...]

The picture presented in this paper is one that is entirely to be expected from an OT perspective. Tone loss results from tonal markedness pressures, but these interact with Faithfulness constraints so that the respective rankings of the two determine whether tones survive or not. Heads enforce more stringent faithfulness, so tones are more likely to survive there. Foot size is controlled by BIN constraints, and these are, as expected, violable, so n-ary feet are optimal in some languages under pressure from prosody–syntax or prosody–prosody (such as ALL-FT-LEFT) alignment constraints. Finally, the striking parallels between tone loss and vowel reduction are clarified by this approach, which builds heavily on earlier OT work on vowel reduction.

Notes

1   Presumably one could admit phonetic interpolation of tone on phonologically toneless syllables, but any kind of phonological tone, even default tone-assignment, would be banned.

2   This constraint will generalize to the vowel-reduction situation, raising the question as to whether HEAD-IDENT is really necessary. The main difference is that only HEAD-IDENT bans the *insertion* of extra features on heads, as in the insertion of H tone on heads in some languages.

3   The other allotonic variation, and its circular nature, is beyond the scope of this paper. See Kirchner 1996 and Moreton 1995 for a recent OT approach.

4   Data do not give tones of each non-final syllable, only the general category "ping/ze". Tones have been reconstructed by comparison with known tones in other dialects, so that if Cantonese has this syllable as "yin qu", it is assumed it is also "yin qu" in Wenzhou, and Zhengzhang gives "yin qu" as 42. Any errors introduced by this procedure do not affect the central generalizations.

5   Note that there is no need for the constraints to refer to the mysterious (and therefore problematic) Ping/Ze contrast directly.

6   Under this approach, these languages have (tT) feet. We must assume the other syllables are unfooted, since otherwise all head syllables would retain tone. Thus the head foot is also the only foot, and the importance of specifying head foot in the constraint remains to be demonstrated.

7   *ALIGN-R(Foot, PrWd) is simply a way of stating extrametricality here; other OT approaches use Nonfinality (Prince and Smolensky 1993).

8   An obvious question for future research is whether there are UG markedness-based rankings of the various tonal faithfulness constraints. I have made use of three: Xiamen: *RISING ≫ *T, Suzhou: *CONTOUR ≫ *T, and Wenzhou: *CONTOUR ≫ *T. Without a precise understanding of what features are behind these cover terms, however, no theory of markedness can be developed, and I leave this topic for future research.

References

Akinlabi, Akinbiyi. 1994. Featural alignment. MS, Rutgers University. ▶

Alderete, John. 1995. Faithfulness to Prosodic Heads. Rutgers Optimality Archive-94. ◀

Bao, Zhi-ming. 1990. *On the Nature of Tone.* PhD dissertation. MIT.

Beckman, Jill. 1995. Shona height harmony: Markedness and positional Identity. *University of Massachusetts Occasional Papers in Linguistics 18: Papers in Optimality Theory,* ed. by Jill Beckman, Laura Walsh Dickey, and Suzanne Urbanczyk, 53–76.

Beckman, Jill. 1996. Positional Faithfulness and the distribution of phonological features. MS, University of Massachusetts, Amherst. ◀

Bickmore, Lee. 1995. Tone and stress in Lamba. *Phonology*, 307–42.

Chen, Matthew. 1987. The syntax of Xiamen tone sandhi. *Phonology Yearbook* 4, 109–50.

Dresher, Bezalel Elan and Harry van der Hulst. 1995. Head-dependent asymmetries in prosodic phonology. MS, University of Toronto and University of Leiden. ▶

Duanmu, San. 1994. Word stress in Mandarin. MS, University of Michigan.

Duanmu, San. 1995. Metrical and tonal phonology of compounds in two Chinese dialects. *Language* 71, 225–59.

Duanmu, San. 1996. Phonology and word order in Chinese compounds. MS, University of Michigan.

Hayes, Bruce. 1995. *Metrical Stress Theory: Principles and Case Studies*. Chicago: University of Chicago Press.

Hewitt, Mark. 1994. Deconstructing foot binarity in Koniag Alutiiq. MS, University of British Columbia. ▶

Hsu, Hui-chuan. 1992. Tonal parsing in idioms: a tug of war between the foot formation rule and the tone group formation. *Proceedings of IsCCL 3*.

Inkelas, Sharon and Draga Zec. 1990. *The Phonology–Syntax Connection*. CSLI.

Kirchner, Robert. 1996. Synchronic chain shifts in Optimality Theory. Paper given at the LSA, San Diego. ◀

Lin, Maochan and JingzhuYan. 1988. The characteristic features of the final reduction in the neutral-tone syllable of Beijing Mandarin. *Phonetic Laboratory Annual Report of Phonetic Research*, Phonetic Laboratory, Institute of Linguistics, Chinese Academy of Social Sciences, Beijing, 37–51.

McCarthy, John. 1995. Extensions of faithfulness: Rotuman revisited. MS, University of Massachusetts, Amherst. ▶

McCarthy, John and Alan Prince. 1995. Faithfulness and reduplicative identity. *University of Massachusetts Occasional Papers in Linguistics 18: Papers in Optimality Theory*, ed. by Jill Beckman, Laura Walsh Dickey, and Suzanne Urbanczyk, 249–384. ◀

Moreton, Elliott. 1995. Noncomputable functions in Optimality Theory. MS, University of Massachusetts. ◀

Myers, Scott. 1993. OCP effects in Optimality Theory. MS, University of Texas, Austin. ◀

Myers, Scott and Troi Carleton. 1996. Tonal transfer in Chichewa. *Phonology*, 39–72.

Noyer, Rolf. 1991. Tone and stress in the San Mateo dialect of Huave. *Proceedings of ESCOL VIII*.

Prince, Alan. 1990. Quantitative consequences of rhythmic organization. *Parasession on the Syllable in Phonetics and Phonology*, ed. by M. Ziolkowski, M. Noske, and K. Deaton, 355–98. Chicago: Chicago Linguistic Society.

Prince, Alan and Paul Smolensky. 1993. *Optimality Theory: Constraint Interaction in Generative Grammar*. ◀

Selkirk, Elisabeth. 1994. Class lectures, University of Massachusetts, Amherst. [not available to the author]

Selkirk, Elisabeth O. and Tong Shen. 1990. Prosodic domains in Shanghai Chinese. *The Phonology–Syntax Connection*, ed. by Sharon Inkelas and Draga Zec, 313–38. CSLI.

Shih, Chilin. 1986. *The Prosodic Domain of Tone Sandhi in Mandarin Chinese*. PhD dissertation, University of California, San Diego.

Shih, Chilin. 1989. Mandarin third tone sandhi and prosodic structure. Paper to appear in Wang Jialing and Norval Smith, eds., *Studies in Chinese Phonology*. Dordrecht: Foris.

Sietsema, Brian. 1988. *Metrical Dependencies in Tone Assignment*. PhD dissertation, MIT.

Xie, Zili. 1982. Suzhou fangyan lianzizu de liandu biandiao [Tone sandhi in Suzhou bisyllables]. *Fangyan*, 245–64.

Ye, Xiangling. 1979. Suzhou fangyan de liandu biandiao [Tone sandhi in the Suzhou dialect]. *Fangyan* 1, 30–46.

Yip, Moira. 1980. *The Tonal Phonology of Chinese*. PhD dissertation, MIT. [New York: Garland Publishing.]

Yip, Moira. 1999. Feet, tonal reduction and speech rate at the word and phrase level in Chinese. In René Kager and Wim Zonneveld, eds., *Phrasal Phonology*. Nijmegen: Nijmegen University Press, 171–94.

Yip, Moira. 2002. *Tone*. Cambridge: Cambridge University Press.

Zhengzhang, Shangfeng. 1964. Wenzhou fangyande liandu shengdiao [Wenzhou dialect tone sandhi]. *Zhongguo Yuwen*, 106–52.

Zoll, Cheryl. 1996. *Parsing Below the Segment in a Constraint-based Framework*. PhD dissertation, University of California, Berkeley. ▶

Study and Research Questions

1   Summarize the argument for why tones must be protected by MAX constraints instead of (or in addition to?) IDENT constraints. Do the examples discussed later in the chapter provide further support for this argument?

2   Summarize the argument for why distinct HEADSYLL-MAX(T) and HEADFOOT-MAX(T) constraints are required (see (18), (19)). Then redo the factorial typology in section 2.3 using these constraints. (To understand the typology, you will need to consider longer inputs like those in (22).)

3   The definition of HEADMAX in (11) is fairly complicated. Analyze the clauses of this definition and explain whether and why this complexity is necessary.

Chapter 13 | Scott Myers

OCP Effects in Optimality Theory

Editor's Note

This chapter shows compellingly how the idea of constraint violability resolves a problem that once seemed intractable. The Obligatory Contour Principle – "adjacent identical tones are prohibited" (so tonal contours are obligatory) – was originally proposed by Goldsmith (1976) as a kind of deduction from Leben's (1973) suprasegmental tone theory. Though initially it was understood as a restriction on underlying tones, it was later argued to trigger and block processes and to affect segments and features as well as tones (Archangeli 1986; Hewitt and Prince 1989; Itô 1984; McCarthy 1986; Mester 1988; Myers 1986; Yip 1988). Despite this explanatory success, though, the OCP has a problem: not every language respects it, and even within a language some phenomena might respect it and others ignore it. This on-again/off-again character of the OCP led to deep skepticism and even outright rejection on the part of some (Goldsmith 1990; Odden 1986, 1988). This chapter resolves the problem and vindicates the OCP: it is not always in force because it is a ranked, violable constraint. Violability of constraints leads to expected non-uniformity of structure, as was first noted by Alan Prince (see McCarthy 2002: 121–9).

After reading this chapter, it may be useful to read chapter 20 and the references there, as well as Keer (1999).

The Obligatory Contour Principle (OCP) forbids representations in which identical elements are adjacent. A sequence of two high tones, for example, is avoided in a variety of ways: one of the tones is deleted or retracted away from the other, or the two are fused into a single high tone. Processes that would create such a sequence are blocked. The problem is how to derive all these different ways of avoiding this configuration from a single principle.

It is argued here that Optimality Theory (OT) provides the means to derive the full range of dissimilatory effects from the OCP, through the ranking of the OCP with Faithfulness constraints.

[...]

Excerpt from:
Myers, Scott (1997) OCP effects in Optimality Theory. *Natural Language and Linguistic Theory* 15: 847–92. [Available on Rutgers Optimality Archive, ROA-6.]

2   The OCP in Three Bantu Tone Systems

Interpreted as an OT constraint, the OCP assigns a violation for each sequence of identical elements. In the case of tone, it assigns a violation for each pair of identical adjacent tones. The effects of this constraint depend on its interaction with other constraints.

I will argue that the ranking of the OCP with respect to the Faithfulness constraints enables us to capture the diverse effects of the OCP, both active and passive. We will look at dissimilatory patterns in tone in three Bantu languages: Shona (Section 2.1), Rimi (Section 2.2), and Kishambaa (Section 2.3) [only Section 2.1 is reprinted here – Ed.]. In each case, we will be looking at what happens when two high tones from different morphemes are brought together through morpheme concatenation.

I focus on what happens when two *high* tones come together because low tone is completely inert in all three languages considered, as in other Bantu languages (Stevick 1969). Tonological patterns in Bantu languages depend on high tones, not low tones. For example, when two high tones are juxtaposed, something generally happens, but nothing happens when two low-toned syllables are juxtaposed. Moreover, low-toned syllables are also phonetically inert. The pitch of low-toned syllables is a function of the pitch of surrounding high tones (Stevick 1969, Myers 1997).

I will therefore assume that the tone contrast in Bantu languages is a privative one between the presence of a high tone and its absence. This is expressed through the following constraint:

(12)   *L

This constraint forbids low tones. It crucially dominates a Faithfulness Constraint in all the Bantu languages under consideration. This insures that no actual output will include a low tone (Prince and Smolensky 1993, pp. 175–196).

2.1   Shona

In this section we will consider tonal alternations in Zezuni Shona, a Bantu language spoken in Zimbabwe, described by Fivaz (1970), Fortune (1985), Myers (1987) and Hewitt (1992). The closely related Karanga dialect has been studied by Odden (1981). Some preliminary assumptions about morphological domains in the language are presented in Section 2.1.1. The configuration of two adjacent high tones, forbidden by the OCP, is avoided in Shona in four different ways, discussed in Sections 2.1.2–2.1.5, respectively.

2.1.1   Domains

In Shona, as in other Bantu languages, tone alternations are often restricted so that they occur in one set of morphological constructions, but not in others. Myers (1987, to appear) argues that this morphological conditioning can be stated in terms of three domains: *stem*, *macrostem*, and *phonological word*.

Only the distinction between the macrostem and the phonological word will be important in the following analysis. The *macrostem* (Hyman and Ngunga 1994, Myers, to appear) consists of the stem (i.e. the root plus suffixes) and optional prefixes, as in (13). The macrostem prefixes include the object marker (as in (13a)), and the subject and tense markers of the subjunctive, participial, and negative inflections (designated Subject$_{macro}$ and Tense$_{macro}$, as in (13b) and (13c)). The minimal macrostem is a stem, as in (13d).

(13)   Macrostem: [(Subject$_{macro}$ – Tense$_{macro}$) – (Object) – Root – (Suffix)* – (Term)]

    a.   . . . [mú-ón-á]   as in kumúóná 'to see him/her'
         him/her-see-term

    b.   [tí-ón-é]
         1stpl/subjunctive-see-term
         we see (subjunctive)

    c.   [va-chí-tárís-a]
         3rdpl-present participial-look-term
         while/if they are seeing

    d.   . . . [gar-o]   as in chigaro 'chair'
         sit-term

In the examples that follow, macrostems will be delimited with square brackets.

The *phonological word* (PW) consists of a lexical macrostem (e.g., noun or verb) preceded by optional clitics, as in (14). The clitics in Shona include the copula, the prepositions ("associative markers"), the class markers, and all the inflectional prefixes that aren't included in the macrostem. Examples are given in (14d–f).

(14)   a.   PW: Macrostem$_{lexical}$
    b.   PW: Clitic PW
    c.   Clitic: Copula, Preposition, Class, Subj$_{clitic}$ + Tense$_{clitic}$, . . .

    d.   [í][banga]
         copula-knife
         (it) is a knife

    e.   [né][banga]
         with-knife
         with a knife

    f.   [ndi-chá][teng-a]
         1stsg-fut-buy-term
         I will buy

Phonological words are marked off in the following examples with spaces, as in the orthography.

I will assume these domains in the following analysis because they simplify the reference to morpheme classes in Shona, but they are not crucial to the analysis. Any analysis, whether derivational or constraint-based, must distinguish the relevant classes of morphological constructions in some way. The skeptical reader can interpret references to the macrostem and phonological word domains as merely referring to the sets of morphological constructions subsumed under those terms, as summarized in (13) and (14).

2.1.2   Meeussen's Rule

The first of the ways in which OCP violations are avoided in Shona is found when a high-tone-initial word is preceded by a high-toned clitic (i.e. a high-toned member of the morpheme classes in (14c)). In this case, there is lowering of the whole high-toned sequence after the clitic, as in (15). The underlyingly high toned vowels are underlined, here and henceforth.[6]

(15)   a.   [í][ba̱nga]
            copula-knife
            (it) is a knife
            cf. báṉgá 'knife'

       b.   [vá] [se̱ku̱ru]
            2a-grandfather
            grandfather (honorific)
            cf. sé̱kú̱ru 'grandfather'

       c.   [ndi-chá̱][te̱ng-es-a]
            1stsg-future-buy-causative-term
            I will sell
            cf. [ku][té̱ng-és-á] 'to sell'[7]

       d.   [v-á̱][te̱ng-es-a]
            3rdpl-past-buy-causative-term
            they sold
            cf. [ku][té̱ng-és-á] 'to sell'

This process is known as Meeussen's Rule (Goldsmith 1984).

In a derivational analysis (e.g., Myers 1987), one would posit a rule deleting a high tone after a high tone, as in (16).

(16)   a. $H \rightarrow \emptyset$ / H __ (Phonological word)
       b.   H   H   H
            | ⋀ |
            i ba   nga   →   i ba nga

The problem with this account is that it does not relate the operation of tone deletion to the crosslinguistic generalization that a sequence of high tones is avoided. It thus does not relate this way of avoiding a sequence of high tones to the other ways discussed above in (4)–(7) [omitted here]. The OT account, on the other hand, can make this connection.

In OT, deletion of a tone occurs if an output constraint dominates MAX-IO (T), the member of the MAX constraint family that requires a tone in the input to have a correspondent in the output. The input in the Meeussen's Rule cases violates the OCP, so we can account for the deletion by ranking the OCP over MAX-IO (T). It is higher priority in Shona to obey the OCP than it is to keep all the underlying high tones.

But what determines that it is the second high tone that is deleted and the first one that survives? I propose that the relevant constraint is of the ALIGN family (McCarthy and Prince 1993b):

(17)   ALIGN-L: ALIGN (H, L, PWd, L)

ALIGN-L requires that the left edge of each tone (defined as the left edge of the leftmost syllable associated with that tone) be aligned with the left edge of the prosodic word. A violation is assessed for each syllable that separates a given tone from that edge.

The influence of this constraint is seen in the tendency of tones in Shona to associate with the leftmost available tone bearer, as illustrated in (18).[8]

(18)   a.   *H of the verb root*
            [téng-és-ér-a]   (*tengésérá)   [kángánw-á]   (*kangánwá)
            buy-causative-applicative-term   *forget-term*
            sell to!   forget!

       b.   *Copula /H/*
            [chí] [gár-o]   cf. [chi][gár-o]
            7/copula-sit-nominalizer   *7-sit-nominalizer*
            (it) is a chair   chair

       c.   *Participial /H/*
            [ndí-cha-téng-a]
            1stsg/participial-future participial-buy-term
            I having bought

            cf. [ndi-chá][teng-a]
                1stsg-future-buy-term
                I will buy

The tone of a verb root is always associated with the first syllable of the verb stem, as in (18a).[9] There is no lexical contrast in the position of tones in verb roots. The floating high tone marking the copular form of a noun, as in (18b), is always associated with the first syllable of the noun (i.e. the first class marker), and the floating high tone marking the participial form of a verb, as in (18c), is always associated with the first syllable of the verb (i.e. the subject marker). ALIGN-L reflects the general crosslinguistic preference for left-to-right association of tones (Pulleyblank 1986), a preference that can be motivated by considerations of speech perception (Myers, in press).

The Meeussen's Rule pattern can be expressed through the following ranking:

(19)   Meeussen's Rule Pattern: OCP ≫ MAX-IO (T) ≫ ALIGN-L

MAX-IO (T) must dominate ALIGN-L, because high tones do occur in non-initial position (e.g., *badzá* 'hoe'). If ALIGN-L dominated MAX-IO (T), then the best way to satisfy alignment in this case would be to delete the offending tone (*badza).[10]

The evaluation of *íbanga* (15a) is as in tableau (20):

(20)   Input: H_1 H_2
             | ∧
             i   banga

Candidates	OCP	Max-IO(T)	Align-L
a. H_1 H_2 	∧ i banga	*!		*
b. H_1 ☞ | i banga		*	
c. H_2 ∧ i banga		*	*!

Candidate (20a) violates the OCP, the highest ranked constraint, and so is less harmonic (optimal) than either of the less faithful candidates (20b) or (20c). Both of these candidates violate Max-IO (T). Candidate (20c), however, violates Align-L as well, which leaves (20b) as the optimal candidate.

In the Meeussen's Rule pattern, the OCP, an output constraint, triggers a dissimilatory change because it dominates a Faithfulness Constraint, Max-IO (T). Other potential ways of avoiding the OCP violation are ruled out by ranking Max-IO (T) below other Faithfulness constraints, so that deletion of the tone is the optimal solution. Consider the candidates in (21), all of which obey the OCP.

(21)   Input: H_1 H_2
             | ∧
             i   banga

Candidates	Violated constraint

a. $H_{1,2}$
         ∧
         i banga
	Uniformity-IO (T)

b. H_1 H_2 	∧ i i banga	Dep-IO (σ)
c. H_1 L H_2 	∧ i banga	Dep-IO (T), *L

Candidate (21a), with fusion of the two input high tones into one output tone, violates UNIFORMITY (T), which requires that correspondence be one-to-one. Candidates (21b) and (21c), with insertion of a buffer syllable or a buffer tone, violate different members of the DEP-IO family. All of these Faithfulness constraints must be ranked above MAX-IO (T) to guarantee that (20b) is the optimal output.

2.1.3   Blocking of tone spread

Another tone pattern in Shona in which a sequence of high tones is avoided is tone spread. A high tone on a syllable followed by a toneless syllable in another morpheme spreads onto that toneless syllable. This occurs, for example, when a high-toned clitic precedes a low-tone-initial word, as in (22a–c).

(22)   a.   [í][sádza]   cf. [sadza] 'porridge'
           copula-porridge
           (it) is porridge

       b.   [ti-chá][véreng-a]   cf. [ku][vereng-a]
           1stpl-future-read-term   *infinitive-read-term*
           we will read   to read

       c.   [ndi-ngá][véreng-e]   cf. (b)
           1stsg-potential-read-term
           I could read

       d.   [bázi]
           branch

       e.   [í][badzá]   cf. [badzá] 'hoe'
           copula-hoe
           (it) is a hoe

However, spread fails to occur if the target syllable is in the same morpheme as the trigger, as in (22d), or if it is followed by a high-toned syllable, as in (22e). Spread in the latter case would create a violation of the OCP.

   To analyze this blocking pattern, we must first account for the spread. In any case of spread, the output has associations that have no counterpart in the input. None of the feature specifications change when a specification is spread, but the position of the specification vis-à-vis other specifications does change. The default, as usual, is to have no change. To express this, we need a Faithfulness constraint that takes as its argument the associations themselves (cf. Pulleyblank 1994):

(23)   DEP-IO (A): An association in the output must have a correspondent in the input.

An association is a binary relation between two elements, so there is no question of a tone association if either the tone or the tone-bearer are missing. Therefore, DEP-IO (A) is violated if and only if (a) there is an output tone T' that has an input correspondent T, (b) there is an output syllable S' that has an input correspondent S, and (c) T' is associated with S' but T is not associated with S.

For there to be spread, this Faithfulness constraint must be dominated. I assume that the basic driving force behind spread is a requirement that syllables bear tones:

(24)   SPECIFY (T): A syllable must be associated with a tone.

This constraint is equivalent to a clause of the Well-Formedness Condition of Goldsmith (1976). McCarthy and Prince (1995, p. 266) note that it can be interpreted as a member of the MAX family of constraints, since it requires an element of one subrepresentation (the tone-bearing tier) to have a correspondent in another subrepresentation (the tone tier). DEP-IO (T), which forbids the insertion of tone, must dominate SPECIFY (T), since otherwise the optimal output for a toneless input would have an inserted high tone associated with all its syllables.[11]

If SPECIFY (T) dominates DEP-IO (A), then the optimal output for an input with a high tone will, all else being equal, have that high tone spread to all the syllables in the form, leaving none unspecified. But the correct output has the high tone spread just one syllable to the right. We therefore need constraints to limit spread.

Consider first the direction of spread. Spread is always rightward in Shona. We can express this with a Faithfulness constraint requiring the preservation of the left edge of a 'tone span', i.e. the string of all the syllables associated with the same (high) tone.

(25)   ANCHOR-L (preliminary formulation): If an output syllable S' is the leftmost syllable in a tone span then its input correspondent S is the leftmost syllable in a tone span.

ANCHOR-L requires that the left edge of any tone in the output correspond to a left edge in the input (cf. ANCHOR-L-FT in McCarthy 1995). Any leftward spread violates this constraint, since in such a case the left edge of the tone span in the output is shifted to the left in comparison to the input.

Now consider the limit of spread to one syllable. It's important to note here that tone spans in Shona are not limited to two syllables. In the phrase *kuténgésá sádza* 'to sell porridge', for example, only the verb root /-téng-/ is underlyingly high-toned.[12] Spread therefore can't be limited by limiting tone spans. Rather, a high tone on a syllable at the end of one macrostem or phonological word spreads onto a syllable in another macrostem or phonological word, but a nonfinal high tone does not spread to another syllable in the same domain. Thus there is no spread within a morpheme such as *bázi* in (22d), and the spread in such a form as [*tichá*][*vérenga*] in (22b) does not continue further into the stem as in *[*tichá*][*véréngá*]. We can express this generalization as in (26).

(26)   BOUND: Successive syllables in a tone span must be in different domains.

Underlying tones within a morpheme are not eliminated, so BOUND must be dominated by MAX-IO (T) and MAX-IO (A). The constraint only has decisive effects on inserted association lines, limiting them to domain edges.[13]

To limit spread, both BOUND and ANCHOR-L must dominate SPECIFY (T). The crucial rankings involved in spread are thus as in (27):

(27) Spread pattern: BOUND, ANCHOR-L ≫ SPECIFY (T) ≫ DEP-IO (A)

Spread is triggered through the domination of the Faithfulness constraint DEP-IO (A) by the output constraint SPECIFY (T). Spread is blocked if it is leftward or unbounded through the domination of that output constraint by the higher constraints BOUND and ANCHOR-L.

The tableau in (28) illustrates how this constraint ranking accounts for the choice of output in the case of *tichávérenga* in (22b).

(28) Input: H_1

|

    [ticha][verenga]

Candidates	ANCHOR-L	BOUND	SPECIFY (T)	DEP-IO (A)
a. H | [ticha][verenga]			****!	
b. ☞ H /\\ [ticha][verenga]			***	*
c. H /\\\\ [ticha][verenga]		*!	**	**
d. H /\\ [ticha][verenga]	*!		***	*

Candidate (28b) is more harmonic than (28a) because it violates SPECIFY (T) less severely. The other candidates violate more highly ranked constraints. Candidate (28c), with the tone spread onto more than one syllable, crucially violates BOUND, since high-toned *ré* is not adjacent to a domain edge. Candidate (28d), with leftward spread of the high tone, violates ANCHOR-L. The optimal candidate is thus (28b), with the high tone of *chá* spread one syllable to the right.

Having outlined an analysis of tone spread, we can now return to the fact that spread is blocked if it would create an OCP violation, as in (22e). We can express this blocking by ranking the OCP above the constraint SPECIFY (T) that motivates spread. We see this in the tableau (29), of example (22e).

(29)   Input: H_1 H_2

         i - badza

Candidates	OCP	Max-IO (T)	Specify (T)	Dep-IO (A)
a. ☞ H_1 H_2 i ba dza			*	

b.
    H_1 H_2
 	
    i ba dza
	*!			*

c.
    H_1
 	
    i ba dza
		*!		**

Candidate (29a) violates SPECIFY (T) because the medial syllable is toneless. This candidate is nevertheless more harmonic than (29b), with spread of the first high tone, because this violates the OCP. Candidate (29c) obeys the OCP, but violates MAX-IO (T) because one of the input high tones has been deleted. The optimal candidate is therefore (29a), without spread.

We have seen the OCP in both an active and a passive role. In the Meeussen's Rule pattern, the OCP triggers tone deletion. In OT, this is expressed through the domination of the OCP over the Faithfulness constraint MAX-IO (T). In the tone spread pattern, on the other hand, the OCP blocks tone spread. Tone spread occurs because the output constraint SPECIFY (T) dominates the Faithfulness constraint DEP-IO (A). Blocking occurs because the OCP in turn dominates SPECIFY (T).

2.1.4   Tone slip

The third tone pattern in Shona that displays an avoidance of a sequence of two high tones is illustrated in (30). Affected vowels are italicized.

(30)   a.   báng*a* g*ú*r*ú*   cf. bángá 'knife', gúrú 'big'
           big knife

       b.   [á-ch*a*][téng-á]   cf. [á-chá][véreng-a]
           3rdsg-future-buy-term   *3sg-future-read-term*
           he/she will buy   he/she will read

c. [á-cha̱] [té̱ng-a] [bá̱ngá]   cf. (a), (b).
    he/she will buy a knife

When a high tone span of more than one syllable precedes another high tone span, the last syllable of the first span is lowered, separating the two spans. One consequence of this is the neutralization of the contrast between word-final HL as in *bázi* 'branch' and word-final HH, as in *bángá* 'knife'. Before a H-initial word, only HL occurs.[14]

This dissimilation process applies wherever the appropriate tone configuration arises, regardless of morphological level. The process affects only one syllable, not a whole high-toned span as in the case of Meeussen's Rule. In a derivational analysis, therefore, we would posit a delinking rule, as in (31) (cf. Myers 1987):

(31) *Tone Slip*: H   H
                   /\ˣ |
                  σ σ σ

This rule, like Meeussen's Rule (16a), takes an input that violates the OCP and converts it into an output that obeys the OCP. Tone deletion (Meeussen's Rule) occurs if the first of the two high tones is associated to only one, and otherwise tone delinking (Tone Slip) occurs.

To distinguish tone deletion from tone delinking in OT we need to distinguish the constraint requiring preservation of underlying tones (MAX-IO (T)) from a constraint requiring the preservation of underlying associations:

(32) MAX-IO (A): A tone association in the input must have a correspondent in the output.

Parallel to DEP-IO (A) in (23), we assume that MAX-IO (A) is only violated when (a) an input tone *T* has an output correspondent *T′*, (b) an input syllable *S* has an output correspondent *S′*, and (c) *T* is associated with *S* but *T′* is not associated with *S′*. Thus if a tone is deleted, that violates MAX-IO (T) but not MAX-IO (A). Only delinking violates MAX-IO (A).

The tone slip pattern arises from the following ranking:

(33) Tone Slip pattern: OCP, ANCHOR-L ≫ MAX-IO (T) ≫ MAX-IO (A)

The OCP dominates both MAX-IO constraints, because deletion of tones or associations is allowed if it alleviates an OCP violation. MAX-IO (T) must dominate MAX-IO (A), because in forms such as those in (30), tone delinking is preferred to tone deletion. Undominated ANCHOR-L captures the fact that it is the left tone that retracts away from the right tone, rather than the reverse. Retraction of a tone rightward would shift the position of the left edge of a tone span, violating ANCHOR-L.

Tableau (34) illustrates the evaluation of example (30a).

(34) Input: H₁   H₂
                 $\wedge$ $\wedge$
             banga guru

Candidates	OCP	ANCHOR-L	MAX-IO (T)	MAX-IO (A)
a. H₁ H₂ $\wedge$ $\wedge$ banga guru	*!			
b. ☞ H₁ H₂ | $\wedge$ banga guru				*
c. H₁ H₂ $\wedge$ | banga guru		*!		*
d. H₁ $\wedge$ banga guru			*!	

The faithful candidate (34a) is less harmonic than (34b) because the former violates the OCP and the latter doesn't. Of the candidates that pass this first test, (34c) is excluded because it violates ANCHOR-L. The output syllable *rú* in this candidate is the left edge of a tone span in the output, but it does not correspond to the left edge of a tone span in the input. Candidate (34d), with deletion of the second tone, is less harmonic than (34b) because it violates MAX-IO (T), which is higher ranked than MAX-IO (A). The optimal output is therefore (34b), with tone slip.

If delinking a tone is preferable to deleting a tone, why is there tone deletion in the Meeussen's Rule cases? In those cases, the first high tone is associated with only one syllable. Thus delinking that tone would yield a floating tone. We can account for the fact that delinking does not happen in this case if we posit a constraint ruling out floating tones:

(35) *FLOAT: A tone must be associated with a syllable.

Such a constraint is part of Goldsmith's (1976) Well-Formedness Conditions. McCarthy and Prince (1995, p. 266) point out that it can be subsumed as a member of the DEP family, since it requires that an element in one representation (the tone tier) have a correspondent in another representation (the tone-bearing tier), the inverse of SPECIFY (T). Given such a constraint, a form such as *íbanga* (15a) is evaluated as in tableau (36).

(36)   Input: H$_1$ H$_2$

        | $\wedge$

        i   banga

Candidates	OCP	*FLOAT	ANCHOR-L	MAX-IO (T)	MAX-IO (A)

a.
 	
☞   H$_1$
 	
      |
 	
   i banga
				*	

b.
 	
   H$_1$ H$_2$
 	
     $\wedge$
 	
   i banga
		*!			*

Candidate (36a), with deletion of the second high tone, is more harmonic than (36b), with delinking of the first high tone, because delinking leaves a floating high tone in violation of *FLOAT.[15]

There is one more candidate that needs to be excluded – *íbánga* – with the high tone of the stem deleted and the high tone of the clitic *í* spread one syllable to the right, as in (37).

(37)   Input: H$_1$ H$_2$

        | $\wedge$

        i   banga

Candidates	OCP	*FLOAT	ANCHOR-L	MAX-IO (T)	MAX-IO (A)	SPECIFY (T)
H$_1$ $\wedge$ i banga				*		*

As the constraints stand, candidate (37) is more harmonic than the actual output (36a), since it ties with that candidate on all the higher constraints, but better satisfies SPECIFY (T). I would suggest that what is wrong with this candidate is that it fails to preserve the left edge of a tone span. The syllable *bá* is at the left edge of a high tone span in the input, but not in the output. We can exclude such a case by revising ANCHOR-L, as in (38):

(38) ANCHOR-L (final formulation): Assign a violation if and only if:
    (a)   there is an output syllable S' that has an input correspondent S,
    (b)   both S and S' bear tone, and
    (c)   either S or S' is the leftmost syllable associated with its tone, and its correspondent syllable is not the leftmost syllable associated with its tone.

According to this formulation, if an input syllable and an output syllable correspond and bear tone, then they must correspond in whether they are a left edge of a tone span.

   Given this reformulation, the candidate in (37), repeated here as (39b), now violates ANCHOR-L, since the syllable *bá* is at the left edge of a tone span in the input, but noninitial in a tone span in the output. The actual output (39a), on the other hand, does not violate ANCHOR-L, since the only syllable that bears tone in both the input and the output, *í*, is a left edge in both.

(39)   Input: H$_1$ H$_2$

                     | /\

                 i banga

Candidates	OCP	*FLOAT	ANCHOR-L	MAX-IO (T)	MAX-IO (A)	SPECIFY (T)

a.
☞ H$_1$
    |
  i banga
				*		**

b.
   H$_1$
   /\\
  i banga
			*!	*		*

Candidate (39a) is now correctly selected as the optimal candidate.[16]

2.1.5 Fusion

The fourth way in which OCP violations are avoided in Shona occurs only within the macrostem. If a high tone on a single syllable is juxtaposed with another high tone within the macrostem, the Meeussen's Rule pattern never results. Both high-toned morphemes remain high-toned, as in (40).[17]

(40)   a.   [ku]-[mú-téng-és-ér-a]
             infinitive-object-buy-causative-applied-term
             to sell to him/her

cf. [ku]-[mú-véréng-er-a]
infinitive-object-read-applied-term
to read to him/her

b.   [tí-téng-és-é]
1stpl/subjunctive-buy-causative-term
we should sell

cf. [tí-tárís-e]
1stpl/subjunctive-look-term
we would look

It might appear that in these constructions violations of the OCP are simply toler-ated. There is evidence, however, that the OCP-violating sequences are subject to a fusion operation, which converts the sequence of two tones into a single multiply-linked high tone. This evidence is provided by hortative constructions in which forms as in (40b) occur after a high-toned clitic (Myers 1987).

(41)   a.   [há][ti-tengese]
hortative-1stpl/subjunctive-buy-causative-term
let us sell

b.   [há][ti-tarise]
hortative-1stpl/subjunctive-look-term
let us look

The hortative form consists of the hortative prefix *há-* followed by the subjunctive form (cf. 40b). All the high tones in the subjunctive macrostem are deleted after the hortative marker – an instance of the Meeussen's Rule pattern. The subjunctive forms that have two underlying high tones pattern with regard to this lowering like the subjunctive forms with just one underlying high tone.

Myers (1987) accounts for these facts by positing a cycle-final operation of OCP Fusion: $\underline{H\ H} \rightarrow \underline{H}$. Such an operation has been motivated in other tone languages (Leben 1978, Kenstowicz and Kidda 1987), and McCarthy (1986) argues that such a fusion is built into Tier Conflation. Once the two high tones have been fused, they act as a single multiply-linked tone.

To account for these facts within OT, we must make some assumptions as to how sensitivity to morphological domains is to be expressed in that model. It is well-established that phonological patterns are different in different morphologically-defined domains. In a derivational model, this is expressed by assigning rules to the appropriate domains (Kiparsky 1985). Following McCarthy and Prince's (1993a) analysis of Axininca Campa, I will assume here that each domain has an independent constraint ranking. In this approach, the output of one domain is taken as the input of the succeeding domain.[18]

Fusion of two input tones to form one output tone is a violation of UNIFORMITY-IO (T), which requires correspondence to be one-to-one (Lamontagne and Rice 1995, McCarthy 1995). The fusion takes an input that violates the OCP and yields an output that obeys the OCP, so we can conclude that the OCP dominates

UNIFORMITY-IO (T) in the macrostem domain in Shona. However, we know that the OCP is dominated by the UNIFORMITY-IO (T) in the phonological word domain, since fusion is never an option when a high-toned clitic is juxtaposed with a high tone (cf. (15)).

The crucial ranking differences, then, are as in (42):[19]

(42) a. Macrostem: OCP ≫ MAX-IO (T) ≫ UNIFORMITY-IO (T) ≫ MAX-IO (A)

      b. Phonological word: UNIFORMITY-IO (T), OCP ≫ MAX-IO (T) ≫ MAX-IO (A)

The evaluation of the subjunctive macrostem *títéngése* in (40b) is then as in (43).

(43) Input: H_1 H_2

      [ti- teng-es-e]

Candidates	OCP	MAX-IO (T)	UNIFORMITY (T)
a. H_1　　H_2 [ti tengese]	*!		
b. H_1 [ti tengese]		*!	
c. ☞ $H_{1,2}$ [ti tengese]			*

Candidate (43a) faithfully preserves the two input tones, but fatally violates the OCP. This renders this candidate less harmonic than candidate (43b), with deletion of the second tone. However, this candidate is in turn less harmonic than candidate (43c) with fusion of the two tones. Candidate (43c) is therefore the optimal output.

The output form of the macrostem (43c) serves as part of the input for the phonological word that is derived from that macrostem: *hátitengese* as in (41a). This form is subject to evaluation against the constraint ranking in (42b), as illustrated in tableau (44). Correspondence indices are assigned by GEN (McCarthy and Prince 1995), and so are not maintained from the macrostem evaluation in (43).

(44)   Input: H₁   H₂

[ha] [ti-teng-es-e]

Candidates	OCP	UNIFORMITY (T)	MAX-IO (T)
a. H₁ H₂ [ha] [ti-teng-es-e]	*!		
b. ☞ H₁ [ha] [ti-teng-es-e]			*
c. H₁,₂ [ha] [ti-teng-es-e]		*!	

The faithful candidate (44a) violates the OCP and so is less harmonic than candidate (44b) with a deleted tone. Candidate (44c), with tone fusion, is also less harmonic than (44b), since in this domain a violation of UNIFORMITY (T) is more serious than one of MAX-IO (T). The optimal form is (44b).[20]

In other forms, tone fusion interacts with tone slip. In the form *áchaténgá* in (45), for example, there are three high-toned morphemes: the subject marker /á/, the future marker /chá/, and the root /-téng-/ 'buy'.

(45)   [á-cha][téng-á]   cf. [ndi-chá][véreng-a]
       3rdsg-future-buy-term   *1stsg-future-read-term*
       he/she will buy   I will read

The input for the inflectional macrostem in (45) would be as in (46a), with two different high tones. The output, by an evaluation entirely parallel to that in (44), would be as in (46b), with one fused tone.

(46)   a.   Input (Stem): H₁ H₂   b.   Output: H₁,₂

              | | /\
            [a-cha]   [a-cha]

This output is a component of the input for (45) in the phonological word level. Tableau (47) illustrates the evaluation of the form in (45), consisting of the inflectional macrostem in (46b) plus a verb macrostem:

(47)   Input (Phonological Word):   H$_1$ H$_2$

[a cha][tenga]

Candidates	OCP	Uniformity (T)	Max-IO (T)	Max-IO (A)
a. H$_1$ H$_2$ [acha] [tenga]	*!			
b. ☞ H$_1$ H$_2$ [acha] [tenga]				*
c. H$_1$ [acha] [tenga]			*!	
d. H$_{1,2}$ [acha] [tenga]		*!		

Given an input derived from two macrostem-level outputs, the optimal output is one with tone slip (47b), rather than an OCP violation (47a), tone deletion (47c), or tone fusion (47d).

2.1.6   Summary of the Shona analysis

The most important constraint rankings in our analysis as far as the OCP is concerned are summarized in (48).

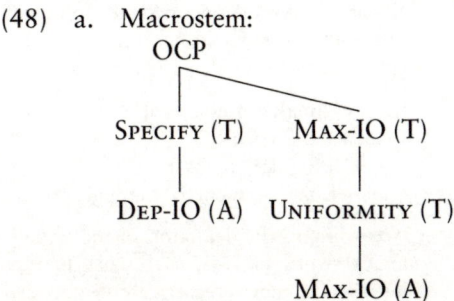

(48)   a.   Macrostem:

OCP

Specify (T)   Max-IO (T)

Dep-IO (A)   Uniformity (T)

Max-IO (A)

b. Phonological word:

$$\text{OCP} \qquad \text{Uniformity (T)}$$

$$\text{Specify (T)} \qquad \text{Max-IO (T)}$$

$$\text{Dep-IO (A)} \qquad \text{Max-IO (A)}$$

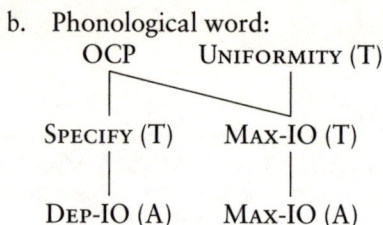

Within the phonological word, the OCP dominates Max-IO (T), yielding the Meeussen's Rule pattern. But tone delinking is the preferred means of avoiding OCP violations where it is possible, so Max-IO (T) dominates Max-IO (A). Spread is due to the domination of Specify (T) over Dep-IO (A). Spread is blocked when it would yield an OCP violation, so the OCP dominates Specify (T). The same rankings hold in the macrostem domain, except that Uniformity (T) is ranked lower than Max-IO (T). This has the consequence that tone fusion is preferred to tone deletion in this domain.[21]

[. . .]

Notes

[. . .]

6   In accordance with Lexicon Optimization (Prince and Smolensky 1993, Inkelas 1995), I assume that the underlying representation is as fully specified as possible. Thus the high tone of the verb root /téng/ in (13c) and (13d) is assumed to be underlyingly associated, although this association is predictable. An input with a floating tone would be mapped to the same output, but would incur violations of Dep-IO (A) that would not be incurred by the alternative input with the associated tone.

7   The high tones on the vowels following /téng/ are due to tone spread. See Sections 2.1.3 and 2.1.5.

8   Tone spread, to be discussed in the next section, is responsible for the strings of high-toned syllables in (18a) and (18b).

9   A high tone within the verb stem occurs on the first syllable of the verb stem, as in [ku][téngéséra] 'to sell to', rather than the first syllable of the phonological word as demanded by Align-L: *[kú][téngéséra]. I assume that there is a dominant constraint requiring that a high tone belonging morphologically to the verb stem must be realized in the verb stem. Satisfying this constraint while minimally violating

Align-L leads to association with the verb-stem-initial position.

10 The output candidate *bádza, with displacement of the tone to satisfy Align-L, violates Max-IO (A) in (32) below.

11 The choice of analysis for spread is not crucial to the argument about OCP blocking effects. One could just as well use an Align constraint to drive spread, as in much recent work in OT (e.g., Cole and Kisseberth 1994).

12 The high tone of the root téng spreads two syllables to the right, as is the usual pattern within a macrostem (see n. 17 below). Then the high tone spreads one syllable further to the right, as is the usual pattern between phonological words.

13 This formulation of Bound allows for spreading beyond one syllable rightward just in the case of a string of monosyllabic clitics, as in (i) (Odden 1981, p. 83):

(i) [Vá][má][zí][mí][chéro]
     2a-6-21-4-fruit
     Mr. Big-ugly-fruits
     (cf. ma-zi-mi-chero 'Big, ugly fruits')

According to the definition of the phonological word in (14), each class marker initiates a new recursively embedded phonological word domain (cf. McCarthy and Prince's (1993a) analysis of Axininca Campa). Thus each syllable in the class markers follows a syllable in another domain, as required by BOUND.

14 Note that because there is a contrast between HH and HL, we cannot derive the alternations in (30) through OCP blocking of spread onto the final syllable. HH words like *bángá* must be distinguished lexically from HL words like *bázi*, and that contrast must be undone in the pre-high-tone context.

15 The candidate in (36b) could also be said to violate another version of the OCP assuming a tier adjacency rather than syllable adjacency (e.g., Myers 1987, Odden 1994).

16 The constraints ANCHOR-L, MAX-IO (A) and DEP-IO (A) are faithfulness constraints requiring preservation of association. An alternative approach would be to use a member of the IDENT-IO family proposed by McCarthy and Prince (1995), requiring that corresponding vowels must have identical tonal specifications. One problem with such a constraint as applied to the pattern we have seen here would be that it would be violated indiscriminately by tone deletion, tone delinking, and tone spread. We have seen, however, these patterns are subject to different conditions in Shona.

Furthermore, such a constraint would treat as equivalent a string with two high tones and a string with one high tone on two syllables. These are not phonetically equivalent representations, however.

17 Within the macrostem, a high tone spreads *two* syllables to the right, rather than one syllable to the right as in the phonological word or between words. The expression of this distinction is not relevant to the issues at hand, so I will not present an analysis here. In tableaux we will consider only candidates with appropriate spreading. On tone spread and tone placement within the macrostem, see Myers (1987) and Hewitt (1992).

18 A promising approach to levels in OT, using output-to-output correspondence, is proposed in Burzio (1994), Benua (1995) and Kenstowicz (1995). We stick to the conservative quasi-serial approach to avoid adding a distracting side issue to the exposition.

19 UNIFORMITY (T) must dominate MAX-IO (A) in the macrostem domain. Fusion occurs only if the first of the two high tones is associated with just one syllable. In cases where the first of the two high tones is associated with more than one syllable, there is tone slip. For examples and discussion, see Myers (1987) and Hewitt and Prince (1989).

20 A reviewer suggests that the lowering in (41a) might just represent a double application of Meeussen's Rule, with lowering of *tí* conditioned by *há* and lowering of *téng* conditioned by *tí*. But Meeussen's Rule applied to three successive high tones generally leads to an alternating HLH output:

(i) [í][mbwa̱][wó]   cf. imbwá̱ 'dog'
     copula-dog-also
     (it) is a dog also

There would also be problems with a rule that lowers all high tones within the macrostem after a high tone. Such a rule would have to apply nonlocally, since the target would often be considerably removed from the trigger. Assuming that phonological processes apply locally, tone fusion is the only way to get the right result in these cases.

21 At the phonological phrase level, where phonological words are juxtaposed with each other, only tone slip occurs and Meeussen's Rule never occurs. There is, for example, no lowering of the tone of *gúrú* in (i), as pointed out by a reviewer:

(i) badzá gúrú
     hoe   big
     a big hoe

Thus at the phonological phrase level, the OCP must dominate MAX-IO (A), but not MAX-IO (T) or UNIFORMITY-IO (T).

References

Beckman, Jill, Laura Dickey, and Suzanne Urbanczyk (eds.): 1995, *Papers in Optimality Theory*, GLSA, Amherst.

Benua, Laura: 1995, 'Identity Effects in Morphological Truncation', in Beckman et al., pp. 77–136.

Burzio, Luigi: 1994, *Principles of English Stress*, Cambridge University Press, Cambridge.

Cole, Jennifer and Charles Kisseberth: 1994, 'An Optimal Domains Theory of Harmony', *Studies in the Linguistic Sciences* 24, 101–14.

Fivaz, Derek: 1970, *Shona Morphophonemics and Morphosyntax*, University of the Witwatersrand Press, Johannesburg.

Fortune, George: 1985, *Shona Grammatical Constructions*, Mercury Press, Harare.

Goldsmith, John: 1976, *Autosegmental Phonology*, Ph.D. dissertation, MIT. Distributed by Indiana University Linguistics Club, Bloomington.

Goldsmith, John: 1984, 'Meeussen's Rule', in M. Aronoff and R. Oehrle, *Language Sound Structure*, MIT Press, Cambridge, MA, pp. 245–59.

Hewitt, Mark: 1992, *Vertical Maximization and Metrical Theory*, unpublished Ph.D. dissertation, Brandeis University.

Hewitt, Mark and Alan Prince: 1989, 'OCP, Locality and Linking: The N. Karanga Verb', in E. Fee and K. Hunt (eds.), *Proceedings of WCCFL 8*, Stanford Linguistics Association, Stanford, pp. 176–91.

Hyman, Larry and Armindo Ngunga: 1994, 'On the Nonuniversality of Tonal Association "Conventions": Evidence from Ciyao', *Phonology* 11, 25–68.

Inkelas, Sharon: 1995, 'The Consequences of Optimization for Underspecification', *NELS* 25, 287–302.

Kenstowicz, Michael: 1995, 'Base-Identity and Uniform Exponence: Alternatives to Cyclicity', in J. Durand and B. Laks (eds.), *Current Trends in Phonology: Models and Methods*, CNRS, Paris, pp. 366–96.

Kenstowicz, Michael and Mairo Kidda: 1987, 'The Obligatory Contour Principle and Tangale Tonology', in D. Odden (ed.), *Current Approaches to African Linguistics, Volume 4*, Foris, Dordrecht, pp. 223–38.

Kiparsky, Paul: 1985, 'Some Consequences of Lexical Phonology', *Phonology Yearbook 2*, 83–138.

Lamontagne, Greg and Keren Rice: 1995, 'A Correspondence Account of Coalescence', in Beckman et al., pp. 221–4.

Leben, Will: 1978, 'The Representation of Tone', in V. Fromkin (ed.), *Tone: A Linguistic Survey*, Academic Press, New York, pp. 177–220.

McCarthy, John: 1986, 'OCP Effects: Gemination and Antigemination', *Linguistic Inquiry* 17, 207–64.

McCarthy, John, 1995, 'Extensions of Faithfulness: Rotuman Revisited', unpublished MS, University of Massachusetts, Amherst. ▶

McCarthy, John and Alan Prince: 1993a, 'Prosodic Morphology I: Constraint Interaction and Satisfaction', MS, University of Massachusetts, Amherst and Rutgers University, New Brunswick. ▶

McCarthy, John and Alan Prince: 1993b, 'Generalized Alignment', in G. Booij and J. van Marle (eds.), *Yearbook of Morphology 1993*, Kluwer, Dordrecht, pp. 79–153. ◀

McCarthy, John and Alan Prince: 1995, 'Faithfulness and Reduplicative Identity', in Beckman et al., pp. 249–384. ◀

Myers, Scott: 1987, *Tone and the Structure of Words in Shona*, Ph.D. dissertation, University of Massachusetts, Amherst. Published 1991 by Garland Press. New York.

Myers, Scott: 1997, 'Surface Underspecification in the Phonetic Implementation of Tone in Chicheŵa', paper presented at the Annual Meeting of the Linguistic Society of America, Chicago, January 2–5, 1997.

Myers, Scott: in press, 'Expressing Phonetic Naturalness in Phonology', in I. Roca (ed.), *Constraints and Derivations in Phonology*, Oxford University Press, Oxford, pp. 125–50. ▶

Myers, Scott: to appear, 'AUX in Bantu Morphology and Phonology', in L. Hyman and C. Kisseberth (eds.), *Theoretical Aspects of Bantu Tone*, CSLI, Stanford. ▶

Odden, David: 1981, *Problems in Tone Assignment in Shona*, unpublished Ph.D. dissertation, University of Illinois at Champaign-Urbana.

Odden, David: 1994, 'Adjacency Parameters in Phonology', *Language* 70, 289–330.

Prince, Alan and Paul Smolensky: 1993, *Optimality Theory: Constraint Interaction in Generative Grammar*, Rutgers Center for Cognitive Science, Piscataway, New Jersey. ◄

Pulleyblank, Douglas: 1986, *Tone in Lexical Phonology*, Reidel, Dordrecht.

Pulleyblank, Douglas: 1994, 'Neutral Vowels in Optimality Theory: A Comparison of Yoruba and Wolof', unpublished MS, University of British Columbia, Vancouver. ►

Stevick, Earl: 1969, 'Tone in Bantu', *International Journal of American Linguistics* 35, 330–41.

Study and Research Questions

1   The constraint ALIGN-L in (17) favors H tone on the initial syllable. In (20), it is used to select which of two adjacent H tones is deleted. Explain how the analysis works when the first H tone is not in the initial syllable, such as (15c).

2   What does factorial typology predict about the candidates in (21)?

3   Could ALIGN-L (17) be substituted for ANCHOR-L in any of the analyses that depend on the latter constraint, such as (34), (36), (37), and (39)?

4   The analysis summarized in (48) presupposes a version of stratal OT, where two different OT grammars (two constraint rankings) are linked serially (see chapter 23). What is the evidence that two different rankings are required? What additional assumptions would be needed to achieve the same results with a single ranking?

5   Read chapter 20, and then reanalyze the tonal OCP in those terms.

Part IV

Segmental Phonology

Chapter 14 | Joe Pater

Austronesian Nasal Substitution and Other NÇ Effects

Editor's Note

It is a fundamental result of OT that the same markedness constraint can be satisfied in different ways in different languages or even under different conditions within a single language (see McCarthy 2002: 93ff for further explanation). This chapter was the first work to exemplify this result for segmental phonology. Moreover, with its attention to the substantive basis for the *NÇ markedness constraint, it helped to initiate the study of functionally based phonological models within OT. It should therefore be read in conjunction with chapter 15, which also addresses this topic.

Introduction

Nasal substitution occurs in Austronesian languages as far flung as Chamorro (Topping 1969, 1973) and Malagasy (Dziwirek 1989), as well as in several African languages (Rosenthall 1989: 50). However, it is most famous for its appearance in the Indonesian *məN*-prefixation paradigm (see e.g., Halle and Clements 1983: 125). Nasal substitution refers to the replacement of a root-initial voiceless obstruent by a homorganic nasal (1a). If the obstruent is voiced, a homorganic cluster results instead (1b). As illustrated by the data in (1c), NÇ (nasal/voiceless obstruent) clusters are permitted root internally:

(1) a. /məN+pilih/   məmilih   'to choose, to vote'
         /məN+tulis/   mənulis   'to write'
         /məN+kasih/   məŋasih   'to give'

     b. /məN+bəli/   məmbəli   'to buy'
         /məN+dapat/   məndapat   'to get, to receive'
         /məN+ganti/   məŋganti   'to change'

Excerpt (with revisions by the author) from:
Pater, Joe (1999) Austronesian nasal substitution and other NÇ effects. In *The Prosody–Morphology Interface*, ed. René Kager, Harry van der Hulst, and Wim Zonneveld, pp. 310–43. Cambridge: Cambridge University Press. [Available on Rutgers Optimality Archive, ROA-160.]

c.   əmpat   'four'
     untuk   'for'
     muŋkin   'possible'

The standard analysis invokes two ordered rules to generate the single nasal from the underlying pair of segments: nasal assimilation, followed by a rule of root-initial, post-nasal, voiceless consonant deletion (e.g., Topping 1973: 49; Onn 1980: 15; Herbert 1986: 252; Teoh 1988: 156; though cf. Lapoliwa 1981: 111, Uhrbach 1987: 72). In this paper, I reanalyze nasal substitution as fusion of the nasal and voiceless obstruent, driven by a phonetically motivated constraint that disallows nasal/voiceless obstruent clusters (*NC̥).

Nasal substitution is just one of a range of processes that languages make use of to rid themselves of NC̥ clusters, which also include post-nasal voicing, nasal deletion, and denasalization. Permutation of the constraint rankings posited for nasal substitution is all that is needed to provide a unified account of these NC̥ effects. Nasal substitution occurs when the anti-fusion constraint LINEARITY is dominated by *NC̥ and the other Faithfulness constraints. Each of the other NC̥ effects is similarly generated when the Faithfulness constraint that it violates falls to the bottom of the hierarchy. Especially strong motivation for a unified treatment of the NC̥ effects comes from the existence of languages in which two of the processes act in a 'conspiracy' (Kisseberth 1970) to eliminate NC̥ clusters. In this paper I provide evidence of conspiracies between nasal substitution and each of nasal deletion and post-nasal voicing, as well as between post-nasal voicing and each of nasal deletion and denasalization.

1   *NC̥

In a wide variety of languages, NC̥ clusters seem to be disfavoured. That is, Input NC̥ (nasal/voiced obstruent) sequences are represented faithfully in the Output, while NC̥'s are somehow altered. The usual result is for the obstruent to be voiced, though there are other possibilities, as enumerated in the Introduction, and below.

The fact that these NC̥ effects, in particular post-nasal voicing, occur with such frequency has long been assumed to stem from the ease of articulation of NC̥ clusters relative to NC̥ (see Kenstowicz and Kisseberth 1979: 37, Herbert 1986), but without a specific hypothesis about the articulatory difficulty inherent in NC̥ being proposed. However, Huffman's (1993: 310) observation that the raising of the velum occurs very gradually during a voiced stop following a nasal segment, with nasal airflow only returning to a value typical of plain obstruents during the release phase, suggests an articulatory basis for an *NC̥ constraint, since an NC̥ cluster allows a more leisurely raising of the velum than an NC̥. Put another way, an NC̥ cluster requires an unnaturally quick velar closure. The fact that this constraint is asymmetrical (i.e. *NC̥, and not *C̥N – see the discussion in section 5) can then be understood in light of Zuckerman's (1972) finding that 'the velum can be lowered more quickly and with greater precision than it can be raised' (Herbert 1986: 195).[1] Ohala and Ohala (1991: 273 – cited in Ohala and Ohala 1993: 239) provide the following complementary perceptually oriented explanation for nasal deletion in the NC̥ configuration:

(2)

    Among the auditory cues for a voiced stop there must be a spectral and amplitude discontinuity with respect to neighbouring sonorants (if any), low amplitude voicing during its closure, and termination in a burst; these requirements are still met even with velic leakage during the first part of the stop as long as the velic valve is closed just before the release and pressure is allowed to build up behind the closure. However, voiceless stops have less tolerance for such leakage because any nasal sound – voiced or voiceless – would undercut either their stop or their voiceless character.

See also Hayes (1999) for a somewhat different hypothesis about the phonetic grounding of *NC̥.

    Additional evidence for the markedness of NC̥ clusters comes from Smith's (1973: 53) observation that they emerged considerably later than NC̥'s in his son's speech, with the nasal consonant of adult NC̥'s being deleted in the child's production. This pattern has also been observed in the speech of learners of Greek (Drachman and Malikouti-Drachman 1973) and Spanish (Vogel 1976). Thus, data from typology, phonetics, and acquisition all converge on the existence of a universal, but violable, *NC̥ constraint:

(3)   *NC̥
    No nasal/voiceless obstruent sequences

One of the primary strengths of a constraint-based theory like Optimality Theory is that phonetically grounded contextual markedness statements like *NC̥ can be directly incorporated into the phonology (Mohanan 1993: 98, Prince and Smolensky 1993: §5, Archangeli and Pulleyblank 1995; see Flemming 1995, Hayes 1999, Jun 1995, Kirchner 1995, and Steriade 1995b for extensive development of this sort of approach within Optimality Theory). In what follows, I demonstrate how the interaction between *NC̥ and constraints on Input–Output Correspondence creates grammars that generate nasal substitution, as well as the other NC̥ effects.[2]

2   *NC̥ and Segmental Correspondence

2.1   Segmental fusion

Rather than positing discrete steps of nasal assimilation and voiceless consonant deletion, or of complete assimilation of the voiceless consonant to the nasal and degemination (Uhrbach 1987: 72; cf. Herbert 1986: 252), I assume that the relationship between Input *maN+pilih* and Ouput *məmilih* is mediated by fusion, or coalescence of segments (Lapoliwa 1981: 111).

To formalize the fusional Input–Output mapping, I draw on McCarthy and Prince's (1994b, 1995, 1999) proposal that the relationship between Input and Output is directly assessed by constraints on Correspondence. In this theory, deletion is penalized by a MAX constraint that demands that every segment in the Input map to a segment in the Output, in other words, that every Input segment have an Output correspondent. Fusion is a two-to-one mapping from Input to Output: two Input segments stand in correspondence with a single Output segment (McCarthy and Prince 1995; see also Gnanadesikan 1995 and Lamontagne and Rice 1995). This mapping satisfies MAX, as shown in (4), where subscripting is used to indicate the crucial correspondence relationship:

(4)   məN$_1$+p$_2$ilih (Input)   məm$_{1,2}$ilih (Output)

Even though fusion satisfies MAX, it does incur violations of other constraints. At the featural level, fusion between non-identical segments violates constraints demanding Identity between Input and Output segments (see section 3 below for elaboration of Identity constraints, and for an example in which NC̥ fusion is over-ruled by a Featural Identity constraint). Because fusion incurs violations of Featural Identity, it tends to occur between segments that are identical, or nearly so (cf. McCarthy and Prince 1993a: 163, where fusion is restricted to identical elements). However, even fusion between identical segments is not automatic or universal, so it must violate at least one constraint other than Featural Identity. One such constraint is LINEARITY, which is independently needed in Correspondence Theory to militate against metathesis.[3] McCarthy and Prince's (1995) formulation of LINEARITY is as in (5), where S$_1$ and S$_2$ refer to Input and Output strings (or any other string of correspondent segments, such as Base and Reduplicant):

(5)   LINEARITY
      S$_1$ reflects the precedence structure of S$_2$, and vice versa.

In the fusional I,O relationship depicted in (4), /N/ precedes /p/ in the Input, but not in the Output, so LINEARITY is violated.[4] To command a violation of LINEARITY, *NC̥ must be ranked above the Faithfulness constraint, as illustrated in the tableau in (6). Unless noted otherwise, all of the following tableaux apply to Indonesian.

(6)   Nasal substitution: *NC̥ ≫ LIN

Input: məN$_1$+p$_2$ilih	NC̥	LIN
a. ☞ məm$_{1,2}$ilih		*
b. məm$_1$p$_2$ilih	* !	

2.2   Morphological conditions on fusion

The fact that fusion violates LINEARITY leads to a straightforward account of the lack of root-internal nasal substitution in Indonesian. McCarthy and Prince (1994b)

and Urbanczyk (1996) show that a large number of disparate phonological phenomena, reduplicative and otherwise, result from stricter Faithfulness requirements
within the root than elsewhere in the word. The ranking of a root-specific LINEAR-
ITY (RootLin) above *NC̥ will block substitution within the root:

(7)   Root-internal NC̥ tolerance: RootLin ≫ *NC̥

əm₁p₂at	RootLin	*NC̥	Lin
a. ☞ əm₁p₂at		*	
b. əm₁,₂at	* !		*

RootLin rules out fusion within the root because fusion destroys the precedence
relationship between Input root segments /m/ and /p/ (7b). Since the nasal in
/məN+pilih/ is not part of the root, nasal substitution across the morpheme boundary does not disturb the precedence structure of root elements, and RootLin is
obeyed.[5]
   RootLin is effective in blocking substitution within the root because it is a constraint on the relationship between Input and Output strings, rather than between
individual Input and Output segments, or features. If we attempted to rule out root-
internal fusion with a root-specific constraint on Identity between Input and Output
correspondents, substitution in the middle of the root and at the beginning of it
would be assessed equally, since both would turn a voiceless obstruent belonging
to the root into an Output nasal. As Donca Steriade (p.c.) has pointed out, it is not
at all clear how a theory with Faithfulness constraints demanding only faithful
segmental and featural parsing would handle these and other segmental 'derived
environment' effects (see Kiparsky 1993 for recent discussion). The main difference
between Indonesian nasal substitution, and more commonly discussed cases such as
the Sanskrit Ruki rule and Finnish assibilation, is that the latter involve segmental
change, rather than segmental fusion. However, if linearity is generalized to sub-
segmental elements, such that it forces their underlying precedence relationship to
be maintained, and if these cases can all be analyzed as involving partial segmental
overlap, then root-specific rankings of sub-segmental linearity would generate non-
derived environment blocking effects. Clearly, a great deal of work needs to be done
to determine the empirical coverage of root-specific LINEARITY constraints, but it
seems plausible that the ranking of morpheme-specific Faithfulness constraints above
phonotactic constraints is the source of this sort of phenomenon.

2.3   Segmental deletion and insertion

So far we have only considered candidates with and without NC̥ fusion. Deletion
and epenthesis could also satisfy *NC̥, without incurring violations of LINEARITY.
This means that in Indonesian, the constraints MAX and DEP, which are violated
by deletion and epenthesis respectively (McCarthy and Prince 1995), must be
ranked above LINEARITY. In fact, these constraints must be placed even higher in

the hierarchy, above *NC̥, since neither deletion nor epenthesis is used to resolve *NC̥ violations root-internally, where fusion is ruled out by RootLin:

(8)   Deletion and epenthesis blocked by Max, Dep ≫ *NC̥

əmpat	Max	Dep	*NC̥
a. ☞ əmpat			*
b. əpat	* !		
c. əməpat		* !	

Though neither deletion nor epenthesis is resorted to in Indonesian to avoid *NC̥ violations, permutation of the rankings of these constraints (Prince and Smolensky 1993: §6) predicts the existence of other languages in which Max and Dep are dominated by *NC̥ and the other Faithfulness constraints, producing NC̥ deletion and NC̥ epenthesis.

Examples of segmental deletion in the NC̥ configuration include the aforementioned cases of child English (Smith 1973: 53), child Greek (Drachman and Malikouti-Drachman 1973), and child Spanish (Vogel 1976). Amongst the adult languages with NC̥ deletion is the Kelantan dialect of Malay, which differs from standard Johore Malay in that it lacks nasals before voiceless obstruents, though it permits homorganic NC̥ clusters (Teoh 1988). This pattern is replicated in African languages such as Venda (Ziervogel, Wetzel, and Makuya 1972: cited in Rosenthall 1989: 47), Swahili, and Maore (Nurse and Hinnebusch 1993: 168), as well as several others cited by Ohala and Ohala (1993: 239).[6]

What unites all of these examples is that the nasal, rather than the obstruent, is deleted. This parallels the nasal/fricative cluster effects detailed in Padgett (1994), which sometimes involve nasal, but never fricative, deletion. One way to capture this is to posit a fixed ranking of an obstruent-specific Max constraint (ObsMax) above the nasal-specific NasMax. Establishing the phonetic basis and typological correctness of this presumed fixed ranking is beyond the purview of this study, but it can be noted that its universality is supported by the observation that a few languages lack nasals, but none are without oral segments (Maddieson 1984, cited in McCarthy and Prince 1994a, who provide a different explanation for this generalization).

The tableau in (9) demonstrates how an /NT/ cluster would be treated in a language such as Kelantan Malay, in which *NC̥ dominates Max (note that all other Faithfulness constraints, including Linearity, are also ranked above Max):

(9)   Tableau for Kelantan-like languages

N_1T_2	*NC̥	ObsMax	NasMax
a. ☞ T_2			*
b. N_1		* !	
c. N_1T_2	* !		

In future tableaux, I will merge the two MAX constraints, and show only the candidate with the deleted nasal.

For some reason, languages seem not to make use of epenthesis to resolve *NC̥ violations. One might stipulate that DEP universally dominates *NC̥, but without any independent motivation for this fixed ranking, such a formalization would remain in the realm of description, rather than explanation. With this potential gap in the typology of NC̥ effects duly noted, I will now turn to the featural changes that can be used to satisfy *NC̥, and propose constraints to rule them out in Indonesian. In these instances, we will see the predicted factorial typology is indeed fulfilled.

3   *NC̥ and Featural Faithfulness

3.1   Denasalization

Instead of completely deleting the nasal, another way to meet the *NC̥ requirement is to change the underlying nasal into an obstruent. There are at least three languages that take this route: Toba Batak (Hayes 1986), Kaingang (Henry 1948; cf. Piggott 1995), and Mandar (Mills 1975). Mandar, a language spoken in South Sulawesi, is particularly interesting because it has a prefixation paradigm that differs minimally from that of Indonesian. A homorganic nasal appears before voiced obstruents (10a), but instead of nasal substitution with the voiceless ones, there is gemination (10b) (in Toba Batak and Kaingang, the resulting obstruent retains its place specification, and can be heterorganic with the following consonant).

(10)   Mandar maN- prefixation
    a.   /maN+dundu/   mandundu   'to drink'
    b.   /maN+tunu/   mattunu   'to burn'

In Mandar, unlike Indonesian, the prohibition against NC̥ extends throughout the language:

(11)
    Nowhere in my material nor in Pelenkahu's extensive lists of minimal pairs is there a single instance of nasal plus voiceless stop. Where such a cluster would be expected, because of cognate items or at certain morpheme boundaries, there is invariably a geminate voiceless stop. In this respect, [Mandar] is far more consistent than [Buginese]; perhaps it reflects greater freedom from outside influence. (Mills 1975: 82)

There are a number of potential constraints, or sets of constraints, that could rule out denasalization in Indonesian, as well as in languages like Kelantan Malay that have nasal deletion. Before turning to them, a short discussion of featural Faithfulness within Correspondence Theory is in order.

To replace the containment-based PARSE FEATURE (see e.g., Itô, Mester, and Padgett 1995) in Correspondence Theory, McCarthy and Prince (1994a, 1995) outline two approaches. One is to extend Correspondence into the featural domain, and require mappings between instances of features such as [voice] in the Input and Output. The one that McCarthy and Prince adopt, however, invokes a set of identity requirements between segmental correspondents. A general formulation for such constraints is given in (12):

(12)   Featural Identity – IDENT-(F)
       Correspondents are identical in their specification for F.

Formulated in this way, featural Faithfulness is not violated if a segment is deleted, since if an Input segment has no Output correspondent, Identity constraints do not come into force.

   In cases of fusion, however, the simple statement of Featural Identity given in (12) leads to some complications. Consider the Input–Output mappings in (13):

(13)   Input   a.   n t   b.   n t
                        \/ | |
       Output   n   t t

Nasal substitution is represented in (13a), and denasalization in (13b). One consequence of the symmetrical nature of Identity is that IDENT[NAS] is violated to the same degree in (13a) and (13b), since in both instances a nasal and a voiceless obstruent stand in correspondence with one another. Nasal substitution also violates LINEARITY, so in terms of the constraints considered thus far, it is impossible for a language to prefer (13a) over (13b), since the Faithfulness violations incurred by (13b) are a subset of those for (13a).

   One might consider ruling out (13b) with constraints against coda obstruents, and/or gemination. By using a syllable structure constraint to rule out denasalization, however, the resulting prediction should be that languages that display nasal substitution have tight restrictions on possible codas. To some extent, this is borne out. However, Chamorro, which has nasal substitution in *man-* and *fan-* prefixation, also has geminates and coda obstruents (Topping 1973: 36–49), even in prefixes, such as *hat-*, *chat-*, and *tak-* (Topping 1973: 66). Thus, nasal substitution does not appear to be driven by a desire to avoid coda obstruents, or gemination.

   Another response to this problem is to elaborate Identity somewhat, so that we have a way of stating that in nasal substitution an Input nasal maps to an Output one, while in denasalization an Input nasal maps to an obstruent. With this shift away from symmetry the theory of featural Faithfulness begins to look more like segmental Correspondence, which could have separate MAX and DEP constraints.

(14)   IDENTI→O[F]
       Any correspondent of an Input segment specified as F must be F.

Nasal substitution does not violate IDENTI→O[NAS], while denasalization does. [NAS] here would refer to the feature [Nasal] in monovalent feature theory, or

[+Nasal] if bivalent features were assumed. The choice is not crucial, but since the feature [−Nasal] seems not to be active in any phonological process, I will assume there is but a single monovalent feature [Nasal] (Piggott 1993, Rice 1993, Steriade 1993, Trigo 1993, cf. Cohn 1993). Note that if bivalent features were used, and Featural Identity were stated without any reference to the value of the feature (i.e. 'any correspondent of Input segment X must be identical to X in its specification for F'), then the effects of this constraint would remain symmetrical, and the problem of differentiating I→O and O→I Identity would remain.

For a language like Mandar, IDENTI→O[NAS] is ranked beneath *NC̥ and the rest of the Faithfulness constraints. In Indonesian, IDENTI→O[NAS] is ranked above LINEARITY, so that fusion is preferred over denasalization. A tableau for Mandar is given in (15):

(15)   Mandar denasalization: *NC̥ ≫ IDENTI→O[NAS]

maN_1+t_2unu	DEP	MAX	LINEARITY	*NC̥	IDENTI→O[NAS]
a. ☞ mat_1t_2unu					*
b. $man_{1,2}unu$			* !		
c. man_1t_2unu				* !	
d. mat_2unu		* !			
e. $maŋ_1at_2unu$	* !				

Some further motivation for the recognition of separate IDENTI→O[NAS] and IDENTO→I[NAS] constraints comes from the fact that there is at least one language in which a geminate nasal is created to avoid an *NC̥ violation (the South Sulawesi language Konjo – Friberg and Friberg 1991: 88). To distinguish Konjo from its near neighbour Mandar, IDENTO→I[NAS] can be ranked beneath IDENTI→O[NAS], so that having an Output nasal in correspondence with an Input obstruent (i.e. NT → NN) is a better resolution of *NC̥ than having an Input nasal in correspondence with an Output obstruent (i.e. NT → TT). In Mandar, of course, the ranking between these constraints would be reversed.[7]

3.2   Post-nasal voicing

The most common, and most widely discussed, NC̥ effect is post-nasal voicing (see Itô, Mester, and Padgett 1995 for another account in Optimality Theory). A particularly relevant, and perhaps less familiar, example is that of the Puyo Pungo dialect of Quechua (Orr 1962, Rice 1993). As shown in (16), post-nasal voicing only affects affixal consonants. Root-internally, post-nasal consonants can remain voiceless.

(16)   Puyo Pungo Quechua
    a.   Root-internal NC̥:
      šiŋki   'soot'   čuntina   'to stir the fire'   pampalʸina   'skirt'

    b.   Suffixal alternations:
      sinik-pa   'porcupine's'   kam-ba   'yours'
      sača-pi   'in the jungle'   hatum-bi   'the big one'
      wasi-ta   'the house'   wakin-da   'the others'

Obviously, post-nasal voicing satisfies *NC̥. Again, the question of what it violates is not as straightforward as it might at first seem. Compare the I,O correspondences for nasal substitution and post-nasal voicing:

(17)   Input   a.   n t   b.   n t
                    \\/ | |
    Output   n   n d

If we assume full specification of the traditional set of features (i.e. those of Chomsky and Halle 1968), IDENT[VOICE] is the only constraint violated in (17b), yet it is also violated in (17a) since Input /t/ corresponds to Output /n/. Nasal substitution violates LINEARITY, while post-nasal voicing does not, so again, there is some difficulty in establishing how Indonesian could prefer (17a) over (17b).

In this case, it is pointless to consider constraints that would rule out the NC̥ configuration itself, since this does occur in Indonesian as the Output of an underlying NC̥ sequence. Nor does the problem lie in the symmetry of Identity, since in both cases a voiceless Input segment stands in correspondence with a voiced Output segment. Rather, it is due to the mistaken assumption that [Voice] on a sonorant, and on an obstruent, are equivalent (see Chomsky and Halle 1968: 300, Lombardi 1991, Rice and Avery 1989, Piggott 1992, Rice 1993, and Steriade 1995a for discussion from a variety of perspectives). Because the exact method adopted for capturing the non-equivalency of sonorant and obstruent [Voice] is of no particular consequence in the present context, I will simply invoke an Identity constraint that specifically targets obstruent [Voice]. There is no need to specify the constraint as applying from I-to-O or O-to-I:

(18)   Obstruent Voice Identity – IDENT[OBSVCE]
    Correspondent obstruents are identical in their specification for [Voice].

As it applies only to obstruents in correspondence, this constraint is not violated by nasal substitution, in which an obstruent is in correspondence with a nasal. For Indonesian, we can thus block post-nasal voicing by ranking IDENT[OBSVCE] above *NC̥. In Puyo Pungo Quechua, a root-specific version of IDENT[OBSVCE] ranks above *NC̥, and the general IDENT[OBSVCE] ranks below it, thus producing affixal post-nasal voicing only.

As this completes the analysis of nasal substitution, it is appropriate to provide an illustrative tableau:

(19)   Final tableau for nasal substitution

/məN₁+p₂ilih/	Dep	Identi→O [Nas]	Max	Ident [ObsVce]	*NÇ̥	Lin
a. ☞ məm₁,₂ilih						*
b. məm₁p₂ilih					* !	
c. məp₁p₂ilih		* !				
d. məm₁b₂ilih				* !		
e. məp₂ilih			* !			
f. məŋ₁əp₂ilih	* !					

Noteworthy in this tableau is the fact that all of the non-optimal candidates, with the exception of the epenthetic (19f), do turn up as optimal in other languages, and that each of these cases can be generated simply by having one of the constraints fall beneath all the others. Candidate (19b) is generated if *NÇ̥ ranks beneath the Faithfulness constraints, as in languages that permit NÇ̥ clusters. With Identi→O[Nas] at the bottom of this hierarchy, candidate (19c) is made optimal, as we have seen in Mandar. Candidate (19d) is preferred when Ident[ObsVce] is lowest ranked, as in Puyo Pungo Quechua. Finally, candidate (19e) wins with Max dominated by the others, as in Kelantan Malay.

With the introduction of constraints such as RootLin that disallow one of the NÇ̥ effects in a particular environment, we would also expect to see cases where an alternate process takes place in the environment in which the usual one is ruled out. Such conspiracies between NÇ̥ effects can be modelled simply by having both of the relevant Faithfulness constraints ranked beneath *NÇ̥. It is a powerful argument for this approach that this expectation is indeed fulfilled.

3.3   NÇ̥ fusion overruled by Featural Identity

In this section, I show how a high ranking Featural Identity constraint can disallow fusion between particular segments. This discussion also serves to introduce evidence of a conspiracy between nasal substitution and nasal deletion. The data to be accounted for involve a parametric difference between Austronesian and African nasal substitution. In all the Austronesian examples of which I am aware, the fricative /s/ undergoes substitution:[8]

(20)   /məN+sapu/   [məɲapu]   'to sweep'   (Indonesian)
       /man+saga/   [maɲaga]   'stay'   (Chamorro: Topping 1973: 50)
       /N+sambuŋ/   [ɲambuŋ]   'to connect'   (Javanese: Poedjosoedarmo
                                                  1982: 51)

African languages with nasal substitution demonstrate a split in behaviour between stops and fricatives, as in the following examples cited by Rosenthall (1989: 49) (see also Odden and Odden 1985 on Kíhehe):

(21) a. /N+tuma/   [numa]   'I send'
          /N+seva/   [seva]   'I cook'   (Umbundu: Schadeberg 1982)

      b. /N+tabi/   [nabi]   'prince'
          /N+supa/   [supa]   'soup'   (Si-Luyana: Givón 1970)

To stem any suspicion that deletion before the fricatives is motivated solely by the markedness of nasal/fricative clusters (see Padgett 1994), note that voiced fricatives undergo post-nasal hardening in Kíhehe (Odden and Odden 1985: 498). This shows that *NC̥ is needed for deletion in a nasal/voiceless fricative sequence, since one would otherwise predict that /ns/ should surface as [nt].

As in Indonesian, fusion with the voiceless stops can be attributed to the ranking of Linearity beneath *NC̥ and the rest of the Faithfulness constraints, including Max. However, unlike Indonesian, deletion occurs with root-initial voiceless fricatives instead of fusion. This indicates that preservation of Input continuancy is more highly valued than preservation of the Input nasal segment in these languages, in other words, that IdentI→O[Cont] dominates Max. The fact that deletion does occur rather than *NC̥ violation places *NC̥ above Max. Combining these rankings, we get *NC̥, IdentI→O[Cont] ≫ Max ≫ Linearity. The following tableaux show how this hierarchy generates the different responses to *NC̥ violations in fricative-initial and stop-initial roots:

(22)   Fusion with stops

N_1+t_2abi	*NC̥	IdentI→O [Cont]	Max	Lin
a. ☞ $n_{1,2}abi$				*
b. n_1t_2abi	* !			
c. t_2abi			* !	

With a stop-initial root, Ident[Cont] is satisfied in fusion, so Max is free to choose fusion (22a) over deletion (22c) as the best alternative to *NC̥ violation (22b).

When the root begins with fricative, as in (23), fusion creates a violation of IdentI→O[Cont], since an Input fricative has a stop as an Output correspondent (assuming an undominated constraint against nasal fricatives in all these languages – see Cohn 1993, Padgett 1994). With IdentI→O[Cont] ≫ Max, the candidate with deletion (23a) becomes optimal in this instance:

(23)   Deletion with fricatives

N_1+s_2upa	*NC̥	IDENTI→O [CONT]	MAX	LIN
a. ☞ $s_2$upa			*	
b. $n_1s_2$upa	* !			
c. $n_{1,2}$upa		* !		*

Austronesian nasal substitution evinces the opposite ranking MAX ≫ IDENT[CONT], since loss of Input continuancy, as in (23c), is preferred to deletion.

4   Other *NC̥ Conspiracies

As Kisseberth (1970) originally pointed out, cases in which two processes conspire to avoid a single configuration provide strong motivation for the formal recognition of output constraints. Under a purely rule-based analysis of nasal substitution, such as the standard one of nasal assimilation followed by voiceless consonant deletion, the functional connection between nasal substitution and nasal deletion would have to be stated independently of the rules themselves; their shared property of eliminating NC̥ clusters is only obliquely retrievable from the rule formulation. This contrasts with the above Optimality Theoretic analysis of African nasal substitution and nasal deletion, in which the functional motivation for these processes is directly incorporated into the formal explanation, thus allowing for a perspicuous account of the conspiracy between them.[9]

There are in fact several other examples of NC̥ conspiracies. OshiKwanyama, a western Bantu language discussed by Steinbergs (1985), demonstrates a conspiracy between nasal substitution and post-nasal voicing. Loanwords are modified by voicing the post-nasal obstruent. The following are borrowings from English:

(24)   Postnasal voicing in OshiKwanyama loanwords
        [sitamba]   'stamp'
        [pelenda]   'print'
        [oinga]   'ink'

Root-initially in native words, nasal substitution, rather than post-nasal voicing, occurs to resolve underlying NC̥ sequences (nasal/voiced obstruent clusters remain intact, though Steinbergs provides no examples):

(25)   Root-initial nasal substitution in OshiKwanyama
        /e:N+pati/   [e:mati]   'ribs'
        /oN+pote/   [omote]   'good-for-nothing'
        /oN+tana/   [onana]   'calf'

A straightforward analysis of OshiKwanyama is obtained under the assumptions of the present study. As in Indonesian, root-internal nasal substitution can be ruled out by a root-specific ranking of LINEARITY above *NC̥, while root-initial substitution is permitted because the general LINEARITY constraint is dominated by *NC̥.[10] However, unlike Indonesian, IDENT[OBSVCE] is also ranked beneath *NC̥, so that post-nasal voicing occurs root-internally.

The phonology of Greek dialects (Newton 1972) provides examples of conspiracies between post-nasal voicing and each of nasal deletion and denasalization. In Modern Greek, post-nasal voicing (26a, c) applies except when the post-nasal obstruent is itself followed by a voiceless obstruent (a fricative). In this situation, nasal deletion applies instead (26b, d), thus avoiding voicing disagreement between obstruents, which is generally prohibited in Greek:

(26) a. /pemp+o/   [pembo]   'I send'
      b. /e+pemp+s+a/   [epepsa]   -aorist
      c. /ton#topo/   [tondopo]   'the place'
      d. /ton#psefti/   [topsefti]   'the liar' (Cypriot)[11]

In the Greek dialect spoken on Karpathos (Newton 1972), post-nasal voicing applies except when the obstruent is word-initial, in which case denasalization occurs instead, as in (27):

(27) /tin+porta/   [tipporta]   'the door'
      /tin+kori/   [tikkori]   'the girl'

In both of these cases, an analysis of the conspiracy can be obtained by having *NC̥ dominate two faithfulness constraints. The choice between the repairs is made by the ranking of the two faithfulness constraints, and by relevant higher ranked constraints (i.e. constraints favouring regressive voicing assimilation, or maintenance of the voicing specification of the stem-initial consonant; see Pater 1996 for details).

5   Conclusions

I have argued that nasal substitution is best analyzed as fusion of a nasal and voiceless obstruent, driven by a phonotactic constraint against this sequence, *NC̥, which can also be satisfied by nasal deletion, denasalization, and post-nasal voicing. The fact that languages exercise a range of options in dealing with *NC̥ violations, along with the existence of conspiracies between these NC̥ effects, provides strong support for the Optimality Theoretic program of decoupling phonotactic constraints from Faithfulness constraints, and allowing them to be freely ranked with respect to one another. However, the apparent lack of NC̥ epenthesis raises an intriguing question for future research: Is it the case that every phonotactic constraint is satisfied in all of the ways predicted by the permutation of the rankings between it and the Faithfulness constraints? Gaps in factorial typologies often serve as indications that constraints must be reformulated, but persistent links between marked configurations and the processes used to repair them would seem to force a more fundamental shift in theoretical assumptions. Either that, or we could settle for a theory of grammar that is in some respects only 'exegetically adequate', as opposed to 'explanatorily adequate', that is, we could rest content with having 'made some progress in understanding the facts as they are, though not in the sense of showing that they could not be otherwise' (Anderson 1979: 18). Such resignation would be disappointing though, in light of the strides that Optimality Theory has made toward predictive explanatory adequacy in many areas of phonology.

There are also some broader conclusions to be drawn from the study of NC̥ effects. Though post-nasal voicing is extremely widespread, there are no reported cases of regressive voicing triggered by nasals only. The progressive nature of nasal-obstruent voicing is particularly striking since more general forms of voicing assimilation tend to be regressive (Lombardi 1991; Mohanan 1993). This directional asymmetry, which is a fundamental property of post-nasal voicing, points to a difficulty for any attempt to construct a restrictive theory of segmental phonology on the basis of a restrictive set of features freely combined with operational parameters (or constraint-based reformulations thereof). If nasal [Voice] can spread right, then why can it not spread left? This asymmetry, along with the NC̥ conspiracies, provides strong support for any theory of segmental phonology based on substantive output constraints, of which Optimality Theory is one instantiation.

Notes

1 I am grateful to John Kingston and Donca Steriade for very helpful discussion of the phonetic facts, though I hasten to claim sole responsibility for any errors of interpretation.

2 The discussion here abstracts from two other NC̥ effects: nasal devoicing and obstruent aspiration. These processes cannot be captured by the simple statement of *NC̥ in (3). It is conceivable that the articulatory or perceptual difficulties of post-nasal voicelessness could be overcome by enhancement with aspiration and/or extension of the duration of voicelessness. However, a proper treatment of these phenomena would force a long digression from the central concerns of this paper, since at least the following rather complex questions would have to be answered: What is the nature of the interaction between these processes: does devoicing result from aspiration, or vice versa (Herbert 1986, Nurse and Hinnebusch 1993)? Are voiceless nasals [−Voice], or [+Aspirated] (Lombardi 1991, Huffman 1994)? Are the voiceless nasals in fact even entirely voiceless

(Maddieson and Ladefoged 1993: 262)? Related to the last question, are these processes categorical or more implementational in nature? Therefore, for present purposes I leave *NC̥ in its perhaps overly simple form.

3 Instead of LINEARITY, one might also invoke a separate UNIFORMITY constraint to block fusion (McCarthy and Prince 1995, 1999).

4 Here I am assuming that the Input is made up of a linearly sequenced set of morphemes. It is not crucial to the analysis that this position be maintained, since it is only LINEARITY within the root that must be obeyed, and there are other ways of ruling out trans-morphemic nasal substitution, such as through the use of DISJOINTNESS constraints (McCarthy and Prince 1995; see the following note).

5 It should be noted that fusion is not free to occur between any two morphemes. Both the prefix+prefix and root+suffix boundaries are impermeable to nasal substitution (e.g., /məN+pər+besar/ → [məmpərbesar] 'to enlarge' and /məN+yakin+kan/ → [məyakinkan] 'to convince'). To encode this

sort of morphological conditioning, constraints are needed to render particular morpheme boundaries opaque to fusion. In particular, McCarthy and Prince's (1995) DISJOINTNESS constraints, which require that the sets of correspondents (or exponents) of morphemes be non-overlapping, could be recruited for this purpose.

6   For ease of exposition, I assume that prenasalized stops are composed of two segments. On two root node theories of prenasalized stops, see Piggott (1988), Rosenthall (1989), Steriade (1993), and Trigo (1993).

7   This leaves a not insignificant problem unresolved. How do we distinguish between nasalization of the voiceless stop, and nasal substitution? In terms of the constraints considered thus far, nasal substitution incurs all the violations that nasalization does, plus a LINEARITY violation that is avoided by nasalization. One possibly key difference is that in fusion, one of the underlying correspondents of the Output nasal is a nasal, while in nasalization the second member of the cluster has as its sole correspondent a voiceless obstruent. I should also note here that Konjo nasalization is subject to considerable morphological conditioning. In fact, the prefix that causes nasalization has a homophonous counterpart that differs only in that it fails to nasalize the following voiceless obstruent.

8   These examples also demonstrate the well-known complication that /s/ becomes a palatal nasal under substitution. The apparent oddness of this alternation is somewhat tempered by the independent evidence from a Javanese morpheme structure constraint that Austronesian /s/ is in fact itself phonologically palatal (Mester 1986). A related complication is that nasal substitution often fails to occur with a /c/ initial root (/c/ is variously described as a palatal stop or an alveo-palatal affricate); see Onn (1980: 62) for discussion.

9   See Pater (1996) for discussion of the inability of Itô, Mester, and Padgett's (1995) analysis of post-nasal voicing to generalize to any of the other NC̥ effects.

10 Steriade (2001) points out that loanwords have post-nasal voicing rather than nasal substitution root-initially. This may indicate the activity of a LINEARITY constraint specific to the loanword stratum (cf. Itô and Mester 1999).

11 In all dialects, the nasal is deleted within the word (26b), and in most dialects, including Cypriot, it is deleted in an article preceding a noun, except in 'slow, deliberate speech' (26d).

References

Anderson, Stephen R. 1979. On the Subsequent Development of the 'Standard Theory' in Phonology. In Daniel A. Dinnsen (ed.) *Current Approaches to Phonological Theory*. Bloomington: Indiana University Press.

Archangeli, Diana and Douglas Pulleyblank. 1995. *Grounded Phonology*. Cambridge, MA: MIT Press.

Beckman, Jill, Laura Walsh, and Suzanne Urbanczyk (eds.) 1995. *Papers in Optimality Theory: University of Massachusetts Occasional Papers* 18. University of Massachusetts, Amherst: GLSA.

Chomsky, Noam and Morris Halle. 1968. *The Sound Pattern of English*. New York: Harper and Row.

Cohn, Abigail C. 1993. The Status of Nasalized Continuants. In Huffman and Krakow, pp. 329–68.

Drachman, Gaberell and Angeliki Malikouti-Drachman. 1973. Studies in the Acquisition of Greek as a Native Language: I. Some Preliminary Findings on Phonology. *Ohio State Working Papers in Linguistics* 15: 99–114.

Dziwirek, Katarzyna. 1989. Malagasy Phonology and Morphology. *Linguistic Notes from La Jolla* 15: 1–30.

Flemming, Edward S. 1995. *Auditory Representations in Phonology*. Doctoral dissertation, University of California, Los Angeles.

Friberg, Timothy and Barbara Friberg. 1991. Notes on Konjo Phonology. In J. N. Sneddon (ed.) *Studies in Sulawesi Linguistics* Part 2. NUSA Linguistic Studies, Jakarta, Indonesia.

Givón, Talmy. 1970. The Si-Luyana language. University of Zambia, Institute for Social Research, Communication 6.

Gnanadesikan, Amalia E. 1995. Markedness and Faithfulness Constraints in Child Phonology. MS, University of Massachusetts, Amherst. ▶

Goldsmith, John (ed.) 1995. *A Handbook of Phonological Theory*. Cambridge, MA: Blackwell.

Halle, Morris and George N. Clements. 1983. *Problem Book in Phonology*. Cambridge, MA: MIT Press.

Hayes, Bruce. 1986. Assimilation as Spreading in Toba Batak. *Linguistic Inquiry* 17: 467–99.

Hayes, Bruce. 1999. Phonetically-Driven Phonology: The Role of Optimality Theory and Inductive Grounding. In M. Darnell, E. Moravscik, M. Noonan, F. Newmeyer, and K. Wheatley (eds.) *Functionalism and Formalism in Linguistics, Volume 1: General Papers*, pp. 243–85. Amsterdam: Benjamins. ◀

Henry, Jules. 1948. The Kaingang Language. *International Journal of American Linguistics* 14: 194–204.

Herbert, Robert K. 1986. *Language Universals, Markedness Theory, and Natural Phonetic Processes*. Berlin: Mouton de Gruyter.

Huffman, Marie K. 1993. Phonetic Patterns of Nasalization and Implications for Feature Specification. In Huffman and Krakow, pp. 303–27.

Huffman, Marie K. 1994. Laryngeal Specifications for the Implementation of Nasals. Handout of paper presented at the University of Delaware, November 14.

Huffman, Marie K. and Rena A. Krakow (eds.) 1993. *Phonetics and Phonology 5: Nasals, Nasalization, and the Velum*. San Diego: Academic Press.

Itô, Junko and Armin Mester. 1999. The Phonological Lexicon. In N. Tsujimura (ed.) *The Handbook of Japanese Linguistics*, pp. 62–100. Oxford: Blackwell. ◀

Itô, Junko, Armin Mester, and Jaye Padgett. 1995. Licensing and Underspecification in Optimality Theory. *Linguistic Inquiry* 26: 571–614. ◀

Jun, Jongho. 1995. *Perceptual and Articulatory Factors in Place Assimilation: An Optimality Theoretic Approach*. Ph.D. dissertation, University of California, Los Angeles.

Kenstowicz, Michael and Charles Kisseberth. 1979. *Generative Phonology: Description and Theory*. New York: Academic Press.

Kiparsky, Paul. 1993. Blocking in Nonderived Environments. In Sharon Hargus and Ellen Kaisse (eds.) *Phonetics and Phonology 4: Studies in Lexical Phonology*, pp. 277–313. San Diego: Academic Press.

Kirchner, Robert. 1995. Contrastiveness is an Epiphenomenon of Constraint Ranking. In *Proceedings of the Berkeley Linguistics Society*.

Kisseberth, Charles. 1970. On the Functional Unity of Phonological Rules. *Linguistic Inquiry* 1: 291–306.

Lamontagne, Greg and Keren Rice 1995. A Correspondence Account of Coalescence. In Beckman et al., pp. 211–23.

Lapoliwa, Hans. 1981. *A Generative Approach to the Phonology of Bahasa Indonesia*. Canberra: Pacific Linguistics D 34.

Lombardi, Linda. 1991. *Laryngeal Features and Laryngeal Neutralization*. Ph.D dissertation, University of Massachusetts, Amherst.

Maddieson, Ian. 1984. *Patterns of Sounds*. Cambridge: Cambridge University Press.

Maddieson, Ian and Peter Ladefoged. 1993. Phonetics of Partially Nasal Consonants. In Huffman and Krakow, pp. 251–301.

McCarthy, John and Alan Prince. 1993a. *Prosodic Morphology I: Constraint Interaction and Satisfaction*. MS, University of Massachusetts, Amherst, and Rutgers University, New Brunswick, NJ. ▶

McCarthy, John and Alan Prince. 1993b. Generalized Alignment. In Geert Booij and Jaap van Marle (eds.) *Yearbook of Morphology 1993*, pp. 79–153. Dordrecht: Kluwer. ◀

McCarthy, John and Alan Prince. 1994a. The Emergence of the Unmarked. *Proceedings of NELS* 24: 333–79. ◀

McCarthy, John and Alan Prince. 1994b. Prosodic Morphology: An Overview. Talks presented at the OTS/HIL Workshop on Prosodic Morphology, University of Utrecht. ▶

McCarthy, John and Alan Prince. 1995. Faithfulness and Reduplicative Identity. In Beckman et al., pp. 249–384. ◀

McCarthy, John and Alan Prince. 1999. Faithfulness and Identity in Prosodic Morphology. In R. Kager, H. van der Hulst, and W. Zonneveld (eds.) *The Prosody–Morphology Interface*, pp. 218–309. Cambridge: Cambridge University Press. ◀

Mester, Armin. 1986. *Studies in Tier Structure*. Doctoral dissertation, University of Massachusetts, Amherst.

Mills, Roger F. 1975. *Proto South Sulawesi and Proto Austronesian Phonology*. Doctoral dissertation, University of Michigan.

Mohanan, K. P. 1993. Fields of Attraction in Phonology. In John Goldsmith (ed.) *The Last Phonological Rule*, pp. 61–116. Chicago: University of Chicago Press.

Newton, Brian. 1972. *The Generative Interpretation of Dialect. A Study of Modern Greek Phonology*. Cambridge: Cambridge University Press.

Nurse, Derek and Thomas J. Hinnebusch. 1993. *Swahili and Sabaki: A Linguistic History*. Berkeley: University of Los Angeles Press.

Odden, David and Mary Odden. 1985. Ordered Reduplication in Kíhehe. *Linguistic Inquiry* 16: 497–503.

Ohala, John J. and Manjari Ohala. 1991. Reply to Commentators. *Phonetica* 48: 271–4.

Ohala, John J. and Manjari Ohala. 1993. The Phonetics of Nasal Phonology: Theorems and Data. In Huffman and Krakow, pp. 225–49.

Onn, Farid M. 1980. *Aspects of Malay Phonology and Morphology*. Bangi: Universiti Kebangsaan Malaysia. [Published version of 1976 University of Illinois dissertation.]

Orr, Carolyn. 1962. Ecuador Quichua Phonology. In Benjamin Elson (ed.) *Studies in Ecuadorian Indian Languages*, pp. 60–77. Norman, OK: Summer Institute of Linguistics.

Padgett, Jaye. 1994. Stricture and Nasal Place Assimilation. *Natural Language and Linguistic Theory* 12: 465–513.

Pater, Joe. 1996. *NC. *Proceedings of NELS* 26: 227–39. Amherst, MA: GLSA.

Piggott, Glyne L. 1988. Prenasalization and Feature Geometry. *Proceedings of NELS* 19: 345–52.

Piggott, Glyne L. 1992. Variability in Feature Dependency: The Case of Nasality. *Natural Language and Linguistic Theory* 10: 33–77.

Piggott, Glyne L. 1993. The Geometry of Sonorant Features. MS, McGill University.

Piggott, Glyne L. 1995. Feature Dependency in Optimality Theory: Optimizing the Phonology of Sonorants. MS, McGill University.

Poedjosoedarmo, Soepomo. 1982. *Javanese Influence on Indonesian*. Canberra: Pacific Linguistics D 38.

Prince, Alan S. and Paul Smolensky. 1993. *Optimality Theory: Constraint Interaction in Generative Grammar*. MS, Rutgers University and University of Colorado at Boulder. ◀

Rice, Keren. 1993. A Reexamination of the Feature [Sonorant]: The Status of 'Sonorant Obstruents'. *Language* 69: 308–44.

Rice, Keren and Peter Avery. 1989. On the Interaction between Sonorancy and Voicing. *Toronto Working Papers in Linguistics* 10: 65–82.

Rosenthall, Samuel. 1989. *The Phonology of Nasal–Obstruent Sequences*. Master's thesis, McGill University.

Schadeberg, T. 1982. Nasalization in Umbundu. *Journal of African Languages and Linguistics* 4: 109–32.

Smith, Neilson V. 1973. *The Acquisition of Phonology: A Case Study*. Cambridge: Cambridge University Press.

Steinbergs, Aleksandra. 1985. The Role of MSC's in OshiKwanyama Loan Phonology. *Studies in African Linguistics* 16: 89–101.

Steriade, Donca. 1993. Closure, Release, and Nasal Contours. In Huffman and Krakow, pp. 401–70.

Steriade, Donca. 1995a. Underspecification and Markedness. In John Goldsmith (ed.) *Handbook of Phonological Theory*, pp. 114–74. Cambridge, MA: Blackwell.

Steriade, Donca. 1995b. Positional Neutralization. MS, University of California, Los Angeles.

Steriade, Donca. 2001. What to Expect From a Phonological Analysis. Handout from the annual meeting of the Linguistic Society of America.

Teoh, Boon Seong. 1988. *Aspects of Malay Phonology – A Non-Linear Approach*. Doctoral dissertation, University of Illinois at Urbana-Champaign.

Topping, Donald M. 1969. A Restatement of Chamorro Phonology. *Anthropological Linguistics* 11: 62–77.

Topping, Donald M. 1973. *Chamorro Reference Grammar*. Honolulu: University of Hawaii Press.

Trigo, R. Lorenza. 1993. The Inherent Structure of Nasal Segments. In Huffman and Krakow, pp. 369–400.

Uhrbach, Amy. 1987. *A Formal Analysis of Reduplication and Its Interaction with Phonological and Morphological Processes*.

Ph.D. dissertation, University of Texas at Austin.

Urbanczyk, Suzanne. 1996. *Patterns of Reduplication in Lushootseed*. Ph.D. dissertation, University of Massachusetts, Amherst.

Vogel, Irene. 1976. Nasals and Nasal Assimilation Patterns, in the Acquisition of Chicano Spanish. *Papers and Reports in Child Language Development*, 201–14.

Ziervogel D., P. J. Wetzel, and T. N. Makuya. 1972. *A Handbook of the Venda Language*. Pretoria: University of South Africa Press.

Zuckerman, Suzanne. 1972. *The Migratory Habits of Nasal Consonants: A Study in Phonological Universals*. M.A. thesis, Ohio State University.

Study and Research Questions

1   Construct tableaux similar to (19) for the other languages discussed. In other words, provide tableaux that dispose of the full range of relevant candidates and include all of the faithfulness constraints discussed in this chapter.

2   Fill in the details of the argument above in (3). Why should children learning English, Greek, or Spanish delete the nasal in NÇ clusters even though these clusters are found in the adult language?

3   Re-read section 2.2 and the associated note, then read about a more recent proposal in Pater (2001: 171ff). Discuss and evaluate the various solutions to the morphological conditioning problem, or develop one of your own.

4   Read and discuss Archangeli et al. (1998), which is a rejoinder to this chapter.

5   Solve the thusfar unsolved problem of why *NÇ never leads to epenthesis (see the end of section 2.3).

Chapter 15 | Bruce Hayes

Phonetically Driven Phonology: The Role of Optimality Theory and Inductive Grounding

Editor's Note

Functionalist approaches to linguistic phenomena look for explanations that are external to formal grammar. In the limit, a radically functionalist view would see formal grammar as completely superfluous, but a much more widely held position is that analyses and explanations should combine formal and functional properties. The possibility of making a solid formal/functional connection was realized from the beginning of OT. Prince and Smolensky (1993: 198) urge reconsideration of strict formalism in the SPE tradition (Chomsky and Halle 1968), where the causes of phonological processes "are placed entirely outside grammar, beyond the purview of formal or theoretical analysis, inert but admired." This chapter is one of the earliest contributions to the emerging research program of using an OT grammar to express functionalist explanations formally. It is closely connected with two topics discussed elsewhere in this book, learning (chapter 5) and the analysis of post-nasal voicing (chapters 14 and 30).

1   Phonological Functionalism and Optimality Theory

The difference between formalist and functionalist approaches in linguistics has taken different forms in different areas. For phonology, and particularly for the study of fully productive sound patterns, the functionalist approach has tradition-ally been phonetic in character. For some time, work in the phonetic literature, such as Ohala (1974, 1978, 1981, 1983), Ohala and Ohala (1993), Liljencrants and Lindblom (1972), Lindblom (1983, 1990), and Westbury and Keating (1986), has argued that the sound patterns of languages are effectively arranged to facilitate

Excerpt (with revisions by the author) from:
Hayes, Bruce (1999) Phonetically driven phonology: the role of Optimality Theory and inductive grounding. In *Functionalism and Formalism in Linguistics*, vol. I: *General Papers*, ed. Michael Darnell, Frederick J. Newmeyer, Michael Noonan, Edith Moravcsik, and Kathleen Wheatley, pp. 243–85. Amsterdam: John Benjamins. [Available on Rutgers Optimality Archive, ROA-158.]

ease of articulation and distinctness of contrasting forms in perception. In this view, much of the patterning of phonology reflects principles of good design.

In contemporary phonological theorizing, such a view has not been widely adopted. Phonology has been modeled as a formal system, set up to mirror the characteristic phonological behavior of languages. Occasionally, scholars have made a nod towards the phonetic sensibleness of a particular proposal. But on the whole, the divide between formal and functionalist approaches in phonology has been as deep as anywhere else in the study of language.

The novel approach to linguistic theorizing known as Optimality Theory (Prince and Smolensky 1993) appears to offer the prospect of a major change in this situation. Optimality Theory has the advantage of allowing us to incorporate general principles of markedness into language-specific analyses. Previously, a formal phonology consisted of a set of somewhat arbitrary-looking rules. The analyst could only look at the rules "from the outside" and determine how they reflect general principles of markedness (or at best, supplement the rules with additional markedness principles, as in Chomsky and Halle (1968, ch. 9), Schachter (1969), or Chen (1973)). Under Optimality Theory, the principles of markedness (stated explicitly and ranked) form the *sole ingredients* of the language-specific analysis. The mechanism of selection by ranked constraints turns out to be such an amazingly powerful device that it can do all the rest. Since rankings are the only arbitrary element in the system, the principled character of language-specific analyses is greatly increased.

2 What is a Principled Constraint?

The question of what qualifies a constraint as an authentic markedness principle, however, is one that may be debated. The currently most popular answer, I think, relies on typological evidence: a valid constraint is one that "does work" in many languages, and does it in different ways.

However, a constraint could also be justified on *functional* grounds. In the case of phonetic functionalism, a well-motivated phonological constraint would be one that either renders speech easier to articulate or renders contrasting forms easier to distinguish perceptually. From the functionalist point of view, such constraints are *a priori* plausible, under the reasonable hypothesis that language is a biological system that is designed to perform its job well and efficiently.

Optimality Theory thus presents a new and important opportunity to phonological theorists. Given that the theory thrives on principled constraints, and given that functionally motivated phonetic constraints are inherently principled, the clear route to take is to explore how much of phonology can be constructed on this basis.

3 Research in Phonetically Driven Optimality-theoretic Phonology

The position just taken regarding phonetics and Optimality Theory is not original with me, but is inspired by ongoing research which attempts to make use of OT to produce phonetically driven formal accounts of various phonological phenomena.

For instance, Steriade (1993, 1997) considers the very basic question of seg-mental phonotactics in phonology: what segments are allowed to occur where? Her perspective is a novel one, taking the line that *perception* is the dominant factor. Roughly speaking, Steriade suggests that segments preferentially occur where they can best be heard. The crucial part is that many segments (for example, voiceless stops) are rendered audible largely or entirely by the contextual acoustic cues that they engender on neighboring segments through coarticulation. In such a situation, it is clearly to the advantage of particular languages to place strong restrictions on the phonological locations of such segments.

Following this approach, and incorporating a number of results from research in speech perception, Steriade is able to reconstruct the traditional typology of "segment licensing," including what was previously imagined to be an across-the-board preference for consonants to occur in syllable onset position. She goes on to show that there in fact are areas where this putative preference fails as an account of segmental phonotactics: one example is the preference for retroflexes to occur postvocalically (in either onset or coda); preglottalized sonorants work similarly. As Steriade shows, these otherwise baffling cases have specific explanations, based on the peculiar acoustics of the segments involved. She then makes use of Optimality Theory to develop explicit formal analyses of the relevant cases.

Phonetically driven approaches similar to Steriade's have led to progress in the understanding of various other areas of phonology: place assimilation (Jun 1995a, b), vowel harmony (Archangeli and Pulleyblank 1994, Kaun 1995a, b), vowel–consonant interactions (Flemming 1995), syllable weight (Gordon 1997), laryngeal features for vowels (Silverman 1995), non-local assimilation (Gafos 1996), and lenition (Kirchner 1998).[1]

4 The Hardest Part

What is crucial here (and recognized in earlier work) is that a research result in phon-etics is not the same thing as a phonological constraint. To go from one to the other is to bridge a large gap. Indeed, the situation facing phonetically driven Optimality-theoretic phonology is a rather odd one. In many cases, the phonetic research that explains the phonological pattern has been done very well and is quite convincing; it is the question of how to incorporate it into a formal phonology that is difficult.

In what follows, I will propose a particular way to attain phonetically driven phonological description.[2] Since I presuppose Optimality Theory, what is crucially needed is a means to obtain phonetically motivated constraints.

In any functionalist approach to linguistics, an important question to consider is: who is in charge? Languages cannot become functionally well designed by themselves; there has to be some mechanism responsible. In the view I will adopt, phonology is phonetically natural because the constraints it includes are (at least partially) the product of *grammar design*, carried out intelligently (that is, unconsciously, but with an intelligent algorithm) by language learners.

Before turning to this design process, I will first emphasize its most important aspect: there is a considerable gap between the raw patterns of phonetics and phonological constraints. Once the character of this divergence is clear, then the proposed nature of the design process will make more sense.

5 Why Constraints Do Not "Emerge" from the Phonetics

There are a number of reasons that suggest that phonetic patterns cannot serve as a direct, unmediated basis for phonology. (For more discussion of this issue, see Anderson 1981 and Keating 1985.

5.1 Variation and gradience

First, phonetics involves gradient and variable phenomena, whereas phonology is characteristically categorial and far less variable. Here is an example: Hayes and Stivers (1996) set out to explain phonetically a widespread pattern whereby languages require postnasal obstruents to be voiced. The particular mechanism is not reviewed here; for now it suffices that it appears to be verified by quantitative aerodynamic modeling and should be applicable in any language in which obstruents may follow nasals.

Since the mechanism posited is automatic, we might expect to find it operating even in languages like English that do not have postnasal voicing as a phonological process. Testing this prediction, Hayes and Stivers examined the amount of closure voicing (in milliseconds) of English /p/ in the environments / m ___ versus / r ___. Sure enough, for all five subjects in the experiment, there was significantly more /p/ voicing after /m/ than after /r/, as our mechanism predicted. But the effect was purely quantitative: except in the most rapid and casual speech styles, our speakers fully succeeded in maintaining the phonemic contrast of /p/ with /b/ (which we also examined) in postnasal position. The phonetic mechanism simply produces a quantitative distribution of voicing that is skewed toward voicedness after nasals. Moreover, the distribution of values we observed varied greatly: the amount of voicing we found in /mp/ ranged from 13 percent up to (in a few cases) over 60 percent of the closure duration of the /p/.

In contrast, there are other languages in which the postnasal voicing effect is truly phonological. For example, in Ecuadorian Quechua (Orr 1962), at suffix boundaries, it is phonologically illegal for a voiceless stop to follow a nasal, and voiced stops are substituted for voiceless; thus *sača-pi* 'jungle-loc.' but *atam-bi* 'frog-loc.'. For suffixes, there is no contrast of voiced versus voiceless in postnasal position. Clearly, English differs from Quechua in having "merely phonetic" postnasal voicing, as opposed to true phonological postnasal voicing.

The Quechua case is what needs additional treatment: it is a kind of leap from simply allowing a phonetic effect to influence the quantitative outcomes to arranging the phonology so that, in the relevant context, an entire contrast is wiped out.[3]

5.2   Symmetry

Let us consider a second argument. I claim that phonetics is asymmetrical, whereas phonology is usually symmetrical. Since the phonetic difficulty of articulation and perception follows from the interaction of complex physical and perceptual systems, we cannot in the general case expect the regions of phonetic space characterized by a particular difficulty level to correspond to phonological categories.

Consider a particular case involving the difficulty of producing voiced and voiceless stops. The basic phonetics (here, aerodynamics) has been studied by Ohala (1983) and by Westbury and Keating (1986). Roughly, voicing is possible whenever a sufficient drop in air pressure occurs across the glottis. In a stop, this is a delicate matter for the speaker to arrange, since free escape of the oral air is impeded. Stop voicing is influenced by quite a few different factors, of which just a few are reviewed here.

(a) *Place of articulation.* In a "fronter" place like labial, a large, soft vocal tract wall surface surrounds the trapped air in the mouth. During closure, this surface retracts under increasing air pressure, so that more incoming air is accommodated. This helps maintain the transglottal pressure drop. Since there is more yielding wall surface in labials (and more generally, at fronter places of articulation), we predict that the voiced state should be relatively easier for fronter places. Further, since the yielding-wall effect actually makes it harder to turn off voicing, we predict that voicelessness should be harder for fronter places.

(b) *Closure duration.* The longer a stop is held, the harder it will be to accommodate the continuing transglottal flow, and thus maintain voicing. Thus, voicelessness should be favored for geminates and for stops in post-obstruent position. (The latter case assumes that, as is usual, the articulation of the stop and the preceding obstruent are temporally overlapped, so no air escape can occur between them.)

(c) *Postnasal position.* As just noted, there are phonetic reasons why voicing of stops should be considerably favored when a nasal consonant immediately precedes the stop.

(d) *Phrasal position.* Characteristically, voicing is harder to maintain in utterance-initial and utterance-final position, since the subglottal pressure that drives voicing tends to be lower in these positions.

As Ohala (1983) and others have made clear, these phonetic factors are abundantly reflected in phonological patterning. (a) Gaps in stop inventories that have both voiced and voiceless series typically occur at locations where the size of the oral chamber makes voicing or voicelessness difficult; thus at *[p] or *[g], as documented by Ferguson (1975), Locke (1983), and several sources cited by Ohala (p. 195). (b) Clusters in which a voiced obstruent follows another obstruent are also avoided, for instance in Latin stems (Devine and Stephens 1977), or in German colloquial speech (Mangold 1962: 45). Geminate obstruents are a similar case: they likewise are often required to be voiceless, as in Japanese (Vance 1987: 42), West Greenlandic (Rischel 1974), or !Xóõ (Traill 1981: 165). (c) Languages very frequently ban voiceless stops after nasals, with varying overt phonological effects depending on how the constraints are ranked (Pater 1996, 1999; Hayes and Stivers 1996). (d) Voicing is favored in medial position, and disfavored in initial and final position, following the subglottal pressure contour (Westbury and Keating 1986).[4]

Plainly, the phonetics can serve here as a rich source of phonological explanation, since the typology matches the phonetic mechanisms so well. However, if we try to do this in a naive, direct way, difficulties immediately set in. Suppose that we concoct a *landscape of stop voicing difficulty* (1) which encodes values for difficulty (zero = maximal ease) on an arbitrary scale for a set of phonological configurations. For simplicity, we will consider only a subset of the effects mentioned above.

(1)   Landscape of Difficulty for Voiced Stops: Three Places, Four Environments

	b	d	g
[−son] ___	43	50	52
# ___	23	27	35
[+son, −nas] ___	10	20	30
[+nas] ___	0	0	0 contour line: 25

The chart in (1) was constructed using a software aerodynamic vocal tract model implemented at UCLA (Keating 1984). The basis of the chart is explained below; for now, it may be considered simply a listing of "difficulty units" for voicing in various phonological configurations. It can be seen that the model has generated patterns that are qualitatively correct: the further back in the mouth a place of articulation is, the harder it is to maintain voicing. Moreover, the rows of the chart reflect the greater difficulty of maintaining voicing after obstruents and initially, as well as the greater ease after nasals.

What is crucial about the chart is that it reflects the *trading relationships* that are always found in the physical system for voicing. One cannot say, for example, that velars are always harder to voice, because velars in certain positions are easier to voice than labials in others. Similarly, the environments / # ___ versus / [+son, −nas] ___ do not define a consistent cutoff in voicing difficulty, since [g] in the environment / [+son, −nas] ___ is harder than [b,d] in the environment / # ___.

The dotted line on the chart represents a particular "contour line" for phonetic "difficulty," analogous to a contour line for altitude on a physical map. A language that truly "wanted" to behave in a phonetically rational way might ban all phonological configurations that exceeded the contour line, as in (2a). Translating this particular contour line into descriptive phonological language, we have the formulation of (2b):

(2)   A Hypothetical Phonological Constraint
    a.   *any voiced stop that characteristically requires more than 25 units of effort
    b.   *post-obstruent voiced stops,
        *[d,g] in initial position,
        *[g] after oral sonorants

Note that [g] is permitted by (2), but only postnasally.

I would contend that a constraint like (2) (however formulated) is unlikely to occur in a real phonology. What occurs instead are constraints that are likewise phonetically sensible, but which possess formal symmetry. Here are some real-world examples, with the languages they are taken from:

(3)   a.   *Voiced obstruent word-finally (Polish)
      b.   *Voiced obstruent after another obstruent (Latin)
      c.   *Voiced obstruent geminate (Japanese)
      d.   *Voiced velar obstruents (Dutch)

These constraints ban symmetrical regions of phonological space, not regions bounded by contour lines of phonetic difficulty. Nevertheless, they are phonetically sensible in a certain way: in the aggregate, the configurations that they forbid are more difficult aerodynamically than the configurations that they allow. Thus constraints like (4) would be quite unexpected:

(4)   a.   *Voiceless obstruent word-finally   (compare (3a))
      b.   *Voiceless obstruent after another obstruent   (compare (3b))
      c.   *Voiceless obstruent geminate   (compare (3c))
      d.   *Voiceless velar obstruents   (compare (3d))

To generalize: I believe that constraints are typically natural, in that the set of cases that they ban is phonetically harder than the complement set. But the "boundary lines" that divide the prohibited cases from the legal ones are characteristically statable in rather simple terms, with a small logical conjunction of feature predicates.

The tentative conclusion is that the influence of phonetics in phonology is not direct, but is mediated by structural constraints that are under some pressure toward formal symmetry. A phonology that was directly driven by phonetic naturalness would, I think, be likely to miss this point.

The gap between the phonetic difficulty patterns and the phonology is thus still there, waiting to be bridged. Clearly, languages are well designed from a phonetic point of view. What is needed, I believe, is a way of accounting for this design that also allows principles of structural symmetry to play a role.

6   A Scheme for Phonological Grammar Design

Grammars could in principle be designed at two levels. Within the species as a whole, it is often held there is a Universal Grammar, invariant among non-pathological individuals, which determines much of the form of possible languages. Another sense in which grammar could be designed, outlined by Kiparsky and Menn (1977: 58), is at the level of the individual, who is engaged from infancy onward in the process of constructing a grammar, one that will ultimately generate the ambient language or something close to it. Could the language learner be a designer of grammars? If so, how might she go about it?

From the discussion above, it would seem plausible that grammatical design within phonology aims at a compromise between formal symmetry and accurate reflection of phonetic difficulty. What follows is a tentative attempt to specify what phonological design could be like.

The task of phonological grammar design, under Optimality Theory, has two parts: gaining access to constraints (here, by inventing them), and forming a grammar by ranking the constraints. The strategy taken is to suppose that constraints are invented in great profusion, but trimmed back by the constraint ranking algorithm.

The particular process whereby constraints are invented I will call *inductive grounding*. The term "grounded," which describes constraints that have a phonetic basis, was introduced by Archangeli and Pulleyblank (1994).

7 Inductive Grounding I: Evaluating Constraint Effectiveness

The language learner has an excellent vantage point for learning phonetically grounded constraints. Unlike any experimenter observing her externally, the child is actually operating her own production and perception apparatus, and plausibly would have direct access to the degree of difficulty of articulations and to the perceptual confusability of different acoustic signals.

Beyond the capacity to judge phonetic difficulty from experience, a language learner would also require the ability to generalize across tokens, creating a *phonetic map* of the range of possible articulations and acoustic forms.

Considering for the moment only articulation, I will suppose that the language learner is able to assess the difficulty of particular phonological configurations, using measures such as the maximum articulatory force needed to execute the configuration. Further, we must suppose that the learner is able to generalize from experience, arriving at a measure of the *characteristic* difficulty of particular phonological configurations, which would abstract away from the variation found at various speaking rates and degrees of casualness, as well as the variable perceptual clarity that different degrees of articulatory precision will produce. Pursuing such a course, the learner could in principle arrive at a phonetic map of the space of articulatory difficulty. A tentative example of a phonetic map is given below under (12).

Given a phonetic map drawn from experience, a language learner could use it to construct phonetically grounded constraints; hence the term "inductive grounding." The inductive grounding algorithm I will suggest here supposes the following.

First, I assume constraints are constructed profusely, as arbitrary well-formed combinations of the primitive elements of phonological theory; thus, with just the features [nasal] and [voice], we would get *[+nasal][−voice], *[+nasal] [+voice], *[−nasal,−voice], *[+nasal], and so on. This involves some risk, sinc. the number of constraints to be considered grows exponentially with the number of formal elements included in their structural descriptions. However, if, as suggested above, constraints are under some pressure toward formal simplicity, it is likely that the size of the search space can be kept under control.

Second, candidate constraints are assessed for their degree of grounding, accessing the phonetic map with a procedure I will now describe.

A grounded constraint is one that is phonetically sensible; that is, it bans things that are phonetically hard, and allows things that are phonetically easy. Taking a given candidate phonological constraint C, and any two entries E_1 and E_2 in the phonetic map, there are four logical possibilities:

(5)   a.   Both E_1 and E_2 violate C.
      b.   Both E_1 and E_2 obey C.
      c. E_1 violates C and E_2 obeys C.
      d. E_1 obeys C and E_2 violates C.

We will ignore all pairs of types (a) and (b) (same-outcome) as irrelevant to the assessment of C. Among the remaining possibilities, we can distinguish cases where the constraint makes an error from those in which it makes a correct prediction.

(6)   a.   Correct predictions
           E_1 violates C and E_2 obeys C; E_1 is harder than E_2.
           E_1 obeys C and E_2 violates C; E_1 is easier than E_2.

      b.   Errors
           E_1 obeys C and E_2 violates C; E_1 is harder than E_2.
           E_1 violates C and E_2 obeys C; E_1 is easier than E_2.

Since the goal of a constraint is to exclude hard things and include easy things, we can establish a simple metric of constraint effectiveness simply by examining all possible pairs $\{E_1, E_2\}$ drawn from the phonetic map. The definition below presumes a particular phonological structural description defining a constraint, and a phonetic map against which the constraint may be tested:

(7)   Constraint effectiveness
      Effectiveness = Correct predictions / (Correct predictions + Errors)

On this scale, "perfect" constraints receive a value of 1, since they always ban things that are relatively harder, and never things that are relatively easier. Useless constraints, which ban things in an arbitrary way with no connection to their phonetic difficulty, receive a value of 0.5; and perverse constraints, which ban only relatively easy things, get a value of 0. Clearly, the language learner should seek constraints with high effectiveness values.

It is more complicated to define constraint effectiveness for perceptual distinctness. Flemming (1995) has argued persuasively that perceptual distinctness can only be defined *syntagmatically* in perceptual space: for instance, [ɨ] is a fine vowel, indeed the preferred high vowel in a vertical vowel system such as Marshallese, where it is the only high vowel (Choi 1992). But where [i] and [u] occur as phonemes, as in most languages, [ɨ] is a poor vowel, due to its acoustic proximity to (thus, confusability with) [i] and [u]. Assuming the correctness of Flemming's position, we must evaluate not individual entries in the phonetic map, but *pairs* of entries. And since constraint effectiveness is determined by comparing cases that a constraint treats differently, we must deal with pairs of pairs. In various cases I have explored, this procedure leads to coherent results, but as there are further complications, I will consider only articulation here, with the intent of dealing with perception elsewhere.

8   Inductive Grounding II: Selecting the Grounded Constraints

Merely defining constraint effectiveness does not provide an explicit definition of a grounded constraint. If we only allowed constraints that showed a maximally good fit to the phonetic map (effectiveness value 1), then only a few simple constraints would be possible, and most of the permitted constraints would be very complex, like the "contour line constraint" in (2) above. This would be wrong on both counts. First, my judgment, based on experience in phonological typology, is that there are *many* constraints, in fact, dismayingly many, unless we come up with a reasonable source for them. Thus, we want the inductive grounding algorithm to generate a very rich (but thoroughly principled) constraint set. Second, as already argued, we want to keep constraints from being heavily "tailored" to fit the phonetic pattern. Real constraints seldom achieve such a perfect fit; rather, they deviate in the direction of structural simplicity.

A simple way to accomplish this deviation, as well as to provide a rich constraint set, is to rely on the notion of *local maximum*; in particular, local maxima of constraint effectiveness. To make the idea explicit, here are some definitions:

(8)   *Constraint space* is the complete (infinite) set of possible constraints. It is generated by locating all legal combinations of the primitive formal elements of a particular phonological theory.

(9)   Two constraints are *neighbors* in constraint space if the structural description of one may be obtained from that of the other by a single primitive formal substitution (switching a feature value; addition or loss of a feature or association line, etc.; the exact set of substitutions will depend on the phonological theory employed).

(10)   Constraint C_1 is said to be *less complex* than constraint C_2 iff the structural description of C_1 is properly included in the structural description of C_2 (cf. Koutsoudas et al. 1974: 8–9).

Using these definitions, we can now state an explicit characterization of phonetic grounding:

(11)   Defn.: *grounded*
Given a phonological constraint C and a phonetic map M, C is said to be *grounded* with respect to M if the phonetic effectiveness of C is greater than that of all neighbors of C of equal or lesser complexity.

Definition (11) uses the notion of local maximum, by requiring that C only exceed its neighbors in effectiveness. But (11) also goes beyond local maxima in a crucial sense: the neighbors that one must consider are only neighbors of equal or lesser complexity. It is this bias that permits the system to output relatively simple constraints even when their match to the phonetic map is imperfect.

The definition of phonetic grounding in (11) has the following virtues: (a) Assuming that a reasonably accurate phonetic map can be constructed, it specifies precisely which constraints are grounded with respect to that map, thus satisfying the requirement of explicitness. (b) The formally simple constraints that a given map yields are not just a few phonetically perfect ones, but a large number, each a local effectiveness maximum within the domain of equally or less complex constraints. (c) Constraints are able to sacrifice perfect phonetic accuracy for formal symmetry, since the competitors with which they are compared are only those of equal or lesser complexity.

9   An Application of Inductive Grounding

Here is a worked out example. To begin, we need a plausible phonetic map, for which I propose (12):

(12)   A Phonetic Difficulty Map for Six Stops in Four Environments

	p	t	k	b	d	g
[−son] ___	7	0	0	43	50	52
# ___	10	0	0	23	27	35
[+son,−nas] ___	45	28	15	10	20	30
[+nas] ___	155	135	107	0	0	0

I obtained this map by using a software aerodynamic vocal tract model. This model was developed originally by Rothenberg (1968) as an electrical circuit model, and is currently implemented in a software version in the UCLA Phonetics Laboratory. This version (or its close ancestors) are described in Westbury (1983), Keating (1984), and Westbury and Keating (1986). Roughly, the model takes as input specific quantitative values for a large set of articulations, and outputs the consequences of these articulations for voicing, that is, the particular ranges of milliseconds during which the vocal folds are vibrating. The units in chart (12) represent articulatory deviations from a posited maximally easy average vocal fold opening of 175 microns; these deviations are in the positive direction for voiceless segments (since glottal abduction inhibits voicing) and negative for voiced (since glottal adduction encourages it).

I used the model in an effort to give plausible quantitative support to the scheme to be followed here. However, it should be emphasized that obtaining reasonable estimates of articulatory difficulty from the model requires one to make a large number of relatively arbitrary assumptions, reviewed in the note below.[5] What makes the procedure defensible is that the outcomes that it produces are qualitatively reasonable: examining the map, the reader will find that all the relevant phonetic

(13)

Constraint	Effectiveness	Neighbors
a. *[+nasal][+voice]	0.000	*[+nasal][−voice], *[−nasal][+voice], *[+voice], *[+nasal]
b. *[+nasal][−voice]	1.000	*[+nasal][+voice], *[−nasal][−voice], *[−voice], *[+nasal]
c. *[−nasal][+voice]	0.701	*[−nasal][−voice], *[+nasal][+voice], *[+voice], *[−nasal]
d. *[−nasal][−voice]	0.357	*[−nasal][+voice], *[+nasal][−voice], *[−voice], *[−nasal]
e. *[+son][+voice]	0.500	*[+son][−voice], *[−son][+voice], *[+voice], *[+son]
f. *[+son][−voice]	0.861	*[+son][+voice], *[−son][−voice], *[−voice], *[+son]
g. *[−son][+voice]	0.841	*[−son][−voice], *[+son][+voice], *[+voice], *[−son]
h. *[−son][−voice]	0.094	*[−son][+voice], *[+son][−voice], *[−voice], *[−son]
i. *[LAB, +voice]	0.425	*[LAB, −voice], *[COR, +voice], *[DORS, +voice], *[LAB], *[+voice]
j. *[LAB, −voice]	0.633	*[LAB, +voice], *[COR, −voice], *[DORS, −voice], *[LAB], *[−voice]
k. *[COR, +voice]	0.500	*[COR, −voice], *[LAB, +voice], *[DORS, +voice], *[COR], *[+voice]
l. *[COR, −voice]	0.443	*[COR, +voice], *[LAB, −voice], *[DORS, −voice], *[COR], *[−voice]
m. *[DORS, +voice]	0.608	*[DORS, −voice], *[LAB, +voice], *[COR, +voice], *[DORS], *[+voice]
n. *[DORS, −voice]	0.371	*[DORS, +voice], *[LAB, −voice], *[COR, −voice], *[DORS], *[−voice]
o. *[+voice] unless LAB	0.568	*[−voice] unless LAB, *[+voice] unless COR, *[+voice] unless DORS, *[ ] unless LAB, *[+voice]
p. *[−voice] unless LAB	0.388	*[+voice] unless LAB, *[−voice] unless COR, *[−voice] unless DORS, *[ ] unless LAB, *[−voice]
q. *[+voice] unless COR	0.521	*[−voice] unless COR, *[+voice] unless LAB, *[+voice] unless DORS, *[ ] unless COR, *[+voice]
r. *[−voice] unless COR	0.513	*[+voice] unless COR, *[−voice] unless LAB, *[−voice] unless DORS, *[ ] unless COR, *[−voice]
s. *[+voice] unless DORS	0.453	*[−voice] unless DORS, *[+voice] unless LAB, *[+voice] unless COR, *[ ] unless DORS, *[+voice]
t. *[−voice] unless DORS	0.556	*[+voice] unless DORS, *[−voice] unless LAB, *[−voice] unless COR, *[ ] unless DORS, *[−voice]
u. *[LAB]	0.541	*[COR], *[DORS]
v. *[COR]	0.466	*[LAB], *[DORS]
w. *[DORS]	0.491	*[LAB], *[COR]
x. *[ ] unless LAB	0.459	*[ ] unless COR, *[ ] unless DORS
y. *[ ] unless COR	0.534	*[ ] unless LAB, *[ ] unless DORS
z. *[ ] unless DORS	0.509	*[ ] unless LAB, *[ ] unless COR
aa. *[+voice]	0.519	*[−voice]
bb. *[−voice]	0.481	*[+voice]
cc. *[+nasal]	Undef.	*[−nasal]
dd. *[−nasal]	Undef.	*[+nasal]
ee. *[+son]	Undef.	*[−son]
ff. *[−son]	Undef.	*[+son]

tendencies described above in section 5.2 are reflected quantitatively in the map. Thus, voiced stops are most difficult after an obstruent, somewhat easier in initial position, easier still after sonorants, and easiest postnasally. The reverse pattern holds for voiceless stops. Further, for any given environment, stops are easier to produce as voiced (and harder as voiceless) when they are in fronter places of articulation.

I will now derive a number of phonological constraints from the phonetic map of (12) by means of inductive grounding. The chart in (13) lists some of the work that must be done. The first column gives what I take to be a fairly substantial list of the most plausible constraints (given what the chart is suitable for testing), along with all of their neighbors that are equally simple or simpler. I have imposed a relatively arbitrary limit of formal complexity on this candidate set, under the assumption that language learners either cannot or will not posit extremely complex constraints. The second column gives the phonetic effectiveness value for the candidate constraints, calculated by the method laid out in sections 7 and 8 and exemplified below. Finally, the third column lists all the neighbor constraints for each main entry that are equally or more simple, taking the assumption that these neighbors are obtained by either a feature value switch or by deletion of single elements from the structural description.

Here is an example of how effectiveness was computed for individual constraints. The constraint *[LAB, −voice] bans [p]; this ban is phonetically natural (for reasons already given) and would thus be expected to have a reasonably high effectiveness value. I repeat the phonetic map below, this time with letters a–x, permitting reference to the entries:

(14)

	p	t	k	b	d	g
[−son] ___	a: 7	b: 0	c: 0	d: 43	e: 50	f: 52
# ___	g: 10	h: 0	i: 0	j: 23	k: 27	l: 35
[+son,−nas] ___	m: 45	n: 28	o: 15	p: 10	q: 20	r: 30
[+nas] ___	s: 155	t: 135	u: 107	v: 0	w: 0	x: 0

*[LAB, −voice] bans the shaded region of the map. If it is to be effective, then pairwise comparisons between banned cells and unbanned ones should predominantly come out with the banned cells being more difficult. Here is the outcome; ">" means "is harder than":

(15) a. Correct Predictions: 50   b. Incorrect Predictions: 29
          a > b, c, h, i, v–x   a < d–f, j–l, n–r, t, u
          g > b, c, h, i, v–x   g < d–f, j–l, n, o, q, r, t, u
          m > b, c, d, h–l, n–r, v–x   m < e, f, t, u
          s > b–f, h–l, n–r, t–x   s < (none)

The computed effectiveness value is 50/(50 + 29), or 0.633, which is what was listed in (13j).

The neighbors of *[**LAB, −voice**] that have equal or lesser complexity are listed below with their effectiveness values:

(16)

Constraint	Effectiveness	Justification for neighbor status
*[LAB, +voice]	0.425	switch value of [voice]
*[COR, −voice]	0.443	switch value of PLACE
*[DORS, −voice]	0.371	switch value of PLACE
*[LAB]	0.541	delete [+voice]
*[−voice]	0.481	delete [LAB]

Since *[**LAB, −voice**] at 0.633 exceeds all of its neighbors in effectiveness, the definition (11) designates it as phonetically grounded with respect to the phonetic map (12).

Repeating this procedure, we find that the constraints listed in (17) emerge as phonetically grounded. In the chart below, I give some mnemonic labels, often embodying a particular effect that a constraint might have. However, the reader should bear in mind that in Optimality Theory the empirical effects of a constraint can range much more widely than the label indicates; see for example Pater (1996, 1999).

(17)

Constraint		Effectiveness	Characteristic effect
a.	*[+nasal][−voice]	1.000	postnasal voicing
b.	*[+son][−voice]	0.861	postsonorant voicing
c.	*[−son][+voice]	0.841	postobstruent devoicing
d.	*[−nasal][+voice]	0.701	postoral devoicing
e.	*[LAB, −voice]	0.633	*p
f.	*[DORS, +voice]	0.608	*g
g.	*[+voice] unless LAB	0.568	/b/ is the only voiced stop
h.	*[−voice] unless DORS	0.556	/k/ is the only voiceless stop
i.	*[LAB]	0.541	*labials
j.	*[ ] unless COR	0.534	COR is the only place
k.	*[+voice]	0.519	voicing prohibited

The other constraints are designated by the algorithm as *not* grounded, because they are not local effectiveness maxima:

(18)

Constraint	Effectiveness	Characteristic effect
a. *[+voice] unless COR	0.521	/d/ is the only voiced stop
b. *[−voice] unless COR	0.513	/t/ is the only voiceless stop
c. *[ ] unless DORS	0.509	DORS is the only place
d. *[COR, +voice]	0.500	*d
e. *[+son][+voice]	0.500	postsonorant devoicing
f. *[DORS]	0.491	*dorsals
g. *[−voice]	0.481	voicing obligatory
h. *[COR]	0.466	*coronals
i. *[ ] unless LAB	0.459	LAB is the only place
j. *[+voice] unless DORS	0.453	/g/ is the only voiced stop
k. *[COR, −voice]	0.443	*t
l. *[LAB, +voice]	0.425	*b
m. *[−voice] unless LAB	0.388	/p/ is the only voiceless stop
n. *[DORS, −voice]	0.371	*k
o. *[−nasal][−voice]	0.357	postoral voicing
p. *[−son][−voice]	0.094	postobstruent voicing
q. *[+nasal][+voice]	0.000	postnasal devoicing

The neighbor constraint that "defeats" each of (18) may be determined by consulting chart (13).

Lastly, there are four constraints (*[+nasal], *[−nasal], *[+son], and *[−son]) for which the algorithm makes no decision, since the candidates either all obey or all violate them. These constraints were included simply to provide neighbors for the truly relevant constraints; I assume they could be evaluated by a more comprehensive map.

Did the simulation work? If the map in (12) is valid, and if languages adopt only grounded constraints, then the constraints of (17) should be empirically attested, and those of (18) not.

(a) The "finest" grounded constraint, with effectiveness value 1, is (17a), *[+nasal][−voice]. This constraint is indeed widely attested, with noticeable empirical effects in perhaps 7.6 percent of the world's languages (estimate from Hayes and Stivers 1996). Voicing in sonorant-adjacent positions ((17b), *[+son][−voice]) and devoicing in obstruent clusters ((17c), *[−son][+voice]) is also quite common.

(b) The chart also includes all the characteristic place-related voicing patterns: the bans on fronter voiceless stops and on backer voiced ones (17e–h).

(c) Two of the simpler constraints, (17i) *[LAB] and (17j) *[ ] **unless COR,** do play a role in phonologies (see Rood 1975 and Smolensky 1993), but their appearance in the chart is accidental. The phonetic map used here is suitable only for testing constraints on obstruent voicing, not place inventories. A legitimate test of the constraints that target place would require a much larger phonetic map.

(d) Likewise, the blanket ban on voicing ((17k) *[+voice]) makes sense only if one remembers that the map (12) only compares obstruents. Since voicing in sonorants is very easy, it is likely that in a fuller simulation, in which the map included sonorants, the constraint that would actually emerge is *[−sonorant, +voice]. This is well attested: for example, 45 of the 317 languages in Maddieson's (1984) survey lack voiced obstruents.

(e) The only non-artifactual constraint designated as grounded that probably is not legitimate is (17d), *[−nasal][+voice], which would impose devoicing after oral segments. It has been suggested by Steriade (1995) and others that [nasal] is a privative feature, being employed in phonological representations only to designate overt nasality. If this is so, then *[−nasal][+voice] would not appear in the candidate set.

(f) We can also consider the constraints of (18), which emerge from the simulation designated as not grounded. My impression, based on my own typological experience, is that these constraints are indeed rare or unattested in actual languages. Obviously, careful typological work would be needed to affirm this conclusion.

I would conclude that the inductive grounding procedure, applied in this narrow domain, does indeed single out the phonologically stated constraints that match typology. It is interesting that some of the constraints (for example (17e) *[LAB, −voice]) do not record extremely high effectiveness scores, but are nevertheless fairly well attested (19 languages of the 317 in Maddieson (1984) show a stop gap at [p]). This suggests, as before, that formal symmetry, and not just phonetic effectiveness, plays a role in constraint creation.

10   The Remainder of the Task of Phonological Acquisition

Above I have outlined a procedure that, equipped with full-scale phonetic maps, could generate large numbers of grounded constraints. What are we to do with them, in order to obtain actual grammars?

In Optimality Theory, the answer is simply: rank them. Tesar and Smolensky (1993, 1995, 1996) have demonstrated an algorithm, called Constraint Demotion, that ranks constraints using input data, with high computational efficiency. I suggest that the promiscuously generated constraints from inductive grounding could simply be fed into the Constraint Demotion algorithm. The algorithm will rank a few of them high in the grammar, the great majority very low. In Optimality Theory, a constraint that is ranked low enough will typically have no empirical effects at all. Thus, the Constraint Demotion algorithm can weed out the constraints that, while grounded, are inappropriate for the language being learned.

The combined effect of inductive grounding and the Constraint Demotion algorithm is in principle the construction of a large chunk of the phonology. The further ingredients needed would be constraints that have non-phonetic origins. These include: (a) the Faithfulness constraints: these perhaps result from their own inductive procedure, applied to the input vocabulary; (b) functionally based constraints that are not of phonetic origin: for example, rhythmically based constraints (Hayes 1995), or constraints on paradigm uniformity. Moreover, the child must also learn the phonological representations of the lexicon, a task that becomes non-trivial when these diverge from surface forms (Tesar and Smolensky 1996). Even so, I believe that getting the phonetic constraints right would be a large step towards phonology.

11   Conclusion

I have suggested, following much earlier work, that phonological constraints are often phonetic in character. They are not phonetics itself, but could in principle be "read off" the phonetics. Most of what I have said has been an effort to specify what this "reading off" could consist of. The hypotheses considered have been, in increasing order of specificity: (a) learners extract phonological constraints from their own experience; (b) in constructing constraints, learners execute a trade-off between phonetic accuracy and formal simplicity; (c) learners go through the logical space of possible phonological constraints, seeking local maxima of good phonetic fit, and at each point comparing candidate constraints only with rivals of equal or greater simplicity.

Notes

1   A number of these areas are also addressed in the related "Functional Phonology" of Boersma (1997).

2   Since this is only one approach among many, the reader is urged to compare it with Steriade's work, as well as Flemming (1995), Boersma (1997), and Kirchner (1998).

3   Actually, this paragraph slights the complexity of phonetic implementation. Following Pierrehumbert (1980) and Keating (1985), I assume that there is also a phonetic component in the grammar, which computes physical outcomes from surface phonological representations. It, too, I think, is Optimality-theoretic and makes use of inductive grounding (below). I cannot address these issues here for lack of space.

4   Interestingly, Westbury and Keating's (1986) modeling work found no articulatory support for the large typological difference between final devoicing (ubiquitous) and initial devoicing (somewhat unusual; see Westbury and Keating for cases). Recent work by Steriade (in progress) that relates the phonology of voicing to its *perceptual* cues at consonant releases would appear to fill this explanatory gap.

5   (a) In real life, numerous articulations other than glottal adduction influence voicing (Westbury 1979, 1983); I have used glottal adduction alone, despite the lack of realism, to reduce phonetic difficulty to a single physical scale. To permit a uniform criterion of perceptual adequacy, the right-side environment for all stops was assumed to be prevocalic, which of course adds another caveat to the results.

(b) Inputs to the aerodynamic model were as in Keating (1984), modified for the postnasal environment as in Hayes and Stivers (1996).

(c) The criterion for adequate perceptual voicelessness was that the release of the stop should be voiceless and there should be at least a 50 msec voiceless interval (half of the stop's 100 assumed msec closure duration). The criterion for perceptual voicing was that the release of the stop should be voiced, and at least half of the stop closure should be voiced. Preceding obstruents and nasals were assumed to overlap with the target stop, so they added only 50 msec to the total consonant closure.

(d) Since I had no basis for assessing what the true maximally easy vocal fold opening is, I was forced (for this one parameter) to "let the theory decide"; picking the value of 175 as the one that best matched observed phonological typology.

References

Anderson, Stephen R. 1981. "Why phonology isn't 'natural'". *Linguistic Inquiry* 12: 493–539.

Archangeli, Diana and Douglas Pulleyblank. 1994. *Grounded Phonology*. Cambridge, MA: MIT Press.

Boersma, Paul. 1997. "The elements of functional phonology." ROA-173, Rutgers Optimality Archive, http://ruccs.rutgers.edu/roa.html.

Chen, Matthew. 1973. "On the formal expression of natural rules in phonology." *Journal of Linguistics* 9: 223–49.

Choi, John-Dongwook. 1992. *Phonetic Underspecification and Target-interpolation: An Acoustic Study of Marshallese Vowel Allophony*. Ph.D. dissertation, University of California, Los Angeles.

Chomsky, Noam and Morris Halle. 1968. *The Sound Pattern of English*. New York: Harper and Row.

Devine, A. M. and Laurence D. Stephens. 1977. *Two Studies in Latin Phonology*. Saratoga, CA: Anma Libri.

Ferguson, Charles. 1975. "Sound patterns in language acquisition." In Daniel P. Dato (ed.), *Developmental Psycholinguistics: Theory and Applications*. Georgetown University Round Table on Languages and Linguistics, 1975. Washington, DC: Georgetown University Press, 1–16.

Flemming, Edward. 1995. *Perceptual Features in Phonology*. Ph.D. dissertation, University of California, Los Angeles. [Published 2002: New York: Routledge.]

Gafos, Adamantios. 1996. *The Articulatory Basis of Location in Phonology*. Ph.D. dissertation, Johns Hopkins University.

Gordon, Matt. 1997. "A phonetically-driven account of syllable weight." MS, Dept. of Linguistics, University of California, Los Angeles. [Published 2002: *Language* 78: 51–80.]

Hayes, Bruce 1995. *Metrical Stress Theory: Principles and Case Studies*. Chicago: University of Chicago Press.

Hayes, Bruce and Tanya Stivers. 1996. "The phonetics of postnasal voicing." MS, Dept. of Linguistics, University of California, Los Angeles. http://www.linguistics.ucla.edu/people/hayes/phonet.htm.

Jun, Jongho. 1995a. "Place assimilation as the result of conflicting perceptual and articulatory constraints." *Proceedings of the West Coast Conference on Formal Linguistics* 14. Stanford, CA: Center for the Study of Language and Information, 221–37.

Jun, Jongho. 1995b. *Perceptual and Articulatory Factors in Place Assimilation: An Optimality Theoretic Approach*. Ph.D. dissertation, University of California, Los Angeles.

Kaun, Abigail. 1995a. *The Typology of Rounding Harmony: An Optimality-Theoretic Approach*. Ph.D. dissertation, University of California, Los Angeles.

Kaun, Abigail. 1995b. "An Optimality-Theoretic account of rounding harmony typology." *Proceedings of the Thirteenth West Coast Conference on Formal Linguistics*. Stanford, CA: Center for the Study of Language and Information, 78–92.

Keating, Patricia. 1984. "Aerodynamic modeling at UCLA." *UCLA Working Papers in Phonetics* 54: 18–28.

Keating, Patricia A. 1985. "Universal phonetics and the organization of grammars." In Victoria Fromkin (ed.), *Phonetic Linguistics: Essays in Honor of Peter Ladefoged*. Orlando, FL: Academic Press, 115–32.

Kiparsky, Paul and Lisa Menn. 1977. "On the acquisition of phonology." In J. Macnamara (ed.), *Language Learning and Thought*. New York: Academic Press.

Kirchner, Robert. 1998. *An Effort-based Approach to Consonant Lenition*. Ph.D. dissertation, University of California, Los Angeles. ROA-276, Rutgers Optimality Archive, http://ruccs.rutgers.edu/roa.html.

Koutsoudas, Andreas, Gerald Sanders, and Craig Noll. 1974. "The application of phonological rules." *Language* 50: 1–28.

Liljencrants, Johan and Björn Lindblom. 1972. "Numerical simulation of vowel systems: the role of perceptual contrast." *Language* 48: 839–62.

Lindblom, Björn. 1983. "Economy of speech gestures." In Peter F. MacNeilage (ed.), *The Production of Speech*. New York: Springer, 217–45.

Lindblom, Björn. 1990. "Explaining phonetic variation: a sketch of the H&H theory." In William J. Hardcastle and Alain Marchal (eds.), *Speech Production and Speech Modelling*. Dordrecht: Kluwer, 403–39.

Locke, John L. 1983. *Phonological Acquisition and Change*. New York: Academic Press.

Maddieson, Ian. 1984. *Patterns of Sounds*. Cambridge: Cambridge University Press.

Mangold, Max. 1962. *Duden Aussprachewörterbuch*. Mannheim: Bibliographisches Institut.

Ohala, John J. 1974. "Phonetic explanation in phonology." In *Papers from the Parasession on Natural Phonology*. Chicago: Chicago Linguistic Society, 251–74.

Ohala, John J. 1978. "Production of tone." In Victoria Fromkin (ed.), *Tone: A Linguistic Survey*. New York: Academic Press, 5–39.

Ohala, John. 1981. "The listener as a source of sound change." *Papers from the Parasession on Language and Behavior*. Chicago: Chicago Linguistic Society, 178–203.

Ohala, John J. 1983. "The origin of sound patterns in vocal tract constraints." In Peter F. MacNeilage (ed.), *The Production of Speech*. New York: Springer, 189–216.

Ohala, John J. and Manjari Ohala. 1993. "The phonetics of nasal phonology: theorems and data." In Marie K. Huffman and Rena A. Krakow (eds.), *Nasals, Nasalization, and the Velum*. San Diego: Academic Press.

Orr, Carolyn. 1962. "Ecuadorian Quichua phonology." In Benjamin Elson (ed.), *Studies in Ecuadorian Indian Languages I*. Norman, OK: Summer Institute of Linguistics.

Pater, Joe. 1996. "*NC." *Proceedings of the North East Linguistic Society* 26. Graduate Linguistic Student Association, University of Massachusetts, Amherst, 227–39.

Pater, Joe. 1999. "Austronesian nasal substitution and other NC effects." In René Kager, Harry van der Hulst, and Wim Zonneveld (eds.), *The Prosody–Morphology Interface*. Cambridge: Cambridge University Press, 310–43. ◄

Pierrehumbert, Janet B. 1980. *The Phonology and Phonetics of English Intonation*. Ph.D. dissertation, Massachusetts Institute of Technology. Distributed 1987 by Indiana University Linguistics Club, Bloomington.

Prince, Alan and Paul Smolensky. 1993. *Optimality Theory: Constraint Interaction in Generative Grammar*. ◄

Rischel, Jørgen. 1974. *Topics in West Greenlandic Phonology*. Copenhagen: Akademisk Forlag.

Rood, David. 1975. "The implications of Wichita phonology." *Language* 51: 315–37.

Rothenberg, Martin. 1968. *The Breath-Stream Dynamics of Simple-Released-Plosive Production*. Bibliotheca Phonetica, no. 6. Basel: Karger.

Schachter, Paul. 1969. "Natural assimilation rules in Akan." *International Journal of American Linguistics* 35: 342–55.

Silverman, Daniel. 1995. *Acoustic Transparency and Opacity*. Ph.D. dissertation, University of California, Los Angeles.

Smolensky, Paul. 1993. "Harmony, markedness, and phonological activity." ROA-37, Rutgers Optimality Archive, http://ruccs.rutgers.edu/roa.html.

Steriade, Donca. 1993. "Positional neutralization." Presentation at the 23rd meeting of the North East Linguistic Society, University of Massachusetts, Amherst.

Steriade, Donca. 1995. "Underspecification and markedness." In John Goldsmith (ed.), *The Handbook of Phonological Theory*. Oxford: Blackwell, 114–74.

Steriade, Donca. 1997. "Phonetics in phonology: the case of laryngeal neutralization." MS, University of California, Los Angeles. [http://mit.edu/linguistics/www/steriade.home.html]

Steriade, Donca. 1999. "Phonetics in phonology: the case of laryngeal neutralization." In

Matthew Gordon (ed.), *Papers in Phonology 3* (UCLA Working Papers in Linguistics 2). Los Angeles: Department of Linguistics, University of California, 25–145.

Tesar, Bruce and Paul Smolensky. 1993. "The learning of Optimality Theory: an algorithm and some basic complexity results." ROA-52, Rutgers Optimality Archive, http:// ruccs.rutgers.edu/roa.html.

Tesar, Bruce and Paul Smolensky. 1995. "The learnability of Optimality Theory." *Proceedings of the Thirteenth West Coast Conference on Formal Linguistics*. Stanford, CA: Center for the Study of Language and Information, 122–37.

Tesar, Bruce B. and Paul Smolensky. 1996. "Learnability in Optimality Theory." ROA-110, Rutgers Optimality Archive, http:// ruccs.rutgers.edu/roa.html. ◄

Traill, Anthony. 1981. *Phonetic and Phonological Studies of !Xóõ Bushman*. Ph.D. dissertation, University of the Witwatersrand, Johannesburg.

Vance, Timothy J. 1987. *An Introduction to Japanese Phonology*. Albany: State University of New York Press.

Westbury, John R. 1979. *Aspects of the Temporal Control of Voicing in Consonant Clusters in English*. Texas Linguistic Forum 14, Department of Linguistics, University of Texas at Austin.

Westbury, John. 1983. "Enlargement of the supraglottal cavity and its relation to stop consonant voicing." *Journal of the Acoustical Society of America* 74: 1322–36.

Westbury, John and Patricia Keating. 1986. "On the naturalness of stop consonant voicing." *Journal of Linguistics* 22: 145–66.

Study and Research Questions

1 Consider some of the markedness constraints used in other chapters of this book. Are they plausibly phonetically grounded as well? Try to apply the proposals in this chapter to another case of a phonetically grounded markedness constraint.

2 This chapter argues that markedness constraints are phonetically grounded and learned. It is at least logically possible, however, that markedness constraints are phonetically grounded and innate. If the constraints are indeed innate, how could their phonetic grounding be explained?

3 Compare the account of post-nasal voicing in this chapter with the one in chapter 14. What about the other ways, besides voicing, in which languages deal with NÇ clusters?

4 There are many other recent works on functional phonology in OT: Boersma 1998, to appear; Crosswhite 1999; Flemming 1995; Gafos 1996; Gess 1998; Gordon 1999; Jun 1995, 1996; Kaun 1995; Kirchner 1998a, 1998b; MacEachern 1997; Myers 1997; Ní Chiosáin and Padgett 2001; Silverman 1995; Steriade 1995, 1997; Walker 1998. Read one of these and discuss its proposals.

Chapter 16 | Jill Beckman

Positional Faithfulness

Editor's Note

Faithfulness constraints are unique to OT, and so it is not surprising that exploration of faithfulness can offer a new perspective on familiar problems. In this chapter, the theory of faithfulness is extended to deal with positional neutralization phenomena. Positional neutralization is one of the topics of Trubetzkoy's *Grundzüge*, where it is called "structurally conditioned suspension of distinctive contrasts"; his examples include final consonant devoicing and reduction of vowels in unstressed syllables. The idea behind positional faithfulness is that the generalizations underlying these phenomena are best expressed by identifying the positions where neutralization does not occur, rather than where it does.

This chapter can be read in conjunction with chapters 11, 12, 17, and 18, which also deal with aspects of positional faithfulness and an alternative to it. For further references, see McCarthy (2002: 179).

[. . .]

2   Root-initial Faithfulness

2.1   Introduction

Positional asymmetries in feature distribution at the syllabic level are well known from the work of Steriade (1982), Itô (1986, 1989), Goldsmith (1989, 1990) and Lombardi (1991), among others. Syllable onsets typically permit more, and more marked, segments than do syllable codas. While investigations of syllable-level asymmetries have been numerous and fruitful, phonological asymmetries associated with other structural positions have largely been overlooked.

Excerpt from:
Beckman, Jill (1998) *Positional Faithfulness*. Doctoral dissertation. Amherst, MA: University of Massachusetts, Amherst. [Available on Rutgers Optimality Archive, ROA-234.]

Root-initial syllables constitute one such case. Phonologically, initial syllables exhibit all of the asymmetrical behaviors typical of "strong licensors": they permit a wide range of marked segments, trigger directional phonological processes, and resist the application of otherwise regular alternations. In this chapter, I will argue that the phonologically privileged status of root-initial syllables arises from high-ranking initial-syllable faithfulness constraints. Such constraints encompass all three aspects of phonological privilege which are displayed by initial syllables. I begin with a survey of initial syllable privilege effects.

2.2   Initial syllable privilege

2.2.1   Psycholinguistic evidence

One source of evidence for initial-syllable positional privilege may be found in the domain of lexical access and language processing. There is a considerable body of psycholinguistic research which indicates that word-initial material, either spoken or written, plays a key role in lexical access, word recognition and speech production. Some of this evidence is outlined in (1) below. (See Hall 1988, 1992; Hawkins & Cutler 1988 for further examples and discussion of the relevant literature.)

(1)   Initiality effects in processing[1]
  • Utterance-initial portions make better cues for word recognition and lexical retrieval than either final or medial portions (Horowitz et al. 1968; Horowitz et al. 1969; Nooteboom 1981)
  • Initial material is most frequently recalled by subjects in a tip-of-the-tongue state (Brown & McNeill 1966)
  • Word onsets are the most effective cues in inducing recall of the target word in tip-of-the-tongue states (Freedman & Landauer 1966)
  • Mispronunciations are detected more frequently in initial positions than in later positions (Cole 1973; Cole & Jakimik 1978, 1980)
  • Mispronunciations in word onsets are less likely to be fluently replaced in a speech shadowing task than errors in later positions (Marslen-Wilson 1975; Marslen-Wilson & Welsh 1978)

From evidence of this type, Hawkins and Cutler (1988: 299) conclude that the temporal structure of lexical entries is "of paramount importance" in the lexicon. They further "suggest that the pervasiveness of onset salience, expressing itself not only in auditory comprehension but in reading as well, and in parallel effects in speech production, argues that the importance of the temporal structure of words in their mental representation extends beyond the auditory access code." In this context, the predictions of Nooteboom (1981: 422) take on particular significance: ". . . lexical items will generally carry more information early in the word than late in the word. In phonological terms one would predict that (i) in the initial position there will be a greater variety of different phonemes and phoneme combinations than in word-final position, and (ii) word initial phonemes will suffer less than word final phonemes from assimilation and coarticulation rules."

Nooteboom's predictions appear to be borne out cross-linguistically. There are many examples of phonological behavior which turn on the root-initial/non-initial syllable distinction. I turn to an overview of such examples in §2.2.2.

2.2.2   Phonological evidence of positional privilege

Phonological asymmetries between root-initial and non-initial syllables are well documented in the descriptive and generative phonological literature. Positional neutralization of vocalic contrasts outside of the root-initial syllable is particularly common in languages which exhibit vowel harmony, and is robustly attested in a variety of languages and language families including Turkic, Tungusic, Mongolian, Finno-Ugric, and Bantu. (Many cases of non-initial vowel neutralization are documented and/or discussed in Trubetzkoy 1939; Bach 1968; Haiman 1972; Ringen 1975; Kiparsky 1981, 1988; Clements & Sezer 1982; Goldsmith 1985; Steriade 1979, 1993, 1995; Hulst & Weijer 1995, to mention only a few.) In languages that exhibit non-initial neutralization of vowel contrasts, the vowel inventory in non-initial syllables is typically a subset of the full vowel inventory appearing in root-initial syllables. Furthermore, membership in the non-initial inventory is not random: non-initial vowels are generally less marked than, or identical to, the members of the vowel inventory which appear in root-initial syllables.

One language which exhibits this pattern of positional neutralization is Shona, a Bantu language of Zimbabwe. In Shona verbs, vowel height may vary freely in root-initial position, as in (2). However, vowel height in non-initial syllables is severely restricted; non-initial mid vowels may surface only if preceded by an initial mid vowel.

(2)   Initial vowel height varies freely
      pera   'end'
      tsveta   'stick'
      sona   'sew'
      ipa   'be evil'
      ɓuɗa   'come out'
      bvuma   'agree'
      ɓata   'hold'
      shamba   'wash'

(3)   Non-initial height is restricted
      tonhor-   'be cold'
      pember-   'dance for joy'
      bover-   'collapse inwards'

      buruk-   'dismount'
      simuk-   'stand up'
      turikir-   'translate'

      charuk-   'jump over/across'
      tandanis-   'chase'

There are no Shona verbs in which mid vowels follow either low or high vowels. Only the peripheral vowels *i*, *u* and *a* are contrastive in non-initial syllables.

Positional restrictions on inventory are not limited to the realm of vowel features. In many languages, consonantal contrasts are confined to root-initial syllables. Representative examples of both vocalic and consonantal positional neutralization are displayed in (4). Further examples may be found in many languages of diverse genetic affiliation.

(4) Root-initial/non-initial inventory asymmetries

Language	Inventory includes	Initial σ	Non-initial σ
Tuva (Turkic) (Krueger 1977)	Plain & glottalized vowels	Both plain & glottalized vowels	No glottalized vowels
Turkic family (Comrie 1981; Kaun 1995)	Round & unround vowels	Round & unround vowels	Round vowels only via harmony with a round initial
Hungarian (C. Ringen, personal communication)	High & mid front rounded vowels	High & mid front rounded vowels	Mid front rounded vowels only after front rounded vowels
!Xóõ (Bushman) (Traill 1985)	Click & non-click consonants	Click & non-click consonants	No clicks
Tamil (Dravidian) (Christdas 1988; Bosch & Wiltshire 1992)	High, mid & low vowels Round & unround vowels Linked & independent POA in coda position	High, mid & low vowels Round & unround vowels Linked & independent POA in coda position	No mid vowels No round vowels Only linked POA in coda position
Malayalam (Dravidian) (Wiltshire 1992)	Labial, dorsal & a variety of coronal consonants	Independent POA in coda position	POA in coda must be shared by following onset
Dhangar-Kurux (Dravidian) (Gordon 1976)	Oral & nasal vowels Long & short vowels	Oral & nasal vowels Long & short vowels	No nasal vowels No long vowels
Shona (Bantu) Fortune 1995) (many other Bantu languages exhibit parallel facts)	High, mid & low vowels	High, mid & low vowels	Mid only via harmony with a mid in the initial syllable
Shilluk (Nilotic) (Gilley 1992)	Plain, palatalized & labialized consonants	Plain, palatalized & labialized consonants	No palatalized or labialized consonants
Doyayo (Niger-Congo) (Wiering & Wiering 1994)	Voiceless, voiced & implosive consonants Labiovelar stops (k͡p, ĝb)	Voiceless, voiced & implosive consonants Labiovelar stops	No implosives (ɓ. ɗ) No labiovelar stops
Bashkir (Turkic) (Poppe 1964)	High, mid & low vowels	High, mid & low vowels	No high vowels

In addition to permitting a wider range of more marked segments, root-initial syllables frequently act as triggers of phonological processes such as vowel harmony, or preferentially fail to undergo an otherwise regular process. Palatal and/or rounding harmony in many Altaic languages can be characterized as spreading triggered by the root-initial syllable. Shona height harmony (and numerous other examples of height harmony in Bantu languages) also falls into this category; harmony is initiated by a segment in the privileged root-initial syllable. The second phenomenon, in which segments in the root-initial syllable fail to undergo a process, is instantiated in Tamil, where codas of initial syllables do not undergo place assimilation, and in Zulu, in which root-initial consonants fail to undergo an otherwise regular process of dissimilation. Further examples of initial syllable resistance can be found in Leti, an Austronesian language, and Korean. Hume (1996) discusses the occurrence of metathesis in the Austronesian language Leti. In Leti, metathesis is a pervasive strategy employed in the satisfaction of a variety of phrase-level prosodic structure constraints. However, while metathesis applies freely to word-final sequences, it never applies in root-initial environments. Finally, Kang (in preparation) (cited in Hume 1996) reports on a process of glide deletion in Seoul Korean which applies at a significantly higher rate in non-initial syllables than in initial syllables.

In this chapter, I will argue that both initially determined positional neutralization and initially triggered or blocked phonological processes result from a high-ranking positional faithfulness constraint, IDENT-σ_1(F), formulated as in (5).

(5) IDENT-σ_1(F)
     Let β be an output segment in the root-initial syllable, and α its input correspondent.
     If β is [γF], then α must be [γF].
     "An output segment in σ_1 and the input correspondent of that segment must have identical feature specifications."

This constraint belongs in the same family as the familiar IDENT(F) of McCarthy & Prince (1995), and universally dominates it, as shown in (6).

(6) Universal ranking, initial syllable faithfulness subhierarchy
     IDENT-σ_1(F) ≫ IDENT(F)

Non-initial neutralization of contrast arises when some markedness constraint or constraints intervene in the ranking shown in (6). For example, the absence of mid vowels outside of root-initial syllables results from the ranking shown in (7), where the intervening markedness constraint is *MID (*[−high, −low]).

(7) Positional limitations on phonemic mid vowels
     IDENT-σ_1(high) ≫ *MID ≫ IDENT(high)

The ranking of IDENT-σ_1(high) ≫ *MID will result in the preservation of underlying height contrasts in root-initial syllables. Conversely, the ranking *MID ≫

IDENT(high) prohibits preservation of input mid vowels outside of the root-initial syllable.

The other two privileged behaviors exhibited by root-initial syllables, triggering of phonological processes and blocking of phonological processes, derive from the same basic pattern of ranking shown in (7). In an OT grammar, phonological processes are manifested when some markedness constraint dominates a faithfulness constraint, thereby forcing an alternation. For example, nasal harmony may result from the ranking of ALIGN(nasal) ≫ IDENT(nasal), place assimilation from the ranking SPREAD(Place) ≫ IDENT(Place) (Padgett 1995b), and so on.

Initial-syllable triggering *and* blocking of phonological processes such as nasal harmony and place assimilation derive from the ranking schema in (8) below, where $\mathbb{M}$ represents any markedness constraint.

(8) Initial-syllable triggering and blocking schema
     IDENT-σ_1(F) ≫ $\mathbb{M}$ ≫ IDENT(F)

The ranking of IDENT-σ_1(F) ≫ $\mathbb{M}$ renders any element in the root-initial syllable immune to the application of the phonological process characterized by the ranking of $\mathbb{M}$ ≫ IDENT(F). An example of this type will be presented in §2.3 below.

The remainder of the chapter is organized as follows. In §2.3, I examine the role of IDENT-σ_1(F) in characterizing Shona height harmony. In Shona, contrastive mid vowels occur only in root-initial syllables; elsewhere, they arise predictably through harmony. This pattern derives from the ranking schema in (8). Section 2.4 [omitted here – Ed.] provides an analysis of Tamil, a language which exhibits multiple reflexes of high-ranking IDENT-σ_1(F). In Tamil, as in Shona, mid vowels are limited to root-initial syllables. Furthermore, coda consonants in initial syllables may have an independent place of articulation, though codas of non-initial syllables may not. We will see that high-ranking IDENT-σ_1(F) constraints are again the key to characterizing both the distribution of vowel height in Shona and of coda place of articulation in Tamil.

2.3   Positional neutralization and harmony in Shona

2.3.1   Data and generalizations

Shona is a Bantu language spoken primarily in Zimbabwe; it belongs in Area S, according to the classification system of Guthrie (1967). The descriptive and generative literature on Shona is extensive, particularly in the realm of tonal phonology. (Notable generative works on Shona tone include Myers 1987 and Odden 1981.) Our focus here will not be on the tonal properties of Shona, but rather on the distribution of vowel height in the verbal system.

The distribution of the feature [high] in Shona verbs is a classic example of positional neutralization accompanied by vowel harmony: the mid vowels *e* and *o* in Shona verbs are contrastive only in root-initial syllables.[2] They appear in subsequent syllables only when preceded by a mid vowel in root-initial position. A string of height-harmonic Shona vowels is therefore firmly anchored in the root-initial syllable.[3]

Shona has a three-height vowel system composed of five surface vowels. The vowels of Shona and the surface feature specifications assumed are shown in (9) below. (Unless otherwise noted, the data and generalizations which follow are drawn from Fortune 1955, who describes the Zezuru dialect of Shona. Tone and vowel length have been omitted throughout; length occurs only in penultimate syllables, as a reflex of stress.)

(9)   Distinctive features of Shona vowels

	[back]	[round]	[high]	[low]
i	–	–	+	–
u	+	+	+	–
e	–	–	–	–
o	+	+	–	–
a	+	–	–	+

In Shona, as in most languages with triangular vowel systems, the low vowel is inert with respect to vowel harmony; *a* systematically fails to pattern with the [–high] vowels *e* and *o*. The appearance of a root-initial *a* does not permit subsequent mid vowels (indicating that the [–high] specification of *a* is not available for linkage to a subsequent non-low vowel). Furthermore, the distribution of [–high] *a* is free, not restricted to the initial syllable as are the [–high] mid vowels. The relative freedom of the low vowel will emerge from constraint interaction, as shown in §2.3.3 below.[4]

While the distribution of *a* is free in Shona verbs, the occurrence of high and mid vowels is subject to certain limitations. Verb *stems* are composed of a verb *root* and any number of optional derivational *extensions*; verb roots are primarily CVC in shape, but polysyllabic roots are not uncommon. In the initial syllable of a verb stem, there are no restrictions on the occurrence of vowel features. However, in non-initial syllables (whether in the root or in an extension), only [round], [back] and [low] may vary freely. The value of the feature [high] is determined by the height of a preceding vowel: mid vowels may appear non-initially only if preceded by a mid vowel. In order for a string of mid vowels to be licit, the left-most vowel must appear in a root-initial syllable. (Thus, a sequence *CeCe*, where C = any consonant, is not possible if preceded by a root-initial high or low vowel: *$CiCeCe$, *$CaCeCe$.) High vowels may appear non-initially if the vowel of the preceding syllable is either high or low, but never if the preceding vowel is mid. This is summarized for #$\sigma_1\sigma_2$ sequences in (10), where #σ_1 indicates a root-initial syllable.

(10) $\sigma_2 \rightarrow$

		i	u	e	o	a
$\#\sigma_1$ ↓	i	✓	✓	▓	▓	✓
	u	✓	✓	▓	▓	✓
	e	▓	✓	✓	▓	✓
	o	▓	▓	✓	✓	✓
	a	✓	✓	▓	▓	✓

Shaded cells in the table indicate non-occurring vowel sequences. Mid vowels may not follow either high or low vowels, while high vowels may not follow mid. This is true both within verb roots and between roots and extensions in derived forms. (The sole exception to this generalization is found in the sequence #CeCu; non-initial round vowels harmonize in height with a preceding vowel only if the vowels agree in rounding. This is manifested in the absence of #CeCo sequences and the presence of #CeCu, as indicated in (10). I will ignore this gap in the remaining discussion; a full analysis is provided in Beckman 1997.)

Data instantiating these distributional generalizations are given in (11)–(16) below. In (11), representative examples of polysyllabic verb roots are provided. (Many of the polysyllabic roots in the language are likely to have been derived from root + extension combinations at an earlier point in the history of the language; such forms appear to have been lexicalized to varying degrees in the synchronic grammar. Others are related to nouns or ideophones. Wherever possible, I have excluded transparently derived roots from the list in (11).) There are no polysyllabic roots which fail to conform to the generalizations shown in (10) above.

(11)   Polysyllabic roots exhibit vowel harmony[5]

tonhor-	'be cold'	Fi	chenjer-	'be wise'	M
nonok-	'dally, delay'	Fo7	chember-	'grow old'	M
nonot-	'scold, abuse'	H	verer-	'move stealthily'	M
korokod-	'itch (nostril)'	H	vereng-	'read; count'	M
gobor-	'uproot'	Fo7	pember-	'dance for joy'	H
bover-	'collapse inwards'	H	nyemwerer-	'smile'	Fo7
kobodek-	'become empty'	H			
pofomadz-	'blind (trans.)'	Fo5	zendam-	'lean w/support at side or back'	H
pofomar-	'be blind'	H	chenam-	'bare teeth angrily'	H
chonjomar-	'sit w/buttocks & soles of feet on ground'	H			

fungat-	'embrace'	D	bvinar-	'fade'	H
pfugam-	'kneel'	Fo7	findam-	'tangle (intr.)'	H
ruram-	'be straight'	Fo7	minaik-	'wriggle'	H
buruk-	'dismount'	Fo7	simuk-	'stand up'	Fo7
dukup-	'to be small'	H	simudz-	'lift'	Fi
kumbir-	'ask for'	M	kwipur-	'uproot'	H
turikir-	'translate'	Fi	svetuk-	'jump'	Fo5
			serenuk-	'water (gums of mouth)'	H
charuk-	'jump over/across'	H	tandanis-	'chase'	Fi
ganhur-	'limit, demarcate'	H	kwazis-	'greet'	Fo7
katuk-	'flicker (flame)'	H			

An exhaustive list of the verbal extensions, both productive and unproductive, is given in (12).

(12)   Shona verbal extensions (Doke 1967: 66–7)

-w, -iw/-ew	Passive
-ir/-er	Applicative
-ik/-ek	Neuter
-is/-es, -y	Causative
-idz/-edz	"
-is/-es, -isis/-eses	Intensive
-irir/-erer	Perfective (from Fortune 1955; Doke says that the perfective does not exist in Shona)
-an	Reciprocal
-uk/-ok, -uruk/-orok	Reversive
-ur/-or, -urur/-oror	"
-aur	Extensive
-at	Contactive (not productive)
-am, -ar	Stative (not productive, according to Doke)

In (13)–(16), I give examples of derived root + extension combinations, taken from Fortune (1955). The (a) forms show surface mid vowels in extensions, while the (b) forms give extensions with surface high vowels. Alternating vowels are italicized.

(13)   Root + applicative extension

a.
pera	'end'	per-*era*	'end in'
tsveta	'stick'	tsvet-*era*	'stick to'
sona	'sew'	son-*era*	'sew for'
pona	'give birth'	pon-*era*	'give birth at'

b.
ipa	'be evil'	ip-*ira*	'be evil for'
ɓata	'hold'	ɓat-*ira*	'hold for'
vava	'itch'	vav-*ira*	'itch at'
svetuka	'jump'	svetuk-*ira*	'jump in'
pofomadza	'blind'	pofomadz-*ira*	'blind for'

(14)   Root + neuter extension
   a.   gona   'be able'   gon-eka   'be feasible'
         verenga   'count'   vereng-eka   'be numerable'
         chengeta   'keep'   chenget-eka   'get kept'

   b.   kwira   'climb'   kwir-ika   'easy to climb'
         bvisa   'remove'   bvis-ika   'be easily removed'
         tarisa   'look at'   taris-ika   'easy to look at'

(15)   Root + perfective suffix
   a.   pota   'go round'   pot-erera   'go right round'
         cheka   'cut'   chek-erera   'cut up small'
         seka   'laugh'   sek-erera   'laugh on and on'

   b.   pinda   'pass'   pind-irira   'to pass right through'
         ɓuɗa   'come out'   ɓuɗ-irira   'to come out well'

(16)   Root + causative suffix
   a.   tonda   'face'   tond-esa   'make to face'
         shonga   'adorn self'   shong-esa   'make adorn'
         oma   'be dry'   om-esa   'cause to get dry'

   b.   bvuma   'agree'   bvum-isa   'make agree'
         shamba   'wash'   shamb-isa   'make wash'
         pamha   'do again'   pamh-isa   'make do again'
         cheyama   'be twisted'   cheyam-isa   'make be twisted'

The data in (11)–(16) demonstrate that high and mid vowels in Shona are not freely distributed in the verbal system. Rather, the height of the root-initial vowel determines the height of any subsequent non-low vowels. If the initial vowel is [–high, +low], following [–low] vowels must share that [–high] specification; if the initial vowel is [+high], only the [+high] vowels *i* and *u* may appear subsequently. Forms such as *cheyamisa* 'make be twisted' and *pofomadzira* 'blind for' demonstrate that the low vowel *a* is opaque to harmony, constituting a barrier to the extension of a multiply-linked [high]. Following a low vowel, no further mid vowels may appear; instead, the typologically less marked high vowels are invariably found. The analysis of these facts is given in section 2.3.2.

2.3.2   Preliminaries: markedness and faithfulness constraints in OT

The distribution of vowel height in Shona, and in many other Bantu languages with comparable harmony systems, is characteristic of positional neutralization. The distinction between high and mid vowels is maintained in root-initial syllables, giving a three-way height contrast, but high and mid vowels are not contrastive outside of the root-initial syllable. This positional restriction on segmental contrastiveness results from the interaction of featural markedness and faithfulness constraints, in the same way that language-wide inventory restrictions arise through markedness/faithfulness interaction (Prince & Smolensky 1993: chapter 9).

I follow the proposals of Prince & Smolensky (1993) and Smolensky (1993), who argue that universal harmony scales, each of which encodes the relative markedness of all features along a particular dimension such as place of articulation or height, are reflected in the grammar by means of corresponding constraint subhierarchies. Various surveys of vowel inventory structure (Crothers 1978, Disner 1984) indicate that the presence of mid vowels in an inventory implies the presence of high and low vowels, while the reverse is not true. The universal harmony scale which reflects this implication is given in (17), with the corresponding constraint dominance hierarchy in (18).

(17)   Height markedness: Harmony Scale
       High, Low > Mid

(18)   Height markedness: Dominance Hierarchy[6]
       *MID ≫ *HIGH, *LOW

The constraints in (18) are instantiated as in (19)–(21) below.[7]

(19)   *MID: *[–high, –low]

(20)   *HIGH: *[+high, –low]

(21)   *LOW: *[–high, +low]

In addition to featural markedness constraints, UG includes a set of faithfulness constraints which regulate exactness of input–output identity in vowel height specifications. The faithfulness constraints relevant to the analysis of Shona are divided into two distinct types. The first type is instantiated in the context-free IDENT constraints of (22).

(22)   IDENT(high)
       Let α be an input segment and β its output correspondent.
       If α is [γhigh], then β must be [γhigh].
       "An input segment and its output correspondent must have identical specifications for the feature [high]."

       IDENT(low)
       Let α be an input segment and β its output correspondent.
       If α is [γlow], then β must be [γlowl.
       "An input segment and its output correspondent must have identical specifications for the feature [low]."

The second type of featural faithfulness constraint is a root-initial faithfulness constraint, as shown in (23). It is the dispersion of height faithfulness according to position which is responsible for the asymmetrical distribution of high and mid vowels in Shona.

(23) IDENT-σ_1(high)
Let β be an output segment in the root-initial syllable, and α its input correspondent.
If β is [γhigh], then α must be [γhigh].
"An output segment in G_1, and the input correspondent of that segment must have identical specifications for the feature [high]."

Because syllabification is reliably present only in output strings, the constraint is formulated with an output "focus", in contrast to the context-free constraints of (22). In both cases, however, violations are incurred by any input–output mismatch in feature specifications; IDENT(high) and IDENT-σ_1(high) are both violated equally by deletion of underlying specifications and by insertion of non-input values. Through interaction with the markedness constraints in (19)–(21), the constraints in (22)–(23) generate the surface patterns of height distribution which are attested in Shona.

2.3.3 Analysis: positional neutralization and harmony

The positional restrictions on phonological inventory which are characteristic of positional neutralization result from the ranking schematized in (24).

(24) Positional neutralization ranking schema
IDENT-*Position*(F) ≫ *F ≫ IDENT(F)

This simple ranking permits the contrastive occurrence of a feature, F, in some prominent position; outside of that position, the ranking of *F above IDENT(F) rules out contrastive occurrences of F. In Shona, all three vowel heights are contrastive in root-initial syllables, calling for the ranking in (25).

(25) IDENT-σ_1(high), IDENT(low) ≫ *MID ≫ *HIGH, *LOW

The context-free IDENT(low) is high-ranking because (i) low vowels are free to occur in initial syllables, and (ii) in non-initial syllables, only the low vowel *a* is completely unfettered in its distribution. Low vowels do not raise, and non-low vowels do not lower; IDENT(low) is always satisfied.[8]

High and mid vowels are not distinctive non-initially; instead, they are predictable according to the height of a preceding vowel. Verbs containing a mid vowel in the root-initial syllable consist entirely of mid vowels, while the vowels in verbs whose initial syllable contains a high vowel are uniformly high. There are no verbs of the shape *CiCeC* or *CeCiC* in Shona. Further, if the root-initial syllable contains a low vowel, subsequent vowels may not be mid: **CaCeC*.[9] These facts, taken together, argue for the ranking in (26).

(26)   IDENT-σ_1(high), IDENT(low) ≫ *MID ≫ *HIGH ≫ IDENT(high)

The correctness of these rankings will be demonstrated in the following sections.

2.3.3.1   Vowel height in initial syllables

I begin by demonstrating that the proposed ranking permits the full range of height contrasts in root-initial syllables. Because IDENT-σ_1(high) and IDENT(low) dominate all of the featural markedness constraints, height specifications in the initial syllable will never deviate from their input values in order to better satisfy featural markedness constraints. This is shown in tableaux (27)–(29) below, where only the initial syllable is evaluated against the constraint hierarchy. Tableau (27) shows that mid vowels are permitted in initial syllables.[10]

(27)   Initial mid vowels are permitted

/cheyam-a/	IDENT-σ_1 (high)	IDENT (low)	*MID	*HIGH	*Low
a. ☞ cheyama ／\ –hi \ –lo			*		
b. chiyama ／\ +hi \ –lo	*!			*	
c. chayama ／\ –hi \ +lo		*!			*

IDENT(low) must dominate *MID in order to prevent lowering of an input mid vowel, as in (27c). Note that the lowered output satisfies IDENT-σ_1(high), as the mid and low vowels are both [–high]. Now we turn to an initial high vowel example in (28).

Here again, the ranking prohibits deviations from underlying height specifications in the initial syllable; the fully faithful (28b) is optimal. Finally, the case of an initial low vowel is illustrated in (29).

As expected, the faithful (29c) is optimal. Vowel height ranges freely over high, mid and low in the root-initial syllable, due to high-ranking initial syllable faithfulness.

(28)   Initial high vowels are permitted

/bvis-a/	IDENT-σ_1(high)	IDENT(low)	*MID	*HIGH	*LOW
a. bvesa (−hi −lo)	*!		*		
b. ☞ bvisa (+hi −lo)				*	
c. bvasa (−hi +lo)		*!			*

(29)   Initial low vowels are permitted

/shamb-a/	IDENT-σ_1(high)	IDENT(low)	*MID	*HIGH	*LOW
a. shemba (−hi −lo)		*!	*		
b. shimba (+hi −lo)	*!	*!		*	
c. ☞ shamba (−hi +lo)					*

2.3.3.2   *Height in non-initial syllables*

The ranking displayed in (27)–(29) generates the full range of height contrasts in the initial syllable, but it does not characterize the neutralization of the high–mid contrast in non-initial syllables. The latter arises from the ranking *MID ≫ *HIGH ≫ IDENT(high). This ranking, when combined with the higher-ranking faithfulness constraints IDENT-σ_1(high) and IDENT(low), will ensure that only low or high vowels may follow an initial syllable containing a low or high vowel. This is illustrated with initial low vowels in (30) and (31), where hypothetical inputs are assumed.

(30)   No mid vowels after initial low

/CaCeC/	IDENT-σ_1(high)	ID(low)	*MID	*HIGH	*Low	ID(high)
a. C a C e C [−hi] [−hi] +lo −lo			*!		*	
b. C a C e C [−hi] +lo −lo			*!		*	
c. ☞ C a C i C [−hi] [+hi] +lo −lo				*	*	*
d. C a C a C [−hi] [−hi] +lo +lo		*!			**	

The input low–mid sequence is prohibited, whether the low and mid vowels have separate specifications of [−high] (30a) or share a single [−high] (30b). This is due to the marked character of mid vowels. Each of the two candidates fatally violates *MID, by virtue of the [−high, −low] combination instantiated on the second vowel; the parasitism of the mid vowel on the [−high] of initial *a* cannot rescue it from a violation of *MID. This is because *MID penalizes a feature combination, rather than an individual feature; in each case, the marked combination of [−high, −low] is instantiated. Candidate (30d), in which the non-initial vowel surfaces as low *a*, is also ruled out, in this case by IDENT(low).[11] This leaves (30c), in which "default" [+high] is specified on the non-initial vowel, as optimal. Mid vowels may not follow a low vowel; an input mid vowel in this position will be realized as a [+high] vowel. Given an input with a low–high sequence, the candidate (30b) will also be preferred by the grammar. Of the non-low vowels, only those which are [+high] may follow *a*.

A non-initial low vowel is also permitted after an initial low vowel, as shown in (31).

(31)   Low vowel licit after initial low

/CaCaC/	IDENT-σ_1(high)	ID(low)	*MID	*HIGH	*Low	ID(high)
a. Ca CeC −hi −hi +lo −lo		*!	*		*	
b. Ca CiC −hi +hi +lo −lo		*!		*	*	*
c. Ca CaC −hi −hi +lo +lo					**!	
d. ☞ Ca CaC Aperture −hi +lo					*	
e. Ca CaC −hi +lo					**!	

Any deviation from the input low vowels incurs a fatal violation of IDENT(low), as in candidates (31a, b). A comparison of (31c–e) reveals that multiple-linking of identical specifications under a single Aperture node is preferred to a sequence of independent Aperture nodes. "Vacuous" vowel harmony is optimal, because IDENT(low) is not violated by multiple-linking, and because multiple-linking of the Aperture node better satisfies the markedness constraint *Low. Such markedness constraints, which penalize feature combinations, are best satisfied when only a single token of the feature combination is instantiated in the representation, as in (31d). In such a configuration, there is a single class node which dominates the complex of features under consideration.

The feature-driven character of *F constraint evaluation was pointed out in McCarthy & Prince (1994), and plays an important role in the Itô & Mester (1994) analysis of Lardil. In Shona, markedness reduction is also achieved via multiple-linking, though the linking in question involves superordinate class nodes, rather than single features such as Coronal or Labial. This is because the markedness constraints which drive multiple-linking are sensitive to the presence of multiple cooccurring features, and multiple features are organized according to feature class.[12] To give a unified formal characterization of constraint violation and satisfaction for featural markedness constraints of both the Lardil and Shona types, I propose the principle of Feature-Driven Markedness, as in (32). (See also Beckman 1997.)

(32) Feature-Driven Markedness
      Let S denote a set of features $\{\alpha, \beta, \gamma, \ldots\}$ and *S a markedness constraint prohibiting the cooccurrence of the members of S.
      *S receives one violation-mark for each node N, where
      • N dominates all features in S *and*
      • there is no node M such that N dominates M and M also dominates all features in S.

For a singleton feature markedness constraint such as *CORONAL, where S = {Coronal}, the node N in (32) = Coronal, on the assumption that domination is a reflexive relation (Wall 1972, Bach 1974, Cushing 1978, Johnson 1978, Pullum & Zwicky 1978). One violation-mark for *CORONAL would therefore be assessed for each occurrence of the feature Coronal in an output form; multiple feature specifications incur multiple violations of markedness constraints, while multiple linkings of a single feature do not. For example, a place-linked nasal + consonant cluster such as *nd* incurs only one violation of *CORONAL; the same cluster, when not place-linked, will incur two *CORONAL violations.

(33) a.   One *CORONAL violation   b.   Two *CORONAL violations
              n   d   n   d
               \ / | |
            Coronal   Coronal   Coronal

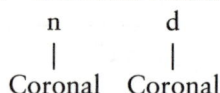

This is exactly the sense in which place markedness violations are assessed in Itô & Mester (1994) and a host of other recent works, including Alderete et al. (1996), Beckman (1995, 1996), Lombardi (1995a, b) and Padgett (1995a, b).

In the case of markedness constraints which evaluate feature combinations, such as *[−high, +low] (*LOW), *[−high, −low] (*MID), etc., (32) calls for violations to be assessed for each discrete node which immediately dominates the relevant feature set. In the case of *LOW, the dominant node in question is the Aperture node. This distinguishes the harmonizing (31d) from the sequence of singly linked identical vowels in (31c), and from the candidate with multiple Aperture nodes (31e). Feature-driven markedness effectively favors multiple-linking at higher levels of structure, in the case of feature cooccurrence constraints.[13]

With this understanding of featural markedness constraints, we turn to examples in which the initial syllable contains a high vowel. We saw above that the presence of a preceding low vowel will permit only high or low vowels in subsequent syllables. The same is true when the initial vowel is high; the constraint hierarchy permits only high or low vowels following an initial high vowel.

(34)   Low vowel licit after initial high

/CiCaC/	IDENT-σ_1(high)	ID(low)	*MID	*HIGH	*Low	ID(high)
a. ☞ CiCaC +hi \−hi −lo +lo				*	*	
b. CiCeC +hi \−hi −lo −lo		*!	*	*		
c. CiCiC +hi \+hi −lo −lo		*!		**		*
d. Ci CiC Aperture +hi −lo		*!		*		*

Here, the identity of the input low vowel is protected by high-ranking IDENT(low). Because the constraint dominates *Low, no change in underlying [+low] specifications is possible, regardless of their position within the word. With an input low vowel in the second syllable, only an output low vowel in that position is possible.

A high vowel is also permitted after a high vowel in the initial syllable. Consider the tableau in (35), where a sequence of input high vowels is examined.

No deviation from the input high–high sequence is permitted. (35d) is ruled out by the violation of IDENT(low) incurred by the output a, and (35c) fatally violates *MID. Because *MID dominates the context-free IDENT(high), mid vowels are generally ruled out, unless protected by IDENT-σ_1(high). Of the remaining candidates, (35b) is favored by virtue of the single *HIGH violation it incurs. Due to the feature-driven nature of markedness assessment (32), multiple-linking is again favored.

Because IDENT(high) is very low-ranking, the ranking of *MID shown in (35) will rule out full faithfulness to an input high–mid sequence, just as it ruled out (35c). This is demonstrated in (36).

(35)   High vowel licit after initial high

/CiCiC/	IDENT-σ_1(high)	ID(low)	*MID	*HIGH	*LOW	ID(high)
a. Ci CiC +hi +hi –lo –lo				**!		
b. ☞ Ci CiC Aperture +hi –lo				*		
c. Ci CeC +hi –hi –lo –lo			*!			*
d. Ci CaC +hi –hi –lo +lo		*!			*	*

Here, just as in (35), the output candidate with two high vowels which share an Aperture node (36b) is optimal, even though the input here includes a mid vowel. The height of the initial vowel is never subject to change (as in (36e)), due to undominated IDENT-σ_1(high). With a necessarily invariant vowel in the initial syllable, height harmony is forced in subsequent syllables by the ranking of the markedness constraints in the midst of the IDENT(high) subhierarchy.

There are three consequences of the proposed constraint ranking that have been established thus far. First, vowel height in initial syllables is fully contrastive and may vary freely. Second, height in non-initial syllables is limited to high or low when preceded by a low initial vowel. This is a kind of "emergence of the unmarked" effect (McCarthy & Prince 1994): if the vowels cannot be of identical height (i.e., if the input contains a low–high or low–mid sequence), then only the less marked of the non-low vowels may occur in non-initial position. (Recall that complete identity of height features is prevented in such cases by high-ranking IDENT(low).) Finally, height in non-initial syllables is restricted to high or low when preceded by a high initial vowel. Input mid vowels may not surface in this environment because of the ranking of *MID ≫ IDENT(high); height harmony is the result.

(36)   Mid vowel illicit after initial high

/CiCeC/	IDENT-σ_1(high)	ID(low)	*MID	*HIGH	*Low	ID(high)
a. Ci CiC /\ /\ +hi +hi −lo −lo				**!		*
b. ☞ Ci CiC Aperture /\ +hi −lo				*		*
c. Ci CeC /\ /\ +hi −hi −lo −lo			*!			
d. Ci CaC /\ /\ +hi −hi −lo +lo		*!			*	
e. Ce CeC Aperture /\ −hi −lo	*!			*		*

Now we can turn to the distribution of vowel height following an initial mid vowel. Only mid or low vowels may immediately follow an initial mid vowel; high vowels do not appear in this position.[14] Thus, we find forms such as *cheŋeta* 'keep', *shoŋgesa* 'make adorn', *ponera* 'give birth at', *pofomadza* 'blind' and *cheyama* 'be twisted', but not *chengita*, *ponira*, or other comparable examples. It is clear that non-low vowels must agree in height, while the low vowels may occur freely. These restrictions also follow from the constraint hierarchy presented above. The tableau in (37) illustrates the simple case of a low vowel appearing after an initial mid vowel.

(37) Low vowel licit after initial mid

/CeCaC/	IDENT-σ_1(high)	ID(low)	*MID	*HIGH	*Low	ID(high)
a. ☞ C e C a C −hi −hi −lo +lo			*		*	
b. C e C e C Aperture −hi −lo		*!	*			
c. C e C i C −hi +hi −lo −lo		*!	*	*		*
d. C i C a C +hi −hi −lo +lo	*!			*	*	*

High-ranking IDENT(low) and IDENT-σ_1(high) combine forces to rule out any un-faithful surface rendering of the input vocalism in this case. The low vowel may not be raised, as in (37b, c), due to undominated IDENT(low); the initial mid vowel cannot be raised because of undominated IDENT-σ_1(high). (The initial vowel cannot be lowered, either, again because of IDENT(low).) The fully faithful (37a) is optimal – low vowels may occur freely after mid vowels.[15]

The more interesting case to examine is the prohibition on a high vowel follow-ing an initial mid. The constraint ranking established above will correctly gen-erate height harmony, given an input sequence of mid + high. This is illustrated in (38).

Candidates (38a, e) fail on undominated height faithfulness constraints, (38a) because the input high vowel is lowered in the output, thereby violating IDENT(low). (38e) fails because the initial mid vowel surfaces as a high vowel in the output, thus incurring a violation of IDENT-σ_1(high). This leaves (38b, c, d) as contenders. Can-didate (38d) exhibits apparent height harmony, in that the input high vowel has been lowered to mid. However, the existence of two discrete height specifications in this candidate results in a fatal violation of *MID. (38b) and (38c) tie on *MID, but

(38)   Height harmony from a mid + high sequence

/CeCiC/	IDENT-σ₁(high)	ID(low)	*MID	*HIGH	*Low	ID(high)
a. C e C a C (–hi / –lo ; –hi / +lo)		*!	*		*	*
b. ☞ C e C e C (Aperture: –hi –lo)			*			*
c. C e C i C (–hi / –lo ; +hi / –lo)			*	*!		
d. C e C e C (–hi / –lo ; –hi / –lo)			**!		*	
e. C i C i C (Aperture: +hi –lo)	*!			*		*

the fully faithful (38c) incurs a fatal violation of *HIGH that (36b) does not suffer. This establishes the crucial ranking *HIGH ≫ IDENT(high).

   In order to complete the analysis of the distribution of height following initial mid vowels, we must examine forms such as *pofomadzira* 'blind for' and *cheyamisa* 'make be twisted'. In these words, a high vowel appears in the verbal extensions after the low *a*, although the initial vowel is mid; the pattern *CeCaCe* does not occur. This is a regular property of height distribution in Shona, and is explained in much the same way as the absence of *CaCeC* sequences in general. This is shown in (39).[16]

(39)   Low vowels are opaque to harmony

/CeCaCiC/	ID-σ_1(high)	ID(low)	*MID	*HIGH	*Low	ID(high)
a. ☞ Ce Ca CiC −hi −hi +hi −lo +lo −lo			*	*	*	
b. Ce Ca CeC −hi −lo +lo −lo			**!		*	*
c. Ce Ce CeC Aperture −hi −lo		*!	*			*

Either candidate in which the [−high] of the initial mid vowel is multiply linked to the rightmost vowel fatally violates some high-ranking constraint. In the case of (39c), the relevant constraint is IDENT(low); raising the intervening vowel from low to mid minimizes violations of *MID, but fails on the higher-ranking faithfulness constraint. The linking in (39b) incurs two violations of *MID, as there are two distinct instances of [−high, −low], dominated by two Aperture nodes. Candidate (39a), with only one *MID violation, is optimal; only [+high] non-low vowels may follow *a*. Low vowel opacity results from high-ranking IDENT(low), and from the role of *MID in limiting the distribution of mid vowels. Sharing only [−high] with a preceding low vowel does not save a mid vowel from fatally violating *MID.

2.3.4   Conclusions and implications

The preceding discussion has demonstrated that positional neutralization of height contrasts in Shona verbs arises through the interaction of markedness and faithfulness constraints. The privileged licensing status of the root-initial syllable results from high-ranking IDENT-σ_1(high), which forces input–output correspondence in the root-initial position, even for the more marked mid vowels. This is due to the ranking of IDENT-σ_1(high) above both of the featural markedness constraints *MID and *HIGH.

The crucial role of the positional faithfulness constraint IDENT-σ_1(high) emerges most clearly when we compare the effects of the proposed ranking on two similar classes of input, shown in (30) and (37). In one case, that of (30), a low–mid sequence (*CaCeC*) occurs in the input. Such inputs can never surface intact; the non-initial vowel must emerge as a high vowel. (Thus, the language includes roots such as *charuk-*, *tandanis-* and *ganhur-*, but no comparable forms containing mid vowels: **charok-*, **tandanes-*, **ganhor-*, etc.) By contrast, the opposite ordering of vowels (mid–low) may surface without incident: for example, input /cheyam-/ corresponds to output *cheyam-*. Each of the faithful output types, schematically *CaCeC* and *CeCaC*, fares equally well on the markedness constraints *MID and *LOW. It is the *location* of the marked mid vowel which is crucial in differentiating the two forms: a free-standing mid vowel is permitted if and only if it occurs in the root-initial syllable.

Positional faithfulness is crucial to an account of this difference; it cannot be derived by replacing IDENT-σ_1(high) with a high-ranking ALIGN(high) constraint. To see this, consider the constraint in (40) below, and its application in tableaux (41) and (42). (For the purposes of demonstration, I assume that the remaining constraints and their rankings are fixed.)

(40) ALIGN([high], L, Root, L)[17]
      "Every [high] specification must be left-aligned with a root."

Such a constraint will favor sharing of [–high] between mid and low vowels, regardless of their input position. This derives the correct results in the case of a mid–low input, as in (41).

(41) [–high] is multiply linked

	ALIGN-L(high)	ID(low)	*MID	*HIGH	*LOW	ID(high)
Input: C e C a C, –hi, –hi, –lo +lo						
a. C e C a C, –hi, –hi, –lo +lo	*!		*		*	
b. C e C e C, Aperture, –hi, –lo		*!	*			
c. ☞ C e C a C, –hi, –lo +lo			*		*	

Candidate (41c), in which [–high] is shared by all output vowels, fares best in this circumstance, as there are no [high] specifications which are not left-aligned. Each of the other plausible output candidates fails on a high-ranking constraint, either ALIGN-L or IDENT(low).

Now consider a case in which the order of the two input vowels is reversed, as in (42).

(42) Low–mid input sequence

C a C e C	ALIGN-L(high)	ID(low)	*MID	*HIGH	*LOW	ID(high)
a. C a C e C (–hi, –hi / +lo, –lo)	*!		*		*	
b. C e C e C Aperture (–hi / –lo)		*!	*			
c. 💣 C a C e C (–hi / +lo, –lo)				*	*	

In this scenario, the constraint hierarchy incorrectly selects candidate (42c). There is no possible ranking of the constraints which can correctly select (41c), but rule out (42c). By contrast, positional faithfulness accounts for the asymmetry, protecting a free-standing mid vowel if and only if it originates in the root-initial syllable.[18]

Turning now to inputs containing only mid or high vowels, I have shown that the persistence of initial values of [high] through vowel harmony follows from the ranking of both of the markedness constraints *MID and *HIGH above IDENT(high), and from the feature-driven character of markedness constraint evaluation. Following the principle of Feature-Driven Markedness (32), multiple instances of a node or feature incur more violations than a single instance of a node or feature. In Shona, a single multiply linked Aperture node dominating some combination of [high] and [low] is more harmonic than two or more individual Aperture nodes dominating the same feature specifications. Thus, feature sharing occurs whenever possible, resulting in uniform height in the output; input $e \ldots i$ surfaces as $e \ldots e$ (38), while underlying $i \ldots e$ surfaces as $i \ldots i$ (36).

The markedness constraints themselves, rather than a harmony-favoring constraint such as ALIGN(high) or SHARE(high), favor multiple-linking in Shona. The key role of the markedness constraints in Shona harmony highlights an important point: the absence of feature-sharing in languages which do not exhibit vowel harmony cannot be derived simply by assuming low-ranking ALIGN(F) constraints. Other constraints in the grammar, such as featural markedness constraints, will also favor multiple-linking as a means of best satisfaction of the constraint hierarchy; this is the case in Shona. Low-ranking of ALIGN(F) alone cannot guarantee that feature-sharing will be ruled out. Rather, UG must contain a constraint or constraints banning multiple-linking; when such constraints dominate the relevant markedness constraints (such as *LOW, *CORONAL, ALIGN(high), etc.), we have a language which does not permit multiple-linking as a means of reducing featural markedness. With the opposite ranking, multiple-linking is allowed, in order to minimize violation of featural markedness or alignment constraints.

Following Benua (1996), I assume that the constraint which penalizes multiple-linking is UNIQUE, shown in (43) below.[19]

(43) UNIQUE
$\forall x$, x a feature or class node, x must have a unique segmental anchor y.

In a language such as Shona, which permits multiple-linking of features, UNIQUE is dominated by the harmony-driving constraints, as shown in (44) below.

(44) Dominated UNIQUE permits multiple-linking

/CeCiC/	ID-σ_1(high)	*MID	*HIGH	*Low	UNIQUE	ID(high)
a. ☞ Ce CeC / Aperture / −hi \ −lo		*			*	*
b. Ce CiC / −hi \ +hi / −lo −lo		*	*!			
c. Ce CeC / −hi \ −hi / −lo −lo		**!				*

In candidate (44a), one violation is incurred by each Aperture node which is multiply linked; because there is one Aperture node which is shared, one violation is assessed. By contrast, there are no UNIQUE violations in candidates (44b, c). Candidate (44a) is optimal because UNIQUE is dominated by both *MID and *HIGH; multiple-linking is optimal.

Conversely, if UNIQUE ≫ *HIGH, multiple-linking will be prohibited. Under such a ranking (characteristic of a language other than Shona), candidate (44b), with the unmarked [+high] vowel in the non-privileged position, is optimal. This is shown in (45).

(45)   High-ranking UNIQUE prohibits multiple-linking

/CeCiC/	ID-σ_1(high)	*MID	UNIQUE	*HIGH	*Low	ID(high)
a. Ce CeC / Aperture / –hi / –lo		*	*!			*
b. ☞ Ce CiC / –hi +hi / –lo –lo		*		*		
c. Ce CeC / –hi –hi / –lo –lo		**!				*

Candidate (45b) is optimal, due to the absence of multiply linked nodes; (45a) fatally violates UNIQUE. The pattern of vowel height distribution in (45b) is typical of positional neutralization without harmony: a relatively marked element is permitted in a privileged position, such as the initial syllable, but cannot be created in other positions via multiple-linking. Such patterns are common cross-linguistically, and arise from high-ranking markedness constraints, along with high-ranking UNIQUE. One example of such a system, Tamil, is examined in detail in §2.4 [omitted here – Ed.]. In Tamil, as in Shona, mid vowels are contrastive only in root-initial syllables. However, Tamil does not permit multiple-linking of height features, by virtue of high-ranking UNIQUE.

[. . .]

Notes

1 In the literature cited here, the distinction between word-initial and root-initial is not systematically explored – in many cases, it is difficult to determine whether only unprefixed forms, or both prefixed and unprefixed words, were used as stimuli. The processing of prefixal morphology is an interesting and complex matter. See Hall (1992) for a useful summary and discussion of the issues.

2 In the interest of internal consistency, I have adopted the term "root" in the discussion of Shona, rather than "radical", which is commonly used in the Bantuist literature.

3 The discussion and analysis which follow are restricted to Shona, for largely practical reasons. The same basic pattern of height distribution occurs in many other Bantu languages which have a five-vowel inventory (e.g., Kinyarwanda (Kimenyi 1979), Lamba (Kenstowicz & Kisseberth 1979: 72)), and the analysis presented here can be extended to such cases straightforwardly.

4 No phonological theory of vowel height features that I am aware of can adequately explain the widespread failure of low vowels to interact with high or mid vowels in height-sensitive processes. (Rare exceptions include various examples of vowel coalescence (de Haas 1988), Romance metaphony (Calabrese 1988, Hualde 1989), and Woleian raising (Sohn 1971, 1975).) If the low vowels are represented with the same features as vowels of other heights, this asymmetry in behavior is unexpected. The issue of vowel height representation is, however, orthogonal to the characterization of non-initial neutralization. See Clements (1991), Steriade (1995) for relevant discussion of this issue.

5 Data sources are abbreviated as follows: D = Doke (1967), Fi = Fivaz (1970), Fo5 = Fortune (1955), Fo7 = Fortune (1967), H = Hannan (1981), M = Myers (1987). Data are given in the Standard Shona Orthography of Hannan (1981), though phonetic transcription is retained for the implosives and the velar nasal. The correspondence between orthography and pronunciation is generally very close. However, note that sv = labialized alveolar fricative [sʷ], tsv =

labialized alveolar affricate [tsʷ], sh = voiceless palato-alveolar fricative [ʃ], ch = voiceless palato-alveolar affricate [tʃ] and v = voiced bilabial continuant [β] (described as a fricative by Fortune 1955, but as an approximant by Hannan 1981 and Pongweni 1990). Vowel length (which is noncontrastive and appears only in the penultimate syllable, as a reflex of stress) and tone are omitted throughout.

Not all of these sources focus on the Zezuru dialect, but all of the roots cited are found in Zezuru, according to Hannan (1981).

6 The relative markedness of high and low vowels is not clear. Jakobson (1941) and Greenberg (1966) both propose an $a > i > u$ implicational hierarchy, with the low vowel implied by the high front vowel. However, Disner (1984) suggests a hierarchy of $\{i, a\} > \{e, o\} > u$, based on the frequency of missing vowels in the 43 defective vowel systems in the UPSID inventory (Maddieson 1984); here there is no implicational relationship between the high front and low vowels. Also, both high and low vowels are found as default segments cross-linguistically. (For example, a is the epenthetic vowel in Axininca Campa (Payne 1981) and Makkan Arabic (Abu-Mansour 1987), while high vowels are epenthetic or default segments in a variety of languages, including Yoruba(Pulleyblank 1988), Zulu (Beckman 1992), Nancowry (Radhakrishnan 1981) and various Arabic dialects (Itô 1989).) Given this indeterminacy, it seems likely that the ranking of *HIGH and *LOW must be subject to cross-linguistic variation.

7 For the sake of convenience, I adopt the Chomsky & Halle (1968) features for vowel height. For alternatives, see Clements (1991), Schane (1984), Selkirk (1991a, b). Steriade's (1995) discussion of Bantu height harmony is also relevant; she proposes a perceptual feature [nonperipheral] (supplementary to the articulatory features [high] and [low]) which characterizes mid vowels. [nonperipheral] may be indirectly licensed in non-initial syllables, via multiple linking.

8   For the sake of simplicity, I have omitted the positional constraint IDENT-σ_1(low) throughout the discussion. Under the ranking in (25), positional IDENT-σ_1(low) can have no visible effect in the grammar.

9   The Final Vowels constitute an exception to this generalization: a mid vowel *e may appear after a low or high vowel just in case* it is the mood-marking Final Vowel characteristic of Bantu verbal morphology. In Shona, final *-e* marks a number of different moods, including subjunctive, negative habitual and potential. The resistance of the Final Vowels to height harmony may reflect a high-ranking constraint which penalizes the loss of morphological distinctions (see the discussion of MORPHDIS in McCarthy & Prince 1995), or a domain restriction on constraint applicability. I will not attempt to resolve this issue here.

10 I assume that vowel features are organized along the lines suggested in Odden (1991), Clements (1991) and Clements & Hume (1995), with a vowel place node that dominates two dependent class nodes, Color and Aperture. Where relevant to constraint satisfaction, I will explicitly show an Aperture node (Clements 1991, Clements & Hume 1995); otherwise, I omit it in the interest of simplicity.

11 A candidate parallel to (30d), but with a single, multiply-linked VPlace or Aperture node, would fare just as poorly on IDENT(low). In both cases, the input [−low] of the second vowel is changed to [+low] in the output form.

12 A treatment of Shona which adheres to the Feature Class Theory of Padgett (1995a, b), in which there are no geometric class nodes, will be somewhat different in character. Combinatory featural markedness constraints (*[F,G]) cannot be better satisfied by multiple-linking of a superordinate class node (versus multiple-linking at the level of the individual features F, G), as there are no superordinate class nodes in FCT. A comparison of the two approaches is orthogonal to the matter at hand.

13 See also the UNIQUE family of constraints proposed by Benua (1996), discussed in §2.3.4 below. UNIQUE constraints prohibit multiple-linking of phonological elements at various levels of structure from feature to class node. For example, UNIQUE(high) is violated by a multiply linked [high] specification, while UNIQUE(Aperture) is violated by a shared Aperture node.

14 With the exception noted above, that round *u* does not harmonize with a preceding *e*. An analysis of this gap is presented in Beckman (1997).

15 Here, as in (30), the outcome is not affected if the mid and low vowel share only [−high].

16 Candidates which incur violations of the No Crossing Constraint (Goldsmith 1976) are not considered; I assume that line crossing is universally ill-formed and therefore not admitted in any candidates.

17 For representative examples of the use of ALIGN(F) constraints in the analysis of harmony phenomena, see Kirchner (1993), Akinlabi (1994, 1995), Pulleyblank (1993, 1994), Ringen & Vago (1995a, b), Beckman (1994) and Cole & Kisseberth (1995a, b).

I consider only ALIGN-LEFT here, as the initial position of the mid vowel is what is at issue.

18 Positional faithfulness differs from positional licensing in this regard, in that a positional licensing approach favors movement of offending features or segments to privileged positions without regard for their place of origin.

19 Because a language may prohibit one type of multiple-linking, such as the linking of vowel features in vowel harmony, but permit another (e.g., coda place assimilation), different UNIQUE(F) constraints may be required to regulate the linking of different feature classes. This is the approach adopted in Benua (1996), where both UNIQUE(F) and UNIQUE(Class) constraints are proposed.

UNIQUE differs from earlier proposals in which multiple-linking is regulated (e.g. the Multiple Linking Constraint of Selkirk 1991a and the UNIFORM(F) constraint of Kaun 1995), in that UNIQUE is not sensitive to the featural content of the segments to which a feature is linked.

References

Abu-Mansour, Mahasen Hasan. 1987. *A Nonlinear Analysis of Arabic Syllabic Phonology, with Special Reference to Makkan*. Ph.D. dissertation, University of Florida.

Akinlabi, Akinbiyi. 1994. Featural alignment. MS, Rutgers University. ▶

Akinlabi, Akinbiyi. 1995. Kalabari vowel harmony. MS, Rutgers University. ▶

Alderete, John, Jill N. Beckman, Laura Benua, Amalia Gnanadesikan, John J. McCarthy, and Suzanne Urbanczyk. 1996. Reduplication and segmental unmarkedness. MS, University of Massachusetts, Amherst. ▶

Bach, Emmon. 1968. Two proposals concerning the simplicity metric in phonology. *Glossa* 2.2, 128–49.

Bach, Emmon. 1974. *Syntactic Theory*. New York: Holt, Rinehart and Winston.

Beckman, Jill N. 1992. Minimality, epenthesis, and the Zulu passive. MS, University of Massachusetts, Amherst.

Beckman, Jill N. 1994. Fill 'er up: An Optimality Theory analysis of Shona height harmony. Talk presented at the annual meeting of the Linguistic Society of America, Boston.

Beckman, Jill N. 1995. Shona height harmony: Markedness and positional identity. In *University of Massachusetts Occasional Papers in Linguistics 18: Papers in Optimality Theory*, ed. Jill N. Beckman, Laura Walsh Dickey, and Suzanne Urbanczyk, 53–75. Amherst: GLSA.

Beckman, Jill N. 1996. Labial opacity as labial attraction. Talk presented at the annual meeting of the Linguistic Society of America, San Diego.

Beckman, Jill N. 1997. Positional faithfulness, positional neutralization and Shona height harmony. *Phonology* 14.1, 1–46.

Benua, Laura. 1996. Case studies in transderivational identity I: Javanese. MS, University of Massachusetts.

Bosch, Anna and Caroline Wiltshire. 1992. The licensing of prosodic prominence in Tamil. In *Papers from the Third Annual Meeting of the Formal Linguistics Society of Midamerica*, ed. Laurel Smith Stvan et al., 1–15. Bloomington: Indiana University Linguistics Club.

Brown, R. and D. McNeill. 1966. The "tip-of-the-tongue" phenomenon. *Journal of Verbal Learning and Verbal Behavior* 5, 325–37.

Calabrese, Andrea. 1988. *Towards a Theory of Phonological Alphabets*. Ph.D. dissertation, MIT.

Chomsky, Noam and Morris Halle. 1968. *The Sound Pattern of English*. New York: Harper and Row.

Christdas, Prathima. 1988. *The Phonology and Morphology of Tamil*. Ph.D. dissertation, Cornell University.

Clements, G. N. 1991. Vowel height assimilation in Bantu languages. In *Working Papers of the Cornell Phonetics Laboratory 5*, 37–76. Ithaca: DMLL Publications.

Clements, G. N. and Elizabeth V. Hume. 1995. The internal organization of segments. In *The Handbook of Phonological Theory*, ed. John Goldsmith, 245–306. Oxford: Blackwell.

Clements, G. N. and Engin Sezer. 1982. Vowel and consonant disharmony in Turkish. In *The Structure of Phonological Representations Part II*, ed. Harry van der Hulst and Norval Smith, 213–55. Dordrecht: Foris.

Cole, Jennifer S. and Charles W. Kisseberth. 1995a. Nasal harmony in Optimal Domains Theory. MS, University of Illinois. ▶

Cole, Jennifer S. and Charles W. Kisseberth. 1995b. An Optimal Domains Theory of harmony. MS, University of Illinois. ▶

Cole, R. A. 1973. Listening for mispronunciations: a measure of what we hear during speech. *Perception and Psychophysics* 11, 153–6.

Cole, R. A. and J. Jakimik. 1978. Understanding speech: How words are heard. In *Strategies of Information Processing*, ed. G. Underwood. London: Academic Press.

Cole, R. A. and J. Jakimik. 1980. A model of speech perception. In *Perception and Production of Fluent Speech*, ed. R. A. Cole. Hillsdale, NJ: Erlbaum.

Comrie, Bernard. 1981. *The Languages of the Soviet Union*. Cambridge: Cambridge University Press.

Crothers, John. 1978. Typology and universals of vowel systems. In *Universals of Human Language, Volume 2: Phonology*, ed. Joseph H. Greenberg, 93–152. Stanford: Stanford University Press.

Cushing, Steven. 1978. A note on node self-dominance. *Linguistic Inquiry* 9.2, 327–30.

Disner, Sandra. 1984. Insights on vowel spacing. In *Patterns of Sound*, ed. Ian Maddieson. Cambridge: Cambridge University Press.

Doke, Clement M. 1967. *The Southern Bantu Languages*. London: Dawsons of Pall Mall.

Fivaz, Derek. 1970. *Shona Morphophonemics and Morphosyntax*. Ph.D. dissertation, University of the Witwatersrand.

Fortune, G. 1955. *An Analytical Grammar of Shona*. London: Longmans, Green and Co.

Fortune, George. 1967. *Elements of Shona* (2nd edn.). Harare, Zimbabwe: Longman Zimbabwe Limited.

Freedman, J. L. and T. K. Landauer. 1966. Retrieval of long-term memory: 'Tip-of-the-tongue' phenomenon. *Psychonomic Science* 4, 309–10.

Gilley, Leoma G. 1992. *An Autosegmental Approach to Shilluk Phonology*. Arlington, TX: Summer Institute of Linguistics.

Goldsmith, John. 1976. *Autosegmental Phonology*. Ph.D. dissertation, MIT.

Goldsmith, John. 1985. Vowel harmony in Khalkha Mongolian, Yaka, Finnish and Hungarian. *Phonology Yearbook* 2, 253–75.

Goldsmith, John. 1989. Licensing, inalterability, and harmonic rule application. In *CLS 25*, ed. Caroline Wiltshire et al., 145–56. Chicago: Chicago Linguistic Society.

Goldsmith, John. 1990. *Autosegmental and Metrical Phonology*. Oxford: Blackwell.

Gordon, Kent H. 1976. *Phonology of Dhangar-Kurux*. Kathmandu: Tribhuvan University Press.

Greenberg, Joseph H. 1966. *Language Universals, with Special Reference to Feature Hierarchies*. The Hague: Mouton.

Guthrie, Malcolm. 1967. *Comparative Bantu*. London: Gregg International.

Haas, Wim de. 1988. *A Formal Theory of Vowel Coalescence: A Case Study of Ancient Greek*. Dordrecht: Foris.

Haiman, John. 1972. Phonological targets and unmarked structures. *Language* 48.2, 365–77.

Hall, Christopher J. 1988. Integrating diachronic and processing principles in explaining the suffixing preference. In *Explaining Language Universals*, ed. J. A. Hawkins. Oxford: Blackwell.

Hall, Christopher J. 1992. *Morphology and Mind: A Unified Approach to Explanation in Linguistics*. New York: Routledge.

Hannan, M. 1981. *Standard Shona Dictionary* (revised edn.). Harare, Zimbabwe: The Literature Bureau.

Hawkins, L. A. and Anne Cutler. 1988. Psycholinguistic factors in morphological asymmetry. In *Explaining Language Universals*, ed. J. A. Hawkins. Oxford: Blackwell.

Horowitz, L. M., M. A. White, and D. W. Atwood. 1968. Word fragments as aids to recall: The organization of a word. *Journal of Experimental Psychology* 76, 219–26.

Horowitz, L. M., P. C. Chilian, and K. P. Dunnigan. 1969. Word fragments and their redintegrative powers. *Journal of Experimental Psychology* 80, 392–4.

Hualde, Jose. 1989. Autosegmental and metrical spreading in the vowel-harmony systems of northwestern Spain. *Linguistics* 27, 773–805.

Hulst, Harry van der and Jeroen van der Weijer. 1995. Vowel harmony. In *The Handbook of Phonological Theory*, ed. John Goldsmith, 494–534. Oxford: Blackwell.

Hume, Elizabeth. 1996. A non-linearity based account of metathesis in Leti. MS, The Ohio State University, Columbus. ▶

Itô, Junko. 1986. *Syllable Theory in Prosodic Phonology*. Ph.D. dissertation, University of Massachusetts, Amherst.

Itô, Junko. 1989. A prosodic theory of epenthesis. *Natural Language and Linguistic Theory* 7, 217–59.

Itô, Junko and Armin Mester. 1994. Reflections on CodaCond and Alignment. In *Phonology at Santa Cruz 3*, ed. Rachel Walker, Jaye Padgett, and Jason Merchant, 27–46. Santa Cruz: Linguistics Research Center.

Jakobson, Roman. 1941. Kindersprache, Aphasie und allgemeine Lautgesetze. In *Selected Writings I*, 328–401. The Hague: Mouton.

Johnson, David E. 1978. A note on self-dominance. *Linguistic Inquiry* 9.2, 325.

Kang, Hyeon-Seok. In preparation. *Phonological Variation and Change in Seoul Korean: A Sociolinguistic Study*. Ph.D. dissertation, The Ohio State University. ▶

Kaun, Abigail. 1995. *The Typology of Rounding Harmony: An Optimality Theoretic Approach*. Ph.D. dissertation.

Kenstowicz, Michael and Charles Kisseberth. 1979. *Generative Phonology*. San Diego: Academic Press.

Kimenyi, Alexandre. 1979. *Studies in Kinyar-wanda and Bantu Phonology*. Edmonton, Alberta: Linguistic Research.

Kiparsky, Paul. 1981. Vowel harmony. MS, MIT.

Kiparsky, Paul. 1988. Phonological change. In *Linguistics: The Cambridge Survey, Volume I*, ed. Frederick J. Newmeyer, 363–415. Cambridge: Cambridge University Press.

Kirchner, Robert. 1993. Turkish vowel dishar-mony in Optimality Theory. Talk presented at the Rutgers Optimality Workshop, New Brunswick, NJ. ▶

Krueger, John. 1977. *Tuvan Manual*. Bloomington: Indiana University Publications.

Lombardi, Linda. 1991. *Laryngeal Features and Laryngeal Neutralization*. Ph.D. dissertation, University of Massachusetts, Amherst.

Lombardi, Linda. 1995a. Positional faithfulness and the phonology of voicing in Optimality Theory. MS, University of Maryland, College Park. ◀

Lombardi, Linda. 1995b. Why Place and Voice are different: Constraint interactions and featural faithfulness in Optimality Theory. MS, University of Maryland, College Park. ▶

Maddieson, Ian. 1984. *Patterns of Sounds*. Cambridge: Cambridge University Press.

Marslen-Wilson, William. 1975. Sentence per-ception as an interactive parallel process. *Science* 189, 226–8.

Marslen-Wilson, William and A. Welsh. 1978. Processing interactions and lexical access during word recognition in continuous speech. *Cognitive Psychology* 10, 29–63.

McCarthy, John J. and Alan Prince. 1994. The emergence of the unmarked: Optimality in prosodic morphology. In *Proceedings of the North East Linguistic Society*, ed. Mercè Gonzàlez, 333–79. Amherst: GLSA. ◀

McCarthy, John J. and Alan Prince. 1995. Faith-fulness and reduplicative identity. In *Univer-sity of Massachusetts Occasional Papers in Linguistics 18: Papers in Optimality Theory*, ed. Jill Beckman, Laura Walsh Dickey, and Suzanne Urbanczyk, 249–384. Amherst: GLSA. ◀

Myers, Scott. 1987. *Tone and the Structure of Words in Shona*. Ph.D. dissertation, Univer-sity of Massachusetts, Amherst.

Nooteboom, Sieb G. 1981. Lexical retrieval from fragments of spoken words: Beginnings vs. endings. *Journal of Phonetics* 9, 407–24.

Odden, David A. 1981. *Problems in Tone Assignment in Shona*. Ph.D. dissertation, University of Illinois.

Odden, David A. 1991. Vowel geometry. *Phonology* 8, 261–89.

Padgett, Jaye. 1995a. Feature classes. In *Univer-sity of Massachusetts Occasional Papers in Linguistics 18: Papers in Optimality Theory*, ed. Jill Beckman, Laura Walsh Dickey, and Suzanne Urbanczyk, 385–420. Amherst: GLSA.

Padgett, Jaye. 1995b. Partial class behavior and nasal place assimilation. In *Coyote Working Papers in Linguistics*. Tucson: University of Arizona. ◀

Payne, David. 1981. *The Phonology and Morphology of Axininca Campa*. Arlington, TX: Summer Institute of Linguistics.

Pongweni, A. J. C. 1990. *Studies in Shona Phon-etics: An Analytical Review*. Harare, Zim-babwe: University of Zimbabwe Publications.

Poppe, Nicholas. 1964. *Bashkir Manual*. Bloomington: Indiana University.

Prince, Alan S. and Paul Smolensky. 1993. Optimality Theory: Constraint Interaction in Generative Grammar. MS, Rutgers Univer-sity and University of Colorado, Boulder. ◀

Pulleyblank, Douglas. 1988. Vocalic under-specification in Yoruba. *Linguistic Inquiry* 19, 233–70.

Pulleyblank, Douglas. 1993. Vowel harmony and Optimality Theory. In *Proceedings of the Workshop on Phonology, University of Coimbra, Portugal*. University of Coimbra, Portugal.

Pulleyblank, Douglas. 1994. Neutral vowels in Optimality Theory: A comparison of Yoruba and Wolof. MS, University of British Columbia.

Pullum, Geoffrey K. and Arnold M. Zwicky. 1978. Self-domination. *Linguistic Inquiry* 9.2, 326–7.

Radhakrishnan, R. 1981. *The Nancowry Word: Phonology, Affixal Morphology and Roots of a Nicobarese Language*. Edmonton, Alberta: Linguistic Research.

Ringen, Catherine O. 1975. *Vowel Harmony: Theoretical Implications*. Ph.D. dissertation, Indiana University.

Ringen, Catherine O. and Robert Vago. 1995a. Hungarian vowel harmony in Optimality The-ory. Paper Presented at the Linguistic Society of America Annual Meeting, New Orleans.

Ringen, Catherine O. and Robert M. Vago. 1995b. A constraint based analysis of Hungarian vowel harmony. In *Approaches to Hungarian, Volume 5: Levels and Structures*, ed. István Kenesei, 309–19. Szeged: JATE.

Schane, Sanford. 1984. The fundamentals of particle phonology. *Phonology Yearbook 1*, 129–55.

Selkirk, Elisabeth O. 1991a. Major place in the vowel space. MS, University of Massachusetts, Amherst.

Selkirk, Elisabeth O. 1991b. Vowel height features: Evidence for privativity and dependency. Handout from a talk presented at Université du Québec à Montréal.

Smolensky, Paul. 1993. Harmony, markedness, and phonological activity. Talk presented at ROW I, New Brunswick, NJ. ▶

Sohn, Ho-Min. 1971. a-raising in Woleaian. *University of Hawaii Working Papers in Linguistics* 3.8, 15–35.

Sohn, Ho-Min. 1975. *Woleaian Reference Grammar*. Honolulu: University of Hawaii Press.

Steriade, Donca. 1979. Vowel harmony in Khalkha Mongolian. In *Papers on Syllable Structure, Metrical Structure and Harmony Processes*, ed. Ken Safir, 25–50. Cambridge, MA: MITWPL.

Steriade, Donca. 1982. *Greek Prosodies and the Nature of Syllabification*. Ph.D. dissertation, MIT.

Steriade, Donca. 1993. Positional neutralization. Talk presented at NELS 24, University of Massachusetts, Amherst.

Steriade, Donca. 1995. Underspecification and markedness. In *The Handbook of Phonological Theory*, ed. John Goldsmith, 114–74. Oxford: Blackwell.

Traill, Anthony. 1985. *Phonetic and Phonological Studies of !Xóõ Bushman*. Hamburg: Helmut Buske Verlag.

Trubetzkoy, N. S. 1939. *Grundzüge der Phonologie*. (1969 translation by C. A. M. Baltaxe.) Berkeley: University of California Press.

Wall, Robert. 1972. *Introduction to Mathematical Linguistics*. Englewood Cliffs, NJ: Prentice-Hall.

Wiering, Elisabeth and Marinus Wiering. 1994. Phonological description of Doyayo (Poli dialect). In *The Doyayo Language: Selected Studies*, ed. Elisabeth Wiering and Marinus Wiering, 1–51. Arlington, TX: Summer Institute of Linguistics.

Wiltshire, Caroline R. 1992. *Syllabification and Rule Application in Harmonic Phonology*. Ph.D. dissertation, University of Chicago.

Study and Research Questions

1 According to (32), featural markedness constraints assign a violation-mark for each token of the offending feature, rather than for each segment bearing the offending feature. By examining the tableaux, determine what crucial work this assumption is doing in the analysis. Can you formulate an alternative? (Cf. chapter 17.)

2 Consult the original source for one of the examples in (4) and construct an analysis using the theory proposed in this chapter. Discuss any issues that arise.

3 Alignment-based approaches to Shona are critiqued in the conclusion of this chapter. Read chapter 18 and determine whether or not it answers these objections.

4 This chapter proposes that initial syllables have special faithfulness status because of their special role in lexical access. In other words, the special status of initial syllables is justified on functional grounds. Read chapter 15 and discuss the proposals there in relation to this functional justification for positional faithfulness.

Chapter 17 | Linda Lombardi

Positional Faithfulness and Voicing Assimilation in Optimality Theory

Editor's Note

Factorial typology is a central property of OT. It is the claim that every ranking of the universal constraints in CON is a possible grammar of a human language. Factorial typology is also an essential discipline for practitioners of OT. Whenever constraints are proposed, their consequences under ranking permutation must be checked. Correlatively, a factorial typology that is, within some reasonable limits, fully worked out analytically and fully instantiated empirically provides a compelling argument for the rightness of an analysis. (See McCarthy 2002: 114ff. for an example.)

This chapter develops a factorial typology of voicing assimilation and neutralization. One important aspect of the typology is that it seeks to explain why voicing assimilation is nearly always regressive, and to that end it employs the positional faithfulness constraint IDENT-ONSET. This chapter can be read in conjunction with chapters 11, 12, 16, and 18.

1 Introduction

Much work in autosegmental phonology, although assuming a derivational theory relying heavily on phonological rules, recognizes that wellformedness constraints are crucial to constructing explanatory analyses. For example, many languages restrict laryngeally marked segments from appearing syllable-finally; a familiar example is German, which devoices obstruents in this position. Lombardi (1991, 1995a) argues that such laryngeal neutralization is the result of a licensing constraint active in some languages which allows laryngeal features only in the following configuration:

Excerpt from:
Lombardi, Linda (1999) Positional faithfulness and voicing assimilation in Optimality Theory. *Natural Language and Linguistic Theory* 17: 267–302.

(1)   The Laryngeal Constraint

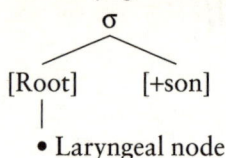

```
            σ
          /   \
   [Root]      [+son]
      |
    • Laryngeal node
```

The relevant position is before [+son] to include both vowels and sonorant consonants, since distinctions are maintained in onset clusters like /tr, dr/ in the relevant languages.

The constraint-based analysis is argued to have several advantages over a solely rule-based one. One is specific to laryngeal phonology, regarding the impossibility of stating the proper environment for a neutralization rule, but others are more general. For example, there are languages that do not show active devoicing alternations because no underlying forms have final voiced obstruents; a rule is unsuitable to analyzing such cases. But we do want to account for the fact that such languages have the same distribution as German, with voiced obstruents allowed initially but not finally, and the constraint is true of both types. Another goal of the constraint-based analysis was a better account of typology. If any rule affecting Lar that can be constructed with the available rule-writing devices is permitted, the grammar overgenerates. Proposing instead that Universal Grammar (UG) provides the constraint in (1), and that languages choose to obey it or not, narrows down the possibilities.

Such an analysis that incorporates constraints into a derivational theory must also account for how the rules and constraints interact. Lombardi (1991, 1995a), following a suggestion of Mester and Ito (1989), argues that delinking is the default repair strategy, since it introduces no new information. This gives the correct result that laryngeal distinctions are lost in unlicensed positions and, combined with autosegmental spreading, accounts for the following typology:

(2)   a.   Syllable-final neutralization
                German

      b.   Voice unrestricted
                English level II, Georgian, Coeur d'Alene
                Kannada, Tulu (Cho 1990)

      c.   No voicing in obstruents
                Maori, Ainu, etc.: see Maddieson (1984)

      d.   Voicing assimilation in obstruent clusters with word-final neutralization
                Polish, Dutch, Catalan, Sanskrit

The addition of a word-edge licensing constraint is argued to account for a final type of language:

      e.   Voicing assimilation in obstruent clusters with word-final voicing contrast
                Yiddish, Romanian, Serbo-Croatian

Other logically possible patterns do not occur: for example, languages which preserve voicing in coda but not in onset, or languages which devoice word-final but not word-internal syllable-final consonants.

The interaction of rules and constraints in the Laryngeal Constraint analysis works because it happens that violations of this constraint are always resolved by neutralization. However, in many other cases in segmental phonology the interaction of rules and constraints is not so simple. Ito's (1986) Coda Condition, which restricts Place syllable-finally, is enforced by a variety of rules both across languages and within the same language: epenthesis, deletion, and assimilation can all be used to yield Coda Condition-obeying surface structures. But none of these rules are formally connected to the constraint itself. This is an example of the well-known 'conspiracy' problem of Kisseberth (1970). This more general problem is concealed by the neat nature of the laryngeal facts, so that while the Laryngeal Constraint analysis is largely successful for the particular data, the flaw is that it cannot be extended to other rather similar cases in segmental phonology.

In response to the problems faced by grammars that attempt to combine rules and constraints, Optimality Theory (Prince and Smolensky 1993, McCarthy and Prince 1993) proposed that grammars consist of constraints alone. However, this founding work in Optimality Theory concentrated mainly on prosodic aspects of phonology, such as syllable structure and prosodic morphology. Given the previous work on constraints in autosegmental phonology, it seemed clear that Optimality Theory could be extended to cover segmental alternations, but the details remained to be worked out.

More recently there has been some attention paid to how to analyze segmental alternations in OT, and this paper falls into that category. I will propose an OT analysis of the laryngeal neutralization and assimilation typology. I will show that these alternations can be seen, in the standard OT manner, to be the result of conflicts between faithfulness and markedness; these conflicts are resolved differently in languages due to different constraint rankings. The position of licensing in Lombardi's (1991, 1995a) constraint will be shown in this analysis to be a position of special faithfulness to underlying laryngeal distinctions. This analysis will thus fit in with recent work that shows that positional faithfulness constraints are important to analyzing the distribution of segmental contrasts in OT (Beckman 1995, 1996; Selkirk 1995; Padgett 1995).

A few more specific contributions will also be made. First, no special licensing is needed for the cases in (2e); they will be seen to fall out from rerankings of the basic constraints, which is appropriate since they are an equally common and natural type of grammar. Second, an additional type of grammar is predicted, which I will argue is seen in Swedish; thus this account results in superior typological coverage. Finally, I will argue that the crosslinguistic restrictions on direction of assimilation – that it is normally regressive – are better handled by this approach.

2 The Constraints and Interactions in Outline

2.1 Faithfulness constraints

I will employ the following two faithfulness constraints for laryngeal features in this analysis:

(3)   IDENTONSET(Laryngeal) (abbreviated IDONSLAR and IDONS in tableaux)
      Consonants in the position stated in the Laryngeal Constraint (1) should be
      faithful to underlying laryngeal specification

(4)   IDENT(Laryngeal) (IDLAR)
      Consonants should be faithful to underlying laryngeal specification

These constraints belong to the IDENT(F) family of Correspondence constraints
proposed by McCarthy and Prince (1995). IDENT(F) constraints check that input
and output *segments* agree in featural specification. I will assume privative [voice]
(see Lombardi 1995c for an argument within OT that [voice] must be privative).
Although the main definition of Ident in McCarthy and Prince (1995) assumes
binary features, there is also discussion of its application with privative features (see
section 3.8, p. 71), and the assessment of violations is straightforward: two consonants without Laryngeal features are identical in Laryngeal specification; two
consonants marked [voice] are likewise identical; in contrast, a consonant without
Laryngeal features and one marked [voice] differ in laryngeal specification, and so
incur a violation of the IDENT constraint.

   One of the proposed IDENT constraints, IDONSLAR, is relativized to position,
'Onset' obviously being used only as a shorthand for the Laryngeal Constraint
position. Such constraints are suggested by Selkirk (1995) and Beckman (1995,
1996) as a way of accounting for the observation (which goes back at least as far as
Trubetzkoy 1939; see also, for example, Goldsmith 1989, 1990, Steriade 1995) that
languages may maintain a distinction only in prominent positions and neutralize it
elsewhere. The 'prominent' position differs for different features (see Beckman 1996
for a number of different types of examples); as shown by Lombardi (1991, 1995a),
the position in (1) is the important one in the case of Laryngeal distinctions. This
position has also been shown to be important for laryngeal features in work by
Kingston (1985, 1990) and Steriade (1993, 1995), and is also relevant for other
consonant features; see Padgett (1995) on Place assimilation; and cf. the work of Ito
(1986) on Place restrictions in coda as well as Goldsmith (1989, 1990) on onset/
coda asymmetries.

2.2   Markedness

Following Prince and Smolensky (1993), I assume a family of markedness constraints on feature specifications, of which *LAR is a member.

(5)   *LAR: do not have Laryngeal features

This constraint will be interpreted to give one mark for each voiced obstruent; that
is, an assimilated cluster incurs two violations of *LAR. The evidence for this will be
presented in section 3.1.

   I assume that [voice] is a privative feature, following Lombardi (1991, 1995b)
and references therein; see also arguments in Lombardi (1995c) that this assumption is required to explain certain asymmetries in the phonology of Place and Voice.[1]

The assumption of privative features is also crucial to the interpretation of this constraint: A voiced consonant will receive one mark for *LAR, and a voiceless one no marks, as it bears no laryngeal feature.[2]

I also assume a constraint that enforces voicing assimilation in obstruent clusters:

(6)   AGREE: Obstruent clusters should agree in voicing

As stated, AGREE applies only to obstruent clusters and thus will only be able to trigger assimilation of obstruent voicing.

As stated, sonorants are unaffected by this constraint by definition. This may actually be a result of a constraint interaction effect; I return to this in section 5 [omitted here – Ed.]. However, the restriction to clusters appears to be fundamental. Voicing assimilation never crosses vowels, unlike other kinds of assimilation (vowel harmonies, for example) that show long-distance effects. If the blocking of voice assimilation across vowels were a constraint interaction effect, we would expect to see crosslinguistic variation, with some languages spreading consonant voicing to consonants across vowels and some not, due to constraint reranking. This variation does not occur, so it seems that the impetus to agree in voicing really only applies to the cluster situation. Therefore, this is definitional for the constraint I am proposing: it is only concerned with a string of adjacent consonants.

An important point is that this constraint is not inherently directional: direction of assimilation will be a constraint interaction effect. This will be discussed further in section 3.6.

In the next section the examples will be confined to those without complex onsets or codas, in order to simplify the presentation of the main constraint interactions. Tautosyllabic clusters will then be discussed in section 4 [omitted here – Ed.].

3   Factorial Typology of Constraints

Note that in this section, to facilitate comparison across different grammars, I will use the same lettering of inputs in examples where possible, as follows:

(7)   a.   Word-final voiced obstruent
      b.   Voiced-voiceless obstruent cluster
      c.   Voiceless-voiced obstruent cluster
      d.   Voiced-voiced obstruent cluster

3.1   Syllable-final neutralization

Syllable-final laryngeal neutralization is a common phenomenon crosslinguistically. A familiar example is standard German. Morphemes may end in voiced obstruents, but such consonants devoice if they surface in the syllable coda. This is seen in the alternations in (8) (Wiese 1996, p. 200):[4]

(8) German syllable-final neutralization

Lo[p]	– Lo[b]es	'praise	– gen.'
Ra[t]	– Ra[d]es	'advise	– gen.'
Sar[k]	– Sär[g]e	'coffin	– plu.'
Gra[s]	– Grä[z]er	'grass	– plu.'
Re[g]en	– re[k]nen	'rain	– to rain'
ja[g]en	– Ja[k]den	'to hunt	– hunts'
	Ja[kt]	'hunt'	

The interaction of *LAR with the positional faithfulness constraint can result in voiced obstruents being possible in the onset and not the coda, as in German. This is the result of the ranking IDONSLAR ≫ *LAR ≫ IDLAR. Consider first a simple monosyllable:

(9) Syllable-Final Neutralization Ranking (German)

	a. /rad/	IDONS	*LAR	IDLAR
	rad		*!	
☞	rat			*
	b. /gut/			
☞	gut		*	
	kut	*!		*

As we see in tableau (9), this ranking gives devoicing syllable-finally, but faithfulness in onset position. For an onset consonant, it is more important to obey IDONSLAR (Onsets should be faithful to underlying voicing) than to obey *LAR (Do not be voiced). But for a coda, markedness outranks the only relevant faithfulness constraint, so it will devoice. It is more important to obey *LAR (Do not be voiced) than to obey IDLAR (Be faithful to input voicing).

Next, consider alternations in word-internal syllables. Most of these examples are straightforward given the discussion so far, but (10c) crucially demonstrates the importance of the interpretation of *LAR.

As in tableau (9), syllable-final consonants devoice, allowing satisfaction of *LAR at the expense only of lower-ranked IDLAR; but voiced syllable-initial consonants remain voiced, since satisfying IDONSLAR (by retaining underlying voicing) is more important than satisfying *LAR (which assigns a mark to each voiced consonant). So far this is the same as we saw in (9). But now (10c) also shows the importance of the interpretation of the markedness constraints as I have described them, where each voiced *segment* receives a mark. Given the assumption of the richness of the base in OT, we must be able to handle the possible input with a cluster with doubly linked [voice]. If *LAR counted [voice] autosegments instead of voiced segments, such a cluster would get only one mark for *LAR.

The outcome would be that (a) is optimal, so that voiced clusters would remain so, but syllable-final consonants would devoice in all other environments. The

(10)   Word-Internal Clusters (German)

		IdOns	*Lar	IdLar
a.	/sagte/			
	sa[gt]e		*!	
☞	sa[kt]e			*
	sa[gd]e	*!	**	*
b.	/ratgeber/			
☞	ra[tg]eber		*	
	ra[dg]eber		*!*	*
	ra[tk]eber	*!		*
c.	/rundgang/			
	run[dg]ang		*!*	
☞	run[tg]ang		*	*
	run[tk]ang	*!		**

'said, 1st person sg.'

'adviser'

'stroll'

(11)   Incorrect Interpretation of *Lar

/rundgang/ $\bigvee$ [voice]	IdOns	*Lar	IdLar
a. rundgang		*	
b. runtgang		*	*!
c. runtkang	*!		**

language would thus have voiced-voiced, voiceless-voiceless, and voiceless-voiced clusters, but no voiced-voiceless clusters. There appears to be no such language. Thus, to rule out this possibility and to achieve the result that neutralization is a direct result of markedness, it must be the case that each voiced consonant receives a mark for *Lar, not each [voice] autosegment. The markedness constraint, then, is interpreted in the way that is most similar to the Ident faithfulness constraints, which calculate faithfulness based on the segment rather than autosegments.

Finally, Agree is low ranked in such a language. As long as Agree is at least lower than *Lar, assimilating [voice] will be impossible, since this induces additional *Lar violations, as seen in (12).

(12)

		IdOns	*Lar	Agree	IdLar
a.	/rat.geber/				
☞	ra[tg]eber		*	*	
	ra[dg]eber		*!*		*
	ra[tk]eber	*!			*
b.	/rundgang/				
	run[dg]ang		*!*		
☞	run[tg]ang		*	*	*
	run[tk]ang	*!			**

(13) Ranking for syllable-final devoicing:[7]
IdOnsLar ≫ *Lar ≫ Agree, IdLar

(14) Voice in Obstruents Unrestricted (English)

		IdOns	IdLar	*Lar	Agree
a.	/pig/				
☞	pig			*	
	pik		*!		
b.	/pigpen/				
☞	pigpen			*	*
	pikpen		*!		
	pigben	*	*!	**	
c.	/catbird/				
☞	catbird			*	*
	cadbird		*!	**	
	catpird	*	*!		
d.	/pegboard/				
☞	pegboard			**	
	pekboard		*!	*	*
	pekpoard	*	*!		

3.2 Voice unrestricted

As long as IDLAR outranks both *LAR and AGREE, there will be faithfulness to under-lying voicing in all positions. *LAR and AGREE are the constraints that could prompt violations of faithfulness; if they are lower ranked than IDLAR, faithfulness will have priority. Note that since IDONSLAR violations are a subset of IDLAR violations, the ranking of IDONSLAR will make no difference as long as IDLAR dominates AGREE and *LAR. The reader can easily see that if the IDONSLAR column were moved to the bottom of the ranking in the above tableau, the result would be no different.

(15) Ranking for unrestricted voicing:
IDLAR ≫ *LAR, AGREE
Ranking of IDONSLAR irrelevant

3.3 No voicing in obstruents

Languages with *LAR ranked above faithfulness will be the common type with no voiced obstruents. (See Maddieson 1984 for many examples, including Maori, Ainu, Arabela (Peru), Maung and many other Australian languages, etc.)

(16) No Voiced Obstruents (hypothetical inputs)

/big/	*LAR	IDONS	IDLAR
☞ pik		*	**
big	*!*		
bik	*!		*
pig	*!	*	*

Summing up these first three grammars, then, we see that it is possible for a language to permit voicing anywhere, to prohibit voicing anywhere, or to allow voicing in the onset but not in the coda. However, the opposite pattern – voicing in the coda but not in the onset – is impossible, which is correct since there are no such languages. Even if we reverse the ranking of the IDLAR and IDONS constraint there would be no ranking that gives this pattern; either we get voicing possible every-where (17), or voicing prohibited entirely (18).

(17)   Voicing Unrestricted (English)

/big/	IdLar	*Lar	IdOns
pik	*!*		*
☞ big		* *	
bik	*!	*	
pig	*!	*	*

(18)   No Voiced Obstruents (hypothetical inputs)

/big/	*Lar	IdLar	IdOns
☞ pik		* *	*
big	*!*		
bik	*!	*	
pig	*!	*	*

Agree will have no effect even if it is ranked above the faithfulness constraints as well. Since voiceless clusters obey both Agree and *Lar, even high-ranked Agree will not motivate retention of voiced obstruents.

(19)   No Voiced Obstruents (hypothetical inputs)

/pik.ben/	*Lar	Agree	IdOns	IdLar
pik.ben	*!	*		
pig.ben	*!*			*
☞ pik.pen			*	*

Relative rankings of constraints lower than *Lar make no difference. Note that there are no languages with alternations like those shown in this tableau; since [voice] never surfaces, it would be impossible for a language with *Lar highest ranked to maintain underlying voiced consonants. By Prince and Smolensky's (1993) principle of Lexicon Optimization, the learner presented with the surface data of the language in (19) will postulate voiceless underlying forms. Nevertheless, given the assumption of richness of the base in OT, we must examine how a grammar handles all possible inputs (Prince and Smolensky 1993, Smolensky 1993, 1996). The treatment of voiced inputs in (19) argues that this is the correct grammar for a language with no voicing distinctions.

(20)   Ranking for language without voicing distinctions:
       *LAR ≫ IdOnsLar, IdLar
       Ranking of AGREE irrelevant

3.4   Voice assimilation in obstruent clusters

Many languages show assimilation to the voicing of the last obstruent in a cluster. Sonorants do not participate in such assimilation.

(21)   Yiddish voicing assimilation (Katz 1987)
       [vog]   'weight'   [vokšoi]   'scale'
       [briv]   'letter'   [briftreger] 'mailman'
       [ayz]   'ice'   [ayskastn]   'icebox'
       [bak]   'cheek'   [bagbeyn]   'cheekbone'
       [zis]   'sweet'   [zizvarg]   'candy products'
       [kop]   'head'   [kobveytik]   'headache'

The behavior of word-final consonants is an issue of considerable relevance to the analysis of voicing assimilation. The most well-known cases of these languages also have word-final neutralization. This allowed Mester and Ito (1989) to suggest that voicing assimilation was a combination of syllable-final neutralization and spread of [voice], thus allowing us to maintain that [voice] is a privative feature – a desirable result for other reasons. This idea was taken up and elaborated by Lombardi (1991, 1995a) and Cho (1990). Because these theories all achieve 'assimilation' to voicelessness as a consequence of syllable-final devoicing, rather than spread of a value [–voice], they predict languages with voicing assimilation to always have word-final devoicing, since word-final consonants are syllable-final; Polish and Dutch are languages of this type. However, as Cho and Lombardi both found, this correlation does not always hold. It is not uncommon for a language to have voicing assimilation yet retain word-final voice, as seen in the Yiddish data above and in other type (e) languages from Lombardi (1991, 1995a).

   Both Cho and Lombardi need some additional mechanism to account for this; for example, Lombardi (1991, 1995a) proposes Final Exceptionality, a feature-level analog of final extrametricality, as a way of retaining otherwise illicit [voice] in word-final position. As I will show, the present analysis can handle these cases by constraint reranking without any such additional stipulation. Languages with assimilation may either devoice or be faithful in this position; the proposed analysis will get the result that both are equally natural, while still allowing us to maintain the result that [voice] is privative.

3.4.1   Assimilation in clusters

As described earlier, the constraint AGREE requires obstruent clusters to agree in voicing. This constraint will of course be in conflict with the faithfulness constraints, which prefer underlying specifications to remain the same. But not all faithfulness constraints are equal. The subset relationship between IdOnsLar and IdLar has the result that it is more important to be faithful to onset laryngeal specification than to coda (or elsewhere) specification. Thus, where the members of an input cluster disagree in voicing, the only way to satisfy AGREE will be for the coda to assimilate to the voicing of the onset:

(22)   Direction of Voicing Assimilation (Yiddish)

/bakbeyn/	AGREE	IDONS	IDLAR
a. bak.beyn	*!		
☞ b. bag.beyn			*
c. bak.peyn		*!	*

In the tableau above, candidate (a) violates AGREE because it has an obstruent cluster that is not uniform in voicing. The cluster in candidate (c) is uniformly voiceless and so satisfies AGREE; but it has done this at the expense of being unfaithful to the onset's laryngeal specification, violating IDONSLAR and IDLAR. Thus, both (a) and (c) will lose to (b), where the coda has assimilated to the onset, satisfying both AGREE and IDONSLAR, and violating only IDLAR.

Like the neutralization and spread analysis of Lombardi (1991, 1995a), Cho (1990), Mester and Ito (1989), this analysis achieves assimilation to voicelessness without use of a feature [−voice], also due to the interaction of AGREE and the faithfulness constraints, as we see in (23).

(23)   Assimilation to Voicelessness (Yiddish)

/vogšoi/	AGREE	IDONS	IDLAR
a. vogšoi	*!		
☞ b. vokšoi			*
c. vogžoi		*!	*

Candidate (a) violates AGREE, since the cluster does not agree in voicing. Candidate (c), with progressive assimilation, obeys AGREE, but has done so at the expense of violating both IDONSLAR and IDLAR, as it has voiced an underlyingly voiceless onset. Therefore, the winner will be (b). By devoicing the coda, this candidate has achieved satisfaction of AGREE – the whole cluster is voiceless – and it has achieved this by violating only IDLAR (the coda has changed from voiced to voiceless) but not IDONSLAR (the onset has not changed). This shows that we can maintain privative [voice] in OT under this analysis; the value [−voice] is not needed to account for voicing assimilation, as also argued in various pre-OT works (Cho 1990, Mester and Ito 1989, Lombardi 1991, 1995a). (See Lombardi 1995c for another argument for privative [voice] in OT.)

3.4.2 Word-final phonology in languages with voicing assimilation

As we have seen, then, for a language to have regressive obstruent voicing assimilation, the ranking will be AGREE, IdOnsLar ≫ IdLar, *Lar. The relative ranking of IdLar and *Lar will not be relevant for clusters, where high-ranking AGREE must be satisfied.

However, word-final consonants are not in an environment where AGREE can have an effect; thus, ranking of the other constraints will be crucial. As we saw above, IdLar ≫ *Lar will result in coda faithfulness, and *Lar ≫ IdLar will result in coda devoicing. Either one of these rankings of *Lar and IdLar is possible in a language that has high-ranked AGREE and IdOnsLar, so both treatments of word-final consonants will be possible in languages that have voicing assimilation, as I will now show.

(24) Voice Assimilation, Final Neutralization (Polish)

		AGREE	IdOns	*Lar	IdLar	
a.	/klub/					'club'
	klub			*!		
☞	klup				*	
b.	/żabka/					'frog, dim.'
	żabka	*!		*		
☞	żapka				*	
	żabga		*!	**	*	
c.	/prosba/					'request (noun)'
	prosba	*!		*		
☞	proźba			**	*	
	prospa		*!		*	
d.	/nigdy/					'never'
☞	nigdy			**		
	nikdy	*!		*	*	
	nikty		*!		**	

As we see in this tableau, where there is no obstruent cluster, AGREE is irrelevant, so in word-final position (a) there is devoicing as a consequence of *Lar ≫ IdLar. AGREE ≫ IdLar means that there will be assimilation to voicelessness in (b): IdOnsLar is high ranked, so AGREE cannot be satisfied by spreading [voice] to the onset; however, AGREE can be satisfied, at the cost only of a low-ranked IDLAR violation, by devoicing the coda. However, we do get syllable-final voiced consonants where they are a consequence of assimilation, in (c, d): Satisfying *LAR (by leaving the coda voiceless) is not possible because it is more important to satisfy AGREE and IDONSLAR: thus we get a cluster that shares the [voice] of the onset.

(25)   Ranking for assimilation and word-final devoicing:
IDONSLAR, AGREE ≫ *LAR ≫ IDLAR

Next, we turn to the Yiddish type of language. To have word-final faithfulness the language must have IDLAR ≫ *LAR; this does not conflict with the ranking that gives assimilation:

(26)   Voice Assimilation, Word-Final Faithfulness (Yiddish)

		AGREE	IDONS	IDLAR	*LAR
a.	/vog/				
☞	vog				*
	vok			*!	
b.	/vogšoi/				
	vogšoi	*!			*
☞	vokšoi			*	
	vogžoi		*!	*	**
c.	/bakbeyn/				
	bakbeyn	*!			*
☞	bagbeyn			*	**
	bakpeyn		*!	*	
d.	/ayzbarg/				
☞	ayzbarg				**
	aysbarg	*!		*	*
	aysparg		*!	**	

The majority of the interactions are the same here as in the last tableau: In both rankings, obeying AGREE is more important than avoiding additional *LAR violations, due to AGREE ≫ *LAR, and assimilation is regressive due to the relationship between IDONSLAR and IDLAR, which favors preserving onset voicing over preserving coda voicing. Thus, we get regressive voicing assimilation in clusters (b, c). But for obstruents that are not in clusters, where AGREE is not at issue, the rankings differ. In (24), *LAR ≫ IDLAR, so we have word-final devoicing. But here, as we see in (a), since IDLAR ≫ *LAR, voiced word-final consonants remain: it is more important to be faithful to an underlying [voice] specification than to obey *LAR by eliminating it.

(27)   Ranking for assimilation and word-final faithfulness:
       IDONSLAR, AGREE ≫ IDLAR ≫ *LAR

Thus, under this analysis assimilation combines equally naturally with either word-final devoicing or word-final faithfulness by simple constraint reranking. No additional mechanisms are required for either type of language, which correctly reflects the fact that they seem to be equally natural.

3.4.3   Phonology of word-medial CN clusters in languages with voicing assimilation

Another issue in a language with obstruent voicing assimilation is what happens in medial obstruent-sonorant clusters. In previous neutralization and spreading analyses of voicing assimilation, if a consonant + nasal (CN) cluster were heterosyllabic, it was predicted that it had to contain a voiceless obstruent, since the first consonant was syllable-final. However, languages like Yiddish and Serbo-Croatian allow a voicing distinction in medial CN clusters:

(28)   Yiddish CN clusters
       [mitniten]   'co-respondent'   [nudnik]   'boring person'
       [žukmaxer]   'bugmaker'   [zegmaxer]   'sawmaker'
       [overzmanik]   'obsolete'   [aropnemen]   'take off'

Lombardi (1991, 1995a) argues that these clusters are onsets, and thus are predicted to allow voicing distinctions. An advantage of the present analysis is that this assumption about syllabification is no longer necessary. In fact, languages like Yiddish will retain voicing in such clusters even if heterosyllabic, due to the ranking IDLAR ≫ *LAR:

(29)   Behavior of CN Clusters

		IDLAR	*LAR
a.	/mitniten/		
☞	mit.niten		
	mid.niten	*!	*
b.	/nudnik/		
☞	nud.nik		*
	nut.nik	*!	

Thus, again the predictions of this theory seem to be correct. The presence of voicing assimilation is not erroneously predicted to cooccur only with devoicing in CN clusters.

3.5   Swedish

There is one remaining ranking that has not yet been addressed, and one language appears to exemplify this grammar. Swedish has been described as having bidirectional spread of [–voice]; in other words, a voiced obstruent devoices next to a voiceless obstruent (data from Hellberg 1974, Stephen Anderson p.c.).[9]

(30) a.   Regressive assimilation to voicelessness
hög	[hö:g]	'high'	
högtid	[hœk:ti:d]	'festival'	
högfärdig	[hœk:fæ:dig]	'self-conceited'	
vigsel	[vik:səl]	'marriage'	*viga* 'to marry'
klädsel	[klɛt:səl]	'dressing'	*kläda* 'to dress'

b.   Progressive assimilation to voicelessness
dag	[da:g]	'day'
tisdag	[tis:ta]	'Tuesday'
skog	[sku:g]	'forest'
skogs	[sku:ks]	(genitive)
skogsbrand	[skuk:spran:d]	'forest fire'

Preterite underlying -*de*, devoices to -*te*:
läste	'read'	*sylde*	'covered'
stekte	'fried'		

c.   Voiced clusters: no change
äga	'to own'	*ägde*	(preterite)
väve	'to weave'	*vävde*	(preterite)

(Hellberg refers to the geminate consonants as tense; some of these forms also have a variant with a short, lax devoiced consonant and a preceding long vowel.)

In a rule-based framework, a mirror image rule is needed to account for this pattern. Under the present analysis no special mechanism is required. This pattern will be found when the constraints are ranked as in the following tableau. (I abstract away from the variation in consonant tenseness/gemination; *LAR violations are noted for the clusters only.)

As we see in (a), word-final consonants remain voiced, since IDLAR is high ranked. When two voiced consonants come together, as in (d), the faithful output obeys both AGREE and IDLAR, so there is no high-ranked motivation to be unfaithful to the underlying specifications. The interesting cases are (b), with a voiced–voiceless sequence, and (c), voiceless–voiced. High-ranked AGREE rules out the faithful outputs. Either kind of assimilation – to voicelessness or to voicing – will change one of the consonants in the cluster, resulting in one IDLAR violation. Thus, the decision

(31)   Bidirectional Cluster Devoicing (Swedish)

		Agree	IdLar	*Lar	IdOns
a.	/sku:g/				
☞	sku:g			*	
	sku:k		*!		
b.	/vigsəl/				
	vigsəl	*!		*	
☞	viksəl		*		
	vigzəl		*	*!*	*
c.	/stekde/				
	stekde	*!		*	
	stegde		*	*!*	
☞	stekte		*		*
d.	/ägde/				
☞	ägde			**	
	äkde	*!	*	*	
	äkte		*!*		*

must be passed on to *Lar, which decides in favor of the voiceless cluster in both cases. Because IdOnsLar is lowest ranked, there is no constraint that favors one *direction* of assimilation over another; instead, *Lar favors assimilation to the unmarked state, voicelessness, regardless of direction.

The rarity of this pattern may be of significance. This is the only known pattern that requires IdLar to be ranked above IdOnsLar. All other languages discussed have rankings that fall into the following categories:

1   The relative ranking of IdOnsLar and IdLar does not matter;
2   IdOnsLar and IdLar are separated by another constraint, and IdOnsLar is higher: IdOnsLar ≫ C ≫ IdLar.

The grammars in the first category would give the same results if there were a strict ranking IdOnsLar ≫ IdLar, although this ranking cannot be proven from the voicing assimilation data. Swedish is the only language I have found that *requires* the opposite ranking of these two constraints. The rarity of this type of assimilation suggests that although the ranking IdLar ≫ IdOnsLar is not impossible, perhaps there is something marked about it. Such a ranking does seem somewhat counterintuitive given the general picture elsewhere that onset voicing is more important than voicing in other positions. Absent a theory of the markedness of rankings, this must remain speculative, but it suggests that such a theory may be required.

To sum up so far, the proposed constraints account for all the types of languages described in Lombardi (1991, 1995a, b, c). They do so without the need for special devices for the Yiddish type of pattern. They also predict the existence of a pattern not discussed in earlier work, which is exemplified by Swedish. I will now turn to the question of how the analysis handles generalizations about the direction of assimilation.

3.6   Direction of assimilation

The licensing analysis of Lombardi (1991, 1995a, b, c) goes some way towards explaining the dominance of laryngeal contrasts in the onset over those in the coda. However, in that analysis the rule of voicing assimilation still must stipulate direction. The wellformedness constraints alone could not prevent coda voiced obstruents from spreading [voice] to an onset, as this would result on the surface in the same well-formed doubly linked structure that results from regressive assimilation.

Thus, the earlier analysis still needs to resort to stipulation to account for the fact that voicing assimilation is overwhelmingly regressive in direction. (As do all previous analyses; see, for example, Mohanan 1993 for discussion.) In contrast, the present analysis predicts that when only these basic constraints are sufficiently high ranked to be active, only regressive assimilation will be possible.

However, because the Agree constraint is not inherently directional, progressive assimilation will still be possible, but only if higher-ranked constraints intervene to override the effects of IdOnsLar. This appears to make the correct empirical predictions. In all languages I know of where voicing assimilation simply applies to all clusters with no further restrictions on environment, it is regressive. All the cases of progressive assimilation I have found, in contrast, have some further morphological or phonological restrictions on the context of assimilation, showing the action of additional constraints. For reasons of space I cannot give detailed analyses of all of these examples, but I will present one and describe others.

The English plural provides a simple case of progressive voicing assimilation. I will account for this alternation by formalizing within OT the analysis proposed by Mester and Ito (1989; see also Lombardi 1991). Mester and Ito assume that the underlying form is voiced /z/ and so need to account for progressive voicing assimilation after voiceless consonants as in *cats*, and the retention of voicing in *pigs*. They propose that this is due to a universal syllable-wellformedness condition noted by Harms (1973) and by Greenberg (1978):

(32)   Harms' generalization:
       Voiced obstruents must be closer than voiceless to the syllable nucleus.

Thus, a form like the following is universally ruled out:

(33)   *[kætz]

Adding this as a top-ranked constraint to the ranking already required for English will account for these facts. English after Level I has no restrictions on the distribution of voiced and voiceless obstruents, and so has the ranking IDONSLAR, IDLAR ≫ *LAR ≫ AGREE (only the relevant constraints for this example are shown in the following tableau).

(34)

/kæt+z/	Harms' genl.	IDLAR	*LAR
a. kætz	*!		*
b. kædz		*	*!*
☞ c. kæts		*	

Candidate (a) violates the universal Harms' generalization, so the only possibilities are the voice-agreeing candidates (b, c). Both of these violate voice faithfulness for a single segment, so the decision falls to *LAR, which chooses the voiceless cluster.

(35)

/pɪg+z/	Harms' genl.	IDLAR	*LAR
☞ a. pɪgz			**
b. pɪks		*!*	
c. pɪgs		*!	*

In this tableau we see that, correctly, when the voiced ending is added to a voiced consonant there is no change. There is no motivation to change from the faithful candidate (a), since it does not violate top-ranked Harms' generalization. Because faithfulness to voicing is higher than *LAR, the faithfulness violations in (b, c) are fatal.

The English example, then, shows the action of an additional high-ranked constraint. Other cases of progressive voicing assimilation similarly show restrictions to special circumstances. Yiddish shows progressive assimilation with only one suffix, for example, and Dutch only when the second consonant is a fricative (see Lombardi 1997 for data and analyses). Polish [r], where it is subject to a palatalization requirement which also results in change to an obstruent, undergoes progressive voicing assimilation (see Bethin 1992 and Lombardi 1991 for data). In all of these languages assimilation is regressive in all other contexts.
[. . .]

Notes

1   However, see Inkelas, Orgun, and Zoll (1994) where an argument for ternary voice specification is presented, in an OT context, to solve a problem in Turkish phonology.

2   A question that I will leave open about this constraint is whether it applies to sonorants. In fact, it is not marked for a sonorant to be voiced; rather it is the normal situation. This could be handled by having *LAR defined as "Obstruents should not have Laryngeal features." However, the more general form of the constraint would allow us to extend it to neutralization of other Laryngeal features: not only do these tend also to neutralize in the same position, but both sonorants and obstruents are affected (see Lombardi 1991, 1995a, b). It could be the case that *LAR is violated by voiced sonorants, but that they must nevertheless retain [voice] in most situations due to a dominant constraint demanding sonorant voicing. Also, given that only one laryngeal feature is at issue in the examples in this paper, we cannot distinguish whether violations are counted on the Laryngeal node (if any) or individual features. See Lombardi (to appear) for discussion of both issues. For simplicity I omit *LAR marks for sonorants.

[. . .]

4   There are a number of words with voiced stops in problematic positions, with variable pronunciations for at least some speakers, such as Han[d]lung-Han[t]lung. The simplest solution is to assume, along with Wiese (1996, p. 202), that this is due to variability in syllabification: that in Han.[d]lung, the voiced obstruent is not in the coda. (Wiese cites Vennemann 1968 and also gives an argument based on the interaction of devoicing and g-spirantization.) This requires that we recognize some onset clusters word-internally that do not occur word-initially. Other approaches to these examples are surveyed by Brockhaus (1995). Earlier work by Wiese claims that these consonants are ambisyllabic, in which case they could escape devoicing by something like the Linking Condition; this would seem to also nicely account for Brockhaus' observation (p. 76) that speakers do not give consistent judgments regarding which syllable the questionable obstruent belongs to. Finally, see Levy

(1997) for an OT account of these forms which invokes output–output correspondence. There are also studies that have claimed to show that laryngeal distinctions are not fully neutralized in languages including German and Polish, but Fourakis and Iverson (1984) show that these effects are due to experimental flaws; their arguments also apply to similar later studies (Slowiaczek and Dinnsen 1985, Charles-Luce 1985).

[. . .]

7   Note that this ranking will also account for the many languages that prohibit laryngeal distinctions syllable-finally but do not show alternations. In OT, where constraints are on outputs only, these must have the same phonological analysis as German; they cannot be the result of a constraint on underlying forms, due to the assumption of the richness of the base. The lack of underlying voiced-final morphemes in, for example, Thai, is a result of unrelated facts about the morphology of the language (words are mostly monosyllabic, and thus do not show alternations that would lead to the positing of final voiced consonants in underlying forms), not something truly different about its phonology.

[. . .]

9   In previous work I argued that Swedish word-internal clusters show assimilation to [+voice] only, following the description in Sigurd (1965). But Hellberg (1974) claims that orthographic mixed-voice word-internal clusters show the same devoicing as the examples in (31). I assume now that Hellberg is the more accurate source, since a more careful transcription is used and there is explicit discussion of the morpheme boundary facts. Assimilation to [+voice] only is predicted not to exist under the present analysis. The only other possible case is Ukrainian. Bethin (1987) argues following work by Andersen that voicing assimilation in Ukrainian is a purely phonetic process following from a rule that laxes syllable-final consonants. However, see also Butska (1998), who provides an OT analysis of Ukrainian assuming that the relevant feature is [voice] and that the constraints proposed in this paper should be modified to include a MAXVOICE constraint, which is also argued to exist by Lombardi (1995c, 1998).

References

Beckman, Jill: 1995, 'Shona Height Harmony: Markedness and Positional Identity', *University of Massachusetts Occasional Papers* 18, GLSA, Amherst, pp. 53–75.

Beckman, Jill: 1996, *Positional Faithfulness*, unpublished Ph.D. dissertation, University of Massachusetts, Amherst. ◀

Bethin, Christina Y.: 1987, 'Syllable Final Laxing in Ukrainian', *Folia Slavica* 81, 185–97.

Bethin, Christina Y.: 1992, *Polish Syllables: The Role of Prosody in Phonology and Morphology*, Slavica, Columbus, Ohio.

Brockhaus, Wiebke: 1995, *Final Devoicing in the Phonology of German*, Niemeyer, Tübingen.

Butska, Luba: 1998, 'Faithfulness of [Voice] in Ukranian: An Analysis of Voicing Alternations within Optimality Theory', unpublished manuscript, Rutgers University.

Charles-Luce, Jan: 1985, 'Word-Final Devoicing in German: Effects of Phonetic and Sentential Context', *Journal of Phonetics* 13, 309–24.

Cho, Young-Mee Yu: 1990, *Parameters of Consonantal Assimilation*, unpublished Ph.D. dissertation, Stanford University.

Fourakis, Marios and Gregory K. Iverson: 1984, 'On the "Incomplete Neutralization' of German Final Obstruents', *Phonetica* 41, 140–9.

Goldsmith, John: 1989, 'Licensing, Inalterability, and Harmonic Rule Application', *Proceedings* of CLS 25, Chicago Linguistic Society.

Goldsmith, John: 1990, *Autosegmental and Metrical Phonology*, Blackwell, Oxford.

Greenberg, Joseph: 1978, 'Some Generalizations Concerning Initial and Final Consonant Clusters', *Universals of Human Language*, vol. 2, *Phonology*, Stanford University Press, Stanford.

Harms, Robert T.: 1973, 'Some Nonrules of English', paper distributed by Indiana University Linguistics Club, Bloomington.

Hellberg, Staffan: 1974, *Graphonomic Rules in Phonology: Studies in the Expression Component of Swedish*, Acta Universitatis Gothoburgensis, Göteborg.

Inkelas, Sharon, Orhan Orgun, and Cheryl Zoll: 1994, 'The Big Bang: Subregularities as Cogrammars', unpublished manuscript, University of California, Berkeley. ◀

Ito, Junko: 1986, *Syllable Theory in Prosodic Phonology*, unpublished Ph.D. dissertation, University of Massachusetts, Amherst.

Katz, Dovid: 1987, *A Grammar of the Yiddish Language*, Duckworth, London.

Kingston, John: 1985, *The Phonetics and Phonology of the Timing of Oral and Glottal Events*, unpublished Ph.D. dissertation, University of California at Berkeley.

Kingston, John: 1990, 'Articulatory Binding', in John Kingston and Mary Beckman (eds.), *Papers in Laboratory Phonology I: Between the Grammar and Physics of Speech*, Cambridge University Press, Cambridge, pp. 406–34.

Kisseberth, Charles: 1970, 'On the Functional Unity of Phonological Rules', *Linguistic Inquiry* 1, 291–306,

Levy, Erika: 1997, 'Identity-Driven Syllabification in German Surface Forms', unpublished manuscript, New York University, New York.

Lombardi, Linda: 1991, *Laryngeal Features and Laryngeal Neutralization*, Ph.D. dissertation, University of Massachusetts, Amherst. [Published in 1994 by Garland, New York.]

Lombardi, Linda: 1995a, 'Laryngeal Neutralization and Syllable Wellformedness', *Natural Language and Linguistic Theory* 13, 39–74.

Lombardi, Linda: 1995b, 'Laryngeal Features and Privativity', *The Linguistic Review* 12, 35–59.

Lombardi, Linda: 1995c, 'Why Place and Voice are Different: Constraint-specific Alternations in Optimality Theory', unpublished manuscript, University of Maryland. ▶

Lombardi, Linda: 1997, 'Restrictions on Direction of Voicing Assimilation: An OT Account', *Maryland Working Papers in Linguistics* 4, Linguistics Department, University of Maryland, College Park.

Lombardi, Linda: 1998, 'Evidence for MaxFeature Constraints from Japanese', paper presented at Linguistic Society of America Annual Meeting, New York, January. ▶

Lombardi, Linda: to appear, 'Constraints Versus Representations: Some Questions from Laryngeal Phonology', *Maryland Working Papers in Linguistics* 7, Linguistics Department, University of Maryland, College Park. ▶

Maddieson, Ian: 1984, *Patterns of Sounds*, Cambridge University Press, Cambridge.

McCarthy, John J. and Alan Prince: 1993, 'Prosodic Morphology I: Constraint Interaction and Satisfaction', unpublished manuscript,

University of Massachusetts, Amherst, and Rutgers University.

McCarthy, John J. and Alan Prince: 1995, 'Faithfulness and Reduplicative Identity', *University of Massachusetts Occasional Papers* 18, GLSA, Amherst, pp. 249–384. ◄

Mester, Armin and Junko Ito: 1989, 'Feature Predictability and Underspecification: Palatal Prosody in Japanese Mimetics', *Language 65*, 258–93.

Mohanan, K. P.: 1993, 'Fields of Attraction in Phonology', in John Goldsmith (ed.), *The Last Phonological Rule*, University of Chicago Press, Chicago.

Padgett, Jaye: 1995, 'Partial Class Behavior and Nasal Place Assimilation', *Proceedings of Southwestern Optimality Theory Workshop* (Arizona Phenology Conference, 5), Coyote Working Papers in Linguistics, Department of Linguistics, University of Arizona, pp. 145–83. ◄

Prince, Alan and Paul Smolensky: 1993, 'Optimality Theory: Constraint Interaction in Generative Grammar', unpublished manuscript, Rutgers University and Johns Hopkins. ◄

Selkirk, Lisa: 1995, Class handout, University of Massachusetts, Amherst.

Sigurd, Bengt: 1965, *Phonotactic Structures in Swedish*, Uniskol, Lund.

Slowiaczek, Louisa M. and Daniel A. Dinnsen: 1985, 'On the Neutralizing Status of Polish Word-final Devoicing', *Journal of Phonetics* 13, 325–41.

Smolensky, Paul: 1993, 'Harmony, Markedness, and Phonological Activity', handout, Rutgers Optimality Workshop, Rutgers University. ►

Smolensky, Paul: 1996, 'The Initial State and Richness of the Base in Optimality Theory', unpublished manuscript, Johns Hopkins University. ►

Steriade, Donca: 1993, 'Closure, Release and Nasal Contours', in Marie K. Huffman and Rena A. Krakow (eds.), *Phonetics and Phonology 5, Nasals, Nasalization and the Velum*, Academic Press, New York.

Steriade, Donca: 1995, 'Underspecification and Markedness', in John Goldsmith (ed.), *The Handbook of Phonological Theory*, Blackwell, Cambridge, Massachusetts.

Trubetzkoy N. S.: 1939, *Principles of Phonology*, reprinted in 1969, University of California Press, Berkeley.

Wiese, Richard: 1996, *The Phonology of German*, Clarendon Press, Oxford.

Study and Research Questions

1   Show that the factorial typology is indeed complete. That is, list all 24 permutations of the four constraints AGREE, *LAR, IDENT-ONSET(Lar), and IDENT(Lar) and show that each corresponds to one of Lombardi's language types. There is considerable overlap because not all constraints are in conflict; identify the non-conflicting constraints and relate them to the ranking permutations that give identical results.

2   The pattern found in Swedish has been called "assimilation to the unmarked" (Baković 1999): if a cluster contains at least one unmarked voiceless consonant, then the entire cluster is voiceless. Explain how the ranking in (31) produces this effect.

3   It is sometimes suggested that featural faithfulness involves MAX(feature) and DEP(feature) constraints instead of IDENT(feature) (see chapter 3). Redo Lombardi's analysis under this different assumption and determine whether any differences arise. (Swedish is an interesting place to start.)

4   Read Mascaró and Wetzels (2001). Can their observations be incorporated into the theory proposed here, perhaps with modifications?

Chapter 18 | Cheryl Zoll

Positional Asymmetries and Licensing

Editor's Note

This chapter proposes an alternative to positional faithfulness: positional markedness. The focus is on a case where a marked structure has a restricted distribution even when it is derived by an unfaithful mapping. Positional faithfulness can also limit marked structures to certain positions – but only marked structures that are already present in the input.

This chapter also introduces a new constraint family, COINCIDE. It is related to the alignment family (see chapter 2), but there is an important difference: COINCIDE constraints do not distinguish different degrees of misalignment.

Introduction

There have been two major approaches to licensing in Optimality Theory. The first, Positional Markedness (1), dictates that certain marked structures either must or cannot occur in particular positions (Ito and Mester 1994, Lombardi 1995, Zoll 1996, 1997, Steriade 1997, inter alia). These go under many different names. Negative Positional Markedness constraints such as NoCODA(Labial) ban labial consonants from the weak coda position, while positive Positional Markedness constraints such as COINCIDE(complex segment, σ_1) specifically restrict complex consonants to strong positions such as the initial syllable.

(1) Positional Markedness
      e.g., NoCODA(Labial): No labial consonants in coda position
            COINCIDE(complex segment, σ_1): A complex segment is word initial

The negative Positional Markedness constraint NoCODA(Labial), for example, rules out segments that are both marked and in a weak position such as the coda,

Excerpt from:
Zoll, Cheryl (1998) Positional asymmetries and licensing. Unpublished manuscript. Cambridge, MA: MIT. [Available on Rutgers Optimality Archive, ROA-282.]

but has no effect on marked segments in stronger positions such as the onset, as illustrated by the tableau in (2). The candidate in (2a), with coda *m*, fatally violates this constraint. The optimal (2b) passes on this constraint because its only labial consonant, *p*, is in the onset. IDENT(Seg), ranked above *LABIAL, prohibits the neutralization of onset labial consonants, so the labial-less (2c), in which the initial consonant has reduced to a /t/, also fails.

(2)   Hypothetical /pum-sa/ → pun.sa

	/pum-sa/	NoCoda(Lab)	Ident(Seg)	NoCoda	*Labial
a.	pum.sa	*! (m)		* (m)	** (m, p)
b. ☞	pun.sa		* (n)	* (n)	* (p)
c.	tun.sa		** (t, n)		

Recent work by Selkirk 1994, Alderete 1995, Jun 1995, Steriade 1995, Beckman 1995, 1997a, 1997b, Casali 1996 and others introduces a potential alternative to licensing known as *Positional Faithfulness* or *Positional Identity*. Positional Faithfulness constraints are parameterizable constraints, as shown in (3). Here a faithfulness constraint is specified to apply only in a particular strong position.

(3)   Positional Faithfulness Constraints
    a.   IDENT-x| x ∈ {onset, stressed syllable, root, other strong constituent . . . }
    b.   MAX-x| x ∈ {onset, stressed syllable, root, other strong constituent . . . }
    c.   DEP-x| x ∈ {onset, stressed syllable, root, other strong constituent . . . }

The Positional Faithfulness constraint IDENT(Onset) in (4), for example, demands that an onset be identical to its input correspondent, but is indifferent to correspondence relations in weak positions (Beckman 1997b). This constraint allows codas to neutralize because no high-ranking faithfulness constraint uniquely refers to the coda. But it specifically protects onsets from alteration.

(4)   IDENT(ONSET): A syllable onset is identical to its input correspondent

The tableau in (5) evaluates the same three candidates as above, this time using Positional Faithfulness. In the optimal (5b) the coda consonant has lost its labiality, thereby reducing the number of violations of the context-independent markedness constraint *LABIAL. Under this account the unsuccessful competitor in (5c) loses because high IDENT(ONSET) blocks neutralization in the onset.

(5)

	/pum-sa/	Ident(Onset)	*Labial	Ident(Seg)
a.	pum.sa		**! (p, m)	
b. ☞	pun.sa		* (p)	* (n)
c.	tun.sa	*! (t)		** (t, n)

The table in (6) summarizes the major differences between the two approaches. Both utilize markedness and faithfulness constraints, but differ in the kind of positional statements they use. In a Positional Markedness account, faithfulness is context-independent, but higher-ranking Positional Markedness constraints force faithfulness violations by directly prohibiting marked structure in weak positions. Positional Faithfulness, on the other hand, restricts identity statements to a particular context, but uses context-independent markedness constraints. With Positional Faithfulness, the context-independent markedness constraints like *LABIAL call for reduction everywhere, but the higher-ranking Positional Faithfulness constraints proscribe neutralization in strong positions.

(6)   The differences:

	Markedness	Faithfulness
Positional Markedness	positional	context-independent
Positional Faithfulness	context-independent	positional

In the simple case of coda neutralization used as an example here, the two approaches appear to be roughly equivalent. This paper demonstrates, however, that Positional Faithfulness is not an adequate substitute for Positional Markedness. First, Positional Faithfulness is too limited in its scope. The theory is designed specifically to account for the overall reduction of marked structure in a word. The candidate in (5b) is optimal, for example, because this form has fewer place features than the unassimilated (5a). However, the range of data previously accounted for with licensing constraints extends far beyond reduction of overall markedness. Marked structures often arise through the addition of structure to an input. Positional Faithfulness does not have the resources to account for these cases. As sketched in (7), Positional Faithfulness constraints prohibit change in strong positions. While this correctly prevents reduction of underlying marked structure, it necessarily blocks augmentation in these contexts as well. Likewise, since no constraint refers specifically to weak positions, a Positional Identity analysis correctly allows neutralization in non-prominent contexts, but it also permits augmentation there for the same reason. In cases where augmentation results in marked structures, Positional Faithfulness therefore makes the erroneous prediction that while lexical marked structure will be limited to strong contexts, marked structure that arises due to augmentation of the input will be drawn to weak positions. For such cases Positional Markedness remains absolutely essential. Case studies of long vowel distribution in Guugu Yimidhirr, an Australian language analyzed by Kager 1996a, and of restrictions on palatalization in Japanese demonstrate the necessity of Positional Markedness constraints for licensing of both underlying and derived marked structures.

(7)   Positional Faithfulness predicts that derived marked structure will be drawn to weak positions

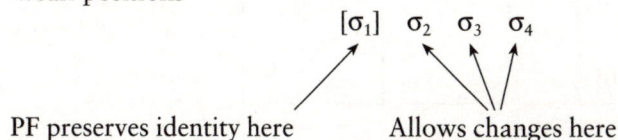

$$[\sigma_1] \quad \sigma_2 \quad \sigma_3 \quad \sigma_4$$

PF preserves identity here   Allows changes here

A second difference between the two theories involves the way in which directionality of assimilation in the repair of illicit clusters is established. Beckman 1997b argues for the superiority of Positional Faithfulness because it determines the directionality of assimilation without additional stipulation. Consider the analysis laid out in (8) for the hypothetical /kun-fa/, where a Positional Markedness constraint forces assimilation in a nasal + consonant cluster. This approach correctly rules out (8c), but cannot decide between progressive (8b) and regressive (8a) assimilation. With Positional Markedness, an independent constraint must determine the direction of spreading. No prediction is made with regard to directionality here.

(8)   /kun-fa/ → [kumfa]

		/kun-fa/	NoCoda(Place)	Ident(Place)
a.	☞	kum.fa V [lab]		*
b.	☞	kun.sa V [cor]		*
c.		kun.fa | | [cor][lab]	*!	

Now compare the Positional Faithfulness account shown in the tableau in (9). A markedness constraint against place features, *CPlace, drives assimilation in the medial cluster, and eliminates (9c).[1] The assimilated clusters both better satisfy the markedness constraint, but Ident(Onset) forces regressive assimilation (9a), since spread of the coda [coronal] feature here (9b) causes the onset of the last syllable to be non-identical to its input correspondent. Positional Faithfulness predicts that spreading will always be from a strong to a weak position, in this case from onset to coda.

(9)   /kun-fa/ → [kumfa]

		/kun-fa/	Ident(Onset)	*CPlace
a.	☞	kum.fa V [lab]		*
b.		kun.sa V [cor]	*!	*
c.		kun.fa | | [cor][lab]		**!

The second problem with Positional Identity arises, however, when cluster conditions in a language are enforced by a variety of conflicting repair strategies. By encapsulating the repair within the positional constraint, even indirectly, cases like Hamer in (10) – where ill-formed clusters succumb to a variety of repair strategies including progressive assimilation, regressive assimilation, and metathesis – are now out of reach. This paper demonstrates that such cases require independent constraints: (i) a Positional Markedness constraint to motivate the variety of strategies, and (ii) a separate constraint to determine directionality.

(10)   Hamer (South Omotic)   (Lydall 1976)
Regressive Assimilation	kʊm- sa	[kʊn.sʌ]	'cause to eat'
Progressive Assimilation	om- na	[om.ma]	'bows'
Metathesis	ep- sa	[es.pa]	'cause to cry'
Metathesis & Assimilation	ʌtʌb- na	[ʌtʌm.ba]	'tongues'

I   Heavy Syllable Licensing in Guugu Yimidhirr

The first problem with licensing as Positional Faithfulness is that Positional Faithfulness constraints protect the integrity of prominent positions by blocking alterations between input to output in these positions. Positional Faithfulness is motivated by cases where reduction fails to occur in positions such as onsets, initial syllables, and heads of feet, but the constraints apply to prevent augmentation in those positions as well. The prediction that both reduction and augmentation will occur only in weak positions, however, is false. Consider the distribution of long vowels in Guugu Yimidhirr (Kager 1996a) in (11). Long vowels are allowed only in the first two syllables of a word. They may occur in the first syllable, the second syllable, or in both the first and second syllables. In (11a), *waaṛigan*, for example, has an initial heavy syllable; in (11f), *ḍamaaṛbina*, the second syllable is heavy; and in (11i), *muuluumul*, both the first and second syllable contain long vowels.

(11)   Vowel length distribution in Guugu Yimidhirr (Kager 1996a: 8)

- Only the first two syllables support a contrast between light and heavy (CVV) syllables

   1st σ heavy
   a.   waaṛigan   'moon'
   b.   waaḍa   'crow'
   c.   guuṛumugu   'meat hawk'

   2nd σ heavy
   d.   dawaaṛ   star'
   e.   gambuugu   'head'
   f.   ḍamaaṛbina   'magpie goose'
   g.   buduunbina   'thunder'

1st and 2nd σ heavy

h. buuɾaay   'water'
i. muuluumul   'dove'
j. daaɾaalŋan   'kangaroo'
k. ɗiiɾaayŋguɾ   'old man'

The distributional restriction extends to derived length as well, as shown in (12). In Guugu Yimidhirr, some suffixes, exemplified here by *-nda*, trigger vowel length on the final vowel of their base. In (12a), the last syllable, which is also the second syllable of the word, lengthens to accommodate the prosodic requirement imposed by the suffix. (12b) shows that lengthening does not take place if the syllable abutting the suffix is not one of the first two syllables of the word. The restriction on the distribution of long vowels holds therefore for both underlying and derived length.

(12)   Restriction holds for derived length as well

- Some suffixes lengthen their base (Kager 1996a: 8)
  Lengthening is blocked outside of first two syllables

  a. /maŋal-nda/   ma.**ŋaal**.nda   'clay'
  b. /wuluŋguɾ-nda/   wu.luŋ.**guɾ**.nda   'lightning, flame-ERG'
  c.   (*wu.luŋ.**guuR**.nda)

The diagnostics for strong positions, shown in (13), have been well established in the literature.[2] Chief among them is that prominent positions maintain more contrasts than weak positions do. Here, because a weight contrast is supported only in the first two syllables, Kager argues that the first two syllables constitute a prominent domain that he calls the Head Prosodic Word (14). Syllables with long vowels are found only in this constituent.

(13)   Diagnostics for prominent positions

		Strong position	*Weak position*
I.	*Contrast*	Supports more contrast	Supports less contrast
II.	*Reduction*	Resists reduction	Yields to reduction
III.	*Stress*	Attracts stress	Does not attract stress
IV.	*Tone*	Attracts H tone	Does not attract H tone
V.	*Harmony*	Triggers harmony	Target of harmony
		May resist assimilation	

(14)   Heavy syllables (CVV) belong to the innermost prosodic word (the Head PWd)

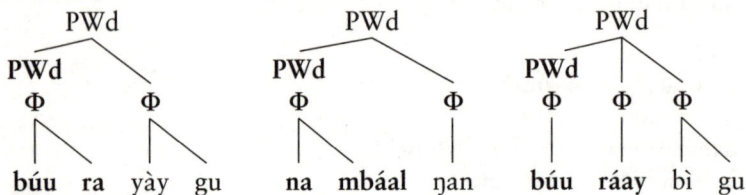

1.1 Positional Markedness

The restriction of CVV to the first two syllables of a word constitutes the primary generalization that any analysis must be able to account for. An analysis of Guugu Yimidhirr utilizing Positional Markedness is uncomplicated. In (15), Positional Markedness is expressed as a COINCIDE constraint that dictates that a heavy syllable should belong to the Head Prosodic Word. An additional constraint, IDENT(mora), hereafter IDENT(μ), which is a context-independent faithfulness constraint, favors identity of vowel length between input and output in all positions.

(15) Licensing as Positional Markedness
      Positional (un)markedness:
      - COINCIDE(heavy syllable, Head PWd):[3] A heavy syllable belongs to the Head PWd (Zoll 1996)
        (i) $\forall x$(x is a heavy syllable) $\rightarrow \exists y$(y= Head PWd $\wedge$ COINCIDE (x,y))
        (ii) Assess one mark for each value of x for which (i) is false

      Faithfulness:
      - IDENT(μ):[4] Input length is preserved in the output (Urbanczyk 1995)

        If α (an integer) weight bearing units dominate a segment in S1 then α weight bearing units dominate its correspondent in S2.

The tableau in (16) shows how these two constraints together preserve lexical vowel length in the first two syllables. (16a), with underlying long vowels retained, is optimal. Since neither of the heavy syllables violates COINCIDE, any reduction of underlying length, as in (16b) and (16c), results in a fatal violation of IDENT(μ).

(16) *muuluu*mul: Heavy syllables are licensed only in the Head PWd

		Candidates	COINCIDE (σ_H, Head PWd)	IDENT(μ)
a.	☞	PWd[muuluu]mul		
b.		PWd[muluu]mul		*!
c.		PWd[muulu]mul		*!

(17) illustrates how this ranking prohibits the surfacing of long vowels outside the Head Prosodic Word. From the hypothetical underlying form with a long vowel in the third syllable, /mulu*buulu*l/, the perfectly faithful (17a) fatally violates the high-ranking Positional Markedness constraint. Candidate (17b) is optimal, despite the difference in vowel length between input and output, since by shortening the vowel of the third syllable, Positional Markedness violations are avoided.

(17)   Hypothetical /mulubuulu/ → [mulubulu]

		Candidates	COINCIDE (σ_H, Head PWd)	IDENT(μ)
a.		$_{PWd}$[mulu]*buulu*	*!	
b.	☞	$_{PWd}$[mulu]*bulu*		*

- COINCIDE ≫ IDENT(μ) because long vowels outside of the Head PWd must shorten

Restrictions on derived length also follow from Positional Markedness. Positional Markedness must dominate the constraint that causes vowel lengthening when the suffix -*nda* attaches to a disyllabic base. (18) presents an alignment constraint that fulfills this function.[5] This constraint requires that the suffix -*nda* attach itself to a heavy syllable.

(18)   ALIGN(-nda, L, heavy σ, R): The suffix -*nda* is affixed to a heavy syllable

As shown by the tableau in (19), COINCIDE crucially outranks ALIGN(nda). For the trisyllabic base, *wuluŋguɾ-*, COINCIDE penalizes lengthening (19b) because the derived long vowel would fall outside the Head Prosodic Word. Since the prosodic requirement of the suffix is less compelling than the need to obey considerations of Positional Markedness, (19a), with no additional vowel length, is optimal.

(19)   Positional Markedness constraint blocks derivation of long vowels in weak position

		/wuluŋguɾ-nda/	COINCIDE (σ_H, Hd PWd)	ALIGN(nda)	IDENT(μ)
a.	☞	$_{PWd}$[wu.luŋ].guɾ.nda		*	
b.		$_{PWd}$[wu.luŋ].guuɾ.nda	*! (*guuR)		*

- COINCIDE ≫ ALIGN(nda) since winner fails to satisfy the prosodic requirements of affix
- Violations of ALIGN(nda) must be categorical to prevent lengthening further to the left

Finally, the tableau in (20) demonstrates that Positional Markedness will not block lengthening within the Head PWd. The lengthened (20b) best satisfies the hierarchy because it manages to meet the length requirements of the suffix without violating the Positional Markedness constraint.

(20) Derived length is permissible in the Head PWd

	/maɲal-nda/	COINCIDE (σ$_H$, Hd PWd)	ALIGN(nda)	IDENT(μ)
a.	$_{PWd}$[ma.ɲal].nda		*!	
b. ☞	$_{PWd}$[ma.ɲaal].nda			*

- ALIGN(nda) ≫ IDENT(μ) since lengthening does take place

The Positional Markedness account of Guugu Yimidhirr is summarized in (21). COINCIDE restricts heavy syllables to the Head Prosodic Word regardless of their source. Furthermore, as it places no specific faithfulness restrictions on the Head Prosodic Word, it allows vowel lengthening to occur there to satisfy the needs of an affix.

(21) Positional Markedness Hierarchy for Guugu Yimidhirr

Restricts heavy syllables, derived and lexical, to the Head Prosodic Word

COINCIDE(σ$_H$, Hd PWd) ≫ ALIGN(nda) ≫ IDENT(μ)

1.2 Comparison with Positional Faithfulness

If Positional Faithfulness constitutes a valid alternative to Positional Markedness then it should be able to account for the licensing of heavy syllables in Guugu Yimidhirr. A Positional Faithfulness account for Guugu Yimidhirr is outlined in (22). IDENT-Head Prosodic Word preserves identity between elements in the first two syllables of the word and their output correspondents. The context-independent *LONG VOWEL proscribes long vowels wherever they are found.

(22) Constraints
Positional faithfulness:
IDENT-HEAD PWD(μ): A syllable in the Head PWd is identical to its input correspondent with respect to weight

Markedness:
*LONG VOWEL: No long vowels (Rosenthall 1994: 42)

With these constraints, ranked as in (23), heavy syllables survive in the Head Prosodic Word because the high-ranking IDENT-Head PWord prohibits vowel shortening in the first two syllables of a word. Candidates (23b) and (23c) are less marked with respect to vowel length, since they contain fewer long vowels, but (23a) is optimal because the prominent syllables have not been reduced.

(23)   *muuluu*mul: Heavy syllables survive in the Head PWd

	Candidates	IDENT-HD PWD(μ)	*LONG VOWEL	IDENT(μ)
a. ☞	PWd[muuluu]mul		**	
b.	PWd[muluu]mul	*! (mu)	*	*
c.	PWd[muulu]mul	*! (lu)	*	*

- IDENT-HdPWd ≫ *LONG VOWEL since long vowels do survive in the first two syllables

As shown in (24), because the Positional Faithfulness constraint says nothing about the less prominent syllables outside the Head Prosodic Word, *LONG VOWEL will compel shortening of long vowels in the third (or a subsequent) syllable. Change in a weak syllable violates only the lowest-ranked general IDENT(μ) constraint (24b), so *LONG VOWEL can be satisfied in this position.

(24)   Input heavy syllables will be shortened outside the Head PWd
       Hypothetical /mulubuulu/ → [mulubulu]:

	Candidates	IDENT-HD PWD(μ)	*LONG VOWEL	IDENT(μ)
a.	PWd[mulu]buulu		*!	
b. ☞	PWd[mulu]bulu			*

- *LONG VOWEL ≫ IDENT(μ) since long vowels shorten outside the Head PWd

Turning now to the case of suffix-induced vowel lengthening in (25), ALIGN(nda) must outrank IDENT-Head Prosodic Word, since lengthening occurs in the optimal candidate (25b) despite the resulting Positional Faithfulness violation. (25a), while perfectly faithful to its input, fails because lengthening has not taken place.

(25)   High-ranking prosodic requirement forces weight change in Head PWd

	/maŋal-nda/	ALIGN(nda)	IDENT-HD PWD(μ)	*LONG VOWEL	IDENT(μ)
a.	PWd[ma.ŋal].nda	*!			
b. ☞	PWd[ma.ŋaal].nda		*	*	*

This ranking makes the wrong prediction about the possibility of lengthening outside of the Head PWd, however, as shown by the tableau in (26). The hierarchy incorrectly selects (26b) with vowel lengthening outside of the Head PWd, because no constraint specifically bans vowel lengthening in a weak position. Positional

Faithfulness entails that if a strong position can be altered, weak ones must be mutable as well.

(26) [💣 indicates an ill-formed candidate wrongly selected by the proposed ranking]

	/wuluŋguɾ-nda/	ALIGN(nda)	IDENT-HD PWD(μ)	*LONG VOWEL	IDENT(μ)
a.	pwd[wu.luŋ]guɾ.nda	*!			
b. 💣	pwd[wu.luŋ]guuɾ.nda			*	*

There is an alternative ranking that does block lengthening outside the Head PWd. The analysis in (27) ranks the context-independent IDENT(μ) above ALIGN(nda). This correctly prevents lengthening outside of the Head PWd (27a). However, it necessarily blocks lengthening within the Head PWd as well, as shown in (28). In addition, this hierarchy allows underlying long vowels to surface in any position, both inside and outside the Head PWd (29).

(27) IDENT(μ) ≫ ALIGN(nda)
blocks lengthening outside of the Head PWd

	/wuluŋguɾ-nda/	IDENT(μ)	ALIGN(nda)	IDENT-HD PWD(μ)	*LONG VOWEL
a. ☞	pwd[wu.luŋ].guɾ.nda		*		
b.	pwd[wu.luŋ].guuɾ.nda	*!			*

(28) IDENT(μ) ≫ ALIGN(nda)
also blocks lengthening within the Head PWd

	/maɲal-nda/	IDENT(μ)	ALIGN(nda)	IDENT-HD PWD(μ)	*LONG VOWEL
a. 💣	pwd[ma.ɲal].nda		*		
b.	pwd[ma.ɲaal].nda	*!		*	*

(29) IDENT(μ) ≫ *LONG VOWEL
also prohibits shortening outside of the Head PWd

	Candidates	IDENT(μ)	IDENT-HD PWD(μ)	*LONG VOWEL
a. 💣	pwd[mulu]buulu			*
b.	pwd[mulu]bulu	*		

To summarize, to account for the lexical distribution of long vowels in Guugu Yimidhirr requires the ranking IDENT-Head PWd(μ) ≫ *LONG VOWEL ≫ IDENT(μ). On the other hand, to block lengthening outside of the Head PWd it must be the case that IDENT(μ) dominates *LONG VOWEL. This ranking paradox cannot be resolved if we rely on Positional Faithfulness to govern the licensing of heavy syllables in Guugu Yimidhirr. Positional Faithfulness is concerned only with preserving input/output correspondence in strong positions. Therefore it favors changes, including the creation of marked structure, only in weak positions. As a result, it wrongly predicts that where there is an asymmetry between positions, derived marked structures preferably arise in weak positions. Without Positional Markedness there is no way to limit derived marked structure to exclusively strong positions.

[. . .]

Notes

1 *PLACE is also violated by the place features on the initial onset, but since this is a constant for the three candidates I have left out that violation for the purposes of this illustration. The [dorsal] place here is likewise protected by IDENT(Onset).

2 See Trubetzkoy 1939/1969, Garde 1967, Hooper 1972, 1976, Vennemann 1972, Haiman 1972, Paulian 1975, Foley 1977, Brasington 1982, Cairns and Feinstein 1982, Goldsmith 1985, Ito 1986, Hyman 1987, 1989, 1990, Goldsmith 1990, Ito and Mester 1993, Bosch 1993, Mohanan 1993, Selkirk 1994, Dresher and van der Hulst 1995, Alderete 1995, Beckman 1995, 1997a, 1997b, Casali 1996, Zoll 1996, 1997, inter alia.

3 Kager derives licensing from a Weight to Stress Principle that states that "heavy syllables have maximal prominence" (p. 13). (This WSP expands upon the original constraint proposed by Prince 1990.) For Kager, to have "maximal prominence" means that a syllable belongs to the head of the word, in this case the first two syllables, which comprise the head of the prosodic word. In other words, Kager's WSP amounts to a constraint which calls for coincidence of a heavy syllable with the Head PWd. The COINCIDE constraint therefore is just a restatement in current terms of Kager's original insight.

4 Urbanczyk 1995: 512 calls this constraint TRANSFER.

5 See Rosenthall 1995 and Kager 1996b, inter alia, for affixes that impose prosodic requirements on their bases; see McCarthy and Prince 1993 for alignment constraints in morpheme subcategorization.

References

Alderete, J. (1995). Faithfulness to prosodic heads. ◀

Beckman, J. (1995). Shona height harmony: Markedness and positional identity. *Papers in Optimality Theory* 18. J. Beckman, L. W. Dickey, and S. Urbanczyk, eds. University of Massachusetts, Amherst, GLSA.

Beckman, J. (1997a). Positional Faithfulness. Hopkins Optimality Theory Workshop, Baltimore, MD.

Beckman, J. (1997b). *Positional Faithfulness*. Doctoral dissertation, Amherst, University of Massachusetts. ◀

Bosch, A. R. K. (1993). *The Licensing of Prosodic Prominence in Tamil*. FLSM, Northwestern University, IULC.

Brasington, R. W. P. (1982). Markedness, strength, and position. *Linguistic Controversies: Essays in Linguistic Theory and Practice in Honour of F. R. Palmer*. D. Crystal, ed. London, Edward Arnold: 81–94.

Cairns, C. and M. Feinstein (1982). 'Marked-ness and the theory of syllable structure.' *LI* 13: 193–226.

Casali, R. F. (1996). 'Vowel elision in hiatus contexts.' *UCLA Working Papers in Phonology* 1: 18–56.

Dresher, E. and H. van der Hulst (1995). Head dependent asymmetries in prosodic phonology. ▶

Foley, J. (1977). *Foundations of Theoretical Phonology*. Cambridge, Cambridge University Press.

Garde, P. (1967). *L'Accent*. Paris, Presses Universitaires de France.

Goldsmith, J. (1985). 'Vowel harmony in Khalka Mongolian, Yaka, Finnish and Hungarian.' *Phonology Yearbook* 2: 253–75.

Goldsmith, J. (1990). *Autosegmental and Metrical Phonology*. Oxford, Blackwell.

Haiman, J. (1972). 'Phonological targets and unmarked structures.' *Language* 48: 365–77.

Hooper, J. (1972). 'The syllable in phonological theory.' *Language* 48: 525–40.

Hooper, J. (1976). *An Introduction to Natural Generative Phonology*. New York, San Francisco, London, Academic Press.

Hyman, L. (1987). 'Prosodic domains in Kukuya.' *NLLT* 5: 311–33.

Hyman, L. (1989). 'Accent in Bantu: An appraisal.' *Studies in the Linguistic Sciences* 19: 111–28.

Hyman, L. (1990). Non-exhaustive syllabification: Evidence from Nigeria and Cameroon. *Papers from the 26th Regional Meeting of the Chicago Linguistic Society: The Parasession on the Syllable in Phonetics and Phonology*. M. Ziolkowski, M. Noske, and K. Deaton, eds. Chicago, Chicago Linguistic Society, 2: 175–96.

Ito, J. (1986). *Prosodic Constituency in the Lexicon*. New York, Garland.

Ito, J. and A. Mester (1993). Licensed segments and safe paths. *Constraints, Violations, and Repairs in Phonology*. C. Paradis, D. LaCharite and E. Nikiema, eds. Special issue of the *Canadian Journal of Linguistics*.

Ito, J. and A. Mester (1994). Realignment. University of California, Santa Cruz. ▶

Jun, J. (1995). *Perceptual and Articulatory Factors in Place Assimilation: An Optimality Theoretic Approach*. Doctoral dissertation, University of California, Los Angeles.

Kager, R. (1996a). Stem Disyllabicity in Guugu Yimidhirr. *UiL OTS Working Papers of Theoretical Linguistics*. Utrecht, Universiteit Utrecht.

Kager, R. (1996b). On affix allomorphy and syllable counting. Utrecht. ▶

Lombardi, L. (1995). Why place and voice are different: Constraint interaction and featural faithfulness in OT. University of Maryland. ▶

Lydall, J. (1976). Hamer. *The Non-Semitic Languages of Ethiopia*. M. L. Bender, ed. East Lansing, Michigan State University: 393–438.

McCarthy, J. and A. Prince (1993). Generalized alignment. University of Massachusetts, Amherst and Rutgers University. ◀

Mohanan, K. P. (1993). Fields of attraction in phonology. *The Last Phonological Rule*. J. Goldsmith, ed. Chicago and London, University of Chicago Press.

Paulian, C. (1975). *Le Kukuya: langue teke du Congo*. Paris, SELAF.

Prince, A. (1990). Quantitative consequences of rhythmic organization. *Papers from the 26th Regional Meeting of the Chicago Linguistic Society: The Parasession on the Syllable in Phonetics and Phonology*. M. Ziolkowski, M. Noske, and K. Deaton, eds. Chicago, Chicago Linguistic Society: 355–98.

Prince, A. and P. Smolensky (1993). Optimality theory: Constraint interaction in generative grammar. Rutgers University and the University of Colorado. ◀

Rosenthall, S. (1994). *Vowel/Glide Alternation in a Theory of Constraint Interaction*. Doctoral dissertation, University of Massachusetts, Amherst.

Rosenthall, S. (1995). The prosodic base of the Hausa plural. *Papers in Optimality Theory* 18. J. Beckman, L. W. Dickey, and S. Urbanczyk, eds. University of Massachusetts, Amherst, GLSA.

Selkirk, E. (1994). Class lecture notes. Dept. of Linguistics, University of Massachusetts, Amherst.

Steriade, D. (1995). Neutralization and the expression of contrast. University of California, Los Angeles.

Steriade, D. (1997). Phonetics in phonology: The case of laryngeal neutralization. Department of Linguistics, University of California, Los Angeles.

Trubetzkoy, N. S. (1939/1969). *Principles of Phonology*. Berkeley and Los Angeles, University of California Press.

Urbanczyk, S. (1995). Double reduplication in parallel. *Papers in Optimality Theory* 18. J. Beckman, L. W. Dickey, and S. Urbanczyk, eds. University of Massachusetts, Amherst, GLSA: 499–532. ▶

Vennemann, T. (1972). 'On the theory of syllabic phonology.' *Linguistische Berichte* 18: 1–18.

Zoll, C. (1996). *Parsing Below the Segment in a Constraint Based Framework*. Stanford, CA, CSLI. ▶

Zoll, C. (1997). 'Conflicting Directionality.' *Phonology* 14: 263–86.

Study and Research Questions

1   The Editor's Note at the beginning of the chapter mentions the similarity and difference between COINCIDE and ALIGN. Explain this difference with an example, then discuss whether both COINCIDE and ALIGN are needed. You will need to look at some of the alignment chapters to answer this question.

2   Re-examine some of the phenomena in chapters 11, 12, 16, and 17 that were adduced in support of positional faithfulness. Discuss which can and cannot be reanalyzed in terms of positional markedness and why.

3   Instead of the constraint ALIGN(nda) (18), suppose that this suffix is represented lexically with a preposed floating mora /μ + nda/. (This is analogous to some treatments of preaccentuation.) Work out the analysis and the argument under this assumption.

4   Construct a hypothetical example that could not be analyzed with positional markedness or positional faithfulness. (Hint: think about the distribution of *unmarked* structures.)

Chapter 19 | Jaye Padgett

Partial Class Behavior and Nasal Place Assimilation

Editor's Note

The theory of feature geometry was one of the most productive and interesting lines of analysis in non-linear phonology. This chapter proposes an alternative to the central representational construct of feature geometry, the class node.

Toward the end, the chapter also draws some conclusions with broader applicability to OT. Properties of language that are encoded in representations are all or nothing. The chapter's argument against the class node is that the phenomena it is intended to explain are not all or nothing, but rather show the characteristics of violable constraints. The broader questions this leads to are these: When are representational theories appropriate? Are they ever appropriate? Should all the work of phonological representations now be accomplished with substantive constraints?

1   Introduction

This paper has two goals. The first is to pursue and further motivate some ideas developed in Padgett (1995a) on the status of the notion *feature class* in phonological theory. The second is to explore the phenomenon of place assimilation. These goals are brought together in an exploration of facts involving nasal place assimilation to complex segments: assimilation in such cases is often partial in the sense that only one articulator of the complex segment spreads under a general process of place assimilation. As we will see, partial assimilation of this sort bears in an important way on our understanding of feature classes.

The notion 'feature class' makes general reference to familiar categories like *Place*, *Laryngeal*, *VPlace*, and so on, classifications of features instantiated most notably in work within Feature Geometry theory (henceforth FG, Clements 1985). FG seeks

Excerpt from:
Padgett, Jaye (1995) Partial class behavior and nasal place assimilation. In *Proceedings of the 1995 Southwestern Workshop on Optimality Theory (SWOT)*, ed. Keiichiro Suzuki and Dirk Elzinga. Tucson, AZ: Department of Linguistics, University of Arizona. [Available on Rutgers Optimality Archive, ROA-113.]

to explain recurrent copatternings of features according to these categories, by means of the representational device *class node*: constraints can target a node *Place* (for example), and thereby indirectly affect all dependent features as a group. Padgett (1995a) explores an alternative understanding of feature classes, called Feature Class Theory (FCT), in which classes are defined instead as sets of features (having no tree-theoretic instantiation). Features pattern into sets according to properties shared by their members – place-hood, laryngeality, and so on. Constraints can make mention of these sets, so that the central insight of FG is preserved, but they thereby target *individually* the member features having the right properties.

FCT finds key motivation in a certain brand of *partial class behavior* first noted by Sagey (1987) under the rubric 'non-constituent' behavior. The phenomenon is illustrated below with an example involving Turkish and the feature class *Color* = {back, round}. The example and argument come from Padgett (1995a); on the class *Color* see also Odden (1991) and Selkirk (1991a). Turkish vowel harmony amounts to an imperative that this class of features span a word, as shown in (1a). (For the facts of Turkish vowel harmony and a classical autosegmental analysis see especially Clements and Sezer 1982.) However, harmony cannot establish a link between [round] and a non-high vowel, due to an independent segmental markedness condition disfavoring such linkage. Resulting from this prohibition are instances of partial class behavior, in which only one member of the targeted class *Color* – namely [back] – conforms to the harmony imperative, shown in (1b). (−*b* and *r* are [−back] and [round] respectively.)

(1)   Full (a) and partial (b) class behavior: Turkish and *Color*

    a. y ü z ü n   'face (gen.)'

           −b r

    b. y ü z d e n   'face (abl.)'

           r −b

Such partial class behavior is surprising from the perspective of FG, because of the way that feature classes like *Color* are represented and understood. They are embodied as elements of a tree representation, the class nodes, upon which rules operate directly, affecting the relevant dependent features only indirectly. These nodes have always been interpreted to function in an all-or-nothing fashion: if color harmony results from the linkage of a node *Color*, as in (2), then the invariant expectation has been that both [back] and [round] will be linked, or failing that, neither one will be linked (unless a separate rule is invoked). Such a theory makes no provision for the intermediate possibility of partial class behavior.

Apparently for this reason, the FG literature has failed to call on the robust evidence of Turkish and other (especially Altaic and Uralic) color harmonies as evidence for a class *Color* – though this class has ample precedent in phonological theory, and has been argued for within FG itself (Odden 1991). Though FG can be recast so as to accommodate partial class behavior, the required alteration essentially

(2)   Total class behavior in FG: *yüzdön or *yüzdAn (no harmony)

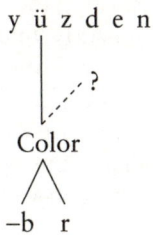

y ü z d e n

Color
/\
−b   r

strips the class nodes of their function of capturing feature classes, and entails something like the FCT point of view, as we will see.

FCT therefore extends the explanatory role of the feature class idea to empirical areas otherwise untraversed. The case of color harmony outlined above is explored in detail in Padgett (1995a). The present paper instead concentrates on facts of nasal place assimilation by consonants (henceforth: NPA), and considers a range of partial assimilation data involving diverse complex segment types. The first goal of the paper, then, is to demonstrate the pervasiveness of partial class behavior with reference to another well-known phenomenon, NPA, and so further motivate FCT.

Exploration of this territory requires some reckoning with the facts of place assimilation very generally, and a theoretical discussion of this phenomenon forms the second goal of the paper. Foremost among the themes here is the important role given to the notion *segmental release* (McCawley 1967, Selkirk 1982, Steriade 1993a, b, 1994), seen here as a featural property that lends great prominence to a segment's other featural distinctions. Such prominence exerts its influence through release-sensitive faithfulness constraints; this builds on the more general idea of position- or prominence-sensitive faithfulness (Selkirk 1994, Beckman 1995). It emerges from these findings that positional categories like 'onset' and 'coda' are often only indirectly relevant to feature licensing, and hence assimilations, contrary to the prevalent view. Further, motivation is found for a feature spreading imperative in assimilations, a surprising fact from the perspective of accounts appealing solely to featural licensing in order to achieve multiple linkage of place.

This work is inspired by central tenets of Optimality Theory (henceforth OT, Prince and Smolensky 1993), calling in particular on those of constraint ranking and (minimal) violability. The representational issue aside, the central point of FCT is that constraints mentioning classes like *Place* and *Laryngeal* are *gradiently violable*, a claim that informs the upcoming account of partial class behavior. Such behavior ensues most commonly under the scenario C ≫ CONSTRAINT(CLASS), where C is any constraint, CONSTRAINT(CLASS) is a constraint targeting any class of features, and the two constraints conflict for some proper subset of the set *Class*. In the case of Turkish above, C prohibits the output of (non-initial) non-high round vowels, and CONSTRAINT(CLASS) is a constraint requiring harmony (treated as alignment in Padgett 1995a, and called ALIGN(COLOR)); these constraints conflict with respect to the feature [round] (a proper subset of *Color*) in forms where harmony would effect linkage of [round] to a non-high vowel. The harmony imperative is therefore violated – but not fully, since [back] conforms.

OT provides a theoretical context in which FCT is essentially necessitated. Once we cast an informed eye on traditional rule-specific stipulations, factoring them out by appeal to the interaction of independent constraints, we frequently find the scenario C ≫ CONSTRAINT(CLASS) (understood as above) as a matter of course. In some cases this factoring will propel us to unify processes once thought of as separate, as when [back] and [round] harmonies are united in *Color* harmony (see Padgett 1995a). In all cases, including those explored below involving *Place*, the notion class *node* is reduced in content to mere feature class label, doing no real work in the theory.[1]

Section 2 below explicates the essential properties of FCT and argues for it on the basis of the partial NPA phenomenon. In section 3 we turn our attention to the task of finding a general account of place assimilations in OT. Section 4 provides empirical substance for uniting these separate expositional strands, briefly surveying a range of data involving partial NPA to various complex segment types, and analyzing a case from Gã, calling on ideas just developed. [Sections 3 and 4 are not reprinted here. – Ed.]

2   Feature Class Theory

2.1   Capturing feature classes

It is now a familiar observation that some phonological features pattern together recurrently in processes of assimilation, dissimilation, neutralization, and so on. Feature classes similar to *Laryngeal* and *Place* achieved a formal status within generative phonology first in the work of Dependency phonologists (Lass and Anderson 1975, Lass 1976, Anderson and Ewen 1987), and later most prominently in Feature Geometry theory (Clements 1985, cf. Mascaró 1983, Mohanan 1983). Within FG, the feature class promise is fulfilled by means of ontological entities known as class nodes, incorporated into a tree representation; these are directly targeted by phonological rules/constraints. The following FG representation, a pared-down adaptation from McCarthy (1988), serves to anchor the discussion.

(3)   The classes *Place* and *Laryngeal* in FG

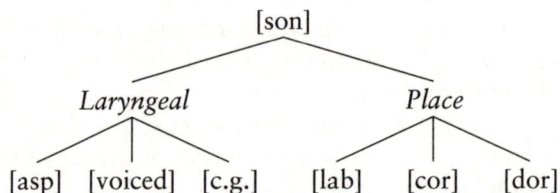

```
                          [son]
                  _____/    _____
                 /                      \
            Laryngeal                   Place
           /    |    \                 /   |   \
          /     |     \               /    |    \
       [asp] [voiced] [c.g.]       [lab] [cor] [dor]
```

Class nodes in FG (like those italicized above) are central to that theory, serving as key *mediators* of feature class behavior. Thus a rule demanding the spreading of *Place* is understood to target the relevant class node; entailments attributed to featural dependency ensure that the actual place features themselves will be affected at the same time. These latter features are therefore affected only indirectly. We will return to this fact and explore its significance in section 2.2.

FCT is a less 'syntactic' and more 'semantic' approach to the feature class insight: terms like *Place* and *Laryngeal* stand for *sets* of features, as shown below. These sets have their basis in the properties that their members share: here, place-hood and laryngeality respectively. (For a precedent involving syntactic feature classes, see Gazdar et al. 1985: 23)

(4)   The classes *Place* and *Laryngeal* in FCT
      Place $=_{\text{def}}$ {labial, coronal, dorsal . . . }
      Laryngeal $=_{\text{def}}$ {aspirated, voiced, constricted glottis}

Naturally, constraints must be able to refer to these classes; FCT maintains the important feature class insight of FG.[2] However, there are now no objects in the representation (class nodes) to mediate feature class behavior in the way seen in (2). By hypothesis we are reverting to a simplified structure most reminiscent of 'bottlebrush' theories (see Hayes 1990 on these theories). In the representation below, feature order is randomized to emphasize the point: classes are understood as sets of features that share the relevant property. The intuition we are developing is straightforward: constraints *mention* classes like *Place* and *Laryngeal*, but they thereby *target*, directly and individually, the features in the respective extensions of these classes, defined in (4).

(5)   FCT representation

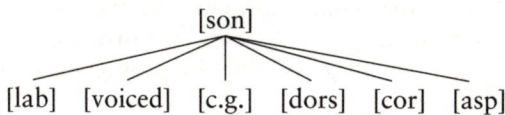

```
                      [son]
          _____/ /|\ _____
         /      /     |    \      \     \
      [lab] [voiced] [c.g.] [dors] [cor] [asp]
```

For the sake of discussion, let us consider a provisional constraint demanding NPA, in the formulation given below. This formulation is a temporary convenience; in section 3 we will inquire more seriously into the nature of the phenomenon.

(6)   Npa: In every sequence NC, every *Place* linked to C is linked to N, and vice versa

This constraint must be understood to bear on the feature [labial] in the representation in (7), by virtue of this feature's status as a place feature. More generally, it must require double linkage of *every* individual feature of the set *Place* in the right (NC) configuration.

(7)   [labial] targeted as a *Place* feature

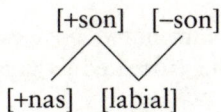

```
          [+son]   [-son]
            /  \   /
           /    \ /
       [+nas]  [labial]
```

An understanding of feature class behavior more or less along these lines is advocated in Selkirk (1991a, b) and Padgett (1991); Hayes (1990) represents a move in the same direction, maintaining the class nodes of FG while essentially motivating individual feature behavior in various 'diphthongization paradoxes'. Sagey (1987) argues for a limited use of individual feature spreading in order to capture class behavior, viewing it as a marked option within FG; Halle (1995) picks up Sagey's argument (though cf. Ní Chiosáin 1995), but advocates individual feature targeting as the only possibility in the theory, as we do here. Differences among these various proposals for individual feature targeting are discussed in the next section.

In order to ensure class behavior as informally illustrated above, we simply capitalize on the postulated sets rather than on postulated nodes. Terms like *Place, Laryngeal* and *Color* are convenient stand-ins for these sets in constraint formulations. However, a look at various possible constraint types reveals a fact worth keeping in mind: different constraints will quantify over these sets in different ways. Thus the intent of our constraint NPA is to quantify universally over the place features, and a rendition with the relevant portion formalized might be the following (where x ranges over features, and F(S) means 'feature F is contained in segment S', i.e., dominated by the same Root node = [son] feature):

(8) NPA redux: For every sequence NC, $\forall_x$, $x \in$ *Place*, $x(N) \Leftrightarrow x(C)$

It should still be clear that this constraint is satisfied by the representation in (7). We will further explore its interpretation momentarily. First, to see how a different quantificational force can arise from another constraint, consider the formulation below of a constraint banning placeless segments, again with the portion of interest formalized below it (see Itô and Mester 1993, Lombardi 1995, among others, on such a constraint).

(9) HAVEPLACE: Every segment must have some *Place*
                 For every segment S, $\exists_x$, $x \in$ *Place*, $x(S)$

This constraint requires *existential* quantification over the feature class. This is the result we want; we do not intend that every Root must dominate all places, for instance. One need not endorse the particular constraints just considered in order to see the point: constraints will differ in the sort of quantificational restrictions they place on their variables. Terms like *Place* and *Laryngeal* in an informally stated constraint actually stand in conveniently for these variables and the relevant sets.[3]

Returning to our provisional NPA, let us run it by a few more representations for completeness. The following summary rates the success of several representations with respect to this constraint, and provides explanatory commentary. The representations have been minimized: L, C, D stand for [labial], [coronal] and [dorsal] respectively.

As can be seen from the violations marked and the commentary, NPA can be violated more than once in a representation. The constraint is treated as gradient

(10)   How NPA rates representations

	Representation	NPA	Commentary

a.	p a ŋ g u r
	   \∨/
	   D
		✓	One NC sequence, one place, doubly linked.

b.	m p a ŋ g u r ∨ ∨ L D	✓	In every NC sequence, every place is doubly linked.
c.	N p a ŋ g u r | ∨ L D	*	In one NC sequence, one place is not doubly linked. (HavePlace is also violated.)
d.	n p a ŋ g u r | | ∨ C L D	**	In one NC sequence, two places are not doubly linked. (Note the biconditional in (8).)
e.	n p a m g u r | | | | C L L D	****	In two NC sequences, two places are not doubly linked.
f.	p a g u r	✓	Constraint vacuously satisfied.

– it is worse to have four place features in the relevant configuration fail to be doubly linked than to have only two place features fail in this way, (10d) vs. (10e), and so on. That is, *every x, x ∈ Place* is not interpreted in the most straightforward truth-conditional way, such that one, or many, failures translates simply as 'false'. Gradience of this sort is now familiar in the OT literature; for general discussion see Prince and Smolensky (1993) and McCarthy and Prince (1993). Gradience will be important to our understanding of partial class behavior later.

Though we will soon revise our understanding of nasal place assimilation, the discussion here illustrates very generally how any constraint mentioning a feature class is to be constructed and understood. Before we move on, it is worth making another point concerning FCT. Like FG, FCT postulates *partitionings* of sets of features; thus, the classes *Place* and *Laryngeal*, for example, do not intersect. This move addresses an empirical claim that no feature could belong to both classes; if correct, a formal statement to this effect is required in either FG or FCT.[4] As for substantive questions like why non-intersection seems (at least largely) correct, or why the sets are divided up precisely as they are and not some other way, the general answer is again theory-neutral: feature classes seem to have their basis in phonetic parameters, whether articulatory or acoustic. (See for example Clements 1985, Sagey 1986, McCarthy 1988, Padgett 1991, 1995c and Zsiga 1993 on this.) Thus while the extension of the set *Place* is a mere list {labial, coronal, dorsal . . . }, the intension is revealed by the phonetic term *Place* itself. Presumably a fuller understanding of this basis will shed some light on the issues raised here.

2.2   Partial class behavior

Suppose we compare accounts within FCT and FG for a straightforward case of NPA, such as that of Spanish (see especially Harris 1984 for an analysis and discussion of the Spanish facts). NPA obtains within words in Spanish, across all places, giving forms like the following:

(11)   NPA in Spanish

sie[m]pre	'always'	pre[n]sa	'press'
á[m]fora	'amphora'	co[n̪]cha	'shell'
a[n̪]dar	'to walk'	á[ɲ]gel	'angel'

Assimilation involves at the least all of the major articulator features required for Spanish, [labial], [coronal] and [dorsal], and so the generalization is over the category *Place*. In many instances, including this one, FCT and FG will be empirically indistinguishable. The former will target every member of a set of features, as outlined in the last section; the result will be linkage of any such feature found in a particular representation, as shown in (12a). FG instead targets a node *Place* in the representation, demanding linkage of this entity, (12b); the logic of dependency entails that any features dependent on *Place* will be interpreted as extending over both segments now also.[5]

(12)   *Place* assimilation in FCT and FG – two representations of [nt]

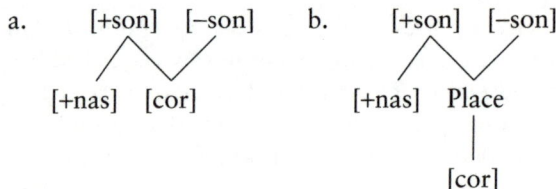

a.   [+son]   [−son]   b.   [+son]   [−son]

          [+nas]   [cor]   [+nas]   Place

                                                      |

                                                    [cor]

One benefit of FG noted by Sagey (1986) involves its straightforward handling of assimilation to complex segments like [gb] of Kpelle. Like Spanish, Kpelle evinces NPA across all places, e.g., [m]*bolu* 'my back', [n]*dia* 'my tattoo', [ŋ]*gɔɔ* 'my foot' (Welmers 1962). Tones are omitted from the cited forms; the assimilating nasal is syllabic. As is true in many West African languages, assimilation to [gb] yields [ŋ͡mg͡b], a homorganic sequence of a doubly articulated nasal followed by the doubly articulated stop, e.g., [ŋ͡m]*gbiŋ* 'myself'. If [gb] is a single segment represented as in (13a), then linkage of the node *Place* will entail this fact without further ado, (13b).

(13)   Assimilation to complex segment in FG

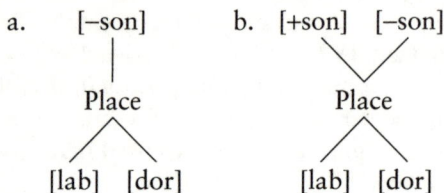

a.   [−son]   b.   [+son]   [−son]

          | \\ /

        Place   Place

          /\   /\

    [lab] [dor]   [lab] [dor]

FCT retains this benefit, if NPA (however conceived) requires linkage of all members of *Place* in the NC configuration, as suggested in our provisional constraint NPA above. In this case the relevant features are targeted directly, by virtue of their status as place features, without the mediation of a mother node:

(14)   Individual feature targeting via the feature class *Place* in FCT

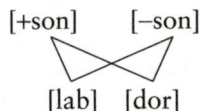

[+son]   [−son]

[lab]   [dor]

However, another outcome of NPA before complex segments is observed in some languages. Deferring full discussion of the facts to section 4 [omitted – Ed.], we simply note the result here to pursue the point: assimilation to [gb] can give simple [ŋ], as in Gã, another language of West Africa. This difference is contrastive within the language: NPA to labiovelars within morphemes is total in Gã, e.g., [ŋm]*kpai* 'libation'. Across a morpheme boundary, in contrast, we see the partial assimilation, e.g., [ŋ]-*kpai* 'my cheeks' (Kropp 1966, Kotey 1974, Ryder 1987). Here, as in Kpelle, the assimilating nasal is syllabic. The outcome [ŋgb] is an example of partial class behavior, shown below.

(15)   Partial NPA to [gb] in FCT

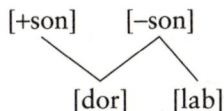

[+son]   [−son]

[dor]   [lab]

Assimilation is partial here in much the same way it is partial in the case of the English prefix *in-*, which gives *i[m]portant* and *i[n]delible* etc., but fails to assimilate before velars, as in *i[n]competent* (careful speech). In both cases NPA requires NC double linkage of every place feature in an NC configuration. This constraint is violated in English by forms such as *incompetent*, due to a higher-ranking markedness prohibition against ŋ. In Gã we similarly see a violation of the constraint, due again to reasons of markedness – a ban on doubly articulated ŋm (see below). In neither language is NPA violated completely or wantonly; in fact it is otherwise obeyed. However, while FG has no problem with partial class behavior like that of English, that of Gã causes trouble. The reason is simple: in Gã one need not look across forms or even different NC clusters to see that assimilation is partial. Rather we find partial class behavior arising within a single NC cluster in (15): some, but not all, of the *Place* features of *gb* spread. Partial class behavior in such cases finds no home in FG (see also Padgett 1995a on this point). Because in FG constraints target actual place features only indirectly, via a mother *Place* node and dependency entailments, we essentially expect one of two outcomes: either all place features will assimilate, or, if assimilation is impossible, no features will assimilate. These outcomes are contrasted below.

(16)   No partial class behavior in FG – constraints/rules target node *Place*

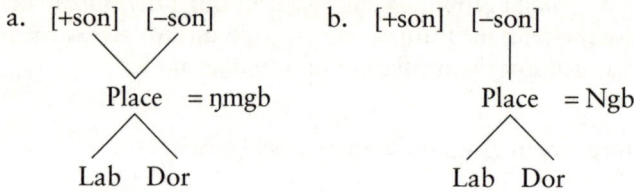

a.   [+son]   [–son]   b.   [+son]   [–son]

Place   = ŋmgb   Place   = Ngb

Lab   Dor   Lab   Dor

In contrast, a central claim of FCT is that constraints mentioning feature classes are gradiently violable. FCT makes no formal distinction between the English and Gã cases, allowing their similarity to emerge naturally. The tableau in (17) anticipates the fuller discussion in section 4. Assuming that the higher-ranked constraint ruling out the doubly articulated nasal is one of segmental markedness, called *COMPSEG ('no complex segments'), candidate (17a) is eliminated from consideration. Yet only this candidate fully satisfies NPA, and so this latter constraint must be violated. Violation is not total, however, as in candidate (17c); this total failure of assimilation is unmotivated (and indeed will normally violate another important markedness constraint, HAVEPLACE). The optimal candidate (17b) violates NPA minimally, that is, only to the extent required by the posited ranking of constraints. This understanding of the facts therefore rests on two important tenets of Optimality Theory (Prince and Smolensky 1993): constraints are violable, and violation is minimal.

(17)   NPA is gradiently violable

/N + gb/	*COMPSEG	NPA
a. ŋmgb	**!	
b. ☞ ŋgb	*	*
c. Ngb	*	**!

It is easy to see that under the reverse ranking, NPA ≫ *COMPSEG, the fully assimilated candidate (17a) would emerge as optimal. The analysis therefore correctly predicts the existence of both full and partial assimilation, and does so with a minimum of assumptions: markedness constraints against complex and placeless segments are required by any theory, as is some account of NPA. Partial assimilation falls out for free, given the existence of constraint (re)ranking, the quite general means of language variation in OT.

The failure of FG resides in its understanding of the representational entity *class node*: this entity and its interpretation together translate essentially into a hard, 'sour grapes' constraint: in effect, either assimilate all features (of some category), or assimilate none. It is worth emphasizing that it is this interpretation of the representation that is at the heart of the failure, rather than the representation itself considered in a theoretical vacuum, if such a thing is possible. Indeed, Halle (1995) argues for individual class feature spreading while retaining class nodes,

see below. The argument here is against hard or 'sour grapes' feature class generalizations, in whatever guise, in favor of their soft understanding illustrated above.
FG is indeed such a 'hard' theory. Presenting the facts of Kpelle, in which assimilation to labiovelars is total (see above), Sagey (1986: 101) provides a telling quote:
"Given the representation of /kp/ . . . there would be no way for place assimilation
spreading the place node to spread just the dorsal, or just the labial, articulation."
Clearly Sagey is not alone in this understanding of FG; in the wake of her important work, the relatively widespread phenomenon of just such partial assimilations
has gone largely unnoticed (though see Ryder 1987); it is hard to avoid the conclusion that theoretical expectations have themselves constrained perception of the
data. In fact, FG has failed to reveal some genuine feature class generalizations
entirely, because of its promotion of hard feature class constraints (see the discussion of *Color* harmony in the introduction and in Padgett 1995a). These failings
point up the two-edged nature of the strategy by which rules (and more generally our understanding of phonology) follow from (interpreted) representations
themselves.

Some possible objections arise at this point. First, suppose FG is correct to regard
feature class generalizations as categorical rather than gradiently violable. Perhaps
NPA in Gã should be supplemented with another rule/constraint effecting linkage
of the feature [dorsal] in just the context $N + gb$. This view might share one aspect
of our account: regular NPA is not possible before labiovelars for reasons of
markedness (though it turns out that some such languages allow *underlying* /ŋm/
to surface, so the generalization might elude some surface-true theories). Either
[dorsal] assimilation follows as a 'repair' (Paradis 1988) to avoid the surfacing of
a placeless segment, or else a rule/constraint of [dorsal] assimilation *preempts* NPA
by the Elsewhere Condition (Kiparsky 1973, 1982, cf. Scobbie 1993). It is hard to
see the appeal of such an approach over that advocated here. The activity of a
constraint targeting [dorsal] must be separately postulated, having no formal connection to the more general constraint that targets a class *Place*, and so seems purely
coincidental. As we saw above in contrast, a form like [ŋgb] falls within the scope of
a general NPA in the FCT account, given the interaction between this constraint and
that of markedness.

Consider instead an attempt within FG to embrace partial class behavior of this
kind, by postulating the following principle guiding feature class generalizations:

(18) FG with a 'resort' strategy
      To target a set of features *Class*,
         a. Target the node *Class*; **unless** targeting this node will fail, in which
             case:
         b. Target individually as many features dominated by node *Class* as
             possible

Whether understood processually or not, any resort strategy of this kind has the 'do
this unless that in which case . . .' quality that Optimality Theory seeks to redress,
and seems unappealing on the face of it. In fact, once we allow for (18b), the theory
has no place for (18a): surely a constraint always targets as many features as possible. FG recast in this way is now an ungainly kin to FCT.

Finally, we might preserve the FG representation while abandoning its tradi-tional interpretation, incorporating something in the spirit of (18b) into the theory, and dispensing with (18a), as in Halle (1995), who builds on Sagey (1987). This view shares with FCT the assumption that feature class constraints target the relevant features directly and individually as a matter of course. The class nodes are now reduced in content to the status of feature class *labels*, having a function similar to that attributed to sets in FCT. The version of this theory suggested by Halle (1995) differs significantly from FCT, however. First, FCT is explicitly committed to the idea of gradient violability of constraints at the surface, and it is couched therefore within OT. Halle (1995) is instead cast within a framework employing ordered rules (as in Bromberger and Halle 1989), and the theoretical implications of the conflicts that inevitably arise between feature class constraints and other constraints are not explored. Halle's example of partial class behavior comes from Barra Gaelic, and tacitly calls on a ranking of the Line Crossing Pro-hibition over a rule requiring that vowel place features (classed as *Place* by Halle) spread. The analysis of Barra posited is not fully secure (see Ní Chiosáin 1995), but another example here serves to illustrate the idea. Vowel harmony in Turkish involves the class *Color* = {back, round}, and may be treated as alignment of this class to prosodic word edges (see Padgett 1995a). The focus here is on the right-ward spreading required of features in forms like that shown below. There is a contrast in Turkish stem-finally between plain and palatalized *l*, the latter bearing the feature [–back] and interacting with the spreading of this feature through har-mony. In the word *petrolʸ-ü* 'petrol (acc.sg.)', the final suffixal vowel receives its [back] specification from the preceding palatalized lateral (cf. *okul-u* 'school', with a non-palatalized lateral); but it receives its [round] specification from the preceding *vowel*. (See Clements and Sezer for discussion.) Neither of the preceding vowels of this disharmonic form is capable of transmitting its [back] value (shown bolded in (19) below) to this suffixal vowel. This is a line crossing or locality issue in one sense – the [back] value of the lateral intervenes, and so blocks any such spreading. Thus rightward alignment of *Color* is violated by these [back] features. There is of course a faithfulness issue here as well: harmony is not fully obeyed at the expense of the loss of any [back] specifications. Obviously *Color* harmony seen as the linkage of a superordinate *node* bearing this name will encounter difficulty with examples like this one.

(19)   Partial class spreading due to line crossing/locality – Turkish

The analysis of Barra Gaelic due to Sagey and Halle is similar: it posits a rule spreading a class of place features from a vowel; [back] cannot spread, due to an intervening palatalized consonant, and spreads from this consonant instead. It is not clear, though, why line crossing (or the equivalent of faithfulness, protecting the disharmonic [back] values) prevails, or why a rule spreading vowel place features is allowed to succeed only partially, since no concrete views on constraint conflict are assumed. The general point here is that the predictions of FCT depend in part on the tenets of Optimality Theory; those of Halle (1995) will depend on how the relevant issues pan out in the framework in which that theory is embedded.[8]

[...]

Notes

1   An interesting question then follows: do class nodes qua representational entities play any role in the theory, other than that of capturing feature class behavior? Assertions that they do are uncommon in the literature, though class nodes have been called on in order to explain facts of segment transparency and opacity, and to illuminate facts of place feature interaction more generally. See Padgett (1995a, b) for respective critical discussion.

2   The classes are assumed to be fixed and universal as well, in the usual way. The makeup of *Laryngeal* and especially *Place* in (4) is obviously not intended to be either exhaustive or definitively accurate; these substantive issues cross-cut the choice of theory.

3   Padgett (1995a) attempts a general definition of CONSTRAINT (CLASS) that seems to wrongly usurp the freedom of a constraint to choose its own quantifiers and variables in this way. The discussion here is meant to supersede that attempt.

4   It is a common perception that FG makes this partitioning seem more natural; we are presumably not allowed to link [labial], say, to both *Place* and *Laryngeal* in a tree. The

implicit tree-theoretic notion here is the Single Mother Condition. In truth, such a condition must either be stipulated or derived in FG.

5   This logic of dependency fails us when confronted with feature class generalizations involving phenomena other than assimilation or positional neutralization, providing arguments for FCT considered in Padgett (1995b). These include dissimilatory OCP effects and constraints like HAVEPLACE seen earlier.

[...]

8   For example, Halle posits a separate rule spreading [back] from the intervening consonant in Barra; [back] spreading from l^y in Turkish instead falls out directly from a requirement of alignment of *Color* to the prosodic word edge, and so is unified with harmony. Whether this disadvantage is intrinsic to the framework assumed in Halle (1995) is unclear. As a separate matter, Halle (1995) allows individual feature targeting only for assimilations (p. 20); FCT is intended to cover all feature class behavior, involving dissimilations, neutralizations, and so on as well.

References

Anderson, John and Colin Ewen. (1987). *Principles of Dependency Phonology*. Cambridge University Press, Cambridge.

Beckman, Jill N. (1995). Shona Height Harmony: Markedness and Positional Identity. MS, University of Massachusetts, Amherst.
◄

Bromberger, Sylvain and Morris Halle. (1989). 'Why Phonology is Different'. *LI* 20.1, 51–70.

Clements, G. N. (1985). 'The Geometry of Phonological Features'. *Phonology Yearbook* 2, 225–52.

Clements, G. N. and Engin Sezer. (1982). 'Vowel and Consonant Disharmony in Turkish'. In Harry van der Hulst and Norval Smith (eds.), *The Structure of Phonological Representations*, Part II, Foris, Dordrecht, 213–55.

Gazdar, Gerald, Ewen Klein, Geoffrey Pullum, and Ivan Sag. (1985). *Generalized Phrase*

Structure Grammar. Harvard University Press, Cambridge, MA.

Halle, Morris. (1995). 'Feature Geometry and Feature Spreading'. *LI* 26.1, 1–46.

Harris, James W. (1984). 'Autosegmental Phonology, Lexical Phonology, and Spanish Nasals'. In Mark Aronoff and Richard T. Oehrle (eds.), *Language Sound Structure*, MIT Press, Cambridge, MA, 67–82.

Hayes, Bruce. (1990). 'Diphthongisation and Coindexing'. *Phonology* 7.1, 31–71.

Itô, Junko and R. Armin Mester. (1993). 'Licensed Segments and Safe Paths'. In C. Paradis and D. LaCharité (eds.), *Constraint-Based Theories in Multilinear Phonology*, special issue of the *Canadian Journal of Linguistics*.

Kiparsky, Paul. (1973). ' "Elsewhere" in Phonology'. In Stephen R. Anderson and Paul Kiparsky (eds.), *A Festschrift for Morris Halle*, Holt, Rinehart and Winston, New York, 93–106.

Kiparsky, Paul. (1982). 'Lexical Phonology and Morphology'. In I. S. Yang (ed.), *Linguistics in the Morning Calm*, vol. 2, Hanshin, Seoul, 3–91.

Kotey, Paul F. Amon. (1974). 'Consonantal Labialization and Consonant Clusters in Gã'. *The Journal of West African Languages* 9.1, 49–56.

Kropp, M. E. (1966). 'The Morphology of the Gã Aspect System'. *Journal of African Languages* 5.2, 121–7.

Lass, Roger. (1976). *English Phonology and Phonology Theory*. Cambridge Studies in Linguistics 14, Cambridge University Press.

Lass, Roger and John Anderson. (1975). *Old English Phonology*. Cambridge Studies in Linguistics 17, Cambridge University Press.

Lombardi, Linda. (1995). 'Positional Faithfulness and the Phonology of Voicing in Optimality Theory'. MS, University of Maryland, College Park. ◄

McCarthy, John J. (1988). 'Feature Geometry and Dependency: A Review'. *Phonetica* 43, 84–108.

McCarthy, John J. and Alan Prince. (1993). Generalized Alignment. MS, University of Massachusetts, Amherst, and Rutgers University, New Brunswick. ◄

McCawley, James. (1967). 'The Role of a Phonological Feature System in a Theory of Language'. *Languages* 8, 112–23.

Mascaró, Joan. (1983). 'Phonological Levels and Assimilatory Processes'. MS, Universitat Autònoma de Barcelona.

Mohanan, K. P. (1983). The Structure of the Melody. MS, MIT, Cambridge, MA.

Ní Chiosáin, Máire. (1995). 'Barra Gaelic Vowel Copy and (Non-)Constituent Spreading'. In *Proceedings of WCCFL* 13.

Odden, David. (1991). 'Vowel Geometry'. *Phonology* 8, 261–90.

Padgett, Jaye. (1991). *Stricture in Feature Geometry*. Doctoral dissertation, University of Massachusetts, Amherst.

Padgett, Jaye. (1995a). 'Feature Classes'. In *Papers in Optimality Theory*, University of Massachusetts Occasional Papers (UMOP) 18, GLSA, University of Massachusetts, Amherst.

Padgett, Jaye. (1995b). 'Feature Classes II'. Paper presented at the Holland Institute of Linguistics Phonology Conference, Amsterdam. [MS in progress.]

Padgett, Jaye. (1995c). *Stricture in Feature Geometry*. CSLI Publications, Stanford, CA. [Revision of Padgett 1991.]

Paradis, Carole. (1988). 'On Constraints and Repair Strategies'. *Linguistic Review* 6, 71–97.

Prince, Alan and Paul Smolensky. (1993). Optimality Theory: Constraint Interaction in Generative Grammar. MS, Rutgers University, New Brunswick, and University of Colorado, Boulder. ◄

Ryder, Mary Ellen. (1987). 'An Autosegmental Treatment of Assimilation to Labiovelars'. In *Proceedings of CLS 23 Part Two: Parasession on Autosegmental and Metrical Phonology*, Chicago Linguistic Society.

Sagey, Elizabeth. (1986). *The Representation of Features and Relations in Non-Linear Phonology*. Doctoral dissertation, MIT, Cambridge, MA.

Sagey, Elizabeth. (1987). Non-Constituent Spreading in Barra Gaelic. MS, School of Social Sciences, University of California, Irvine.

Scobbie, James M. (1993). 'Constraint Violation and Conflict from the Perspective of Declarative Phonology'. *Canadian Journal of Linguistics* 38, 155–67.

Selkirk, Elisabeth. (1982). 'The Syllable'. In Harry van der Hulst and Norval Smith (eds.), *The Structure of Phonological Representations*, Part II, Foris, Dordrecht, 337–84.

Selkirk, Elisabeth. (1991a). 'Major Place in the Vowel Space. Vowel Height'. Paper presented at the Workshop on Feature Organization, Linguistic Society of America Institute, Santa Cruz, CA. [MS, University of Massachusetts, Amherst.]

Selkirk, Elisabeth. (1991b). 'A Two-Root Theory of Length'. In E. Dunlap and J. Padgett (eds.), *Papers in Phonology*, University of Massachusetts Occasional Papers in Linguistics 14, GLSA, University of Massachusetts, Amherst.

Selkirk, Elisabeth. (1994). Class notes, Linguistics 730, University of Massachusetts, Amherst.

Steriade, Donca. (1993a). 'Closure, Release and Nasal Contours'. In M. K. Huffman and R. A. Krakow (eds.), *Phonetics and Phonology 5: Nasals, Nasalization and the Velum*, Academic Press, New York, 401–70.

Steriade, Donca. (1993b). 'Positional Neutralization'. Paper presented at *NELS* 24.

Steriade, Donca. (1994). 'Complex Onsets as Single Segments: The Mazateco Pattern'. In Jennifer Cole and Charles Kisseberth (eds.), *Perspectives in Phonology*, CSLI Publications, Stanford, CA, 203–91.

Welmers, W. E. (1962). 'The Phonology of Kpelle'. *Journal of African Languages* 1, 69–93.

Zsiga, Elizabeth. (1993). *Features, Gestures, and the Temporal Aspects of Phonological Organization*. Doctoral dissertation, Yale University, New Haven, CT.

Study and Research Questions

1 Apply the theory proposed here to the class of *Color* features (see (1, 2)). In other words, work out the details of the analysis of Turkish vowel harmony under the assumptions of this chapter.

2 Flesh out the analysis of Gã. That is, build on (17) but include other relevant constraints and candidates. Try also to deal with the difference between hetero- and tautomorphemic sequences noted above (15).

3 Halle, Vaux, and Wolfe (2000) present a feature-geometry model in which only terminal features spread. (This is similar to the Halle (1995) model discussed at the end of the chapter.) Compare an analysis of Gã constructed using their model with the one in the chapter.

Chapter 20 | John Alderete

Dissimilation as Local Conjunction

Editor's Note

Local constraint conjunction, due originally to Smolensky (1995), is a way of combining two constraints to form a third. (Also see chapters 21 and 29 for other applications of local conjunction.) An extension of the basic idea, also suggested by Smolensky, is local conjunction of a constraint with itself. This chapter argues that dissimilation is to be analyzed in these terms. The idea is that dissimilation is the result of activity by a markedness constraint that is conjoined with itself, prohibiting two instances of the marked structure while allowing just one. The prediction: dissimilation only affects structures that are, on independent grounds, marked.

It may make sense to read this chapter with chapter 13, which deals with tonal dissimilation under the rubric of the OCP.

1   Introduction

The Obligatory Contour Principle (1) has played a significant role in formal phonology. The OCP has been called upon in many language-particular analyses to describe the distribution of phonological units like Place features and tone, and it has provided the basis for explaining many phonological processes, both in motivating the application of the process and restricting its output.

(1)   The Obligatory Contour Principle (Leben 1973, Goldsmith 1976, McCarthy 1986)
      Adjacent identical autosegments are prohibited.

While the OCP has proved to be a useful tool, a fundamental problem arises when it is applied to the analysis of dissimilation and segmental cooccurrence restrictions.

Excerpt from:
Alderete, John (1997) Dissimilation as local conjunction. In *Proceedings of the North East Linguistic Society 27*, ed. Kiyomi Kusumoto, pp. 17–32. Amherst, MA: GLSA Publications. [Available on Rutgers Optimality Archive, ROA-175.]

Such phenomena typically rule out more than one *marked* element in some domain. But the OCP, as a bald declarative statement, says nothing about the markedness of the elements involved. To account for the correlation between activity in a dissimilatory process and the markedness of target and trigger, adjunct theories of feature specification are required. These theories, however, have been shown to have a number of unsatisfactory consequences, essentially because unmarked segments can be active in ways that do not involve the OCP (Mohanan 1991, McCarthy & Taub 1992, Smolensky 1993, Steriade 1995, Itô, Mester & Padgett 1995 (= IMP henceforth)).

Consider the well-known case of Lyman's Law in Japanese as an example of the general problem. This cooccurrence restriction rules out more than one voiced obstruent in a stem, as shown by the blocking of a regular pattern of rendaku (sequential voicing) in stems with voiced obstruents: /kami+kaze/ → kami-_kaze_ 'divine wind'. Voiced obstruents can occur with voiced sonorants, however, e.g., /ori+kami/ → ori-_gami_ 'folding paper', showing that voiced obstruents are 'active', while unmarked voiced sonorants are 'inactive'. If sonorants are unspecified for [voice] underlyingly, this accounts for the inactivity of sonorants. But derived obstruent voicing in post-nasal obstruents is also active in Lyman's Law, indicating that sonorant voicing is active in a limited way and must therefore be specified for [voice] (see IMP for more detailed argumentation). This example, and many others like it, suggest that alternative approaches to predicting the correlation between phonological activity and markedness are warranted, and this paper will develop one such alternative.

I propose to deal with this problem by developing the following hypothesis.

(2)   Dissimilation as Local Conjunction (DLC)
      OCP effects are derived by markedness constraints, doubled in a local context.

The hypothesis is that OCP effects, broadly conceived to encompass segmental processes of dissimilation and restrictions on segment cooccurrence, are the result of markedness constraints that are strengthened by the operation of Local Conjunction (see below). Because of the role of markedness in the proposal, it will be possible to derive the relationship between phonological activity and markedness in a direct way, following a proposal first put forth in Smolensky 1993. The core assumptions embodied in the DLC thesis are given below:

A.   *The inventory derived by constraint interaction* (Prince & Smolensky 1993, = P&S): Inventory patterns are characterized through the interaction of faithfulness and markedness constraints.

B.   *Markedness through constraint satisfaction* (P&S, Smolensky 1993, McCarthy 1993): If property P is marked in structural inventories, then there is a constraint in Universal Grammar that marks forms bearing P.

C.   *Local Conjunction* (Smolensky 1993, Kirchner 1996, cf. Hewitt & Crowhurst 1996): Multiple constraint violations in a local context are categorically worse than the same violations in a nonlocal context.

Following P&S, I assume that the inventory of a language is a matter of markedness–faithfulness interactions (A). Roughly speaking, if faithfulness to property P dominates the markedness constraint for P, then P is part of the inventory. Conversely, if markedness to P is ranked above faithfulness, P is not part of the inventory.

The second crucial assumption is that observations about markedness are characterized by the constraint system as well (B). Thus, if property P is marked in inventories, there is a constraint in UG that marks forms bearing P with a "*". That is, principles of phonological markedness are encoded directly in the grammar as well-formedness constraints and as inherent orderings among these constraints.

Finally, I assume, following Smolensky 1993, that well-formedness constraints can be combined through a process of Local Conjunction (LC). In particular, LC provides an account of the systematic avoidance of multiple constraint violations in a local context. In this article, I only use LC of a constraint with itself, local 'self-conjunction' in Smolensky's formal system. The meaning of the self-conjoined constraint C^2_L is simply that more than one violation of C is not allowed in the local context L.

These assumptions combine to provide an explanation for why marked elements are active in dissimilation. Returning to Lyman's Law, the constraint responsible for blocking rendaku is built up from an independently necessary markedness constraint NoVoicedObstruent (= *[+VOI, −SON] below). The markedness of voiced obstruents is shown by their behavior in inventories and alternations: the existence of a voiced obstruent series implies the presence of a voiceless series (Maddieson 1984) and a host of phonological processes resolve obstruent voicing (see Lombardi 1999). The markedness of voiced obstruents is also evident in Lyman's Law: more than one voiced obstruent is not allowed. This observation is explained in DLC by performing local self-conjunction on the constraint against voiced obstruents and ranking it above RENDAKU, a constraint that may call for the presence of more than one of these marked structures:

(3)   Dissimilation as Local Conjunction

Input	Output	*[+VOI, −SON]²	RENDAKU	*[+VOI, −SON]
a. /kami+kaze/	→ kami-kaze		*	*
	kami-gaze	*!		**
b. /ori+kami/	→ ori-gami			*
	ori-kami		*!	

It is immediately apparent above why specifically voiced obstruents block rendaku voicing: only voiced obstruents incur violations of *[+VOI, −SON]. Since Lyman's Law is encoded as a self-conjoined version of this constraint, only double occurrences of these marked structures will be avoided (3a), cf. (3b).[1] The DLC account differs, therefore, from the analysis of dissimilation offered by the OCP in that, under DLC, the positive correlation between markedness and phonological activity is an unavoidable consequence of the constraints motivating dissimilation.

The rest of this paper elaborates on the role of markedness in the proposal and shows how DLC resolves two additional problems for the standard characterization of the OCP. First, the possibility of dissimilatory effects outside the domain of autosegmental phonology poses a problem for the OCP (see e.g., Yip 1988). As a constraint on features linearized on an autosegmental tier, the OCP fails to generalize to cases of dissimilation that involve prosodic categories, e.g., moraic units or grid marks. However, if dissimilation is the result of self-conjoined markedness constraints, constraints outside the domain of autosegmental phonology can drive dissimilation. In section 2, I show how this hypothesis can be applied to just such a case, namely length dissimilation on Oromo.

A second problem addressed below involves the viability of the OCP for Place cooccurrence restrictions, especially for the behavior of coronals. As evidenced in Semitic languages, partially dissimilar coronals may cooccur in a root, but the same is not true for dorsals and labials, showing that the OCP does not apply across the board in all members of a feature class (Yip 1989, Padgett 1991 [1995]). DLC gives a natural account of the aberrant behavior of coronals in cooccurrence restrictions, an account that also stems from the role of markedness. In section 3, I demonstrate how coronal inertness in a pattern of Berber labial dissimilation derives from the equation, marked segments = active in dissimilation, where the relative unmarkedness of coronals is expressed on a harmony scale.

2   Disharmony outside of Autosegmental Phonology

It is a common observation in languages with vowel length that long vowels dissimilate in adjacent syllables. Languages that exhibit this type of length dissimilation include the Australian language Gidabal (Geytenbeek & Geytenbeek 1971), Slovak (Kenstowicz & Rubach 1987), and the Cushitic language Oromo (Gragg 1976, Lloret-Romanyach 1988). The basic observation in these languages is that, given a sequence of two consecutive syllables, only one syllable can have a long vowel. This pattern is illustrated in (4) and (5) with morpho-phonemic alternations from Oromo. As shown in (4), the form of the plural suffix -(o)ota is predictable from the stem it attaches to. Thus, the suffix shortens only when it attaches to a base that ends with a long vowel, as in the example gaal-ota. The allomorphy of the causative suffix in (5) also supports this observation and extends the domain of shortening to sequences of suffixes (5c).

(4)   Plural suffix alternations: -oota ~ -ota
   a.   nama   nam-oota   'person'
        harree   harr-oota   'donkey'
        k'ottuu   k'ott-oota   'farmer'
        fardda   fardd-oota   'horse'

   b.   gaala   gaal-ota   'camel'
        loomi   loom-ota   'lemon tree'
        ʔadaadaa   ʔadaad-ota   'aunt'
        adaammi   adaamm-ota   'cactus'

(5) Causative suffix alternations: *-siis ~ -sis*
    a.   argisiis-   agarsiis-   √arg 'see'
         gufacciis-   √gufadd'- 'stumble'

    b.   adeemsis-   √adeem- 'go'
         teesis   √taaʸ- 'sit'

    c.   fiig-a   fiig-sis-a   fiig-sis-iis-a   'drink'
         ɪug-a   ɪug-siis-a   ɪug-siis-is-a   'run'

I assume, following the researchers mentioned above, that these suffixes are underlyingly long and that they shorten because of a general ban on adjacent long vowels. These researchers stress that this pattern also holds of lexical forms, showing that length dissimilation is a general pattern in the language that is independent of syllable parity.[2]

The central thesis of DLC is that dissimilation is driven by markedness. To understand its application to length dissimilation, therefore, the markedness for vowel length needs to be considered. The relevant markedness and faithfulness constraints are given below.

(6) Markedness and Faithfulness for Vowel Length

    a. NoLongVowel (Rosenthall 1994)
        Avoid vowels dominated by more than one mora.

    b. WeightIdent (McCarthy 2000)
        If α and β are correspondent segments in input and output,
            and α is monomoraic, then β is monomoraic (= no lengthening)
            and α is bimoraic, then β is bimoraic (= no shortening)

The markedness constraint in (6a) is a context-free constraint that bans long vowels. It yields a star for every long vowel in a surface form. The faithfulness constraint in (6b) has the effect of preserving underlying length properties at the surface.

The length markedness constraint asserts that long vowels are marked in segmental inventories. The observation characterizing length dissimilation in Oromo is that long vowels are active in the process. The conclusion we can draw from this, therefore, is the following. Long vowels dissimilate because of a locally conjoined markedness constraint banning more than one long vowel in a local context, as formalized below.

(7) NoLongVowel$^2_{SA}$
    In adjacent syllables, avoid two vowels each dominated by more than one mora.

As the product of self-conjunction, this constraint rules out more than one long vowel. Long vowels must also be in adjacent syllables in order to be local for this constraint.[3] Consequently, NoLongVowel$^2_{SA}$ is violated only by forms with two adjacent syllables containing long vowels, exactly the dispreferred sequence in Oromo.

The effects of NoLongVowel$^2_{SA}$ can be seen when it assumes high rank in the constraint system, as illustrated in (8) with the plural suffix.

(8)   Length Dissimilation: /gaal-oota/ → gaal-ota, *gaal-oota

Candidates	NoLongVowel$^2_{SA}$	WeightIdent	NoLongVowel
☞ gaal-ota		*	*
gaal-oota	*!		**

The failed candidate above violates NoLongVowel twice in adjacent syllables, and so it violates NoLongVowel$^2_{SA}$. The optimal candidate is therefore the one that violates WeightIdent to achieve the requisite length alternation. Therefore, consistent with the DLC thesis, long vowels are active in dissimilation, because they are doubly marked by the length markedness constraint in UG.

We are now in a position to make a second argument in favor of the DLC hypothesis. The OCP fails to derive results like this, because the marked structures in this case are not autosegments in the correct sense. Timing units such as moras do not figure in the representations worked on by the OCP, and so the OCP cannot generalize to these cases. On the other hand, if dissimilation is generally the effect of locally conjoined markedness constraints, there is no implication that the units targeted by dissimilation rules must be represented in autosegmental structure. The only requirement is that the target and trigger of the dissimilatory process be marked, and in this example, long vowels are marked by the length markedness constraint.

When one ponders the possibility of dissimilatory patterns outside of autosegmental phonology, extensions of the main idea fleshed out here are not hard to come by. For example, complex segments like pre-nasalized stops are marked in segmental inventories, and as sketched below in (A), self-conjunction of the constraint behind this observation will directly account for dissimilation of pre-nasalized stops. A second case, given in (B), involves self-conjunction of a syllable structure constraint NoCoda: NoCoda$^2_{SA}$ prohibits two neighboring closed syllables, causing degemination of voiceless obstruent geminates in the context of an adjacent closed syllable. A third example suggests a self-conjoined ParseSyll to characterize the fact that stress systems generally avoid leaving two adjacent syllables unfooted (C).

A. *Dissimilation of complex segments.* The Ganda Law (Meinhof 1932): "When two successive syllables both begin with a nasal plus following voiced plosive, the plosive of the first syllable is lost". General constraints on Luganda syllable structure require NC sequences to be syllabified as complex segments, permitting the following analysis: PreNasal$^2_{SA}$ ≫ Max$_{IO}$ ≫ PreNasal.

B. *Dissimilation of marked syllable structure.* Consonant Gradation in Finnish (Keyser & Kiparsky 1984): geminate voiceless stops degeminate when the second member is the onset of a closed syllable. Assuming voiceless obstruents may only occupy the coda position as the first member of a geminate suggests the following: NoCodA$^2_{SA}$ ≫ Max$_{IO}$ ≫ NoCoda.

C. *Disharmony of strict layering violations.* Underparsing in ternary stress systems (Kager 1994) and stress–epenthesis interaction (Alderete 1999): these researchers find that two adjacent unfooted syllables are categorically worse than two nonadjacent unfooted syllables: PARSESYLL$^2_{SA}$ ≫ ALIGNRIGHT, HEADDEP ≫ PARSESYLL.

The abundance of examples presented above suggests that disharmony phenomena are well-attested outside the domains operated on by the OCP. I have sketched here how DLC generalizes to such cases, which distinguishes this theory from an account that employs the standard version of the OCP.

3   Coronal Unmarkedness in Dissimilation

In the examples examined thus far, markedness has been correlated with phonological activity, while unmarked structures have been inactive. In this section, I will derive a similar set of results, but in this case markedness is defined relative to a harmony scale.

Markedness can be derived by meta-constraints on constraint rankings. For example, P&S claim that coronals are unmarked relative to dorsals and labials, as encoded in the meta-constraint below.

(9)   Place markedness subhierarchy (P&S, Alderete et al. 1999, Lombardi 2001)
      *PL/LAB, *PL/DORS ≫ *PL/COR

This markedness relation explains an array of phenomena in which coronals are ignored in phonological processes, i.e., well-known cases of 'coronal transparency' (see Smolensky 1993 and McCarthy 1993). If coronals are unmarked relative to noncoronals, we also expect that they will be inactive in dissimilation. I will argue below that the inactivity of coronals in Tashlhiyt Berber dissimilation follows from this assumption.

Derived stems in Tashlhiyt Berber may have at most one primary labial consonant, i.e., /b f m/ (Boukous 1987, Lasri 1991, Elmedlaoui 1992 [1995], Selkirk 1993). One reflex of this restriction is that derivational prefixes containing *m* delabialize when they combine with a root that also contains a labial, as exemplified by the data in (10) and (11).

(10)   Reflexive prefix alternation: *m-* ~ *n-* (C! is an emphatic consonant)
      a.   m-xazar   √xzr   'scowl'
           m-saggal   √siggl   'look for'
           m-!ʃawar   √!ʃawr   'ask advice'
           mm-ʒla   √ʒla   'lose'

      b.   n-fara   √fra   'disentangle'
           n-ħaʃʃam   √ħʃʃm   'be shy'
           n-xalaf   √xalf   'place crosswise'
           n-kaddab   √kddb   'consider a liar'

(11)   Agentive prefix alternation: *am-* ~ *an-*
  a.   am-las   √las   'shear'
       am-krz   √krz   'plow'
       am-agur   √agur   'remain'
       am-zug   √sug   'abscond'

  b.   an-!rmi   √!rmi   'be tired'
       an-bur   √bur   'remain celibate'
       an-!dfur   √!dfur   'follow'
       an-!azum   √!azum   'fast'

The output of delabialization is a coronal nasal, so I assume, following the authors listed above, that the underlying form for e.g. *n-fara* is /*m-fara*/, and that the default coronal is the output of dissimilation. Note that the prefixes with *m* default to a coronal nasal, even if the root also contains a coronal, as supported by the data in (12).

(12)   a.   /a-m-bdad/   anbdad   'pélier, colonne'
            /a-m-rzif/   anrzif   'l'invité'
            /a-m-jdam/   anjdam   'le contaminé'
            /a-m-!dalab/   an!dalab   'mendiant'

       b.   /m-fa!sal/   nfa!sal   's'arranger'
            /m-ʕajab/   nʕajab   's'apprécier'
            /m-b!dan/   nb!dan   'se séparer'
            /m-xalaf/   nxalaf   'se differencier'

We can think of delabialization as a dissimilation process for identical Place features. This assumption is sensible, because delabialization is part of a larger pattern of Place cooccurrence restriction in stems, a pattern that extends to dorsal sounds as well (Selkirk 1993). An analysis along these lines leads to the following question: why do labials and dorsals dissimilate, but not coronals?

I will give an answer to this question, but first we must show what drives dissimilation in the first place. Labial dissimilation is the result of the constraint interaction employed thus far where the labial markedness constraint is strengthened by the operation of LC, resulting in the constraint given below.

(13)   *$\text{PL}/\text{LAB}^2_{\text{Stem}}$
       Ban any stem containing two segments with independent [labial] specifications.

Ranking the complex constraint above the faithfulness constraint for Place features, as in the tableau given below, produces the dissimilatory pattern on a par with the cases examined thus far.

(14)   Delabialization as a result of *$\text{PL}/\text{LAB}^2_{\text{Stem}}$

Input: m-kaddab	*$\text{PL}/\text{LAB}^2_{\text{Stem}}$	IDENT[Place]	*PL/LAB
☞ [n-kaddab]$_{\text{Stem}}$		*	*
[m-kaddab]$_{\text{Stem}}$	*!		**

The failed candidate incurs two violations of *Pl/Lab within the stem, and so it also incurs a fatal violation of $\text{*Pl/Lab}^2_{\text{Stem}}$. The optimal candidate is therefore the one that delabializes to satisfy the labial cooccurrence constraint.[4]

Now that we have accounted for what drives labial dissimilation, we are in a position to account for the inactivity of coronals in this pattern. Remember that labial prefixes default to coronals, even if there is a coronal in the root. In sum, more than one labial or dorsal is out, but more than one coronal is okay. I propose to deal with this pattern by extending P&S's meta-constraint to the locally conjoined Place markedness constraints:

(15)   Meta-constraint on self-conjoined Place markedness constraints
*Pl/Lab^2_L, $\text{*Pl/Dor}^2_L \gg \text{*Pl/Cor}^2_L$, where L is some local context.

By extending the subhierarchy in this way, coronal inactivity can receive a very general explanation, as illustrated in the following tableau. The root *kaddab* contains a Place specification for all three of the relevant Place features, so no matter how the prefix is realized, an OCP violation will result. But given the ordering of the self-conjoined Place markedness constraints above, the form with the coronal prefix best satisfies the constraint hierarchy.

(16)   Deriving the coronal default[5]

Input: m-kaddab	$\text{*Pl/Lab}^2_{\text{Stem}}$	$\text{*Pl/Cor}^2_{\text{Stem}}$
☞ [n-kaddab]$_{\text{Stem}}$		*
[m-kaddab]$_{\text{Stem}}$	*!	

The coronal nasal violates the dissimilation constraint for coronals, but that's okay, because it is the best of all possible alternatives.

The inactivity of coronals in this case could be accounted for with [coronal] underspecification (see Paradis & Prunet 1991 and references cited therein), but such an analysis is complicated considerably by the exceptions to delabialization reported in Elmedlaoui 1995 for the Imdlawn variety of Tashlhiyt. Imdlawn Tashlhiyt has delabialization too, but delabialization is blocked when the base begins with a coronal sonorant. In such a context, the nasal prefix either retains its [labial] specification, e.g., /m-laqqaf/ → *mlaqqaf* 'attraper en l'air', or it delabializes and epenthetic *ya* separates the prefix from the coronal sonorant, as in /m-lkm/ → *nyalkam* 'atteindre'. The underspecification approach to coronal inactivity is thus confronted with the now classic problem that coronals are indeed active in specific contexts and must therefore be specified. In the current model, this problem can be handled straightforwardly with the assumption that blocking effects are the result of a higher-ranking dissimilation constraint that prohibits strictly adjacent coronal sonorants (along the lines of Walsh-Dickey 1997 and Steriade 1995).

This approach to the output of labial dissimilation has some further advantages. To conceive of the coronal default in terms of relative unmarkedness paves the way for relating this example to coronal defaults elsewhere in phonology. For example, the explanation for the output of delabialization is treated by a markedness sub-hierarchy related to the one responsible for deriving coronals as a preferred output in epenthesis and as a default segment in neutralization processes (Smolensky 1993, McCarthy 1993, cf. Lombardi 2001). Furthermore, this approach has clear implications for the behavior of coronals in segment cooccurrence restrictions generally. The Theorem of Coronal Unmarkedness, given below, and proven in (18), fleshes these implications out in detail.

(17)   **Theorem.** A segmental cooccurrence restriction on [coronal] entails the same cooccurrence restriction for [labial] and [dorsal].

(18)   Re-ranking of Place faithfulness relative to the self-conjoined Place subhierarchy
       (i) $\gg$ *PL/LAB^2_L, *PL/DOR^2_L $\gg$ (ii) $\gg$ *PL/COR^2_L $\gg$ (iii)
       $\uparrow$ $\uparrow$ $\uparrow$

       IDENT[Place]   IDENT[Place]   IDENT[Place]

The ranking permutation for Place faithfulness within the self-conjoined Place subhierarchy yields a restricted typology of segmental cooccurrence restrictions: (i) no segmental cooccurrence restrictions, (ii) cooccurrence restrictions for [labial] and [dorsal] but not [coronal], or (iii) cooccurrence restrictions for all Place features. The general prediction is that, all things being equal, a restriction on coronals will always be matched by a parallel restriction on noncoronals. This prediction accords nicely with the general tendency for root cooccurrence restrictions on coronals to be weaker than those on noncoronals. For example, in Russian all labials form an identity class for the purpose of root cooccurrence restrictions, but coronal identity classes are split up into stops, fricatives, and sonorants (Padgett 1991 [1995]). Furthermore, examination of the cases presented in Yip 1989, Mester 1986, Pierrehumbert 1993, and Kawasaki 1989 reveals a strong bias towards weaker cooccurrence restrictions on coronals than noncoronals.

To summarize the main features of the analysis, the language-particular rankings needed for Tashlhiyt Berber are given below.

(19)   Delabialization in Berber: *PL/PLACE$^2_{Stem}$ $\gg$ IDENT[Place] $\gg$ *PL/PLACE

The ranking of the universal *PL/PLACE^2 subhierarchy above IDENT[Place] yields the observed delabialization and cooccurrence restrictions within the stem, and the inherent rankings within the *PL/PLACE$^2_{Stem}$ subhierarchy derive the coronal default in the process.

4   Conclusion

In conclusion, I have developed a proposal in this article that roots dissimilatory phenomena within a theory of the inventory in Optimality Theory. In this theory, OCP effects are the result of a richly articulated constraint component governing phonological markedness. From this hypothesis, I derive a number of consequences.

First, the proposal provides a direct explanation for the correlation between phonological activity and the markedness of target and trigger. Second, the theory generalizes to cases of dissimilation that are not represented in autosegmental phonology. Lastly, the hypothesis provides an avenue for explaining the output of dissimilation in a way that generalizes to other areas of phonology.

Notes

1   It is also clear why derived obstruent voicing blocks rendaku: whether voiced obstruents arise from lexical specification or a phonological process, their cooccurrence with another voiced obstruent incurs a violation of the self-conjoined markedness constraint.

2   There is one important exception to this surface-true constraint, namely that the final two syllables can both contain long vowels, e.g., ʔadaadaa. This looks like a case of classic extrametricality in the sense that the final syllable both fails to undergo shortening and fails to condition the process in the preceding syllable.

3   The characterization of locality here is akin to the notion of Head Adjacency employed in Archangeli & Pulleyblank 1987 and Syllable Adjacency in Odden 1994. This constraint therefore requires a relational characterization of locality, which is an enrichment of the locality conditions proposed in Smolensky 1993 (see Alderete 1996 for motivation and analyses of particular examples).

4   The prefixal target for delabialization can be analyzed as an effect of McCarthy & Prince's 1995 meta-constraint Root Faith ≫ Affix Faith: the [labial] feature is preserved in the root, because failing to do so would violate high-ranking featural faithfulness for roots (Selkirk 1995).

5   We cannot test the effects of $*\text{Pl}/\text{Dor}^2_{\text{Stem}}$ in this case, because Tashlhiyt does not have a velar nasal, so an independent constraint must rule out this realization of the nasal prefix.

References

Alderete, J. 1996. A formal theory of dissimilation. Handout to talk presented at Rum J. Clam II, University of Massachusetts, Amherst, May. (Available on ROA)

Alderete, J. 1999. Head dependence in stress–epenthesis interaction. In B. Hermans and M. van Oostendorp (eds.), *The Derivational Residue in Phonological Optimality Theory*, pp. 29–50, Amsterdam: John Benjamins. (Available on ROA) ◀

Alderete, J., J. Beckman, L. Benua, A. Gnanadesikan, J. McCarthy, and S. Urbanczyk. 1999. Reduplication with fixed segmentism. *Linguistic Inquiry* 30: 327–64. (Available on ROA)

Archangeli, D. and D. Pulleyblank. 1987. Maximal and minimal rules: the effects of tier scansion. *NELS* 17: 16–35.

Boukous, A. 1987. *Phonotactiques et domains prosodiques en Berbère (Parler Tachelhit d'Agadir, Maroc)*. Thèse d'etat, Université de Paris VIII, Vincennes à Saint Denis.

Elmedlaoui, M. 1992 [1995]. *Aspects des representations phonologiques dans certaines langues chamito-semitiques*. Thèse de doctorat d'état, Université Mohamad V, Rabat.

Elmedlaoui, M. 1995. Géométrie des restrictions de cooccurrence de traits en sémitique et en Berbère: synchronie et diachronie. *Canadian Journal of Linguistics* 40: 39–76.

Geytenbeek, B. and H. Geytenbeek. 1971. *Gidabal Grammar and Dictionary*. Canberra: AIAS.

Goldsmith, J. 1976. *Autosegmental Phonology*. Doctoral dissertation, MIT.

Gragg, G. 1976. Oromo of Wellegga. In M. L. Bender (ed.), *The Non-Semitic Languages of Ethiopia*, pp. 166–93, East Lancing: Michigan State University Press.

Hewitt, M. and M. Crowhurst. 1996. Conjunctive constraints and templates in Optimality Theory. *NELS* 26: 101–16.

Itô, J., A. Mester, and J. Padgett. 1995. Licensing and underspecification in Optimality

Theory. *Linguistic Inquiry* 26: 571–614. (Available on ROA) ◄

Kager, R. 1994. Ternary rhythm in alignment theory. MS, Utrecht University. (Available on ROA)

Kawasaki, N. 1989. Cooccurrence restrictions on consonants in some Polynesian languages. MS, University of Massachusetts, Amherst.

Kenstowicz, M. and J. Rubach. 1987. The phonology of syllabic nuclei in Slovak. *Language* 63: 463–97.

Keyser, S. and P. Kiparsky. 1984. Syllable structure in Finnish phonology. In M. Aronoff and R. Oehrle (eds.), *Language Sound Structure*, pp. 7–31, Cambridge, MA: MIT Press.

Kirchner, R. 1996. Synchronic chain shifts in Optimality Theory. *Linguistic Inquiry* 27: 341–50. (Available on ROA) ◄

Lasri, A. 1991. *Aspects de la phonologie non-linéaire du parler Berbère Chleuh de Tidli*. Thèse de doctorat, Université de la Sorbonne Nouvelle, Paris III.

Leben, W. 1973. *Suprasegmental Phonology*. Doctoral dissertation, MIT.

Lloret-Romanyach, M. R. 1988. *Gemination and Vowel Length in Oromo Morphophonology*. Doctoral dissertation, Indiana University.

Lombardi, L. 1999. Positional faithfulness and voicing assimilation in Optimality Theory. *Natural Language and Linguistic Theory* 17: 267–302. ◄

Lombardi, L. 2001. Why place and voice are different: constraint-specific alternations in Optimality Theory. In L. Lombardi (ed.), *Segmental Phonology in Optimality Theory*, pp. 13–45, Cambridge: Cambridge University Press. (Available on ROA)

Maddieson, I. 1984. *Patterns of Sounds*. Cambridge: Cambridge University Press.

McCarthy, J. 1986. OCP effects: gemination and antigemination. *Linguistic Inquiry* 17: 207–63.

McCarthy, J. 1993. The parallel advantage: containment, consistency, and alignment. Handout to talk presented at Rutgers Optimality Workshop I, October.

McCarthy, J. 2000. Faithfulness and prosodic circumscription. In J. Dekkers, F. van der Leeuw, and J. van de Weijer (eds.), *Optimality Theory, Phonology, Syntax, and Acquisition*, pp. 151–89, Oxford: Oxford University Press. (Available on ROA)

McCarthy, J. and A. Prince. 1995. Faithfulness and reduplicative identity. *University of*

Massachusetts Occasional Papers in Linguistics 18: 249–384. (Available on ROA) ◄

McCarthy, J. and A. Taub. 1992. Review of Paradis and Prunet 1991. *Phonology* 9: 363–70.

Meinhof, C. 1932. *Introduction to the Phonology of the Bantu Languages*. Berlin: Dietrich Reimer.

Mester, A. 1986. *Studies in Tier Structure*. Doctoral dissertation, University of Massachusetts, Amherst.

Mohanan, K. 1991. On the bases of radical underspecification. *Natural Language and Linguistic Theory* 9: 285–325.

Odden, D. 1994. Adjacency parameters in phonology. *Language* 70: 289–330.

Padgett, J. 1991 [1995]. *Stricture in Feature Geometry*. Doctoral dissertation, University of Massachusetts, Amherst [Chicago: University of Chicago Press].

Paradis, C. and J. F. Prunet. 1991. Introduction: asymmetry and visibility in consonant articulations. In C. Paradis and J. F. Prunet (eds.), *The Special Status of Coronals: Internal and External Evidence*, pp. 1–28, San Diego: Academic Press.

Pierrehumbert, J. 1993. Dissimilarity in the Arabic verbal roots. *NELS* 23: 367–81.

Prince, A. and P. Smolensky. 1993. *Optimality Theory: Constraint Interaction in Generative Grammar*. Report no. 2, Rutgers University Center for Cognitive Science, Piscataway, New Jersey. ◄

Rosenthall, S. 1994. *Vowel/Glide Alternations in a Theory of Constraint Interaction*. Doctoral dissertation, University of Massachusetts, Amherst. (Available on ROA)

Selkirk, E. 1993. Labial relations. MS, University of Massachusetts, Amherst.

Selkirk, E. 1995. Language-particular violation of a universal constraint: the OCP from the perspective of Optimality Theory. MS, Marrakech.

Smolensky, P. 1993. Harmony, markedness, and phonological activity. Handout to talk presented at Rutgers Optimality Workshop I, October. (Available on ROA)

Steriade, D. 1995. Underspecification and markedness. In J. Goldsmith (ed.), *Handbook of Phonological Theory*, pp. 114–74, Cambridge, MA: Blackwell.

Walsh-Dickey, L. 1997. *The Phonology of Liquids*. Doctoral dissertation, University of Massachusetts, Amherst.

Yip, M. 1988. The obligatory contour principle and phonological rules: a loss of identity. *Linguistic Inquiry* 19: 65–100.

Yip, M. 1989. Feature geometry and co-occurrence restrictions. *Phonology* 6: 349–74.

Study and Research Questions

1   This theory predicts that many imaginable types of dissimilation do not exist. Present hypothetical examples of two of them.
2   Think of other kinds of markedness constraints that, when conjoined with themselves, might produce novel or unexpected dissimilation effects.
3   Find another example of dissimilation and reanalyze it with local conjunction.
4   If you are familiar with underspecification theory, explain how it would account for the unmarkedness of coronals in dissimilation. Does underspecification theory offer a general explanation for the main claim of this chapter, that only marked structures dissimilate?
5   A constraint that is derived by local conjunction is itself a constraint, and so it too can be combined with a constraint by local conjunction. Smolensky (1995) observes that, when constraints are self-conjoined, recursive conjunction produces the "power hierarchy" ... $\gg$ $C^4 \gg C^3 \gg C^2 \gg C$. Legendre, Smolensky, and Wilson (1998) use such a power hierarchy as a theory of barriers in syntax – it crucially treats movement that crosses three barriers as worse than movement that crosses two barriers. Do distinctions like this exist in phonology? If so, give an example. If not, explain how they might be ruled out.
6   Compare the analyses in this chapter with some of the other recent literature on dissimilation in OT, such as Itô and Mester (1998), Fukazawa (1999), and Suzuki (1998).

Chapter 21 | Robert Kirchner

Synchronic Chain Shifts in Optimality Theory

Editor's Note

In a synchronic chain shift, underlying /A/ becomes surface [B], while underlying /B/ becomes surface [C]. In OT, some high-ranking markedness constraint must force the /B/ → [C] mapping. But then why does the same constraint allow /A/ to shift to [B], instead of making it go all the way to [C]? The answer can only be found in the theory of faithfulness. The argument in this chapter is that the faithfulness constraint responsible for this aspect of a chain shift is derived by the local conjunction of two other, simpler constraints. Local conjunction, due originally to Smolensky (1995), also figures prominently in chapters 20 and 29. See chapter 6 on why there can be no circular chain shifts.

Synchronic chain shifts, whereby certain sounds are promoted (or demoted) stepwise along some phonetic scale in some context, are one of the classic cases of opaque rule interactions. If, for example, /a/ raises to [e], and /e/ raises to [i], it would appear that the /e/ → [i] raising must precede /a/ → [e] raising in the derivation; otherwise, /a/ and /e/ would both neutralize to [i].[1] These cases therefore pose a challenge for nonserial theories of phonology, including strongly parallel versions of Optimality Theory (OT) (Prince and Smolensky 1993).[2] McCarthy (1993) and Orgun (1995) have given OT analyses of a particular chain shift, namely, $a \rightarrow i \rightarrow \emptyset$ reduction in Bedouin Hijazi Arabic; however, these solutions are limited to chain shifts with no more than two "steps," where one of the steps involves deletion. I show that a more general solution to the chain shift problem can be obtained using *local conjunction* (Smolensky 1995) of featural faithfulness constraints, the effect of which is to constrain the "distance" between input and output values along some phonetic scale. As an illustration, I analyze a three-step nondeletional chain shift in Nzɛbi (Guthrie 1968).

Excerpt from:
Kirchner, Robert (1996) Synchronic chain shifts in Optimality Theory. *Linguistic Inquiry* 27: 341–50. [Available on Rutgers Optimality Archive, ROA-66.]

Let us begin with the previous treatments of vowel reduction in the Ḥarb dialect of Bedouin Hijazi Arabic (BHA) (Al-Mozainy 1981). In nonfinal open syllables, short /a/ raises to a high vowel (transcribed [i], realized as [i], [u], or [ɨ] depending on adjacent consonants), whereas short /i/ syncopates (short /u/ is marginal, and in any case behaves like /i/ in this regard).

(1) $i \rightarrow \emptyset$ /ʕarif-at/   ʕarfat   'she knew'
                  /kitil/   ktil   'he was killed'
                  /kitil-at/   kitlat   'she was killed'
                  /kitil-na/   ktilna   'we were killed'
                  /yaskin-uun/   yasknuun   'they (m.) dwell'
                  /yaskin-in/   yasknin   'they (f.) dwell'

      $a \rightarrow i$ /katab/   kitab   'he wrote'
                  /samiʕ/   simiʕ   'he heard'
                  /rafaagah/   rifaagah   'companions'

In classical rule-based theories, such cases were handled by breaking the chain shift into distinct rules, one rule for each step, and imposing a counterfeeding order on the rule set.

(2)   Rule 1: $a \rightarrow i$ / ___ σ
      Rule 2: $i \rightarrow \emptyset$ / ___ σ
      Rule 2 precedes Rule 1

However, as McCarthy (1993) observes, this shift constitutes a unified phenomenon of vowel reduction.[3] It should therefore not be decomposed into a set of formally unrelated rules. McCarthy attributes the vowel reduction to a constraint prohibiting place feature specifications in a short vowel in an open syllable, No-V-Place. He further assumes the following faithfulness constraints:

(3)   Parse$_{hi}$: The feature [high] is parsed (by a vocalic Root node).
      Parse$_{low}$: The feature [low] is parsed (by a vocalic Root node).
      Parse$_V$: A vocalic Root node is parsed (by a mora).

In this view of faithfulness, stray elements are automatically deleted post-phonologically; therefore, failure to parse (indicated by angle brackets in tableau 1) amounts to deletion. (The restriction to nonfinal syllables is the result of interaction with alignment constraints, which are not relevant to this discussion.) Note that in the winner in part (b) of tableau 1, Parse$_{hi}$ is satisfied by linking the [high] feature to the Root node, even though the Root node itself is unparsed. As Orgun (1995) notes, this interpretation of featural faithfulness is problematic with respect to the phenomenon of autosegmental stability (Goldsmith 1976). An example of this is Rotuman umlaut under deletion of a front vowel.

(4)   *Complete phase*   *Incomplete phase*
      f u t i   f ü t ⟨ i ⟩   'to pull'
          | |
      −back   −back

Tableau 1

	No-V-Place	Parse$_{hi}$	Parse$_V$	Parse$_{low}$

a. /{V,low}/ → V
   | (= a)
   low
	*!			

/{V,low}/ → ⟨V⟩
   | (= Ø)
   low
			*!	

☞ /{V,low}/ → V
         (= i)
   ⟨low⟩
				*

b. /{V,hi}/ → V
   | (= i)
   hi
	*!			

☞ /{V,hi}/ → ⟨V⟩
         (= Ø)
   hi
			*	

/{V,hi}/ → V
         (= i)
   ⟨hi⟩
		*!		

If Parse$_{back}$ can be satisfied by linking the [−back] feature to the unparsed Root node, it is unclear why [−back] reassociates to the preceding (parsed) vowel.

Orgun instead handles the BHA facts by splitting the faithfulness constraints into two distinct families, as shown in tableau 2: the CORRESPONDENCE constraints, which require the presence of corresponding segments in the input and output; and the MATCH constraints, which require corresponding input and output segments to be featurally identical. Observe, however, that both McCarthy's and Orgun's analyses capture the chain shift effect by exploiting the distinction between failure to parse a feature and failure to parse a segment: McCarthy's does this by treating the top-ranked faithfulness constraint, Parse$_{hi}$, as satisfied in an unparsed segment; Orgun's, by distinguishing a violation of CORRESPONDENCE (which is fatal in part (a) of tableau 2) from a violation of MATCH (nonfatal). For this reason, neither McCarthy's nor Orgun's approach can be extended to chain shifts that are richer than the one found in BHA – namely, chain shifts with more than two steps – or where none of the steps involve segment deletion.

A three-step nondeletional chain shift is found in Nzɛbi, a Bantu language spoken in Gabon (Guthrie 1968, Clements 1991).

Tableau 2

CORR(/a/):   Every input /a/ has an output correspondent.
No[a]:   No [a] in open syllables.
NoV: No V in open syllables.
MATCH(V):   Output correspondents of input V are featurally identical to it.

		CORR(/a/)	No[a]	NoV	MATCH(V)
a.	/a/ → a		*!	*	
	/a/ → Ø	*!			
	☞ /a/ → i			*	*
b.	/i/ → i			*!	
	☞ /i/ → Ø				

(5)

	Unraised	Raised	
i → i	bis	bis[-i]	'to refuse'
u → u	suɛm	suem[-i]	'to hide self'
o → u	kolən	kulin[-i]	'to go down'
ə → i			
e → i	bet	bit[-i]	'to carry'
ɛ → e	βɛɛd	βeed[-i]	'to give'
ɔ → o	tɔɔd	tood[-i]	'to arrive'
a → ɛ	sal	sɛl[-i]	'to work'

The raised form of the verb appears to be selected by certain tense and aspect affixes. The suffix -i in the raised form is omitted except in extremely careful speech; moreover, there does not appear to be a general phonological process of vowel raising before a high vowel (e.g., *banzix* 'oranges'). Therefore, it appears that the raising is morphologically rather than phonologically conditioned. Nevertheless, there exist other cases of nondeletional chain shifts that are clearly phonologically conditioned, for example, Basque vowel raising under hiatus (Hualde 1991). Therefore, I believe that the Nzɛbi chain shift warrants a general phonological solution, albeit one involving a morphologically conditioned constraint.

(6) RAISING
    Maximize vowel height (in verbs when occurring with certain tense and aspect affixes).[4]

For the sake of concreteness, I assume the following vowel height features:

(7)

	low	high	ATR
i, u	–	+	+
e, o, ə	–	–	+
ɛ, ɔ	–	–	–
a	+	–	–

I further posit feature-specific faithfulness constraints, of the following form:

(8) PARSE$_F$
     For all $\alpha \in \{+, -, 0\}$, if feature F is specified α in the input, it is specified α in the output.

The obvious problem is that (as illustrated in tableau 3) there appears to be no way to rank RAISING relative to the PARSE$_F$ constraints to permit raising of the nonhigh vowels without raising /a/ all the way to [i] (the ☞ here indicates the incorrectly predicted winner; the true winner appears in boldface).

Tableau 3
RAISING ≫ PARSE$_{low}$ (otherwise no /a/ → [ɛ] raising)
RAISING ≫ PARSE$_{ATR}$ (otherwise no /ɛ/ → [e] raising)
RAISING ≫ PARSE$_{hi}$ (otherwise no /e/ → [i] raising)

		RAISING	PARSE$_{low}$	PARSE$_{ATR}$	PARSE$_{hi}$
	a → a	*!**			
	a → ɛ	*!*	*		
	a → e	*!	*	*	
☞	a → i		*	*	*

The crucial observation is that, to satisfy RAISING, the input–output mapping for a given vowel can violate any one vowel height faithfulness constraint, *but it cannot violate more than one*. This prohibition on outputs that contain compounded violations of a single constraint (or closely related constraints) within a single domain (in this case, within a given vowel) is not unique to this problem. To handle similar constraint interactions that enforce sonority distance requirements in syllabification, Smolensky (1995) posits an operation on the constraint set, local conjunction, whereby two or more constraints may be conjoined to form a derived constraint, which is violated just in case all the conjoined constraints are violated within the relevant domain.[5] Similarly, Donca Steriade (personal communication) observes that local conjunction is required to account for languages that permit stress clash but ban double-sided clash.

For Nzɛbi, the correct result is obtained by conjoining the faithfulness constraints as shown in tableau 4.

An alternative approach is to build the stepwise condition into the raising constraint itself, by allowing the constraint to refer to the underlying height of the vowel (i.e., "Raise a vowel one step from its underlying height value"). Note, however, that vowel raising in Basaa (Guthrie 1953) is essentially identical to vowel raising in Nzɛbi, except that /a/ and /ɛ/ both raise to [e]. Under the "built-in stepwise" approach, Basaa would require a distinct raising constraint that is neutralizing with respect to /a/ and /ɛ/ but stepwise with respect to the other vowels. If this approach is extended to chain shift phenomena generally, we must, for example, posit distinct

Tableau 4

PARSE_low & (violated iff PARSE_low and PARSE_ATR are violated with respect to a given vowel)
PARSE_ATR

PARSE_hi & (violated iff PARSE_hi and PARSE_ATR are violated with respect to a given V)
PARSE_ATR

	PARSE_low & PARSE_ATR	PARSE_hi & PARSE_ATR	RAISING
a → a			***!
☞ a → ε	(only PARSE_low)		**
a → e	*!		*
a → i	*!	*	
ε → a	(only PARSE_low)		***!*
ε → ε			**!
☞ ε → e	(only PARSE_ATR)	(only PARSE_ATR)	*
ε → i		*!	
e → a	*!		****
e → ε	(only PARSE_ATR)	(only PARSE_ATR)	*!*
e → e			*!
☞ e → i		(only PARSE_hi)	
i → a	*!		***
i → ε		*!	**
i → e		(only PARSE_hi)	*!
☞ i → i			

constraints for stepwise versus neutralizing applications (or combinations thereof) of vowel reduction, thereby losing a unified treatment of vowel reduction phenomena; likewise for all other phonological processes that can apply in chain shift fashion. Under the local conjunction approach, however, the Basaa facts can be handled straightforwardly, *pace* Schmidt (1994), using the same constraint hierarchy as in Nzɛbi, modulo the ranking of PARSE_low (and any conjoined constraints containing PARSE_low) below RAISING.[6]

The local conjunction approach can readily be extended to handle the BHA facts as well. I posit the following vowel reduction constraint:

(9)   REDUCE
Minimize the duration of a short vowel in an open syllable.

High vowels are phonetically shorter than low vowels (Lehiste 1970), and of course
Ø has zero duration. As demonstrated in Kirchner 1995a, b, such subphonemic
durational distinctions are relevant in conditioning various phonological phenomena and must therefore be represented. For the sake of concreteness, I will assume
the following (privative) durational features for BHA:[7]

(10)   [duration > 0 msec]   [duration > 150 msec]
        a   +   +
        i   +
        Ø

Thus, [a] incurs a greater violation of REDUCE than [i], and Ø incurs no violation at
all. As illustrated in tableau 5, the conjunction of the corresponding faithfulness
constraints, ranked above REDUCE, yields the correct results for BHA.

Tableau 5

		$\text{PARSE}_{dur>0}$ & $\text{PARSE}_{dur>150}$	REDUCE
	a → a		**!
☞	a → i	(only $\text{PARSE}_{dur>150}$)	*
	a → Ø	*!	
	i → a	(only $\text{PARSE}_{dur>150}$)	*!*
	i → i		*!
☞	i → Ø	(only $\text{PARSE}_{dur>0}$)	

More generally, for any constraint that militates in favor of maximal (or minimal) values of features with respect to some phonetic dimension, that constraint
applies in chain shift fashion just in case it is outranked by locally conjoined PARSE
constraints for features in that dimension. More generally still, for any case previously characterized as a rule application of "counterfeeding in the focus" (Kenstowicz
and Kisseberth 1977) (whether or not the counterfeeding rules appear to constitute
a unified phenomenon; cf. n. 3), the counterfeeding effect follows from domination
of the constraints that give rise to the alternations by some conjunction of PARSE
constraints.[8]
    A remaining question concerns the class of constraints that may be conjoined
with one another. Unrestricted local conjunction would appear to result in excessive
descriptive power. For example, if it is possible to conjoin a constraint on complex
onsets with a constraint on heavy syllables, we wrongly predict sound systems
in which only light syllables may have complex onsets. Although it is certainly

premature to attempt to formulate restrictions on local conjunction, I tentatively observe that the cases motivating local conjunction appear to be limited to conjunction of a constraint with itself (e.g., self-conjoined *CLASH to ban double-sided stress clash) or with closely related constraints (e.g., faithfulness constraints for features within the same phonetic dimension, in the chain shift cases).[9]

It is unclear whether the approach proposed here will be sufficient for the reanalysis of all phenomena previously characterized as opaque rule interactions. Cole and Kisseberth (1995), for example, account for the counterbleeding/counterfeeding interaction of Yawelmani vowel lowering and harmony in terms of the notion of feature domains, and the distinction between existence of a domain and its featural expression. To handle other opacity cases, McCarthy (1995) tentatively abandons the condition that well-formedness constraints are exclusively stated over output representations. I have shown, however, that a substantial class of opaque rule interactions – namely, synchronic chain shifts – can be handled insightfully within a strongly parallel theory of phonology, using local conjunction of faithfulness constraints.

Notes

1 In *diachronic* chain shifts, of course, this is not a problem, since the ordering of the sound changes presumably corresponds to distinct historical stages.

2 This assumes the standard conception wherein well-formedness constraints are stated exclusively over output representations, and only the faithfulness constraints can refer to underlying properties (this conception is implicit in McCarthy and Prince 1995, and explicit in Orgun 1995). As an anonymous reviewer notes, opacity phenomena pose no formal problem if structural descriptions of well-formedness constraints can refer to underlying as well as surface environments (see McCarthy 1995), though the resulting theory is much less restrictive.

3 An anonymous reviewer points out that in a similar chain shift in Kashgar Uighur (Orgun 1994), the environment for deletion is more restricted than the environment for raising, and concludes from this that deletion and raising really are two unrelated phenomena. Whether or not this conclusion is warranted, for Uighur or BHA, McCarthy's general point is clearly valid for numerous other chain shifts, including the Nzɛbi vowel raising examined below.

4 For an explicit treatment of the notion of a phonetic dimension, such as vowel height, see Flemming 1995a.

5 This operation was originally proposed in Smolensky 1993. Note that Hewitt and Crowhurst (1995) have proposed a similar operation, which they also call conjunction, whereby the derived constraint is violated just in case *any* of the component constraints is violated. See also Suzuki 1995.

6 Flemming (1995b) gives yet another OT analysis of Nzɛbi, relying on constraints that refer directly to the preservation of contrasts within a given phonetic dimension. That is, the raising is constrained by the need to maintain at least two vowel height contrasts. However, the MAINTAIN CONTRAST constraints say nothing about the mapping between particular vowels in the unraised and raised forms. To rule out mappings such as $i \rightarrow \varepsilon$, $\{a,e\} \rightarrow i$, $\varepsilon \rightarrow e$, local conjunction of faithfulness constraints is required. But as shown herein, locally conjoined faithfulness constraints are sufficient to account for chain shifts (whether or not the MAINTAIN CONTRAST constraints are motivated by other phenomena).

7 If this feature were not privative, $i \rightarrow \emptyset$ would violate PARSE$_{dur>150}$ ($-dur>150 \rightarrow$ 0dur>150) and so would violate the conjoined constraint, yielding the wrong result in tableau 5.

8 It is not immediately apparent how to handle circular chain shifts such as Xiamen tone

sandhi (Chen 1987, wherein a 53 contour tone lowers to 44, 44 → 22, 22 → 21, but 21 raises all the way to 53) in this or any other approach. Perhaps a solution lies in the idea that the points at opposite extremes of a phonetic dimension are in some sense perceptually closer to each other than to the intermediate points; in other words, the perceptual "space" is curved. If this idea has merit, the 21 → 53 alternation would traverse *less* perceptual distance than 21 → 44, thereby falling into line with the distance-based effects attributed to conjoined faithfulness constraints above.

9 Paul Smolensky (personal communication) suggests that local conjunction, even in the chain shift cases, can be formally reduced to self-conjunction, by allowing faithfulness constraints to refer to "feature classes" (Padgett 1995). Thus, assuming that the vowel height features ([high], [low], [ATR]) constitute a class, the active conjoined constraint in Nzɛbi is $\text{PARSE}_{\text{V-height}} \& \text{PARSE}_{\text{V-height}}$, or in Smolensky's notation, $\text{PARSE}_{\text{V-height}}^2$. However, this approach cannot handle the Basaa chain shift, without invoking an ad hoc class of vowel height features that excludes [low].

References

Al-Mozainy, Hamza, Q. 1981. *Vowel Alternations in a Bedouin Hijazi Arabic Dialect: Abstractness and Stress.* Doctoral dissertation, University of Texas, Austin.

Chen, Matthew. 1987. The syntax of Xiamen tone sandhi. *Phonology Yearbook* 4: 109–49.

Clements, G. N. 1991. Vowel height assimilation in Bantu languages. In *Proceedings of the Special Session on African Language Structures*, 25–64. Berkeley Linguistics Society, University of California, Berkeley.

Cole, Jennifer, and Charles Kisseberth. 1995. Levels of representation in nonderivational phonology: Opaque rule interaction in Yawelmani vowel harmony. Paper presented at Arizona Phonology Conference, University of Arizona, April 1995.

Flemming, Edward. 1995a. *Auditory Representations in Phonology.* Doctoral dissertation, University of California, Los Angeles.

Flemming, Edward. 1995b. Evidence for constraints on contrast. Paper presented at the 14th West Coast Conference on Formal Linguistics, University of California, Los Angeles, March 1995.

Goldsmith, John. 1976. *Autosegmental Phonology.* Doctoral dissertation, MIT, Cambridge, Mass.

Guthrie, Malcolm. 1953. *The Bantu Languages of Western Equatorial Africa.* London: Oxford University Press.

Guthrie, Malcolm. 1968. Notes on Nzɛbi (Gabon). *Journal of African Languages* 7: 101–29.

Hewitt, Mark, and Megan Crowhurst. 1995. Conjunctive constraints and templates in Optimality Theory. MS, University of British Columbia, Vancouver; University of North Carolina, Chapel Hill.

Hualde, José Ignacio. 1991. *Basque Phonology.* London: Routledge.

Kenstowicz, Michael, and Charles Kisseberth. 1977. *Topics in Phonological Theory.* New York: Academic Press.

Kirchner, Robert. 1995a. Contrastiveness and faithfulness. MS, University of California, Los Angeles. ▶

Kirchner, Robert. 1995b. Contrastiveness is an epiphenomenon of constraint ranking. Paper presented at the 21st Annual Meeting of the Berkeley Linguistics Society, University of California, Berkeley, February 1995.

Lehiste, Ilse. 1970. *Suprasegmentals.* Cambridge, Mass.: MIT Press.

McCarthy, John. 1993. The parallel advantage: Containment, consistency, and alignment. Paper presented at Rutgers Optimality Workshop-1, Rutgers University, October 1993.

McCarthy, John. 1995. Remarks on phonological opacity in Optimality Theory. MS, University of Massachusetts, Amherst. ▶

McCarthy, John, and Alan Prince. 1995. Faithfulness and reduplicative identity. MS, University of Massachusetts, Amherst; Rutgers University, New Brunswick, N.J. ◀

Orgun, C. Orhan. 1994. Monotonic cyclicity and Optimality Theory. In *Proceedings of*

NELS 24, 461–74. GLSA, University of Massachusetts, Amherst.

Orgun, C. Orhan. 1995. Correspondence and identity constraints in two-level Optimality Theory. MS, University of California, Berkeley. ▶

Padgett, Jaye. 1995. Feature classes. In *University of Massachusetts Occasional Papers in Linguistics 18: Papers in Optimality Theory*. GLSA, University of Massachusetts, Amherst. ◀

Prince, Alan, and Paul Smolensky. 1993. Optimality Theory: Constraint interaction in generative grammar. MS, Rutgers University, New Brunswick, N.J.; University of Colorado, Boulder. ◀

Schmidt, Deborah. 1994. Vowel raising in Basaa. MS, University of Georgia, Athens.

Smolensky, Paul. 1993. Harmony, markedness, and phonological activity. Paper presented at Rutgers Optimality Workshop-1, Rutgers University, October 1993. ▶

Smolensky, Paul. 1995. On the internal structure of the constraint component of UG. Colloquium presented at University of California, Los Angeles, April 7, 1995. ▶

Suzuki, K. 1995. Vowel raising in Woleaian: Adjacency and precedence in OT. Paper presented at Arizona Phonology Conference, University of Arizona, April 1995.

Study and Research Questions

1   Reformulate the constraint in (9) so it can be evaluated unambiguously. That is, reformulate it to read "Assign one violation-mark for each . . .".

2   This chapter mentions the possibility of "build[ing] the stepwise condition into the raising constraint itself, by allowing the constraint to refer to the underlying height of the vowel (i.e., 'Raise a vowel one step from its underlying height value')." This possibility is rejected for empirical reasons. Are there also reasons of principle for rejecting it? (Chapter 6 is relevant.)

3   Gnanadesikan (1997) has a different approach to chain shifts. Her idea is that, instead of local conjunction, there are faithfulness constraints against two-step moves on a phonetic scale. Review her proposal and compare it to the one in this chapter.

4   Compare this chapter's analysis of Nzɛbi with the one proposed by Clements (1991). If Clements's representational assumptions are adopted, how does the OT analysis change?

Part V

Interfaces

Chapter 22 | Laura Benua

Transderivational Identity: Phonological Relations Between Words

Editor's Note

The phonological cycle is one of the central insights of Chomsky and Halle (1968). This insight was developed further in the theory of Lexical Phonology (Kiparsky 1982; Mohanan 1986). The idea is that phonological rules first apply to simple words and then apply again to morphologically complex words derived from them.

   The cycle and like notions were worked out within a rule-based framework, and so it is natural to re-examine these ideas within OT. The proposal in this chapter is that effects formerly attributed to the cycle or lexical strata should be analyzed in terms of faithfulness constraints – not the familiar input–output faithfulness, but rather faithfulness between different output forms of related words.

   This chapter should be read after chapter 3, which it relies on. It would be profitable to read it in conjunction with chapter 23, which argues instead for incorporating the Lexical Phonology model into OT. For related work, see Buckley (1999), Burzio (1994b, 1996, 1997a, 1997b, 1999, 2000), Crosswhite (1998), Itô, Kitagawa, and Mester (1996), Itô and Mester (1997), Kager (1997), Kenstowicz (1996, 1997), Kraska-Szlenk (1995), Orgun (1996b), and Pater (2000).

[...]

2 Transderivational Correspondence

2.1 Transderivational correspondence theory

In an early exposition of Correspondence Theory, McCarthy & Prince (1994) suggest that correspondence relations hold not only between input–output and

Excerpt from:
Benua, Laura (1997) *Transderivational Identity: Phonological Relations Between Words*. Doctoral dissertation: University of Massachusetts, Amherst. [Available on Rutgers Optimality Archive, ROA-259.]

base–reduplicant pairs, but also between independent words. This dissertation develops that suggestion into Transderivational Correspondence Theory (TCT). The core of the proposal is that words in a paradigm are required to be phonologically identical by constraints on an identity relation between two surface words. This is a transderivational or output–output (OO) correspondence relation, linking words across their individual input–output mappings. The related words are evaluated simultaneously, in parallel, against the constraint hierarchy. Through ranking, OO-correspondence constraints produce misapplication effects – or "cyclic" effects – without a cyclic derivation.

Related words are required to be identical by OO-correspondence constraints, and they are also required to be identical on an input–output (IO) correspondence relation. This complex of relations is represented schematically in (11).

(11)   Transderivational (Output–Output) Correspondence

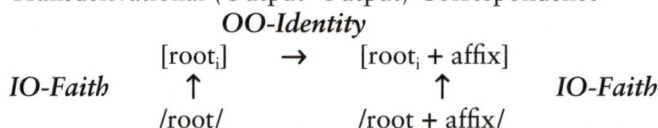

$$\text{IO-Faith} \quad \begin{array}{ccc} & OO\text{-}Identity & \\ [root_i] & \rightarrow & [root_i + affix] \\ \uparrow & & \uparrow \\ /root/ & & /root + affix/ \end{array} \quad \text{IO-Faith}$$

Each output word is linked to an input by an IO-correspondence relation, and the two words are related to each other by a transderivational OO-correspondence relation. Through these relations, each word is evaluated for faithfulness to its input by IO-Faith constraints (IO-MAX, IO-DEP, IO-IDENT[F], etc.) and the two outputs are compared by OO-Identity constraints (OO-MAX, OO-DEP, OO-IDENT[F], etc.). The two types of faithfulness requirements are distinct and separately rankable. IO-Faith and OO-Identity constraints coexist in the hierarchy, and interact with one another and with a fixed ranking of markedness constraints.

When a derived word and its base differ in some way relevant to a phonological process observed in the language, permuting the ranking of IO-Faith and OO-Identity with respect to markedness constraints produces one of three patterns: *overapplication*, in which the process applies where it is not phonologically conditioned; *underapplication*, in which the process is conditioned but fails to apply; and *normal application*, in which the process applies always and only where it is properly conditioned. In §2.4 [omitted here – Ed.], each pattern is introduced, together with the ranking that generates it. But first, §2.2 explains how correspondence-governed paradigms are defined, and §2.3 discusses how they are evaluated by constraints.

2.2   Phonological paradigms

Transderivational OO-correspondence relations are the phonological reflex of a morphological relation between two words. All types of morphological derivation are mirrored by a transderivational correspondence relation; affixation, truncation, reduplication, ablaut, consonant mutation, mapping to a template, compounding, or any other type of word formation requires an OO-correspondence relation between the derived word and an output base.[22] Although I adopt an item-and-arrangement approach to word formation, my proposals are also consistent with an item-and-process view (see, e.g., Hockett 1954; Anderson 1992). It makes no difference whether affixes are objects or operations, as long as morphological derivation is concomitant with a phonological identity relation.

The identity relation triggered by morphological derivation holds between the derived word and an output base. The base is the independent word identified with the string that undergoes morphological derivation; in affixation, the base is the word identified with the string adjacent to the affix. A precise definition is difficult to formulate, because the relevant base can be identified only with respect to a specific derived word. For example, the base can be morphologically simplex (as in *sign* ≈ *signer*) or complex (as in *original* ≈ *originality*). Often, the base is the word that is minimally less morphologically complex than the derived word, so that the base consists of a subset of the derived word's morphemes. But this kind of subset relation does not always hold. An obligatorily-inflected word can serve as the base of another inflected word, and the base's inflection is neither morphologically nor phonologically present in the derived word.[23] Given these kinds of cases, there can be no formal requirement of a morphological subset relation between the derived word and its base.

The base of an OO-correspondence relation is a licit output word, which is both morphologically and phonologically well-formed. Morphological well-formedness constraints are important. In inflectional languages, morphology requires OO-correspondence relations to hold between two fully-inflected words (and it also prevents the base's inflection from appearing in the derived form). In derivational systems, the fact that the base must be morphologically well-formed entails that bound roots are not cyclic domains. The minimal domain of phonology is the word.[24] The base of an OO-correspondence relation is also phonologically well-formed, in that it conforms to the language's canonical surface patterns. This is not a definitional characteristic of the base, however, because maximal base harmony is entailed by the recursive evaluation of paradigms performed by the grammar, as set out in §2.3 below.

Every affix or morphological operation requires a transderivational relation to be established between the derived output and an output base. To formalize this, I adopt the familiar subcategorization frames of Lieber (1980). In addition to their segmental content (if any), affixal morphemes are supplied with a subcategorization frame that specifies idiosyncratic information about the affix, such as its selectional restrictions, and whether it is a prefix or a suffix. I propose that the affix's subcategorization frame also specifies the OO-correspondence relation that links the affixed output in a paradigmatic identity relation. This provides a direct connection between morphological derivation and phonological identity relations, preventing identity relations between randomly selected words. Because of their link with morphological subcategorization frames, OO-correspondence relations compare a morphologically derived word and its base, and not other kinds of word pairs. Subcategorization also provides a ready explanation of phonological class behavior: individual affixes may be subcategorized by distinct OO-correspondence relations.

Each affix or morphological operation invokes an OO-correspondence relation. Consequently, phonological paradigms are constructed as a linear array, as in (12). In a multiply-affixed word like *originálity*, each affix triggers an OO-correspondence relation between the affixed output and an output base. The resulting linear paradigm reflects the increasing complexity of morphological structure.

(12)   Multiple Affixation

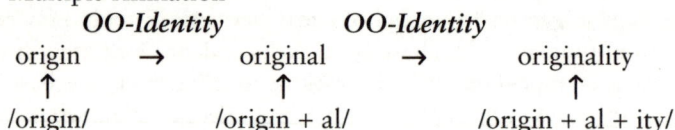

$$\begin{array}{ccccc} & \textit{OO-Identity} & & \textit{OO-Identity} & \\ \text{origin} & \rightarrow & \text{original} & \rightarrow & \text{originality} \\ \uparrow & & \uparrow & & \uparrow \\ \text{/origin/} & & \text{/origin + al/} & & \text{/origin + al + ity/} \end{array}$$

With each affix triggering an OO-relation, words in an extended paradigm are related two at a time, in SUBPARADIGMS, and paradigmatic identity is evaluated in a strictly local way. The goodness of correspondence between *originálity* and its base *original* is reckoned separately from the goodness of correspondence between *original* and its base *órigin*. This is a useful result, since paradigmatic identity is observed in only one of these pairs – *originálity* mimics the stress feet of its base *original*, but *original* is not faithful to the footing of *órigin*. The linear phonological paradigms built by subcategorization are local, in the sense that a derived word is linked to its base only.

   With these linear and local paradigms, TCT predicts the phenomena attributed to *bracket erasure* in cyclic theories (e.g., Chomsky & Halle 1968; Pesetsky 1979; Kiparsky 1982a). Bracket erasure is the mechanism that erases morphological brackets after each cycle of phonological rules, thereby preventing the derivation of a multiply-affixed word from making crucial reference to the derived phonology of embedded constituents. By the time phonology applies on the outermost cycle of *originálity*, bracket erasure has rendered the initial cycle on *órigin* indistinguishable from the intermediate cycle on *original*. In effect, multiply-affixed *originálity* cannot rely on information contained in *órigin* if that information is not also present in *original* (for example, word-initial stress). TCT explains bracket erasure effects differently. *Originálity* is not phonologically related to the unaffixed word *órigin*, so *originálity* cannot mimic the stress pattern in *órigin* – it can only be influenced by the stress of its base *original*. The derived phonology of embedded constituents is not available because OO-correspondence relations link only the most morphologically similar words in local subparadigms.[25] [. . .]

2.3   Evaluation of paradigms

2.3.1 Recursive evaluation

Words in a phonological paradigm are evaluated in parallel against a recursive constraint hierarchy. The language-particular hierarchy is duplicated, and the recursions are ranked with respect to one another. The optimal form of each word in the paradigm is determined by one of the recursions of the constraints, so that the base is evaluated against a higher-ranked recursion, and the derived word is evaluated against a lower-ranked recursion of the hierarchy. This recursive evaluation mechanism enforces the "bottom-up" character of word formation by restricting misapplication identity effects to the derived word in the subparadigm.

To show how the recursive system works and why I propose it, it is helpful to have a real example at hand. Consider an identity effect involving morphological truncation in English described by Kahn (1976).[27] In paradigms like L[æ]rry ≈ L[æ]r, the truncated diminutive satisfies an OO-Identity constraint by violating a phonotactic constraint against tautosyllabic ær sequences. All other English words must have a back low vowel before a tautosyllabic r (c[a]r, h[a]rd), and not a front one (*c[æ]r, *h[æ]rd). Neutralization of the a/æ contrast before tautosyllabic r fails to apply, or underapplies, to preserve identity in the L[æ]rry ≈ L[æ]r paradigm.

For present purposes, the phonotactic constraint that drives neutralization is called *ær]$_\sigma$.[28] This constraint must outrank input–output faithfulness: *ær]$_\sigma$ ≫ IO-IDENT[BK] prevents any possible input from giving rise to an optimal output with a tautosyllabic ær sequence (c[a]r, *c[æ]r). Truncated words violate *ær]$_\sigma$ in order to respect identity with the base – the nickname is L[æ]r, not *L[a]r, because the base name L[æ]rry has a front vowel. My proposal is that a dominant OO-Identity constraint forces violation of *ær]$_\sigma$, blocking neutralization in the truncated word. The ranking is (15).

(15)   OO-IDENT[BK] ≫ *ær]$_\sigma$ ≫ IO-IDENT[BK]

Optimal paradigms are selected by recursions of this ranking. Evaluation of candidates is represented in complex tableaux like (16). Candidates are subparadigms, represented discontinuously across the tableau. In paradigm (a), both words have a back vowel. In candidates (b) and (c), the related words have different vowels. Candidate (d) is the optimal paradigm with two front vowels. Because the OO-Identity constraint is at the top of the hierarchy, it is more harmonic to achieve identity than to obey the phonotactic constraint.

(16)   Recursive Evaluation
       candidate (a)   L[a]rry ≈ L[a]r   *overapplication*
       candidate (b)   L[a]rry ≈ L[æ]r   *"backwards" application*
       candidate (c)   L[æ]rry ≈ L[a]r   *normal application*
☞   candidate (d)   L[æ]rry ≈ L[æ]r   *underapplication*

Recursion (A)   Recursion (B)

/læri/		OO-Id	*ær]$_\sigma$	IO-Id	≫	/læri + Trunc/		OO-Id	*ær]$_\sigma$	IO-Id
a.	la.ri			*!		a′.	lar			*
b.	la.ri			*!		b′.	lær	*	*	
c.	læ.ri					c′.	lar	*!		*
d. ☞	læ.ri					d′. ☞	lær		*	

The truncatory diminutive morphology triggers an OO-correspondence relation and a recursion of the constraint hierarchy, and each word in the subparadigm is evaluated against one of the recursions. The base is evaluated by the dominant recursion, so paradigms with non-canonical phonology in the base are eliminated. Paradigms (16a) and (16b) are ruled out by the violation of IO-IDENT[BK] incurred by *L[a]rry*, the base common to them.[29] The choice between the remaining candidates falls to the lower-ranked recursion of the constraints, where OO-Identity is decisive. Paradigm (16d) is optimal in spite of its **ær]$_\sigma$* violation.

By taking into account *where* in a paradigm constraint violations are incurred – in the base or in the derived word – recursive evaluation makes paradigmatic underapplication possible. Without it, underapplication of phonology in the derived word would be ruled out in favor of overapplication in the base. In (16a), overapplication of the [æ]-to-[a] change[30] in the base of the paradigm satisfies both OO-Identity and markedness, and violates only IO-Faithfulness. And since IO-Faith has to rank below **ær]$_\sigma$* to drive the canonical neutralization pattern, overapplication is expected to win. Recursive evaluation ensures that it does not. The IO-Faith violation incurred by the base in (16a) is more costly, because it is higher-ranked, than the **ær]$_\sigma$* violation in the derived word in the optimal paradigm (16d).

Underapplication requires a low-ranking constraint to compel violation of a dominant one. Recursive evaluation resolves this paradox by invoking a second order of evaluation of paradigms, differentiating (through ranking) the violations incurred by each member. Thus, a lower-ranked constraint can compel violation of a higher-ranked one if and only if the lower-ranked constraint is violated in a word with RANKING PRIORITY in a subparadigm. The idea is that the base is morphologically prior to or less complex than the derived word, so it is endowed with ranking priority, and subjected to a higher-ranked recursion of the constraints. The base is therefore maximally harmonic, satisfying the language-particular ranking as best it can by conforming to canonical surface patterns.[31] Since the base has to show canonical phonology, high-ranking OO-Identity can be only satisfied by misapplying phonology in the paradigm's derived word. Underapplication *L[æ]rry ≈ L[æ]r* is optimal, even though it violates a dominant constraint, because overapplication **L[a]rry ≈ L[a]r* violates the PRIORITY OF THE BASE generalization enforced by the recursive evaluation.

Another way to resolve the ranking paradox in underapplication is to re-rank constraints, so that some part of the English grammar forces low vowel neutralization by the ranking **ær]$_\sigma$* ≫ IO-IDENT[BK] (hence *c[a]r, *c[æ]r*), while another part of the grammar, relevant to truncated words, has the opposite ranking and no neutralization (*L[æ]r, *L[a]r*). The idea that multiple grammars coexist in one language is familiar from cyclic and stratal theories like Lexical Phonology (Pesetsky 1979; Kiparsky 1982a, b, 1985; Mohanan 1982, 1986; Borowsky 1986, 1993), as well as from OT subgrammar theories (McCarthy & Prince 1993a; Inkelas 1994; Kenstowicz 1995; Itô & Mester 1995; Kiparsky 1997). But note that distinguishing between levels or subgrammars (by constraint re-ranking or otherwise) is by itself insufficient to model the base-priority asymmetry in paradigms. The levels or subgrammars also have to be chained together in serial order.

In a re-ranking analysis of misapplication, serialism has two functions. First, when misapplication involves mimicry of a phonologically predictable property, as in the English stress case *original ≈ originálity*, the derived word has to be related to a form that has already undergone some phonological derivation. This entails (at least) two derivational steps. Serialism also enforces the PRIORITY OF THE BASE generalization. The base is derived first in a bottom-up construction of the complex word, and the base's derivation cannot look ahead to anticipate later events. It follows that the less-complex base can never copy the phonology of the derived word.

Recursive evaluation supplants serialism's "no look-ahead" function (its other job, relating outputs, is assigned to the OO-Identity constraints). Identity relations between words are asymmetrical – the base can never copy the derived word – because each word is evaluated individually, and violations in the base are more costly than violations in the derived word. There is no need to invoke a serial derivation, so I propose that words are evaluated in parallel by OO-Identity (and other) constraints. This has the added benefit of obviating the other leg of the serial analysis: re-ranking. A parallel theory is necessarily monostratal, with fixed constraint ranking, so only a limited variety of patterns can be produced in the same language. By allowing constraints to re-rank, subgrammar theory makes much broader typological predictions. These and other points of comparison between TCT and serial theory are developed throughout this thesis.

[. . .]

3   Sundanese

3.1   Introduction

Paradigmatic OO-Identity constraints force overapplication of phonology in the Austronesian language Sundanese. In plurals created by infixation, progressive nasal assimilation applies where it is not conditioned, nasalizing vowels that are not in a post-nasal context: [ɲ-āl-īār] 'seek (pl.)'. Nasalization overapplies in the plural to achieve identity with the singular base, where corresponding vowels are predictably nasal in post-nasal context, [ɲīār] 'seek'. This Sundanese case study demonstrates that the paradigmatic OO-Identity requirements responsible for misapplication are distinct from IO-Faith constraints on input–output relations, and that the two sets of faithfulness constraints coexist in the same markedness hierarchy.

The Sundanese facts are laid out in (37–39). Nasality is not contrastive in vowels. Predictable harmony spreads nasality onto vowels and vowel sequences that follow primary nasal consonants. The laryngeals [h, ʔ] are transparent to nasal spread (37a), but oral consonants and glides block it (37b). Thus, nasal vowels appear in post-nasal context, and oral vowels appear elsewhere.

(37)   Sundanese Nasal Assimilation

	a.			b.		
	ɲīār	'seek'		ɲãtur	'arrange'
	bɨŋhãr	'to be rich'		ɲīsər	'displace'
	ɲãũr	'say'		ɲũliat	'stretch'
	nīʔīs	'relax in a cool place'		mãrios	'examine'
	nãʔãtkɨn	'dry'		ɲīwat	'elope'

Certain plural words deviate from the canonical pattern, and have nasal vowels in oral context. The plural affix, which is realized as either *ar* or *al*, is prefixed to vowel-initial roots, as in (38a), and infixed if the root begins with a consonant or consonant cluster, as in (38b).[42]

(38)   Sundanese Plurals
   a.   Plural Prefixation
       Singular   *Plural*
       alus   ar-alus   'be pleasant'
       ala   ar-ala   'take'
       omoŋ   ar-omoŋ-an   'say, their (our, your) words'

   b.   Plural Infixation
       Singular   *Plural*
       bawa   b-ar-awa   'carry'
       dahar   d-al-ahar   'eat'
       hormat   h-al-ormat   'honor'

In (39), the plural marker is infixed after a root-initial nasal consonant. Unexpectedly, nasality spreads over the infix's liquid onto the following vowels (Robins 1957; Anderson 1972; Stevens 1977; Hart 1981; van der Hulst and Smith 1984; Cohn 1990).

(39)   Plural Infixation after Nasal Consonants: Overapplication of Nasal Spread
       Singular   *Plural*
       ɲĩãr   ɲ-ãl-ĩãr   'seek'
       ɲãũr   ɲ-ãl-ãũr   'say'
       mãhãl   m-ãr-ãhãl   'expensive'
       ɲãʔãtkɨn   ɲ-ãr-ãʔãtkɨn   'dry'

Nasal harmony applies where its phonological conditions are not met to preserve identity in the plural paradigm. This is overapplication, forced by a high-ranking constraint on an OO-correspondence relation.

   Cohn (1990) presents a cyclic analysis of Sundanese overapplication. The nasalization pattern presents an ordering paradox, in that the nasalization rule has to apply both before and after infixation of the plural morpheme. Cycles resolve the paradox, allowing the nasal spread rule to apply more than once in the derivation of the plural word. Nasal spread applies on the first cycle, nasalizing the root vowels in [ɲĩãr] while they are in post-nasal context, and applies again on the second cycle, after bracket erasure brings the infix into the derivation, to nasalize the infixal vowel.

(40)   Cyclic Nasal Spread
       Input   [al [ɲiar]]
       Cycle 1 nasal spread   ɲĩãr
       Bracket erasure   ɲ-al-ĩãr
       Cycle 2 nasal spread   ɲ-ãl-ĩãr

The nasal spread rule is properly conditioned each time it applies. Morphology excluded from the first cycle destroys the conditioning environment of the first application of nasal spread, but since subsequent derivation does not denasalize the root's vowels, nasal vowels appear in oral context in the plural word. With cycles, nasality in the plural's root vowels is not enforced by any rule of grammar; it is simply a by-product of the serial derivation of the plural word.

Transderivational Correspondence Theory (TCT) gives the Sundanese pattern a different explanation: nasality in the plural is enforced grammatically, by OO-Identity constraints. The plural word and its singular base are linked phonologically by an OO-correspondence relation. Through ranking, constraints on this relation force plural paradigms to violate canonical phonotactics.

(41)   Transderivational Identity

$$OO\text{-}Identity$$

	[ɲĩãr]	→	[ɲ-ãl-ĩãr]	
IO-Faith	↑		↑	*IO-Faith*
	/ɲiar/		/aR + ɲiar/	

The misbehavior of nasal harmony in Sundanese is overapplication: nasalization applies in both words, even though it is properly conditioned only in the base. A constraint demanding identity of nasality in the paradigm, ranked above a constraint against nasal vowels, produces the overapplication effect. Because OO-IDENT[NAS] ≫ *V$_{NAS}$, it is better to achieve identity than to avoid marked vocalic nasality.

Like all constraints, OO-Identity constraints are ranked and violable under domination. In the paradigms in (42), an affix introduces nasality, and satisfaction of OO-IDENT[NAS] is not optimal. Instead, harmony applies normally, affecting all and only post-nasal vowels.

(42)   Paradigmatic Identity Failure: Normal Application of Nasal Spread

gəde ≈ g-um-ə̃de	*gəde ≈ g-um-əde
'big/be conceited'	*gə̃de ≈ g-um-ə̃de
rasa ≈ r-um-ãsa	*rasa ≈ r-um-asa
'feel/admit to'	*rãsa ≈ r-um-ãsa
indit ≈ paŋ-ĩndit	*indit ≈ paŋ-indit
'to leave/reason for leaving'	*ĩndit ≈ paŋ-ĩndit

Corresponding vowels in related words in (42) do not match in nasality, because OO-Identity is dominated by constraints that ban oral vowels from post-nasal context, abbreviated here as *NV$_{ORAL}$.[43] This prohibition is always obeyed – oral vowels never appear after nasals in Sundanese – so *NV$_{ORAL}$ must outrank all conflicting constraints. In (42), *NV$_{ORAL}$ conflicts with the paradigmatic identity requirement, and the markedness constraint is satisfied because it is dominant: *NV$_{ORAL}$ ≫ OO-IDENT[NAS].

Together, overapplication in (39) and normal application in (42) show that OO-IDENT[NAS] ranks between two markedness constraints: it dominates *V$_{NAS}$ and is dominated by *NV$_{ORAL}$. Thus, identity in paradigms is optimal unless it would produce an oral vowel in a post-nasal context. The markedness hierarchy of *NV$_{ORAL}$ ≫ *V$_{NAS}$ entailed by the OO-Identity effect is independently motivated in Sundanese, by the canonical distribution of oral and nasal vowels in (37). Ranked above faithfulness to the rich input, this markedness hierarchy ensures that nasal vowels appear, violating *V$_{NAS}$, only if dominant *NV$_{ORAL}$ demands them – that is, nasal vowels appear only after nasals, even if nasal vowels are assumed to be present underlyingly (see §3.2). Thus, the *NV$_{ORAL}$ ≫ *V$_{NAS}$ ranking is constant, and two distinct faithfulness constraints, OO-Ident[nas] and IO-Ident[nas], interact with it. This case is evidence, then, that OO-Identity and IO-Faith coexist in a single hierarchy, and all words are derived by the same grammar.

Since a single total ordering of constraints is responsible for both the canonical nasal harmony pattern in (37) and (42) and the overapplication identity effect in (39), the Sundanese analysis begins with an examination of canonical allophonic nasality (§3.2). Once the basic constraint ranking is established, OO-Identity constraints are introduced to explain overapplication of nasal spread in plural infixation paradigms (§3.3) and normal application in other paradigms (§3.4). The transderivational approach is compared to various alternatives (§3.5) [3.4 and 3.5 are omitted here – Ed.]. In addition to the cyclic model in (40), three alternatives are considered: one based on underspecification of the plural morpheme's consonant, another that invokes underlying nasalization in Sundanese roots (derived by Prince & Smolensky's *Lexicon Optimization*), and a third that relies on a serial elaboration of an OT grammar. For various reasons, each of these analyses fails to improve on the transderivational approach.

3.2   Allophonic nasal harmony

In monomorphemic Sundanese words, nasality in vowels is predictable from the vowel's phonological environment. Nasal vowels appear after nasal segments, and oral vowels appear elsewhere.

(43)   Allophonic Nasal Harmony

ɲĩãr	'seek'	ŋãtur	'arrange'
bɨŋhãr	'to be rich'	ɲĩsər	'displace'
ŋãũr	'say'	ŋũliat	'stretch'
nĩʔĩs	'relax in a cool place'	mãrios	'examine'
nãʔãtkɨn	'dry'	ŋĩwat	'elope'

This is a simple allophonic alternation, predictable from phonological context alone. My analysis of allophonic nasality in Sundanese follows McCarthy & Prince's (1995) treatment of a similar pattern in the related language Madurese. The focus of the analysis is on the distribution of oral and nasal vowels, and not on the nature of the nasalization process itself.

[. . .]

The first step in identifying the markedness constraints that force an allophonic alternation is to determine the relative markedness of the allophones. In the Sundanese case this is simple: nasal vowels are more marked than oral vowels. Traditionally, (universal) implicational statements encode the relative markedness of segment types; for example, any system that admits nasal vowels must also allow oral vowels. OT allows a precise characterization of relative markedness: more-marked elements violate higher-ranked constraints (Smolensky 1993). Nasal vowels are more marked than oral vowels because the constraint against nasal vowels is higher-ranked than the constraint against oral vowels.[44]

(44)   Relative Markedness of Allophones
    $*V_{NAS}$ "No nasal vowels."
    $*V_{ORAL}$ "No oral vowels."
    $*V_{NAS} \gg *V_{ORAL}$ "Nasal vowels are more marked than oral vowels."

The markedness hierarchy in (44) captures the correct implicational relation. A grammar that admits nasal vowels also has oral vowels, because any constraint ranked high enough to compel nasal vowels, in violation of $*V_{NAS}$, must also outrank $*V_{ORAL}$. Conversely, domination of $*V_{ORAL}$ does not entail domination of $*V_{NAS}$, so a system with oral vowels will not necessarily have nasal vowels too.

By itself, the ranking $*V_{NAS} \gg *V_{ORAL}$ bans nasal vowels. In Sundanese, nasal vowels do appear, but only in a specific context, after nasal consonants. Markedness constraints ban less-marked oral allophones from this specific environment, and force more-marked nasal allophones to appear. Nasal harmony is characterized here as a simple ban on oral vowels in post-nasal context, but is certainly enforced by a complex of constraints, including constraints that generalize over all types of assimilation and constraints on nasality in particular. The $*NV_{ORAL}$ constraint in (45) stands in for this set of harmony constraints (McCarthy & Prince, 1995).

(45)   Context-Sensitive Markedness
    $*NV_{ORAL}$ "No oral vowels in post-nasal context."

The prohibition against oral vowels in post-nasal context outranks the ban on nasal vowels: $*NV_{ORAL} \gg *V_{NAS}$. These constraints logically conflict, and with the opposite ranking nasal vowels would never surface. Since $*NV_{ORAL}$ forces nasal spread and not any other possible alternation, $*V_{NAS}$ has to be dominated by certain other constraints, so that denasalization of consonants, deletion of either the nasal or the following vowel, or any other possible repair of a $*NV_{ORAL}$ violation is dispreferred to nasal spread. To simplify matters, the only repair of $*NV_{ORAL}$ violation considered here is nasalization of vowels.

The ranking $*NV_{ORAL} \gg *V_{NAS}$ forces canonical nasal spread. When a vowel follows a nasal segment, $*NV_{ORAL}$ forces nasality. When $*NV_{ORAL}$ is irrelevant, lower-ranked $*V_{NAS}$ demands less-marked oral vowels. Faithfulness constraints play no role in the alternation. The crucially dominated IO-Faith constraint regulates nasality.

(46)   IO-IDENT[NAS]   "Correspondents in input–output pairs agree in nasality."

The low rank of IO-IDENT[NAS] in Sundanese is demonstrated by the four tableaux in (47), which evaluate candidates generated from four possible inputs for [nãtur] 'arrange'. In tableau (i) both input vowels are oral, in tableaux (ii–iii) the input contains one oral and one nasal vowel, and in tableau (iv) the input vowels are nasal. In each case, the grammar selects the optimal form (d) [nãtur], with a nasal vowel after the nasal and an oral vowel after the oral consonant. IO-IDENT[NAS] ranks below the markedness hierarchy, and all of these inputs converge on a single optimal output.

(47)   Allophonic Nasal Harmony
       *NV$_{ORAL}$ ≫ *V$_{NAS}$ ≫ IO-IDENT[NAS]

   (i)   input vowels are oral

/ŋatur/	*NV$_{ORAL}$	*V$_{NAS}$	IO-IDENT[NAS]
a. ŋatur	*!		
b. ŋatũr	*!	*	*
c. ŋãtũr		**!	**
d. ☞ ŋãtur		*	*

   (ii)   input vowels are oral and nasal

/ŋãtur/	*NV$_{ORAL}$	*V$_{NAS}$	IO-IDENT[NAS]
a. ŋatur	*!		*
b. ŋatũr	*!	*	**
c. ŋãtũr		**!	*
d. ☞ ŋãtur		*	

   (iii)   input vowels are oral and nasal

/ŋatũr/	*NV$_{ORAL}$	*V$_{NAS}$	IO-IDENT[NAS]
a. ŋatur	*!		*
b. ŋatũr	*!	*	
c. ŋãtũr		**!	*
d. ☞ ŋãtur		*	**

(iv)   input vowels are nasal

/ŋãtũr/		*NV$_{ORAL}$	*V$_{NAS}$	IO-IDENT[NAS]
a.	ŋatur	*!		**
b.	ŋatũr	*!	*	*
c.	ŋãtũr		**!	
d. ☞	ŋãtur		*	*

The tableaux evaluate the same candidate set, and each tableau correctly selects optimal candidate (d). Candidates (a) and (b) have an oral vowel in a nasal context, and are eliminated by top-ranked *NV$_{ORAL}$. In candidate (c) both vowels are nasal, incurring gratuitous and fatal violation of *V$_{NAS}$. Optimal (d) violates *V$_{NAS}$ minimally, just enough to satisfy higher-ranked *NV$_{ORAL}$.

The four tableaux in (47) differ only in the input vowels assumed. Because output-based OT cannot require vowels to be either oral or nasal in input forms, the grammar has to get the right result from any possible input vowel. It follows that IO-IDENT[NAS] is low-ranking. Comparison of candidates (c) and (d) in tableau (iii) demonstrates the ranking *V$_{NAS}$ ≫ IO-IDENT[NAS]. With this particular input, suboptimal (c) fares better on faithfulness than the optimal form does, but incurs worse violation of dominant *V$_{NAS}$.

So far, I have shown that predictable nasal harmony in Sundanese is produced by the interaction of markedness constraints, which crucially rank above an IO-Faith requirement.

(48)   Summary Ranking
         *NV$_{ORAL}$ ≫ *V$_{NAS}$ ≫ IO-IDENT[NAS]

With this basic ranking established, I turn now to the forms that disobey the canonical pattern, and show how paradigmatic identity constraints force over-application of nasalization in infixed plurals. Nasal vowels appear in oral contexts – that is, *V$_{NAS}$ is violated even though *NV$_{ORAL}$ is not relevant – when *V$_{NAS}$ violation increases phonological identity of morphologically related words.

3.3   Overapplication of nasal spread in infixed plurals

Infixed plural words do not conform to the canonical nasal harmony pattern. Instead, they surface with nasal vowels in oral context.[45]

(49)   Overapplication of Nasal Spread

Singular	*Plural*	
ɲĩar	ɲ-ãl-ĩar	'seek'
ɲãũr	ɲ-ãl-ãũr	'say'
mãhãl	m-ãr-ãhãl	'expensive'
ɲãʔãtkɨn	ɲ-ãr-ãʔãtkɨn	'dry'

The infixed plural words mimic nasality in their unaffixed bases. Nasal vowels correspond to nasal vowels, even though nasalization is phonologically conditioned only in the base. This overapplication of nasalization preserves identity in plural paradigms.

(50)   *OO-Identity*
                  [ɲĩãr]   →   [ɲ-ãl-ĩãr]
   IO-Faith   ↑   ↑   *IO-Faith*
                  /ɲiar/   /ar + ɲiar/

The plural in (49) is faithful to a surface property of its base, the nasal vowel allophones. Since OT cannot make stipulations about input vowels, they must be allowed to be rich in noncontrastive nasality. The distribution of allophones is reliably determined only in surface representations, where it is enforced by output constraints. If nasal vowels are reliably present only in the output [ɲĩãr], and the related infixed word is faithful to those nasal vowels, then the responsible constraints must compare two surface words. Paradigmatic identity is enforced by constraints on an output–output relation, the OO-Identity constraints.

IO-Faith and OO-Identity are distinct sets of constraints that can be ranked separately in the Sundanese grammar. The IO-Faith constraint on nasality is low-ranking; tableau (47) established that $*V_{NAS} \gg$ IO-IDENT[NAS]. The overapplication pattern in plurals shows that OO-IDENT[NAS] is ranked higher; in (49–50), achieving identity of corresponding vowels takes precedence over avoiding nasal vowels: OO-IDENT[NAS] $\gg *V_{NAS}$. Putting this all together gives the ranking in (51). Two faithfulness constraints, governing different types of relations, coexist in the nasalization hierarchy.

(51)   Overapplication
       $*NV_{ORAL}$, OO-IDENT[NAS] $\gg *V_{NAS} \gg$ IO-IDENT[NAS]

No ranking between $*NV_{ORAL}$ and OO-IDENT[NAS] can be established on the basis of the plural paradigms. With respect to these data, $*NV_{ORAL}$ and the OO-Identity constraint do not conflict – optimal overapplication satisfies both constraints, as shown in (52).

Paradigms are evaluated as units, in parallel, against ranked recursions of the language-particular hierarchy. To simplify the discussion and focus in on the relevant interaction, the candidate paradigms in tableau (52) vary in a limited way: root vowels are either both oral or both nasal in a given word, and the infix's vowel is always nasalized (as required by undominated $*NV_{ORAL}$). Also, the inputs shown have nasal vowels (irrelevantly, since IO-IDENT[NAS] is bottom-ranked). Four competitive candidate paradigms are listed above the tableau.

(52)   Overapplication of Nasal Spread
       $*NV_{ORAL}$, OO-IDENT[NAS] $\gg *V_{NAS} \gg$ IO-IDENT[NAS]
       candidate (a)   ɲiar ≈ ɲ-ãl-iar
       candidate (b)   ɲiar ≈ ɲ-ãl-ĩãr
       candidate (c)   ɲĩãr ≈ ɲ-ãl-iar
☞   candidate (d)   ɲĩãr ≈ ɲ-ãl-ĩãr

Recursion (A)

/ɲĩãr/		*NV$_{ORAL}$	OO-Id[NAS]	*V$_{NAS}$	IO-Id[NAS]	≫
a.	ɲiar	*!			**	
b.	ɲiar	*!			**	
c.	ɲĩãr			**		
d. ☞	ɲĩãr			**		

Recursion (B)

/ãl + ɲĩãr/		*NV$_{ORAL}$	OO-Id[NAS]	*V$_{NAS}$	IO-Id[NAS]
a′.	ɲ-ãl-iar			*	**
b′.	ɲ-ãl-ĩãr		**	***	
c′.	ɲ-ãl-iar		**!	*	**
d′. ☞	ɲ-ãl-ĩãr			***	

Candidates are represented discontinously across the recursive tableau, and the base is evaluated against the dominant recursion of constraints. In (52), candidates (a) and (b) are eliminated by the upper recursion of the hierarchy, by the *NV$_{ORAL}$ violation incurred by the base [ɲiar]. Because other candidates have a more harmonic base, and better satisfy constraints in the dominant recursion, paradigms (a–b) are out of the running. In paradigm (c), nasal harmony applies normally, and all and only post-nasal vowels are nasalized, but corresponding vowels are in different environments, so (c) fatally violates the OO-Identity constraint. Candidate (d) fares worse on *V$_{NAS}$ than (c) does, but OO-IDENT[NAS] is dominant, and (d) is the optimal paradigm.

Recursive evaluation of paradigms plays no crucial role in overapplication patterns, because overapplication is the most harmonic way to satisfy paradigmatic identity constraints. In (52), optimal overapplication violates only *V$_{NAS}$, and all other candidates violate one of the higher-ranked constraints. In particular, the identity-satisfying candidate (52a), which underapplies nasalization in the base, is ruled out by its *NV$_{ORAL}$ violation, rather than by the recursive evaluation mechanism. As discussed in §2, the local evaluation of each paradigm member in a recursive system is essential when underapplication is optimal. It also plays a crucial role in the evaluation of certain paradigms in Sundanese, as set out shortly below.

To summarize, the allophonic oral/nasal alternation in vowels overapplies in infixed plurals under the force of an OO-Identity constraint. It is more harmonic to achieve identity of corresponding vowels in related words than to avoid marked nasality. The overapplication hierarchy is repeated in (53).

(53)   Overapplication
$$*NV_{ORAL}, \text{OO-IDENT[NAS]} \gg *V_{NAS} \gg \text{IO-IDENT[NAS]}$$

Two faithfulness constraints coexist in the ranking. IO-Faith is bottom-ranked, and the canonical nasalization pattern is produced from rich inputs by a dominant markedness ranking $*NV_{ORAL} \gg *V_{NAS}$. OO-Identity is higher-ranking, and can force markedness violations. Nasal vowels are forced to appear in non-nasal context, violating $*V_{NAS}$, if nasalization satisfies the dominant OO-Identity constraint.

A ranking between OO-IDENT[NAS] and $*NV_{ORAL}$ can be established by looking at nasality in other Sundanese words. In particular, paradigms produced by affixes that contain nasal consonants show that the top-ranked markedness constraint, $*NV_{ORAL}$, can force violation of the OO-Identity constraint. [. . .]

Notes

[. . .]

22   In compounding, the derived word has two output bases. Compounding is not analyzed in this thesis, but see Allen (1975) on Welsh, Mohanan (1982, 1986) on Malyalam and Duanmu (1995) on Chinese for examples of transderivational identity effects in compounding.

23   Cases in which an obligatorily-inflected word functions as the base of an OO-correspondence relation are discussed in §4.2 and §6.3 [both omitted here – Ed.]. The base's inflectional morphology is not present in the derived word (in either its input string or its output form), but it can nevertheless affect the derived word's surface phonology by altering neighboring stem segments in the base.

24   Compare this result with the proposal in Kiparsky (1982a) that the minimal domain of rule application is the *lexeme*, a category that includes both full words and a special subset of bound roots – those that can be made into full words by obligatory inflection.

25   Although the phonology of embedded constituents is not available to a multiply-affixed word, the complete morphological structure is accessible from the input string. This makes it possible to violate bracket erasure with respect to morphological information, as when an affix selects for a base that contains another specific affix (see Williams 1981; Fabb 1988; Hammond 1991; among others).

[. . .]

27   According to Kahn, the misapplication effect described here occurs in English dialects that maintain a *Mary* ≈ *marry* ≈ *merry* distinction.

28   This constraint is just a brute-force convenience. A more refined understanding of *a/æ* neutralization would probably relate it to the dorsality of English bunched *r*.

29   The underlying form of the base *Larry* must have a front *æ* because backness is contrastive before heterosyllabic *r* (cf. *sorry*). I assume that low vowels contrast in backness in the general case, which means that IO-IDENT[BK] is dominated only by context-sensitive constraints like $*ær]_\sigma$. All other conflicting markedness constraints, in particular context-free bans on each vowel or feature combination ($*æ$, or $*a$), rank lower than IO-Faith. Thus, it is IO-IDENT[BK] that requires a front vowel in *Larry*, as shown in (16).

30   The procedural terminology over- and underapplication gets in the way here. I do not claim that there is a productive [æ]-to-[a] process in English. Rather, a contrast between *a* and *æ*, observed in open syllables, is neutralized in syllables that are closed by *r*, as demanded by $*ær]_\sigma$. While it is accurate to say that the $*ær]_\sigma$ constraint underapplies in the diminutive *L[æ]r*, in that it has no effect in that word, it is difficult to characterize the overapplication candidate other than by reference to an *æ/a* alternation.

31 The base of an OO-correspondence relation can show non-canonical phonology if it is itself morphologically complex, and its deviant features increase identity with its output base.

[. . .]

42 The plural morpheme alternates predictably between *al* and *ar* under the influence of liquids in the root (Robins 1957; Cohn 1992; Holton 1995). It has the same distribution as other Austronesian VC prefixes (e.g., Tagalog *um*), infixing after a root-initial consonant. Infixation optimizes syllable structure (Anderson 1972), and is forced by the constraint against coda consonants NoCoda ranked above the EdgeMost or Align constraint that requires prefixes to be leftmost in the word (Prince & Smolensky 1993; McCarthy & Prince 1993a, b).

43 A serious theory of nasal harmony would require a typological study that is not within the scope of this work. The $*NV_{ORAL}$ constraint, which is borrowed from McCarthy & Prince (1995), is only a stand-in for whatever constraint or set of constraints is responsible for harmony in post-nasal context.

44 The apparent universality of the markedness ranking in (44) suggests that there is no constraint against oral vowels, so that $*V_{NAS}$ alone determines the relative markedness of oral and nasal vowels.

45 Robins (1957) reports that the vowel immediately following the plural infix is not nasal, although subsequent vowels are, as in [m-ār-ahāl] or [ɲ-āl-iār]. However, in nasal airflow studies Cohn (1990) found orality only in vowels that immediately follow the trilled *ar* allomorph; vowels that follow the *al* alternant are nasalized. Orality after *ar* could be phonological – Cohn formulates a rule of denasalization, which spreads a [−nasal] feature from the trill onto the immediately following vowel. Cohn's denasalization rule could be recast in OT as a high-ranking constraint forbidding a nasal vowel after a trill. Alternatively, orality in vowels after *ar* could be a phonetic effect – lack of nasality in the vowel might reflect the lag time in lowering the velum after production of the trill. I leave this question aside, and abstract away from vocalic orality after the *ar* allomorph. This simplification of the data is irrelevant, because the second root vowel in [m-ār-ahāl] is still forced to be nasal by the high-ranking paradigmatic identity requirement.

References

Allen, Margaret. 1975. Vowel mutation and word stress in Welsh. *Linguistic Inquiry* 6: 181–201.

Anderson, Stephen. 1972. On nasalization in Sundanese. *Linguistic Inquiry* 3: 253–68.

Anderson, Stephen. 1992. *A-morphous Morphology*. Cambridge: Cambridge University Press.

Borowsky, Toni. 1986. *Topics in the Lexical Phonology of English*. Doctoral dissertation, University of Massachusetts, Amherst.

Borowsky, Toni. 1993. On the word level. In S. Hargus and E. Kaisse (eds.). *Phonetics and Phonology 4: Studies in Lexical Phonology*, 199–234. New York: Academic Press.

Chomsky, Noam and Morris Halle. 1968. *The Sound Pattern of English*. New York: Harper and Row.

Cohn, Abigail. 1990. *Phonetic and Phonological Rules of Nasalization*. Doctoral dissertation, University of California, Los Angeles [UCLA Working Papers in Phonetics 76].

Cohn, Abigail. 1992. The consequences of dissimilation in Sundanese. *Phonology* 9: 199–220.

Duanmu, San. 1995. Alignment and the cycle are different. Talk presented at the Tilburg Conference on the Derivational Residue in Phonology, Tilburg University. ▶

Fabb, Nigel. 1988. English suffixation is constrained only by selectional restrictions. *Natural Language and Linguistic Theory* 6: 527–39.

Hammond, Michael. 1991. Morphemic circumscription. In G. Booij and J. van Marle (eds.). *Yearbook of Morphology*, 195–210. Dordrecht: Kluwer.

Hart, George. 1981. Nasality and the organization of autosegmental phonology. Bloomington: Indiana University Linguistics Club.

Hockett, Charles. 1954. Problems of morphemic analysis. *Language* 23: 321–43.

Holton, David. 1995. Assimilation and dissimilation of Sundanese liquids. In J. Beckman, L. Walsh-Dickey and S. Urbanczyk (eds.). *University of Massachusetts Occasional Papers in Linguistics: Papers in Optimality Theory*, 167–80. Amherst: GLSA.

Hulst, Harry van der and Norval Smith. 1984. Prosodic domains and opaque segments in autosegmental theory. In H. van der Hulst and N. Smith (eds.). *The Structure of Phonological Representations*, vol. 2, 311–36. Dordrecht: Foris.

Inkelas, Sharon. 1994. Exceptional stress-attracting suffixes in Turkish: Representations versus the grammar. MS, University of California, Berkeley. ▶

Itô, Junko and R. Armin Mester. 1995. The core-periphery structure of the lexicon and constraints on reranking. In J. Beckman, L. Walsh-Dickey and S. Urbanczyk (eds.). *University of Massachusetts Occasional Papers in Linguistics: Papers in Optimality Theory*, 181–209. Amherst: GLSA.

Kahn, Daniel. 1976 [1980]. *Syllable-Based Generalizations in English Phonology*. Doctoral dissertation, MIT [New York: Garland].

Kenstowicz, Michael. 1995. Cyclic vs. non-cyclic constraint evaluation. *Phonology* 12.

Kiparsky, Paul. 1982a. Lexical morphology and phonology. In I.-S. Yang (ed.). *Linguistics in the Morning Calm*, vol. 2, 3–91. Seoul: Hanshin.

Kiparsky, Paul. 1982b. From Cyclic Phonology to Lexical Phonology. In H. van der Hulst and N. Smith (eds.). *The Structure of Phonological Representations*, vol. 1, 131–75. Dordrecht: Foris.

Kiparsky, Paul. 1985. Some consequences of Lexical Phonology. *Phonology* 2: 85–138.

Kiparsky, Paul. 1997. Output–output constraints vs. cyclicity. Handout from LSA Summer Institute, Cornell University.

Lieber, Rochelle. 1980. *On the Organization of the Lexicon*. Doctoral dissertation, MIT.

Bloomington: Indiana University Linguistics Club.

McCarthy, John and Alan Prince. 1993a. Prosodic Morphology I: Constraint interaction and satisfaction. MS, University of Massachusetts, Amherst and Rutgers University. Rutgers Center for Cognitive Science (RuCCs) technical report 3. ▶

McCarthy, John and Alan Prince. 1993b. Generalized alignment. In G. Booij and J. van Marle (eds.). *Yearbook of Morphology*, 79–153. Dordrecht: Kluwer. ◀

McCarthy, John and Alan Prince. 1994. An overview of prosodic morphology. Lectures presented at the OTS/HIL Workshop on Prosodic Morphology, University of Utrecht. ▶

McCarthy, John and Alan Prince. 1995. Faithfulness and reduplicative identity. In J. Beckman, L. Walsh-Dickey and S. Urbanczyk (eds.). *University of Massachusetts Occasional Papers in Linguistics: Papers in Optimality Theory*, 249–384. Amherst: GLSA. ◀

Mohanan, K. P. 1982. *Lexical Phonology*. Doctoral dissertation, MIT.

Mohanan, K. P. 1986. *The Theory of Lexical Phonology*. Dordrecht: Reidel.

Pesetsky, David. 1979. Russian morphology and lexical theory. MS, MIT.

Prince, Alan and Paul Smolensky. 1993. Optimality Theory: Constraint interaction in generative grammar. MS, Rutgers University and University of Colorado, Boulder. Rutgers Center for Cognitive Science (RuCCs) technical report 2. ◀

Robins, R. H. 1957. Vowel nasality in Sundanese. *Studies in Linguistic Analysis; Special Volume of the Philological Society*, 87–103. Reprinted in *Diversions of Bloomsbury, Selected Writings in Linguistics*, Amsterdam: North-Holland, 1970.

Smolensky, Paul. 1993. Harmony, markedness, and phonological activity. Talk presented at ROW I. Rutgers University. ▶

Stevens, Alan M. 1977. On local ordering in Sundanese. *Linguistic Inquiry* 8: 155–62.

Williams, Edwin. 1981. On the notions "lexically related" and "head of a word". *Linguistic Inquiry* 12: 245–74.

Study and Research Questions

1   By positing appropriate stress constraints, including OO-IDENT, work out an analysis of the "origin/original/originality" relation in (12).
2   In the Boston-area dialect spoken by the editor of this book, coda [ɹ] is not pronounced: 'Park your car in Harvard yard" [pɑk jə kɑɹ ɪn hɑvəd yɑd]. Yet he pronounces the shortened form of the name Barry [bæɹij] as Bar' [bæɹ] Mary [mejɹij] as Mar' [mejɹ], and Jerry [ʤɛɹij] as Jer' [ʤɛɹ]. Explain.
3   Work out the analysis sketched in note 45. How convincing is it?
4   Consult a phonology textbook or other source for an example of cyclic or stratal ordering of phonological rules, and reanalyze it in OO faithfulness terms.

Chapter 23 | Jerzy Rubach

Backness Switch in Russian

Editor's Note

Rule-based phonology uses rule ordering as a way of capturing generalizations that are not surface-true: a rule states a generalization that is true at the derivational instant when it applies, but subsequent rules can obscure that rule's effects. Rule ordering is also used to express precedence relations among rules: except for the Elsewhere Condition (Kiparsky 1973a), the last rule to apply takes precedence, in the sense that it is assured of stating a truer generalization.

OT treats surface-trueness and precedence very differently. In OT, if a generalization is not surface-true, then this is usually an indication that the constraint expressing that generalization is crucially dominated. And if one constraint takes precedence over another, then the first dominates the second. Since constraint interaction can reproduce these effects of rule ordering, so the reasoning goes, then maybe it can reproduce all of the effects of rule ordering (McCarthy 2002: 138–42).

This reasoning is the basis for the strong parallelism hypothesis in OT: the entire phonology is done in one pass through EVAL, mapping directly from the input to the surface form. Many analysts, though, have opted for a weaker parallelism hypothesis: the phonology of a language involves several passes through EVAL. (See the Study and Research Questions for references.) The idea is that several OT grammars, each of them parallel in itself, are arranged serially like the strata or levels of the theory of Lexical Phonology. This chapter argues for just such a model.

Russian exhibits several different types of palatalisation. These are exemplified in (1), where we look at voiceless stops and affricates.

(1)   a.   *Velar Palatalisation*[1] (velars change into postalveolars): $k \rightarrow č$
ruk+a 'hand (FEM NOM SG)' – ruč+išč+a (AUG NOM SG), ruč+en'k+a (DIM NOM SG)

Excerpt from:
Rubach, Jerzy (2000) Backness switch in Russian. *Phonology* 17: 39–64.

b. *Affricate Palatalisation* (affricates become postalveolar): *ts* → *č*
   konets 'end' – konč+i+t' 'to finish'
   otets 'father' – otč+estv+o 'patronymic'

c. *Iotation* (many disparate changes of consonants):[2] *t* → *č*
   šut 'joker' – šuč+u 'I joke'

d. *Surface Palatalisation* (consonants become [−back, +high]): *t* → *t'*
   xvost 'tail' – xvost+ik [t'] (DIM), xvost+e [t'] (LOC SG)
   brat 'brother' – brat+j+a [t'] 'brothers (COLL)'

A coherent analysis of these disparate effects is a formidable task, but one process seems to be easy: Surface Palatalisation is a straightforward spreading change. This change is particularly simple in the context of *i* and *j* since not only the feature [−back] but also the feature [+high] is spread from the triggering context onto the input consonant. In the following, I will restrict the scope of analysis to this simple case. That is, I will look at Surface Palatalisation applying in the context of *i* and *j*. I will demonstrate that standard Optimality Theory (henceforth OT: Prince & Smolensky 1993, McCarthy & Prince 1995), with its insistence on parallel evaluation, cannot offer an adequate analysis of Surface Palatalisation. I will suggest that standard OT needs to be modified and to admit the possibility of a level distinction (a derivational step) in the evaluation of output forms.[3]

This paper is organised as follows. §1 introduces the basic generalisations. It looks at the interaction between consonants and high vowels, showing that, on the one hand, /i/ affects consonants (Palatalisation: C → C') and, on the other hand, consonants affect /i/ and /ɨ/ (Retraction: /i/ → /ɨ/ and Fronting: /ɨ/ → /i/, respectively). §2 presents an OT analysis of Palatalisation, Retraction and Fronting, arguing that these disparate processes are in fact a single generalisation. The generalisation is that consonants and vowels must agree in backness, so either consonants and vowels are made [−back] (Palatalisation and Fronting, respectively) or vowels are made [+back] (Retraction). I call these two strategies a backness switch, and demonstrate that, contrary to appearances, they can be reconciled if we adopt the insight of Lexical Phonology that lexical and postlexical operations may have different effects due to a change of focus, which is expressed formally by the reordering of generalisations (Kiparsky 1982, Halle & Mohanan 1985, Booij & Rubach 1987). In the instance at hand, the focus is on [−back] at the lexical level and on [+back] at the postlexical level. The analysis of backness switch in §2 is then contrasted with the OT handling of the same or similar problems in the past literature (§3). It is shown that the earlier analysis in terms of syllable domains is descriptively incorrect and must be rejected. A further claim is that the problem can be solved neither by Output–Output Theory nor by Sympathy Theory. §4 refines the analysis by introducing Palatalisation-j, a generalisation that has never been observed in the generative literature on Russian to date (§4.1), and by looking at Hardening (§4.2), which strengthens the conclusions of §2. §5 is a summary of the main results. We begin with the presentation of the facts and the basic generalisations in the section that follows below. [§§3–5 are not reprinted here. – Ed.]

I   Basic Generalisations

Russian is a typical language in the sense that it draws a distinction between [−back] and [+back] vowels, which include [i e] and [ɨ u o a], respectively. Less typical is the fact that backness is also a parameter for consonants, which are either [−back] (palatalised) or [+back] (velarised). This means that there are no 'plain' consonants. That is, every consonant is articulated with one of the following two tongue-body positions: forward movement and raising towards the hard palate (palatalisation) or backward movement and raising towards the velum (velarisation). These are the so-called secondary articulation effects, because the gesture performed by the tongue body is simultaneous with but independent of the primary gesture that is responsible for determining the place of articulation. For example, the primary gesture for *m* is the closure of the lips, hence the place of articulation is bilabial. The secondary gesture is executed by the tongue body, which is raised and moved forwards or backwards, with the consequence being that we have either [m'] (palatalised bilabial nasal) or [mˠ] (velarised bilabial nasal), where the apostrophe means palatalisation and the superscript [ˠ] denotes velarisation.

The palatalised–velarised distinction, which is characterised in traditional grammars as a distinction between soft and hard consonants, has been known about Russian for more than a hundred years (Sweet 1879, Broch 1911, Halle 1959). The soft series includes [p' b' m' f' v' t' d' s' z' r' l' n' č' k' g' x']. All other consonants are hard: [pˠ bˠ mˠ fˠ vˠ tˠ dˠ sˠ zˠ tsˠ rˠ nˠ lˠ šˠ žˠ kˠ gˠ xˠ].[4] It is the occurrence of [±back] in consonants and vowels that is the source of the three basic generalisations: Palatalisation, Fronting and Retraction. These generalisations are illustrated below by looking at a sample of representative alternations.

Front vowels and [j] trigger Palatalisation.

(2)   *Palatalisation*

otvet[6] [tˠ] 'answer'	otvet+i+t' [t'] 'to answer'
voz [zˠ] 'cart'	voz+i+t' [z'] 'carry'
golos [sˠ] 'voice'	golos+in+a [s'] (DIM)
stol [lˠ] 'table'	stol+ik [l'] (DIM)
dub [bˠ] 'oak'	dub+ik [b'] (DIM)
sestr+a [rˠ] 'sister'	sestr+ic+a [r'] (DIM)
žen+a [nˠ] 'wife'	žen+i+t' [n'] 'marry'
nog+a [gˠ] 'leg'	dvu+nog+ij [g'] 'two legged'
tix [xˠ] 'silent'	tix+ij [x'] 'silent (INFL)'
kolos [sˠ] 'ear of corn'	kolos+j+a [s'] 'ears of corn (COLL)'
ofitser [rˠ] 'officer'	ofitser+j+o [r'] 'officers (PEJOR)'
bab+a [bˠ] 'woman' (PEJOR)	bab+j+o [b'] 'women (COLL)'

Schematically, the generalisation can be stated as follows:

(3)   *Palatalisation*

$$C \rightarrow \begin{bmatrix} C \\ -back \end{bmatrix} / \underline{\quad} i/j$$

The data in (4) below make two points. First, an underlying //i//[8] surfaces as [ɨ] after a hard consonant (4a). Second, if the consonant is soft, the //i// fronts to [i] (4b). Our example is the nominative plural ending //i//.[9]

(4) NOM SG NOM PL

   a. *Hard C+//i//*

šut	šut+y [tᵛɨ]	'joker'
nos	nos+y [sᵛɨ]	'nose'
zub	zub+y [bᵛɨ]	'tooth'
stol	stol+y [lᵛɨ]	'table'
zakon	zakon+y [nᵛɨ]	'law'

   b. *Soft C+//i//*

gost'	gost+i [t'i]	'guest'
los'	los+i [s'i]	'moose'
golub'	golub+i [b'i]	'pigeon'
nol'	nol+i [l'i]	'zero'
slovar'	slovar+i [r'i]	'dictionary'

The standard analysis is to assume that the underlying //i// exemplified in (4a) is fronted to [i] after a soft consonant.

(5) *Fronting*

$$ɨ \rightarrow i \ / \begin{bmatrix} C \\ -\text{back} \end{bmatrix} —$$

Finally, //i// is retracted to [ɨ] after a hard consonant. This happens at the juncture between the prefix and the stem (6a), and between two words which may (6b) but need not (6c) constitute a clitic phrase, that is, a phrase involving a preposition (Avanesov 1968).

(6) *Retraction*
   a. iskat' 'look for' – *perfective forms*: raz+yskat'[11] [zᵛɨ], ob+yskat' [bᵛɨ], ot+yskat' [tᵛɨ], s+yskat' [sᵛɨ], pod+yskat' [dᵛɨ], iz+yskat' [zᵛɨ]
      igrat' 'play' – *perfective forms*: s+ygrat' [sᵛɨ], raz+ygrat' [zᵛɨ], ot+ygrats'a [tᵛɨ], ob+ygrat' [bᵛɨ], pod+ygrat' [dᵛɨ]

   b. ot instituta [tᵛ ɨ] 'from the institute', k invalidu [kᵛ ɨ] 'to the invalid', pod izboj [dᵛ ɨ] 'under the room', s igloj [sᵛ ɨ] 'with the needle'

   c. brat id'ot [tᵛ ɨ] 'my brother is going', mal'čik igrajet [kᵛ ɨ] 'a boy is playing', dom iskustva [mᵛ ɨ] 'art gallery', golos Ivana [sᵛ ɨ] 'Ivan's voice'

Needless to say, Retraction does not occur after a soft consonant. Such consonants exist independently of Palatalisation, that is, they are palatalised in the underlying representation since, for example, they occur word-finally, as in (7).

(7) gost'   'guest'   gost' iz Moskvy [t' i]   'a guest from Moscow'
     bukvar'   'dictionary'   bukvar' Ivana [r' i]   'Ivan's dictionary'
     rol'   'role'   rol' instituta [l' i]   'the role of the institute'
     los'   'moose'   los' id'ot [s' i]   'the moose is going'

The alternations in (6) are standardly analysed as instances of Retraction, which is motivated by the fact that the [i] variants occur in isolation: *iskat'* 'look for', *institut* 'institute', *Ivan* 'Ivan', *iz* 'from' and so forth. Since consonants are velarised in Russian, Retraction is no less of an assimilation than Fronting (5) is.

(8) *Retraction*

$$ \dot{\text{i}} \rightarrow \text{i} \, / \begin{bmatrix} \text{C} \\ +\text{back} \end{bmatrix} — $$

The coexistence of Palatalisation, Fronting and Retraction presents quite a challenge for a phonological analysis. This is illustrated, among other things, by the phrase *ot instituta* 'from the institute', which is standardly analysed as derivable from the underlying representation //ot^{v}in^{v}s^{v}t^{v}it^{v}ut^{v}a//.[12] The first occurrence of //t^{v} i// is subject to Retraction, while the second occurrence of //t^{v}i// undergoes Palatalisation: [ot^{v}in^{v}s^{v}t'it^{v}ut^{v}a]. How can these facts be analysed in Optimality Theory? It is this question that we address in the next section.

2   OT Analysis

We begin with a summary of various consonant–vowel configurations and the changes that these configurations induce. Taking the voiceless dental stop as an example, we obtain the following schema. (The glide /j/ is discussed later.)

(9) a.   t^{v}i → t'i   examples in (2)
     b.   t'ɨ → t'i   examples in (4b)
     c.   t^{v}ɨ → t^{v}ɨ (*no change*)   examples in (4a)
     d.   t^{v}i → t^{v}ɨ   examples in (6)
     e.   t'i → t'i (*no change*)   examples in (7)

An overarching generalisation is that consonants and vowels agree in backness. An OT treatment of this generalisation is due to Zubritskaya (1995), who suggests the following constraint:

(10)   CV LINK: In CV all features linked to a vowel must also be linked to a consonant.

Now, with the credit having been given, in what follows I will depart in significant ways from Zubritskaya's analysis. I will suggest an alternative analysis, which crucially bears on the modification of the OT assumption about parallel derivation. In §3, I will show that Zubritskaya's account is in fact incorrect.

The agreement of consonants and vowels in backness cannot be plausibly accounted for in terms of a single constraint. Rather, we have a set of constraints which differ in scope, much as classical rules differ in their degree of generality. Thus there is a difference between the backness agreement of consonants and high vowels and the backness agreement of consonants and mid vowels. Viewed from the perspective of Palatalisation, this difference manifests itself as an asymmetry in the ability of front vowels to palatalise consonants. The implicational generalisation is that a language that palatalises consonants before mid vowels will also palatalise consonants before high vowels, but the reverse is not true (see Chen 1973). The matter is highly complicated and cannot be adequately discussed here, so let us merely point to two examples and add some subtlety to the generalisation just stated.

In Ukrainian, consonants are palatalised before [i] but not before [e] (Bilodid 1969). Similarly, Polish Surface Palatalisation, a postlexical generalisation, affects consonants before *i* and *j* but not before *e* (Rubach 1984).

(11) a. *Ukrainian*
          syn [n] 'son' (NOM SG) – syn+iv [n'] (GEN PL) *vs.* syn+e [n] (VOC SG)

      b. *Polish*
          głos Ireny [s' i] 'Irene's voice', głos Janka [s' j] 'John's voice' *vs.*
          głos Ewy [s e] 'Eve's voice'

In fact, Russian is a language that palatalises consonants before high vowels and glides (the data in (2)) as well as before the mid vowel *e*. The latter environment has crept surreptitiously into some of our earlier examples. For instance, in *otvetit'* 'answer', we have palatalisation not only on the penultimate *t* but also on the *v*: [at^{y}v'et'it']. Similarly, the *s* is palatalised not only in *golos+in+a* 'voice (DIM)' but also in *golos+e* 'voice (LOG SG)'. There is a distinction, however. While Palatalisation may have exceptions (Avanesov 1968, Holden 1976), my inspection of the data shows that all exceptions occur only in the environment of *e* and none are found in the environment of *i*. This is best illustrated by words which have both *i* and *e*. The examples in (12), from Avanesov (1968), have been confirmed by my Russian consultants.

(12) tenisist   'tennis player'   [t^{y}en'is'is^{y}t^y]
      xrizantema   'chrysanthemum'   [x^{y}r'iz^{y}an^{y}t^{y}em^{y}a]
      sintetika   'acrylic material'   [s'in^{y}t^{y}et'ik^{y}a]

We conclude that the backness agreement between consonants and high vowels is different from the backness agreement between consonants and mid vowels. In what follows, we limit our discussion to consonants followed by high vowels. The relevant constraint is PALATALISATION-i:[14]

(13) PALATALISATION-i (PAL-i)
      A consonant and a following high vowel agree in backness.

In terms of the melodic tier, PAL-i looks at the Root nodes and thus does not distinguish between real vowels (nuclear Root nodes, here *i*) and glides (Root nodes occurring in syllable margins, here *j*), which is exactly what is required by the data in (2).

Returning to the schema in (9), we are now in a position to account for the changes in (9a–c). PAL-i is the only new constraint. All other constraints are the familiar input–output faithfulness constraints of McCarthy & Prince (1995) and the inventory markedness constraints of Prince & Smolensky (1993). The constraints relevant at this stage are summarised in (14).

(14) a. IDENT-C$_{[+back]}$
          Input [+back] on consonants must be preserved as output [+back] on consonants.

   b. IDENT-C$_{[-back]}$
       Input [−back] on consonants must be preserved as output [−back] on consonants.

   c. IDENT-V$_{[+back]}$
       Input [+back] on vowels must be preserved as output [+back] on vowels.

   d. *ü: don't be a high front rounded vowel.
   e. *ɨ: don't be a high back unrounded vowel.
   f. *i: don't be a high front unrounded vowel.

Palatalisation, //tʸ// → [t'], is a violation of (14a) because a hard consonant is turned into a soft consonant. Since this is the desired effect, PAL-i must outrank IDENT-C$_{[+back]}$. Furthermore, PAL-i in //tʸi// → [t'i] strings should not be satisfied by retracting the vowel: *//tʸi// → [tʸɨ]. This follows from the ranking *ɨ ≫ *i, which is expected, because [i] is universally a less marked segment than [ɨ].[15] We summarise this reasoning in (15).

(15)

//tʸ+i//	PAL-i	*ɨ	*i	ID-C$_{[+bk]}$
☞ a. t'+i			*	*
b. tʸ+ɨ		*!		
c. tʸ+i	*!		*	

The surfacing of //tʸɨ// as [tʸɨ] shows that [ɨ] is preferred to [i] when it comes from the underlying //ɨ//. This is a straightforward instance of faithfulness that is enforced by the high ranking of IDENT-V$_{[+back]}$.

(16)

//tʸ+ɨ//	PAL-i	ID-V$_{[+bk]}$	*ɨ	*i	ID-C$_{[+bk]}$
☞ a. tʸ+ɨ			*		
b. t'+i		*!		*	*
c. tʸ+i	*!	*		*	

The fronting of //t'ɨ// to [t'i] in (9b) shows that underlying soft consonants are never sacrificed in order to obey the [+back] faithfulness on vowels. This is guaranteed by IDENT-C$_{[-back]}$.

(17)

//t'+ɨ//	ID-C$_{[-bk]}$	PAL-i	ID-V$_{[+bk]}$	*ɨ	*i	ID-C$_{[+bk]}$
☞ a. t'+i			*		*	
b. t^ɣ+ɨ	*!			*		
c. t^ɣ+ɨ		*!		*		

The fronting effect shown in (17) should not extend to the rounded vowel *u* because *put'+u*, the accusative singular of *put'* //p^{ɣ}ut'// 'journey', should not surface as *[p^{ɣ}ut'+ü], with the front rounded vowel [ü]. This is easily prevented by assuming that *ü is an undominated constraint.

Finally, for completeness, we look at one further configuration: an underlying soft consonant followed by *i*, as in *put' is Moskvy* 'a journey from Moscow'.[18]

(18)

//t'+i//	ID-C$_{[-bk]}$	PAL-i	ID-V$_{[+bk]}$	*ɨ	*i	ID-C$_{[+bk]}$
☞ a. t'+i					*	
b. t^ɣ+ɨ	*!			*		
c. t'+ɨ		*!		*		

The overall picture that has emerged from (15)–(18) is as follows. Underlying //t^ɣ+ɨ// and //t'+i// have fully faithfully optimal outputs because they are a perfect fit from the perspective of PAL-i: there is no disagreement in backness between the consonant and the vowel. Where such a disagreement occurs, that is, in //t^ɣ+i// and //t'+ɨ//, the resolution of the conflict is always in favour of [–back], regardless of whether this would impinge on the faithfulness of the consonant (//t^ɣ// → [t']) or the vowel (//ɨ// → [i]). This strategy is contradicted by (9d), //t^{ɣ}i// → [t^{ɣ}ɨ], exemplified in (6). How can this reversal be accounted for? The answer is simple if we permit a derivational step.

Observe that the strings analysed in (15)–(18) share a morphological property: they are all words. Let us therefore assume that words are analysed at level 1. Level 2 adds further structure: it looks not only at words (see §4.2 [omitted here – Ed.]) but also at clitic phrases and other combinations of words. That is, level 2 is much like the postlexical level in Lexical Phonology.[19] The distinction between levels 1 and 2, while grounded in morphology, has a beneficial effect for the understanding of phonology, because a reranking of constraints becomes possible. All that is required is a simple move: at level 2 IDENT-C$_{[+back]}$ is upgraded to the echelon of high-ranking constraints.[20] Specifically, it is ranked above *ɨ. The effect is that the retraction of the vowel rather than the palatalisation of the consonant becomes optimal. In (19) we look at the evaluation of *brat Ivana* 'Ivan's brother'. The outputs of level 1, here the unchanged /bˠrˠatˠ/ and /ivˠanˠa/, are now a phrase, and this phrase constitutes an input to level 2. That is, the phrase is an 'underlying representation' for level 2 evaluation: /bˠrˠatˠ ivˠanˠa/ → [bˠrˠatˠ ɨvˠanˠa].

(19)

level 2 /tˠ i/	ID-C$_{[-bk]}$	ID-C$_{[+bk]}$	PAL-i	ID-V$_{[+bk]}$	*ɨ	*i
☞ a. tˠ ɨ					*	
b. t' i	*!					*
c. tˠ i			*!			*

When a soft consonant and [i] become adjacent in a phrase at level 2, there is no incentive to alter representations, because PAL-i is satisfied. Consequently, /pˠut' ivˠanˠa/ *put' Ivana* 'Ivan's journey', is both the input and the optimal output. The evaluation is the same as the word-internal evaluation of //t'+i// shown in (18).[21]

An apparent complication arises with prefixes. Prefix-final consonants remain unpalatalised and trigger Retraction, for example, *raz+yskat'* 'look for (PERFECTIVE)' and *s+ygrat'* 'play (PERFECTIVE)':

(20)   rˠazˠ+isˠkˠat' → rˠazˠ+isˠkˠat'   (*not* *rˠaz'+isˠkˠat')
       sˠ+igˠrˠat'   → sˠ+igˠrˠat'   (*not* *s'+igˠrˠat')

However, prefix-internal consonants palatalise, for example, *pri+gotovit'* 'prepare': //pˠrˠi// → [pˠr'i]. This suggests that prefixes are in the purview of level 1 evaluation. How can we reconcile Palatalisation and Retraction in prefixes? The answer lies in further details of Russian phonology.

Prefixes which in the surface representation end in a hard consonant (hence those that cause Retraction) are derived from underlying representations that have a prefix-final back vowel. This is shown by alternations. For example, the prefixes *raz* and *s* of *raz+yskat'* and *s+ygrat'*, respectively, appear as *razo* and *so* in *razo+brat'* 'take apart' and *so+brat'* 'collect'. These vowels alternating with zero are called yers in Slavic phonology, and they are represented as floating segments, that is, as segments without a mora or an X-slot.[22] The underlying representations of *raz/razo* and *s/so* are therefore //rˠazˠO// and //sˠO//, respectively, where O denotes a floater (here the back yer *o*). Now the strategy of accounting for the absence of palatalisation is clear.[23] At level 1 the yer //O// is present in the output, so the prefix-final consonants are not adjacent to the vowel *i*: /rˠazˠO+isˠkˠat'/ and /sˠO+igˠrˠat'/. The result is that Palatalisation is blocked. At level 2 floaters are not permitted since this level is the final phonological output representation. Consequently, unvocalised yers are deleted and hence the prefix-final consonant is adjacent to the stem-initial vowel *i*.[24] With Retraction being the dominant strategy at level 2, the candidates [rˠaz'+isˠkˠat'] and [s'+igˠrˠat'] lose to the candidates [rˠazˠ+isˠkˠat'] and [sˠ+igˠrˠat'] in the same way as the candidate [t'i] loses to the candidate [tˠɨ] in tableau (19). Prefix-internally, as in *pri* of *pri+gotovit'* 'prepare', the optimal output of level 1 is [pᵞr'i], with a palatalised *r*. The string [pᵞr'i] does not violate PAL-i when it enters level 2, because [r'] and [i] agree in backness. The level 2 evaluation is then the same as that for //t'i// given in (18).

The behaviour of prefixes strengthens our argument for level distinction. The reason is that the pattern of Palatalisation *vs.* Retraction shown in prefixes requires an intermediate stage at which the underlying back yer //O// occurs in the output representation and thus blocks Palatalisation. At level 2 the yer is deleted but then Palatalisation has already lost force. Bill Idsardi points out to me that this analysis is further strengthened by the fact that the front yer //E// results in Palatalisation not only when //E// is vocalised as [e] but also when //E// cannot vocalise and deletes. For example, the dark *l* of *komsomol* [lᵞ] 'komsomol [youth organisation in the Soviet Union]' is palatalised to [l'] in the derived noun meaning 'member of komsomol', which is formed by adding //Ets'//.[25] Palatalisation is found not only in the nominative singular, where the yer is vocalised and surfaces as [e], but also in the inflected forms, where the yer does not vocalise: *komsomol+ets* [l'] (NOM SG) and *komsomol'+ts+a* [l'] (GEN SG). The occurrence of [l'] in *komsomol'+ts+a* (GEN SG) is unproblematic if yers are not deleted at level 1 since then the level 1 output representation still has the surface-covert front vowel that triggers Palatalisation: /kᵞomᵞsᵞomᵞol'+Ets'+a/. The yer //E//, like the yer //O// in *raz+yskat'* and *s+ygrat'* cited earlier, deletes at level 2 and we obtain the correct output form [kᵞomᵞsᵞomᵞol'+tsᵞ +a].[26]

In sum, the distinction between level 1 and level 2 gains additional support from the behaviour of the yers. This behaviour is of two types: back yers block Palatalisation (*raz+yskat'* and *s+ygrat'*), while front yers trigger it (*komsomol'+ts+a* (GEN SG)). These effects are understandable if we can access the representation at level 1 showing the structure prior to the surface representation in which the yers are not present.

Pulling together the facts analysed in this section, we conclude that the conflicts between Palatalisation, Fronting and Retraction are resolved in a straightforward way by recognising that the analysis proceeds in two steps and that we have an intermediate derivational level (word level) between the underlying representation and the final output representation.[27] This conclusion is unacceptable from the point of view of standard OT, whose founding principle is that all evaluation is done in parallel and that there cannot be any derivational steps calling for the reranking of constraints.

[. . .]

Notes

1 For a recent analysis of Velar Palatalisation, see Plapp (1996).

2 From a synchronic point of view, Iotation is an extremely opaque process, because its trigger, the *j*, is present neither in the underlying representation nor in the surface representation. Thus, synchronically, the effects of Iotation are probably best treated as instances of allomorphy, as originally suggested by Spencer (1986).

3 Some early work in OT permitted a derivational step (serial evaluation) between morphologically defined domains, in particular between prefixes and stems (McCarthy & Prince 1993). However, this stance was later abandoned, in spite of

some papers that argued for the distinction between the word level and the sentence level (see, for example, Booij 1997). Current work in OT, especially McCarthy (1999), rejects any form of serialism. The belief is that all arguments for serial OT have been made invalid by Sympathy Theory. This is not so, as this paper will show.

4   With [k g x], velarisation is the primary place of articulation. When palatalised, the velars are fronted and become [–back].

[. . .]

6   The transliteration used in this paper is close to the phonetic transcription. Palatalisation, marked by an apostrophe, is indicated in contexts other than before front vowels. Note also that x stands for [x], a voiceless velar fricative, and y for [ɨ], a high back unrounded vowel.

[. . .]

8   I use double slashes for underlying representations, single slashes for intermediate representations and square brackets for phonetic representations.

9   In surface terms, the nominative plural ending [i] occurs after palatalised stems while [ɨ] occurs after hard stems. This complementary distribution of [i] and [ɨ] is standardly analysed as stemming from the underlying //i// that is fronted to [i] after [–back] segments. One reason is that the nominative plural ending contrasts with affixes such as -ist in that it does not trigger Palatalisation; compare *volos* [sʸ] 'hair' – *volos+y* [sʸ] (NOM PL) with *Marks* [sʸ] – *Marks+ist* [sʲ] 'Marxist'. Let us add that -ist does not have an alternant with [ɨ]. See Rubach (1984) for an analysis of the nominative plural ending in Polish.

[. . .]

11   In prefix–stem words, the *i* is shown in the spelling by the letter *y*, which denotes [ɨ].

12   The basic generalisations are due to Halle (1959) and Lightner (1965, 1972).

[. . .]

14   I retain the traditional name 'Palatalisation', even though (13) extends to the assimilation of both consonants to vowels (classical Palatalisation) and vowels to consonants (classical Fronting and Retraction).

15   As pointed out by Zubritskaya (1995), this markedness relationship accounts for the

absence of [ɨ] word-initially in the citation form where it is not in the purview of PAL-i (Zubritskaya's CV LINK). The lexical gap that Russian has no word-initial [ɨ] is best treated in terms of underspecification.

[. . .]

18   PAL-i requires agreement in backness and is satisfied regardless of whether the agreement comes from spreading or not. The latter situation is found when the consonant and the vowel happen to have the same value for backness in the underlying representation, as in this example and in the configuration considered in (16).

19   This line of thinking is in keeping with Kiparsky's (1997) work, whose goal is to reconcile OT with Lexical Phonology.

20   Note that at level 2 (postlexical level) IDENT-C$_{[+back]}$ and IDENT-C$_{[-back]}$ are ranked together. While OT has no evaluation metric to prefer the same ranking of two related constraints that differ just in the plus and minus value, the intuition is that such ranking is natural. Since this natural ranking is found at the postlexical level but not at the lexical level, the postlexical level comes across as less marked than the lexical level. Thanks to Bill Idsardi for drawing my attention to this point.

21   Since [ɨ] does not occur word-initially (see note 15), the configurations /tʸ ɨ/ and /t' ɨ/ are not inputs at level 2.

22   The representation of the yers as well as their pattern of vocalisation *vs.* deletion has received extensive coverage in the literature, beginning with Lightner (1965, 1972), who introduced the idea of yers into the phonology of modern Slavic languages. A number of further studies made use of this idea in a variety of ways, see especially Rubach (1986), Kenstowicz & Rubach (1987), Halle & Vergnaud (1987) and Melvold (1990). Yearley (1995) has offered an OT analysis of this problem.

23   Thanks to Bill Idsardi for drawing my attention to this strategy.

24   The pattern of retention and deletion of unvocalised yers at level 1 and level 2, respectively, can be accounted for in terms of PARSE$_{seg}$ (parse segments into syllables) and MAX$_{seg}$ (don't delete segments). At level 1, MAX$_{seg}$ ≫ PARSE$_{seg}$ keeps the unvocalised yers in place since it is worse to delete a

segment than to have an unparsed segment. (Recall that yers cannot be parsed because they are moraless vowels.) At level 2, the constraints are reranked: $\text{PARSE}_{seg} \gg \text{MAX}_{seg}$. The consequence is that unparsed segments (here unvocalised yers) are deleted.

25 At the underlying level, the *ts* is soft; see §4.2 and note 41 [omitted here – Ed.].

26 Phonetically, the *ts* is hard; see §4.2 [omitted].

27 The behaviour of prefixes *vis-à-vis* the process of Yer Vocalisation suggests that there is a level prior to our level 1 (word level). The point is that the vocalisation of the yer in the prefix depends on whether the yer has vocalised in the stem (Pesetsky 1979). This earlier level would thus need to encompass roots and suffixes but not prefixes, a suggestion made originally by Halle & Vergnaud (1987). Since, in spite of the progress made by Yearley (1995), it is unclear how Yer Vocalisation should be handled in OT, investigation of the stem level is a matter of future research.

References

Avanesov, Ruben I. (1968). *Russkoye literaturnoye proiznoshenie*. Moscow: Prosveshchenie.

Bilodid, I. K. (1969). *Suchasna ukrains'ka literaturna mova*. Kiev: Naukova Dumka.

Booij, G. E. (1997). Non-derivational phonology meets Lexical Phonology. In Iggy Roca (ed.) *Derivations and Constraints in Phonology*. Oxford: Oxford University Press, 261–88.

Booij, G. E. and J. Rubach (1987). Postcyclic versus postlexical rules in Lexical Phonology. *Linguistic Inquiry* 18. 1–44.

Broch, Olaf (1911). *Slavische Phonetik*. Heidelberg: Carl Winter.

Chen, Matthew (1973). Predictive power in phonological description. *Lingua* 32. 173–91.

Halle, Morris (1959). *The Sound Pattern of Russian*. The Hague: Mouton.

Halle, Morris and K. P. Mohanan (1985). Segmental phonology of modern English. *Linguistic Inquiry* 16. 57–116.

Halle, Morris and Jean-Roger Vergnaud (1987). *An Essay on Stress*. Cambridge, Mass.: MIT Press.

Holden, Kyril (1976). Assimilation rates of borrowings and phonological productivity. *Language* 52. 131–47.

Kenstowicz, Michael and Jerzy Rubach (1987). The phonology of syllabic nuclei in Slovak. *Language* 63. 463–97.

Kiparsky, Paul (1982). From cyclic to lexical phonology. In Harry van der Hulst and Norval Smith (eds.) *The Structure of Phonological Representations*. Part 1. Dordrecht: Foris, 131–75.

Kiparsky, Paul (1997). LP and OT. Handout, Cornell Linguistic Institute.

Lightner, Theodore M. (1965). *Segmental Phonology of Contemporary Standard Russian*. PhD dissertation, MIT.

Lightner, Theodore M. (1972). *Problems in the Theory of Phonology: Russian Phonology and Turkish Phonology*. Edmonton, Alberta: Linguistic Research Inc.

McCarthy, John J. (1999). Sympathy and phonological opacity. *Phonology* 16. 331–99.

McCarthy, John J. and Alan Prince (1993). *Prosodic Morphology: Constraint Interaction and Satisfaction*. MS, University of Massachusetts, Amherst and Rutgers University. ►

McCarthy, John J. and Alan Prince (1995). Faithfulness and reduplicative identity. MS, University of Massachusetts, Amherst and Rutgers University. ◄

Melvold, Janis L. (1990). *Structure and Stress in the Phonology of Russian*. PhD dissertation, MIT.

Pesetsky, David (1979). Russian morphology and Lexical Phonology. MS, MIT.

Plapp, Rosemary K. (1996). Russian /i/ and /ɨ/ as underlying segments. *Journal of Slavic Linguistics* 4. 76–108.

Prince, Alan and Paul Smolensky (1993). *Optimality Theory*. MS, Rutgers University and University of Colorado. ◄

Rubach, Jerzy (1984). *Cyclic and Lexical Phonology: The Structure of Polish*. Dordrecht: Foris.

Rubach, Jerzy (1986). Abstract vowels in three-dimensional phonology: the yers. *The Linguistic Review* 5. 247–80.

Spencer, Andrew (1986). A non-linear analysis of vowel–zero alternations in Polish. *Journal of Linguistics* 22. 249–80.

Sweet, Henry (1879). Russian pronunciation. *Transactions of the Philological Society 1877–79*. 543–60.

Yearley, Jennifer (1995). Jer vowels in Russian. In Jill N. Beckman, Laura Walsh Dickey and Suzanne Urbanczyk (eds.) *Papers in Optimality Theory*. Amherst: GLSA, 533–71.

Zubritskaya, Ekaterina L. (1995). *The Categorical and Variable Phonology of Russian*. PhD dissertation, University of Pennsylvania.

Study and Research Questions

1   Proceed systematically through the tableaux and locate all the ranking arguments. That is, find all of the cases where a pair of candidates prove the ranking of a pair of constraints, and present them in the form of 2 × 2 ranking tableaux.

2   On the basis of your answer to question (1), construct two diagrams, one for level 1 and one for level 2, showing the ranking relationships for all of the constraints. Use this diagram to determine exactly how the ranking must differ between levels 1 and 2. In other words, exactly which pairs of constraints must be re-ranked?

3   An important issue in the context of theories like this one is the range of permissible differences between levels within a single language. An OT grammar is a ranking of CON. Can any ranking of CON be combined with any other ranking of CON to form two levels of a single language? If not, what are some plausible restrictions?

4   There is a very large literature discussing proposals for combining OT with Lexical Phonology: Bermúdez-Otero (1999), Cohn and McCarthy (1994/1998), Hale and Kissock (1998), Hale, Kissock, and Reiss (1998), Itô and Mester (2003), Kenstowicz (1995), Kiparsky (2003, to appear), McCarthy (2000), McCarthy and Prince (1993), Potter (1994), and many of the contributions to Hermans and van Oostendorp (1999) and Roca (1997). Look up one of these works and evaluate the arguments.

Chapter 24 | John J. McCarthy and Alan Prince

Generalized Alignment: The Prosody–Morphology Interface

Editor's Note

Morphological structure has significant impact on prosodic structure, but how is this mediated? For example, why is it that many languages resist "resyllabification" at /CVC+V . . . / prefix+root boundary? In rule-based phonology, the cycle produces indirect effects of morphology on prosody. In OT, however, alignment constraints establish a direct relation between the edges of morphological constituents and the edges of prosodic constituents. Crucial to the OT account is the violability of alignment constraints; for instance, ONSET can compel /CVC+V . . . / to be syllabified as [CV. CV . . .], even though this is ill-aligned.

Other excerpts from "Generalized alignment" are reprinted as chapters 2 and 7.

[. . .]
The interface constraints we have just examined are of the general form Align(GCat, Edge, PCat, Edge); they require that the edge of any instance of the morphological constituent GCat align with the corresponding edge of some prosodic constituent PCat. For example, ALIGN-ROOT in Dakota requires that the left edge of the root coincide with the left edge of the prosodic word (PrWd), leading to an infixed locus for formal prefixes. But similar Alignment constraints on the morphology–prosody interface can have effects other than infixation when embedded in different systems of interacting constraints. In this section, we will show that Align(GCat, Edge, PCat, Edge) can have profound consequences for the prosody of a language in relation to its morphology. We will focus specifically on the following two constraints of this type:

(68) ALIGN-LEFT
    Align(Stem, L, PrWd, L)

Excerpt from:
McCarthy, John J. and Prince, Alan (1993) Generalized alignment. In *Yearbook of Morphology*, ed. Geert Booij and Jaap van Marle, pp. 79–153. Dordrecht: Kluwer. [Available on Rutgers Optimality Archive, ROA-7.]

(69) ALIGN-RIGHT
      Align(Stem, R, σ, R)

These constraints demand, respectively, that every stem begin at the left edge of a PrWd and that it end at the right edge of a syllable.[27] Phenomena variously attributable to the cycle, to domains of rule application, and to extrametricality can all be subsumed under this rubric, within OT.

Many of the consequences of ALIGN-LEFT and ALIGN-RIGHT for prosody and especially segmental phonology derive ultimately from a property of Gen dubbed Consistency of Exponence (McCarthy and Prince 1993: section 2). This condition places a fundamental limit on Gen's freedom to hypothesize output candidates: it cannot alter the grammatical analysis of the input. The input consists of various morphemes, root or affix, arranged into stems. The input also includes the lexical specifications of the phonological segments making up its constituent morphemes. Gen takes this input and, respecting Containment, posits various candidate output forms. Under Consistency of Exponence, the affiliations of segments with particular morphemes cannot change in the output, nor can segments be added to or subtracted from a morpheme.

This is, however, not to say that all and only the segments of the input are actually pronounced; what is actually pronounced is determined by the prosody of the optimal output form. Epenthesis and deletion phenomena are simply special situations in prosodic parsing. For epenthesis, the syllable parse posits segmentally unfilled structural positions, which receive a default interpretation as some actual segment, such as *a* or *i*, *t* or *ʔ* (Selkirk 1981, Archangeli 1984, Itô 1986, 1989). For deletion, the syllable parse is incomplete, leaving some segments crucially unparsed, to be ignored in the subsequent interpretation (McCarthy 1979, Steriade 1982, Itô 1986, 1989). Unfilled structural positions in candidate output forms are indicated by □, and unparsed segments are bracketed with '⟨...⟩'. Gen supplies output candidates with various combinations of unfilled and unparsed elements, and their distribution in actual languages is controlled by the following two fundamental constraints (Prince and Smolensky 1991a, 1991b, 1992, 1993), which for present purposes can be stated like this:

(70) PARSE
      ⟨α⟩ is prohibited.

(71) FILL
      □ is prohibited.

The ranking of PARSE and FILL relative to each other and to the constraints on syllable well-formedness like ONSET and NO-CODA characterizes the basic syllabic typology of the world's languages (Prince and Smolensky 1993: section 6).

With this much technical development in hand, we can see how two important Alignment effects come to affect the assignment of syllable structure. In Axininca Campa, an Arawakan language of Peru,[29] hiatus at /V+V/ juncture is prohibited. Potential hiatus leads to surface consonant epenthesis, shown by the element □ (interpreted as *t*) in (72).

(72)   Epenthetic Examples in Axininca Campa

/i-N-koma-i/	iŋ.ko.ma.□i	'he will paddle'
/i-N-koma-aa-i/	iŋ.ko.ma.□aa.□i	'he will paddle again'
/i-N-koma-ako-i/	iŋ.ko.ma.□a.ko.□i	'he will paddle for'
/i-N-koma-ako-aa-i-ro/	iŋ.ko.ma.□a.ko.□aa.□i.ro	'he will paddle for it again'
/i.N-čʰik-i/	iñ.čʰi.ki	'he will cut'
/i.N-čʰik-aa-i/	iñ.čʰi.kaa.□i	'he will cut again'
/i-N-čʰik-ako-i/	iñ.čʰi.ka.ko.□i	'he will cut for'
/i-N-čʰik-ako-aa-i-ro/	iñ-čʰi.ka.ko.□aa.□i.ro	'he will cut for it again'

The constraint implicated here is obviously ONSET. When morphemic combination brings together /V+V/, the heterosyllabic parse [V.V] produces an onsetless
syllable. All such faithfully-parsed candidates are sub-optimal; competing with them
are *unfaithful* candidate forms, which satisfy ONSET by positing FILL violation (that
is, the empty consonant □ in (72)) or unparsed segments. Of these, PARSE violators
– with phonetic loss of one or the other of the V's – are never found. Thus, PARSE is
undominated and so unviolated. FILL-violation is the pattern seen in (72).

The appearance of □ satisfies the requirement that syllables have onsets. This means
that ONSET dominates FILL in the constraint ranking, as the following tableau shows:

(73)   ONSET ≫ FILL, from/iN-koma-i/

Candidates	ONSET	FILL
☞ .iŋ.ko.ma.□i.	*	*
.iŋ.ko.ma.i.	**!	

The comparison between candidates here shows that FILL conflicts with ONSET.
Since performance on ONSET is decisive, and FILL violation or satisfaction is irrelevant, we conclude that ONSET ≫ FILL.

Tableau (73) establishes the ranking of ONSET and FILL, but it is not a complete
account of the optimality of candidates like *iŋ.ko.ma.□i*. Two problems remain.
First, tableau (73) completely disregards the initial violation of ONSET in *iŋ.ko.ma.□i*;
surely *□iŋ.ko.ma.□i*. should be more harmonic, since it contains no violations of
ONSET at all. Second, because *ai* is a permissible diphthong of Axininca Campa, it is
logically possible to parse /a+ i/ as tautosyllabic, escaping the consequences of both
FILL and ONSET, yielding *iŋ.ko.mai*. Given the constraints we have in hand, this
output should beat FILL-violating *iŋ.ko.ma.□i*.

We record these two observations as follows:

(74)   Initial V
        Axininca Campa has no word-initial epenthesis and freely tolerates initial
        onsetless syllables.

(75)   Non-coalescence of /V+V/
        Underlying /V – V/ sequences at stem-suffix juncture are never parsed as
        tautosyllabic; they always correspond to V.□V in the output.

The first observation bans epenthesis; the second requires it. Nevertheless, both observations devolve from conditions on GA, requiring coincidence of the edges of prosodic and morphological constituents.

We begin with the Initial V phenomenon. Axininca surface structures are replete with vowel-initial words, in flagrant violation of ONSET. This mode of departure from strict ONSET obedience is common in other languages as well, so it is no mere fluke of Axininca Campa. As a bare-faced fact, this observation would seem to require parametrizing ONSET, to exclude PrWd-initial syllables from its purview:

(76) 'NO-HIATUS' (Hypothetical Constraint, Parametrizing ONSET)
       *[σV except word-initially.

The codicil is specifically crafted so that 'NO-HIATUS' cannot compel FILL-violation in initial position. This will eliminate initial epenthesis.

Parametrizing ONSET by adding 'NO-HIATUS' to the panoply of universal constraints is obviously unsatisfactory. It does not explain why just exactly word-initial position is special, and it compromises the claim of OT that languages differ principally in how they rank a fixed set of universal constraints. It would be far better to retain the original, simple version of ONSET, without parametrization via 'NO-HIATUS', as the only possibility permitted by phonological theory.

Another approach to the Initial-V phenomenon, this time a more familiar one, is to say that initial onsetless syllables are extrametrical, therefore outside the purview of ONSET. This is the tack taken by Spring (1990: 37–44) and Black (1991). It has both local and global problems. Within Axininca Campa grammar, there is no other good evidence that initial onsetless syllables are extrametrical, and there is much evidence, from word minimality, stress, allomorphy, and reduplication, showing that they are actually intrametrical (McCarthy and Prince 1993: section 6). We return to the broader issue of extrametricality below, in the discussion of example (97).

Rejecting these alternatives, we propose that the Initial-V phenomenon arises from the interaction of ONSET and ALIGN-LEFT (68), which says that the left edge of any stem must coincide with the left edge of a PrWd. ALIGN-LEFT is unviolated and therefore undominated in the constraint hierarchy of Axininca Campa. ONSET is violated when it conflicts with ALIGN-LEFT; therefore ONSET cannot dominate ALIGN-LEFT. This gives us ALIGN-LEFT ≫ ONSET. The effects on initial C-epenthesis are shown in (77), where the symbol '|' marks the relevant GCat-edge (here, [Stem) and the PrWd-edge is shown by '[':

(77) Failure of Prothesis, from /i-N-koma-i/

Candidates	ALIGN-LEFT	ONSET	FILL
a. [.|iŋ.ko.ma.i.		**!	
b. ☞ [.|iŋ.ko.ma.□i.		*	*
c. [.□|iŋ.ko.ma.□i.	*!		**

The initial □ in the losing candidate (77c) shifts the PrWd-edge away from the stem-edge, causing misalignment of the leading edges of the PrWd and the stem. This means that all V-initial stems of Axininca must be parsed with an Onset violation, to satisfy dominant Align-Left. In contrast, both (77a) and (77b) are well-aligned, but the former contains multiple Onset violations, in contravention of the Optimality-Theoretic imperative of minimal violation.

The application of Align-Left in this example relies crucially on Consistency of Exponence, as explicated above. Specifically, the epenthetic element □ is part of the prosodic constituent PrWd, but it is not part of the stem, since 'stem' is a morphological notion, pertaining to the input, while an epenthetic segment is purely phonological, pertaining to the output only. Gen is denied the power to add elements like □ to a morpheme – indeed to add anything at all to a morpheme – so the segmental composition of root, affix, or stem is the same in the output as in the input. Thus, epenthetic elements have no morphological affiliation whatsoever. In this way, satisfaction of Align-Left demands a faithful parse at the left edge of the stem, as in (77a, b); in (77c) the element □ at the left edge of PrWd, belonging to PrWd but not to stem, is sufficient to de-align the PrWd and stem edges.

An alternative to Fill-violation is Parse-violation, leading to non-pronunciation of initial vowels. This alternative fares no better in the face of undominated Align-Left, however, since an unparsed segment is still a part of the morpheme (and hence the stem) that sponsors it:

(78)   De-Alignment by Unparsed Initial Syllable
       *|⟨iŋ⟩[koma□i

Underparsing can never bring a form into agreement with Align-Left. For Align-Left to be satisfied, the stem-initial segment, vowel or consonant, must occupy initial position in a PrWd. Consequently, an unparsed initial vowel, which occupies no position at all in any syllable, will de-align a stem.

Word-initial Onset-violation could also be avoided by trans-junctural syllabification, parsing the final consonant of one word as the onset of the following word. Again, unviolated Align-Left excludes this possibility, as the following schema shows:

(79)   De-Aligning Trans-Junctural Syllabification
       /matan iŋkomai/   →   *mata[.n|iŋkoma□i
                             *mata.n|iŋ[koma□i

The example is purely hypothetical, since Axininca Campa, with a strict constraint on possible codas (82), does not permit any word-final consonants whatsoever. Still, this effect of Align-Left is real, and it is important in other languages discussed below.

In sum, Align-Left explains why word-initial position should be an apparent exception to Onset in terms of constraint interaction and the general theory of the prosody–morphology interface. Moreover, Align-Left makes predictions beyond allowing initial onsetless syllables: it forbids all initial epenthesis – vocalic, consonantal, or syllabic – and forbids it for all stems, whether they begin with C or V.

This broader prediction holds without exception, and it is equally important in the grammar of augmentation to bimoraicity (*v.* below (89) [omitted here – Ed.]). For purely empirical reasons, then, it's correct to reject No-Hiatus and preserve the pristine constraint Onset, abetted by Align-Left.

The Axininca data in (72) also exhibit another phenomenon, Non-Coalescence of /V + V/. A further constraint is required, Align-Right (69). It must dominate Fill, because it compels Fill-violation. Observe how, in the following examples, epenthesis guarantees alignment of the end of the stem and the end of a syllable, whereas coalescence places the morphological stem-edge internal to a syllable:[30]

(80)   Stem–Syllable Alignment

    a. /iN-koma-i/   .iŋ.ko.ma.|□i.
                               * .iŋ.ko.ma|i.

    b. /iN-koma-ako-i/   .iŋ.ko.ma.|□a.ko.|□i.
                               * .iŋ.ko.ma|a.k.o|i.

Each suffix is assumed to create a new stem category recursively, and the right edge of each such stem lies at a syllable boundary, in accordance with Align-Right. GA quantifies universally over its first argument and existentially over its second [see chapter 2 – Ed.]; hence, Align-Right asserts that every right stem-edge coincides with a right syllable-edge. Thus, Align-Right does not demand that every syllable-edge coincide with a stem-edge (which would say that roots and affixes must be monosyllabic).

As noted, Align-Right is ranked above Fill, forcing the appearance of empty structure even where a faithful, non-epenthetic parse would meet the purely phonological requirements on Axininca syllables. The following tableau makes this clear:

(81)   Align-Right ≫ Fill, from /iN-koma-i/

Candidates	Align-Right	Fill
a. ☞ .iŋ.ko.ma|.□i.		*
b. .iŋ.ko.ma|i.	*!	

With this ranking, failure to meet Align-Right dooms the coalescent form.

These facts have been regarded previously as evidence of cyclic syllabification (Spring 1990: 52–53, 161–162; Black 1991: 205). The idea is that a syllable formed on one cycle is closed to the addition of further segments on later cycles. For example, in *iŋkoma□i*, the cyclic domain *iŋ.ko.ma* is fully syllabified as shown. When the suffix *i* is added on the next cycle, it cannot be joined to the syllable *ma*, which is now closed to the addition of further segments.

The cyclic analysis encounters various difficulties. For one thing, the failure of coalescence at morpheme juncture is the only evidence for cyclic rule application in the language.[31] For another, the specific details of the account are not compatible with any general theory of the cycle to be found in the literature. Steriade (1988:

309–10) has argued that closure is not true of cyclic syllabification (though she holds that it is true of cyclic foot assignment). Furthermore, Inkelas (1989: 59–66) and others have argued that bound roots are not cyclic domains. Axininca Campa verbal roots are bound (Payne 1981: 19), yet they would have to be cyclic domains, since they show closure just like affixes. Thus, cyclic syllabification in Axininca would be very much an isolated peculiarity, both within the language and within linguistic theory as a whole.

ALIGN-RIGHT is a dominated constraint, so it is violated elsewhere in the language. The circumstance where this is most obvious is /C + V/ juncture, as in /i-N-čʰik-i/ → iñ.čʰi.ki (72). The dominant constraint here is a 'coda condition', to use Itô's (1986) term, which bars k (and most other consonants) from syllable-final position. We state it informally here:

(82)   CODA-COND (Axininca Campa)
       A coda consonant can only be a nasal homorganic to following stop or
       affricate.

The following ranking argument establishes this result:

(83)   CODA-COND ≫ ALIGN-RIGHT, from /iñ-čʰik-i/

Candidates	CODA-COND	ALIGN-RIGHT
a. ☞ .iñ.čʰi.k|i.		*
b. .iñ.čʰik|.□i.	*!	

The failed candidate in (83) is a FILL-violator too, but irrelevantly, since FILL is ranked below ALIGN-RIGHT, as (81) shows. Other possible candidate analyses fare no better than this:

(84)   Further Failures of ALIGN-RIGHT in /C + V/ Juncture

Candidates	CODA-COND	ONSET	ALIGN-RIGHT	FILL
a. ☞ .iñ.čʰi.k|i.		*	*	
b. .iñ.čʰik|.□i.	*!	*		*
c. .iñ.čʰi.k|□.i.		**!	*	*
d. .iñ.čʰi.k|□.□i.		*	*	*!*
e. .iñ.čʰik|.i.	*!	**		

Under the ranking CODA-COND ≫ ALIGN-RIGHT, no amount of artifice can achieve satisfactory right Alignment in /C + V/ juncture.

In sum, ALIGN-RIGHT, crucially ranked below CODA-COND and above FILL, yields exactly the correct pattern of faithful versus epenthetic syllabic parsing at stem/suffix juncture. It is paralleled by the nearly symmetric constraint ALIGN-LEFT, which yields a very different phonological pattern: the possibility of initial onsetless syllables. This difference in the effects derived from the two Alignment constraints of Axininca Campa – ALIGN-RIGHT favors an epenthetic parse stem-finally, while ALIGN-LEFT favors a faithful one stem-initially – follows from a crucial differenceʾ in ranking. ALIGN-RIGHT pertains to the right edge of the syllable, and it is dominated by CODA-COND, which regulates the segments that can appear at the right edge of the syllable. ALIGN-LEFT pertains to the left edge of the PrWd, hence the left edge of the syllable, and it itself dominates ONSET, which regulates the segments that can appear at the left edge of the syllable. Because they interact differently with these other constraints, ALIGN-RIGHT and ALIGN-LEFT lead to these quite distinct effects on the surface. This is a frequently encountered situation in OT: similar constraints, when embedded in different ranking contexts, can lead to very different empirical results. [...]

Our goal now is to survey some of the diversity of effects that Alignment constraints on the morphology–prosody interface can lead to, given OT with Gen subject to Consistency of Exponence.

The original case of Alignment, from Prince and Smolensky's (1991b, 1993) analysis of Lardil, is identical to ALIGN-RIGHT in Axininca. In Lardil, prosodic minimality requires that words contain at least two syllables, forcing empty structure in the optimal analysis of a too-small base. The constraint ALIGN-RIGHT functions to regulate the extent of augmentation, explaining the contrast between the patterns in (92).

(92)   Align in Lardil

	Root	*CV-augment*	*V-augment*	
a.	/yak/		.ya.k|□. ($\to$ *yaka*)	'fish'
b.	/maṛ/	.maṛ|.□□ ($\to$ *maṛta*)	*.ma.ṛ|□. ($\to$ **maṛa*)	'hand'

Lardil syllables cannot end in *k*, forcing misalignment of /yak/ in (92a). The root /maṛ/ in (92b), by contrast, is susceptible to syllabification in its entirety. As a consequence, augmentation is driven beyond the absolute minimum: we find a whole CV syllable .□□ where just a vowel would suffice to provide the basis for the required second syllable. Formally, we have ALIGN-RIGHT ≫ FILL, so that double FILL-violation is compelled when it yields proper right-alignment. [...]

[Another] application of ALIGN-RIGHT is in phenomena usually attributed to final-consonant extrametricality.[38] Consider a language like Kamaiurá (Everett and Seki 1985), in which syllables are strictly open except word-finally, where a single consonant can occur: *apot*. This is standardly analyzed with a maximal CV syllable and final-consonant extrametricality (*cf.* e.g., Borowsky 1986, Itô 1986, 1989, Rice 1989). Alignment theory permits an alternative conception.

In Kamaiurá, the basic syllable pattern is set by No-Coda, which must dominate either Parse or Fill, so that CVC strings can never be faithfully parsed as coda-containing syllables (*cf.* Prince and Smolensky 1993: section 6). Let us assume for the sake of illustration that Parse is crucially dominated. Then a hypothetical input like /hutka/ yields the Parse-violating, codaless output *huka*:[39]

(96)   No-Coda ≫ Parse, from /hutka/

Candidates	No-Coda	Parse
a. ☞ .hu.⟨t⟩ka.		*
b. .hut.ka.	*!	

But No-Coda is itself crucially dominated by Align-Right. This means that the rightmost segment of the stem must be faithfully parsed even if it leads to a No-Coda violation:

(97)   Align-Right ≫ No-Coda, from /apot/

Candidates	Align-Right	No-Coda	Parse
a. ☞ .a.pot|.		*	
b. .a.po.⟨t⟩|	*!		*
c. .a.po.t|□.	*!		

The final consonant of the optimal candidate (97a) is actually parsed as a syllable coda, in violation of No-Coda. It is not 'extrametrical' in any sense. The final consonant of the failed candidate (97b) is worse than extrametrical: it is not parsed at all, leading to erasure and non-pronunciation when this representation is interpreted. Failure to parse the final consonant, as in (97b), or parsing it with a final epenthetic vowel, as in (97c), de-aligns the stem. In this way dominant Align-Right yields the pattern of codaless medial syllables combined with the possibility of a coda word-finally.[40]

Align-Left in Axininca Campa and Align-Right in Kamaiurá illustrate a general approach to so-called edge-of-constituent effects, where expected phonotactic patterns are disrupted in peripheral position. These effects arise when Align(GCat, E, PCat, E) ≫ P, where P stands for some phonotactic constraint that affects the composition of the edge E of PCat. For Align-Left in Axininca Campa, P = Onset, and for Align-Right in Kamaiurá, P = No-Coda. Obviously, additional cross-linguistic possibilities can be obtained with other values of GCat and PCat, as well as other choices of P, such as constraints regulating the complexity of onset or coda clusters or the maximum weight of syllables.

In standard accounts, the phenomena in Axininca Campa and Kamaiurá would be (and are) analyzed by extrametricality. Inkelas's (1989: 144ff.) influential proposal is that extrametricality is just exactly a *misalignment* of prosodic and morphological constituents. Here, though, we have argued that some phenomena that have been analyzed by extrametricality actually reflect constraints on the *alignment* of prosodic and morphological categories. More broadly, results in OT suggest that proposed mechanisms of 'extrametricality' or 'invisibility' attempt (less than successfully) to conflate unrelated empirical phenomena, which can be seen to fall out from distinct substantive constraints (Prince and Smolensky 1993: section 4.3).

Another class of Alignment effects derives from the Prosodic Hierarchy, and subsumes traditional statements to the effect that a morphological boundary is 'opaque' to prosodification. A constraint of the ALIGN-LEFT type requires that the left edge of each stem coincide with the left edge of a PrWd. But it also entails that the left edge of the stem not lie *within* a syllable or *within* a foot, since σ and Ft are subordinate to PrWd in the Prosodic Hierarchy. Thus, a well-aligned stem-edge is opaque to syllable-parsing and to foot-parsing.

Polish is a case of this type, exhibiting phenomena that have been analyzed in terms of the domains of prosodization rules or the opacity of morphological constituents to prosodization. Rubach and Booij (1990: 442) (see also Szpyra 1989: 178f.) observe that Polish does not permit syllabification between words or in prefix + stem juncture, as in (98).

(98)   Impossibility of Junctural Syllabification in Polish

    a.   mechanizm.|obronny   'defense mechanism'
       *mechaniz.m|obronny

    b.   roz.|ognić   'heat'
       *ro.z|ognić

They propose that this syllabification is required by a Prosodification Constraint, according to which 'Derivation of prosodic structure is blocked by the constituency bracket [.' Their '[' corresponds to our left stem-edge '|'.

Rubach and Booij's Prosodification Constraint, though cast within a rule-based theory, translates directly into ALIGN-LEFT: Align(Stem, L, PrWd, L). Because PrWd dominates σ in the Prosodic Hierarchy, the stem-edge cannot lie within a syllable, if ALIGN-LEFT is to be satisfied. Thus, syllabification across /C|V/ juncture is fatally de-aligning, as the tableau (99) demonstrates:[41]

(99)   ALIGN-LEFT ≫ ONSET, from /mechanizm obronny/

Candidates	ALIGN-LEFT	ONSET
a. ☞ [.|mechanizm][.|obronny]		*
b. [.|mechaniz][.m|obronny]	*!	

In (99a), each stem-edge '|' aligns with a PrWd-edge '['. But in (99b), the second stem-edge lies inside a syllable. Since, by the Prosodic Hierarchy, a PrWd-edge cannot occur inside a syllable, (99b) violates ALIGN-LEFT, with deadly results. Thus, undominated ALIGN-LEFT bans trans-junctural syllabification. This is identical to the result shown for the hypothetical Axininca Campa example in (79).

ALIGN-LEFT also has consequences for stress in Polish, through interaction with other constraints. By the Prosodic Hierarchy, no foot can straddle two PrWd's, so each stem is a separate domain for foot-parsing, as shown by examples like the following (Rubach and Booij 1990: 443):

(100)   Foot-Parsing in Polish Stems

   [|nor(wésk-o)][|(pólsk-i)]   'Norwegian-Polish'

The prosodic constraint responsible here is Align(PrWd, R, Ft, R), which requires that each right PrWd-edge coincide with a right foot-edge. Thus, each stem begins with a Prosodic Word, and each Prosodic Word ends with a foot, just as in (100). [. . .]

Notes

[. . .]

27   The asymmetry between PrWd-demanding ALIGN-LEFT and σ-demanding ALIGN-RIGHT is worthy of scrutiny. We return to ·this matter at the end of this section [omitted here – Ed.] after exploring the empirical sense of the constraints as formulated.

[. . .]

29   Axininca Campa is the subject of a comprehensive analysis by Payne (1981), from which most of our data and generalizations come. (Some additional forms are taken from Spring (1990).) The discussion here is drawn from a near-complete Optimality-Theoretic account of Axininca Campa prosody and prosodic morphology in McCarthy and Prince (1993).

30   Yip (1983: 244–5) proposes that Axininca epenthesis is 'morphological' because it is limited to verb suffixation and because it breaks up syllables that would otherwise be permissible. The morphological condition is encoded by repeating an ALIGN-like restriction in the contexts of two separate epenthesis rules.

31   Another potential case, involving the phonology of the velar glide, is discussed in McCarthy and Prince (1993: section A.3).

[. . .]

38   Thanks to Greg Iverson and Kelly Lietz for pointing this out.

39   Of course, in such conditions a form like /hutka/ will never be posited as a lexical entry in the absence of evidence from alternations that the /t/ is there. The principle of *Lexicon Optimization* in Prince and Smolensky (1993: section 9, p. 192) militates against choosing underlying forms that lead to gratuitous constraint violations, formalizing a theme from the work of Stampe (1969, 1973/9).

40   Other accounts of Kamaiurá are possible under Generalized Alignment. The analysis in the text assumes that the final *t* of *apot* is a coda, but suppose it could be established on phonological grounds that it is actually an appendix (a segment parsed directly by PrWd (Rubach and Booij 1990)). Then the dominant alignment constraint must be Align(Stem, R, PrWd, R), which requires coincidence of stem-edge and PrWd-edge (not syllable-edge). This crucially dominates a constraint NO-APPENDIX, which prohibits appendices (cf. Sherer 1994).

41   Satisfaction of ALIGN-LEFT entails that prefixed forms are parsed with PrWd-recursion: [|roz[|ognić]]. That is, both the stem *rozognić* and the stem *ognić* are PrWd's. The effects of this are roughly equivalent to Rubach and Booij's (1990: 459–61) derivational account, in which prefixes are adjoined to PrWd postcyclically.

References

Archangeli, D. 1984. *Underspecification in Yawelmani Phonology and Morphology*. Ph.D. dissertation, MIT.

Black, H. 1991. "The Phonology of the Velar Glide in Axininca Campa". *Phonology 8*, 183–217.

Borowsky, T. 1986. *Topics in the Lexical Phonology of English*. Ph.D. dissertation, University of Massachusetts, Amherst.

Everett, D. and L. Seki 1985. "Reduplication and CV Skeleta in Kamaiurá". *Linguistic Inquiry 16*, 326–30.

Inkelas, S. 1989. *Prosodic Constituency in the Lexicon*. Ph.D. dissertation, Stanford University.

Itô, J. 1986. *Syllable Theory in Prosodic Phonology*. Ph.D. dissertation, University of Massachusetts, Amherst.

Itô, J. 1989. "A Prosodic Theory of Epenthesis". *Natural Language and Linguistic Theory 7*, 217–60.

McCarthy, J. 1979. *Formal Problems in Semitic Phonology and Morphology*. Ph.D. dissertation, MIT.

McCarthy, J. and A. Prince 1993. *Prosodic Morphology I: Constraint Interaction and Satisfaction*. MS, University of Massachusetts, Amherst, and Rutgers University. ▶

Payne, D. 1981. *The Phonology and Morphology of Axininca Campa*. Arlington, TX: Summer Institute of Linguistics.

Prince, A. and P. Smolensky 1991a. "Optimality". Paper given at Arizona Phonology Conference.

Prince, A. and P. Smolensky 1991b. "Notes on Connectionism and Harmony Theory in Linguistics". In *Technical Report CU-CS-533-91*, Department of Computer Science, University of Colorado, Boulder.

Prince, A. and P. Smolensky 1992. "Optimality: Constraint Interaction in Generative Grammar". Paper read at 12th West Coast Conference on Formal Linguistics, Los Angeles.

Prince, A. and P. Smolensky 1993. *Optimality Theory: Constraint Interaction in Generative Grammar*. MS, Rutgers University, New Brunswick, and University of Colorado, Boulder. ◀

Rice, K. 1989. "On Eliminating Resyllabification into Onsets". In E. Fee and K. Hunt (eds.), *Proceedings of the Eighth West Coast Conference on Formal Linguistics*. Stanford, CA: Stanford Linguistics Association, 331–46.

Rubach, J. and G. Booij 1990. "Edge of Constituent Effects in Polish". *Natural Language and Linguistic Theory 8*, 427–63.

Selkirk, E. 1981. "Epenthesis and Degenerate Syllables in Cairene Arabic". In H. Borer and J. Aoun (eds.), *Theoretical Issues in the Grammar of the Semitic Languages*. Cambridge: MIT (MIT Working Papers in Linguistics, Vol. 3).

Sherer, T. 1994. *Prosodic Phonotactics*. Ph.D. dissertation, University of Massachusetts, Amherst.

Spring, C. 1990. *Implications of Axininca Campa for Prosodic Morphology and Reduplication*. Ph.D. dissertation, University of Arizona, Tucson.

Stampe, D. 1969. "The Acquisition of Phonetic Representation". In *Papers from the Fifth Regional Meeting of the Chicago Linguistic Society*.

Stampe, D. 1973/9. *A Dissertation in Natural Phonology*. New York: Garland Publishing Co.

Steriade, D. 1982. *Greek Prosodies and the Nature of Syllabification*. Ph.D. dissertation, MIT.

Steriade, D. 1988. "Greek Accent: A Case for Preserving Structure". *Linguistic Inquiry 19*, 271–314.

Szpyra, J. 1989. *The Phonology–Morphology Interface*. London: Routledge.

Yip, M. 1983. "Some Problems of Syllable Structure in Axininca Campa". In P. Sells and C. Jones (eds.), *Proceedings of NELS 13*, Graduate Linguistic Student Association, University of Massachusetts, Amherst, 243–51.

Study and Research Questions

1 Work out the details of a cyclic, rule-based analysis of Axininca Campa, along the lines suggested in the text below (81).
2 Re-analyze the examples in this chapter using the MAX and DEP constraints of correspondence theory (see chapter 3). Discuss any issues that arise.
3 Re-analyze the examples in this chapter using OO faithfulness (see chapter 22). Can OO faithfulness subsume all of the effects of (GCat, PCat) alignment?
4 Read and evaluate Itô and Mester's (1994) argument for a distinction between "crisp" and "non-crisp" alignment.

Chapter 25 | Elisabeth Selkirk

The Prosodic Structure of Function Words

Editor's Note

Lexical and functional elements differ not only grammatically but also phonologically. Across languages, there is a fairly consistent pattern: lexical elements are free-standing phonological words, but functional elements are phonologically dependent – that is, they are clitics. This pattern is not entirely consistent, however, since functional elements are sometimes promoted to the status of phonological words. The conditions under which functional elements are promoted, as well as the prosodic structure assigned to clitics, differ from language to language.

In short, the phonological disposition of functional elements follows a strong but not omnipotent cross-linguistic tendency, and there is a range of variation in when the tendency is violated and how it is obeyed. Situations like this make for ideal applications of OT, as this chapter shows.

1   Introduction

It seems likely that all languages make a distinction between words belonging to *functional* categories and those belonging to *lexical* categories, a distinction which roughly coincides with the sets of open and closed class items. Nouns, verbs and adjectives constitute the class of lexical categories in English, while determiners, prepositions, auxiliaries, modals, complementizers, conjunctions and other sorts of particles fall into the class of functional categories. The distinction between lexical and functional categories plays an important role in characterizing the syntactic properties of sentences (Jackendoff 1977, Chomsky 1986, Fukui and Speas 1986, Abney 1987, Pollock 1989, Grimshaw 1991). Now it happens that words belonging to functional categories display phonological properties significantly different from those of words belonging to lexical categories (Selkirk 1972, 1984, 1986,

Excerpt from:
Selkirk, Elisabeth (1996) The prosodic structure of function words. In *Signal to Syntax: Bootstrapping from Speech to Grammar in Early Acquisition*, ed. James L. Morgan and Katherine Demuth, pp. 187–214. Mahwah, NJ: Lawrence Erlbaum Associates. Also appeared (1995) in Jill Beckman, Laura Walsh Dickey, and Suzanne Urbanczyk (eds.) *Papers in Optimality Theory*. Amherst, MA: GLSA Publications, pp. 439–70.

Kaisse 1985, Berendsen 1986, Nespor and Vogel 1986, Kanerva 1989, Inkelas 1989, Zec 1993). For example, in English, monosyllabic function words may appear in either a stressless 'weak' form or a stressed 'strong' form, depending on their position in the sentence, whereas a lexical category word always appears in a stressed unreduced form. In standard Serbo-Croatian, a lexical word always bears a high tone accent on one of its syllables, whereas a function clitic does not. In Tokyo Japanese, a function word will lose its high tone accent if it is preceded by another accented word in the same phrase, but in the same circumstances a lexical word will not lose its accent. The mere fact of a systematic phonological difference between words belonging to lexical and functional categories raises the possibility that this distinction might be exploited by the language learner in their acquisition of the syntactic distinction between lexical and functional categories, where what needs to be learned as the first order of business is which words are functional and which lexical. The aim of this paper is to lay out the elements of a theory that will provide some insight into the lexical/functional contrast in phonology. Such a theory can provide a framework for discussion of a possible relation between the learning of the phonology of the functional/lexical distinction in a language and the acquisition of syntax in this domain.

A phrase consisting of a sequence of lexical words (Lex)[1] in morphosyntactic representation (S-structure) is characteristically prosodized as a sequence of prosodic words (PWd) in phonological representation (P-structure):

(1) S-structure   [Lex Lex]
     P-structure $((lex)_{PWd} (lex)_{PWd})_{PPh}$

(Italicized *lex* stands for the phonological content of Lex.) The PWd structure of phrases with function words, by contrast, is more various. In this paper evidence will be presented that a function word (Fnc) may be prosodized either as a PWd, or as one of three different types of prosodic clitic. The term *prosodic clitic* will be taken to stand for a morphosyntactic word which is not itself a PWd. It will be argued that options in the surface prosodization of function words simply reflect the manner in which function words are organized into *prosodic words* in the sentence (see Berendsen 1986, Selkirk 1986, Zec 1988, 1993, Inkelas 1989, Kanerva 1989 who also argue for this position). Corresponding to a syntactic phrase [Fnc Lex], for example, four different organizations into prosodic word are in principle available:[2]

(2) S-structure   [Fnc Lex]
     P-structure   (i) $((fnc)_{PWd} (lex)_{PWd})_{PPh}$ ***Prosodic Word***
                                                             Prosodic Clitics:
                  (ii) $(fnc (lex)_{PWd})_{PPh}$ *free clitic*
                  (iii) $((fnc lex)_{PWd})_{PPh}$ *internal clitic*
                  (iv) $((fnc (lex)_{PWd})_{PWd})_{PPh}$ *affixal clitic*

(Italicized *fnc* stand for the phonological content of Fnc.) In (ii), the *free clitic* case, the function word is sister to PWd and daughter to phonological phrase (PPh). In (iii), where the function word is an *internal clitic*, it is dominated by the same PWd that dominates its sister lexical word. In the *affixal clitic* case, (iv), the function word is located in a nested PWd structure, both sister to PWd and dominated by PWd. The claim is that these and only these prosodic structures for function word are motivated by the facts of the two languages to be examined here – English and Serbo-Croatian [the section on Serbo-Croatian has been omitted here – Ed.].

A goal of this paper is to explain *why* it is that function words appear in this array of prosodic structures, and under what circumstances. I will argue that whether a function word in a particular syntactic configuration in a particular language is a prosodic word or not, and if not, what type of prosodic clitic it is, depends crucially on the interaction of various well-attested types of constraints on prosodic structure. That diverse families of constraints – both morphosyntactic and phonological – contribute to defining the prosodic organization of function words lends support to the modular theory of prosodic structure expounded in work by Selkirk 1989, 1993, Selkirk and Tateishi 1988, 1991, Selkirk and Shen 1990, Prince and Smolensky 1993 and McCarthy and Prince 1993a, b. That an appeal to constraint interaction bears considerable fruit in this area lends support to Optimality Theory (Prince and Smolensky 1993, McCarthy and Prince 1993a, b), which holds that the relative ranking of constraints constitutes a central aspect of grammatical description.

1.1   Constraints on prosodic structure

Prosodic structure theory holds that a sentence is endowed with a hierarchically organized prosodic structure that is distinct from the morphosyntactic structure of the sentence and that phenomena of sentence phonology and phonetics are defined in terms of units of prosodic structure, not morphosyntactic structure. According to prosodic structure theory, in any language sentences are organized into a structure whose categories are drawn from the set defined in the Prosodic Hierarchy:

(3)   The Prosodic Hierarchy (Selkirk 1978)
     Utt   Utterance
     IP   Intonational Phrase
     PPh   Phonological Phrase
     PWd   Prosodic Word
     Ft   Foot
     σ Syllable

This hierarchy of prosodic categories forms the core of the theory of phonological constraints on prosodic structure. It is in terms of this hierarchy that certain fundamental constraints on prosodic structure are defined:

(4)   Constraints on Prosodic Domination
    (where C^n = some prosodic category)

    (i)   *Layeredness*   No C^i dominates a C^j, $j > i$,
        e.g., "No σ dominates a Ft."

    (ii) *Headedness*   Any C^i must dominate a C^{i-1} (except if $C^i = \sigma$),
        e.g., "A PWd must dominate a Ft."

(iii)   *Exhaustivity*   No C^i immediately dominates a constituent C^j, $j < i - 1$,
        e.g., "No PWd immediately dominates a σ."

(iv)   *Nonrecursivity*   No C^i dominates C^j, $j = i$,
       e.g., "No Ft dominates a Ft."

For ease of reference I will call these *constraints on prosodic domination*.

According to the Strict Layer Hypothesis (Selkirk 1981, 1984, Nespor and Vogel 1986) these constraints on prosodic domination universally characterize prosodic structure. Expressed as a monolithic whole, the Strict Layer Hypothesis reads as a single constraint requiring that a prosodic constituent of level C^i immediately dominate only constituents of the next level down in the prosodic hierarchy, C^{i-1}. That the Strict Layer Hypothesis should instead be factored out into more primitive component constraints, each with an independent status in the grammar, is argued by Inkelas 1989 and Itô and Mester 1992. The set of constraints on prosodic domination given above constitutes just such a decomposition of the Strict Layering.

Layeredness and Headedness, which together embody the essence of the Strict Layer Hypothesis, appear to be properties that hold universally, in all phonological representations. In optimality theoretic terms the inviolability of these constraints implies that they are undominated in the constraint ranking of every language. Exhaustivity and Nonrecursivity, on the other hand, turn out not to hold of all instances of P-structure. For example, it has been widely observed that there exist cases where a syllable is immediately dominated by a prosodic word, in violation of Exhaustivity (see e.g., Inkelas 1989, Kanerva 1989, Hayes 1991, McCarthy and Prince 1991, 1993a, b, Itô and Mester 1992, Kager 1993, Mester 1994, Prince and Smolensky 1993). The inviolability of Nonrecursivity has been challenged as well (Ladd 1986, 1992, Inkelas 1989, McCarthy and Prince 1993a, b). Below we will see additional evidence in favor of viewing Nonrecursivity and Exhaustivity as constraints on prosodic structure that may be violated. In particular, free clitics (cf. (2-ii)) violate Exhaustivity-with-respect-to-Phonological Phrase (Exh_{PPh}) and affixal clitics (cf. (2-iv)) violate Nonrecursivity-with-respect-to-Prosodic Word ($NonRec_{PWd}$), and Exhaustivity-with-respect-to-Prosodic Word (Exh_{PWd}) as well.

The class of constraints on prosodic domination constitute one, central, class of constraints on prosodic structure. Another significant class is constituted by *constraints on alignment* of edges of constituents (Selkirk 1986, Selkirk and Tateishi 1988, 1991, Selkirk and Shen 1990, McCarthy and Prince 1993a, b). Selkirk 1986 and related works argues that the relation between syntactic structure and prosodic structure is to be captured by constraints on the alignment of the two structures, ones which require that, for any constituent of category α in syntactic structure, its R (or L) edge coincides with the edge of a constituent of category β in prosodic structure:

(5)   The Edge-based Theory of the Syntax–Prosody Interface (e.g., Selkirk 1986)
      Right/Left edge of α ⇒ edge of β,
      α is a syntactic category, β is a prosodic category

Edge-alignment constraints of this type have been shown to allow an insightful characterization of the influence of sentential phrase structure on prosodic structure in a wide array of languages, and have been argued to play a role in characterizing the influence of word-internal structure on prosodic structure as well (see e.g., Myers 1987, Cohn 1989, Rice 1991, Kang 1992a, b, and McCarthy and Prince 1993a, b). In recent work, McCarthy and Prince 1993a, b have argued that the notion of edge alignment should be generalized; they show that a remarkable range of phonological phenomena yield to analysis in terms not only of constraints on grammatical structure–prosodic structure alignment but also in terms of constraints on the alignment of edges of various sorts of prosodic entities within phonological representation. The class of alignment constraints is enlarged to include constraints of the following general types:

(6)   Generalized Alignment (McCarthy and Prince 1993b):
        Align (αCat, E; βCat, E)
   a.   Align (GCat, E; PCat, E)
   b.   Align (PCat, E; GCat, E)
   c.   Align (PCat, E; PCat, E)
   (GCat ranges over morphological and syntactic categories; PCat ranges over the prosodic categories; E = Right or Left)

These all state: "For any αCat in the representation, align its edge (R,L) with the edge (R,L) of some βCat." We will see that alignment constraints of the various subclasses defined here arguably play a role in the characterization of the prosodic structure of function words.

   Central to our concerns in this paper, then, is the alignment of words in morphosyntactic representation with the prosodic words of phonological representation. It is here that the morphosyntactic distinction between function words and lexical words comes into play. My proposal, one which echoes the position taken in Selkirk 1984, 1986 and Selkirk and Shen 1990, is that *the set of constraints governing the interface between morphosyntactic and prosodic structure makes no reference to functional categories at all*. Rather, it is only lexical categories and their phrasal projections which would figure in the statement of morpho-syntactic constraints on prosodic structure; GCat would stand only for 'LexCat' in any constraint of the Align (GCat; PCat) variety. The proposed form of the constraints which align grammatical words with prosodic words is accordingly as in (7):

(7)   The Word Alignment Constraints (WdCon)
        (i)   Align (Lex, L; PWd, L)   (= WdConL)
        (ii) Align (Lex, R; PWd, R)   (= WdConR)

We will see that it is the restriction of word alignment constraints to lexical cat-egory words that is responsible for the availability of prosodic clitic analyses for function words.

   The generalized alignment theory also sanctions word-level alignment constraints of the Align (PCat; GCat) type in (8), where the category types are reversed:

(8)   The Prosodic Word Alignment Constraints (PWdCon)
       (i)   Align (PWd, L; Lex, L)   (= PWdConL)
       (ii) Align (PWd, R; Lex, R)   (= PWdConR)

The PWdCon constraints say that, for any PWd in the representation, its L (or R) edge must coincide with the L (or R) edge of some Lex. A representation in which *both* were respected would contain no function word which itself had the status of a prosodic word. Thus, the PWdCon constraints form part of the explanation for the fact that function words typically do not have the status of PWd.

Summarizing briefly, the analysis of function word prosodization to be offered in what follows gives crucial roles to constraints on prosodic structure from two well-known families: constraints on prosodic domination such as Exhaustivity and Nonrecursivity and constraints on the alignment of prosodic structure and morphosyntactic structure such as WdCon and PWdCon. We will see that the precise manner in which these constraints are ranked in the grammar of a particular language provides the basis for explaining which of the variety of function word prosodizations is realized in a particular morphosyntactic configuration in that language.

[. . .]

2   Weak and Strong Forms of Function Words in English

In English, a large number of the monosyllabic function words – prepositions, determiners, complementizers, auxiliary verbs, personal pronouns – may appear in either a 'weak', i.e. stressless and reduced, or a 'strong', i.e. stressed and unreduced, form (Sweet 1891, 1908, Jones 1964, Gimson 1970, Zwicky 1970, Selkirk 1972, 1984, Kaisse 1985, Berendsen 1986). This simple fact presents a challenge to any theory of syntax–phonology interaction: it needs to be explained why, in the same language, function words appear with different surface prosodizations. What I want to show is that these different surface prosodizations result from different underlying input structures, and that one and the same English-particular ranking of constraints is responsible for deriving the variety of surface prosodic structures attested.

Pronounced in isolation, function words appear in strong form and are indistinguishable stress-wise and vowel quality-wise from monosyllabic lexical category items:

(9)   for   [fɔr]   four
       can   [kæn]   (tin) can
       him   [hɪm]   hymn
       at   [æt]   hat

Strong forms also appear when the function word is focussed (see 2.1), and when it is phrase-final (see 2.4). Weak forms appear when the function word is nonfocussed and not phrase-final (see 2.3), and also when phrase-final but object of a verb or preposition (see 2.5 [omitted here – Ed.]). In their weak form(s), illustrated in (10), monosyllabic Fnc words display the properties of stressless syllables: vowel reduction, appearance of syllabic sonorants, loss of onset *h*, etc.

(10) for   [fr̩]   for Timothy (cf. fertility)
      căn   [kən], [kn̩], [km̩]   can pile   (cf. compile)
      hĭm   [ɨm], [m̩]   need him   (cf. Needham)
      ăt   [ət]   at home   (cf. atone)

Prosodic theory analyzes stressed syllables as the prominent, or only, syllable of the prosodic constituent *foot*. Thus, the strong forms of monosyllabic function words in English have the status of a head of a foot and the weak forms do not. We will see that the foot-head status of strong forms is in most instances the consequence of the assignment of Prosodic Word status to the Fnc. Weak forms, by contrast, are prosodic clitics.

2.1 Focussed Fnc

When focussed, a function word always appears in strong form:

(11) She spoke AT the microphone not WITH it.
      Bettina CAN speak, but refuses to.
      We need HER, not HIM.

It is a fact that, whether a Fnc or a Lex, a focussed word is assigned a pitch accent in the morphosyntactic structure of the sentence in English (cf. Pierrehumbert 1980, Selkirk 1984, ch. 5). The presence of that pitch accent is arguably responsible for the strong form of focussed Fnc. It has been widely observed that pitch accents in English are associated only with stressed syllables (Liberman 1975, Ladd 1980, Pierrehumbert 1980, 1994, Selkirk 1984, Hayes 1991).

(12) Association of Pitch Accent (AssocPA)
      A pitch accent associates to (aligns with) a stressed syllable (i.e. the head of a foot).

Such a constraint guarantees that the pitch accent which is assigned to a word in morphosyntactic representation will never be realized on a stressless syllable in prosodic structure, and thus rules out *ASSign, *strucTURE, *PROsodic, *foCUS. Compare the grammatical forms asSIGN, STRUCture, proSODic, FOCus, which respect this constraint. This same constraint allows us to explain why the morphosyntactic assignment of a pitch accent to a monosyllabic function word entails the strong form foot-head status of *fnc* in P-structure. For a syllable to carry stress it must be the head of a Foot. Thus the presence of pitch accent in the input structure in effect induces the presence of the prosodic structure required in order for the constraint AssocPA to be satisfied in English:

(13) $[can]_{Mod}$ ⇒ $(can)_{Ft}$
      H*   AssocPA   H*

The proposal, then, is that the strong form of a function word that is in focus is called for by an independently required constraint on the relation between tonal structure and prosodic structure. The surface form of a nonfocussed function word, by contrast, arguably results from the interplay of constraints on prosodic domination and constraints on the alignment of morphosyntactic and prosodic structure.

2.2   Fnc in isolation

A function word uttered in isolation appears in strong form, cf. (9). Its foot-head status falls out immediately from the basic prosodic structure principle of Headedness. An isolation pronunciation is an utterance; an utterance is analyzed at the highest level of prosodic structure, the prosodic category Utterance (Utt). Assuming the Prosodic Hierarchy in (3), by Headedness, Utt must dominate an Intonational Phrase (IP), IP must dominate a Phonological Phrase (PPh), a PPh must dominate a PWd, and a PWd a Ft, hence the strong form of the isolation pronunciation of a monosyllabic Fnc:

(14) $((((((fnc)_\sigma)_{Ft})_{PWd})_{PPh})_{IP})_{Utt}$

This representation violates PWdCon, the pair of constraints which require that for every L/R edge of PWd in P-structure there is a L/R edge of some Lex in S-structure. Given an optimality-theoretic approach, the violation of PWdCon is ascribed to the higher ranking of Headedness in the constraint hierarchy. Indeed, since Headedness is a defining property of prosodic structure, it may be considered to be inviolable, more highly ranked than any other violable constraint.

(15)   Headedness $\gg \ldots \gg$ PWdCon $\ldots$

Quite generally, the inviolability of Headedness makes the prediction that any word pronounced in isolation would have the prosodic properties of entities at all the levels of the Prosodic Hierarchy. This prediction appears to be borne out in English and elsewhere.

2.3   Nonfinal Fnc

It is a fact that, in the absence of pitch accent, the prosodic structure of a Fnc word correlates with the position in which that Fnc is embedded in the sentence. A Fnc followed by a Lex within the same syntactic phrase standardly appears in weak form:

(16)   Diane căn paint hěr portrait ŏf Timothy ăt home.
       Bŭt shě found thăt thě weather wăs too hot fŏr painting.

I will assume that such Fnc–Lex sequences appear in the phrase structure configuration in (17a), one in which the function word heads a functional phrase FncP within which it is followed by a phrase LexP that is itself headed by Lex. The structures in (17b) and (17c) are representative examples.

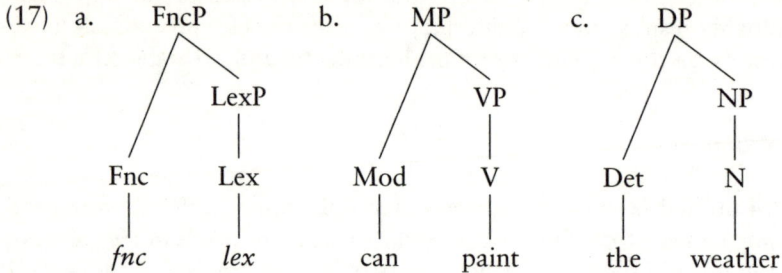

(17)   a.   FncP   b.   MP   c.   DP

The structures show tree diagrams:

- (17a) FncP with Fnc (fnc) and LexP → Lex (lex)
- (17b) MP with Mod (can) and VP → V (paint)
- (17c) DP with Det (the) and NP → N (weather)

It is on the basis of such inputs, then, that the grammar of constraints on prosodic structure must derive the weak prosodic clitic form of the function word in the output.

As pointed out in the introduction, there are in principle a number of different prosodic structures in which a function word in structures like (17) may appear. So the first question to be addressed here is an empirical one. Which prosodic structure correctly represents the structure of non-phrase-final weak function words in English like these? The candidates in (18a–d) represent the four different possible organizations of function words into PWd given above in (2). They have in common that the function word has the representation of a stressless syllable (one which does not head a foot).

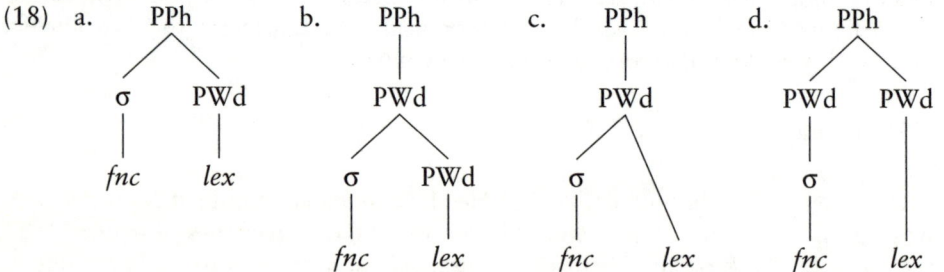

(18)   a.   PPh   b.   PPh   c.   PPh   d.   PPh

The structures show tree diagrams:

- (18a) PPh with σ (fnc) and PWd (lex)
- (18b) PPh with PWd → σ (fnc) and PWd (lex)
- (18c) PPh with PWd → σ (fnc) and lex
- (18d) PPh with PWd (fnc) and PWd (lex)

In (18a) *fnc* is a free clitic; in (18b) it is an affixal clitic; in (18c) it is an internal clitic; and in (18d) it is a prosodic word.

Example (18d) violates the inviolable constraint Headedness, which calls for every PWd to dominate at least one Ft, and therefore is excluded. Note that if *fnc* in (18d) were also to be a foot, in accordance with Headedness, then it would have the status of a stressed syllable, contrary to fact. So (18d) is not a possible prosodization for a weak form Fnc.

Neither is (18c) a possible representation of non-phrase-final stressless monosyllabic function words. In this representation, that of an internal clitic, *fnc* and *lex* are dominated by the same, single, PWd. This representation implies that a Fnc–Lex combination should display phonological behavior identical to that of PWd constituted of a single Lex alone, and this is arguably not correct. It is a well known fact about patterns of English stress that at most one stressless syllable may occur at the left edge of a Lex:

(19) mằsságe   Màssăchúsĕtts, *Mắssăchúsĕtts
      tĕnácity   Tènnĕssée, *Tĕnnĕssée
      tĕlépathy   tèlĕpáthic, *tĕlĕpáthic

McCarthy and Prince 1993b suggest that this fact argues for the existence of an alignment constraint of the Align (PCat; PCat) variety, whereby the left edge of any PWd is required to coincide with the left edge of a Foot:

(20) Align (PWd, L; Ft, L)

If we assume on the basis of the evidence in (19) that this constraint goes unviolated as long as the initial syllable(s) of a PWd can indeed be organized into a well-formed foot, then it follows that non-phrase-final function words do not have the structure of (18c). This is because sequences of stressless syllables made up wholly or in part by non-phrase-final function words are systematically possible, in violation of (20).

(21) (i)   ă méssage   ă mằsságe
            hĕr áptitude   hĕr ăbílities
            căn pérch   căn pĕrtúrb

      (ii) fŏr ă méssage   fŏr ă mằsságe
            ăt hĕr áptitude ăt hĕr ăbílities
            yŏu căn pérch   yŏu căn pĕrtúrb

Therefore, (18c) is not a possible representation for a non-phrase-final Fnc. Anticipating the discussion below, note that the presence of aspiration in a Lex-initial stressless syllable following a Fnc, e.g., *a cʰonversion, in Tʰoronto*, provides additional evidence against an internal clitic analysis of the function words. This structure would lack the aspiration-triggering PWd edge at the left edge of the Lex.

In contrast, either of the representations (18a) or (18b) would allow for sequences of stressless syllables such as those in (21) without incurring a violation of constraint (20). In (18a), the *fnc* is not PWd-initial, and hence would not be subject to the constraint Align (PWd, L; Ft, L) in the first place. In (18b), the *fnc* is PWd-initial, but so is any syllable that follows it (because of the recursive PWd structure there). In this case no Ft could dominate the two, since the resulting structure would not constitute a well-formed bracketing. Which means that positing (18b) would not lead to the prediction that the *fnc* should be stressed if followed by a stressless syllable. What further empirical considerations, then, might decide between these two remaining structures?

Initial position in PWd is often associated with effects involving the phonetic realization of segments. In English, a word-initial voiceless stop is aspirated, even when the syllable to which it belongs is stressless.

(22) grow tʰomatoes, grow pʰetunias, grow cʰalendula

Cooper 1991, 1994 shows that there is a distinct word-initial aspiration effect (one which cannot be reduced to a simple syllable-initial effect). Prosodic structure theory takes such 'word-initial' effects to be PWd-initial effects. It is significant, therefore, that aspiration does not appear to be attested in initial position in weak non-phrase-final function words, as shown, among other things, by the appearance of the flapped version of *t* (impossible in word-initial position):

(23)   They grow to the sky. So can delphiniums. Take Grey to London.

It can therefore be concluded that function words in this position do not initiate PWds, as (18b) would have it, and instead that they are immediately dominated by PPh, as in (18a), and illustrated here:

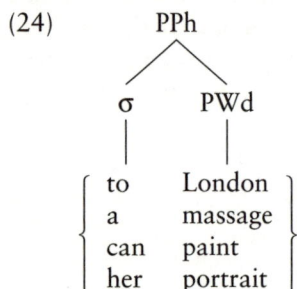

(24)

$$
\begin{array}{cc}
& \text{PPh} \\
& \diagup \diagdown \\
\sigma & \text{PWd} \\
| & | \\
\left\{
\begin{array}{ll}
\text{to} & \text{London} \\
\text{a} & \text{massage} \\
\text{can} & \text{paint} \\
\text{her} & \text{portrait}
\end{array}
\right\}
\end{array}
$$

The next question to ask, the analytical one, is *why* it is (18a) rather than one of the set (18b–d) which is the optimal (grammatical) representation of non-phrase-final function words in English. It is here that optimality theory comes crucially into play. Note that *all* of the representations in (18a–d) violate *some* constraint. (25) lists the representations and the constraints they violate. We saw above that the optimal output representation is (18a)/(25i), which violates only Exh_{PPh}. Optimality theory holds that constraints on phonological representation are violable. That is, the grammatical, optimal, output prosodic representation that the constraint hierarchy of a grammar defines based on a particular input morphosyntactic representation may violate some constraint. Such surface violations in an optimal output form are claimed to occur under two circumstances: (i) when the alternative, non-optimal, output representations that could be constructed (based on the same input) violate a constraint that is higher ranked than the constraint violated in the optimal representation, or (ii) when the alternative candidates contain *more* violations of the same constraint, or of some other same-ranked constraint(s).

(25)   *Output representation*   *Constraint violated*

(i) $_{PPh}(\text{fnc }_{PWd}(\text{lex})_{PWd})_{PPh}$ Exh_{PPh}
[since PPh immediately dominates σ]

(ii) $_{PPh}(_{PWd}(\text{fnc }_{PWd}(\text{lex})_{PWd})_{PWd})_{PPh}$ $NonRec_{PWd}, PWdCon$
[$NonRec_{PWd}$ since PWd dominates PWd; $PWdCon$ since L edge of PWd not aligned with L edge of a Lex]

(iii) $_{PPh}(_{PWd}(fnc\ lex)_{PWd})_{PPh}$ *WdCon, PWdCon*
[WdCon since L edge of Lex not aligned with
L edge of some PWd; PWdCon since L edge
of PWd not aligned with L edge of some Lex]

(iv) $_{PPh}(_{PWd}(fnc)_{PWd}\ _{PWd}(lex)_{PWd})_{PPh}$ *PWdCon (twice), Headedness*
[PWdCon since L and R edges of the lefthand
PWd not aligned with L/R edges of some Lex;
Headedness since one PWd lacks a Foot head]

No clear indication of the relative ranking of the constraints at issue emerges from the observations in (25). The fact that the optimal candidate (18a)/(25i) incurs just a single constraint violation while the other non-optimal candidates incur violations of at least two other constraints is consistent with a variety of possible constraint rankings. Only examination of further data will enable us to decide on the correct ranking. Given the data at hand, it could simply be that Exh$_{PPh}$ is dominated by all the other constraints at issue: Headedness, NonRec$_{PWd}$, WdCon, PWdCon$_L$ and PWdCon$_R$. This would explain why the free clitic candidate violating Exh$_{PPh}$ is the optimal one. On the other hand, it could also be that, except for the undominated Headedness, all the constraints have the same rank. In this case, the mere fact that the free clitic candidate has the fewest violations would decide in its favor. It could also be that Exh$_{PPh}$ is ranked lower than, say, NonRec$_{PWd}$ and WdCon (as well as Headedness), but same ranked with respect to PWdCon. In this latter case, the violations of Headedness, WdCon and NonRec$_{PWd}$ seen in each of the other respective candidates would be fatal to them. The evidence we will consider in the sections to follow gives support for ranking both Exh$_{PPh}$ and PWdCon below NonRec$_{PWd}$ and WdCon, and is thus consistent with the latter ranking.[3]

2.4 Final Fnc

Consider next the case of monosyllabic Fnc appearing in phrase-final position. The italicized function words in (27) appear in strong form, and can *not* appear in the weak form they may adopt when not phrase-final.

(27) I can eat more than Sara *cán*.   [kæn], *[kən], *[kn̩]
      If you think you *cán*, go ahead and do it.
      I don't know whether Ray *ís*.   [ɪz], *[z]
      Wherever Ray *ís*, he's having a good time.
      What did you look *át* yesterday?   [æt], *[ət]
      Who did you do it *fór* that time?   [fɔr], *[fr̩]

Given that they are stressed we know that these monosyllables have at least the status of a foot, i.e. ((fnc)_)$_{Ft}$. Further evidence suggests that phrase-final Fnc elements are final in a PWd. The evidence comes from the behavior of intrusive *r* in the Eastern Massachusetts dialect described by McCarthy (1991, 1993).

Intrusive *r* is inserted after a word-final low vowel when the following word begins with a vowel. Significantly, McCarthy shows, intrusive *r* appears in just two contexts: at the right edge of Lex, (28i-a), and at the right edge of a phrase-final Fnc, (28i-b). It never appears at the right edge of non-phrase-final Fnc, (28ii).[4]

(28)   (i) Presence of Intrusive *r*
    a.   After Lex
          saw-r-ing
          rumba-r-ing
          guffaw-r-ing
          The spa-r is broken.
          He put the tuna-r on the table.
          The boat'll yaw-r a little.
    b.   After phrase-final Fnc (compare to examples in (ii))
          I said I was gonna-r and I did.
          Did you-r, or didn't you.
          We oughta-r if we're asked.
          If you hafta-r, I'll help.

    (ii) Lack of Intrusive *r* after Non-phrase-final Fnc
    a.   Modal + reduced *have*
          should have (shoulda), could have (coulda), might have (mighta)
          He shoulda eaten already   [ʃʊdə(*r) ijʔən]
    b.   Fnc-like verbs + reduced *to*
          going to (gonna), ought to (oughta), have/has to (hafta, hasta), got to
          (gotta), used to (useta), supposed to (supposta)
          I'm gonna ask Adrian.   [gənə(*r) æsk]
    c.   Auxiliary + reduced *you*
          did you, should you, would you, could you
          Did **you** answer him?   [dɪdʒə(*r) ænsər ɪm]
    d.   Reduced *to, do, of*
          To add to his troubles   [tə(*r) æd tə(*r) ɪz trəbəlz]
          Why do Albert and you   [wɑj də(*r) ælbət ən juw]
          A lotta apples   [ə lɔtə(*r) æpəlz]

The McCarthy analysis is that PWd-final position defines the locus of intrusive *r* insertion. This analysis assumes, and at the same time gives crucial support for, the generalization that a phrase-final function word is PWd-final. An additional set of examples shows that a phrase-final Fnc is preceded by a PWd as well:

(29)   It's more scary than a subpoena-r is.
      What did they convict Wanda-r of?
      That's nothing to guffaw-r at!

The appearance of intrusive *r* at the end of the lexical word preceding the phrase-final *fnc* indicates that the *lex* is PWd-final.

This evidence from intrusive *r* is consistent with two possible surface prosodic structures for phrase-final *fnc*: $(lex)_{PWd}$ $(fnc)_{PWd}$, in which the *fnc* is a PWd on its own, and $((lex)_{PWd}$ $fnc)_{PWd}$, in which the *fnc* is located in a nested PWd structure. In both cases the phrase-final *fnc* is PWd-final, and so is the preceding *lex*. But only the analysis of the *fnc* as a PWd itself will explain why it is always stressed. By assuming that the *fnc* is a PWd (rather than just as the end of one), its stressedness simply falls out from Headedness, which entails its foot-head status. So we conclude in the PWd status of phrase-final *fnc*.

The question then is *why* phrase-final function words have the status of PWd, in violation of PWdCon. Why aren't they simply one of the variety of prosodic clitics that are in principle available? In particular, why aren't they free clitics, just like the non-phrase-final *fnc* are? This is what the grammar as currently constituted would predict. Explaining the asymmetry in the prosodic status of phrase-final and non-phrase-final *fnc* will therefore require appeal to some constraint(s) that have not yet had a crucial role to play. I believe the relevant constraints concern prosodic structure at the level of the phonological phrase.

It has often been observed that phonological phrase breaks typically occur at the edges of morphosyntactic phrases. Investigation of the sentence phonology of a variety of languages has led to the conclusion that there are alignment constraints requiring that the Right, or Left, edge of a maximal phrasal projection coincide with the edge of a phonological phrase (PPh). More specifically, the phrasal alignment appears to be defined with respect to Lex^{max}, the maximal phrase projected from a Lex (Selkirk and Shen 1990). These constraints are expressed in the generalized alignment format as (30):

(30)   a.   Align (Lex^{max}, R; PPh, R)
       b.   Align (Lex^{max}, L; PPh, L)

They state that the right (resp. left) edge of any Lex^{max} in morphosyntactic structure coincides with the right (resp. left) edge of some phonological phrase in prosodic structure. The two constraints, available universally, must be independently rankable, for it has been shown that languages may show either predominantly right edge or left edge effects. As for English, the PWd status of phrase-final Fnc suggests very strongly that the constraint (30a) calling for the alignment of a PPh edge with the right edge of a maximal projection is higher ranked than any of the other constraints under consideration.

If we assume that Align (Lex^{max}; PPh) is for all intents and purposes an undominated constraint in English, this means any element that is final in a morphosyntactic phrase will also be final in a phonological phrase. The sentence in (31a), with its morphosyntactic phrase-final Fnc *át*, will be parsed into phonological phrases as in (31b) in all of the candidate output representations, putting *át* in PPh-final position.

(31)   a.   [What did you $_{VP}$[look $_{PP}$[at___]$_{PP}$]$_{VP}$ last time]
       b. $_{PPh}$(What did you look át)$_{PPh}$ $_{PPh}$(last time)$_{PPh}$

Observe that the candidates for the output representation of *look at* which satisfy Align (Lex^{max}; PPh), as well as Headedness, include the following:

(32) a. PPh   b. PPh   c. PPh   d. PPh

PWd		PWd		PWd		PWd	PWd
Ft		Ft		PWd		Ft	Ft
σ	σ	σ	σ	Ft		σ	σ
look	at	look	at	σ	σ	look	át
				look	at		

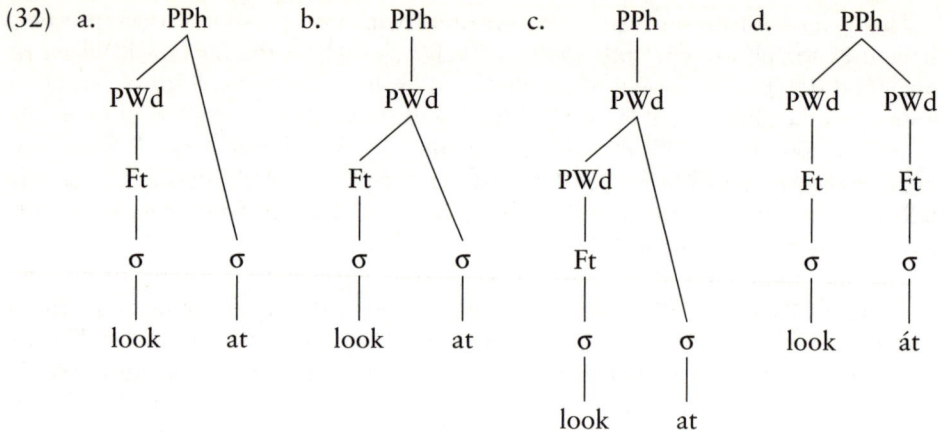

An explanation for the non-optimality of the free clitic case in (32a) now suggests itself, namely that there is a constraint that calls for the right edge of a PPh to be aligned with the right edge of a PWd, and that it is violated in candidate (a). This is just the sort of constraint that alignment theory claims will be typically seen to play a role in grammars, a constraint of the Align (PCat; PCat) family:

(33)   Align (PPh, R; PWd, R)

If unviolated, this constraint ensures that, given the presence of a PPh edge after *át* (itself called for by Align (Lex^{max}, R; PPh, R)), there must be also a PWd edge after *át*. It excludes the free clitic candidate (a), and provides the basis for an explanation for the asymmetry between phrase-final and non-phrase-final prosodizations in English. The ordering of Align (Lex^{max}; PPh) and Align (PPh; PWd), the constraints violated in (b–c), is all that it takes to render the free clitic candidate non-optimal:

(34)   Align (Lex^{max}; PPh), Align (PPh; PWd) ≫ WdCon, NonRec$_{PWd}$, PWdCon

Assuming these phrasal alignment constraints and the constraint hierarchy in (34) doesn't, however, provide an explanation for why the optimal candidate is (d), rather than the affixal or internal clitic candidates (b–c), since in them *at* is also PWd-final in PPh. But the explanation is readily available. In order that (d) be chosen instead of (b, c) we need only assume that WdCon and NonRec$_{PWd}$ are ranked higher than PWdCon:

(35)   WdCon, NonRec$_{PWd}$ ≫ PWdCon

(Recall that no ranking amongst these constraints was earlier established.) The optimality theoretic ranking of WdCon above PWdCon means that the candidate violating WdCon, (b), is "less well-formed" than the candidate violating PWdCon, (d). ((b) violates WdCon since there is no PWd edge at the right edge of *look*.) And the ranking of NonRec$_{PWd}$ above PWdCon rules (c) "less well-formed" than (d).

(The nested PWd structure of (c) violates $NonRec_{PWd}$.) So despite the violations of PWdCon seen in it, (d) is the "best-formed" candidate relative to the others, i.e. the optimal one.

Putting together the assumptions about constraint rankings that have been posited thus far (in (34), (35) and the final paragraph of section 2.3), we see they are consistent with each other, and give the amalgamated ranking in (36):

(36)   Align Lex^{max}, Align PPh $\gg$ WdCon, $NonRec_{PWd}$ $\gg$ PWdCon, Exh_{PPh}

(This ranking mentions only constraints that are assumed to be violable. A full ranking statement would include Headedness and Layeredness, universally undominated constraints, at the left extreme.)
[. . .]

4   Conclusion

Summing up, we have seen that functional category words are distinguished from lexical category words in that (i) they need not have the status of prosodic word in phonological representation, and (ii) they may appear in a variety of distinct prosodic clitic structures, both cross-linguistically and in the same language. It was proposed that the first property follows from the invisibility of function words (and functional projections) to constraints governing the interface of prosodic structure and morphosyntactic structure. Of central importance is the notion that the constraint WdCon requires only that the L/R edges of word-level Lex items align with PWd edges; words of the Fnc variety suffer no such requirement and hence are free to be otherwise organized. The second property, namely the variety in prosodization of function words, can come about in just two different ways, given an optimality theoretic perspective: through differences in the morphosyntactic input structure in which the Fnc is located and/or differences in the ranking of the relevant constraints. The constraints themselves are held to be universal. In English we saw that the same ranking of constraints on prosodic structure will give rise to differences in the prosodic structure of function words when the morphosyntactic input structures differ in relevant ways.

Notes

1   The X-bar theory of phrase structure (Jackendoff 1977) is assumed in this paper. The theory distinguishes three levels of morphosyntactic category: *word*, designated by X^0, or simply X; *maximal projection*, designated by X^{max}; and intermediary projections, designated by X$'$. **Lex** designates a morphosyntactic word belonging to a lexical category, i.e. N, V, or A. **Fnc** designates a morphosyntactic word belonging to a functional category.

2   Berendsen 1986 sorts weak, clitic, function words into those incorporated into an adjacent prosodic word, type (iii) here, and those immediately dominated by a phonological phrase, type (ii) here. Neijt 1985 argues for the recursive PWd type in (iv) as a candidate structure. The Zec 1993 proposal for

Serbo-Croatian presupposes all three possibilities, see below.

3 There is a class of candidate output structures for a [[*fnc*][*lex*]] input that were not considered above: ones with a Foot dominating the monosyllabic *fnc*, where the *fnc* would therefore be interpreted as stressed. The absence of Foot dominating the monosyllabic *fnc* in the optimal candidate is arguably a consequence of the general principle calling for a minimization of structure (cf. Selkirk and Shen 1990), codified in optimality theory as the constraint *Struc (Prince and Smolensky 1993). *Struc says, in effect,

all else being equal, 'less is best'. Thus, if the constraints and their ranking do not call for the presence of Foot dominating the monosyllabic *fnc*, then no Foot will appear.

Actually, *Struc could also provide an explanation for the lack of a PWd dominating the monosyllabic *fnc* in the optimal output of a [[*fnc*][*lex*]] input, thereby depriving PWdCon of some of its motivation. In what follows I will assume a role for PWdCon, but keep in mind the possibility that it might be supplanted by *Struc.

4 This table of facts is due to McCarthy 1991, 1993 and to a 1994 class lecture handout.

References

Abney, Steven (1987) *The English Noun Phrase in its Sentential Aspect*. Ph.D. dissertation, MIT.

Berendsen, E. (1986) *The Phonology of Cliticization*. Ph.D. dissertation, Utrecht.

Chomsky, Noam (1986) *Barriers*. Linguistic Inquiry Monograph 13. Cambridge, Mass.: MIT Press.

Cohn, Abigail (1989) Stress in Indonesian and bracketing paradoxes. *Natural Language and Linguistic Theory* 7, 167–216.

Cooper, André (1991) *An Articulatory Account of Aspiration in English*. Doctoral dissertation, Yale University, New Haven.

Cooper, André (1994) Aspiration in English: How should it be defined and where should it be described? Unpublished MS, University of Michigan, Ann Arbor.

Fukui, Naoki and M. Speas (1986) Specifiers and Projection. In N. Fukui, T. Rappaport, and E. Sagey, eds., MIT *Working Papers in Linguistics*. Cambridge, Mass.: MIT.

Gimson, A. C. (1970) *An Introduction to the Pronunciation of English*. 2nd edn. London: Edward Arnold.

Grimshaw, Jane (1991) Extended Projection. MS, Brandeis University and Rutgers University.

Hayes, Bruce (1991) *Metrical Stress Theory: Principles and Case Studies*. Draft manuscript, UCLA. [Published 1995, Chicago: University of Chicago Press.]

Inkelas, Sharon (1989) *Prosodic Constituency in the Lexicon*. Doctoral dissertation, Stanford University.

Itô, Junko and Armin Mester (1992) Weak layering and word binarity. MS, University of California, Santa Cruz.

Jackendoff, Ray (1977) *X-bar Syntax*. Cambridge, Mass.: MIT Press.

Jones, Daniel (1964) *Outline of English Phonetics*. 9th edn. Cambridge: Heffer.

Kager, René (1993) Alternatives to the Iambic-Trochaic Law. *Natural Language and Linguistic Theory* 11(2), 381–432.

Kaisse, Ellen (1985) *Connected Speech*. New York: Academic Press.

Kanerva, Jonni (1989) *Focus and Phrasing in Chichewa Phonology*. Ph.D. dissertation, Stanford University.

Kang, Ongmi (1992a) Word internal prosodic words in Korean. *Proceedings of the North East Linguistic Society*, 22.

Kang, Ongmi (1992b) *Korean Prosodic Morphology*. Ph.D. dissertation, University of Washington.

Ladd, D. Robert (1980) *The Structure of Intonational Meaning*. Bloomington: Indiana University Press.

Ladd, D. Robert (1986) Intonational phrasing: The case for recursive prosodic structure. *Phonology* 3, 311–40.

Ladd, D. Robert (1992) Compound prosodic domains. Occasional Paper, Linguistics Department, University of Edinburgh.

Liberman, Mark (1975) *The Intonational System of English*. Ph.D. dissertation, MIT. [Published 1979, New York: Garland].

McCarthy, John (1991) Synchronic rule inversion. In L. A. Sutton, C. Johnson, and R. Shields, eds., *Proceedings of the 17th Annual Meeting of the Berkeley Linguistics Society*, 192–207. Berkeley: Berkeley Linguistics Society.

McCarthy, John (1993) A case of surface constraint violation. *Canadian Journal of Linguistics/Revue canadienne de linguistique* 38(2), 169–95.

McCarthy, John and Alan Prince (1991) Prosodic minimality. Lecture presented at University of Illinois conference The Organization of Phonology.

McCarthy, John and Alan Prince (1993a) *Prosodic Morphology I: Constraint Interaction and Satisfaction.* New Brunswick, NJ: Rutgers University Center for Cognitive Science Technical Report 3. ►

McCarthy, John and Alan Prince (1993b) Generalized Alignment. In G. Booij and J. van Marle, eds., *Yearbook of Morphology 1993*, 79–153. Dordrecht: Kluwer. ◄

Mester, Armin (1994) The quantitative trochee in Latin. *Natural Language and Linguistic Theory* 12(1), 1–61.

Myers, Scott (1987) *Tone and the Structure of Words in Shona.* Ph.D. dissertation, University of Massachusetts, Amherst.

Neijt, Anneke (1985) Clitics in arboreal phonology. In H. van der Hulst and N. Smith, eds., *Advances in Nonlinear Phonology*. Dordrecht: Foris.

Nespor, Marina and Irene Vogel (1986) *Prosodic Phonology.* Dordrecht: Foris.

Pierrehumbert, Janet (1980) *The Phonetics and Phonology of English Intonation.* Doctoral dissertation, MIT; distributed by Indiana University Linguistics Club, Bloomington.

Pierrehumbert, Janet (1994) Alignment and prosodic heads. In Andreas Kathol and Michael Bernstein, eds., *Proceedings of the Eastern States Conference on Linguistics 1993*, 268–86. Ithaca, NY: Cornell Linguistics Circle.

Pollock, Jean-Yves (1989) Verb movement, universal grammar, and the structure of IP. *Linguistic Inquiry* 20(3).

Prince, Alan and Paul Smolensky (1993) *Optimality Theory: Constraint Interaction in Generative Grammar.* New Brunswick, NJ: Rutgers University Center for Cognitive Science Technical Report 2. ◄

Rice, Keren (1991) Word-internal prosodic words in Slave. MS, University of Toronto.

Selkirk, Elisabeth O. (1972) *The Phrasal Phonology of English and French.* Ph.D. dissertation, MIT.

Selkirk, Elisabeth O. (1978/81) On prosodic structure and its relation to syntactic structure. In T. Fretheim, ed., *Nordic Prosody II.* Trondheim: Tapir, 111–40.

Selkirk, Elisabeth O. (1981) On the nature of phonological representation. In J. Anderson, J. Laver, and T. Meyers, eds., *The Cognitive Representation of Speech.* Amsterdam: North Holland.

Selkirk, Elisabeth O. (1984) *Phonology and Syntax: The Relation Between Sound and Structure.* Cambridge, Mass.: MIT Press.

Selkirk, Elisabeth O. (1986) On derived domains in sentence phonology. *Phonology* 3, 371–405.

Selkirk, Elisabeth O. (1989) Parameterization in the syntax–phonology mapping: The case of Chinese dialects. Paper presented at the 12th GLOW Colloquium, Utrecht.

Selkirk, Elisabeth O. (1993) Constraints on prosodic structure – A modular approach. Paper presented at ESCA Workshop on Prosody, Lund University, September 1993.

Selkirk, Elisabeth O. and Koichi Tateishi (1988) Constraints on minor phrase formation in Japanese. In *Papers from the 24th Annual Meeting of the Chicago Linguistic Society*, 316–36. Chicago: Chicago Linguistic Society.

Selkirk, Elisabeth O. and Koichi Tateishi (1991) Syntax and downstep in Japanese. In C. Georgopoulos and R. Ishihara, eds., *Interdisciplinary Approaches to Language: Essays in Honor of S.-Y. Kuroda*, 519–44. Dordrecht: Kluwer.

Selkirk, Elisabeth O. and Tong Shen (1990) Prosodic domains in Shanghai Chinese. In S. Inkelas and D. Zec, eds., *The Phonology–Syntax Connection.* Chicago: University of Chicago Press, 313–38.

Sweet, Henry (1891) *A Handbook of Phonetics.* Oxford: Henry Frowde.

Sweet, Henry (1908) *The Sounds of English – An Introduction to Phonetics.* Oxford: Clarendon Press.

Zec, Draga (1988) *Sonority Constraints on Prosodic Structure.* Ph.D. dissertation, Stanford University.

Zec, Draga (1993) Rule domains and phonological change. In S. Hargus and E. Kaisse, eds., *Studies in Lexical Phonology.* New York: Academic Press.

Zwicky, Arnold (1970) Auxiliary reduction in English. *Linguistic Inquiry* 1, 323–36.

Study and Research Questions

1   Summarize and evaluate the phonological diagnostics used to determine which of the structures in (18) is the right one for English. Can you think of some additional diagnostics?

2   Figure out and compare the prosodic structures of (28i-b) "I said I was gonna-r and I did" and (28ii-b) "I'm gonna ask Adrian".

3   A function word in isolation is, all by itself, a syllable, a foot, a PWd, a PPh, etc., as in (14). Think of as many diagnostics for this structure as you can and show whether or not they hold for the utterance "Him" (e.g., as a response to the question "Did you see him or her?").

4   Describe the phonology of clitics in another language. Attempt to analyze it in terms of the proposal in this chapter.

Chapter 26 | John J. McCarthy and Alan Prince

The Emergence of the Unmarked

Editor's Note

A key difference between OT and many other linguistic theories is the absence of parametrization. In OT, languages differ in constraint ranking and not in parameter values. This distinction is important because a low-ranking constraint is not the same as a parameter whose value is "off"; even a low-ranking constraint can emerge under the right circumstances, making a crucial choice when no higher-ranking constraint is able to. (See the end of section 6.1 in chapter 1 for an example and McCarthy 2002: 129–34 for further explanation.)

This chapter identifies this prediction of OT and argues that emergence of low-ranking markedness constraints is responsible for the structure of reduplicative morphemes. It antedates chapter 3, so it assumes a mixed theory of faithfulness relations: the PARSE and FILL constraints control input–output faithfulness (as in chapter 1), while the correspondence constraint MAX is responsible for the reduplicative copying relation. See chapter 28 for related work.

1 Introduction

The distinction between marked and unmarked structures has played a role in the development of phonology and of linguistics generally. Optimality Theory (Prince and Smolensky 1993) offers an approach to linguistic theory that aims to combine an empirically adequate theory of markedness with a precise formal sense of what it means to be "unmarked".

In Optimality Theory, forms are marked with respect to some constraint $\mathbb{C}$ if they violate it – indeed, as Smolensky (1993) emphasizes, they are *literally* marked in that they incur violation-marks for constraint $\mathbb{C}$ as part of their grammatical derivation. But whether or not $\mathbb{C}$ is categorically true in some particular language is a separate matter from the statement of $\mathbb{C}$ itself; it depends instead on how $\mathbb{C}$ is

Excerpt from:
McCarthy, John J. and Prince, Alan (1994) The emergence of the unmarked: Optimality in prosodic morphology. In *Proceedings of the North East Linguistic Society* 24, ed. Mercè Gonzàlez, pp. 333–79. Amherst, MA: GLSA Publications. [Available on Rutgers Optimality Archive, ROA-13.]

ranked with respect to other constraints in that language. For instance, suppose that ℂ is itself top-ranked and dominates some constraint that requires faithful parsing of elements relevant to ℂ: then no structure violating ℂ can find its way into the output. Instead, parsing will be unfaithful to preserve ℂ. If, however, in some other grammar ℂ is itself crucially dominated by another constraint, violations of ℂ will indeed be found in some output forms. In cases like this, OT recovers exactly the standard notion of implicational markedness: some languages have only the ℂ-unmarked structure, some languages have both the ℂ-marked and ℂ-unmarked structures, and (absent a congeries of independent principles amounting to a denial of ℂ) no grammar can require that only the ℂ-marked structure be admitted. (See, e.g., Prince & Smolensky 1993: chs. 6, 8 for demonstration of these constraint interaction patterns.)

An essential property of this conception of markedness is that within OT there is no *parametrization* in the usual sense: even in the languages where ℂ is crucially dominated, it is not "turned off" or banished from consideration. Rather, it is fully present in the grammar, even though it is violated, under domination, in some output forms. This property of OT, fundamental to the theory, extends the traditional notion of markedness in a significant way. Even in languages where ℂ is crucially dominated and therefore violated, the effects of ℂ can still be observed under conditions where the dominating constraint is not relevant. Thus, in the language as a whole, ℂ may be roundly violated, but in a particular domain it is obeyed exactly. In that particular domain, the structure unmarked with respect to ℂ emerges, and the structure marked with respect to ℂ is suppressed. This *emergence of the unmarked* is quite conspicuous in the prosodic morphology of reduplication, and here we will be focusing on that empirical domain.

[. . .]

3   Syllable Unmarkedness

For our first example, we turn to a reduplicative pattern in the Wakashan language Nootka, coming from work by Stonham (1990) and Shaw (1992), based on Swadesh (1937) and Sapir & Swadesh (1939, 1955):

(1)   Nootka CV(:) Reduplication (Stonham 1990: 19, 131; Shaw 1992)

    a.   Root [CV, *Reduplicant* CV-

        <u>ʔu</u>- ʔu- ʕiːħ   'hunting it'

        <u>či</u>- čims- ʕiːħ   'hunting bear'

    b.   Root [CV:, *Reduplicant* CV:-

        <u>waː</u>- waːs- čiɬ   'naming where . . .'

        <u>taː</u>- taːkʷa- ʕiːħ   'hunting only that'

According to Stonham and Shaw, vowel length is transferred from base to reduplicant, but the reduplicant never ends in a consonant. As Shaw argues, a templatic weight restriction cannot explain the absence of a coda, since the reduplicant is sometimes heavy and sometimes light.

The structure of the reduplicant in Nootka is unmarked relative to the language as a whole. Nootka syllables can have codas, as is apparent from most of the examples cited, but the reduplicant can not. Not having a coda is one aspect of universal syllable unmarkedness (Jakobson 1962, Clements & Keyser 1983, Steriade 1982): there exist languages where *no* syllables have codas and there exist languages where *some* syllables have codas, but no language obliges syllables to have codas.

Prince and Smolensky (1993) provide a formal account of this and other aspects of syllable unmarkedness within Optimality Theory. The key idea is that constraints like the following are part of Universal Grammar:

(2)   No-Coda
        *C]$_\sigma$
        "Syllables may not have codas."

The constraint No-Coda demands the structure that is unmarked in this respect; when undominated in the grammar of some particular language, it will ensure that *only* the unmarked structure is observed in output forms of that language. If, however, No-Coda is crucially dominated, then it will be violated in some output forms, and both the marked CVC and the unmarked CV syllable structures will be found.

Since Nootka has some syllables with codas, No-Coda is crucially dominated. The dominating constraints are those that require faithful parsing of input representations in the output. For present purposes, we will state them entirely informally as follows (Prince and Smolensky 1993):

(3)   Parse-Seg
        "Unsyllabified segments are prohibited."

(4)   Fill
        "Epenthetic structure is prohibited."

To show that Parse-Seg and Fill dominate No-Coda, we need to exhibit a case where faithful parsing of the input leads to a coda in the output, where unfaithful parsing would avoid a coda. Any of the examples in (1) would do:

(5)   Parse-Seg, Fill ≫ No-Coda, in Nootka

Candidates	Parse-Seg	Fill	No-Coda
a. ☞ .ʔu.ʔu.'iːħ.			*
b. .ʔu.ʔu.'iːħə.		* !	
c. .ʔu.ʔu.'iː.⟨ħ⟩	* !		

Syllable-edges are shown by a period; the epenthetic vowel is here assumed to be ə; an unparsed segment is bracketed. The faithful parse in (5a) is optimal, though one of its syllables has a coda. The alternatives in (5b) and (5c) are less harmonic because they posit unfaithful parses, either epenthetic or incomplete.

This much is a straightforward application of familiar aspects of Prince and Smolensky's theory of syllable structure. But, as we noted just above, Nootka has a particular class of syllables that cannot have a coda: syllables in the reduplicative formation exemplified in (1). Significantly, faithfulness – obedience to Parse-Seg and Fill – is not an issue in the reduplicant, because the content of the reduplicant is freely chosen. Rather, the issue is exactness of correspondence between a freely chosen reduplicant and its base: "copying". The constraint of greatest relevance here is Max, which requires that every element of the base be echoed in the reduplicant. When Max is dominated, copying is less than complete. Max is obviously dominated by the templatic constraint $R = \sigma$, which limits the reduplicant to a single syllable. (The reduplicant R is the surface expression of the input reduplicative morpheme RED.) In addition, Max is crucially dominated by No-Coda, which leads directly to non-copying of a potential syllable coda:

(6)   No-Coda ≫ Max, in Nootka, from /RED+čims/

Candidates	No-Coda	Max
a. .čim. – čim.s~	** !	*
b. ☞ .či. – čim.s~	*	**

We emphasize that there is no question of a Parse-Seg violation in (6b) – only Max is violated by incomplete copying in the reduplicant. Unlike accounts of reduplication in which a complete copy of the base is made and then shortened to fit the template (e.g., Marantz 1982, Steriade 1988), the theory laid out in Section 2 above [omitted here – Ed.] evaluates each candidate reduplicant in its *actual output form*, asking only how successfully it duplicates the base to which it is attached. In this respect, the approach developed here is perhaps closest to the suprafixational models of reduplication in Clements (1985) and Mester (1986).

Nootka is a typical case of emergence of the unmarked. It has codas generally, but not in the reduplicant. This follows from a ranking in which the general faithfulness constraints Parse-Seg and Fill stand at the top of the hierarchy, dominating the syllable-structure constraint No-Coda, which itself dominates the parochial reduplicative constraint Max. Indeed, the analysis of Nootka provides a general model for emergence of the unmarked in the reduplicant: a structural constraint ℂ is ranked *below* the relevant faithfulness constraints but *above* some copying constraint, normally Max. In just that case, ℂ will be obeyed in the reduplicant, but violated in the language as a whole.

We have shown how syllabic unmarkedness is responsible for the coda-less reduplicant in Nootka. It has been recognized previously that the unmarked structure of syllables plays a role in reduplication. In McCarthy and Prince (1986), we hypothesized a template-type consisting of the unmarked "core syllable" structure

CV, with simple onset and rhyme, to account for the reduplicative pattern of Sanskrit (_du-druv-_) and other languages. Steriade (1988) proposes to generalize Prosodic Morphology to include reference to a full range of syllabic markedness parameters which, in her account, govern truncation operations that apply to a full copy of the base. For example, Sanskrit _du-druv_ is derived by first making a full copy of the base (_druv-druv_) and then subjecting it to truncation operations that correspond to the syllabic markedness parameters that militate against a filled coda (yielding _dru-druv_) and a complex onset (yielding _du-druv_).

But in Steriade's operational approach, syllabification itself is _not_ done with reference to syllabic markedness parameters, and the truncation operations, which are peculiar to reduplication, play no role in ordinary syllabification either. As a consequence, the theory does not formally relate the markedness structure of syllables in general to the markedness structure of syllables in the reduplicant. The underlying insight is important, but a new approach is needed to capture it.

Optimality Theory provides the desired coherence. Exactly the same constraint, No-Coda, is implicated in the theory of syllable markedness, in the actual syllabification of words, and in the emergence of the syllabically unmarked structure of the Nootka reduplicant. Through this single constraint, these various threads are all joined into a unified conception of syllable markedness and syllabification, within and without reduplication.

[. . .]

4   The Unmarked Prosodic Word

Consider the pattern of reduplication observed in Diyari, a language spoken in Australia:

(7)   Diyari (Austin 1981, Poser 1982, 1989, McCarthy and Prince 1986)

wiḻa	wiḻa- wiḻa	'woman'
kanku	kanku- kanku	'boy'
kuḻkuŋa	kuḻku- kuḻkuŋa	'to jump'
tʲilparku	tʲilpa- tʲilparku	'bird sp.'
ŋankaṉṯi	ŋanka- ŋankaṉṯi	'catfish'

Descriptively, the reduplicant is identical to the first syllable of the base plus the initial CV of the second syllable. This description raises a couple of questions: Why must the reduplicant end in a vowel? Why must it be disyllabic, and not shorter or longer?

The answer to the first question is that the reduplicant is a free-standing Prosodic Word (PrWd), and all PrWd's of Diyari are vowel-final. According to Austin, both the reduplicant and the base bear their own primary word-stresses: _kánku-kánku, tʲílpa-tʲílparku_. This is determined impressionistically and confirmed by the fact that they each have vowel and consonant allophones that are diagnostic of primary stress. Therefore, the structure of a typical Diyari reduplicated word is as follows:

(8)   [tʲilpa]ₚᵣwd [tʲilparku]ₚᵣwd

The reduplicant is vowel-final because it is a PrWd, and must therefore conform to any unviolated requirement on PrWd's of Diyari.[1]

Several different answers have been given to the second question, about the disyllabic target. According to Poser, the templatic target in Diyari reduplication is a foot. The stress pattern of simplex words locates main stress on the initial syllable and secondary stress on every odd non-final syllable thereafter. This pattern is typical of a trochaic, disyllabic foot, as in the following examples:

(9)   (kána)   'man'
      (pína)du   'old man'
      (ŋánda)(wàlka)   'to close'

With a syllabic trochee foot in the language as a whole, a foot template correctly entails disyllabicity of the reduplicant.

A somewhat more abstract account of the Diyari template is given in our earlier work, which proposes that the template is a *minimal word* of the language. This subsumes the requirement that it be a free-standing PrWd together with the requirement that it be disyllabic. Every PrWd must contain a foot – this is demanded by the Prosodic Hierarchy (Selkirk 1980a, b, McCarthy and Prince 1986, Itô and Mester 1992). Every foot is minimally binary, as the following constraint ensures:

(10)   FT-BIN (Prince 1980, McCarthy and Prince 1986, Hayes 1995)
       "Feet are binary under syllabic or moraic analysis."

With no distinctions of weight, feet are *syllabically* binary. That is the case in Diyari.

This still leaves unanswered the question of *why* the minimal word should be a possible reduplicative template. Linguistic theory ought to provide more than a heterogenous list of the reduplicative templates that happen to be observed in various languages. We propose here to explain why the Diyari reduplicant is identical to the minimal word of the language, without invoking the notion of minimality at all.

To do this, we require some background about a particular aspect of prosodic theory as developed within OT (Robert Kirchner, p.c.; McCarthy and Prince 1993b). In Diyari, syllables are parsed into trochaic feet from left to right: (σσ)(σσ)σ. The following constraints are responsible for this effect:

(11)   ALL-FT-LEFT
       Align(Ft, L, PrWd, L)
       "Every foot stands in initial position in the PrWd."

(12)   PARSE-SYLL[2]
       "Every syllable belongs to a foot."

With the ranking PARSE-SYLL ≫ ALL-FT-LEFT, the pattern of directional footing observed in Diyari is obtained. According to ALL-FT-LEFT, all feet should be *at* the left edge. But dominance of PARSE-SYLL requires that the form be fully footed (subject only to FT-BIN). Under minimal violation of ALL-FT-LEFT, a multi-foot form must have its feet *as close to* the left edge as possible. In right-to-left footing, ALL-FT-RIGHT – the symmetric counterpart of ALL-FT-LEFT – is the active constraint. (See McCarthy and Prince 1993b, elaborating on the proposal of Kirchner 1993, for further development.)

In a form like $(\sigma\sigma)(\sigma\sigma)\sigma$, both PARSE-SYLL and ALL-FT-LEFT are violated. PARSE-SYLL is violated because there is always an unparsed syllable in odd-parity words, to preserve FT-BIN, which is undominated in this language. ALL-FT-LEFT is violated because the non-initial foot is misaligned. Both constraints can, however, be obeyed fully. In that case,

- every syllable is footed, and   (PARSE-SYLL is obeyed)
- every foot is initial.   (ALL-FT-LEFT is obeyed)

Only one configuration meets both of these requirements, the minimal word, since it has a single foot that parses all syllables and is itself properly left-aligned:

$[Ft]_{PrWd}$ i.e. $[(\sigma\sigma)_{Ft}]_{PrWd}$ or $[(\mu\mu)_{Ft}]_{PrWd}$

Thus, the minimal word is the most harmonic PrWd possible, with respect to PARSE-SYLL and ALL-FT-LEFT – indeed, with respect to every form of Ft/PrWd alignment.[3] Of course, the single foot contained within the minimal word is optimally binary, because of FT-BIN. Hence, the most harmonic PrWd (with respect to these metrical constraints) is a disyllable in any language that does not make quantitative distinctions.

We return now to Diyari. Recall that the reduplicant is a free-standing PrWd, as evidenced by its stress behavior and vowel-final status. This is, in fact, *all* that needs to be said about the Diyari reduplicant:

(13)   Templatic Constraint
       R = PRWD
       "The reduplicant is a prosodic word."

There is no mention of the "minimal word" in this *or in any other* templatic requirement. Rather, minimalization follows from the high rank of PARSE-SYLL and ALL-FT-LEFT/RIGHT. If the base of reduplication is greater than a minimal word, the reduplicant will contain a less-than-complete copy, violating MAX but obeying high-ranking PARSE-SYLL and ALIGN-FT.

Consider first MAX-violation under domination by PARSE-SYLL:

(14)   PARSE-SYLL ≫ MAX, from /RED+tʲilparku/

		PARSE-SYLL	MAX
a. ☞	$[(\underline{tʲilpa})_{Ft}]_{PrWd}$ – $[(tʲilpar)_{Ft}\ ku]_{PrWd}$	*	***
b.	$[(\underline{tʲilpar})_{Ft}\ \underline{ku}]_{PrWd}$ – $[(tʲilpar)_{Ft}\ ku]_{PrWd}$	** !	

Form (14b) is a perfect copy, but it also involves an extra PARSE-SYLL violation. Less-than-full copying is available that avoids this unparsed syllable, and, as (14a) shows, this is more harmonic.

The "minimalization" of the reduplicant follows from this ranking. Other seemingly plausible candidates fare no better against (14a). Consider these, for example, which violate undominated constraints:

▸[(ṯʲil)]-[(ṯʲilpar)ku]   violates FT-BIN.
▸[(ṯʲilpar)]-[(ṯʲilpar)(ku)]   violates the requirement, unviolated in Diyari, that all PrWd's are V-final.
▸[(ṯʲil-ṯʲil)(parku)]   violates the templatic constraint R = PRWD.
▸[(ṯʲilpar)(ku-ṯʲil) (parku)]   violates the templatic constraint R = PRWD.
▸[ṯʲil]-[(ṯʲilpar)ku]   contains a foot-less (hence head-less) PrWd, contrary to the requirements of the Prosodic Hierarchy.

The failure of such candidates ensures the validity of the ranking argument just given.

A parallel ranking argument can be constructed for ALL-FT-LEFT and MAX, using a quadrisyllabic root as input. (Unfortunately, no reduplicated quadrisyllables are cited by Austin, so this example is hypothetical.)

(15)   ALL-FT-LEFT ≫ MAX, from (hypothetical) /RED+ŋandawalka/

	ALL-FT-LEFT	MAX
a. ☞ [(ŋanda)$_{Ft}$]$_{PrWd}$ − [(ŋanda)$_{Ft}$ (walka)$_{Ft}$]$_{PrWd}$	*	*****
b. [(ŋanda)$_{Ft}$ (walka)$_{Ft}$]$_{PrWd}$ − [(ŋanda)$_{Ft}$ (walka)$_{Ft}$]$_{PrWd}$	** !	

In (15b), the reduplicant fatally violates ALL-FT-LEFT, since it contains an unaligned foot, while form (15a) spares that violation by less-than-full copying. Another failed candidate, *(ŋanda)wa-(ŋanda)(walka), incurs a fatal violation of PARSE-SYLL, which also dominates MAX, as was just demonstrated.

Both ALL-FT-LEFT and PARSE-SYLL are fully obeyed by the reduplicant, and this explains why it is minimal-word-sized. There is no need for a minimal-word template; rather, the templatic requirement is simply the Prosodic Word, with "minimalization" obtained from constraint interaction, via the ranking PARSE-SYLL, ALL-FT-LEFT ≫ MAX.

In contrast to the reduplicant, ordinary stems of Diyari (including the base of reduplication) may violate PARSE-SYLL and/or ALL-FT-LEFT. Ordinary stems must honor the commitment to their underlying segmentism – that is, they must obey the constraint PARSE-SEG, which requires faithful parsing of the input segments, even at the expense of metrical imperfection. This is a far more weighty matter than incomplete copying, which is only a violation of low-ranking MAX. Schematically, the ranking is as follows;

(16)   Schematic Ranking and Illustration

    a.   Ranking
    PARSE-SEG ≫ PARSE-SYLL, ALL-FT-LEFT ≫ MAX

    b.   Illustration[4]

	PARSE-SEG	PARSE-SYLL	MAX
a. ☞ $[(t^{j}ilpa)_{Ft}]_{PrWd} - [(t^{j}ilpar)_{Ft} ku]_{PrWd}$		*	***
b. $[(t^{j}ilpa)_{Ft}]_{PrWd} - [(t^{j}ilpar)_{Ft}]_{PrWd} \langle ku \rangle$	** !		*

Non-parsing of the segmental string *ku* in (16b) spares a PARSE-SYLL violation, but is nonetheless fatal, since it violates dominant PARSE-SEG. As usual, low-ranking MAX is irrelevant. A parallel argument can be constructed involving ALL-FT-LEFT, which could also be obeyed, in principle, by failing to parse strings of segments that would amount to an entire non-initial foot.

This, then, is a paradigm case of the emergence of the unmarked. In the Diyari language as a whole, the constraints PARSE-SYLL and ALL-FT-LEFT are violated freely, under compulsion of higher-ranking constraints. In particular, violation of PARSE-SYLL and ALL-FT-LEFT is inevitable in the face of the higher-ranking faithfulness constraint PARSE-SEG. Yet in the reduplicant, PARSE-SYLL and ALL-FT-LEFT are obeyed strictly, forcing disyllabicity. That is, in the reduplicant, where only low-ranking MAX is at stake, the structure that is unmarked with respect to PARSE-SYLL and ALL-FT-LEFT emerges, revealing itself under just these conditions.

These observations emphasize an important point about OT: there is no "parametrization" in the usual sense, where constraints can be shut off, all or nothing in particular grammars. Though PARSE-SYLL and ALL-FT-LEFT are false as statements about Diyari as a whole, they are true in the limited domain of the reduplicant, precisely where they can be true, given the interaction with PARSE-SEG and MAX. Second, the optimal candidate is in no sense literally perfect – to achieve the most harmonic PrWd with respect to syllabic parsing and foot alignment, it is necessary to accept an untrue copy of the base. From the perspective of theories with inviolable principles rather than violable constraints, this imperfection is deeply puzzling: if the reduplicant is unmarked, then reduplication must surely be total; and if grammar demands the optimal PrWd whenever a PrWd is needed, then surely the perfect disyllabic PrWd must be everywhere required in the language. But, as we have emphasized, markedness is reckoned along many dimensions and, with ranking, one dimension is favored over another when conflict develops. The fallacious claims proceed from focusing exclusively, and unsupportably, on a single dimension of evaluation and forgetting all the rest. In the case at hand, the fallacious claim ignores the structural constraints on the reduplicant, seeing only MAX; and, in complementary fashion, it overlooks the faithfulness constraints on the general parse, seeing only the structural constraints assessing prosody.
[. . .]

Notes

1 This requirement is itself an interesting one. One possible analysis involves the following constraint-ranking for Diyari:

OUTPUT-CONTIGUITY ≫ NO-CODA ≫ PARSE-SEG

By Output-Contiguity, we mean *x⟨y⟩z (cf. Kenstowicz 1994, Rosenthall 1994). This is the converse of the anti-medial-epenthesis sense of contiguity in McCarthy and Prince (1993a: 50) and Kenstowicz (1994). In input/output terms, it is cognate to the "No-Skipping" clause of reduplicative CONTIGUITY.

2 Cf. the account of exhaustivity requirements in Liberman and Prince (1977: 266, 294), Prince (1980: 535), Halle and Vergnaud (1987), and Hayes (1987).

3 Some additional refinements are possible, leading to further results. First, under Align (Stem, E, PrWd, E), the *stem* must match the PrWd. Hence, the most harmonic *stem* with respect to alignment is MinWd-sized. This effect is commonly seen in phenomena analyzed as prosodic circumscription, prosodic delimitation, and root-and-pattern morphology (McCarthy and Prince 1990a, b, 1993a, c). It can also be compared to an analysis of Sino-Japanese stems presented by Junko Itô and Armin Mester in class lectures: ALIGN-LEFT(Stem, Ft) & ALIGN-RIGHT(Stem, Ft) & ALIGN-LEFT(σ, Stem) ≈ stem consists of whole number of feet and is monosyllabic.

Another refinement: Suppose ALL-FT is obeyed fully, and PARSE-SYLL is violated minimally. The resulting configuration is [Ft σ]_{PrWd} or [σ Ft]_{PrWd}, depending on whether ALL-FT-LEFT or ALL-FT-RIGHT is active. This is the *loose minimal word* of McCarthy and Prince (1993c) (cf. also Itô, Kitagawa, and Mester 1992, Hewitt 1992).

4 Form (16b) incurs one MAX violation under the assumption that only parsed segments of the base must be copied. This assumption is obviously not essential to the argument, since MAX plays no crucial role in determining the outcome in this case.

References

Austin, Peter. 1981. *A Grammar of Diyari, South Australia*. Cambridge: Cambridge University Press.

Clements, G. N. 1985. The problem of transfer in nonlinear morphology. In *Cornell Working Papers in Linguistics* 7, 38–73. Department of Linguistics, Cornell University, Ithaca, N.Y.

Clements, G. N. and S. J. Keyser. 1983. *CV Phonology*. Cambridge, Mass.: MIT Press.

Halle, Morris and Jean-Roger Vergnaud. 1987. *An Essay on Stress*. Cambridge, Mass.: MIT Press.

Hayes, Bruce. 1987. A revised parametric metrical theory. In *Proceedings of NELS 17*. GLSA, University of Massachusetts, Amherst.

Hayes, Bruce. 1995. *Metrical Stress Theory: Principles and Case Studies*. Chicago: University of Chicago Press.

Hewitt, Mark. 1992. *Vertical Maximization and Metrical Theory*. Doctoral dissertation, Brandeis University, Waltham, Mass.

Itô, Junko and Armin Mester. 1992. Weak layering and word binarity. Unpublished MS, University of California, Santa Cruz.

Itô, Junko, Yoshihisa Kitagawa, and R. Armin Mester. 1992. Prosodic type preservation in Japanese: evidence from *zuuja-go*. Report SRC-92-05, Syntax Research Center, University of California, Santa Cruz. Available on Rutgers Optimality Archive.

Jakobson, Roman. 1962. *Selected Writings I: Phonological Studies*, expanded edn. The Hague: Mouton. [Reference is to: Typological studies and their contribution to historical comparative linguistics. Report in the First Plenary Session of the Eighth International Congress of Linguists, Oslo, 5 August 1957.]

Kenstowicz, Michael. 1994. Syllabification in Chukchee: a constraints-based analysis. In *Proceedings of Formal Linguistics Society of Mid-America* 4. Available on Rutgers Optimality Archive. ▶

Liberman, Mark and Alan Prince. 1977. On stress and linguistic rhythm. *Linguistic Inquiry* 8: 249–336.

Marantz, Alec. 1982. Re reduplication. *Linguistic Inquiry* 13: 435–82.

McCarthy, John and Alan Prince. 1986. Prosodic morphology. MS, University of Massachusetts, Amherst, and Brandeis University, Waltham, Mass. ▶

McCarthy, John J. and Alan Prince. 1990a. Foot and word in prosodic morphology: The Arabic broken plural. *Natural Language and Linguistic Theory* 8: 209–83.

McCarthy, John J. and Alan Prince. 1990b. Prosodic morphology and templatic morphology. In Mushira Eid and John J. McCarthy (eds.), *Perspectives on Arabic Linguistics II: Papers from the Second Annual Symposium on Arabic Linguistics*, Amsterdam: John Benjamins, 1–54.

McCarthy, John and Alan Prince. 1993a. *Prosodic Morphology I: Constraint Interaction and Satisfaction.* Technical Report #3, Rutgers University Center for Cognitive Science. Available on Rutgers Optimality Archive. ▶

McCarthy, John and Alan Prince. 1993b. Generalized Alignment. In Geert Booij and Jaap van Marle (eds.), *Yearbook of Morphology 1993*, Dordrecht: Kluwer, 79–153. Technical Report #7, Rutgers University Center for Cognitive Science. Available on Rutgers Optimality Archive. ◀

McCarthy, John and Alan Prince. 1993c. [Publ. 1995] Prosodic morphology. In John Goldsmith (ed.), *A Handbook of Phonological Theory*, Oxford: Blackwell, 318–66.

Mester, R. Armin. 1986. *Studies in Tier Structure.* Doctoral dissertation, University of Massachusetts, Amherst.

Poser, William. 1982. Why cases of syllable reduplication are so hard to find. MS, MIT, Cambridge, Mass.

Poser, William. 1989. The metrical foot in Diyari. *Phonology* 6: 117–48.

Prince, Alan. 1980. A metrical theory for Estonian quantity. *Linguistic Inquiry* 11: 511–62.

Prince, Alan and Paul Smolensky. 1993. Optimality Theory: constraint interaction in generative grammar. MS, Rutgers University, New Brunswick, N.J., and University of Colorado, Boulder. ◀

Rosenthall, Samuel. 1994. *Vowel/Glide Alternations in a Theory of Constraint Interaction.* Doctoral dissertation, University of Massachusetts, Amherst. Available on Rutgers Optimality Archive.

Sapir, Edward and Morris Swadesh. 1939. *Nootka Texts, Tales, and Ethnological Narratives.* Philadelphia: Linguistic Society of America. [Not seen.]

Sapir, Edward and Morris Swadesh. 1955. *Native Accounts of Nootka Ethnography.* Bloomington: Indiana University Press. [Not seen.]

Selkirk, Elisabeth. 1980a. Prosodic domains in phonology: Sanskrit revisited. In Mark Aronoff and Mary-Louise Kean (eds.), *Juncture*, Saratoga, Calif.: Anma Libri, 107–29.

Selkirk, Elisabeth. 1980b. The role of prosodic categories in English word stress. *Linguistic Inquiry* 11: 563–605.

Shaw, Patricia. 1992. Templatic evidence for the syllable nucleus. In *Proceedings of NELS 23.* GLSA, University of Massachusetts, Amherst.

Smolensky, Paul. 1993. Harmony, markedness, and phonological activity. Handout from talk presented at Rutgers Optimality Workshop I, Rutgers University, New Brunswick, N.J. Available on Rutgers Optimality Archive. ▶

Steriade, Donca. 1982. *Greek Prosodies and the Nature of Syllabification.* Doctoral dissertation, MIT, Cambridge, Mass.

Steriade, Donca. 1988. Reduplication and syllable transfer in Sanskrit and elsewhere. *Phonology* 5: 73–155.

Stonham, John. 1990. *Current Issues in Morphological Theory.* Doctoral dissertation, Stanford University.

Swadesh, Morris. 1937. Nootka phonology and morphology. MS 30(W2a. 10) in the Boas Collection of the American Philosophical Society. [Not seen.]

Study and Research Questions

1   Update the analysis to reflect the assumptions about correspondence theory in chapter 3.
2   Substituting other markedness constraints for PARSE-SYLL and ALL-FT-LEFT in the ranking (16a) predicts various other patterns of reduplication. Work out some of those predictions and comment on their plausibility. (Cite examples if you know of any.)
3   Construct a parametric theory that is able to account for the examples in this chapter. What are its advantages or disadvantages in comparison with emergence of the unmarked?
4   Find another case of reduplication and analyze it in these terms. Discuss any issues that arise.
5   Can all templatic effects in reduplication be reduced to emergence of the unmarked? To begin to answer this question, read one or more other papers on this research program, called Generalized Template Theory: Alderete et al. (1999), Carlson (1998), Chung (1999), Downing (1999), Gafos (1998), Hendricks (1999), Itô, Kitagawa, and Mester (1996), McCarthy (2000), McCarthy and Prince (1994), Spaelti (1997), Struijke (1998, 2000a, 2000b), Urbanczyk (1996, 1999b), Ussishkin (1999), and Walker (2000). (Cf. Hyman and Inkelas 1997, Inkelas 1999a for another view.)

Chapter 27 | Paul de Lacy

Maximal Words and the Maori Passive

Editor's Note

There was a time – indeed, there may still be a time – when every phonology student on the planet had seen Hale's (1973) famous problem of the Maori passive. It was deeply perplexing, since the obvious solution that every good student was expected to find was arguably not the way that Maori speakers had internalized their knowledge.

This chapter revisits the Maori passive and proposes an analysis that may be the last word on the problem. The analysis is connected deeply with the proposals in chapters 24 and 26 about the relationship between prosodic and morphological constituents.

I Introduction

Many languages exhibit Minimal Word conditions: restrictions on the smallest possible Prosodic Word (PrWd) in a language (McCarthy & Prince 1986). In this paper, I propose that there are also restrictions on the maximum size of PrWds – i.e. 'maximal word' effects. Since very little has been written about maximal word conditions, one of the two aims of this paper is to show that such restrictions exist. The other aim is to show that upper bounds on PrWd size reduce to general constraints on prosodic structure.

The empirical focus of this paper is the Polynesian language Māori [má:oɾi], spoken in New Zealand. I show that PrWds in this language are allowed to contain at most one trochaic foot and no other unfooted footable sequences. This restriction allows bimoraic and trimoraic PrWds – {(húka)}, {(táŋa)ta}, {ku(ríː)} – and four-mora PrWds with a medial foot – {ta(mái)ti} – or an initial uneven trochee – {(kóːre)ro}. However, it bans all other PrWd types, such as those with four light syllables or two light syllables and a heavy.[1]

Excerpt (with revisions by the author) from:
de Lacy, Paul (2002) Maximal words and the Maori passive. In *Proceedings of the Austronesian Formal Linguistics Association (AFLA) VIII*, ed. Norvin Richards. Cambridge, MA: MIT Working Papers in Linguistics.

Since there is pressure for PrWd and root edges to coincide, the restriction on PrWds translates into severe limitations on root and word size in Māori. The PrWd limits are also argued to be responsible for a famous problem of allomorphy – the many realizations of the Māori passive suffix (Hohepa 1967, Hale 1968, Kenstowicz & Kisseberth 1979: 171–4, McCarthy 1981). Representative examples are given in (1).

(1) | | Active (root) | Passive | Gloss |
|---|---|---|---|
| a. | horo | horo-a | 'fall in fragments' |
| b. | kopou | kopou-a | 'appoint' |
| c. | hoka | hoka-ia | 'run out' |
| d. | mahue | mahue-tia | 'put off' |
| e. | arihi | arihi-tia | 'chop' |

The short forms of the passive -a and -ia are shown to appear only when they can form an acceptable PrWd with the root. For example, {(hóro)a}, {ko(póu)a}, and {ho(kái)a} are within the maximal word limit: they contain only one foot and no other footable sequences. In contrast neither of the short forms could appear with a longer root in the same PrWd: both *{(ári)hi-a} and *{(ári)(hì-a)} are unacceptable since the former contains an unfooted footable sequence and the latter has too many feet. In such cases, the passive is forced to form a PrWd on its own, with attendant consonant epenthesis: {(ári)hi} {(tía)}.

The maximal word limit is argued to be the primary factor in controlling the passive's realizations. I will argue that other forms of the passive follow from general conditions on Māori phonology. A number of new observations about the data are also presented.

The theoretical aim of this paper is to show that the maximal word limit observed in Māori follows from general constraints on prosodic structure. This proposal ties in with McCarthy & Prince's (1994a) Generalized Template Theory – a reductionist approach to templatic restrictions.

Section 2 presents an outline of the theoretical approach and identifies the primary constraints used to effect the maximal word limits. The theory is applied to Māori's PrWd size restrictions in section 3. Typological predictions of the theory are discussed in section 4, and conclusions in section 5.

2   Theory

The theory of maximal word effects proposed in this paper is a reductionist one: no special devices effect maximal word limits. Instead, maximal word limits appear when general prosodic constraints outrank faithfulness constraints.

The work that is most relevant for present concerns is found in McCarthy & Prince (1994b). The authors argue that there is no need for constraints that baldly state reduplicant form, such as 'RED = CVCV'. Instead, the emergent effect of prosodic constraints determines reduplicant shape. They illustrate with an analysis of Diyari reduplication, showing that the constraints ALLFTL and PARSE-σ ensure that reduplicants are maximally bimoraic in this language.

(2) PARSE-σ "Every syllable belongs to a foot."
ALLFTL "Every foot appears at the left edge of a PrWd." (McCarthy & Prince 1993b)

These constraints outrank MAX-BR, a constraint that requires reduplicants to contain their base's material. The reduplicant is underlined in the candidates below; foot boundaries are not marked because they have no bearing on the result.

(3)

/RED+ŋandawalka/	ALLFTL	PARSE-σ	MAX-BR
a. {(ŋanda)(walka)}{ŋandawalka}	* *		
b. {(ŋanda)wa}{ŋandawalka}		*!	* * *
☞ c. {(ŋanda)}{ŋandawalka}			* * * * *

Despite the fact that (c)'s reduplicant is the least faithful copy of the base, it forms the most unmarked PrWd. The other candidates are ruled out because they are relatively more marked – (a) contains too many feet while (b) has a stray syllable.

Such size limits apply not only to reduplicants: Ito & Mester (1992, 1994) point out that Japanese loanword truncations place upper limits on their size, and Mester (1994) argues that cretic shortening in Latin may be seen as an imposition of a word size limit.

Since Optimality Theory allows free ranking permutation, analyses like that in (3) imply that prosodic constraints can limit the size of other morphological elements, not just reduplicants. If MAX-IO (every input segment is preserved in the output) replaces MAX-BR, all morphemes will be maximally bimoraic or split between PrWds. In such a language, the root /takapa/ would surface as {taka}, {kapa}, or be split into two PrWds – the faithful {takapa} would fatally violate one of the foot-related constraints. In the following sections I argue that this prediction is borne out in Māori; its maximal word limit is produced by ranking constraints on footing above faithfulness constraints.

Apart from the constraints already mentioned, the following footing constraints will be employed:

(4) LAPSE_FT "Adjacent unstressed moras must be separated by a foot boundary." (Green & Kenstowicz 1995, Prince 1983, Selkirk 1984)
*FT- "Incur a violation for every non-head foot."

LAPSE_FT is violated when a footable sequence is not parsed into feet. *FT- bans every foot except for the head foot, effectively preventing PrWds with more than one foot. The constraints in (4) together favour small PrWds – ones that contain a single foot and no unfooted but footable sequences.

3   The Māori Passive

In this section I show that there is an active restriction on the maximum size of PrWds in the Polynesian language Māori. While the main focus of this section is the passive suffix, some background to Māori phonology will first be presented.

Māori has the consonant phonemes /p t k f/ φ h m n ŋ ɾ w/ and vowels /i e a o u i: e: a: o: u/. Syllable structure is (C)V(V). Syllable rhymes may contain either a long vowel or a diphthong. In all diphthongs the second vowel is equally or less sonorous than the first: i.e., [ai ae ao au eo ei oe ou iu ui].[2] Other vowel sequences (e.g., [oa io]) form separate syllables.

Bimoraic syllables contain either a long vowel or a diphthong. For present purposes, it is enough to say that stress falls on a bimoraic syllable, otherwise the initial.

(5)   [táma]   'boy'
      [táŋata]   'man'
      [maráe]   'meeting area'
      [kurí:]   'dog'

Content words – nouns, verbs, and adjectives – are minimally bimoraic. In foot terms, Māori employs trochaic feet and aims to have them at the left edge of the PrWd if possible (i.e., {(táŋa)ta}, *{ta(ŋáta)}).

Every bimoraic root or affix is contained inside its own PrWd. Standard diagnostics for PrWd boundaries are syllabification and stress (Nespor & Vogel 1986). For example, the compound /taka afe/ 'circuitous' ('go'+ 'encircle') is stressed as [tákaáfe], not *[taká:fe], indicating that there is a PrWd break – and therefore a syllable break – between the medial [a]'s: [{táka}{áfe}]. Similarly, the prefix *taki-* (numeral modifier) forms its own PrWd: [{táki}{íwa}] 'by nine', *[{takí:wa}].

Monomoraic affixes appear inside the PrWd of their root. For example, the monomoraic prefixal reduplicant clearly falls inside the same PrWd as its root since it bears the stress: e.g., {híhiŋa} 'fall in a large amount' (< híŋa 'fall').

The affixes that are of most interest in this paper are those that have both bimoraic and monomoraic realizations – i.e., the passive and gerund. Their varying realizations will eventually be argued to be conditioned by the maximal word limit. The first step, though, is to identify the size restrictions on Māori PrWds.

3.1   Maximal words

Māori roots may contain two, three, or four moras. Four-mora roots only come in two types: with an initial heavy syllable followed by two light syllables (HLL) and with a medial heavy syllable surrounded by two light syllables (LHL).

(6) (a) Bimoraic roots: LL, H

[tá.ma]	'boy'	[héu]	'eaves'
[ú.a]	'be rained upon'	[ú:]	'bite, gnaw'
[kái]	'food'	[pá:]	'fortified village'

(b) Trimoraic roots: LLL, HL, LH

[ká.ra.ŋa]	'sing'	[káu.ri]	'type of tree'
[á.mi.o]	'roam'	[te.káu]	'ten'
[á:.mi]	'gather'	[ku.rí:]	'dog'

(c) Four-mora roots: HLL, LHL; *LLLL, *LLH, *HH

(i) HLL		(ii) LHL	
[má:.o.ri]	'Maori, normal'	[ta.mái.ti]	'child'
[kó:.re.ro]	'tie'	[ta.rái.wa]	'driver'
[pá:.ke.ha]	'Caucasian'	[ma.ná:.ki]	'show kindness'

Many of the LHL roots are historically derived from bimorphemic forms (e.g., *tamaiti* 'child' < *tama* 'boy' + *iti* 'small'). Nevertheless, they are now single roots, with meanings that are often unrelated to their (historically) component morphemes. It is clear that four-mora roots are a recent addition to Māori, and it is likely that they were once prohibited. In fact, the earlier restriction will be shown to persist in modern Māori, though in a covert way – while four-mora PrWds are tolerated, they are avoided when possible.[3]

I propose that the limits on root shape are due to restrictions on the size of PrWds: PrWds may contain only one foot and no unfooted but footable sequences. This requirement affects roots because each root is required to be contained inside a single PrWd.

As mentioned above, feet are trochaic; they may consist of one heavy syllable ($\acute{\sigma}_{\mu\mu}$), two light syllables ($\acute{\sigma}_{\mu}\sigma_{\mu}$), or a heavy–light sequence ($\acute{\sigma}_{\mu\mu}\sigma_{\mu}$). The constraints introduced in section 2 (*Fт- and Lapse$_{FT}$) are used here to require only one foot per PrWd. Either one or both of these constraints are violated by PrWds that contain more than one foot or have unfooted sequences of moras. For example, the four-mora PrWd {karaŋata} cannot help but contain a non-head foot {(kára)(ŋàta)} – violating *Fт- – or an unfooted sequence {(kára)ŋata}, so violating Lapse$_{FT}$.[4]

The two foot-related constraints conflict with the requirement that root material be preserved: Max$_{Root}$ (McCarthy & Prince 1994b). With this ranking, roots are forced to truncate if they get too large.

(7) Lapse$_{FT}$, *Fт- ≫ Max$_{Root}$

/karaŋata/	*Fт-	Lapse$_{FT}$	Max$_{Root}$
a. {(kára)ŋata}		*!	
b. {(kára)(ŋàta)}	*!		
☞ c. {(kára)ŋa}			*

The faithful candidates (a) and (b) fail because they violate one of the footing constraints. Candidate (a) manages to avoid violating *FT- by having one foot, but in doing so it ends up with two unfooted syllables, fatally violating LAPSE$_{FT}$. Candidate (b) satisfies LAPSE$_{FT}$, but can do so only by fatally violating *FT-. In short, four-mora roots of this type will inevitably violate a footing constraint, dooming them to loser status.

The same ranking rules out almost all other roots with four or more moras. The two exceptions are PrWds with a medial foot, as in {ta(mái)ti}, and those with an initial uneven trochee {(kó:re)ro}. Neither of these forms violate *FT- or LAPSE$_{FT}$ since both contain a single foot and no unfooted footable sequences. The following tableau illustrates this situation with *ko:rero*. As shown, the winning form (a) must contain an uneven trochee; those with even trochees – (b), (c) – violate one of the foot constraints.

(8)

/ko:rero/	*FT-	LAPSE$_{FT}$	MAX$_{Root}$
☞ a. {(ko:re)ro}			
b. {(kó:)rero}		*!	
c. {(kó:)(rèro)}	*!		
d. {(kó:)re}			**!

The following section shows that the PrWd size restrictions are not just a historical accident, but are active in the phonology of Māori.

3.2   The passive: Introduction

The Māori passive has received a great deal of attention (Williams 1971[1844]; Biggs 1961; Pearce 1964; Hohepa 1967; Hale 1968, 1973, 1991; Kiparsky 1971; Kenstowicz & Kisseberth 1979: 171–4; McCarthy 1981; Sanders 1990, 1991; Harlow 1991; Bauer 1993; Blevins 1994; Kibre 1998). The key data are the following:

(9)

Active	*Passive*	*Gloss*
afi	afitia	'embrace'
hopu	hopukia	'catch'
aru	arumia	'follow'
mau	mauria	'carry'
kite	kitea	'see, find'
hoka	hokaia	'run out'
tahu	tahuna	'light'

Hale (1968) pointed out that the data allow for two types of analysis. A purely morphological analysis would have a large number of passive allomorphs: *-kia, -mia,*

-ria, *-tia*, and so on; each root would specify which passive allomorph it took. In contrast, a phonological analysis would have consonants be part of the root: i.e., *hopu* is /hopuk/, and the passive is /ia/. The final consonant would delete when the root appears on its own because codas are banned (i.e., /hopuk/ → [hopu]), but the consonant can appear when it is an onset – i.e., with the passive: /hopuk+ia/ → [hopukia].

Here, I aim to show that the passive's realization is determined by the PrWd size limit. Certainly, some other conditions do influence the output form of the passive, but these will be shown to reduce to general prosodic restrictions that are visibly active in other processes in Māori. In short, a basically phonological approach is viable and does not require any devices that find their sole support in the passive's alternations.

3.3   Generalizations

This section presents a brief statement of the passive's various realizations. The following sections will analyze different aspects of the description. I must note that the following generalizations made about the data do not entirely agree with previous descriptions. The generalizations presented below were based on an exhaustive search of two Māori dictionaries – Williams (1971) and Ngata (1993). I also checked the forms with my consultants.[5]

The table in (10) summarizes the generalizations. One example form is given for each root shape; further examples are given in the following sections when appropriate. The number of examples that support each generalization are given after the gloss.

Since the prosodic form of the output proves significant, stress, syllable, and PrWd boundaries are marked in the examples. Evidence that forms such as {ínu} {mía} and {tápuhi} {tía} form separate PrWds comes from stress placement and intonation; specifically, the H* of the declarative tune falls on the rightmost PrWd's stressed syllable, and the pitch rise occurs over the passive suffix in just these words.

(10)	Root shape	Root	Passive	Root+Passive	Gloss	Num.
	(a) C-final					
	/an/-final	/epan/	ina	{e.pái.na}	'throw'	22
	other n-final	/taon/	a	{táo.na}	'cook in oven'	54
	other C-final	/inum/ } /koharak/ }	ia	{í.nu}{mí.a} {ko.ha.ra}{kí.a}	'drink' 'split open'	} 137
	(b) Bimoraic V-final					
	(C)i:	/pi:/	a	{pí:.a}	'bathe'	6
	other (C)V:	/pu:/	ia	{pú:.i.a}	'bundle'	12
	(C)V(C)a	/hika/	ia	{hi.kái.a}	'plant'	41
	other (C)V(C)V	/horo/	a	{hó.ro.a}	'fall down'	434
	(c) Larger V-final					
	HL	/taute/	a	{táu.te.a}	'consider'	13
	LH	/kopou/	a	{ko.póu.a}	'appoint'	13
	LLL	/tapuhi/ } /ko:rero/ }	tia	{tá.pu.hi}{tí.a} {kó:.re.ro}{tí.a}	'sort out' 'talk, say'	} 81
	LHL, HLL					

One other realization of the passive is found with 26 roots: these lengthen their initial syllable as well as suffixing a passive form (e.g., /kume/ → [ku:mea] 'be angry, fight'). I have discussed this pattern elsewhere, so I will leave it aside here (de Lacy 1999; also see Harlow 1991).

One important issue relates to the claim that trimoraic and four-mora vowel-final forms take -tia.[6] Evidence for this claim comes from two sources. One is that trimoraic and longer loanwords take -tia in the passive (Hale 1968, Blevins 1994: 41). The other is that no trimoraic form takes -ia or -a.[7] Since the majority of trimoraic roots take -tia, it is therefore difficult to imagine that V-final trimoraic forms take anything but this form of the passive.

The following analysis takes the underlying form of the passive to be /ia/; arguments for this proposal are provided in section 3.7.

3.4   Maximal words and the passive

The realizations of the passive are primarily controlled by the maximal word limit. If it is possible to create the least marked PrWd – a trimoraic one – the passive will truncate from /ia/ to [a] to do so: /horo+ia/ → {hóroa}. Failing that, the aim will be to create an admissible four-mora PrWd: e.g., /kopou+ia/ → {ko(póu)a}. When truncation cannot produce the right result, the passive is placed in its own PrWd, with attendant epenthesis: /mahue+ia/ → {máhue}{tía}.

I will start by showing that the passive truncates when necessary, and that the PrWd size limit determines when this truncation takes place. Evidence comes from trimoraic roots that contain a heavy syllable; such roots take -a in the passive:

(11)   *Trimoraic roots with a heavy syllable*

(i) $\sigma_\mu\sigma_{\mu\mu}$ roots
horoi   {ho(rói)a}   'clean'
kopou   {ko(póu)a}   'appoint'
tapae   {ta(páe)a}   'present'
tapi: {ta(pí:)a}   'mend'

(ii) $\sigma_{\mu\mu}\sigma_\mu$ roots
keue   {(kéue)a}   'move'
haere   {(háere)a}   'go over/for'
a:mi   {(á:mi)a}   'gather'
hu:hi   {(hú:hi)a}   'cover'

The reason that these roots take -a is because the more faithful alternative [ia] violates the maximal word limit: e.g., *{ko(póu)ia}, *{(háere)ia}. So, the passive will truncate if doing so is the only way to form an admissible PrWd:

(12)   Truncation under duress

/kopou+ia/	*FT-	LAPSE_FT	MAX
☞ a. {ko(póu)a}			*
b. {ko(póu)ia}		*!	
c. {ko(póu)(ìa)}	*!		

The alternative realization – -*tia* – is ruled out because it contains an epenthetic consonant [t]. The constraint against consonant epenthesis – DEP-C – outranks MAX, so banning the form *{ko(póu)}{(tía)}. The -*tia* realization and epenthesis will be discussed in more detail in section 3.6.

3.5   The emergent maximal word

The maximal word limit that affects affix form is more stringent than the one imposed on roots. While four-mora roots are tolerated in Māori, they are avoided in affixed forms. Specifically, the passive will truncate to form a three-mora PrWd in order to avoid a four-mora one. Such truncation takes place with bimoraic roots that end in a non-low vowel.

(13)   *Bimoraic V^{-low} roots*

hori	{hória}	'cut'
huke	{húkea}	'excavate'
moe	{móea}	'marry, beget'
miro	{míroa}	'twist'
ehu	{éhua}	'bail'
hau	{háua}	'strike'

The alternative to the trimoraic output forms above is a four-mora PrWd: e.g., *{hu(ké-i)a}. The avoidance of such PrWds is due to the constraint ALLFTL (see (2)). With ALLFTL outranking MAX, the passive will truncate to avoid four-mora PrWds with the form $\{\sigma_\mu(\sigma_{\mu\mu})\sigma_\mu\}$.

(14)   Avoidance of {LHL}

/huke/	ALLFTL	MAX
☞ a. {(húke)a}		*
b. {hu(kéi)a}	*!	

Importantly, the constraint MAX$_{Root}$ outranks ALLFTL; since MAX$_{Root}$ specifically preserves root material, it keeps roots like *tamáiti* from being eliminated:

(15)   LHL roots

/tamaiti/	MAX$_{Root}$	ALLFTL
☞ a. {ta(mái)ti}		*
b. {(táma)}	***!	

With the ranking MAX$_{Root}$ ≫ ALLFTL ≫ MAX, the ban on four-mora PrWds only emerges in affixation. In other words, the most desirable PrWd is bi- or trimoraic, with four-mora PrWds only possible under duress.

3.6   The last resort

So far I have argued that the maximal word limit forces the passive to truncate when necessary. However, there is one situation where truncation does not achieve the right result. With trimoraic roots that consist entirely of light syllables, neither -*a* nor -*ia* will form an acceptable PrWd: e.g., /mahue+ia/ → *{mahu(é-i)a}, *{(máhu)ea}. In this situation, there is only one remaining option: the passive must appear inside its own PrWd, resulting in {(máhu)e}{(tía)}.

The reader will no doubt have noticed that a [t] appears in the output form; the passive is not *{(máhu)e}{(ía)}. The appearance of the [t] relates to an independent restriction in Māori: if an affix starts a PrWd, that PrWd must begin with a consonant. The effect of this restriction is seen in two facts: (i) all prefixes begin with consonants and (ii) prefixal reduplicants cannot reduplicate vowel-initial words (Keegan 1996: 36).[8] So, *{máhue}{ía} is ruled out by the affix restriction; the only way for an affix to appear in its own PrWd is for a consonant to be epenthesized, hence {máhue}{tía}.

Consonant epenthesis violates the constraint DEP-C. Since avoidance of a maximal word violation is clearly preferable to avoiding epenthesis, *FT- and LAPSE$_{FT}$ must both outrank DEP-C:

(16)   Epenthesis as a last resort

/mahue+ia/	*FT-	LAPSE$_{FT}$	DEP-C
☞ a. {(máhu)e}{(tía)}			*
b. {mahu(éi)a}		*!	
c. {(máhu)(èa)}	*!		

In short, placing the passive in its own PrWd with attendant epenthesis is a last resort; it only takes place when truncation cannot satisfy the maximal word limit.

The fact that /kopou+ia/ surfaces as {kopóua} and not *{kopóu}{tía} shows that DEP-C outranks MAX. With this ranking, even admissible four-mora PrWds are more harmonic than epenthesis.

(17)   {σ$_μ$σ$_{μμ}$σ$_μ$} is preferable to epenthesis

/kopou+ia/	DEP-C	MAX
☞ a. {ko(póu)a}		*
b. {ko(póu)}{(tía)}	*!	

While this concludes the discussion of the primary effects of the maximal word limit, there are still several realizations of the passive that require further comment. These include the forms found with C-final roots, [a]-final roots, and long vowels.

3.7   Epenthesis and the last resort

Epenthesis forms an important part of the analysis presented above: it is the constraint against epenthesis – Dep-C – that renders the -*tia* realization least harmonic. So, the form *{kopóu}{tía} is not rejected because it has two PrWds, but rather because it has an epenthetic consonant. In fact, epenthesis is the only reason that the -*tia* realization is ruled out in this situation; apart from epenthesis, output forms with -*tia* satisfy all the other constraints, obeying the maximal word limit.

This approach makes an important prediction: if -*ia* can appear in its own PrWd without epenthesis, no constraint will prevent it from surfacing faithfully. This prediction is borne out in C-final roots: these all end up with -*ia* in a separate PrWd:

(18)   *C-final roots*

Underlying form	Passive	Gloss
inum	{ínu}{mía}	'drink'
monok	{móno}{kía}	'prepare food'
fauf	{fáu} {fía}	'tie'
nekeh	{néke}{hía}	'move'
ku:ŋ	{kú:}{ŋía}	'nip'
apur	{ápu}{ría}	'heap upon'
koharak	{kóhara}{kía}	'split open'
manakoh	{mánako}{hía}	'accept'
matakur	{mátaku}{ría}	'be feared'

The competing form is one with a single PrWd and the realization -*a* (e.g., *{(móno)ka}). This form is ruled out by Max since the passive's [i] is deleted. In comparison, forms with the passive in a separate PrWd do not violate any of the constraints identified so far: {(móno)} {(kía)} does not violate LAPSE_{FT} or *Ft-, and does not violate Dep-C. The latter fact is crucial – it shows that the {tia} realization is not avoided because it appears in a separate PrWd, but because it has an epenthetic consonant.

The form {(móno)} {(kía)} gives some insight into requirements on root–PrWd containment. Some constraint must require roots to appear inside a single PrWd – this is dubbed Wrap(Root, PrWd) after Truckenbrodt (1995). This constraint requires every vocalic element of a root to be contained inside the same PrWd, preventing roots from forming two separate PrWds to satisfy the maximal word limit: i.e. /karaŋata/ → *{(kára)} {(ŋáta)}. Wrap(Root, PrWd) must at least outrank MAX_{Root}.

(19) WRAP ≫ MAX$_{Root}$

/karaŋata/	WRAP(Root, PrWd)	MAX$_{Root}$
☞ a. {(kára)ŋa}		*
b. {(kára)}{(ŋáta)}	*!	

In the present analysis, WRAP(Root, PrWd) must only apply to the vocalic members of roots, otherwise [{mono}{kia}] would be banned.

The C-final forms are important in determining the input's form. I have assumed that the passive is underlyingly /ia/. The alternative – that it is /a/ – incorrectly predicts that /inum+a/ should surface as *{(ínu)ma}. This form does not violate the maximal word conditions, so it is difficult to see what would rule it out in favour of {ínu}{mía}, a form that (at least) violates DEP-V.

3.8   Violability

The preceding sections have argued that the maximal word limit is imposed by constraints on footing, and not some independent templatic requirement. If the limit is truly imposed by constraints, though, one would expect these to be violable. The violability of the maximal word limit is shown in three realizations of the passive. In these cases, the form of the passive that is most harmonic in terms of the maximal word limit is ruled out by higher ranking constraints.

One case involves the OCP (Goldsmith 1976). The OCP bans adjacent identical elements within the same PrWd in Māori, ruling out $[V_i:V_i]$ sequences (e.g., *[a:a]). The OCP also influences the passive's realization with bimoraic long-vowel roots. Although most roots of this shape take the passive form [ia], those with an [i:] take -a.

(20) Roots with long vowels

    (i) [(C){e,a,o,u}:]
    ko: {kó:.i.a}   'dig with kō'
    a: {á:.i.a}   'drive, urge'
    pu: {pú:.i.a}   'make into bundle'

    (ii) [(C)i:]
    hi: {hí:.a}   'raise'
    ki: {kí:.a}   'mention'
    pi: {pí:.a}   'bathe'

The reason that non-[i:] long vowels take -ia follows from the ranking presented so far. The candidate {(kó:.i).a} does not exceed the maximal word limit, nor does it violate ALLFTL. Its competitor {(kó:)a} fatally violates MAX, and {(kó:)}{(tía)} violates DEP-C:

(21)   The HLL output

/ko:+ia/	DEP-C	MAX
☞ a. {(kó:i)a}		
b. {(ko:)a}		*!
c. {(kó:)}{(tía)}	*!	

However, *-ia* is not the most harmonic form for [(C)i:] roots: i.e., *{(pí:i)a}. The reason is that the output clearly violates the OCP.

(22)

/pi:+ia/	OCP	MAX
a. {(pí:i)a}	*!	
☞ b. {(pí:)a}		*

The OCP also affects roots that end in [a]. While most bimoraic roots take *-a* as their passive form (see (13)), those that end in [a] take *-ia*.

(23)   [a]-final bimoraic roots

hika   {hikáia}   'plant'
pona   {ponáia}   'tie'
tia   {tiáia}   'paddle vigorously'

The alternative would have adjacent [a]'s: *[hi.ka.a]. Again, the OCP can be used to rule this form out:

(24)

/hika+ia/	OCP	ALLFTL
☞ a. {hi(kái)a}		*
b. {(híka)a}	*!	

One other candidate deserves further comment: the form *{hi(ká:)}, with a long vowel, does not violate the OCP and so should be the winner.[9] I suggest that such forms are ruled out by a constraint that requires the passive to have some unique output exponent. Such a constraint is proposed by McCarthy & Prince (1995) – MORPHDIS prevents all the passive's melodic elements from coalescing, as is the case in *hiká:.

In any case, a similar constraint is needed to explain why the passive does not delete entirely with trimoraic forms. Given the input /mahue +ia/, the output form {máhue} – where the passive has deleted entirely – wins out over {máhue}{tía} since the latter violates DEP-C while the former only violates the lower-ranked MAX. Some constraint that requires the passive to have an output exponent must therefore outrank DEP-C.

Another case involves /n/-final roots. Such roots do not behave like other C-final roots; roots that end in /an/ metathesize the /n/ with the passive's [i], while other /n/-final roots take -a, not -ia.

(25)   /an/-final roots [22 forms]
     /epan/   {e(pái)na}   'throw'
     /huan/   {hu(ái)na}   'determine'
     /weran/   {we(rái)na}   'burn'

     /n/-final roots [54 forms]
     /akon/   {(áko)na}   'learn'
     /takin/   {(táki)na}   'stick in'
     /wao/   {(wáo)na}   'part combatants'

To deal with [n]'s behavior, I suggest that there is a constraint against [ni] sequences, which I will call *ni here. Admittedly, this constraint is ad hoc; I expect that the real reason behind avoidance of [ni] can be related to the plethora of cooccurrence conditions found in Māori (Kawasaki 1990, de Lacy 1998). However, developing this line of research would go beyond the scope of this paper. For present purposes, it is enough that some constraint that bans [ni] sequences at least outranks MAX:

(26)

/takon+ia/	*ni	ALLFTL	MAX
a. {(táko)}{(nía)}	*!		
☞ b. {(táko)na}			*
c. {ta(kói)na}		*!	

As for the metathesized candidate, it is as if the [n] did not exist: the OCP sees right through it, effectively banning [a(n)a] sequences:

(27)

/epan+ia/	*ni	OCP	ALLFTL
a. {(épa)}{(nía)}	*!		
☞ b. {e(pái)na}			*
c. {(épa)na}		*!	

Of course, more must be said about these roots. For example, why does only /n/ undergo metathesis? An adequate response would need to invoke separate constraints on order preservation (i.e., LINEARITY), a step that is unfortunately beyond the scope of the present work.

Despite the remaining questions about the /n/-final forms, it is clear that the maximal word condition still determines the outcome of passivization of these forms. In fact, the *ni constraint acts much like the OCP: it bans the most harmonic form in terms of the maximal word limit. Even so, the footing constraints are still crucial in picking the winning form.

4   Typology

This section aims to identify general properties of prosodic constraints that have a bearing on maximal word restrictions. One is minimality: markedness constraints generally militate against proliferation of structure. The other is binarity: prosodic constraints often promote binary structures, as for feet (e.g., FTBIN) and often in stressed syllables.

Apart from constraints requiring binarity – discussed below – markedness constraints prefer less structure over more. For example, the constraint ALLFTL can only be satisfied if a PrWd contains a single foot. Since a PrWd size limit comes about when a prosodic constraint outranks a faithfulness constraint and prosodic constraints promote the minimum structure, size restrictions must therefore promote some prosodically minimal structure.

For example, the Māori maximal word limit requires the minimum number of feet in a PrWd. Similarly, it minimizes the number of unfooted sequences: none are allowed. Other maximal word limits support the idea that maximal word limits must promote prosodic minimality. For example, Ura – spoken in Vanuatu – allows only two- and three-mora roots (Crowley 1999: 116–17). Ura's restriction can also be seen as minimizing the number of feet in a word, but to a slightly stricter extent than in Māori. The maximal word limits that emerge in many reduplications impose an even stronger minimality requirement: root reduplicants are maximally bimoraic, minimizing both feet and stray syllables.

The minimization effect of prosodic constraint rules out many types of PrWd size restriction. For example, no maximal word limit can allow PrWds with three feet but prohibit larger ones since there is no imaginable sense in which a tri-podal PrWd is prosodically minimal or unmarked.

On the other hand, some prosodic constraints promote increased structure, though in a very restricted way. FTBIN, for example, favors bimoraic feet over monomoraic ones. Similarly, ONSET prefers a bisegmental $[CV]_\sigma$ syllable over a monosegmental $[V]_\sigma$ one.

Binarity requirements could also produce maximal word effects. For example, Ito & Mester (1992, 1994) argue that there is a size restriction on the output of Japanese loanword truncation. The condition allows binary branching PrWds, but no larger; they can contain a single foot and an unfooted syllable or two feet, but no other structure. In terms of binarity, this structure is unmarked and so can potentially be an upper bound on PrWds. Similarly, Selkirk & Tateishi (1988) have argued that Major Phrases in Japanese are maximally binary.

So, there are two general properties of prosodic constraints that can affect maximal word limits: minimality and binarity. Together, these predict that maximal word limits will place a rather strict upper bound on PrWd size. In effect, maximal word conditions will require PrWds to be prosodically minimal or maximally binary. Finally, as in Māori maximal word limits may vary in their domain of application. For example, root-faithfulness may be ranked so highly that roots are unaffected by maximal word conditions; in such a case, maximal word effects may only emerge in affixation or reduplication.

5   Conclusions

The aims of this paper were to show that maximal word limits exist and that such conditions reduce to general prosodic constraints. To that end I showed that PrWd size limits control the Māori passive suffix's realizations.

The analysis of the passive also showed that the maximal word limit is effected by several separate, violable constraints. The most important part of the analysis, though, was that the constraints make no mention of PrWd size; they are general prosodic constraints, requiring footing (LAPSE_FT, *Ft-) and foot alignment (ALLFTL). In short, maximal word limits can be subsumed under the general enterprise to reduce all size-related restrictions to general properties of CON, providing a single theory to cover reduplication, truncation, and templatic morphology.

Notes

1   . marks syllable boundaries, ( ) foot boundaries, { } PrWd boundaries, and - indicates morpheme breaks.

2   The status of [iu] and [ui] as diphthongs varies across dialects; in any case, they are rare and do not prove to be significant in the following discussion.

3   Many names are exceptions to the generalizations made above. These are either morphologically complex or onomatopoeic. For example, the name {tú:i:} 'parson bird' consists of two heavy syllables, and derives from the sound of its call. This fact is unsurprising: even English names exhibit prosodic structures not found in other words (Liberman & Prince 1977).

4   The candidate {ka(ráŋa)ta} is ruled out by constraints requiring initial stress, also responsible for initial stress in {(táŋa)ta}, *{ta(ŋáta)}.

5   My consultants were unfamiliar with a number of the forms from Williams. In those

cases, I asked them to comment on the naturalness of the passive termination.

6   Blevins (1994), citing Ray Harlow, reports that some dialects have -hia and some -ŋia as the default passive form.

7   There are about 21 apparent exceptions to this claim: e.g., kohuki~kohukia 'impel', tapahi~tapahia 'stamp (foot), disobey'. However, Williams points out that most of these forms end in a fossilized suffix, -i. I suggest that this suffix is still recognized as distinct from the root, so tapahi is underlyingly /tapah-i/. In passivization, the fossilized suffix is eliminated and the passive concatenates as expected: /tapah-ia/ → {tapa}{hia}. Support for this approach comes from the gerund: /tapahi + aŋa/ appears as [tapahaŋa], not *[tapahiŋa] (cf. /hoki+aŋa/ → [hokiŋa] 'return').

8   This restriction can be analyzed as due to the emergent effect of ONSET, outranked by (i) a condition on root contiguity – ruling

out root-medial epenthesis – and (ii) PrWd–root alignment, ruling out epenthesis at the left edge of roots.

9 In fact, I found 12 [a]-final forms that take -a (e.g., raŋa~raŋa: 'charge', tara~tara: 'gossip'). However, all the forms are from Williams' dictionary alone, and he offers alternative forms with -ia or -ina for six of them. For the seven forms for which Ngata provided the passive, all were recorded as taking -ia or -ina, not -a. So, the -a termination for [a]-final roots is very marginal.

References

Bauer, W. (1993). *Maori*. London and New York: Routledge.

Biggs, B. (1961). The structure of New Zealand Maaori. *Anthropological Linguistics* 3: 1–53.

Blevins, J. (1994). A phonological and morphological reanalysis of the Maori passive. *Te Reo* 37: 29–53.

Crowley, T. (1999). *Ura: A Disappearing Language of Southern Vanuatu*. Canberra: Australian National University.

de Lacy, P. (1998). A cooccurrence restriction in Maori. *Te Reo* 40: 10–44.

de Lacy, P. (1999). Circumscriptive morphemes. In C. Smallwood and C. Kitto (eds.), *Proceedings of the Meeting of the 4th Austronesian Formal Linguistics Association (AFLA IV)*. Toronto: University of Toronto.

Goldsmith, J. (1976). *Autosegmental Phonology*. Doctoral dissertation, MIT.

Green, T. and M. Kenstowicz. (1995). The lapse constraint. MS, MIT. Rutgers Optimality Archive #101.

Hale, K. (1968). Review of Hohepa (1967), *A Profile Generative Grammar of Maori*. *Journal of the Polynesian Society* 77: 83–99.

Hale, K. (1973). Deep–surface canonical disparities in relation to analysis and change: an Australian example. In T. Sebeok (ed.), *Current Trends in Linguistics 11*. The Hague: Mouton.

Hale, K. (1991). Remarks on G. Sanders, "Levelling and reanalysis in the history of Polynesian passive formations". *Journal of the Polynesian Society* 100: 99–101.

Harlow, R. (1991). Consonant dissimilation in Maori. In R. Blust (ed.), *Currents in Pacific Linguistics: Papers on Austronesian Languages and Ethnolinguistics in Honour of George W. Grace*. Pacific Linguistics Series C, no. 117. Canberra: Australian National University, pp. 117–28.

Hohepa, P. (1967). *A Profile Generative Grammar of Maori*. Bloomington: Indiana University Press.

Ito, J. and A. Mester. (1992). Weak layering and word binarity. MS, University of California at Santa Cruz. Linguistic Research Center Report, pp. 92–109.

Ito, J. and A. Mester. (1994). Japanese phonology. In J. Goldsmith (ed.), *The Handbook of Phonological Theory*. Cambridge, MA: Blackwell, pp. 817–38.

Kawasaki, N. (1990). Cooccurrence restrictions on consonants in some Polynesian languages. *University of Massachusetts Occasional Papers (UMOP)* 13. Amherst, MA: GLSA, pp. 49–84.

Keegan, P. (1996). *Reduplication in Maori*. MPhil dissertation, University of Waikato.

Kenstowicz, M. and C. Kisseberth (1979). *Generative Phonology: Description and Theory*. San Diego: Academic Press.

Kibre, N. (1998). Formal property inheritance and consonant/zero alternations in Maori verbs. Rutgers Optimality Archive #285.

Kiparsky, P. (1971). Historical linguistics. In W. Dingwall (ed.), *A Survey of Linguistic Science*. College Park: University of Maryland, pp. 577–649.

Liberman, M. and A. Prince (1977). On stress and linguistic rhythm. *Linguistic Inquiry* 8: 249–336.

McCarthy, J. (1981). The role of the evaluation metric in the acquisition of morphology. In C. L. Baker and J. McCarthy (eds.), *The Logical Problem of Language Acquisition*. Cambridge, MA: MIT Press, pp. 218–48.

McCarthy, J. and A. Prince. (1986). Prosodic morphology. MS, University of Massachusetts, Amherst, and Rutgers University. ▶

McCarthy, J. and A. Prince. (1993a). *Prosodic Morphology I*. Rutgers Technical Reports TR-3. ▶

McCarthy, J. and A. Prince (1993b). Generalized Alignment. In G. Booij and J. van Marle (eds.), *Yearbook of Morphology*. Dordrecht: Kluwer, pp. 79–153. ◀

McCarthy, J. and A. Prince (1994a). Two lectures on prosodic morphology. Rutgers Optimality Archive #59. ▶

McCarthy, J. and A. Prince (1994b). The emergence of the unmarked: Optimality in prosodic morphology. In M. Gonzàlez (ed.), *Proceedings of NELS 24*. Amherst, MA: GLSA, pp. 333–79. ◀

McCarthy, J. and A. Prince. (1995). Faithfulness and reduplicative identity. In J. Beckman, S. Urbanczyk and L. Walsh Dickey (eds.), *University of Massachusetts Occasional Papers in Linguistics (UMOP) 18*. Amherst, MA: GLSA, pp. 249–384. ◀

Mester, A. (1994). The quantitative trochee in Latin. *Natural Language and Linguistic Theory* 12: 1–62.

Nespor, M. and I. Vogel. (1986). *Prosodic Phonology*. Dordrecht: Foris.

Ngata, H. M. (1993). *English–Maori Dictionary*. Wellington, NZ: Learning Media.

Pearce, G. L. (1964). A classification of the forms of the "passive" suffix used with Maori verb-bases. *Te Reo* 7: 51–8.

Prince, A. (1983). Relating to the grid. *Linguistic Inquiry* 14: 19–100.

Sanders, G. (1990). On the analysis and implications of Maori verb alternations. *Lingua* 80: 149–96.

Sanders, G. (1991). Levelling and reanalysis in the history of Polynesian passive formations. *Journal of the Polynesian Society* 100: 71–90.

Selkirk, E. (1984). *Phonology and Syntax: The Relation between Sound and Structure*. Cambridge, MA: MIT Press.

Selkirk, E. and K. Tateishi. (1988). *Minor Phrase Formation in Japanese*. In L. Macleod et al. (eds.), *Papers from CLS 24*. Chicago: Chicago Linguistic Society, pp. 316–36.

Truckenbrodt, H. (1995). *Phonological Phrases: Their Relation to Syntax, Focus, and Prominence*. Doctoral dissertation, MIT.

Williams, H. W. (1971) [1844]. *A Dictionary of the Maori Language*. 7th edn. Wellington, NZ: A. R. Shearer, Government Printer.

Study and Research Questions

1   One of the main reasons that Hale (1973) adopted a morphological analysis (see the text below (9)) is that [-tia] shows up in passives with suspicious frequency and in diverse circumstances. How does the analysis in this chapter account for [-tia]'s special status?

2   Analyze the OCP effect (section 3.8) using the proposal in chapter 20.

3   Through ranking permutation, could languages show word-size limits that are different from Maori's? What are the predicted possibilities?

Chapter 28 | Joan Mascaró

External Allomorphy as Emergence of the Unmarked

Editor's Note

In ordinary phonology, morphemes alternate in phonologically predictable ways under phonologically predictable conditions. In external allomorphy, morphemes alternate in unpredictable ways under predictable conditions. For example, the nominative suffix in Korean has two allomorphs, /-i/ after a consonant and /-ka/ after a vowel. The alternation in the form of the suffix is arbitrary, but the conditions make sense phonologically, since /-i/ after a consonant satisfies No-Coda and /-ka/ after a vowel satisfies Onset.

External allomorphy was not among the phenomena contemplated by Prince and Smolensky when they created OT, so OT's remarkable success in analyzing external allomorphy is quite unexpected. In addition to this chapter, there is now a substantial literature on the topic; see the Study and Research Questions for references.

1 Introduction

This paper is concerned with a long standing theoretical and empirical problem. It is a theoretical problem because it regards the organization of the grammar; in particular it addresses the question of where in the grammar are lexical, impredictable morpheme alternations to be included, and where are phonological regularities to be expressed. It is empirical in the sense that it has to do with a well-defined descriptive phenomenon, commonly referred to as *external allomorphy*, or *phrasal allomorphy*. External allomorphs are allomorphic, lexical variants (hence not determined by phonological processes) whose choice is conditioned outside of the normal domain of allomorphy, the word. The problem leads to two successive paradoxes, that are, we claim, solvable if we appeal to the notion of *emergence of the unmarked* of OT.

Excerpt from:
Mascaró, Joan (1996) External allomorphy as emergence of the unmarked. In *Current Trends in Phonology: Models and Methods*, ed. Jacques Durand and Bernard Laks, pp. 473–83. Salford, Manchester: European Studies Research Institute, University of Salford.

2   An Illustrative Example

Let us first consider a well known case of external allomorphy as a first illustration of the problem. The English indefinite article shows two phonetic forms [ən], [ə], that are not phonologically general (i.e. they are restricted to the lexical item *definite article*), hence not phonologically predictable, as (1a, b, c) show.

(1)   a.   a[n] impossible word   a possible word
       b.   *the[n] impossible word   the possible word
       c.   in impossible word   *i[ ] impossible word

This suggests an allomorphic, i.e. a lexical solution: /a/, /an/ are not retraceable to a single phonological underlying form, but are both listed in the lexicon under the lexical item corresponding to the indefinite article. In other words, the lexical item *definite article* has not a single underlying phonological representation, but two. Now compare this situation to a normal case of allomorphy, i.e. *internal* allomorphy like (2a):

(2)   a.   make made   meɪk   meɪ + d
             say   said   seɪ   se + d
             stand stood   stænd   stʊ + d

       b.   (She) ($_{\alpha}$saɪ+d)$_{\alpha}$ (($_{\beta}$(an)#(impossible))$_{\beta}$ (word)).

In (2a) the domain is the word, a lexical element (in its inflected form), whereas in (1) the domain of allomorphy includes more than one word – more exactly, it corresponds to some prosodic constituent that dominates the prosodic word.[1] The sentence in (2b) contains two domains of allomorphy, a word domain α and a higher prosodic domain β. Since allomorphy is idiosyncratic, it is lexical. That would allow for a lexical solution for the word case (α), since words are lexical elements. But it raises a paradox for the external case (β): the alternation is *lexical*, but it takes place in a *nonlexical* domain.

The second problem appears once the conditioning of the alternation is examined more closely. Recall that cases of external allomorphy like English *a/an* consist of two parts, the allomorphic alternants, i.e. /a/–/an/, and the external conditioning. This external conditioning is not like the alternation itself, which is idiosyncratic, unmotivated. The fact that [ən] appears before a vowel, and [ə] before a consonant in (1) is not a coincidence, it is completely regular. As we will see (section 4), this kind of regularity is not confined to the particular case of *a/an* allomorphy, but it extends homogeneously across languages.

Using informally the notation reserved for derivational processes, we might say that we are confronted with a regularity in (part of) the *structural description*, and an idiosyncrasy in the *structural change*: the irregular, lexically listed forms *a*, *an* alternate (*alternate* is represented by '↔' in (3)) in the regular environments /__C and /__V, respectively:

(3)   a.   a /__C ↔ an /__V

Summing up, we are faced with the following paradoxes:

(4)   a.   Why is external allomorphy *lexically* restricted (e.g., restricted to the indefinite article), but regularly defined in a *nonlexical* context?

     b.   Why is the context of allomorphic choice phonologically regular and at the same time underivable by (postlexical) phonological rules?

3   External Allomorphy and Emergence of the Unmarked

In this section it will be shown that the paradoxes in (4) disappear under the appropriate theoretical assumptions. For the moment I will assume that the features assigned to English *a/an* allomorphy apply also to cases found in other languages; empirical evidence in that direction will be provided in the next section. The theoretical conditions under which a proper analysis of external allomorphy can be developed are provided by some properties of OT. The basic idea is first developed in McCarthy & Prince (1994), in their explication of some crucial properties of reduplication. Consider their analysis of Nootka as an illustration. I reproduce partly their example of Nootka (1) as (5) (I italicize the reduplicant):

(5)   *ʔu- ʔu-*   'iːħ   'hunting it'
     tʃi- tʃims-   'iːħ   'hunting bear'

The syllable structure of Nootka allows codas like [ħ] in (5), which means that PARSE-SEG and FILL dominate NO-CODA (constraints are defined below in (7)). The crucial point, however, is that "there is a particular class of syllables that cannot have a coda: syllables in the reduplicative formation" (McCarthy & Prince 1994: 345). This apparent contradiction dissolves once we realize that faithfulness constraints like PARSE and FILL have a special property, stated in (6): they always evaluate an output of Gen with respect to another form, the underlying form. If there is no underlying form to refer to, a faithfulness constraint cannot be applied, and therefore it cannot be violated.

(6)   *Faithfulness constraints*
     Given an input to Gen which is a lexical entry in_i, and a candidate $cand_j$ ($cand_j \in$ Gen (in_i)), satisfaction or violation(s) of a constraint belonging to the set of faithfulness constraints is a function of both $cand_j$ and in_i.

If faithfulness conditions cannot be violated when there is no underlying form, other constraints which are ranked lower in the hierarchy, and which normally show no effect because they are overpowered by the former, will *emerge* as deciding constraints. One such case, as argued in more detail in McCarthy & Prince (1994), is reduplication, where *faithfulness* of the reduplicant to the base is controlled by MAX (7), a constraint which requires that every element of the base has a correspondent element in the reduplicant. For ease of reference I also list in (7) other constraints that will be considered in this paper (for further details, see McCarthy & Prince (1994), Prince & Smolensky (1993)).

(7) ONSET: Syllables must have onsets.
     NO-CODA: Syllables must not have a coda.
     FILL: Epenthetic structure is prohibited.
     COMPLEX: No more than one C, V can associate to one syllable node.
     PARSE-SEG: Unsyllabified segments are prohibited.
     MAX   Every element of B (the base) has a correspondent in R (the reduplicant).

In the case of Nootka, the ordering NO-CODA $\gg$ MAX determines the choice. Even if the reduplicants *tʃims* (8a) and *tʃim* (8b) satisfy MAX better than *tʃi* (8c), because they diverge less from the base *tʃims*, the coda-less CV form *tʃi* is preferred as the reduplicant because it satisfies better the higher ranked constraint NO-CODA:

(8)

		NO-CODA	MAX
a.	tʃims- tʃims-	**!	
b.	tʃim- tʃims-	**!	*
c.	☞ tʃi- tʃims-	*	**

We can now return to the case of external allomorphy. Assume, for simplification, that we have exactly two allomorphs, /A/ and /B/, and that we divide the set of constraints Con in two subsets Con_1 and Con_2, where no constraint in Con_2 dominates any constraint in Con_1. If some output of Gen (Gen (/A/ ∩ /B/)) is rated as the most harmonic by Con_1, then it will belong either to Gen (/A/) or to Gen (/B/). If, say, it belongs to Gen (/A/), then /A/ will be the allomorph chosen, independently of the evaluation of the lower ranked set of constraints Con_2. If this is not the case, i.e. if there are two candidates $cand_1 \in$ Gen (/A/) and $cand_2 \in$ Gen (/B/) that are equally harmonic with respect to Con_1, then Con_2 will be allowed to decide between them.

In our example if we take $cand_1$ = [ə] and $cand_2$ = [ən] (as in, e.g., [ə.sɪn], [ə.ɪn], [ən.sɪn], [ə.nɪn]), which show no empty (□) or unparsed (<X>) elements added by Gen, both $cand_1$ and $cand_2$ satisfy Con_1, i.e. (among others) faithfulness constraints. But they do not show the same harmonic rating with respect to constraints that relate to syllabic structure. Lower ranked constraints in Con_2 will now *emerge* as decisive constraints and will determine the optimal candidate.

Both in the case of reduplication and in the case of external allomorphy, the fact that lower ranked constraints *emerge* as crucial constraints is due to the fact that the multiplicity of forms to be evaluated does not arise from the effect of Gen only, but also from other sources. In the case of reduplication the additional source is the process of copying from the base (or of the function Gen applied to the reduplicative morpheme RED – see McCarthy & Prince 1994: 340–3). In external allomorphy the source is the multiplicity of underlying forms in a single lexical item.

In the case of English, both /ə/ and /ən/ satisfy faithfulness constraints. After Gen has introduced syllable constituency to Art X sequences like *a(n) impossible word*, *a(n) possible word*, we get, among others, the forms [ə.n ɪ]*mpossible word* and [ə .ɪ]*mpossible word* in the first case, and [ən .p]*ossible word*, [ə .p]*ossible word* in the second case. Faithfulness (and other) constraints being equally satisfied by both candidates in each pair, the burden of choice rests on ONSET and NO-CODA, which filter out the more marked syllabic structures VV ([ə V]) and CC ([ən C]):[2]

(9)   a.

	ONS	NO-CODA
☞ ə.n *impossible*	*	
ə.*impossible*	**!	

b.

	ONS	NO-CODA
ən.*possible*	*	*!
☞ ə.*possible*	*	

4   Three Other Cases

Cases like English /ə/–/ən/ are by no means isolated. Although the existence of external allomorphy in a given language is limited (probably because of general properties of the structure of the lexicon), the phenomenon is quite widespread across languages. We will consider three other illustrative cases. See Mascaró (1996) for more examples.

In Moroccan Arabic the 3rd masc. sg. pronominal enclitic 'him, his' presents two allomorphs, [h]/[u]. Pronominal enclitics appear as objects after verbs, as obliques after prepositions and particles, and as obliques with a genitive reading after nouns. The pronominal enclitic of first person 'me, mine' is also subject to allomorphy; in this case it alternates as [i]/[ja]. The examples in (10), from Harrell (1962), show the differences in allomorphic form of these enclitics when they follow the lexical elements [xtˤˤa] 'error', [ktab] 'book', [mˤa] 'with', [menn] 'from', [ʃafu] 'they saw', [ʃaf] 'he saw'. (10a, c) shows the clitic hosts ending in V, and (10b, d) those ending in C:

(10)   *Moroccan Arabic: 3rd masc. sg. and 1st sg. clitic allomorphs*

   a.   *3rd masc. sg. /* __V   b.   *3rd masc. sg. /* __C
       [xtˤa h] 'his error'   [ktab u] 'his book'
       [mˤa h] 'with him'   [menn u] 'from him'
       [ʃafu h] 'they saw him'   [ʃaf u]   'he saw him'

c. *1st sg. / __V*   d. *1st sg. / __C*
[xtˤa ja] 'my error'   [ktab i] 'my book'
[mˤa ja] 'with me'   [menn i] 'from me'
(No verbal examples because 'me' is [ni] after verbs.)

The allomorph is chosen depending on the phonological shape of an adjacent word (within a certain prosodic domain). In the 3rd masc. sg. pronominal the form [h] appears after vowels, and [u] appears after consonants. In the 1st sg., after a preceding vowel we get [ja], and after a preceding consonant we get [i]. Here again, the generalization is clear: the allomorphic lexical choice is determined by the degree of markedness, in syllabic structure terms, of the resulting combination: the less marked structure is chosen. In the case of the third person clitic, and when the host is vowel final, a structure with a closed syllable ($_\sigma$...Vh) is preferred to a structure ($_\sigma$...V)($_\sigma$u), i.e. a closed syllable fares worse than an onsetless syllable. In the case of consonant final hosts, a CV structure like ($_\sigma$...Ci) is preferred to the structure ($_\sigma$...Ch), in which we get a syllable closed by two consonants.

For the 1st sg. enclitic, the situation is parallel: ($_\sigma$...V)($_\sigma$ja) with a ...V.CV structure is preferred to ($_\sigma$...V)($_\sigma$i) with a ...V.V structure. For hosts ending in a consonant, the ...CV structure of ($_\sigma$...Ci) is preferred to the structure ...C.CV of ($_\sigma$...C)($_\sigma$ja), which contains a closed syllable.

Within OT, we directly derive this descriptive generalization from the multiplicity of underlying phonological forms in the lexical representation of these clitics. We first consider the syllable structure of Moroccan Arabic: multiple onsets, onsetless syllables, and multiple codas are possible (cf. *ktebt* 'I wrote', *aʒi* 'come!-sg.': Harrell 1962: 42, 43). Hence faithfulness constraints must overrank the syllable structure constraints ONSET and NO-CODA. If, as dictated by OT, these two constraints *must* be part of the grammar, and assuming the normal order ONSET ≫ NO-CODA, then whenever faithfulness constraints are not applicable, the syllable structure constraints will determine the allomorphic choice. In the case of *men.n ja / men.n i* we also need the constraint COMPLEX so that the less complex onset is chosen (alternatively, depending on syllabification, the less complex coda in *menn .ja*) over the more complex one.

(11) a.

	ONS	NO-CODA	COMPLEX
☞ xtˤa h		*	*
xtˤa. u	*!		*

b.

	ONS	NO-CODA	COMPLEX
ktab h		*!	* *
☞ kta. b u			*

c.

	Ons	No-Coda	Complex
☞ mˢa. ja			*
mˢa. i	*!		*

d.

	Ons	No-Coda	Complex
men.n ja		*	*!
☞ men.n i		*	

Another well known case of external allomorphy is the alternance found in French words like *nouvel–nouveau, vieil–vieux, fol–fou, cet–ce, mon–ma, ton–ta, son–sa.* When a following word begins with a vowel, the first member of the pair is chosen: if it begins with a consonant, then the second member is chosen.[3]

(12)   *French* Belle *allomorphy: beau ~ bel, nouveau ~ nouvel, etc.*

    a.   / __V   / __C   / __]
       bel ami   beau mari   il est beau
       [bɛl ami]   [bo mari]   [bo]
                                        beau à voir
                                        [bo]

    b.   / __V   / __C   / __]
       nouvel   nouveau   nouveau
       [nuvɛl]   [nuvo]   [nuvo]
       vieil   vieux   vieux
       [vjɛj]   [vjø]   [vjø]

    c.   joli ami   joli mari   joli
       deux [z] amis   deux [Ø] maris   deux [Ø]
       quel ami   quel mari   quel
       petit [t] ami   petit [Ø] mari   petit [Ø]

Belle allomorphy is similar to the English case presented in the second section. Faithfulness constraints being satisfied by both candidates, the candidate that succeeds in obtaining a better syllabification with the following word will be the optimal candidate. Again, Ons and No-Coda are the crucial constraints. Notice that in this case the word subject to allomorphy can be clearly domain final in *beau, nouveau, vieux,* and *fou* (cf. n. 3).

(13)   a.

	Ons	No-Coda
☞ bɛ.l a.mi		
bo .a.mi	*!	

b.

	Ons	No-Coda
bɛl .ma.ri		*!
☞ bo .ma.ri		

c.

	Ons	No-Coda
bɛl		*!
☞ bo		

I will finally present a case in which constraints which are higher ranked than Ons and No-Coda play a role in the evaluation.

In Catalan there are two types of definite articles. The common form is *el/la/els/les*. The so-called *personal* article is used with (unique) proper personal names and has (in Central Catalan) two forms for the masc. sg. One is *en*, the other is identical to the corresponding form of the definite article, *l'*, phonetically [ən] and [l], respectively. Thus whereas *en Wittgenstein* has only a unique interpretation, and *el Wittgenstein* only a nonunique one (as in *el primer Wittgenstein* 'the first Wittgenstein'), *l'Einstein* has both interpretations. This is the reason why the NPs in (14a) cannot pluralize, while the nonunique NPs in (14b) can: *he llegit els Prince (1976 i 1978)* 'I read Prince (1976 and 1978)', *els dos Wittgensteins* 'the two Wittgensteins', *els Einsteins que desconeixem* 'the Einsteins we don't know'.

(14)   a.   *Definite personal*   b.   *Definite nonpersonal*
         en Prince   He llegit el Prince (1976)
         l'Alan Prince   'I read'
         en Wittgenstein   el (primer) Wittgenstein
         l'Einstein   l'Einstein (que desconeixíem) 'we didn't know'

Thus the personal definite article has two allomorphs, /ən/ and /l/, the latter coinciding formally with the morph of the nonpersonal definite article. The choice between the two allomorphs is determined by the shape of the following word, in parallel to the cases examined above: a following vowel causes the appearance of /l/, and a following consonant the appearance of /ən/. It should be noted that l#C as it stands (as in [l prins]) would violate the constraints regulating possible onsets; in such cases insertion takes place, and violation of FILL is circumvented by satisfaction of those constraints that control sonority sequencing in onsets. Therefore the form with *e* to be compared to the form with *en* in (15) is supplied with □, which will show up as an epenthetic schwa:

(15)

	Fill	Ons	No-Coda
☞ ən .prins		*	* *
□l .prins	*!	*	* *

	Fill	Ons	No-Coda
ə.n a.lən prins		*!	**
☞ l a.lən prins			**

In the case of the definite nonpersonal article (as in *He llegit [əl prins] (1976)*), there is no allomorphy. A single underlying form /l/ will show up as [l] before vowels, and as [□l] before consonants. We are therefore faced in this case with a normal instance of multiplicity of forms arising only from applying Gen to a single underlying form.

5 Summary and Conclusion

Two basic properties of OT are that constraints are ranked, and that underlying forms are submitted to Gen, a general function providing a set of possible alternative analyses to its inputs. Given a lexical item L_i with a phonological form ϕ_i, we normally get *Gen* $(\phi_i) = \{cand_1, cand_2, \ldots, cand_n\}$ as the output of Gen. This output is then evaluated by the set of constraints, yielding a single, optimal candidate, $cand_j = Eval$ $(\{cand_1, cand_2, \ldots, cand_n\})$. But under special conditions the output of Gen is not the result of a *single* underlying form. Under such circumstances a subset of higher ranked constraints fails to decide on the optimal output, i.e. it yields the same harmonic rating to two (or more) candidates. This set of tied candidates will be differently rated by lower ranked constraints which will thus *emerge* as crucial for the evaluation. External allomorphy, like reduplication, is an instance of such special conditions. The existence of multiple underlying phonological forms for one lexical item can result in ties of harmonic ratings with respect to faithfulness constraints for several candidates, since each allomorph can be equally faithful to its own under-lying form. When the outputs of Gen are evaluated with respect to constraints that are lower in the hierarchy, these turn out to give a different rating of these candidates. In the examples examined in this paper, OT correctly predicts that the allomorph whose syllabification with an adjacent word results in a less marked syllabic structure will be favored over the rest, and chosen by Eval as the optimal candidate.

Notes

1 I will not address here the problem of determining the domain of external allomorphy, surely an important issue.

2 The analysis predicts that the indefinite article, when appearing with no context to the right (i.e., when final in the prosodic domain), should take the form *a*, and not *an*, the latter violating No-Coda. Although such contexts are not very common, cf. sentences like (i) and (ii):

  (i) I was talking about A, I was not talking about THE optimal candidate.

  (ii) I was talking about *AN, I was not talking about THE optimal candidate.

3 For discussion of other analyses (Piera 1985, Hayes 1990, Tranel 1994), see Mascaró (1996).

References

Harrell, R. S. (1962). *A Short Reference Grammar of Moroccan Arabic*. Washington, D.C.: Georgetown University Press.

Hayes, B. (1990). Precompiled phrasal phonology. In S. Inkelas and D. Zec (eds.) *The Phonology–Syntax Connection*. Chicago: University of Chicago Press, 85–108.

McCarthy, J. and A. Prince (1994). The emergence of the unmarked. Optimality in Prosodic Morphology. *Proceedings of the North East Linguistic Society*, vol. II. Amherst: University of Massachusetts, 333–79. ◀

Mascaró, J. (1996). External allomorphy in Romance. *Probus* 8: 181–205.

Piera, C. (1985). On the representation of higher order complex words. In L. D. King and C. A. Maley (eds.), *Selected Papers from the XIIIth Linguistic Symposium on Romance Languages*. Amsterdam/Philadelphia: John Benjamins, 287–313.

Prince, A. and P. Smolensky (1993). *Optimality Theory: Constraint Interaction and Satisfaction*. University of Massachusetts and University of Colorado. MS. ◀

Tranel, B. (1994). *French Liaison and Elision Revisited: A Unified Account within Optimality Theory*. University of California, Irvine. MS.

Study and Research Questions

1   Why not analyze the English *a/an* alternation as deletion or epenthesis of [n]?

2   Some types of allomorphy have been analyzed using floating or "ghost" segments (Michelson 1986; Szpyra 1992; Tranel 1988; Zoll 1993a, 1993b). Using the examples in this chapter or others you know about, compare the ghost-segment approach with the one advocated here.

3   There are many other works discussing external allomorphy or lexical selection within Optimality Theory. Read one of them, summarize the argument, and discuss any issues that arise. The references are these (drawn from McCarthy 2002: 152–6, 183–4): Alcantará (1998), Anttila (1997), Bresnan (2001, 2003), Burzio (1994a, 1997a), Drachman, Kager, and Drachman (1997), Grimshaw (1997), Hargus (1995), Hargus and Tuttle (1997), Kager (1996), Lapointe and Sells (1997), McCarthy and Prince (1993: chapter 7), Mester (1994), Perlmutter (1998), Russell (1995), Tranel (1996a, 1996b, 1998), and Urbanczyk (1999b).

Chapter 29 | Anna Łubowicz

Derived Environment Effects in Optimality Theory

Editor's Note

Kiparsky's (1973b) Alternation Condition says that neutralization rules can only apply in derived environments – environments created by morpheme concatenation or by prior application of another rule. Later, Mascaró (1976) proposed to replace the Alternation Condition with the Strict Cycle Condition, with approximately the same effect but a very different formal basis. Later still, Kiparsky (1993) developed an underspecificational model of what are now called derived environment effects.

This chapter reveals a very different perspective on the problem – a perspective that only OT can offer. The proposal here is yet another use of Smolensky's important idea of local constraint conjunction (also see chapters 20 and 21).

1 Introduction

The theory of Lexical Phonology limits cyclic rule application to derived environments which are created by either prior rule application (phonologically derived environments) or morpheme concatenation (morphologically derived environments). This restriction to derived environments is achieved by imposing a condition on cyclic rule application, known as the Strict Cycle Condition (SCC) (Chomsky, 1965; Kean, 1974; Mascaró, 1976; Kiparsky, 1982; Rubach, 1984), given in (1).

(1) Strict Cycle Condition (Kiparsky, 1982: 4)

    a. Cyclic rules apply only to derived representations.

    b. *Definition*: A representation ϕ is derived w.r.t. rule R in cycle j iff ϕ meets the structural analysis of R by virtue of a combination of morphemes introduced in cycle j or the application of a phonological rule in cycle j.

Excerpt (with revisions by the author) from:
Łubowicz, Anna (2002) Derived environment effects in Optimality Theory. *Lingua* 112: 243–80. [Available on Rutgers Optimality Archive, ROA-239.]

This paper shows how derived environment effects can be understood within the Optimality Theory framework (OT) of Prince and Smolensky (1993) by making use of local constraint conjunction, which was originally introduced for other reasons by Smolensky (1995, 1997). The proposal is that a markedness constraint is conjoined with a faithfulness constraint, so that the markedness constraint is active, able to compel a phonological alternation, only when the faithfulness constraint is violated. I will argue that this proposal captures all legitimate effects of the Strict Cycle Condition leading to different and arguably superior predictions.

This paper is organized as follows. Section 2 discusses spirantization in Polish as an example of an environment derived by prior rule application and shows why this type of derived environment effect is initially problematic for OT. Section 3 presents the proposal, developing a novel account of this type of derived environment effect that makes use of local conjunction (LC). The LC account is illustrated with spirantization in Polish (section 3.1) and lenition in Campidanian Sardinian (section 3.2) [not reprinted here – Ed.]. Typological predictions are discussed in section 3.3.

2   Phonologically-derived Environments: Statement of the Problem

The interaction of Velar Palatalization and Spirantization in Polish provides an example of an environment derived by prior rule application (Rubach, 1984). In Polish, velars turn into postalveolars before front vocoids (see (2a)). In the very same environment, however, as (2b) shows, a voiced velar /g/ also spirantizes and so turns into a voiced postalveolar fricative ž (/g/→ž, */g/→ǰ). Crucially, ǰ's that are present underlyingly make it to the surface (see (2c)).[1]

(2)   Interaction of First Velar Palatalization and Spirantization in Polish (Rubach, 1984)

a.   First Velar Palatalization: /k, g, x/ → č, ǰ, š / __ [−cons, −back]

kro[k]+i+ć	→	kro[č]+i+ć	'to step'
kro[k]+ĭk+ĭ	→	kro[č]+ek	'step' (dim.)
stra[x]+i+ć	→	stra[š]+i+ć	'to frighten'

b.   Palatalization and Spirantization of underlying /g/

va[g]+i+ć	(→ va[ǰ]+i+č)	→	va[ž]+i+ć	'to weigh'
dron[g]+ĭk+ĭ	(→ dron[ǰ]+ek)	→	drõw̃[ž]+ek (dim.)	'pole'
śńe[g]+ĭc+a	(→ śńe[ǰ]+ic+a)	→	śńe[ž]+ic+a	'snow-storm'

c.   No Spirantization of underlying voiced postalveolar affricates /ǰ/

brĭ[ǰ]+ĭk+ĭ	→	brĭ[ǰ]+ek	'bridge' (dim.)
ban[ǰ]+o	→	ban[ǰ]+o	'banjo'
[ǰ]em+ĭ	→	[ǰ]em	'jam'

The Polish data raise a question: why does underlying /g/ in (2b) undergo both palatalization and spirantization? If it only palatalized it would turn into surface ǰ and surface ǰ's exist in Polish (2c). In response, Rubach (1984) proposes that Polish has a rule of Spirantization (/ǰ/→ž) that is subject to the SCC: it is restricted to apply only in a derived environment which is created by the prior application of the rule of First Velar Palatalization. Hence, ǰ spirantizes if and only if palatalization has taken place. This is illustrated in (3):

(3)   SCC account of Polish (Rubach, 1984)

	a. *derived* ǰ	b. *underlying* ǰ
UNDERLYING FORM	va[g]+i+ć	brɨ[ǰ]+ĭk+ɨ̆
VELAR PALATALIZATION	va[ǰ]+i+ć	does not apply
SPIRANTIZATION	va[ž]+i+ć	blocked by SCC
Other rules	va[ž]+i+ć	brɨ[ǰ]+ek

It seems clear that Rubach's analysis reflects a real insight, an insight that other theories of phonology need to capture. Yet SCC effects like this one are initially problematic for OT. To show this, I will first lay out some representational assumptions, and then I will discuss the constraints and their interaction. Following Clements (1989, 1991) and Hume (1992), I assume that front vowels are coronal. In palatalized sequences the coronal node of the vowel extends to the preceding velar, and so IDENT(coronal) is violated. (Since g is not specified for [coronal], this analysis of palatalization is presented under the assumption that IDENT(coronal) is violated even when an input segment is not specified for coronality.) Furthermore, I follow Rubach (1992) in assuming that Polish affricates are strident stops, [−continuant, strident]. Thus, spirantization involves a change from [−continuant] to [+continuant], violating IDENT(continuant). In this section I discuss spirantization only. Velar palatalization is itself subject to a morphologically derived environment.[2]

We now have the background to see why the Polish case is initially problematic in OT. There are two basic approaches one might take. One approach would be to ban ǰ from outputs generally. But, as I will show in detail below, this general prohibition on ǰ will affect all ǰ's, whether underlying or derived. Another approach would be to permit ǰ generally, but then there is no way to prohibit derived ǰ's. Either way we run into a ranking paradox or a grammar that doesn't work.

To see the problem, let us examine the second of these approaches in more detail. As we recall from (3), underlying g changes to surface ž (it palatalizes and spirantizes), but underlying ǰ is unaffected (it does not spirantize). Since there are ǰ's at the surface in Polish, the markedness constraint against them (*ǰ) must be ranked below the faithfulness constraint that stops ǰ from changing into a fricative:

(4)   IDENT(continuant) ≫ *ǰ

But because *ǰ is low-ranked, both underlying /ǰ/ and ǰ's that come from underlying /g/ should make it to the surface. To put it concretely, we expect *vaǰić in (3a), with the affricate ǰ, and not važić, with the actual fricative ž. In other words, there is nothing to stop ǰ from surfacing as an output in Polish regardless of its source.

Another way to look at this problem is in terms of faithfulness. Mapping underlying /g/ to output ǰ would violate only one faithfulness constraint, IDENT(coronal). (Recall that Polish affricates are strident stops, according to Rubach (1992).) In comparison, the actual output form with ž violates not only IDENT(coronal), but also an additional faithfulness constraint, IDENT(continuant). This is shown in (5).

(5)   Faithfulness violations in Polish

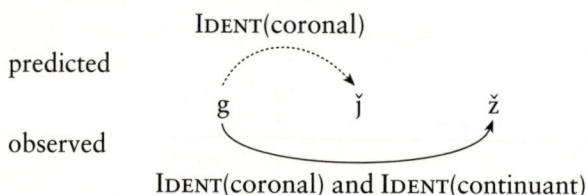

$$\text{predicted} \quad \overset{\text{IDENT(coronal)}}{\underset{}{}}$$

g   ǰ   ž

observed

IDENT(coronal) and IDENT(continuant)

The mapping /g/→ž incurs a double violation of faithfulness, while the mapping /g/→ǰ violates only one faithfulness constraint. The challenge for OT, therefore, is to explain why the mapping with double violation of faithfulness is optimal.

3   The Proposal: Local Conjunction of Markedness and Faithfulness

3.1   Spirantization in Polish

Let's compare the two mappings formally on the example of an underlying form /rog+ek/ ('horn'). The competing candidates are *roǰek* with an affricate (the predicted output) and *rožek* with a fricative (the actual output). As shown in the following tableau, the constraint ranking established so far wrongly chooses as optimal the candidate that incurs a lesser violation of faithfulness, that is, the one with an *affricate* in the output form *(*roǰek)*.

(6)   /g/ in the input – wrong result[3]

/rog+ek/	IDENT(coronal)	IDENT(continuant)	*ǰ
a. ☜ roǰek	*		*
b. ☞ rožek	*	!*!	

Candidate (a) violates the low-ranked markedness constraint *ǰ, but because this constraint is low-ranked it does not rule out this candidate. Both candidates violate IDENT(coronal), since they both palatalize. But the actual output form *rožek*, candidate (b), in addition fatally violates the high-ranked faithfulness constraint IDENT(continuant).

To choose candidate (b) as optimal, the force of the additional faithfulness violation that it incurs, IDENT(continuant), must be rendered irrelevant. Intuitively, it seems that in Polish, though the markedness constraint *ǰ is low-ranked, the affricate *ǰ* cannot surface if it is a result of palatalization. What this amounts to in OT terms is that the low-ranked markedness constraint *ǰ is activated if and only if there is a change from /g/ into a coronal, that is when IDENT(coronal) is violated.

I propose that the markedness constraint against voiced postalveolar affricates (*ǰ) is activated by the violation of the faithfulness constraint IDENT(coronal). This activation of a markedness constraint by the violation of a faithfulness constraint is achieved by locally conjoining them. Local constraint conjunction (LC), which was proposed by Smolensky (1995, 1997), is a way of combining constraints. The formal definition of LC is given in (7) below.

(7)   Definition of LC (Smolensky, 1993)
      The Local Conjunction of C_1 and C_2 in domain D, $[C_1 \& C_2]_D$, is violated when there is some domain of type D in which both C_1 and C_2 are violated.[4]

Let's work through this definition. The locally conjoined constraint is of the form $C = (C_1, C_2, D)$, where C_1 and C_2 are constraints and D is the domain in which C_1 and C_2 are conjoined. Then C is violated if and only if C_1 and C_2 are both violated somewhere in domain D. In other words, the locally conjoined constraint is violated if and only if all of its conjuncts are violated within a single domain. Generally speaking, LC is used to activate constraints that are by themselves dominated in the grammar of a particular language, and so they are otherwise either partially or totally inactive, their force having been vitiated by higher-ranked constraints. LC makes the otherwise low-ranked constraint active by requiring obedience to it when a violation of another constraint occurs within the same domain. The role of the domain is crucial to the concept of LC, and will have important implications below.[5]

In Polish and in other cases of phonologically derived environments, the domain for LC of the markedness constraint and the faithfulness constraint is a segment. In Polish, then, the markedness constraint *ǰ and the faithfulness constraint IDENT(coronal) cannot be violated together within the same segment. The locally conjoined constraint is ranked above IDENT(continuant), so that it can compel violation of IDENT(continuant):

(8) $[*ǰ \& \text{IDENT(coronal)}]_{\text{Segment}} \gg \text{IDENT(continuant)} \gg *ǰ$

To put it differently, the markedness constraint *ǰ is low-ranked, but its conjunction with the faithfulness constraint IDENT(coronal) is high-ranked. As a result, a violation of the faithfulness constraint activates the low-ranked markedness constraint. Because of this conjunction of constraints ranked above IDENT(continuant), there are no surface ǰ's except those already present in the input form.[6]

Let us now apply these ideas to the Polish data. When there is a voiced stop in the input, as in (9), the markedness constraint is activated by the violation of IDENT(coronal), and so the locally conjoined constraint selects candidate (b), notwithstanding the double violation of faithfulness.

(9)   /g/ in the input

/rog+ek/		$[*ǰ \& \text{IDENT(coronal)}]_{\text{Seg}}$	IDENT(continuant)	*ǰ
a.	rojek	*!		*
b. ☞	rožek		*	

Yet, when the affricate ǰ is already in the input, and so there is no violation of IDENT(coronal), then the locally conjoined constraint has no force. In this case, candidate (a), with no spirantization, becomes the winner.

(10) /ǰ/ in the input

/banǰ+o/	[*ǰ & IDENT(coronal)]$_{Seg}$	IDENT(continuant)	*ǰ
a. ☞ banǰo	✓		*
b. banžo	✓	*!	

Consequently, the mapping /g/→ž is forced by the locally conjoined constraint. The local conjunction of *ǰ and IDENT(coronal) compels the otherwise problematic double faithfulness violation. The optimal candidate with the fricative ž violates both IDENT(coronal) and IDENT(continuant) (shown in (5)).

The ranking that has been established is presented in (11).

(11) Established ranking

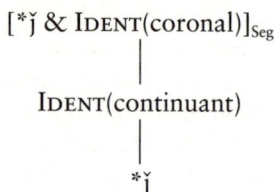

[*ǰ & IDENT(coronal)]$_{Seg}$

|

IDENT(continuant)

|

*ǰ

By virtue of this ranking, *ǰ is only relevant when IDENT(coronal) is violated, and this is so when ǰ is not in the input. That is the effect of local conjunction.

There are three significant observations to be made about the Polish example. These observations are important because they hold of other cases of phonologically derived environments, such as lenition in Campidanian Sardinian (Bolognesi 1998), vowel lowering in Tiberian Hebrew (Prince, 1975), and diphthongization in Slovak (Rubach, 1993).

First, in each of the cases of phonologically derived environments, segments are allowed to surface faithfully if they are underlying but cannot arise as a result of a phonological alternation. To illustrate it, let's look again at the Polish example. As we saw in (2), in Polish underlying ǰ's are allowed on the surface but ǰ's that would be a result of palatalization are banned. This is accounted for by means of a high-ranked locally conjoined constraint *ǰ and IDENT(coronal). The markedness constraint *ǰ is low-ranked but is activated when faithfulness, IDENT(coronal), is violated.

Second, the actual mapping in cases of phonologically derived environments (in Polish, /g/→ž) incurs a seemingly unmotivated double violation of faithfulness. At the same time there is a more faithful hypothetical mapping (/g/→ǰ) which violates one faithfulness constraint less. We know this because the featural composition of a voiced velar stop (g) is more similar to a voiced postalveolar affricate (ǰ), than it is to a voiced postalveolar fricative (ž). Thus, a change from /g/ to ǰ would result in a more faithful mapping and should be preferred for faithfulness reasons, as the discussion of (6) emphasized. The challenge for OT is to explain what forces the less faithful mapping to take place, and the proposal here is that the locally conjoined markedness and faithfulness constraint is responsible.

Third, in each legitimate case of phonologically derived environments, the markedness constraint that results in the unmotivated faithfulness violation (in Polish, the spirantization constraint) is context-free. The context-free property of the markedness constraint allows the domain for LC in cases of phonologically derived environments to be a single segment. It is enough to look at the segment itself to evaluate the context-free markedness constraint.

In summary, there are three characteristics of phonologically derived environments: (i) the special status of underlying segments, (ii) the seemingly unmotivated double violation of faithfulness in the actual mapping, and (iii) the context-free property of the phonological alternation that adds an unmotivated faithfulness violation. The LC proposal takes into account these three characteristics and accounts for each of them using the general tools of OT. In this way the LC proposal provides a general account of all legitimate cases of phonologically derived environments. The idea is straightforward; an otherwise low-ranked markedness constraint is activated, resulting in a phonological alternation, only when a faithfulness constraint is violated within the same segment. [. . .]

3.3   Typological implications

Inherent to Optimality Theory is language typology. The central question that needs to be asked of any OT analysis is what languages are predicted by various re-rankings of the proposed constraints. In this section I examine ranking permutations involving the local conjunction of markedness and faithfulness proposed so far.

When establishing ranking permutations, free permutations may be limited by universally fixed (non-permutable) rankings. One general claim concerning local constraint conjunction is that conjoined constraints universally outrank their component parts, thus the locally conjoined constraint $[F\&^*M]_D$ dominates its components, markedness $^*M$ and faithfulness F, in all grammars (Smolensky 1995, 1997). Predicted grammars are given in (21).

(21)   Predicted Grammars

    a.   Derived environment effect
        $[F\&^*M]_D \gg \textsc{Ident}(M) \gg {}^*M$

    b.   Normal application
        $^*M \gg \textsc{Ident}(M)$

    c.   Blocking in all environments
        $\textsc{Ident}(M) \gg [F\&^*M]_D \gg {}^*M$

The ranking in (a) is a general schema for derived environment effects. The marked segment M surfaces in some environments in the language ($\textsc{Ident}(M) \gg {}^*M$) but is ruled out when faithfulness F is violated in a local domain ($[F\&{}^*M]_D \gg \text{IDENT}(M)$). As argued in this paper, faithfulness violation implies a derived environment effect. Thus, according to this ranking, M-type segments are not allowed in derived environments. The ranking in (b), on the other hand, presents a case where the marked segment is banned from all environments due to the high-ranked markedness $^*M$ ($^*M \gg \text{IDENT}(M)$). In this case, the ranking of the locally conjoined constraint $[F\&{}^*M]_D$ is irrelevant since markedness is active in all environments. Finally, the ranking in (c) is a case where the marked segment is admitted to all environments. Faithfulness to M, IDENT(M), outranks both the locally conjoined constraint and antagonistic markedness. We have seen now that LC theory can account for the range of attested behaviors: derived environment effect, normal application, and blocking in all environments.

[. . .]

Notes

1 The intermediate step shown in (2b) is a convenient way of representing the discrepancy in the underlying–surface mapping and has no formal status in the OT approach taken in this paper.

2 One might wonder why only voiced affricates spirantize. As suggested to me by John Kingston (p.c.), one way to explain this fact is to compare voiced and voiceless stop closures. Voiced stops typically have shorter closures than voiceless stops. (It is difficult to maintain voicing throughout a stop, and so the closure has to be short.) But because the voiced stop closure is so short, speakers do not always achieve complete closure, and so the result is a fricative (Ohala, 1983; Kingston, 1998).

3 In the tableau I consider only candidates that satisfy the constraint demanding palatalization. As for the notation, I use '☞' and '☞' in opposite ways: '☞' marks the observed output form which according to the constraint ranking in (6) is non-optimal, whereas '☞' points to a candidate that does not surface as the output, but is optimal according to the constraint ranking. The input form is simplified for clarity. According to Rubach (1984), the input is /–g+ĭk+ĭ/. This simplification has no effect on the outcome.

4 LC has been employed previously for the analysis of a number of other phonological phenomena. Among others see Alderete (1997), Ito and Mester (1998) for dissimilation as self-conjunction of markedness; Alderete (1999) for transderivational nonidentity effects as local conjunction of an antifaithfulness constraint and anchoring;

Kirchner (1996) for chain-shifts as conjunction of faithfulness; Smolensky (1993), Ito and Mester (2002) for the Coda-Condition; Smolensky (1995) for the Sonority Hierarchy; and Smolensky (1997), Baković (2000) for the typology of Vowel Harmony. For a different understanding of LC see Hewitt and Crowhurst (1996), Crowhurst and Hewitt (1997), Crowhurst (1998).

5 There are limits on what constraints can be conjoined and in what domains. Hewitt and Crowhurst (1996), and Crowhurst and Hewitt (1997) propose that only constraints that share a fulcrum (an argument) can be conjoined. Though I adopt a somewhat different conceptualization of LC than they do, my work supports this view.

As for the domain, I propose that it is the smallest domain within which both of the locally conjoined constraints can be evaluated. In cases of phonologically derived environments the relevant markedness and faithfulness constraints can be assessed within a single segment, and so the segment is the domain for LC.

6 There are cases in Polish where $\check{j}$'s that are a result of palatalization do not spirantize. In all instances where spirantization fails, $\check{j}$'s are preceded by a postalveolar fricative $\check{z}$ (e.g., *musk* 'brain' – *mužǰ+ek* 'dim.', *drob'jask* 'trifle' – *drob'jažǰ+ek* 'dim.', *m'jazg+a* 'pulp' – *m'jažǰ+i+ć* 'to squash'). I postulate that spirantization is blocked here because it would incur a violation of an OCP constraint which in the grammar of Polish dominates the locally conjoined constraint.

References

Alderete, J., 1997. Dissimilation as local conjunction. In: K. Kusumoto (ed.), *Proceedings of the North East Linguistic Society* 27, 17–32. Amherst, MA: GLSA. ◄

Alderete, J., 1999. *Morphologically-governed Accent in Optimality Theory*. Ph.D. dissertation, University of Massachusetts, Amherst.

Baković, E., 2000. *Harmony, Dominance, and Control*. Ph.D. dissertation, Rutgers University, New Brunswick, NJ.

Bolognesi, R., 1998. *The Phonology of Campidanian Sardinian: A Unitary Account of a Self-organizing Structure*. Ph.D. dissertation, Holland Institute of Linguistics, Leiden. [Printed by ICG Printing, Dordrecht.]

Chomsky, N., 1965. *Aspects of the Theory of Syntax*. Cambridge, MA: MIT Press.

Clements, G. N., 1989. A unified set of features for consonants and vowels. MS, Cornell University, Ithaca.

Clements, G. N., 1991. Place of articulation in consonants and vowels. A unified theory. In: G. N. Clements and E. Hume (eds.), *Working Papers of the Cornell Phonetics Laboratory* 5, 77–123. Ithaca: Cornell University.

Crowhurst, M., 1998. Conflicting directionality and tonal association in Carib of Surinam. Paper presented at the West Coast Conference on Formal Linguistics 17, University of British Columbia, Vancouver, BC. ►

Crowhurst, M. and M. Hewitt, 1997. Boolean operations and constraint interactions in Optimality Theory. MS, University of North Carolina at Chapel Hill and Brandeis University. [Rutgers Optimality Archive, http://ruccs.rutgers.edu/roa.html.]

Hewitt, M. and M. Crowhurst, 1996. Conjunctive constraints and templates. In: J. Beckman et al. (eds.), *Proceedings of the North East Linguistic Society* 26, 101–16. Amherst, MA: GLSA.

Hume, E., 1992. *Front Vowels, Coronal Consonants and Their Interaction in Nonlinear Phonology*. Ph.D. dissertation, Cornell University, Ithaca.

Ito, J. and A. Mester, 1998. Markedness and word structure: OCP effects in Japanese. MS, University of California, Santa Cruz. [Rutgers Optimality Archive, http://ruccs.rutgers.edu/roa.html.]

Ito, J. and A. Mester, 2002. On the sources of opacity in OT: Coda processes in German.

In: C. Féry and R. van de Vijver (eds.), *The Optimal Syllable*. Cambridge: Cambridge University Press.

Kean, M-L., 1974. The strict cycle in phonology. *Linguistic Inquiry* 5, 179–203.

Kingston, J., 1998. Introduction to phonetic theory. Class notes: Linguistics 614, University of Massachusetts, Amherst.

Kiparsky, P., 1982. *Explanation in Phonology*. Dordrecht: Foris.

Kirchner, R., 1996. Synchronic chain shifts in Optimality Theory. *Linguistic Inquiry* 27, 341–9. ◄

Mascaró, J., 1976. *Catalan Phonology and the Phonological Cycle*. Ph.D. dissertation, MIT, Cambridge, MA.

Ohala, J., 1983. The origin of sound patterns in vocal tract constraints. In: P. MacNeilage (ed.), *The Production of Speech*, 189–216. New York: Springer Verlag.

Prince, A., 1975. *The Phonology and Morphology of Tiberian Hebrew*. Ph.D. dissertation, MIT, Cambridge, MA.

Prince, A. and P. Smolensky, 1993. *Optimality Theory: Constraint Interaction in Generative Grammar*. Report no. RUCCS-TR-2. New Brunswick, NJ: Rutgers University Center for Cognitive Science. ◄

Rubach, J., 1984. *Cyclic and Lexical Phonology: The Structure of Polish*. Dordrecht: Foris.

Rubach, J., 1992. Affricates as strident stops in Polish. *Linguistic Inquiry* 25, 119–43.

Rubach, J., 1993. *The Lexical Phonology of Slovak*. New York: Oxford University Press.

Smolensky, P., 1993. Harmony, markedness, and phonological activity. Paper presented at Rutgers Optimality Workshop-1, Rutgers University, New Brunswick, NJ. [Rutgers Optimality Archive, http://ruccs.rutgers.edu/roa.html.]

Smolensky, P., 1995. On the internal structure of the constraint component of UG. Colloquium presented at the University of California, Los Angeles. [Rutgers Optimality Archive, http://ruccs.rutgers.edu.html.]

Smolensky, P., 1997. Constraint interaction in generative grammar II: Local conjunction or random rules in Universal Grammar. Paper presented to Hopkins Optimality Theory Workshop/Maryland Mayfest '97. Baltimore, MD.

Study and Research Questions

1 In chapter 20 and in Smolensky (1995), pairs of markedness constraints are conjoined. In chapter 21, pairs of faithfulness constraints are conjoined. In this chapter, markedness is conjoined with faithfulness. Describe any general similarities or differences that emerge in these three circumstances.

2 One of the important issues in the theory of local conjunction is this (Fukazawa 1999; Fukazawa and Miglio 1998; Itô and Mester 1998, 2003): what constraints can be conjoined? Study the examples in this chapter and chapters 20 and 21 and use them as the basis for a restrictive theory of conjoinability. Construct some implausible conjunctions that your theory rules out.

3 Read and evaluate Inkelas's (1999b) alternative proposal. Other approaches can be found in Burzio (1997a, 2000) and Polgárdi (1998).

Chapter 30 | Junko Itô, Armin Mester, and Jaye Padgett

Licensing and Underspecification in Optimality Theory

Editor's Note

One of the core theses of OT is richness of the base, the hypothesis that there are no language-particular restrictions on inputs (see section 9.3 of chapter 1). Instead of input restrictions, there are input→output mappings under the control of the grammar. For example, English has no words with initial nasal + consonant (NC) clusters because any input with such a cluster is treated unfaithfully (/mba/ → [ba]) and not because there is an input restriction, such as a morpheme-structure constraint, against #NC. (For further explication, see McCarthy 2002: 76–81.)

As a consequence of richness of the base, languages are replete with neutralizing mappings: e.g., /mba/ → [ba] and /ba/ → [ba]. Lexicon Optimization, the topic of the current chapter, is a hypothesis about how learning of underlying forms proceeds in the face of such massive neutralization. The discussion is based on the example of post-nasal voicing in the native (Yamato) vocabulary of Japanese (cf. chapters 14 and 15 for other approaches to this phenomenon and chapter 32 for related discussion).

[. . .]

3.2 Underspecification as an Output Property

Consider the connection, often merely implicit in practice and yet clear in principle, between feature redundancy and feature underspecification. Building on a proposal made by Padgett (1991: 56–58), we link the two by means of the notion *licensing*. The hypothesis formulated in (11), as a principle of Universal Grammar, is an

Excerpt (with assistance from the authors) from:
Itô, Junko, Mester, Armin, and Padgett, Jaye (1995) Licensing and underspecification in Optimality Theory. *Linguistic Inquiry* 26: 571–614. [Available on Rutgers Optimality Archive, ROA-38.]

explicit statement of this connection (cf. the redundancy rules and marking conditions of Kiparsky (1985), Archangeli and Pulleyblank (1986), and others).

(11) *Licensing Cancellation*
      If F ⊃ G, then ¬(FλG).
      "If the specification [F] implies the specification [G], then it is not the case that [F] licenses [G]."

The statement in (11) is intended as follows: Suppose a grammar contains a segment structure condition expressing the segment-internal redundancy that a segment that has the feature [F] also has the feature [G]. Then the feature [G] is not licensed within a segment containing [F]. For example, given the redundancy implication [sonorant] ⊃ [voice], a sonorant segment does not license [voice]. The [voice] feature is licensed when linked to obstruents (12a), but not when linked to sonorants (12b).

(12) a. *Licensed [voice]*   b. *Unlicensed [voice]*
          [d]   [n]
           | |
         [voice]   [voice]

[...]
   Thus, given Licensing Cancellation, a redundancy implication [sonorant] ⊃ [voice] means that the feature [voice] is not licensed in a sonorant segment (12b). The absence of [voice] is forced by the relevant member of the family of feature-licensing constraints schematically characterized in (14).

(14) *License(Φ)*
      The phonological feature Φ must be licensed.

In the context of our discussion, the relevant redundancy implication in Japanese (shared by all natural languages) is the one repeated in (15) (we follow the convention in OT of abbreviating constraint names for use in constraint tableaux). This condition in fact represents a whole family of sonorant-voicing conditions (governing nasals, liquids, vocoids, and other sonorants).

(15) SᴏɴVᴏɪ
      [sonorant] ⊃ [voice]

   To illustrate the role of feature licensing in our account of Japanese, we will use the word *kami* 'paper'. The relevant members of the constraint families involved are the voice-licensing constraint Lɪᴄᴇɴsᴇ(Vᴏɪᴄᴇ) (16), where Φ = [voice], and the nasal version of the sonorant-voicing condition NᴀsVᴏɪ (17).

(16) Lɪᴄᴇɴsᴇ(Vᴏɪᴄᴇ)
      The feature [voice] must be licensed.

(17)   NASVOI
       [nasal] ⊃ [voice]

Since LICENSE(VOICE) is the only member of the family of licensing constraints to play a role in our analysis, we will refer to this constraint simply as LICENSE. Focusing on the nasal [m] in *kami*, we have two potential candidate representations: one with the nasal specified for voicing (18a), and one with the nasal unspecified (18b).

(18)   a.
k a m i	→	*LICENSE
v		√NASVOI

       b.
k a m i	→	√LICENSE
		*NASVOI

(18a) fulfills NASVOI but violates LICENSE. (18b), on the other hand, violates NASVOI but fulfills LICENSE. The situation thus looks like a standoff, with each representation violating one constraint, while fulfilling the other. This is the kind of constraint conflict that OT resolves, with its notion of constraint domination. Leaving details to the more technical expositions of the formal theory (see especially Prince and Smolensky (PS) 1993), the central idea is that constraints are ranked in a strict domination order, with higher constraints taking absolute precedence over lower constraints. For the case at hand, we hypothesize that LICENSE is ranked above NASVOI. In the notation of OT, this is written as in (19).

(19)   LICENSE ≫ NASVOI

Given this constraint ranking, (18b) is the winning candidate, with the nasal unspecified for voicing.
[...]
   Building on PS 1993 and on our earlier work in OT (Itô, Mester, and Padgett 1993), as well as that of others (McCarthy and Prince 1993, Myers 1993, Archangeli and Pulleyblank 1993), we extend the faithfulness constraints as in (24). Since the individual constraints shown below need not be distinguished in the ranking hierarchy to be discussed, we group the family of faithfulness constraints into a single collective constraint FAITH.

(24)   FAITH *(Feature Faithfulness)*
       PARSEFEAT
       All input features are parsed.
       FILLFEAT
       All features are part of the input.
       PARSELINK
       All input association relations are kept.
       FILLLINK
       All association relations are part of the input.

[. . .]

Consider now the constraint tableau 7, which evaluates candidates built on the input /tompo/ (for the Japanese form *tombo* 'dragonfly'). As noted earlier, we assume the candidate set to include any autosegmental "improvisation" on the input – insertion and nonparsing of features, and so on. Since our focus is on the medial NC cluster and the feature [voice], we indicate only the presence or absence of relevant voicing specifications in the input and in the candidate forms. The two candidates (b) and (e) of tableau 7 fail for now familiar reasons, falling victim to LICENSE. Candidates (a) and (c) are eliminated by NASVOI. The doubly linked candidate (d) emerges as optimal – though violating faithfulness – since it satisfies both higher-ranked constraints. Here we see the crucial ranking of NASVOI ≫ FAITH: were this ranking reversed, the faithful candidate (a) (having passed licensing) would emerge the winner. Instead, dominant NASVOI forces the insertion of [voice] and double linking, resulting in multiple violations of FAITH. Thus, postnasal voicing depends on the assumption that inserting and spreading [voice] costs less than violating the requirement that nasals be voiced.

Turning now to the question of *input* representations, we will use the same example and consider several alternative input representations for the Japanese form *tombo*. As potential alternative inputs, we choose the five representations in (25) identical to the *output candidates* (a–e) in tableau 7. Anticipating the main result, we will see that all of these possible inputs converge on an output core with double linking of [voice].

Tableau 7

Input: /tompo/ 'dragonfly'

Candidate	LICENSE	NASVOI	FAITH
a. t o m p o		* !	
b. t o m p o 	 υ	* !		*
c. t o m b o 	 υ		* !	*

d. ☞ t o m b o
      V
      υ
			* *

e. t o m b o 		 υ υ	* !		* *

(25) a.   b.   c.   d.   e.
         tompo   tompo   tombo   tombo   tombo
            | | | V | |
            v   v   v   v   v v

We have already evaluated the candidate set associated with input (25a) in tableau 7. Below we establish that double linking for [voice] is the fate of all the other inputs as well. This result follows from the fact that FAITH is outranked by both LICENSE and NASVOI. The latter constraints will always conspire in the way we have shown to effect double linking, regardless of the amount of feature insertion or nonparsing required. Thus, in tableau 8 for input (25b), FAITH tolerates the insertion of another association line on the optimal candidate (d). The faithful candidate (b), on the other hand, fatally violates LICENSE.

In tableau 9 (for input (25c)) the establishment of a new association line is similarly required for candidate (d). In this case the faithful candidate (c) incurs a fatal violation of NASVOI.

In tableau 10 (for input (25d)) we see a happy meeting of the needs of all of our constraints at once: in addition to fulfilling both LICENSE and NASVOI, the optimal form (d) is devoutly faithful to the input, a fact that will become significant in our discussion of lexicon optimization.

Tableau 8

Input: /tompo/ 'dragonfly'
           |
           v

Candidate	LICENSE	NASVOI	FAITH
a. t o m p o (↓ to v̶, deleted)		* !	*
b. t o m p o (— to v)	* !		
c. t o m b o (v̶ v)		* !	* *
d. ☞ t o m b o (double link to v)			*
e. t o m b o (v v)	* !		*

Tableau 9

Input: /tombo/ 'dragonfly'

Candidate	LICENSE	NASVOI	FAITH
a. t o m p o		*!	*
b. t o m p o	*!		* *
c. t o m b o		*!	
d. ☞ t o m b o			*
e. t o m b o	*!		*

Tableau 10

Input: /tombo/ 'dragonfly'

Candidate	LICENSE	NASVOI	FAITH
a. t o m p o		*!	* *
b. t o m p o	*!		*
c. t o m b o		*!	*
d. ☞ t o m b o			
e. t o m b o	*!		* *

Tableau 11

Input: /tombo/ 'dragonfly'

Candidate	License	NasVoi	Faith
a. t o m p o		* !	* *
b. t o m p o	* !		*
c. t o m b o		* !	*
d. ☞ t o m b o			* *
e. t o m b o	* !		

The last input to consider, (25e), starts off with separate [voice] specifications on the members of the NC cluster; again, the optimal form, candidate (d) of tableau 11, shows double linking instead, at a cost to Faith.

This experiment with various possible inputs bears out our earlier claim that there is no need for a separate theory of underlying feature minimization: the constraint hierarchy itself forces the correct output, irrespective of specification in the input. This means that there is no *grammatical* imperative against even a redundantly specified input form as in tableau 10.

However, there may well be *learnability* factors restricting the choice of the underlying form, requiring that the proper underlying representation be inferable, as the "simplest" choice, from the constraint hierarchy. Language learners have at their disposal the strategy of Lexicon Optimization ("Stampean occultation"; see PS 1993: 192, 196 for a full statement).

(26) *Lexicon Optimization*
Of several potential inputs whose outputs all converge on the same phonetic form, choose as the real input the one whose output is the most harmonic.

In order to develop these somewhat abstract considerations into a concrete analytical method, we propose the "tableau des tableaux" technique in tableau 12. Taking up a remark made by PS (1993: 192), we compare each of the winning outputs seen

Tableau 12

Tableau des tableaux: Evaluating outputs of the different inputs

Input	Output	LICENSE	NASVOI	FAITH
a. /tompo/	☞ t o m b o v			* ! *
b. /tompo/ v	☞ t o m b o v			* !
c. /tombo/ v	☞ t o m b o v			* !
d. ☞ /tombo/ v	☞ t o m b o v			
e. /tombo/ v v	☞ t o m b o v v̵			* ! *

above for harmonic status, each in relation to the corresponding input. The tableau des tableaux 12 assembles the input–output pairings established in tableaux 7–11, with the set of violation marks for each constraint. All of the winning outputs are doubly linked for [voice], satisfying both LICENSE and NASVOI; they differ only in violations of low-ranked FAITH. As shown, the "superhand" chooses (d) as the optimal input (i.e., the input associated with the most harmonic of the different outputs).

With Lexicon Optimization and tableau des tableaux as a guideline, the learner chooses the input form that maps onto an output in the way least offensive to the grammar of ranked constraints. For our purposes, this means that the learner will choose the input leading to the fewest faithfulness violations, to wit, the input bearing double linking of redundant [voice]. This conclusion, if correct, points up even more dramatically our basic conclusion: there is no requirement of underlying feature minimization.

To recapitulate this section and the overall analysis, we rely on three broad categories of constraints: redundancy conditions, derivative licensing restrictions, and constraints against input/output disparities. Each of these is largely akin to notions widely held in modern phonology. Our approach to underspecification is novel in two important respects, however. First, our interpretation of licensing puts no penalty on feature cooccurrence per se; rather, a feature is merely required to be licensed in *some* fashion. Second, we rely crucially on the ranking and violability of constraints, notions that form the backbone of OT.

Continuing in this last vein, it may seem odd, even in the context of OT, to propose simultaneous constraints, one *demanding* that nasals be voiced (NasVoi) and the other *blocking* licensing of [voice] by nasal segments (License). Yet as noted at the outset of this section, these are just familiar notions in a new guise, and they must be regarded as two sides of the same coin: the import of NasVoi is that voicing is in a sense *inherent* in nasals (Stevens, Keyser, and Kawasaki 1986); yet it is surely the very redundancy of such voicing that also entails its phonological inertness. Whereas the antagonism between these two constraints has led past theories to assign them to complementary "levels" of the grammar (i.e., underspecification early and presence of redundant values late), we find a new possibility within OT: redundant specification is not irrelevant until "late" in the derivation, but rather is crucially a constant demand. The facts of Japanese provide striking support for this view. Our analysis therefore constitutes an argument in favor of the enforcement of phonological constraints *in parallel*, a notion central to OT.

[. . .]

References

Archangeli, Diana, and Douglas Pulleyblank. 1986. The content and structure of phonological representations. MS, University of Arizona, Tucson, and University of Southern California, Los Angeles.

Archangeli, Diana, and Douglas Pulleyblank. 1993. Optimality, grounding theory, and rule parameters. Handout from talk presented at Rutgers Optimality Workshop I, Rutgers University, New Brunswick, N.J.

Itô, Junko, Armin Mester, and Jaye Padgett. 1993. Licensing and redundancy: Underspecification theory in Optimality Theory. Report LRC-93-07, Linguistics Research Center, University of California, Santa Cruz.

Kiparsky, Paul. 1985. Some consequences of Lexical Phonology. *Phonology Yearbook* 2: 82–138.

McCarthy, John J., and Alan S. Prince. 1993. Prosodic morphology I: Constraint interaction and satisfaction. MS, University of Massachusetts, Amherst, and Rutgers University, New Brunswick, N.J. ▶

Myers, Scott. 1993. OCP effects in Optimality Theory. MS, University of Texas, Austin. ◀

Padgett, Jaye. 1991. *Stricture in Feature Geometry*. Doctoral dissertation, University of Massachusetts, Amherst. ▶

Prince, Alan S., and Paul Smolensky. 1993. Optimality Theory: Constraint interaction in generative grammar. MS, Rutgers University, New Brunswick, N.J., and University of Colorado, Boulder. ◀

Stevens, Kenneth, Samuel Jay Keyser, and Haruko Kawasaki. 1986. Toward a phonetic and phonological theory of redundant features. In *Invariance and Variability in Speech Processes*, (ed.) Joseph S. Perkell and Dennis H. Klatt, 426–49. Hillsdale, N.J.: Lawrence Erlbaum Associates.

Study and Research Questions

1 Compare the licensing approach to post-nasal voicing with the *NC̥ constraint of chapter 14.

2 Find a phonotactic restriction in a language you are familiar with. Show how that observed phonotactic restriction is analyzed in OT under richness of the base, using Lexicon Optimization and the tableau des tableaux.

3 Lexicon Optimization as defined in (26) is not the only imaginable approach to selecting an input. Imagine a different one and compare it with (26).

Chapter 31 | Sharon Inkelas, Orhan Orgun, and Cheryl Zoll

The Implications of Lexical Exceptions for the Nature of Grammar

Editor's Note

This chapter and the next offer somewhat different perspectives on the treatment of lexical exceptions in OT. Lexical exceptions posed no particular challenge to rule-based phonology; diacritic features that controlled rule application were proposed by Chomsky and Halle (1968) and adopted in most subsequent work. OT, with its much more integrated view of what a grammar is, does not lend itself to such an easy solution.

Of course, diacritic features on rules are something of an intellectual dead-end, since they do little more than stipulate that which is observed. If it is necessary to work harder to accommodate lexical exceptions in OT, it is also necessary to work smarter. The result is a theory of lexical exceptions that is not *sui generis*, but rather illuminates other aspects of phonology, as these two chapters show.

1   Introduction

This chapter explores the consequences of lexical exceptions for the nature of grammar, drawing a comparison between two types of phonological theory: rule theory (or derivational theory), which uses rules to capture alternations and constraints to capture static patterns, and Optimality Theory (Prince and Smolensky 1993), which uses constraints to handle alternations as well as static patterns. We conclude that in order to deal with lexical exceptions, rule theory is forced to use morpheme-specific co-phonologies (subgrammars), a practice which engenders such serious

Excerpt from:
Inkelas, Sharon, Orgun, Orhan, and Zoll, Cheryl (1997) The implications of lexical exceptions for the nature of grammar. In *Derivations and Constraints in Phonology*, ed. Iggy Roca, pp. 393–418. Oxford: Oxford University Press.

problems that it must be rejected outright. By contrast, Optimality Theory is capable of avoiding morpheme-specific co-phonologies. The fact that OT has violable constraints allows it to employ a principled prespecification approach to lexical exceptions. As we demonstrate, prespecification has a number of advantages over the co-phonology approach and none of its fatal problems. The chapter concludes with a discussion of the positive implications of OT for a principled underlying representation, and with some speculation on the grammatical status of static patterns.

2 Case Studies

We begin by setting out two case studies which will inform the discussion. (Clearly it would be desirable to consider more examples, but space limitations force us to refer the reader to other, related works; see especially Inkelas 1994, forthcoming, and Inkelas and Orgun 1995, forthcoming for a richer panoply of data). Both examples are from Turkish, and form part of a larger ongoing study by two of the authors on the lexical phonology of Turkish.

2.1 Labial attraction

Our first example of lexical exceptionality involves a static pattern which induces no alternations but has none the less been claimed to have grammatical status in Turkish.

As originally described by Lees (1966) and developed in subsequent work by Itô et al. (1993), Ní Chiosáin and Padgett (1993), and Itô and Mester (1995: 818), Labial Attraction is an alleged root-structure constraint to the effect that if a labial consonant occurs between the vowel /a/ and a following high back vowel, that high vowel must be round, i.e. /u/. (In fact, a consonant may occur immediately adjacent to the labial, on either side, but we omit this immaterial detail for notational ease.)

(1) A root obeys Labial Attraction if the following statement is true:
'∀ /aB[+ bk, + hi]/, [+ bk, + hi] = /u/'
(where 'B' represents any labial consonant)
A root disobeys Labial Attraction if the same statement is false.

Some roots overtly conforming to Labial Attraction are listed in (2):[1]

(2) karpuz   'watermelon'
    sabun   'soap'
    habur   (the place name 'Habur')
    javru   'cub'

As Clements and Sezer (1982) note, Lees's Labial Attraction constraint admits numerous exceptions, some of which are listed below:[2]

(3)   kapɯ   'door'
      kalamuʃ   (the place name 'Kalamış')
      tavɯr   'attitude'

Labial Attraction induces no alternations, holding strictly within roots and never across morpheme boundaries, as shown by the suffixed forms in (4a). The forms in (4b) serve as a control to show that the same suffixes can, elsewhere, appear with round vowels; these result from vowel harmony, which assimilates them to a preceding round vowel.

(4)   a.   i.   kitap   'book'
                 kitab-ɯ   'book-accusative'   *kitabu

           ii.   tambura-m   'stringed instrument-1sg.poss'
                 tambura-m-dɯ   'stringed instrument-1sg.poss-past'   *tamburamdu

      b.   i.   sabun   'soap'
                 sabun-u   'soap-accusative'
                 sabun-du   'soap-past'

2.2   Coda devoicing

Our second example is a pattern which *does* induce alternations. Coda Devoicing is a well-known alternation in Turkish whereby plosives surface as voiced in onset position but as voiceless in coda position (Lees 1961; Lewis 1967; Underhill 1976; Kaisse 1986; Rice 1990; Inkelas and Orgun 1995). An example involving /t ~ d/ is given below:

(5)   a.   ka.nat   'wing'
      b.   ka.nat.-lar   'wing-plural'
      c.   ka.na.d-ɯ   'wing-accusative'

The generalization is described as coda devoicing (Kaisse 1986; Rice 1990) rather than, for example, onset voicing, because of the large number of roots ending in consistently voiceless plosives:

(6)   a.   dev.let   'state'
      b.   dev.let.-ler   'state-plural'
      c.   dev.le.t-i   'state-accusative'

Coda Devoicing admits a small number of lexical exceptions, roots which end in plosives that surface as voiced even in coda position (Kaisse 1986; Hayes 1990; Inkelas and Orgun 1995):[3]

(7)   a.   e.tyd   'study'
           e.tyd.-ler   'study-plural'

b. ka.ta.log   'catalog'
    ka.ta.log.-dan   'catalog-ablative'

[. . .]

5   Lexical Exceptions in Optimality Theory

It is now time to look at lexical exceptions from a different perspective, that of OT, in which constraints are used to handle both static patterns and alternations. The crucial difference, for our purposes, between OT and rule theory is that in OT, constraints are violable. As we will demonstrate, this makes it possible for OT to use the prespecification method for handling lexical exceptions. As a consequence, morpheme-specific co-phonologies, and all the problems that they entail, can be entirely avoided.

That said, morpheme-specific co-phonologies *have* been imported into OT as a means of capturing lexical exceptionality; see e.g. Kisseberth (1993), Kirchner (1993), Pater (1994), Cohn and McCarthy (1994). However, not only do the same problems arise that we discussed in the previous section; in addition, the morpheme-specific co-phonology approach stands in contradiction to the fundamental assumption in OT that constraints are violable. In the case of lexical exceptions, co-phonologies are defined on the basis of a set of morphemes all of which – or none of which – violate a given constraint. By defining away the possibility for constraints to be violated, the morpheme-specific co-phonology approach prevents the analyst from benefiting from constraint violability and from noticing emergent generalizations of the type, called 'emergence of the unmarked', discussed by McCarthy and Prince (1994).

In OT all that is needed in order for a lexical item to resist the effects of a constraint is for the faithfulness constraints which protect the underlying structure of that lexical item to be ranked higher than the constraint in question. This approach has been used by Inkelas (1994; forthcoming) for exceptions to vowel harmony, coda devoicing, and stress in Turkish, and by Roca (1996) for Spanish plural formation.

In the case of Labial Attraction, lexical exceptions to the constraint (which, recall, requires a high vowel to be /u/ if the preceding vowel is /a/ and a labial consonant intervenes) are simply prespecified lexically with an unrounded vowel, /ɯ/. In the case of the morpheme /kapɯ/ 'door', the faithfulness constraint (PARSE, for Prince and Smolensky 1993; MAX, for McCarthy and Prince 1994; MATCH, for Orgun 1995) banning deletion of input material outranks Labial Attraction, preventing the /ɯ/ from surfacing as /u/.

(28)   How prespecification works to characterize exceptions to Labial Attraction

	kapɯ	FAITH	LABIAL ATTRACTION
☞ a.	[kapɯ]		*
b.	[kapu]	*!	

Similarly, prespecification can easily handle exceptions to Coda Devoicing, our example of an alternation admitting lexical exceptions. Plosives which alternate with respect to voicing (e.g. the final consonant of /kanaD/ 'wing') are underspecified for [voice] (29a), while those which always surface as voiced (e.g. in /etyd/ 'study') are prespecified as [+voice] (29b); those which always surface as voiceless (e.g. in /devlet/ 'state') are prespecified as [−voice] (29c). As proposed by Hayes (1990) and Inkelas and Orgun (1995), Coda Devoicing is a purely structure-filling alternation, meaning, in OT, that the requirement that coda plosives be voiceless is dominated by a constraint prohibiting the deletion of input [voice] specifications.

(29)   How prespecification works to characterize Coda Devoicing and its exceptions

a.	/kanaD/	FAITH	CODA DEVOICING
☞ i.	[kanat]	*	
ii.	[kanad]	*	*!

b.	/etyd/	FAITH	CODA DEVOICING
i.	[etyt]	*!	
☞ ii.	[etyd]		*

c.	/devlet/	FAITH	CODA DEVOICING
☞ i.	[devlet]		
ii.	[devled]	*!	*

Prespecification has a number of advantages over the co-phonology approach, the most obvious being that it does not contribute to co-phonology proliferation. When prespecification is the method of capturing lexical exceptions, only one (co-)phonology is needed.

Another advantage of prespecification is that it deals handily with 'mixed' morphemes, those in which one segment is exceptional and another, well-behaved. Recall, for example, the mixed morphemes confronting the Coda Devoicing rule in Turkish, which posed an embarrassing problem for the morpheme-specific co-phonology approach. All that needs to be said in the prespecification approach is that the exceptional, voiced plosives are prespecified for [+voice], while the obedient, alternating ones are underlyingly unspecified, supplied with the appropriate value for [voice] by the structure-filling grammar.

(30)   /edʒda:D/   /istibda:D/   /pɯrelyd/
         | | |
        vd   vd   vd

As long as the grammar is designed such that the faithfulness constraint protecting underlying [voice] specifications outranks the constraint requiring coda plosives to be voiceless, the exact nature of the lexical exceptionality of these morphemes we have discussed is trivially easy to describe.[15]

Similarly, as Harris (1985) shows, prespecification is the solution to the dilemma of mixed morphemes in Spanish. Recall that there are morphemes in which one mid vowel in a morpheme undergoes Diphthongization in the appropriate stress context, but another does not. Harris (1985) proposes a simple prespecification treatment, assigning diphthongizing vowels an unlinked timing unit which gets filled only under stress:

(31)   Short vowel   True diphthong   Alternating vowel
            X   X X   X X
            | | | |
            i   i e   i

As long as Diphthongization is purely structure-filling, meaning that the constraint requiring stressed mid vowels to be diphthongs is ranked below the constraint requiring prelinked vowels to be preserved, there is no need to create two co-phonologies in Spanish, one which forces diphthongization and the other which does not. All morphemes can belong to the same co-phonology, at least as far as Diphthongization is concerned.

To conclude, we have demonstrated that the only alternative to prespecification, namely morpheme-specific co-phonologies, is an untenable approach to lexical exceptionality; moreover, we have shown that prespecification is capable of describing the kinds of intricacy that one actually finds in exceptionality. In sum, prespecification is the most constrained while simultaneously the only descriptively adequate way of handling lexical exceptionality to static patterns and alternations. It is made possible in OT precisely because of the ability of constraints in OT to be violated; lexical resistance (exceptionality) results when faithfulness constraints preserve underlying structure from the ravages of lower-ranked constraints.

Put another way, OT is intrinsically suited to the prespecification approach to exceptions because it is intrinsically suited to capturing the notion of a structure-filling alternation. This notion is what rule theory has been unable to formalize adequately, for good reason: as Kiparsky (1982) notes, the same rule can apply in a structure-filling manner in one instance but in a structure-changing manner in another. Structure-fillingness is best understood as a property of a given input–output mapping, rather than a property of a rule, divorced from the particular forms it is applying to.

6   The Principled Nature of Prespecification

Past proposals to use prespecification to handle lexical exceptionality have often come under criticism for being unprincipled (see e.g., Mester and Itô 1989; Steriade 1995). The principal concern seems to be that if underlying representation can be adjusted to fit the observed data, then no predictions can be made about which forms actually occur in a language. It has even been suggested that the problem is enhanced in OT, whose practitioners typically opt to impose no constraints at all on underlying representation.[16]

However, we would like to argue, with Inkelas (1994), that the situation is exactly the opposite. It is precisely the 'richness of the input' aspect of OT (McCarthy 1995) which makes the prespecification account so successful. In OT, it does not technically matter what underlying representation is given to a morpheme so long as whatever underlying representation is chosen leads to the correct surface form. In fact, it is possible in some cases for any of a variety of possible underlying representations to work in any given case. How, then, is under-lying representation determined? The solution that has been offered within OT by Prince and Smolensky (1993) is Lexicon Optimization. According to Prince and Smolensky (1993) (see also Itô et al. 1993, 1995; and Inkelas 1994), that underlying representation is chosen which leads to the violation of the fewest highly ranked constraints in the generation of surface form (see Pulleyblank and Turkel 1997 for akin discussion). Each morpheme has exactly one best underlying representation. As a result, there is no reason to worry about indeterminacy in underlying representation.

As illustration, a sample Lexicon Optimization tableau with one constraint (adapted from Itô et al.'s (1995: 593) discussion of postnasal obstruent voicing in Japanese) is shown below.[17] All inputs given will yield the same output, according to the grammar postulated by Itô et al. That input is selected to be stored in under-lying representation which violates the fewest high-ranking constraints in grammar. In this simple *tableau des tableaux* (to use the term of Itô et al. 1993, 1995), only FAITH is shown; the optimal input is (d), the most faithful to the output form *tombo*. Even though the shared voicing structure would be assigned by the gram-mar and is thus redundant, Lexicon Optimization causes it to be stored lexically anyway.

(32)

	Input	Output	FAITH	Comments
a.	/toMPo/	tombo	**!	MP specified for voice in output only
b.	/tomPo/ | vd	tombo	*!	P specified for voice in output only
c.	/toMbo/ | vd	tombo	*!	M specified for voice in output only
☞ d.	/tombo/ V vd	tombo		voice faithful between input and output

Not surprisingly, FAITH constraints will always favor a fully specified form in the absence of higher-ranked constraints forcing underspecification. Thus for structures which exceptionally fail to show the expected alternations and instead maintain a constant surface form, Lexicon Optimization will naturally cause them to be stored underlyingly in their surface form – that is, to be prespecified.

Given a theory of Lexicon Optimization and a single grammar, underlying specification is constrained, in fact determined, by the surface forms of morphemes. If *SPEC (Prince and Smolensky 1993) is one of the constraints in the grammar, then the best underlying form is the one that adheres the most closely to *SPEC, all other things being equal (i.e. given that it can generate the correct surface forms). However, underlying form is still principled even if constraints such as *SPEC are not part of the grammar at all. Even if, as explicitly advocated in Inkelas (1994), no constraints at all are dedicated to shaping underlying form, Lexicon Optimization still ensures that underlying representation is deterministic. It provides a principled way of deciding underlying form while allowing exceptionality to be handled using prespecification, precisely the combination of goals that derivational theories have been unable to achieve.

[. . .]

Notes

1   Turkish data are presented in phonemic transcription using IPA symbols (and following the common practice of representing the low back unrounded vowel, [ɑ], as [a]). Syllable boundaries (marked with a dot) are indicated only when directly relevant to the discussion. Upper-case letters stand for archiphonemes, unspecified for alternating features (in the case of low vowels ('E'), [back]; in the case of high vowels ('I'), [back] and [round]; in the case of plosives (e.g. 'B'), [voice]). Data represent the speech of the alphabetically second author, a native speaker of (Standard) Istanbul Turkish.

2   Itô et al. (1993; 1995) have claimed that Labial Attraction is true of the native vocabulary of Turkish. In fact, however, a number of the roots (including some which Itô et al. (1993) list) are loans (e.g. *karpuz* 'watermelon', from Greek, *armut* 'pear', from Persian, *sabun* 'soap', from Arabic, *ʃampuan* 'shampoo', from French and so on), while a number of native roots (e.g. *kapɯ* 'door') are exceptions to the constraint. It may be that the constraint held at one time in the history of the language;

kapɯ used to be pronounced *kapu* (and still is, by some older speakers), and there are a few forms with frozen suffixes whose vowels conform to Labial Attraction (e.g. *yamuk* 'crooked', with a frozen adjective suffix *-uk*), suggesting that the constraint may even have induced alternations at one time.

3   As noted in Lewis (1967), monosyllabic roots follow a different pattern in which it is alternating plosives that are the exception. For an account of this, see Inkelas and Orgun (1995).

[. . .]

15   What to prespecify in the case of exceptions to Velar Deletion is not quite as obvious; Inkelas and Orgun (1995) offer reasons to think that it is syllable structure which is prespecified, and that the Velar Deletion alternation affects only velars which are not syllabified in the input.

16   See, however, Prince and Smolensky (1993), who entertain the possibility of using *SPEC as a constraint whose only effect is on underlying representation.

17   See Inkelas (1994) for discussion of Lexicon Optimization in cases of alternations.

References

Clements, G. N., and Sezer, E. (1982). 'Vowel and consonant disharmony in Turkish', in H. van der Hulst and N. Smith (eds.), *The Structure of Phonological Representations*, pt. II. Dordrecht: Foris, 213–55.

Cohn, A., and McCarthy, J. (1994). 'Alignment and Parallelism in Indonesian phonology'. ROA-25. ▶

Harris, J. (1985). 'Spanish diphthongization and stress', *Phonology Yearbook* 2: 31–45.

Hayes, B. (1990). 'Precompiled lexical phonology', in S. Inkelas and D. Zec (eds.), *The Phonology–Syntax Connection*. Chicago: University of Chicago Press, 85–108.

Inkelas, S. (1994). 'The consequences of optimization for underspecification', in J. Beckman (ed.), *Proceedings of the North East Linguistics Society* 25: 287–302.

Inkelas, S. (forthcoming). 'Exceptional stress-attracting suffixes in Turkish: representations vs. the grammar', in H. van der Hulst, R. Kager, and W. Zonneveld (eds.), *Prosodic Morphology*. Cambridge: Cambridge University Press. ▶

Inkelas, S., and Orgun, C. O. (1995). 'Level ordering and economy in the lexical phonology of Turkish', *Language* 71: 763–93.

Inkelas, S., and Orgun, C. O. (forthcoming). 'Level (non)ordering in recursive morphology: evidence from Turkish', in S. Lapointe (ed.), *Proceedings of the Davis Workshop on Morphology and Its Relations to Syntax and Phonology*. Stanford, Calif.: CSLI. ▶

Itô, J., and Mester, A. (1995). 'Japanese phonology', in J. Goldsmith (ed.), *The Handbook of Phonological Theory*. Cambridge, Mass.: Blackwell, 817–38.

Itô, J., Mester, A., and Padgett, J. (1993). 'Licensing and Redundancy: Underspecification in Optimality Theory'. University of California, Santa Cruz, LRC-93-07.

Itô, J., Mester, A., and Padgett, J. (1995). 'Licensing and underspecification in Optimality Theory', *Linguistic Inquiry* 26: 571–613. ◀

Kaisse, E. (1986). 'Locating Turkish devoicing', in M. Dalrymple et al. (eds.), *Proceedings of the Fifth West Coast Conference on Formal Linguistics*. Stanford, Calif.: Stanford Linguistics Association, 119–28.

Kiparsky, P. (1982). 'Lexical morphology and phonology', in I.-S. Yang (ed.), *Linguistics in the Morning Calm*. Seoul: Hanshin, 3–91.

Kirchner, R. (1993). 'Turkish Vowel Disharmony in Optimality Theory'. ROA-4.

Kisseberth, C. (1993). 'Optimal domains: a theory of Bantu tone. A case study from Isixhosa', Rutgers Optimality Workshop 1.

Lees, R. (1961). *The Phonology of Modern Standard Turkish*. Bloomington: Indiana University Publications.

Lees, R. (1966). 'On the interpretation of a Turkish vowel alternation', *Anthropological Linguistics* 8: 32–9.

Lewis, G. (1967). *Turkish Grammar*. Oxford: Oxford University Press.

McCarthy, J. (1995). 'Extensions of Faithfulness: Rotuman Revisited'. ROA-110. ▶

McCarthy, J., and Prince, A. (1994). 'An overview of Prosodic Morphology', pt. 1: 'Templatic form in reduplication'. Utrecht University Workshop on Prosodic Morphology. ▶

Mester, A., and Itô, J. (1989). 'Feature predictability and underspecification: palatal prosody in Japanese mimetics', *Language* 65: 258–93.

Ní Chiosáin, M., and Padgett, J. (1993). 'On the Nature of Consonant–Vowel Interaction'. Linguistics Research Center publication LRC-93–09, University of California, Santa Cruz.

Orgun, C. O. (1995). 'Correspondence and identity constraints in two-level Optimality Theory', in J. Camacho (ed.), *Proceedings of the Fourteenth West Coast Conference on Formal Linguistics*. Stanford, Calif.: Stanford Linguistics Association.

Pater, J. (1994). 'Against the underlying specification of an "exceptional" English stress pattern', *Proceedings of the Conference on Contrast*, University of Toronto.

Prince, A., and Smolensky, P. (1993). 'Optimality Theory: Constraint Interaction in Generative Grammar'. MS, Rutgers University and the University of Colorado, Boulder. ◀

Pulleyblank, D., and Turkel, W. J. (1997). 'Gradient retreat', in I. Roca (ed.), *Derivations and Constraints in Phonology*. Oxford: Oxford University Press, 153–93.

Rice, K. (1990). 'Predicting rule domains in the phrasal phonology', in S. Inkelas and D. Zec (eds.), *The Phonology–Syntax Connection*. Chicago: University of Chicago Press and CSLI Publications, 289–312.

Roca, I. (1996). 'The phonology–morphology interface in Spanish plural formation', in U. Kleinhenz (ed.), *Interfaces in Phonology*. Berlin: Akademie Verlags, 210–30.

Steriade, D. (1995). 'Underspecification and markedness', in J. Goldsmith (ed.), *A Handbook of Phonological Theory*. Cambridge, Mass.: Blackwell, 114–74.

Underhill, R. (1976). *Turkish Grammar*. Cambridge, Mass.: MIT Press.

Study and Research Questions

1 Explain why OT "is intrinsically suited to capturing the notion of a structure-filling alternation".

2 Compare the approach to devoicing in this chapter with the one in chapter 17.

3 Think about possible challenges to this proposal. Are there imaginable kinds of exceptions that cannot be encoded with prespecification or that might require additional assumptions? (In answering this, you will want to think about diverse phonological processes and the ways in which words might be exceptions to them.) If you can, locate a real-life example.

4 Find your own example of a lexical exception and provide an analysis of it in terms of the proposal here.

Chapter 32 | Junko Itô and Armin Mester

The Phonological Lexicon

Editor's Note

This chapter and the one that precedes it form a unit on the analysis of lexical exceptions in OT. The emphasis in this chapter is on systems of exceptions, as represented by the lexical strata in Japanese. The theory proposed here is particularly interesting because it could only be expressed within OT, since it relies on differentiating faithfulness constraints according to lexical class membership.

Introduction: Stratification and Lexical Subsetting

This chapter presents some recent results on a central aspect of Japanese phonology, namely, the structure of the phonological lexicon. The issue here is the fundamental division of the lexicon into different strata: native (or Yamato), Sino-Japanese, and Western loans at various stages of assimilation. An understanding of such stratification patterns not only is a prerequisite for serious analytical work in Japanese phonology (and elsewhere), but enables us to raise the question of what, if anything, the existence of lexical strata might tell us about the organization of the phonology (and ultimately, the grammar) as a whole. Within Optimality Theory (Prince and Smolensky 1993), as we will see, this issue is intimately connected to the form and function of faithfulness constraints.
[. . .]
   An initial idea might be that stratification can be depicted as in (2), where the lexicon is partitioned into parallel sublexica containing native items, loan items, etc.

Excerpt from:
Itô, Junko and Mester, Armin (1999) The phonological lexicon. In *The Handbook of Japanese Linguistics*, ed. Natsuko Tsujimura, pp. 62–100. Oxford: Blackwell.

(2)

$$\text{Lexicon}$$

Sublexicon-1	Sublexicon-2	Sublexicon-3	Sublexicon-4
Native	Established loans	Assimilated foreign	Unassimilated foreign

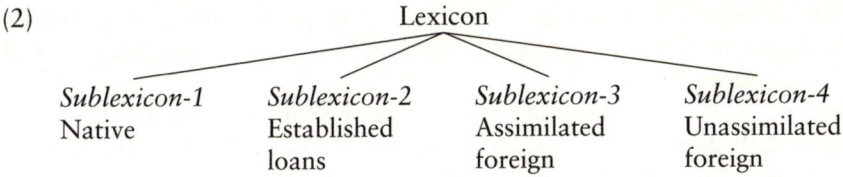

However, a significant finding of Kiparsky (1968), taken up and extended in Saciuk (1969), is that a model like (2) misses two central and interrelated features of lexical structure – the *gradual* and *hierarchical* character of lexical stratification. Lexical items do not come neatly packaged into groups labeled [±foreign]; rather, different degrees of nativization among foreign words are commonplace.[12] Instead of a partitioning into parallel and disjoint [+foreign] and [–foreign] sublexica, we have "a hierarchy of foreignness, with exceptions to one rule always being exceptions to another rule, but not vice versa" (Kiparsky 1968: 20).

On the basis of a detailed investigation of the phonological lexicon of contemporary Japanese, Itô and Mester (1995a, 1995b) take up this idea and argue for a model of the phonological lexicon in which this kind of hierarchy among lexical items plays a central role. In this conception, which is to be further developed and motivated below, the central notion is that of a "lexical constraint domain"; that is, analyzing lexical stratification means analyzing the inclusion and overlap relations between constraint domains. The main result is that lexical items are organized in terms of an overall *core–periphery structure* that can be depicted as in (3).[13]

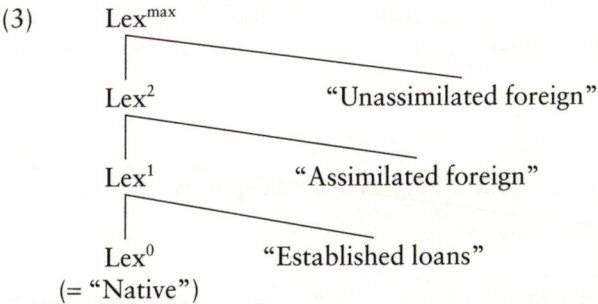

(3) Lex^{max}

Lex^2 "Unassimilated foreign"

Lex^1 "Assimilated foreign"

Lex^0 "Established loans"
(= "Native")

In this model, the relevant structural organization of the lexicon is set inclusion, leading from the innermost lexical core Lex^0 to the most inclusive set Lex^{max} comprising all lexical items. In this set inclusion hierarchy $\text{Lex}^0 \subset \text{Lex}^1 \subset \text{Lex}^2 \subset \ldots \subset \text{Lex}^{max}$, Lex^0 corresponds to what is usually called the "native stratum," Lex^1 includes "native" and "established loans," and so on. Crucially different from the sublexicon model in (2), the (higher) lexical strata do not directly correspond to Lex^1, Lex^2, etc., but are defined by set complementation, following the general schema $\text{Lex}^i - \text{Lex}^{i-1}$ (i.e. Lex^i minus Lex^{i-1}). Thus the stratum of established loans in (3) is the set $\text{Lex}^1 - \text{Lex}^0$, etc. More inclusive sets can be read off the diagram in an analogous way: the set of all non-native items is $\text{Lex}^{max} - \text{Lex}^0$, the complement of Lex^0, etc. The elements of Lex^0 fulfill lexical constraints in the maximal way and form the core of the lexicon. Moving outwards from the core, we encounter items that violate more and more constraints until we encounter, at the periphery, items

fulfilling only a small subset of the constraints. These constraints are truly fundamental in the sense that they define the basic syllable canons and other central
aspects of the language.

Structures as in (3) are built out of a network of implicational relations involving
lexical items and phonological constraints of the following kind: items that are
subject to constraint *A* are also always subject to constraint *B*, but not all items
subject to *B* are also subject to *A*. This makes *A* a constraint with a more restricted
domain than *B* – in fact, *A*'s domain is properly included in *B*'s domain, as
schematically shown in (4).

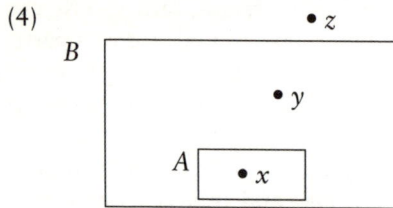

(4)

$$\begin{array}{c} \bullet\, z \\[2pt] B \quad \boxed{\begin{array}{c} \\ \bullet\, y \\[4pt] A \,\boxed{\begin{array}{c}\\ \bullet\, x \\ \end{array}} \\ \end{array}} \end{array}$$

Here *x* is in the domain of *A* and of *B*, *y* is in the domain of *B*, but not of *A*, and *z*
is in the domain of neither *A* nor *B*. It is not possible for an item to be in the domain
of *A* without being in the domain of *B*. If lexical items and constraints consistently
pattern in this way, it makes sense to talk about core–periphery relations, with *x*
being closer to the lexical core than *y*, *z* occupying the periphery, etc.

After exploring the core–periphery relations of the various constraints whose
interaction gives rise to some of the characteristics of the Japanese sound pattern
(section 1), we turn to the formal analysis of the constraint domains in Optimality
Theory (section 2).

I   Phonological Constraints: Canonical Patterns, Alternations, and Domains

We see clear instances of core–periphery relations when we consider how the different
classes of lexical items discussed above (see (2), (3)) behave with respect to the
constraints in (5) (taken from Itô and Mester 1995a, 1995b) operative in the
phonological lexicon of Japanese.

(5)   a.   SYLLSTRUC: Syllable structure constraints (see below)
      b.   NoVoicedGem (No-DD):   "No voiced obstruent geminates" (*bb*,
                                               dd, *gg*, etc.)
      c.   NoVoicelessLab (No-p):   "No singleton-p": a constraint against
                                               nongeminate [p]
      d.   NoNaŝVoiceless (No-nt):   "Postnasal obstruents must be voiced" (*nt*,
                                               mp, *ŋk*)

The set of basic syllable constraints of Japanese collectively referred to as
SYLLSTRUC includes, among others, *COMPLEX (disallowing complex onsets and

complex codas) and CODACOND (limiting codas to place-linked consonants or segments without consonantal place (= nasal glide N)).[14] These constraints are responsible for the well-known verbal paradigm alternations (6), where the gerundive form shows gemination (6a) or epenthesis (6b) to avoid high-ranking CODACOND or *COMPLEX violations.

(6) a. tor-u "take-Present" tot-te "take-Gerundive" *tor-te
     b. kas-u "lend-Present" kaši-te "lend-Gerundive" *kas-te

The pattern is not limited to the verbal paradigm, but is productively found in verbal root compounds (7), where the unsyllabifiable input cluster *kt* is either split by epenthesis or geminated.

(7) fuk- "blow"   tob- "fly"
     fuki-tobu, fut-tobu "blow-away" *fuk-tobu

The constraint against voiced geminates (NO-DD) also plays an active role in verbal root compounding. As shown in (8), the prefixal roots *ow-* and *tsuk-* induce gemination of the following consonant (*ok-kakeru, tsut-tatsu*). When this consonant is a voiced obstruent, the result is not a geminate (*od-dasu, *tsud-dasu) but rather a homorganic nasal + voiced obstruent sequence (*on-dasu, tsun-dasu*).

(8)
ow-	"chase"	kake-	"run"	ok-kakeru	"run after"[15]
		tsuk-	"arrive"	ot-tsuku	"overtake"
		das-	"put out"	on-dasu, *od-dasu	"drive out"
tsuk-	"stab"	kom-	"be full"	tsuk-komu	"cram"
		tat-	"stand"	tsut-tatsu	'stand straight"
		nomer-	"lean"	tsun-nomeru	"lunge forward"
		das-	"put out"	tsun-dasu, *tsud-dasu	"thrust out"

As shown in (9), similar patterns are observed for intensive *-ri* adverbs with internal gemination.[16] The corresponding single consonants are found in the base forms, which occur as reduplicated adverbs (e.g. *zabu-zabu*), or as stems of other lexical formations (*hiso-ka* = adj., *nobi-ru* = verb, etc.).

(9) a. uka(-uka)   ukka(-ri)   "absentmindedly"
         biku(-biku) bikku(-ri)   "surprising, frightening"
         šito(-šito) šitto(-ri)   "wet, rainy"
         hiso(-ka)   hisso(-ri)   "secretly"
         gusa(-ri)   gussa(-ri)   "plunging in (with a dagger)"
         hono(-ka)   honno(-ri)   "dimly, faintly"
         šimi(-ǰimi) šimmi(-ri)   "deeply, heartily"
     b. zabu(-zabu) zambu(-ri) *zabbu(-ri) "raining heavily"
         šobo(-šobo) šombo(-ri) *šobbo(-ri) "lonely"
         koga(-su)   koŋga(-ri) *kogga(-ri) "toasted, roasted"
         nobi(-ru)   nombi(-ri) *nobbi(-ri) "leisurely"
         nodo(-ka)   nondo(-ri) *noddo(-ri) "tranquil, calm"

The voiceless labial restriction (No-P) rules out any *p* that is exclusively linked to onset position (henceforth, "singleton-*p*").[17] An underlying singleton-*p* is debuccalized to [h] and appears allophonically as bilabial [ɸ] and palatal [ç] before high back and high front vowels, respectively. Following standard transcriptional practice, we render these as [fu] and [hi]. Besides the well-known variants *nippo*N and *niho*N "Japan" and the adverb *yappari~yahari* "after all," we find numerous instances of the *p~h* alternation, some of which are listed in (10)–(12).[18]

(10)   Verbal root compounding (cf. (8) above):

hik-	"pull"	har-	"stretch"	hip-paru	"pull strongly"
ow-	"chase"	hajime-	"start"	op-pajimeru	"really start"
tsuk-	"stab"	hašir-	"run"	tsup-paširu	"dash, race"

(11)   *ma-* prefixation:

	hiruma	"daytime"	map-piruma	"broad daylight"
	hadaka	"naked"	map-padaka	"stark naked"
cf.	kuro	"black"	mak-kuro	"pitch black"
	naka	"center"	man-naka	"dead center"

(12)   Sino-Japanese compounding:[19]

hatsu-bai	"sale"	šup-patsu	"departure"
hai-tatsu	"distribution"	šim-pai	"worry"
tai-fuu	"typhoon"	top-puu	"sudden wind"

By adding a voicing feature, Rendaku gives rise to *h~b* alternations in Yamato word compounding.[20]

(13)

hana	"flower"	ike-bana	"flower arrangement"
hata	"side, bank"	kawa-bata	"river bank"
fue	"flute"	kuči-bue	"mouth flute, whistle"
hito	"person"	tabi-bito	"traveller"

Finally, the constraint against nasal voiceless sequences (No-NT) (5d)[21] is responsible for a widespread and fully regular alternation in verbs involving the gerundive ending *-te* and the past tense ending *-ta* (14).[22]

(14)

	Base	Gerundive	Past	
	šin-	šin-de	šin-da	"die"
	in-[23]	in-de	in-da	"leave"
	yom-	yon-de	yon-da	"read"
	susum-	susun-de	susun-da	"progress"
	hasam-	hasan-de	hasan-da	"put between"
cf.	mi-	mi-te	mi-ta	"see"
	hašir-	hašit-te	hašit-ta	"run"
	kaw-	kat-te	kat-ta	"buy"

Verbal root compounding also shows ample evidence for a postnasal voicing alternation, as illustrated in (15), where the first verbal root *fum-* "to step on" ends in a nasal.

(15) tsukeru   "attach"   fun-dzukeru   *fun-tsukeru   "trample on"
      haru   "stretch"   fum-baru   *fum-paru   "resist"
      kiru   "cut"   fuŋ-giru   *fuŋ-kiru   "give up"
      šibaru   "tie"   fun-jibaru   *fun-šibaru   "immobilize"

While the formal structure of these constraints and their phonetic grounding are an interesting topic deserving further exploration, the focus of this chapter is a different one, namely, their systematic patterning in the various lexical strata. Besides leading to a large number of morpheme alternations in Yamato and Sino-Japanese items (see (6)–(15)), the constraints in (5) leave their mark on the phonological lexicon as a whole in a less direct, but equally significant way. They result in static restrictions on morpheme shape, independent of any alternations. The way in which these restrictions are distributed over the lexicon reveals the details of its stratal structure.

The syllable constraints of Japanese collectively referred to as SYLLSTRUC in (5a) are observed in all lexical strata. An item such as *trot*, with a complex onset and non-place-linked consonantal place in the coda, is simply not a viable lexical item in Japanese. While NO-DD (5b) is observed in most of the lexicon, violations are encountered in the unassimilated foreign vocabulary (e.g., *roddo* "rod" or *nobbu* "knob;" cf. the nativized variant *nobu*). NO-P (5c) is frequently violated in all kinds of foreign items (e.g., *peepaa* "paper"), including cases showing effects of nativization (e.g., *sepaado* "German shepherd dog").[24] Finally, while NO-NT (5d) is observed in the Yamato vocabulary, violations are freely found elsewhere in the lexicon, not only in the foreign stratum (e.g., *kompyuutaa* "computer," *santa* "Santa"), but also in Sino-Japanese items (e.g., *sampo* "walk," *hantai* "opposite").[25]

All of this may strike the casual observer as nothing but a collection of random facts and idiosyncracies; in reality, we are dealing with an instance of a simple generalization holding for every stratified lexicon. The table in (16) reveals the systematicity of the pattern, in the form of hierarchical inclusion relations between the domains in the phonological lexicon where the various constraints are active.

(16)

	SYLLSTRUC	NO-DD	NO-P	NO-NT
Yamato	✓	✓	✓	✓
Sino-Japanese	✓	✓	✓	violated
Assimilated foreign	✓	✓	violated	violated
Unassimilated foreign	✓	violated	violated	violated

The situation seen in (16) is an instance of the abstract pattern shown in (4). Everything subject to NO-DD is also subject to SYLLSTRUC, but not vice versa; everything subject to NO-P is also subject to NO-DD, but not vice versa, etc. Given the cross-linguistic frequency of such patterns, it is natural to hypothesize that some fundamental property of lexical constraint systems must be at work here. The nesting of constraint domains is depicted in (17), where in Japanese "Native" is instantiated by Yamato and "Established loans" by Sino-Japanese.

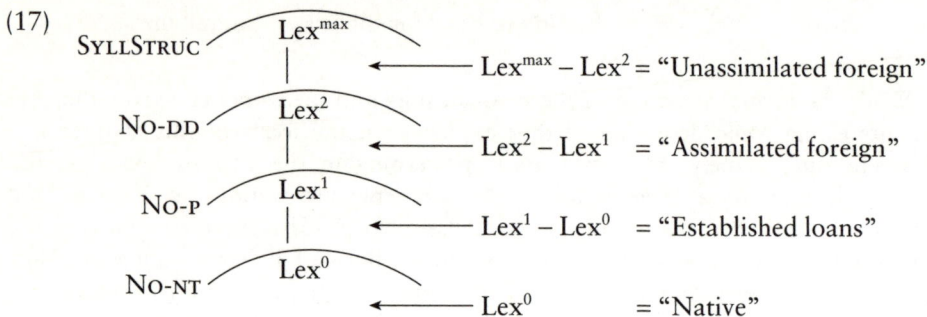

(17)

$$\text{SYLLSTRUC} \diagup \text{Lex}^{max}$$

$\text{Lex}^{max} - \text{Lex}^2$ = "Unassimilated foreign"

$$\text{No-DD} \diagup \text{Lex}^2$$

$\text{Lex}^2 - \text{Lex}^1$ = "Assimilated foreign"

$$\text{No-P} \diagup \text{Lex}^1$$

$\text{Lex}^1 - \text{Lex}^0$ = "Established loans"

$$\text{No-NT} \diagup \text{Lex}^0$$

Lex^0 = "Native"

Several observations can be made about this kind of model. First, viewed as a large set of elements, the whole lexicon is organized as a structure with more and more inclusive subsets: a member of Lex^i is also a member of Lex^{i+1} in that it fulfills all the constraints of Lex^{i+1}.

Second, a consistent pattern of set inclusion of this kind entails the existence of an innermost domain included in all the larger domains – in other words, a core area governed by the maximum set of lexical constraints (and hence "unmarked").

Third, the fundamental structural characteristic of the lexicon is the set-inclusion structure, and not the existence of large, homogeneous, and well-defined strata, which is a secondary phenomenon. It is certainly true that some traditional vocabulary strata emerge as lexical areas that stand out in virtue of serving as the domains for a number of different constraints, somewhat reminiscent of the bundles of isoglosses defining dialect areas in a traditional dialect map. In Japanese, this holds true for Yamato and Sino-Japanese; such groupings constitute genuine morphological classes in the sense of Aronoff (1994), which can be referred to as such in the grammar.[26] On the other hand, a closer inspection (Itô and Mester 1995a: 198–205) also supports the cross-linguistic finding that the class of foreign items does not constitute a uniform stratum, but is best thought of as the cumulative totality of the items occupying less and less central areas of the lexicon.[27] In (17) and elsewhere in this chapter, this nonuniformity is acknowledged by the split into "unassimilated" and "assimilated" foreign items. In reality, many finer distinctions are hidden beneath this coarse classification: the less nativized an item is, the more it disobeys lexical constraints, i.e. the more it falls outside of various constraint domains and is located towards the periphery of the lexical space.
[...]

2   Optimality Theory and Lexical Core–Periphery Relations

Up to this point, our usage of the term "constraint" has been an informal, pretheoretic one. It is now time to be more precise in this respect. In particular, we need to clarify what it means for a given constraint to be "out of force" in certain areas of the lexicon. In Optimality Theory, the traditional notion of a parametrized constraint – something that can be turned "on" or "off" in grammars – is replaced by the notion that a grammar literally consists in imposing a ranking order on a given set of universal and violable constraints.[32] In this view, constraints are universal, uniformly present in all grammars; the effects of a given constraint differ from grammar to grammar depending on the placement of the constraint within the overall ranking. The "on/off" settings approach of earlier theories can be seen as a rough approximation to a more accurate theory based on the notions of ranking and violability.

For the case at hand, the question becomes how the core–periphery structure in (17) can be obtained with a uniform constraint set: how do the various areas of the lexicon differ, if they do not differ in terms of which constraints are "on" and which are "off"? The obvious suggestion is that they differ in the way the constraints are *ranked*. In pursuing this line of investigation, familiar considerations of restrictiveness suggest that we explore the possibility that there are strict limits on such lexicon-internal rerankings.[33] In Optimality Theory crucial aspects of the role of a particular constraint are determined by the way it is ranked with respect to the faithfulness constraints, including the three subfamilies prohibiting segment deletion (MAX), segment insertion (DEP), and change in feature value (IDENT).[34]

For a given wellformedness constraint (say, NOCODA), being ranked above some conflicting faithfulness constraints is roughly equivalent to being "on" in terms of traditional parameter setting; being ranked below all conflicting faithfulness constraints is roughly equivalent to being "off." In Optimality Theory, the "underlying inventory" of a certain language (segments, clusters, syllable types, etc.) is determined indirectly. Inputs themselves are not directly regulated; anything at all can in principle serve as an input; the grammar, as a system of ranked constraints, determines how, if at all, the input gets parsed.

Let us start with Prince and Smolensky's (1993) assumption of strict domination: every optimality-theoretic grammar imposes a total order on the set of constraints. Given constraints A and B, either A ≫ B or B ≫ A must hold. Taking a cue from the relation between the domains seen above in (16) and (17), it is natural to hypothesize that the four constraints under discussion are ranked as in (18).

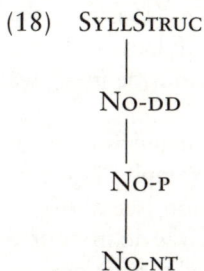

(18)   SYLLSTRUC
         |
        NO-DD
         |
        NO-P
         |
        NO-NT

In order to focus on the essential point, we abstract away from the differentiation between various Input/Output (henceforth, IO) constraints and consolidate the family of faithfulness conditions into a single unit (abbreviated as "FAITH"). Ranking FAITH below some constraint C means that C can command violations of faithfulness – at least one of the relevant faithfulness constraints is ranked below C. Likewise, ranking FAITH above some constraint C means that C cannot command violations of faithfulness – none of the relevant faithfulness constraints is ranked below C.[35]

The hierarchy in (18) suggests a very simple hypothesis about lexical stratification, namely, that it comes about through different rankings of faithfulness within a fixed hierarchy of structural wellformedness constraints. Consider the four wellformedness constraints under discussion. With their relative ranking fixed as in (18) above, there are five niches where FAITH can in principle be located, marked as FAITH$_1$, through FAITH$_5$ in (19). As indicated, FAITH$_1$–FAITH$_4$ indeed characterize the four vocabulary strata of Japanese under discussion.[36]

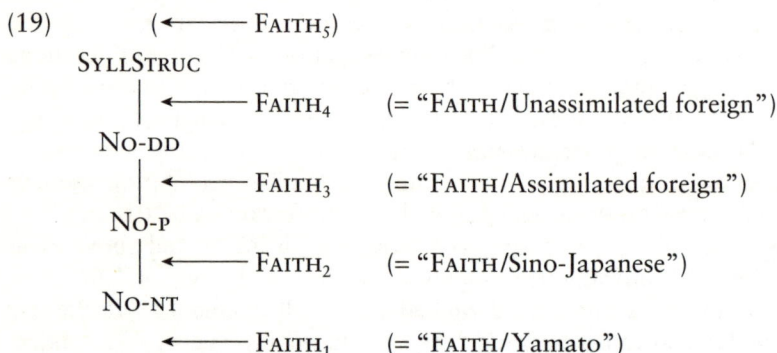

(19)   ($\longleftarrow$ FAITH$_5$)

  SYLLSTRUC

     | $\longleftarrow$ FAITH$_4$ (= "FAITH/Unassimilated foreign")

   NO-DD

     | $\longleftarrow$ FAITH$_3$ (= "FAITH/Assimilated foreign")

   NO-P

     | $\longleftarrow$ FAITH$_2$ (= "FAITH/Sino-Japanese")

   NO-NT

        $\longleftarrow$ FAITH$_1$ (= "FAITH/Yamato")

Working within the original version of Optimality Theory as developed in Prince and Smolensky (1993), Itô and Mester (1995a) conceive of FAITH$_1$–FAITH$_5$ as different rankings of the same block of IO-faithfulness constraints. Different strata involve slightly different grammars, and stratification is thus a form of linguistic variation. A variant of this proposal couched within Correspondence Theory (McCarthy and Prince 1995) posits the different rankings of IO-FAITH as distinct replicas of IO-FAITH, each indexed for a vocabulary stratum (i.e. FAITH/Yamato, etc.). We will here present the theory in the indexed-FAITH format, and will later return to general questions raised by FAITH$_1$, etc.[37]

FAITH/Yamato ranks below all four wellformedness constraints in (19), with the consequence that it cannot interfere with their demands. When a faithfulness violation is preferred over violations of segmental, sequential, or syllabic wellformedness, we have core behavior: in Japanese, a characteristic of Yamato items.[38]

At the other end of the spectrum, top-ranking FAITH/Unassimilated foreign in (19) is subordinate to general syllable structure constraints. For example, Japanese disallows complex onsets and adheres to a very strict coda condition (see above) – hence the appearance of epenthetic vowels in loanwords where the loan source has a consonant cluster or a final coda. But since FAITH/Unassimilated foreign dominates the other three structural wellformedness constraints, faithfulness demands will be met at their cost. As shown in (20), *beddo*, *petto*, and *tento*, while taking a final epenthetic vowel[39] to meet syllable structure demands, faithfully preserve their voiced geminate, singleton-*p*, and nasal + voiceless obstruent cluster, respectively, in violation of the lower-ranking structural constraints.

(20) Unassimilated foreign:
　　　beddo "bed"　　　　　　petto "pet"　　　　tento "tent"
　　　(violation of No-DD)　　(violation of No-P)　(violation of No-NT)

		SyllStruc	Faith/ Unassimilated foreign	No-DD	:	No-P	:	No-NT	:
/bed/ Unassimilated foreign	[bed]	*!							
	☞ [beddo]		* (Dep)	*					
	[betto]		**! (Dep, Ident-F)						
/pet/ Unassimilated foreign	[pet]	*!				*			
	☞ [petto]		* (Dep)			*			
	[hetto]		**! (Dep, Ident-F)						
/tent/ Unassimilated foreign	[tent]	*!						*	
	☞ [tento]		* (Dep)					*	
	[tendo]		**! (Dep, Ident-F)						

The candidate [beddo] is more faithful to /bed/ than [betto], which has an IDENT (i.e. change of feature value) violation in addition to a DEP (epenthesis) violation.[40]

As Katayama (1998) points out for similar cases, nothing much hinges on the choice of underlying forms. Besides /bed/, /pet/, and /tent/, another possibility is /beddo/, /petto/, /tento/, i.e. with lexically encoded epenthetic vowels, as shown in (21). In the absence of alternations, a version of lexicon optimization that puts a higher value on input–output similarity than on input simplicity in fact selects the latter set as the optimal input forms.[41]

One step down the ladder in (19), we find FAITH/Assimilated foreign, which differs from FAITH/Unassimilated foreign only in being subordinate to the voiced geminate obstruent constraint No-DD. Avoidance of voiced obstruent geminates is therefore a high priority, as far as the nativization of loanwords is concerned.[42] The result is illustrated in (22).

With respect to the other two constraints, No-P and No-NT, FAITH/Assimilated foreign remains dominant, thus forestalling any changes leading to the avoidance of singleton-p or of nasal+voiceless obstruent clusters. This is illustrated in (22) for the loanword pabu "pub" with its possible input /pabbu/: while parsing the b non-moraically, which is one way of avoiding the otherwise expected geminate, is legitimized by this ranking of FAITH, debuccalizing p to h, which would lead to a more fully nativized form habu, is forestalled by faithfulness.

(21)

		SyllStruc	Faith/ Unassimilated foreign	No-DD	...	No-P	...	No-NT	...
/beddo/ Unassimilated foreign	☞ [beddo]			*					
	[betto]		*! (Ident-F)						
/petto/ Unassimilated foreign	☞ [petto]					*			
	[hetto]		*! (Ident-F)						
/tento/ Unassimilated foreign	☞ [tento]							*	
	[tendo]		*! (Ident-F)						

(22)   Unassimilated foreign: beddo "bed"   Assimilated foreign: (hando)bakku "handbag"[43]

(violation of No-DD)   (no violation of No-DD, violation of Faith/Assimilated foreign)

		Faith/ Unassimilated foreign	No-DD	Faith/ Assimilated foreign	No-P	...	No-NT	...
/beddo/ Unassimilated foreign	☞ [beddo]		*					
	[betto]	*! (Ident-F)						
/baggu/ Assimilated foreign	[baggu]		*!					
	☞ [bakku]			*! (Ident-F)				
/pabbu/ Assimilated foreign	[pabbu]		*!		*			
	☞ [pabu]			* (Ident-μ)	*			
	[habu]			**! (Ident-F,μ)				
	[habbu]		*!	* (Ident-F)				

In (23), we define the individual faithfulness constraints violated in the tableaux above.

(23)   Let *s* and *s′* be two segments that are correspondents of each other, and let *P(x)* denote the specification status of segment *x* with respect to some property *P* (e.g., [+continuant], [−continuant], or [0continuant]; [0μ], [1μ], or [2μ], etc.).[44]

    a.   IDENT-F: *F(s) = F(s′)*. "Correspondent segments have identical specifications for feature F."

    b.   IDENT-μ: *μ(s) = μ(s′)*. "Correspondent segments have the same moraicity."

Returning to the hierarchy of indexed FAITH (19), we find FAITH/Sino-Japanese ranked below SYLLSTRUC, NO-DD, and NO-P, but still above NO-NT. This means that an input sequence like / . . . nt . . . / will be parsed as such in the output, in violation of NO-NT, but the other three constraints can all command violations of FAITH/Sino-Japanese. In particular, singleton-*p* cannot surface in Sino-Japanese.

(24)   Assimilated foreign: paN "bread"   Sino-Japanese: haN "group"
                               (violation of No-P)   (no violation of No-P)

		...	No-DD	FAITH/ Assimilated foreign	No-P	FAITH/ Sino-Japanese	No-NT	...
/paN/ Assimilated foreign	☞ [paN]				*			
	[haN]			*!				
/paN/ Sino-Japanese	[paN]				*!			
	☞ [haN]					*		

Thus the word for *bread* surfaces as [paN] (cf. Portuguese *pão*), but the Sino-Japanese morpheme /paN/ "group" is realized as [haN] (cf. *ippaN*" group one," *sampaN* "group 3").

Finally, (25) contrasts Sino-Japanese and Yamato items with respect to the low-ranking constraint NO-NT.

Stepping back from the details of this sketch of the stratal grammar of Japanese, we see that the simple hypothesis that stratal variation is due to the ranking of faithfulness and nothing else appears to provide enough descriptive flexibility to account for the empirical facts of stratification while at the same time imposing tight limits on the types of divergence allowed between strata. Ranked and violable faithfulness constraints are essential for this enterprise, just as in other areas. Optimality Theory allows us to reduce what looks like a haphazard application of constraints in different strata to a simple model, viz. a single phonology with a unique set of ranked structural constraints, with stratally indexed faithfulness constraints interleaved at different points.[45]

[. . .]

(25)   Sino-Japanese: šin-tai "body"   Yamato: šin-de "die-Gerund"
                       (violation of No-NT) (no violation of No-NT)

	No-DD		No-P	FAITH/ Sino-Japanese	*No-NT	FAITH/ Yamato
/šiN-tai/ Sino-Japanese ☞ [šiNtai]					*	
[šiNdai]				*!		
/šiN-te/ Yamato [šiNte]					*!	
☞ [šiNde]						*

Notes

[. . .]

12   See, for example, Holden (1976) and Lightner (1972) on Russian, and Nessly (1971) on English.

13   For further developments, see Paradis and Lebel (1994) on Quebec French, Cohn and McCarthy (1994) on Indonesian stress, Pater (1995) on English stress, Davidson and Noyer (1997) on Huave loan phonology, Kubozono (1997) on Japanese compound accent, Shinohara (1997) and Katayama (1998) on Japanese segment inventories and pitch accent, and Karvonen (1998) on Finnish loanwords.

14   Together with most researchers, we are assuming that the complex of conditions collectively referred to as the "Coda Condition" since Itô (1986) need further analysis. An approach that makes the required distinctions (i.e. disallowing non-place-linked codas while permitting geminates and place-assimilated nasals) is the alignment proposal in Itô and Mester (1994, 1999). In light of more recent work, a further reduction to a conjunction of more elementary factors is perhaps feasible – for example, to structural markedness locally conjoined with segmental markedness, as we have argued for coda-devoicing languages like German in other work (see Itô and Mester, 1997: 130–2), building on

Smolensky (1995). Related proposals have been made in Positional Faithfulness Theory, as in the work of Beckman (1998), Lombardi (1999) Padgett (1995), and others.

15   Some of these forms have alternants without gemination (oikakeru, oitsuku, oidasu).

16   For further details regarding the gemination of other sonorant consonants, resulting in forms like huNwari or hiNyari (phonetically, [huw̃wari] and [hiỹyari]), see Mester and Itô (1989: 275).

17   Historically speaking, in forms nowadays pronounced with initial [h] some feature of labial articulation must have persisted until recent times. Thus in the early 1500s the future emperor Gonara is reported to have posed the following riddle:

(i)   haha ni wa ni-do aitare-do mo, čiči ni wa iči-do mo awazu
      "for mother (haha) they meet twice, for father (čiči) not even once"

The intended answer is kučibiru "(the) lips," which only makes sense if haha was still pronounced somewhat like [ɸaɸa]. Martin (1987: 11) comments: "It would seem that in the mainstream of the language, centering on the capital cities, the syllable ha was pronounced Fa from as early as 800 till as late as 1600, at least initially."

18 See Poser (1984) for an illuminating discussion of double-verb compounding (10) and *ma-* prefixation (11), and see Itô and Mester (1996) and works cited there for many other examples of Sino-Japanese compounding (12).

19 For optimality-theoretic analyses of Sino-Japanese compounding, see Sakai (1994), Nasu (1996), and Kurisu (1998).

20 For further examples and discussion, see Itô and Mester (1986).

21 See Itô et al. (1995), Padgett (1995), Suzuki (1995), Pater (1996), and Hayes (1996) for different views regarding the constraints involved in the postnasal voicing syndrome. In order to sidestep unnecessary complications, we simplify the exposition of the analysis by means of the ad hoc constraint NO-NT. Similar remarks hold for NO-P and NO-DD, which can each be reduced to more elementary constraints.

22 See Davis and Tsujimura (1991) for an autosegmental analysis of the verbal alternations.

23 This root is felt to be archaic. Except for *šin-* "die," other *n*-final roots appear almost exclusively with stem-extensions in contemporary Japanese, e.g., *kasan-ar-u* "pile up," *sokon-er-u* "harm" for older †*kasan-u*, †*sokon-u*.

24 This form violates NO-P but obeys the sequential constraint disallowing the sequence *še* (or more generally, "palatal consonant + front mid vowel"). See Itô and Mester (1995a, 1995b) for further analysis and discussion of these sequential restrictions.

25 See the end of this section [omitted here – Ed.] for some discussion of borderline cases.

26 See Itô and Mester (1995a, 1995b) and Tateishi (1989) for details, and Martin (1952) and McCawley (1968) for earlier comprehensive studies.

27 Cf. Saciuk's (1969) [–homogeneous] class. [. . .]

32 See Prince and Smolensky (1993) as well as the large subsequent literature.

33 For a discussion of the limits on positing different "cophonologies" within the same grammar, see Inkelas et al. (1997).

34 We adopt here the correspondence-theoretic version of faithfulness, as developed by McCarthy and Prince (1995).

35 With respect to a more elaborate analysis differentiating between the various aspects of faithfulness, FAITH marks the position of the lowest-ranking relevant faithfulness constraint (MAX, DEP, etc.).

36 Top-ranked FAITH$_S$, which overrides even basic syllable constraints, appears to play no stratificatory role in Japanese, but see Itô and Mester (1995a: 198).

37 The indexed-FAITH format was first used by Pater (1995) for the English lexicon. Later applications include Prince (1996) and Fukazawa (1998) for Japanese. While the two versions of the theory are conceptually quite distinct, we are unaware of any decisive empirical differences between the two versions. As Rachel Walker (personal communication) has pointed out, hybrid formations, such as the cooccurrence of fixed affixes with alternating affixes in Tuyuca discussed and analyzed in Walker (1998: 116–38), are interesting in this regard: here simultaneous access to two rankings would be required (see also Fukazawa et al. 1998 for a case in Japanese) – a situation dealt with straightforwardly in the indexed faithfulness account, but calling for some imaginative development of the technical aspects of the original reranking proposal in Itô and Mester 1995a. Putting aside matters of execution and the technicalia of Correspondence Theory, the larger question for linguistic theory is whether variation *within* a single language is entirely different from – or related to – variation *between* languages, which must be the result of a difference in grammars, i.e. of differential constraint ranking.

38 Instead of FAITH/Yamato, it might be more adequate to make use of general, unindexed, IO-faithfulness. An indexed FAITH/Yamato family for core behavior is in danger of missing the point that core–periphery patterns show "Elsewhere" organization.

39 We are not concerned here with the quality of epenthetic vowels, which are mostly *u*, but *o* after coronal plosives where *u* would trigger major allophony (hence *beddo* instead of *beddzu*), and *i* after *k* in some older loans like *sutoraiki* "labor strike" (vs. *sutoraiku* "a strike in a baseball game").

40 The degeminating candidate [bedo] violates
    another higher-ranking constraint, either
    ALIGN-R (STEM, σ), requiring that the right
    edge of a stem and a syllable coincide
    (Kitahara 1996), or a sympathetic faithful-
    ness constraint requiring the coronal /d/ to
    maintain its syllable role (here: as a coda,
    see Katayama (1998)).

41 See Prince and Smolensky (1993) and Itô
    et al. (1995) for further discussion.

42 Among early loans from Western languages,
    there are a few cases of *p*-replacement, such
    as the word *batereɴ* "padre" (modern
    paadoru) from Portuguese, and in some
    documents from the late Tokugawa period
    the last name of Commander Perry appears
    as *heruri*. But such cases are sporadic.

43 It is unsurprising that we find a consider-
    able amount of variation in this area of the
    lexicon, with some speakers treating the
    loanword for "bed" as Assimilated foreign
    (i.e. *betto*), and the loanword for "bag" as
    Unassimilated foreign (i.e. *baggu*).

44 Further differentiation is of course pos-
    sible and arguably required in terms of
    individual features, feature values, specifica-
    tion/underspecification, insertion/deletion,
    zero-, mono-, and bimoraicity, consonantal
    vs. vocalic moras, etc.

45 For the strata appearing in this model of
    the phonological lexicon, the term
    "cophonologies" (see Inkelas et al. (1997))
    is therefore misleading. Just as for redu-
    plication and other areas where special
    faithfulness relations are involved, we are
    dealing with a single grammar and a single
    phonology.

References

Aronoff, Mark. 1994. *Morphology by Itself*. Cambridge, MA: MIT Press.

Beckman, Jill. 1998. *Positional Faithfulness*. University of Massachusetts, Amherst: doctoral dissertation. ◄

Cohn, Abigail, and John J. McCarthy. 1994/1998. Alignment and parallelism in Indonesian phonology. *Working Papers of the Cornell Phonetics Laboratory* 12: 53–137.

Davidson, Lisa, and Rolf Noyer. 1997. Loan phonology in Huave: nativization and the ranking of faithfulness constraints. In *The Proceedings of the West Coast Conference on Formal Linguistics 15*, eds. Brian Agbayani and Sze-Wing Tang, 65–79. Stanford: CSLI Publications.

Davis, Stuart, and Natsuko Tsujimura. 1991. An autosegmental account of Japanese verbal conjugation. *Journal of Japanese Linguistics* 13: 117–44.

Fukazawa, Haruka. 1998. Multiple input–output faithfulness relations in Japanese. MS, University of Maryland, College Park.

Fukazawa, Haruka, Mafuyu Kitahara, and Mitsuhiko Ota. 1998. Lexical stratification and ranking invariance in constraint-based grammars. In *CLS 32, Part 2: The Panels*, eds. M. Catherine Gruber et al., 47–62. Chicago: Chicago Linguistic Society.

Hayes, Bruce. 1996/1999. Phonetically driven phonology: the role of Optimality Theory and inductive grounding. In *Functionalism and Formalism in Linguistics, Volume I: General Papers*, eds. Michael Darnell et al., 243–85. Amsterdam: John Benjamins. ◄

Holden, K. 1976. Assimilation rates of borrowings and phonological productivity. *Language* 52: 131–47.

Inkelas, Sharon, Orhan Orgun, and Cheryl Zoll. 1997. The implications of lexical exceptions for the nature of grammar. In *Derivations and Constraints in Phonology*, ed. Iggy Roca, 393–418. Oxford: Oxford University Press. ◄

Itô, Junko. 1986. *Syllable Theory in Prosodic Phonology*. University of Massachusetts, Amherst: doctoral dissertation.

Itô, Junko, and Armin Mester. 1986. The phonology of voicing in Japanese: theoretical consequences for morphological accessibility. *Linguistic Inquiry* 17: 49–73.

Itô, Junko, and Armin Mester. 1994. Reflections on CodaCond and Alignment. In *Phonology at Santa Cruz*, eds. Jason Merchant et al., 27–46. Santa Cruz: Linguistics Research Center, University of California, Santa Cruz.

Itô, Junko, and Armin Mester. 1995a. The core–periphery structure of the lexicon and constraints on reranking. In *Papers in Optimality Theory (University of Massachusetts Occasional Papers in Linguistics 18)*, eds. Jill Beckman et al., 181–210. Amherst, MA: GLSA Publications.

Itô, Junko, and Armin Mester. 1995b. Japanese phonology. In *Handbook of Phonological Theory*, ed. John Goldsmith, 817–38. Cambridge, MA: Blackwell.

Itô, Junko, and Armin Mester. 1996. Stem and word in Sino-Japanese. In *Phonological Structure and Language Processing: Cross-Linguistic Studies*, eds. T. Otake and A. Cutler, 13–44. Berlin: Mouton de Gruyter.

Itô, Junko, and Armin Mester. 1997. Sympathy theory and German truncations. In *University of Maryland Working Papers in Linguistics 5. Selected Phonology Papers from Hopkins Optimality Theory Workshop 1997/ University of Maryland Mayfest 1997*, eds. Viola Miglio and Bruce Morén, 117–39.

Itô, Junko, and Armin Mester. 1999. Realignment. In *The Prosody–Morphology Interface*, eds. René Kager et al., 188–217. Cambridge: Cambridge University Press.

Itô, Junko, Armin Mester, and Jaye Padgett. 1995. Licensing and underspecification in Optimality Theory. *Linguistic Inquiry* 26: 571–614. ◄

Karvonen, Daniel. 1998. Finnish loanword phonology and the core–periphery structure of the lexicon. MS, University of California, Santa Cruz.

Katayama, Motoko. 1998. *Optimality Theory and Japanese Loanword Phonology*. Department of Linguistics, University of California, Santa Cruz: doctoral dissertation.

Kiparsky, Paul. 1968/73. How abstract is phonology? In *Three Dimensions of Linguistic Theory*, ed. O. Fujimura, 5–56. Tokyo: TEC.

Kitahara, Mafuyu. 1996. Consonant gemination and accent in Japanese loanwards. In *Formal Approaches to Japanese Linguistics 2* (Working Papers in Linguistics 29), eds. M. Koizumi et al., 61–79. Cambridge, MA: Dept. of Linguistics and Philosophy, MIT.

Kubozono, Haruo. 1997. Lexical markedness and variation: a nonderivational account of Japanese compound accent. In *The Proceedings of the West Coast Conference on Formal Linguistics 15*, eds. Brian Agbayani and Sze-Wing Tang, 273–87. Stanford: CSLI Publications.

Kurisu, Kazutaka. 1998. Richness of the base and root fusion in Sino-Japanese. MS, University of California, Santa Cruz.

Lightner, Theodore. 1972. Some remarks on exceptions and on coexistent systems in

phonology. In *The Slavic Word*, ed. D. S. Worth, 426–42. The Hague: Mouton.

Lombardi, Linda. 1999. Positional faithfulness and voicing assimilation in Optimality Theory. *Natural Language and Linguistic Theory* 17: 267–302. ◄

Martin, Samuel E. 1952. *Morphophonemics of Standard Colloquial Japanese*. Baltimore: Linguistic Society of America.

Martin, Samuel. 1987. *The Japanese Language through Time*. New Haven: Yale University Press.

McCarthy, John J., and Alan Prince. 1995. Faithfulness and Reduplicative Identity. In *Papers in Optimality Theory (University of Massachusetts Occasional Papers in Linguistics 18)*, eds. Jill Beckman et al., 249–384. Amherst, MA: GLSA Publications. ◄

McCawley, James D. 1968. *The Phonological Component of a Grammar of Japanese*. The Hague: Mouton.

Mester, Armin, and Junko Itô. 1989. Feature predictability and underspecification: palatal prosody in Japanese mimetics. *Language* 65: 258–93.

Nasu, Akio. 1996. Niji-kango ni okeru sokuon-ka genshoo: saitekisei-riron niyoru bunseki [Gemination in Sino-Japanese words: an analysis based on Optimality Theory]. *Bulletin of the Phonetic Society of Japan* 213: 27–40.

Nessly, L. 1971. Anglicization in English phonology. In *Papers from the 7th Regional Meeting, Chicago Linguistic Society*, 499–510. Chicago: Chicago Linguistic Society.

Padgett, Jaye. 1995. Partial class behavior and nasal place assimilation. In *Proceedings of the 1995 Southwestern Workshop on Optimality Theory (SWOT)*, eds. Keiichiro Suzuki and Dirk Elzinga. Tucson, AZ: Department of Linguistics, University of Arizona. ◄

Paradis, Carole, and Caroline Lebel. 1994. Contrasts from segmental parameter settings in loanwords: core and periphery in Quebec French. In *Proceedings of the MOT Conference on Contrast in Phonology*, ed. Carrie Dyke, 75–95. Toronto: Department of Linguistics, University of Toronto.

Pater, Joe. 1995. On the nonuniformity of weight-to-stress and stress preservation effects in English. MS, McGill University.

Pater, Joe. 1996. *NC. In *Proceedings of the North East Linguistics Society 26*, ed. Jill Beckman, 227–39. Amherst, MA: GLSA Publications.

Poser, William. 1984. *The Phonetics and Phonology of Tone and Intonation in Japanese.* MIT: doctoral dissertation.

Prince, Alan. 1996. Aspects of mapping under OT. Paper presented at Colloquium, University of California, Santa Cruz.

Prince, Alan and Paul Smolensky. 1993. Optimality Theory: Constraint interaction in generative grammar. MS, Rutgers University and University of Colorado, Boulder. RUCCS-TR-2. ◄

Saciuk, Bohdan. 1969. The stratal division of the lexicon. *Papers in Linguistics* 1: 464–532.

Sakai, Hiromu. 1994. Alignment with place nodes: an analysis of lexical domain distinctions in Japanese. In *The Proceedings of the West Coast Conference on Formal Linguistics 13*, eds. Raul Aranovich et al., 106–21. Stanford, CA: CSLI Publications.

Shinohara, Shigeko. 1997. Analyse phonologique de l'adaptation japonaise de mots étrangers. Université de la Sorbonne nouvelle Paris III: thèse pour le doctorat.

Smolensky, Paul. 1995. On the internal structure of the constraint component Con of UG. Paper presented at University of Arizona.

Suzuki, Keiichiro. 1995. NN: Rendaku and Licensing Paradox. Paper presented at the 6th Annual Japanese/Korean Linguistics Conference, August 8–10, University of Hawaii at Manoa.

Tateishi, Koichi. 1989. Phonology of Sino-Japanese morphemes. In *University of Massachusetts Occasional Papers in Linguistics 13*, 209–35. Amherst, MA: GLSA Publications.

Walker, Rachel. 1998. *Nasalization, Neutral Segments, and Opacity Effects.* University of California, Santa Cruz: doctoral dissertation.

Study and Research Questions

1 According to (19), if a morpheme with the underlying form /paddo/ is pronounced [paddo], what stratum does it belong to? What if it is pronounced [pando]? Or [hando]? Could the input /paddo/ ever become [haddo], if (19) is correct?

2 Explain in your own words what is meant by the following statement (from the end of section 1): "[T]he fundamental structural characteristic of the lexicon is the set-inclusion structure, and not the existence of large, homogeneous, and well-defined strata, which is a secondary phenomenon."

3 Instead of the proposal in (19), one could imagine two alternatives: (i) the lexical strata have different constraint rankings rather than different Faith constraints (Itô and Mester 1995); (ii) the markedness constraints, rather than the faithfulness constraints, are differentiated by lexical strata. Show how tableau (25) would look under these alternatives. Discuss the conceptual and empirical differences among them.

Chapter 33 | Arto Anttila and
Young-mee Yu Cho

Variation and Change in Optimality Theory

Editor's Note

In classic OT, as set forth in chapter 1, a grammar of a language is a total ordering of the constraints in CON. This chapter explores a somewhat different definition of a grammar: it is a partial ordering of CON, which means that some constraints may be formally tied in the ranking. There are many ways to interpret such a tie; the idea in this chapter is that a total ordering compatible with the grammar's partial ordering is selected each time the grammar is employed. This proposal tightly integrates the theory of variation with the theory of grammar and it establishes a direct connection between language variation and language change. Previous theories of variation, particularly the variable-rule theory (see Labov 1997: 148–51 for a concise summary), are not nearly as successful in achieving these aims. For further references on variation and change in OT, see McCarthy (2002: 233–4).

1 Introduction

Variation and change have not been among the leading issues in generative linguistics. While generative grammar is concerned with competence, variation reflects interactions between competence and other cognitive systems, including social systems, whereas change is often manifestly driven by external factors such as language contact. The question arises as to what extent grammars, construed as synchronic, psychological entities, play a role in language variation and change.

One possible approach to variation is to attribute it to performance. In classical generative grammar, genuine optionality can be handled with logical disjunction, either in the rule system (parentheses, curly brackets) or in the lexicon (structurally equivalent formatives, allomorphy), but there is no way to capture preferences which must be explained by extragrammatical factors, such as processing mechanisms and social constraints. However, there is plenty of evidence that the microstructure of

Excerpt from:
Anttila, Arto and Cho, Young-mee Yu (1998) Variation and change in Optimality Theory. *Lingua* 104: 31–56.

variation is not grammatically random, but reflects constraints very similar to those found in the domain of categorical rules. A well-studied example of such "orderly heterogeneity" (Weinreich et al., 1968) is the variable word-final -*t*/*d*-deletion in English words like *lost~los<t>*. Among other things, the rate of deletion depends on the sonority of the following segment (vowel > glide > liquid > obstruent): the more sonorous the following segment, the less frequently -*t*/*d* is deleted (Guy, 1991a, b, 1995). The sonority variable is clearly grammatical in nature, yet its effects are gradient, and thus cannot be derived from a pure optionality model.

Sound changes show similar structure-dependence. While Neogrammarian sound changes, being automatic and structure-blind, may well destroy morphological paradigms and create homonymy through mergers, phonologically they are benign: the result is always a well-behaved phonological system, and not one with, say, only voiced but no voiceless stops. More generally, sound changes do not subvert phonological principles such as implicational universals, which shows that grammar is somehow involved (Jakobson, 1929; Kiparsky, 1995).

Once we accept the fact that grammars impose structural constraints on variation and change, we need no less than a theory which formally connects invariant and variable phenomena, synchrony and diachrony. On the synchronic side, we need an integrated theory of rules and tendencies; on the diachronic side, the theory should predict implicational hierarchies ("Change c_1 must precede change c_2", "If form w_1 has undergone change c_1, then so has form w_2") and changes which manifest themselves only as statistical shifts in an individual's speech. One could also expect such a theory to shed light on the question why change always involves synchronic variation whereas the reverse does not necessarily hold (Weinreich et al., 1968: 188).

Instead of discussing these immensely complex questions at a general level, we choose a very concrete approach. We take up two well-documented diachronic changes: the fall and rise of the English *r* and the analogical levelling of a genitive plural paradigm in Finnish [only the section on English is reproduced here – Ed.]. Both span several centuries and both are still in progress in several dialects. After having shown that these processes are subject to interesting phonological constraints, we use them to illustrate in detail how change, including variation and usage statistics, can be modelled in Optimality Theory (OT) (Prince and Smolensky, 1993).

2   *r*–∅ Alternation in English

The *r*–∅ alternation can be illustrated by the following examples from the Eastern Massachusetts dialect (McCarthy, 1993: 169).

(1)   <r> = *r*-deletion, [r] = *r*-insertion
    (a)   *r-Deletion*   (b)   –
        The spa<r> seems to be broken.   The spa seems to be broken.
        He put the tune<r> down.   He put the tuna down.
        You'<r>e somewhat older.   The boat tends to yaw some.

(c) *Linking-r*
    The spar is broken.
    He put the tuner away.
    You're a little older.

(d) *Intrusive-r*
    The spa[r] is broken.
    He put the tuna[r] away.
    The boat'll yaw[r] a little.

Examples (a) and (c) show that a word-final etymological *r* is deleted before a following consonant, but not before a vowel. In (b) and (d) there is no etymological *r*. Instead, an *r* is inserted between adjacent heterosyllabic vowels, more specifically after [a, ɔ, ə] before V. This happens, not only across words, but also across root–suffix boundaries as in *draw[r]ing, withdraw[r]al*. Insertion does not apply before a consonant as (b) shows. The intuitive generalization is that *r* is favored before vowels, but disfavored before consonants. The concrete result may be deletion or insertion depending on whether there is an underlying /r/ or not, but the fundamental phonological generalization is nondirectional. It is almost universally agreed that this generalization is syllable-based (Johansson, 1973; Kahn, 1976; McCarthy, 1991, 1993). One plausible formulation is that *r* is deleted/not inserted in codas, but preserved/inserted in onsets. For example, in (c) an etymological *r* is saved by resyllabification within the utterance. Since the following word starts with a vowel, *r* ends up in the onset position and is thus not deleted.

The history of r–Ø alternation is roughly as follows (see e.g. Jespersen, 1909; Kurath and McDavid, 1961; Parslow, 1967; Kurath, 1972; Hughes and Trudgill, 1979; Trudgill and Hannah, 1985; Giegerich, 1992; Harris, 1994). In some systems nothing happened: there was neither deletion nor insertion. This situation obtained in all dialects before the 17th century and is currently attested in the basic rhotic dialects: Ireland, Scotland, south-western England, most of the US, Canada and parts of the Caribbean. The weakening of Coda-*r* started by the 17th century and by the 18th century resulted in the loss of *r* in parts of Britain and coastal America. In these dialects, Coda-*r* was deleted either variably or categorically. This is the current situation in South Africa, south-eastern US and formal British Received Pronunciation. Intrusive *r* developed later, yielding a system where the linking *r* is categorically deleted and intrusive *r* is at least variably present. This is currently the basic system in non-rhotic England, parts of the eastern and southern US and the southern hemisphere.[1]

These five systems, three invariant and two variable ones, are summarized below. We call the invariant systems A, B and C. The variable systems (variable deletion, variable insertion) can be viewed as combinations of two systems: A+B and B+C, respectively.[2]

(2) A Wanda left Homer left   Wanda arrived   Homer arrived
    B Wanda left Home<r> left   Wanda arrived   Homer arrived
    C Wanda left Home<r> left   Wanda[r] arrived   Homer arrived

We begin by giving an optimality-theoretic analysis of the three invariant synchronic systems A, B and C. The analysis assumes three constraints: the familiar syllable-structure constraints ONSET = "Syllables have onsets" and *CODA = "Syllables do not have codas" and a faithfulness constraint FAITH = "Don't delete, don't insert". In dialect A, the most important constraint is FAITH, hence there is neither deletion nor insertion. In Dialect B, the syllable structure constraint *CODA has become more important than FAITH which results in the coda deletion pattern. However, FAITH still remains more important than ONSET; witness the fact that there is no *r*-insertion in onset positions yet. Dialect C takes this final step: FAITH submits to both *CODA and ONSET and as a result we see both *r*-deletion in codas and *r*-insertion in onsets.

The three systems differ in the relative placement of FAITH. The overall change can be characterized as the gradual submergence of FAITH and the concomitant emergence of the two syllable structure constraints, *CODA and ONSET. As it stands, the analysis does not predict that the epenthetic onset should be *r* instead of, say, *t* or a glottal stop. However, it seems correct to separate syllable structure which motivates both deletion and insertion from the quality of the epenthetic segment. As

(3)

	Dialect A	FAITH	*CODA	ONSET
a. ☞	Wanda left			
	Wanda[r] left	*!	*	
b. ☞	Homer left		*	
	Home⟨r⟩ left	*!		
c. ☞	Wanda arrived			*
	Wanda[r] arrived	*!		
d. ☞	Homer arrived			
	Home⟨r⟩ arrived	*!		*

	Dialect B	*CODA	FAITH	ONSET
a. ☞	Wanda left			
	Wanda[r] left	*!	*	
b.	Homer left	*!		
☞	Home⟨r⟩ left		*	
c. ☞	Wanda arrived			*
	Wanda[r] arrived		*!	
d. ☞	Homer arrived			
	Home⟨r⟩ arrived		*!	*

	Dialect C	*Coda	Onset	Faith
a. ☞	Wanda left			
	Wanda[r] left	*!		*
b.	Homer left	*!		
☞	Home⟨r⟩ left			*
c.	Wanda arrived		*!	
☞	Wanda[r] arrived			*
d. ☞	Homer arrived			
	Home⟨r⟩ arrived		*!	*

Johansson (1973: 57–58) points out, a glottal stop is indeed sometimes substituted for both intrusive and linking-*r*.

One basic assumption of standard Optimality Theory is that every constraint is ranked with respect to every other. In our example, there are three constraints: Faith, *Coda and Onset. For example, in Dialect C, *Coda is ranked with respect to both Onset and Faith (4a, b), Onset is ranked with respect to both *Coda and Faith (4a, c) and Faith is ranked with respect to both *Coda and Onset (4b, c). This translates into a single tableau.

(4) Ranking: (a) *Coda ≫ Onset (b) *Coda ≫ Faith (c) Onset ≫ Faith

   Tableau: | *Coda | Onset | Faith |

More generally, an optimality-theoretic grammar can be defined as a set of ordered pairs R in the constraint set C, i.e. as a binary relation in C. In standard Optimality Theory, this relation has the following properties.[3]

(5) (a) *Irreflexivity.* R is irreflexive if and only if for every x in C, R contains no ordered pair $\langle x,x \rangle$ with identical first and second members. (No constraint can be ranked above or below itself.)
   (b) *Asymmetry.* R is asymmetric if and only if for any ordered pair $\langle x,y \rangle$ in R the pair $\langle y,x \rangle$ is not in R. (If x is ranked above y, it cannot be ranked below y.)
   (c) *Transitivity.* R is transitive if and only if for all ordered pairs $\langle x,y \rangle$ and $\langle y,z \rangle$ in R, the pair $\langle x,z \rangle$ is also in R. (If x is ranked above y and y is ranked above z, then x is ranked above z.)
   (d) *Connectedness.* R is connected if and only if for every two distinct elements x and y in C, $\langle x,y \rangle \in R$ or $\langle y,x \rangle \in R$. (Every constraint is ranked with respect to every other constraint.)

Properties (5a–d) define a *total order*. Standard Optimality Theory assumes that grammars have all the properties (a–d). We propose that grammars of natural languages are not connected, i.e. they do not have property (d). The remaining properties (a–c) define a more general relation which includes total orders as a special case: a *partial order*.

In (4), every constraint was ranked with respect to every other constraint, satisfying connectedness. If we omit (4c) ONSET ≫ FAITH, we get a relation which is irreflexive, asymmetric and transitive, but no longer connected, because neither ONSET ≫ FAITH nor FAITH ≫ ONSET holds. The constraint *CODA continues to rank above both ONSET and FAITH, but the mutual ranking of the latter two is not defined. This translates into two total orders (tableaux): one with the ranking ONSET ≫ FAITH, the other with FAITH ≫ ONSET.

(6)   Ranking: (a) *CODA ≫ ONSET   (b) *CODA ≫ FAITH

Tableaux:

*CODA	ONSET	FAITH
*CODA	FAITH	ONSET

Removing yet another ranking (b) *CODA ≫ FAITH yields the partial order in (7) which translates into three total orders. This time, the ranking of FAITH is completely free. Removing the last ranking leaves us with all the six logically possible total orders listed in (8).

(7)   Ranking *CODA ≫ ONSET

Tableaux:

*CODA	ONSET	FAITH
*CODA	FAITH	ONSET
FAITH	*CODA	ONSET

(8)   Ranking: Ø

Tableaux:

*CODA	ONSET	FAITH
*CODA	FAITH	ONSET
FAITH	*CODA	ONSET
FAITH	ONSET	*CODA
ONSET	*CODA	FAITH
ONSET	FAITH	*CODA

These examples show that a partial order can be viewed from two different angles: abstractly, as a set of ordered constraint pairs (rankings), or concretely, as a set of total orders (tableaux). The number of rankings is inversely proportionate to the number of tableaux: the fewer rankings, the more tableaux. Choosing between the two points of view is a matter of convenience. However, it is important to see that some sets of tableaux are not partial orders. Consider the two tableaux in (9):

(9)   Tableaux:

*CODA	ONSET	FAITH
FAITH	*CODA	ONSET

What is the corresponding ranking relation? FAITH cannot be ranked with respect to *CODA since both *CODA ≫ FAITH and FAITH ≫ *CODA are allowed. The same holds of FAITH and ONSET. This leaves us with the ranking *CODA ≫ ONSET which is clearly true of both tableaux. Unfortunately, as (7) shows, this ranking includes a third tableau and we have run out of possible rankings. Thus, we conclude that (9) is not a partial order, but a random pair of tableaux.

If the constraint set is small, as in this case, one can with little trouble figure out the partial orders hidden in it. One way to do this is by beginning from the total orders and removing rankings one by one until the set is empty. The resulting inventory of grammars can be pictured as a semilattice where each node is a partial order. The total orders are found at the leaves and the number of rankings decreases towards the root. The six partial orders hidden in the English system are shown in (10).

(10)   Grammar lattice

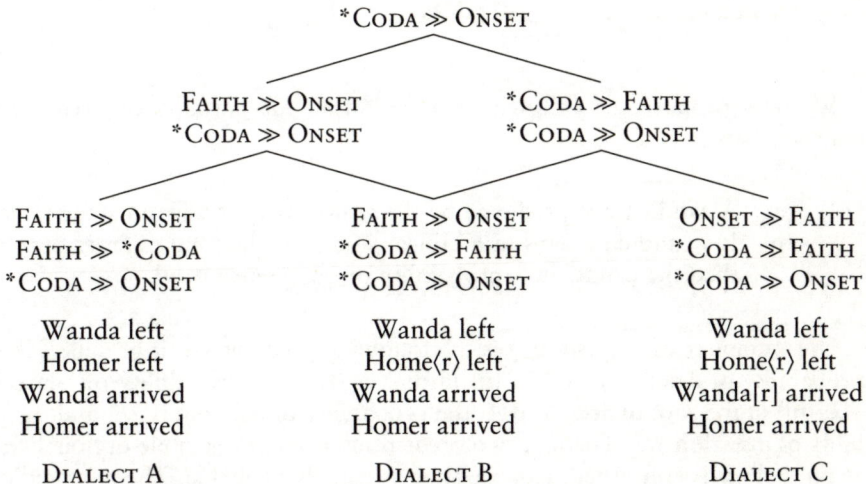

$$*\text{CODA} \gg \text{ONSET}$$

FAITH ≫ ONSET *CODA ≫ ONSET		*CODA ≫ FAITH *CODA ≫ ONSET

FAITH ≫ ONSET	FAITH ≫ ONSET	ONSET ≫ FAITH
FAITH ≫ *CODA	*CODA ≫ FAITH	*CODA ≫ FAITH
*CODA ≫ ONSET	*CODA ≫ ONSET	*CODA ≫ ONSET
Wanda left	Wanda left	Wanda left
Homer left	Home⟨r⟩ left	Home⟨r⟩ left
Wanda arrived	Wanda arrived	Wanda[r] arrived
Homer arrived	Homer arrived	Homer arrived
DIALECT A	DIALECT B	DIALECT C

Each leaf has three binary rankings which equals a single totally ranked tableau. At the upper levels, each mother node contains the intersection of the rankings of its daughters. Thus, for example, the root ranking *CODA ≫ ONSET is a member of every partial order in the lattice. The representation also visualizes the dual nature of partial orders: the nodes are annotated by ranking relations; the corresponding tableaux are the leaves dominated by this node.[4]

The linguistic interpretation of the lattice is straightforward. The three leaves are the invariant grammars: dialects A, B and C. The higher nodes are the variation grammars. For example, the node with the ranking {FAITH ≫ ONSET, *CODA ≫ ONSET} dominates two totally ranked grammars, dialects A and B, one of which predicts *Homer left*, the other *Home<r> left*. This node thus defines a variation dialect with variable *r*-deletion. The root grammar {*CODA ≫ ONSET} dominates three leaves: one predicts neither deletion nor insertion (dialect A), another predicts only deletion (dialect B), the third one predicts deletion as well as insertion (dialect C). The variation dialect predicted by this grammar is given in (11).

(11)

Candidate	Wins in	Result
Wanda left	3 tableaux	no insertion before C
Wanda[r] left	0 tableaux	
Homer left	1 tableau	variable deletion before C
Home[r] left	2 tableaux	
Wanda arrived	2 tableaux	variable insertion before V
Wanda[r] arrived	1 tableau	
Homer arrived	3 tableaux	no deletion before V
Home<r> arrived	0 tableaux	

We now propose the following interpretation for partially ordered grammars (Anttila, 1997):

(12)   (a)   A candidate is predicted by the grammar iff it wins in some tableau.
        (b)   If a candidate wins in n tableaux and t is the total number of tableaux, then the candidate's probability of occurrence is n/t.

Our grammar of English makes the following predictions: (i) in dialect A+B, the probability of *r*-deletion is 1/2; (ii) in dialect B+C the probability of *r*-insertion is 1/2; (iii) in the root dialect A+B+C the probability of deletion is 2/3 and the probability of insertion 1/3. The first two predictions amount to simple optionality; as far as phonology is concerned, either output is equally probable. The last prediction is more interesting: in a dialect where both *r*-deletion and *r*-insertion are optional, the former should be twice as frequent as the latter.[5]

The hypothesis that grammars are partial orders has important theoretical consequences. First, the set of possible grammars includes both invariant and variable systems. Both kinds of grammars are nodes in the grammar lattice. In some nodes, the ranking converges on one winner (invariance), in others several solutions are found (variation). The difference is merely quantitative: variable grammars typically have less ranking information.[6] The approach bears a certain resemblance to the traditional idea that variation is due to multiple grammars in the society or individual (Weinreich et al., 1968; Kroch, 1989; Kroch, 1994). However, while partial orders are representable as sets of totally ordered tableaux, there are many sets of tableaux which are not partial orders and thus not grammars in our sense. This contrasts sharply with the general multiple grammars model where any arbitrary collection of tableaux is as good a grammar as any other. The crucial empirical evidence that distinguishes between the two theories is statistical in nature. In section 3 [omitted here – Ed.], we will see that the partial ordering theory makes certain correct statistical predictions not made by the multiple grammars theory.

Second, the partial ordering theory accommodates both categorical judgments and preferences without abolishing the distinction between grammaticality vs. ungrammaticality. One and the same grammar can predict both statistical preferences observable in usage data and categorical regularities of the familiar kind. Deriving quantitative predictions from grammars may at first appear to deviate from the standard assumption that a grammar is a model of competence, not performance. However, the distinction between competence and performance is clearly independent of the question whether models of competence are categorical or not. Insofar as usage statistics reflect grammatical constraints, such as sonority, stress and syllable structure, they reflect competence and should be explained by the theory of competence, which partial ordering permits us to do. If this is so, then variable phenomena, including statistics, may provide critical evidence for evaluating theories of competence.

In the partial ordering theory, diachronic change can be visualized traversing the grammar lattice. In (13), the observed path of change is indicated by arrows going from the leftmost leaf to the rightmost leaf. Going up, the number of rankings decreases and variation increases. Going down, the number of rankings increases and variation decreases. The path of change passes through two partially ordered grammars with variable outputs.

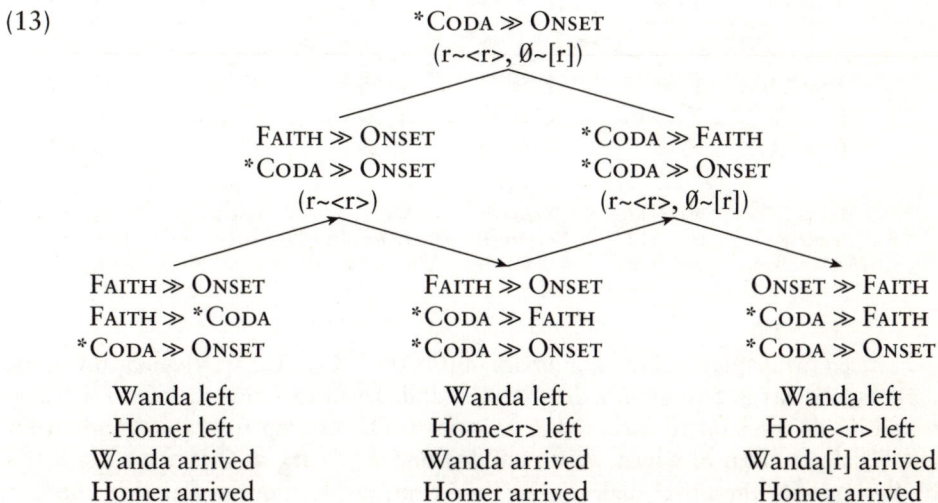

(13)

$$
*\text{CODA} \gg \text{ONSET}
$$
$$
(r\sim\langle r\rangle, \emptyset\sim[r])
$$

FAITH ≫ ONSET	*CODA ≫ FAITH
*CODA ≫ ONSET	*CODA ≫ ONSET
(r~<r>)	(r~<r>, Ø~[r])

FAITH ≫ ONSET	FAITH ≫ ONSET	ONSET ≫ FAITH
FAITH ≫ *CODA	*CODA ≫ FAITH	*CODA ≫ FAITH
*CODA ≫ ONSET	*CODA ≫ ONSET	*CODA ≫ ONSET
Wanda left	Wanda left	Wanda left
Homer left	Home<r> left	Home<r> left
Wanda arrived	Wanda arrived	Wanda[r] arrived
Homer arrived	Homer arrived	Homer arrived

It seems natural that diachronic change should track a connected path within the lattice. Due to external factors such as generational overlap language tends to change, not by quantal leaps from one invariant grammar to another, but glacially, accompanied by centuries of variation, with temporally adjacent dialects differing from each other minimally. In terms of our model, since the totally ordered A diachronically precedes the totally ordered B, it is not surprising to find an intermediary dialect which combines properties of both. However, note that the existence of such a dialect in no way follows from the model. In fact, it should not, since the gradual nature of language change is presumably a reflection of the gradual nature of change in the external world, not a formal property of mental grammars. What would be a problem would be finding a dialect which has no theoretical home in the lattice. Given the root ranking {*CODA ≫ ONSET}, the following dialects are excluded since the lattice contains no nodes with such properties.

(14) (a) Dialects with intrusive-*r* but no *r*-deletion.
      (b) Dialects where intrusive-*r* has a higher probability than *r*-deletion.
      (c) Dialects with intrusive-*r* before a consonant (*Wanda[r] left*).
      (d) Dialects where linking-*r* is deleted before a vowel (*Home<r> arrived*).

The lattice in (13) contains only those six partial orders that satisfy the ranking *CODA ≫ ONSET. We conclude by showing the complete lattice for {ONSET, *CODA, FAITH}, abbreviated O, C and F.

(15)

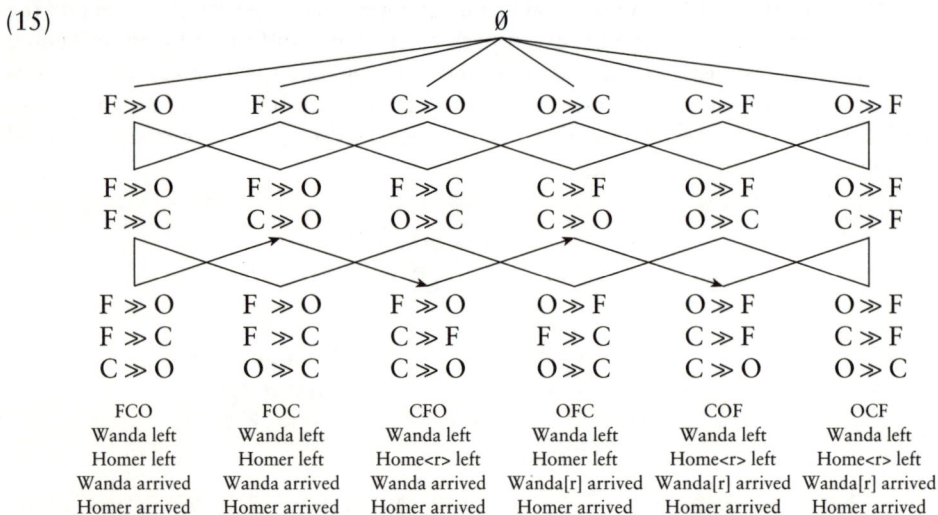

FCO	FOC	CFO	OFC	COF	OCF
Wanda left	Wanda left	Wanda left	Wanda left	Wanda left	Wanda left
Homer left	Homer left	Home<r> left	Homer left	Home<r> left	Home<r> left
Wanda arrived	Wanda arrived	Wanda arrived	Wanda[r] arrived	Wanda[r] arrived	Wanda[r] arrived
Homer arrived	Homer arrived	Homer arrived	Homer arrived	Homer arrived	Homer arrived

Lattice (15) displays all the grammars in {ONSET, *CODA, FAITH}: eight invariant dialects (six leaves, two intermediary nodes) and eleven variation dialects. English is found inside the sublattice rooted at *CODA ≫ ONSET (top row, third node from left). Dialects (14a, b) which were excluded under *CODA ≫ ONSET are predicted by this system; the novel dialect type (insertion, no deletion) is found in the leaf

OFC. The lattice further shows that dialects (14c, d) are still not generated by any ranking. In other words, dialects (14c, d) are excluded on universal grounds, whereas the absence of (14a, b) is an accidental gap, possibly with an historical explanation. [. . .]

Notes

1   This account ignores many fine-grained distinctions among dialects. Brett Kessler (p.c.) points out that there are dialects with intrusive-*r* only after [ə], but not after [aː, ɔ], dialects with intrusive-*r* after both [ə] and [aː, ɔ], but for the latter only between words, not before suffixes, and so on. For the present purposes, we idealize away from vowel quality and morphological structure and concentrate on syllable structure only. Another issue we do not have anything new to say about is the syntactic condition which blocks intrusive-*r* after function words. Thus, we do not get *He shoulda[*r] eaten, I'm gonna[*r] ask Adrian, Did you[*r] answer him?, to[*r] add to[*r] his troubles, why do[*r] Albert and you, a lotta[*r] apples, the[*r] apples* and so on. See McCarthy (1993) for discussion.

2   Harris (1994: 232–239) also mentions dialect D spoken in the Upper South of the United States. In this dialect, *r* may only occur in foot-initial onsets as in *red* and *tray*. The word *star* lacks an *r*-ful alternant, not just pre-pausally and pre-consonantally, but also pre-vocalically: *sta<rr>y, sta<r>of*. This dialect is different from A, B and C in that there is no *r*-Ø alternation and thus no evidence for an underlying *r* in the relevant positions. We assume that in dialect D a static distributional constraint prohibits *r*s everywhere except foot-initially.

3   For properties of relations, see e.g. Partee et al. (1993: 39–53).

4   It is important to see that the lattice is theoretically dispensable: it simply spells out all the possible rankings in terms of set-theoretic inclusion. Similar lattices can be constructed mechanically for any OT grammar. If the constraint set is totally ranked (as is usual in OT practice), the lattice reduces to one leaf.

5   The idea of exploiting partial constraint ranking to derive quantitative predictions goes back to Kiparsky (1993) and has since emerged in various forms for example in Reynolds (1994), Nagy and Reynolds (1995), Anttila (1997) and Ringen and Heinämäki (1997).

6   Total ordering does not necessarily imply invariance since two candidates may violate exactly the same constraints which results in a tie. Conversely, partial ordering does not necessarily imply variability since all the total orderings may converge on one and the same winner.

References

Anttila, A., 1997. Deriving variation from grammar. In: F. Hinskens, R. van Hout, and L. Wetzels (eds.), *Variation, Change and Phonological Theory*. Amsterdam: Benjamins.

Giegerich, H., 1992. *English Phonology*. Cambridge: Cambridge University Press.

Guy, G. R., 1991a. Contextual conditioning in variable lexical phonology. *Language Variation and Change* 3: 223–39.

Guy, G. R., 1991b. Explanation in variable phonology. *Language Variation and Change* 3: 1–22.

Guy, G. R., 1995. Competence, performance, and the generative grammar of variation. Paper presented at the International Workshop on Language Variation and Linguistic Theory, University of Nijmegen, September 5, 1995. ▶

Harris, J., 1994. *English Sound Structure*. Oxford: Blackwell.

Hughes, A. and P. Trudgill, 1979. *English Accents and Dialects*. London: Edward Arnold.

Jakobson, R., 1929. Remarques sur l'évolution phonologique du russe comparée à celle des autres langues slaves. In: *Travaux du Cercle*

Linguistique de Prague 2, 15–16. Prague. Reprinted in *Selected Writings*, vol. 1. The Hague: Mouton.

Jespersen, O., 1909. *A Modern English Grammar on Historical Principles*. Heidelberg: Carl Winter.

Johansson, S., 1973. Linking and intrusive /r/ in English: A case for a more concrete phonology. *Studia Linguistica* 27: 53–68.

Kahn, D., 1976. *Syllable-based Generalizations in English Phonology*. PhD thesis, Massachusetts Institute of Technology, Cambridge, MA.

Kiparsky, P., 1993. Variable rules. Handout distributed at the Rutgers Optimality Workshop (ROW 1).

Kiparsky, P., 1995. The phonological basis of sound change. In: J. A. Goldsmith (ed.), *The Handbook of Phonological Theory*, 640–70. Oxford: Blackwell.

Kroch, A., 1994. Morphosyntactic variation. In: K. Beals, J. Denton, R. Knippen, L. Melnar, H. Suzuki, and E. Zeinfeld (eds.), CLS 30, vol. 2: *The Parasession on Variation in Linguistic Theory*, 180–201. Chicago: CLS.

Kroch, A. S., 1989. Reflexes of grammar in patterns of language change. *Language Variation and Change* 1(3): 199–244.

Kurath, H., 1972. *Studies in Area Linguistics*. Bloomington, IN: Indiana University Press.

Kurath, H. and R. I. McDavid, 1961. *The Pronunciation of English in the Atlantic States*. Ann Arbor, MI: University of Michigan Press.

McCarthy, J., 1991. Synchronic rule inversion. In: L. Sutton, C. Johnson, and R. Shields (eds.), *Proceedings of the 17th Annual Meeting of the Berkeley Linguistics Society*, 192–207. Berkeley, CA: Berkeley Linguistics Society.

McCarthy, J., 1993. A case of surface constraint violation. *Canadian Journal of Linguistics* 169–95.

Nagy, N. and W. Reynolds, 1995. Accounting for variable word-final deletion within Optimality Theory. In J. Arnold, R. Blake, B. Davidson, S. Schwenter, and J. Solomon (eds.), *Sociolinguistic Variation: Theory, Data and Analysis. Selected Papers from NWAV23*. Stanford CA: CSLI Publications.

Parslow, R., 1967. *The pronunciation of English in Boston, Massachusetts*. PhD thesis, University of Michigan, Ann Arbor.

Partee, B. H., A. ter Meulen, and R. E. Wall, 1993. *Mathematical Methods in Linguistics*. Dordrecht: Kluwer Academic. [Corrected first edn.]

Prince, A. and P. Smolensky, 1993. Optimality theory: Constraint interaction in generative grammar. MS, Rutgers University, New Brunswick, and University of Colorado, Boulder. ◄

Reynolds, W. T., 1994. *Variation and Phonological Theory*. PhD thesis, University of Pennsylvania.

Ringen, C. O. and O. Heinämäki, 1997. Variation in Finnish vowel harmony: An OT account. MS, University of Iowa and University of Helsinki. ►

Trudgill, P. and J. Hannah, 1985. *International English. A Guide to Varieties of Standard English*. London: Edward Arnold. [2nd edn.]

Weinreich, U., W. Labov, and M. I. Herzog, 1968. Empirical foundations for a theory of language change. In: W. Lehmann and Y. Malkiel (eds.), *Directions for Historical Linguistics: A Symposium*, 95–195. Austin, TX: University of Texas Press.

Study and Research Questions

1   Choose another set of three or four interacting constraints. Work out the predicted patterns of variation by assuming that only one or two rankings are fixed. Construct a grammar lattice. Using (12), determine the predicted frequency of each variant.

2   Look at Müller (1999), a summary of all the ways that syntactic variation has been (or could be?) addressed within OT. Compare one of the proposals reviewed there with the proposal in this chapter.

3   Boersma and Hayes (2001) propose a theory in which constraints are ranked along a numerical scale, so some constraints can be ranked more closely together than others. Variation comes from "noise" in the system, which can cause constraints to be re-ranked – and the closer two constraints are in the numerical ranking, the more likely they are to be re-ranked. Compare the Boersma–Hayes approach to the one in this chapter.

References

Note

This reference list supplements the bibliographies in each chapter. It includes all works cited in the editor's notes and study questions, and it provides more complete citations for items marked by ▶ in the chapter bibliographies. When a work is available on the Rutgers Optimality Archive (http://roa.rutgers.edu) this has been indicated, but it should be noted that the ROA version may differ from the published version.

Akinlabi, Akinbiyi. 1996. Featural alignment. *Journal of Linguistics* 32: 239–89. [Available on Rutgers Optimality Archive, ROA-185.]

Akinlabi, Akinbiyi. 1997. Kalabari vowel harmony. *The Linguistic Review* 14(2): 97–138.

Alcantará, Jonathan B. 1998. *The Architecture of the English Lexicon*. Doctoral dissertation. Ithaca, NY: Cornell University. [Available on Rutgers Optimality Archive, ROA-254.]

Alderete, John, Beckman, Jill, Benua, Laura, Gnanadesikan, Amalia, McCarthy, John J., and Urbanczyk, Suzanne. 1999. Reduplication with fixed segmentism. *Linguistic Inquiry* 30: 327–64. [Available on Rutgers Optimality Archive, ROA-226.]

Anttila, Arto. 1997. *Variation in Finnish Phonology and Morphology*. Doctoral dissertation. Stanford, CA: Stanford University.

Archangeli, Diana. 1986. The OCP and Nyangumarda buffer vowels. In S. Berman, J.-W. Choe, and J. McDonough (eds.), *Proceedings of the North East Linguistics Society 16*, Amherst, MA: GLSA Publications, 34–46.

Archangeli, Diana, Moll, Laura, and Ohno, Kazutoshi. 1998. Why not *NC. In M. Catherine Gruber, Derrick Higgins, Kenneth S. Olson, and Tamra Wysocki (eds.), *CLS 34, Part 1: The Main Session*, Chicago: Chicago Linguistic Society, 1–26.

Archangeli, Diana and Pulleyblank, Douglas. 1994. *Grounded Phonology*. Cambridge, MA: MIT Press.

Baković, Eric. 1999. Assimilation to the unmarked. In Jim Alexander, Na-Rae Han, and Michelle Minnick Fox (eds.), *University of Pennsylvania Working Papers in Linguistics: Proceedings of the 23rd Annual Penn Linguistics Colloquium*, Philadelphia: Department of Linguistics, University of Pennsylvania. [Available on Rutgers Optimality Archive, ROA-340.]

Bermúdez-Otero, Ricardo. 1999. *Constraint Interaction in Language Change: Quantity in English and Germanic*. Doctoral dissertation. Manchester, UK: University of Manchester.

Boersma, Paul. 1998. *Functional Phonology: Formalizing the Interaction Between Articulatory and Perceptual Drives*. The Hague: Holland Academic Graphics.

Boersma, Paul. to appear. Typology and acquisition in functional and arbitrary phonology. In René Kager, Joe Pater, and Wim Zonneveld (eds.), *Fixing Priorities: Constraints in Phonological Acquisition*, Cambridge: Cambridge University Press.

Boersma, Paul and Hayes, Bruce. 2001. Empirical tests of the gradual learning algorithm. *Linguistic Inquiry* 32: 45–86. [Available on Rutgers Optimality Archive, ROA-348.]

Bresnan, Joan. 2001. The emergence of the unmarked pronoun. In Géraldine Legendre, Jane Grimshaw, and Sten Vikner (eds.), *Optimality-Theoretic Syntax*, Cambridge, MA: MIT Press, 113–42. [Available on Rutgers Optimality Archive, ROA-179.]

Bresnan, Joan. 2003. Explaining morphosyntactic competition. In Mark Baltin and Chris Collins (eds.), *Handbook of Contemporary Syntactic Theory*, Oxford: Blackwell. [Available on Rutgers Optimality Archive, ROA-299.]

Buckley, Eugene. 1999. Uniformity in extended paradigms. In Ben Hermans and Marc van Oostendorp (eds.), *The Derivational Residue in Phonological Optimality Theory*, Amsterdam: John Benjamins, 81–104.

Burzio, Luigi. 1994a. Metrical consistency. In Eric Sven Ristad (ed.), *Language Computations*, Providence, RI: American Mathematical Society, 93–125.

Burzio, Luigi. 1994b. *Principles of English Stress*. Cambridge: Cambridge University Press.

Burzio, Luigi. 1996. Surface constraints versus underlying representation. In Jacques Durand and Bernard Laks (eds.), *Current Trends in Phonology: Models and Methods*, Manchester, UK: European Studies Research Institute, University of Salford, 123–42.

Burzio, Luigi. 1997a. Italian participial morphology and correspondence theory. In Geert Booij, Angela Ralli, and Sergio Scalise (eds.), *Proceedings of the First Mediterranean Conference of Morphology (Mytilene, Greece, Sept. 19–21 1997)*, Patras, Greece: University of Patras, 42–53.

Burzio, Luigi. 1997b. Strength in numbers. In Viola Miglio and Bruce Morén (eds.), *University of Maryland Working Papers in Linguistics 5. Selected Phonology Papers from Hopkins Optimality Theory Workshop 1997 / University of Maryland Mayfest 1997*, College Park, MD: University of Maryland, 27–52.

Burzio, Luigi. 1999. Surface-to-surface morphology: When your representations turn into constraints. Unpublished MS. Baltimore, MD: Johns Hopkins University. [Available on Rutgers Optimality Archive, ROA-341.]

Burzio, Luigi. 2000. Cycles, non-derived environment blocking, and correspondence. In Joost Dekkers, Frank van der Leeuw, and Jeroen van de Weijer (eds.), *Optimality Theory: Phonology, Syntax, and Acquisition*, Oxford: Oxford University Press, 47–87.

Carlson, Katy. 1998. Reduplication and sonority in Nakanai and Nuxalk. In J. Austin and A. Lawson (eds.), *Proceedings of the Fourteenth Eastern States Conference on Linguistics '97*, Ithaca, NY: Cornell Linguistics Circle, 23–33. [Available on Rutgers Optimality Archive, ROA-230.]

Chomsky, Noam. 1995. *The Minimalist Program*. Cambridge, MA: MIT Press.

Chomsky, Noam and Halle, Morris. 1968. *The Sound Pattern of English*. New York: Harper & Row.

Chung, Chin Wan. 1999. *Reduplication in Korean*. Doctoral dissertation. Bloomington, IN: Indiana University.

Clements, G. N. 1991. Vowel height assimilation in Bantu languages. In K. Hubbard (ed.), *BLS 17S: Proceedings of the Special Session on African Language Structures*, Berkeley, CA: Berkeley Linguistics Society, 25–64.

Cohn, Abigail and McCarthy, John J. 1994/ 1998. Alignment and parallelism in Indonesian phonology. *Working Papers of the Cornell Phonetics Laboratory* 12: 53–137. [Available on Rutgers Optimality Archive, ROA-25.]

Cole, Jennifer S. and Kisseberth, Charles. 1995a. Nasal harmony in Optimal Domains Theory. Unpublished MS. Urbana: University of Illinois. [Available on Rutgers Optimality Archive, ROA-49.]

Cole, Jennifer S. and Kisseberth, Charles. 1995b. An Optimal Domains theory of harmony. Unpublished MS. Urbana: University of Illinois. [Available on Rutgers Optimality Archive, ROA-22.]

Crosswhite, Katherine. 1998. Segmental vs. prosodic correspondence in Chamorro. *Phonology* 15: 281–316.

Crosswhite, Katherine. 1999. *Vowel Reduction in Optimality Theory*. Doctoral dissertation. Los Angeles: University of California, Los Angeles.

Crowhurst, Megan. 1999. Conflicting directionality and tonal association in Carib of Surinam. In Kimary N. Shahin, Susan J. Blake, and Eun-Sook Kim (eds.), *Proceedings* of the West Coast Conference on Formal Linguistics 17, Stanford, CA: CSLI Publications.

Downing, Laura. 1999. Verbal reduplication in three Bantu languages. In René Kager, Harry van der Hulst, and Wim Zonneveld (eds.), *The Prosody–Morphology Interface*, Cambridge: Cambridge University Press, 62–89.

Drachman, G., Kager, René, and Drachman, A. 1997. Greek allomorphy: An Optimality account. *Proceedings of the 2nd International Congress on Greek Linguistics*, Salzburg: University of Salzburg, 151–60.

Dresher, B. Elan. 1999. Charting the learning path: Cues to parameter setting. *Linguistic Inquiry* 30: 27–67.

Dresher, B. Elan and van der Hulst, Harry. 1998. Head-dependent asymmetries in phonology: Complexity and Visibility. *Phonology* 15: 317–52.

Duanmu, San. 1999. Alignment and the cycle are different. In Ben Hermans and Marc van Oostendorp (eds.), *The Derivational Residue in Phonological Optimality Theory*, Amsterdam: John Benjamins, 129–52.

Flemming, Edward S. 1995. *Auditory Representations in Phonology*. Doctoral dissertation. Los Angeles: University of California, Los Angeles.

Fukazawa, Haruka. 1999. *Theoretical Implications of OCP Effects on Features in Optimality Theory*. Doctoral dissertation. College Park, MD: University of Maryland. [Available on Rutgers Optimality Archive, ROA-307.]

Fukazawa, Haruka and Miglio, Viola. 1998. Restricting conjunction to constraint families. In Vida Samiian (ed.), *Proceedings of the Western Conference on Linguistics 9 (WECOL 96)*, Fresno, CA: Department of Linguistics, California State University, Fresno, 102–17.

Gafos, Adamantios. 1996. *The Articulatory Basis of Locality in Phonology*. Doctoral dissertation. Baltimore, MD: Johns Hopkins University.

Gafos, Adamantios. 1998. A-templatic reduplication. *Linguistic Inquiry* 29: 515–27.

Gess, Randall. 1998. Phonetics versus phonology in sound change: An Optimality-Theoretic perspective. *Texas Linguistic Forum* 41: 71–86.

Gnanadesikan, Amalia. 1993. The feature geometry of coronal subplaces. *University of Massachusetts Occasional Papers in Linguistics 16*, Amherst, MA: GLSA Publications, 27–67.

Gnanadesikan, Amalia. 1995/to appear. Markedness and faithfulness constraints in child phonology. In René Kager, Joe Pater, and Wim Zonneveld (eds.), *Fixing Priorities: Constraints in Phonological Acquisition*, Cambridge: Cambridge University Press. [Available on Rutgers Optimality Archive, ROA-67.]

Gnanadesikan, Amalia. 1997. *Phonology with Ternary Scales*. Doctoral dissertation. Amherst, MA: University of Massachusetts at Amherst. [Available on Rutgers Optimality Archive, ROA-195.]

Goldsmith, John. 1976. An overview of autosegmental phonology. *Linguistic Analysis* 2: 23–68.

Goldsmith, John. 1990. *Autosegmental and Metrical Phonology*. Oxford and Cambridge, MA: Blackwell.

Gordon, Matthew. 1999. *Syllable Weight: Phonetics, Phonology, and Typology*. Doctoral dissertation. Los Angeles: University of California, Los Angeles.

Grimshaw, Jane. 1997. The best clitic: Constraint conflict in morphosyntax. In Liliane Haegeman (ed.), *Elements of Grammar*, Dordrecht: Kluwer, 169–96. [Available on Rutgers Optimality Archive, ROA-250.]

Guy, Gregory. 1997. Competence, performance, and the generative grammar of variation. In Frans Hinskens, Roeland van Hout, and W. Leo Wetzels (eds.), *Variation, Change, and Phonological Theory*, Amsterdam: John Benjamins, 125–43.

Hale, Kenneth. 1973. Deep-surface canonical disparities in relation to analysis and change: An Australian example. In Thomas Sebeok (ed.), *Current Trends in Linguistics*, The Hague: Mouton, 401–58.

Hale, Mark and Kissock, Madelyn. 1998. The phonology–syntax interface in Rotuman. In Matthew Pearson (ed.), *Recent Papers in Austronesian Linguistics: Proceedings of the Third and Fourth Meetings of the Austronesian Formal Linguistics Society, UCLA Occasional Papers in Linguistics #21*, Los Angeles: University of California, Los Angeles, Department of Linguistics, 115–28.

Hale, Mark, Kissock, Madelyn, and Reiss, Charles. 1998. Output-output correspondence in Optimality Theory. In E. Curtis, J. Lyle, and G. Webster (eds.), *Proceedings of the West Coast Conference on Formal Linguistics 16*, Stanford, CA: CSLI Publications, 223–36. [Available on Rutgers Optimality Archive, ROA-202.]

Halle, Morris. 1995. Feature geometry and feature spreading. *Linguistic Inquiry* 26: 1–46.

Halle, Morris, Vaux, Bert, and Wolfe, Andrew. 2000. On feature spreading and the representation of place of articulation. *Linguistic Inquiry* 31: 387–444.

Halle, Morris and Vergnaud, Jean-Roger. 1987. *An Essay on Stress*. Cambridge, MA: MIT Press.

Hammond, Michael. 1984. *Constraining Metrical Theory: A Modular Theory of Rhythm and Destressing*. Doctoral dissertation. Los Angeles: University of California, Los Angeles. [Published 1988, Outstanding Dissertations in Linguistics series, Garland Press, New York.]

Hargus, Sharon. 1995. The first person plural prefix in Babine-Witsuwit'en. Unpublished MS. Seattle: University of Washington. [Available on Rutgers Optimality Archive, ROA-108.]

Hargus, Sharon and Tuttle, Siri G. 1997. Augmentation as affixation in Athabaskan languages. *Phonology* 14: 177–220. [Available on Rutgers Optimality Archive, ROA-191.]

Hayes, Bruce. 1980. *A Metrical Theory of Stress Rules*. Doctoral dissertation. Cambridge, MA: MIT. [Published by Garland Press, New York, 1985.]

Hayes, Bruce. 1995. *Metrical Stress Theory: Principles and Case Studies*. Chicago: University of Chicago Press.

Hendricks, Sean. 1999. *Reduplication without Templates: A Study of Bare-Consonant Reduplication*. Doctoral dissertation. Tucson, AZ: University of Arizona.

Hermans, Ben and van Oostendorp, Marc (eds.). 1999. *The Derivational Residue in Phonological Optimality Theory*. Amsterdam: John Benjamins.

Hewitt, Mark. 1994. Deconstructing foot binarity in Koniag Alutiiq. Unpublished MS. Vancouver, BC: University of British Columbia. [Available on Rutgers Optimality Archive, ROA-12.]

Hewitt, Mark and Prince, Alan. 1989. OCP, locality and linking: The N. Karanga verb. In E. J. Fee and K. Hunt (eds.), *Proceedings of the West Coast Conference on Formal Linguistics 8*, Stanford, CA: Stanford Linguistic Association, 176–91.

Hume, Elizabeth. 1998. Metathesis in phonological theory: The case of Leti. *Lingua* 104: 147–86. [Available on Rutgers Optimality Archive, ROA-180.]

Hung, Henrietta. 1994. *The Rhythmic and Prosodic Organization of Edge Constituents*. Doctoral dissertation. Waltham, MA: Brandeis University. [Available on Rutgers Optimality Archive, ROA-24.]

Hyman, Larry and Inkelas, Sharon. 1997. Emergent templates: The unusual case of Tiene. In Viola Miglio and Bruce Morén (eds.), *University of Maryland Working Papers in Linguistics 5. Selected Phonology Papers from Hopkins Optimality Theory Workshop 1997 / University of Maryland Mayfest 1997*, College Park, MD: University of Maryland, 92–116. [Available on Rutgers Optimality Archive, ROA-214.]

Inkelas, Sharon. 1999a. Exceptional stress-attracting suffixes in Turkish: Representation vs. the grammar. In René Kager, Harry van der Hulst, and Wim Zonneveld (eds.), *The Prosody–Morphology Interface*, Cambridge: Cambridge University Press, 134–87. [Available on Rutgers Optimality Archive, ROA-39.]

Inkelas, Sharon. 1999b. Phonotactic blocking through structural immunity. Berkeley, CA: University of California, Berkeley. [Available on Rutgers Optimality Archive, ROA-366.]

Inkelas, Sharon and Orgun, C. Orhan. 1998. Level (non)ordering in recursive morphology: Evidence from Turkish. In Steven G. Lapointe, Diane K. Brentari, and Patrick M. Farrell (eds.), *Morphology and its Relation to Phonology and Syntax*, Stanford, CA: CSLI Publications, 360–92.

Ishii, Toru. 1996. An optimality theoretic approach to ternary stress systems. In Brian Agbayani and Naomi Harada (eds.), *UCI Working Papers in Linguistics*, vol. 2: *Proceedings of the South Western Optimality Theory Workshop*, Irvine, CA: Irvine Linguistics Students Association, 95–111.

Itô, Junko. 1984. Melodic dissimilation in Ainu. *Linguistic Inquiry* 15: 505–13.

Itô, Junko, Kitagawa, Yoshihisa, and Mester, Armin. 1996. Prosodic faithfulness and correspondence: Evidence from a Japanese

Argot. *Journal of East Asian Linguistics* 5: 217–94. [Available on Rutgers Optimality Archive, ROA-146.]

Itô, Junko and Mester, Armin. 1994. Reflections on CodaCond and Alignment. In Jason Merchant, Jaye Padgett, and Rachel Walker (eds.), *Phonology at Santa Cruz*, Santa Cruz, CA: Linguistics Research Center, University of California, Santa Cruz, 27–46. [Available on Rutgers Optimality Archive, ROA-141.]

Itô, Junko and Mester, Armin. 1995. The core–periphery structure of the lexicon and constraints on reranking. In Jill Beckman, Laura Walsh Dickey, and Suzanne Urbanczyk (eds.), *Papers in Optimality Theory*, Amherst, MA: GLSA Publications, 181–210.

Itô, Junko and Mester, Armin. 1997. Correspondence and compositionality: The ga–gyo variation in Japanese phonology. In Iggy Roca (ed.), *Derivations and Constraints in Phonology*, Oxford: Oxford University Press, 419–62. [Available on Rutgers Optimality Archive, ROA-145.]

Itô, Junko and Mester, Armin. 1998. Markedness and word structure: OCP effects in Japanese. Unpublished MS. Santa Cruz, CA: University of California at Santa Cruz. [Available on Rutgers Optimality Archive, ROA-255.]

Itô, Junko and Mester, Armin. 1999. Realignment. In René Kager, Harry van der Hulst, and Wim Zonneveld (eds.), *The Prosody–Morphology Interface*, Cambridge: Cambridge University Press, 188–217.

Itô, Junko and Mester, Armin. 2003. On the sources of opacity in OT: Coda processes in German. In Caroline Féry and Ruben van de Vijver (eds.), *The Optimal Syllable*, Cambridge: Cambridge University Press. [Available on Rutgers Optimality Archive, ROA-347.]

Jun, Jongho. 1995. *Perceptual and Articulatory Factors on Place Assimilation*. Doctoral dissertation. Los Angeles: University of California, Los Angeles.

Jun, Jongho. 1996. Place assimilation as the result of conflicting perceptual and articulatory constraints. In Jose Camacho, Lina Choueiri, and Maki Watanabe (eds.), *Proceedings of the West Coast Conference on Formal Linguistics 14*, Stanford, CA: CSLI Publications, 221–37.

Kager, René. 1989. *A Metrical Theory of Stress and Destressing in English and Dutch*. Dordrecht: Foris.

Kager, René. 1992a. Are there any truly quantity-insensitive systems? In Laura Buszard-Welcher, Lionel Wee, and William Weigel (eds.), *Proceedings of the Eighteenth Annual Meeting of the Berkeley Linguistics Society*, Berkeley, CA: Berkeley Linguistics Society, 123–32.

Kager, René. 1992b. Shapes of the generalized trochee. In J. Mead (ed.), *Proceedings of the Eleventh West Coast Conference on Formal Linguistics*, Stanford, CA: CSLI Publications, 298–312.

Kager, René. 1993. Alternatives to the iambic-trochaic law. *Natural Language and Linguistic Theory* 11: 381–432.

Kager, René. 1994. Ternary rhythm in alignment theory. Unpublished MS. Utrecht: Utrecht University. [Available on Rutgers Optimality Archive, ROA-35.]

Kager, René. 1996. On affix allomorphy and syllable counting. In U. Kleinhenz (ed.), *Interfaces in Phonology*, Berlin: Akademie Verlag, 155–71. [Available on Rutgers Optimality Archive, ROA-88.]

Kager, René. 1997. Rhythmic vowel deletion in Optimality Theory. In Iggy Roca (ed.), *Derivations and Constraints in Phonology*, Oxford: Oxford University Press, 463–99.

Kager, René. 1999. *Optimality Theory*. Cambridge: Cambridge University Press.

Kager, René. 2001. Rhythmic directionality by positional licensing. Handout. Fifth HIL Phonology Conference (HILP 5), University of Potsdam. [Available on Rutgers Optimality Archive, ROA-514.]

Kang, Hyeon-Seok. 1997. *Phonological Variation in Glides and Diphthongs of Seoul Korean: Its Synchrony and Diachrony*. Doctoral dissertation. Columbus, OH: Ohio State University.

Kaun, Abigail. 1995. *The Typology of Rounding Harmony: An Optimality Theoretic Approach*. Doctoral dissertation. Los Angeles: University of California, Los Angeles. [Available on Rutgers Optimality Archive, ROA-227.]

Keer, Edward. 1999. *Geminates, the OCP, and the Nature of CON*. Doctoral dissertation. New Brunswick, NJ: Rutgers University.

[Available on Rutgers Optimality Archive, ROA-350.]

Kenstowicz, Michael. 1994. Syllabification in Chukchee: A constraints-based analysis. In Alice Davison, Nicole Maier, Glaucia Silva, and Wan Su Yan (eds.), *Proceedings of the Formal Linguistics Society of Mid-America 4*, Iowa City: Department of Linguistics, University of Iowa, 160–81. [Available on Rutgers Optimality Archive, ROA-30.]

Kenstowicz, Michael. 1995. Cyclic vs. non-cyclic constraint evaluation. *Phonology* 12: 397–436. [Available on Rutgers Optimality Archive, ROA-31.]

Kenstowicz, Michael. 1996. Base-identity and uniform exponence: alternatives to cyclicity. In Jacques Durand and Bernard Laks (eds.), *Current Trends in Phonology: Models and Methods*, Manchester, UK: University of Salford, 363–93. [Available on Rutgers Optimality Archive, ROA-103.]

Kenstowicz, Michael. 1997. Uniform exponence: Exemplification and extension. In Viola Miglio and Bruce Morén (eds.), *University of Maryland Working Papers in Linguistics 5. Selected Phonology Papers from Hopkins Optimality Theory Workshop 1997 / University of Maryland Mayfest 1997*, College Park, MD: University of Maryland, 139–55. [Available on Rutgers Optimality Archive, ROA-218.]

Kiparsky, Paul. 1973a. "Elsewhere" in phonology. In Stephen R. Anderson and Paul Kiparsky (eds.), *A Festschrift for Morris Halle*, New York: Holt, Rinehart and Winston, 93–106.

Kiparsky, Paul. 1973b. Phonological representations. In O. Fujimura (ed.), *Three Dimensions of Linguistic Theory*, Tokyo: TEC, 3–136.

Kiparsky, Paul. 1982. Lexical phonology and morphology. In I. S. Yang (ed.), *Linguistics in the Morning Calm*, Seoul: Hanshin, 3–91.

Kiparsky, Paul. 1993. Blocking in non-derived environments. In Sharon Hargus and Ellen Kaisse (eds.), *Studies in Lexical Phonology*, San Diego, CA: Academic Press.

Kiparsky, Paul. 2003. Syllables and moras in Arabic. In Caroline Féry and Ruben van de Vijver (eds.), *The Optimal Syllable*, Cambridge: Cambridge University Press.

Kiparsky, Paul. to appear. *Paradigmatic Effects*. Stanford, CA: CSLI Publications.

Kirchner, Robert. 1993. Turkish vowel harmony and disharmony: An Optimality Theoretic account. Unpublished MS. Los Angeles: University of California, Los Angeles. [Available on Rutgers Optimality Archive, ROA-4.]

Kirchner, Robert. 1997. Contrastiveness and faithfulness. *Phonology* 14: 83–111.

Kirchner, Robert. 1998a. *An Effort-Based Approach to Consonant Lenition*. Doctoral dissertation. Los Angeles: University of California, Los Angeles. [Available on Rutgers Optimality Archive, ROA-276.]

Kirchner, Robert. 1998b. Preliminary thoughts on "phonologization" within an exemplar-based speech-processing system. Unpublished MS. Edmonton, AB: University of Alberta. [Available on Rutgers Optimality Archive, ROA-320.]

Kraska-Szlenk, Iwona. 1995. *The Phonology of Stress in Polish*. Doctoral dissertation. Urbana, IL: University of Illinois.

Labov, William. 1997. Resyllabification. In Frans Hinskens, Roeland van Hout, and W. Leo Wetzels (eds.), *Variation, Change, and Phonological Theory*, Amsterdam: John Benjamins, 145–79.

Lapointe, Steven G. and Sells, Peter. 1997. Separating syntax and phonology in Optimality Theory: The case of suppletive segment/ø allomorphy. Unpublished MS. Davis, CA, and Stanford, CA: University of California, Davis and Stanford University.

Leben, Will. 1973. *Suprasegmental Phonology*. Doctoral dissertation. Cambridge, MA: MIT.

Legendre, Géraldine, Raymond, William, and Smolensky, Paul. 1993. An Optimality-Theoretic typology of case and voice systems. In Joshua S. Guenter, Barbara A. Kaiser, and Cheryl C. Zoll (eds.), *Proceedings of the Nineteenth Annual Meeting of the Berkeley Linguistics Society*, Berkeley, CA: Berkeley Linguistics Society, 464–78.

Legendre, Géraldine, Smolensky, Paul, and Wilson, Colin. 1998. When is less more? Faithfulness and minimal links in *wh*-chains. In Pilar Barbosa, Danny Fox, Paul Hagstrom, Martha McGinnis, and David Pesetsky (eds.), *Is the Best Good Enough? Optimality and Competition in Syntax*, Cambridge, MA: MIT Press, 249–89. [Available on Rutgers Optimality Archive, ROA-117.]

Liberman, Mark and Prince, Alan. 1977. On stress and linguistic rhythm. *Linguistic Inquiry* 8: 249–336.

Lombardi, Linda. 1998a. Constraints versus representations: Some questions from laryngeal phonology. In Haruka Fukazawa, Frida Morelli, Caro Struijke, and Yi-Ching Su (eds.), *University of Maryland Working Papers in Linguistics*, College Park, MD: Department of Linguistics, University of Maryland.

Lombardi, Linda. 1998b. Evidence for MaxFeature constraints from Japanese. In Haruka Fukazawa, Frida Morelli, Caro Struijke, and Yi-Ching Su (eds.), *University of Maryland Working Papers in Linguistics*, College Park, MD: Department of Linguistics, University of Maryland. [Available on Rutgers Optimality Archive, ROA-247.]

Lombardi, Linda. 2001. Why Place and Voice are different: Constraint-specific alternations in Optimality Theory. In Linda Lombardi (ed.), *Segmental Phonology in Optimality Theory: Constraints and Representations*, Cambridge: Cambridge University Press, 13–45. [Available on Rutgers Optimality Archive, ROA-105.]

MacEachern, Margaret. 1997. *Laryngeal Co-occurrence Restrictions*. Doctoral dissertation. Los Angeles: University of California, Los Angeles.

Mascaró, Joan. 1976. *Catalan Phonology and the Phonological Cycle*. Doctoral dissertation. Cambridge, MA: MIT.

Mascaró, Joan and Wetzels, Leo. 2001. The typology of voicing and devoicing. *Language* 77: 207–44.

McCarthy, John J. 1979. On stress and syllabification. *Linguistic Inquiry* 10: 443–66.

McCarthy, John J. 1986. OCP effects: Gemination and antigemination. *Linguistic Inquiry* 17: 207–63.

McCarthy, John J. 1996. Remarks on phonological opacity in Optimality Theory. In Jacqueline Lecarme, Jean Lowenstamm, and Ur Shlonsky (eds.), *Studies in Afroasiatic Grammar: Papers from the Second Conference on Afroasiatic Linguistics, Sophia Antipolis, 1994*, The Hague: Holland Academic Graphics, 215–43.

McCarthy, John J. 2000. The prosody of phase in Rotuman. *Natural Language and Linguistic Theory* 18: 147–97. [Preliminary version on Rutgers Optimality Archive, ROA-110.]

McCarthy, John J. 2002. *A Thematic Guide to Optimality Theory*. Cambridge: Cambridge University Press.

McCarthy, John J. and Prince, Alan. 1986/1996. *Prosodic Morphology 1986*. New Brunswick, NJ: Rutgers University Center for Cognitive Science. [Available (July, 2002) at http://ruccs.rutgers.edu/pub/papers/pm86all.pdf. Excerpts appear in John Goldsmith (ed.), *Essential Readings in Phonology*, Oxford: Blackwell, 1999, 102–36.]

McCarthy, John J. and Prince, Alan. 1993. *Prosodic Morphology: Constraint Interaction and Satisfaction*. New Brunswick, NJ: Rutgers University Center for Cognitive Science. [Available on Rutgers Optimality Archive, ROA-482.]

McCarthy, John J. and Prince, Alan. 1994. Two lectures on Prosodic Morphology (Utrecht, 1994). Part I: Template form in Prosodic Morphology. Part II: Faithfulness and reduplicative identity. Unpublished MS. Amherst, MA and New Brunswick, NJ: University of Massachusetts, Amherst and Rutgers University. [Available on Rutgers Optimality Archive, ROA-59.]

Mester, Armin. 1988. Dependent tier ordering and the OCP. In Harry van der Hulst and Norval Smith (eds.), *Features, Segmental Structure and Harmony Processes*, Dordrecht: Foris, 127–44.

Mester, Armin. 1994. The quantitative trochee in Latin. *Natural Language and Linguistic Theory* 12: 1–61.

Michelson, Karin. 1986. Ghost R's in Onondaga: An autosegmental analysis of *R-stems. In L. Wetzels and E. Sezer (eds.), *Studies in Compensatory Lengthening*, Dordrecht: Foris, 147–66.

Mohanan, K. P. 1986. *The Theory of Lexical Phonology*. Dordrecht: Reidel.

Müller, Gereon. 1999. Optionality in Optimality-theoretic syntax. *Glot International* 4(5): 3–8. [Available (12 June, 2002) at http://merlin.philosophie.uni-stuttgart.de/~heck/ot/papers/.]

Myers, Scott. 1986. *Tone and the Structure of Words in Shona*. Doctoral dissertation. Amherst, MA: University of Massachusetts, Amherst.

Myers, Scott. 1997. Expressing phonetic naturalness in phonology. In Iggy Roca (ed.), *Derivations and Constraints in Phonology*, Oxford: Oxford University Press, 125–52.

Myers, Scott. 1998. AUX in Bantu morphology and phonology. In Larry Hyman and Charles Kisseberth (eds.), *Theoretical Aspects of Bantu Tone*, Stanford, CA: CSLI Publications.

Ní Chiosáin, Máire and Padgett, Jaye. 2001. Markedness, segment realization, and locality in spreading. In Linda Lombardi (ed.), *Segmental Phonology in Optimality Theory: Constraints and Representations*, Cambridge: Cambridge University Press. [Available on Rutgers Optimality Archive, ROA-503.]

Odden, David. 1986. On the Obligatory Contour Principle. *Language* 62: 353–83.

Odden, David. 1988. Anti Antigemination and the OCP. *Linguistic Inquiry* 19: 451–75.

Orgun, C. Orhan. 1996a. Correspondence and identity constraints in two-level Optimality Theory. In Jose Camacho, Lina Choueiri, and Maki Watanabe (eds.), *Proceedings of the West Coast Conference on Formal Linguistics 14*, Stanford, CA: CSLI Publications, 399–413. [Available on Rutgers Optimality Archive, ROA-62.]

Orgun, C. Orhan. 1996b. *Sign-based Morphology and Phonology, with Special Attention to Optimality Theory*. Doctoral dissertation. Berkeley, CA: University of California, Berkeley. [Available on Rutgers Optimality Archive, ROA-171.]

Padgett, Jaye. 1995. *Stricture in Feature Geometry*. Stanford, CA: CSLI Publications.

Pater, Joe. 2000. Nonuniformity in English secondary stress: The role of ranked and lexically specific constraints. *Phonology* 17: 237–74. [Available on Rutgers Optimality Archive, ROA-107.]

Pater, Joe. 2001. Austronesian nasal substitution revisited: What's wrong with *NC (and what's not). In Linda Lombardi (ed.), *Segmental Phonology in Optimality Theory: Constraints and Representations*, Cambridge: Cambridge University Press, 159–82.

Perlmutter, David. 1998. Interfaces: Explanation of allomorphy and the architecture of grammars. In Steven G. Lapointe, Diane K. Brentari, and Patrick M. Farrell (eds.), *Morphology and its Relation to Phonology and Syntax*, Stanford, CA: CSLI Publications, 307–38.

Polgárdi, Krisztina. 1998. *Vowel Harmony: An Account in Terms of Government and Optimality*. The Hague: Holland Academic Graphics.

Potter, Brian. 1994. Serial optimality in Mohawk prosody. In Katharine Beals, Jeannette Denton, Robert Knippen, Lynette Melmar, Hisami Suzuki, and Erica Zeinfeld (eds.), *Proceedings of the Thirtieth Annual Regional Meeting of the Chicago Linguistics Society*, Chicago: Chicago Linguistics Society, 347–61.

Prince, Alan. 1983. Relating to the grid. *Linguistic Inquiry* 14: 19–100.

Prince, Alan. 1985. Improving tree theory. In M. Niepokuj, M. VanClay, V. Nikiforidou, and D. Jeder (eds.), *Proceedings of BLS 11*, Berkeley, CA: Berkeley Linguistics Society, 471–90.

Prince, Alan. 1990. Quantitative consequences of rhythmic organization. In M. Ziolkowski, M. Noske, and K. Deaton (eds.), *Parasession on the Syllable in Phonetics and Phonology*, Chicago: Chicago Linguistics Society, 355–98.

Prince, Alan and Smolensky, Paul. 1993. *Optimality Theory: Constraint Interaction in Generative Grammar*. New Brunswick, NJ: Rutgers University Center for Cognitive Science. Technical report RuCCS-TR-2. [Available on Rutgers Optimality Archive, ROA-537.]

Pulleyblank, Douglas. 1996. Neutral vowels in Optimality Theory: A comparison of Yoruba and Wolof. *Canadian Journal of Linguistics* 41: 295–347.

Ringen, Catherine O. and Heinämäki, Orvokki. 1999. Variation in Finnish vowel harmony: An OT account. *Natural Language and Linguistic Theory* 17: 303–37.

Roca, Iggy (ed.). 1997. *Derivations and Constraints in Phonology*. Oxford: Oxford University Press.

Russell, Kevin. 1995. Morphemes and candidates in Optimality Theory. Unpublished MS. Winnipeg: University of Manitoba. [Available on Rutgers Optimality Archive, ROA-44.]

Silverman, Daniel. 1995. *Phasing and Recoverability*. Doctoral dissertation. Los Angeles: University of California, Los Angeles.

Smolensky, Paul. 1993. Harmony, markedness, and phonological activity. Handout from Rutgers Optimality Workshop I, New Brunswick, NJ. [Available on Rutgers Optimality Archive, ROA-87.]

Smolensky, Paul. 1995. On the structure of the constraint component Con of UG. Handout.

University of California, Los Angeles. [Available on Rutgers Optimality Archive, ROA-86.]

Smolensky, Paul. 1996. The initial state and "Richness of the Base" in Optimality Theory. Baltimore, MD: Department of Cognitive Science, Johns Hopkins University. [Available on Rutgers Optimality Archive, ROA-154.]

Spaelti, Philip. 1997. *Dimensions of Variation in Multi-Pattern Reduplication.* Doctoral dissertation. Santa Cruz, CA: University of California, Santa Cruz. [Available on Rutgers Optimality Archive, ROA-311.]

Steriade, Donca. 1995. Positional neutralization. Unpublished MS. Los Angeles: University of California, Los Angeles.

Steriade, Donca. 1997. Phonetics in phonology: The case of laryngeal neutralization. Unpublished MS. Los Angeles: University of California, Los Angeles.

Steriade, Donca. 1999. Phonetics in phonology: The case of laryngeal neutralization. In Matthew Gordon (ed.), *Papers in Phonology 3 (UCLA Working Papers in Linguistics 2)*, Los Angeles: Department of Linguistics, University of California, Los Angeles, 25–145.

Struijke, Caroline. 1998. Reduplicant and output TETU in Kwakwala. In Haruko Fukazawa, Frida Morelli, Caro Struijke, and Y. Su (eds.), *University of Maryland Working Papers, vol. 7 (Papers in Phonology)*, College Park, MD: Department of Linguistics, University of Maryland, 150–78. [Available on Rutgers Optimality Archive, ROA-261.]

Struijke, Caroline. 2000a. *Reduplication, Feature Displacement and Existential Faithfulness.* Doctoral dissertation. College Park, MD: University of Maryland.

Struijke, Caroline. 2000b. Why constraint conflict can disappear in reduplication. In Masako Hirotani (ed.), *Proceedings of the North East Linguistics Society 30*, Amherst, MA: GLSA Publications, 613–26. [Available on Rutgers Optimality Archive, ROA-373.]

Suzuki, Keiichiro. 1998. *A Typological Investigation of Dissimilation.* Doctoral dissertation. Tucson, AZ: University of Arizona. [Available on Rutgers Optimality Archive, ROA-281.]

Szpyra, Jolanta. 1992. Ghost segments in nonlinear phonology: Polish yers. *Language* 68: 277–312.

Tesar, Bruce. 1997a. An iterative strategy for learning metrical stress in Optimality Theory.

In Elizabeth Hughes, Mary Hughes, and Annabel Greenhill (eds.), *Proceedings of the 21st Annual Boston University Conference on Language Development*, Somerville, MA: Cascadilla Press, 615–26. [Available on Rutgers Optimality Archive, ROA-177.]

Tesar, Bruce. 1997b. Multi-recursive constraint demotion. Unpublished MS. New Brunswick, NJ: Rutgers University. [Available on Rutgers Optimality Archive, ROA-197.]

Tesar, Bruce. 1998a. Error-driven learning in Optimality Theory via the efficient computation of optimal forms. In Pilar Barbosa, Danny Fox, Paul Hagstrom, Martha McGinnis, and David Pesetsky (eds.), *Is the Best Good Enough? Optimality and Competition in Syntax*, Cambridge, MA: MIT Press, 421–35.

Tesar, Bruce. 1998b. Using the mutual inconsistency of structural descriptions to overcome ambiguity in language learning. In Pius N. Tamanji and Kiyomi Kusumoto (eds.), *Proceedings of the North East Linguistics Society 28*, Amherst, MA: GLSA Publications, 469–83. [Available on Rutgers Optimality Archive, ROA-426.]

Tesar, Bruce. 1998c. An iterative strategy for language learning. *Lingua* 104: 131–45. [Available on Rutgers Optimality Archive, ROA-177.]

Tesar, Bruce. 1999. Robust interpretive parsing in metrical stress theory. In Kimary N. Shahin, Susan J. Blake, and Eun-Sook Kim (eds.), *Proceedings of the West Coast Conference on Formal Linguistics 17*, Stanford, CA: CSLI Publications. [Available on Rutgers Optimality Archive, ROA-262.]

Tesar, Bruce and Smolensky, Paul. 2000. *Learnability in Optimality Theory.* Cambridge, MA: MIT Press.

Tranel, Bernard. 1988. Floating consonants and ghost consonants: French vs. Tiwi. Unpublished MS, University of California, Irvine.

Tranel, Bernard. 1996a. Exceptionality in Optimality Theory and final consonants in French. In Karen Zagona (ed.), *Grammatical Theory and Romance Languages*, Amsterdam: John Benjamins, 275–91. [Available on Rutgers Optimality Archive, ROA-61.]

Tranel, Bernard. 1996b. French liaison and elision revisited: A unified account within Optimality Theory. In Claudia Parodi, Carlos Quicoli, Mario Saltarelli, and Maria Luisa Zubizarreta (eds.), *Aspects of Romance*

Linguistics, Washington, DC: Georgetown University Press, 433–55. [Available on Rutgers Optimality Archive, ROA-15.]

Tranel, Bernard. 1998. Suppletion and OT: On the issue of the syntax/phonology interaction. In E. Curtis, J. Lyle, and G. Webster (eds.), *Proceedings of the West Coast Conference on Formal Linguistics 16*, Stanford, CA: CSLI Publications, 415–29.

Urbanczyk, Suzanne. 1995. Double reduplication in parallel. In Jill Beckman, Laura Walsh Dickey, and Suzanne Urbanczyk (eds.), *Papers in Optimality Theory*, Amherst, MA: GLSA Publications, 499–532. [Available on Rutgers Optimality Archive, ROA-73.]

Urbanczyk, Suzanne. 1996. *Patterns of Reduplication in Lushootseed*. Doctoral dissertation. Amherst, MA: University of Massachusetts.

Urbanczyk, Suzanne. 1999a. Double reduplications in parallel. In René Kager, Harry van der Hulst, and Wim Zonneveld (eds.), *The Prosody–Morphology Interface*, Cambridge: Cambridge University Press, 390–428. [Available on Rutgers Optimality Archive, ROA-73.]

Urbanczyk, Suzanne. 1999b. A-templatic reduplication in Halq'eméylem'. In Kimary N. Shahin, Susan J. Blake, and Eun-Sook Kim (eds.), *Proceedings of the West Coast Conference on Formal Linguistics 17*, Stanford, CA: CSLI Publications, 655–69.

Ussishkin, Adam. 1999. The inadequacy of the consonantal root: Modern Hebrew denominal verbs and output-output correspondence. *Phonology* 16: 401–42.

Walker, Rachel. 1998. *Nasalization, Neutral Segments, and Opacity Effects*. Doctoral dissertation. Santa Cruz, CA: University of California, Santa Cruz. [Available on Rutgers Optimality Archive, ROA-405.]

Walker, Rachel. 2000. Nasal reduplication in Mbe affixation. *Phonology* 17: 65–115. [Available on Rutgers Optimality Archive, ROA-264.]

Wright, W. 1896. *A Grammar of the Arabic Language*. Cambridge: Cambridge University Press. [Third edn.]

Yip, Moira. 1988. The Obligatory Contour Principle and phonological rules: A loss of identity. *Linguistic Inquiry* 19: 65–100.

Zoll, Cheryl. 1993a. Directionless syllabification and ghosts in Yawelmani. Unpublished MS. Berkeley, CA: University of California, Berkeley. [Available on Rutgers Optimality Archive, ROA-28.]

Zoll, Cheryl. 1993b. Ghost segments and Optimality. In Erin Duncan, Michele Hart, and Philip Spaelti (eds.), *Proceedings of the West Coast Conference on Formal Linguistics 12*, Stanford, CA: Stanford Linguistics Association, 183–99.

Zoll, Cheryl. 1996. *Parsing below the Segment in a Constraint-based Framework*. Doctoral dissertation. Berkeley, CA: University of California, Berkeley. [Available on Rutgers Optimality Archive, ROA-143.]

Index of Languages and Language Families

Languages mentioned only in passing (e.g., in long lists of languages exhibiting some phenomenon) are generally not included in this index.

Abaza 59
Aguacatec 203
Ainu 344, 351
Akan 88–90
Algonquian 231
Altaic 314, 380
Amele 203
Arabela 351
Arabic
    Bedouin Hijazi 154, 407–9, 412–13
    Classical 203
    Colloquial 42, 222
    Moroccan 517–19
Au 203
Australian 351
Axininca Campa 41, 79, 452–9, 461

Bakshir 313
Balangao 79
Bantu 232, 312
Barra Gaelic 390
Basaa 411
Basque 410
Berber 7–9, 20–8, 43, 400–3

Campidanian Sardinian 528
Catalan 232, 344, 520–1
Cayuvava 181–3, 186–8
Chamorro 271, 278, 281
Cheremis
    Eastern 203
    Western 203

Chinese
    Chaoyang 231
    Nantong 242
    Shanghai 229, 231–2, 241
    Suzhou 239–42
    Wenzhou 229, 231–2, 237–42
    Xiamen (Taiwanese) 150, 157–60,
        230–2, 236, 242
Chugach Alutiiq 185
Chukchee 79, 196–200
Chuvash 203
Coeur d'Alene 344

Dakota 217–21, 225, 451
Dhangar-Kurux 313
Diyari 79, 487–91, 497
Doyayo 313
Dutch 157, 296, 344, 361
    Flemish Brussels 155–7

English 72, 74, 154, 175, 231–2, 276, 293,
        344, 350–2, 360–1, 387–8, 421–4,
        464–5, 469–80, 514–15, 517, 570–8

Finnish 185, 275, 399
Finno-Ugric 312
French 207, 519–20

Gã 387–9
Garawa 72, 169–75
Georgian 344
German 294, 343–4, 347–50

Germanic 160
Gidabal 397
Golin 203
Greek 273, 276, 284
Guugu Yimidhirr 367, 369–76

Hamer 369
Hebrew, Tiberian 528
Hindi 203
Huasteco 203
Huave 232
Hungarian 313

Icelandic 231
Indonesian 72, 271–7, 279–80, 282, 284
Irish 59
Italian 232

Japanese 152, 294, 296, 367, 395–6, 465,
    497, 509, 534–41, 548, 552–64
Javanese 281

Kaingang 277
Kamaiurá 458–9
Kanakuru 207
Kannada 344
Karanga 247
Kíhehe 282
Kiliwa 153–4
Klamath 203
Kobon 193–5
Komi Yaz'va 203
Konjo 279
Korean 154, 314
Kpelle 386–7, 389
Kuuku-Yaʔu 203, 212
Kwakiutl 160
Kwakw'ala 203

Lardil 29–30, 41, 49–50, 79, 326, 458
Latin 49–50, 294, 296, 497
Lenakel 221–2
Leti 314
Lhasa Tibetan 203
Luganda 399
Lutshootseed 91, 203

Madurese 87–91
Maithili 231
Malagasy 271
Malay 276, 281

Malayalam 313
Mandar 277, 279, 281
Mandarin 230, 241–2
Maore 276
Māori 344, 351, 495–510
Marshallese 298
Maung 351
Mohawk 154, 221
Mongolian 312
    Khalkha 203
Mordwin 203
Murik 203
Muskogean 231

Nootka 484–7, 515–16
Nzɛbi 407, 409–12

Oromo 397–9
OshiKwanyama 283–4

Pintupi 178–80
Polish 169, 174, 296, 344, 355, 361, 443,
    460–1, 524–8

Quechua
    Ecuadorian 284
    Puyo Pungo 279–81

Romanian 344
Rotuman 79
Russian 218–20, 232, 238, 403, 438–47

Sanskrit 275, 344, 487
Sawai 154
Selkup 203
Sentani 185
Serbo-Croatian 344, 357, 465
Shilluk 313
Shona 247–64, 312–36
Si-Luyana 282
Sindhi 203
Slovak 397, 528
Spanish 42, 221, 273, 276, 386, 545,
    547
Sundanese 425–34
Swahili 221, 276
Swedish 358–60

Tagalog 73–5, 88
Tamil 313–15, 336
Tinrin 203

Toba Batak 277
Tübatulabal 80
Tulu 344
Tungusic 312
Turkic 312–13
Turkish 380–1, 390, 543–6
Tuva 313

Ukrainian 443
Ulwa 73–7
Umbundu 282
Ura 509
Uralic 380
Uzbek 203

Venda 276

Wankumara 168
Warao 168, 174, 178–9, 185

!Xóõ 294, 313

Yana 203
Yavapai 203
Yawelmani 86, 203, 414
Yeletnye 203
Yiddish 344, 353–4, 356–7, 360–1
Yidinʸ 51–9
Yimas 216–17, 222–5
Yoruba 79
Yup'ik 160

Zulu 314

Index of Constraints

Because there are no generally accepted conventions for constraint naming, similar constraints may be cross-referenced under different names. In constraint names, the abbreviations A, F, and T usually stand for association lines, features, and tones, respectively.

ALIGN constraints
  ALIGN 73, 74, 459, 468
  ALIGN(Color) 381
  ALIGN(F) 335
  ALIGN(Ft, L, PrWd, L) 173–5, 181, 186–9, 200, 204–11, 220, 223–4, 240, 243, 488–91, 497, 503–4, 506–10; see also ALL-FT-X
  ALIGN(Ft, R, PrWd, L) 175
  ALIGN(Ft, R, PrWd, R) 171–4, 182–3, 188–9, 195, 200, 204–11; see also ALL-FT-X
  ALIGN(Ft, R, ó, R) 192–200
  ALIGN(H, L, PWd, L) 250–1
  ALIGN(Head, R, Ft, R) 236; see also RHTYPE=I
  ALIGN(Lex, L, PWd, L) see WDCON
  ALIGN(Lex, R, PWd, R) 468
  ALIGN(Lex^{max}, L, PPh, L) 477
  ALIGN(Lex^{max}, R, PPh, R) 477
  ALIGN(nasal) 315
  ALIGN(PPh, R, PWd, R) 478
  ALIGN(PrWd, Edge, H(PrWd), Edge), ALIGN-HEAD 175
  ALIGN(PrWd, L, Ft, L) 74, 170–5, 473
  ALIGN(PrWd, L, Ft, R) 175
  ALIGN(PrWd, R, Ft, R) 173–4, 461
  ALIGN(PWd, L, Hd(PWd), L) 208–11
  ALIGN(PWd, L, Lex, L) see PWDCON
  ALIGN(PWd, R, Hd(PWd), R) 208–11

  ALIGN(PWd, R, Lex, R) 469
  ALIGN(Stem, L, PrWd, L) 451, 454–6, 458–61
  ALIGN(Stem, R, ó, R) 452, 456–9
  ALIGN([high], L, root, L) 333–5
  ALIGN([ka]$_{Af}$, L, Ft , R) 74
  ALIGN([um]$_{Af}$, L, Stem, L) 74–5
  ALIGN-BASE-RT 196–7
  ALIGN-FT-LEFT see ALIGN(Ft, L, PrWd, L)
  ALIGN-FT-RIGHT see ALIGN(Ft, R, PrWd, R)
  ALIGN-PRWD see ALIGN(PrWd, L, Ft, L)
  ALIGN-RIGHT 400
  ALL-FT-X 179, 181, 184, 186–7; see also ALIGN(Ft, L, PrWd, L); ALIGN(Ft, R, PrWd, R)
  COINCIDE(complex segment, ó$_1$) 365
  COINCIDE(heavy syllable, Head PWd) 371–3
  EDGEMOST(f;E;D) 170–2
  EDGEMOST(F;L;PrWd) see ALIGN(PrWd, L, Ft, L)
  HEAD-RIGHT 192–200

prosodic Markedness constraints
  *C]$_σ$ see NOCODA
  *CLASH 414
  *CODA see NOCODA
  −CODA see NOCODA
  *COMPLEX 34, 516, 518–19, 555

*Ft- 497, 499–500, 502, 504–5, 510

*FtFt 182–3

*Lapse 178, 182–8; see also Parse-Syll-2

*Long vowel 373–6

*Margin/V 34, 43–5, 50–1, 193

*Peak/C 34, 43–5, 50–1

Coda Devoicing 546

CodaCond 457–8, 555

Exhaustivity 467

Exh_PPh 474–5, 479

Foot-Form(Trochaic) 168

Ft-Bin 50, 168–9, 173, 179–81, 193–6, 200, 220, 488–9, 509

Ft-Bin-Max 240, 243

Ft-Bin-Min 240

Headedness 466, 471–2, 475, 477

HNuc 12–16, 21–7

Lapse_FT 497, 499–500, 502, 504–5, 510

Layeredness 466

Lx≈Pr 41, 50, 62

No-Hiatus 454, 456

NoCoda, 31–6, 39–42, 44, 48, 104, 106, 111–13, 121, 123–4, 128–9, 131–4, 366, 399, 459, 485–7, 515–21, 559, 571–8

NoCoda(Labial) 365–6

NoCoda(Place) 368

NoLongVowel 398–9

Nonfinality 182–3, 196–200

NonRec_pwd 474–5, 478–9

NonRecursivity 467

Nuc 33–4, 38, 53

Onset 12–16, 19, 23–7, 31–8, 40, 42, 44–5, 48, 81, 104, 106, 111–12, 116, 121, 123–4, 128–9, 131–4, 453–60, 509, 516–21, 571–8

Parse-σ see ParseSyll

Parse-Syll-2 224; see also *Lapse

ParseSyll 168–9, 173–5, 179–83, 186–8, 196, 200, 204–11, 400, 488–91, 497

Peak Prominence 45, 192–200

PWdCon 469, 471, 474–5, 477–9

RhType=I (Iamb) 220; see also Align(Head, R, Ft, R)

RhType=T (Trochee) 223–4

SyllStruc 554, 557–62

Trough 193

WdCon 468, 475, 478–9

Wrap 505–6

WSP 206–7, 211

other Markedness constraints

*[+high, –low] see *High

*[–high, +low] see *Low

*[+voi, –son] see NoVoicedObstruent

*ær]_σ 423–4

*CompSeg 388

*Contour 238–42

*[COR] see *Coronal

*Coronal 326, 335

*CPlace 368

*Float 257–9

*g, *Voiced velar obstruents 294, 296

*H 235

*High 320, 322–5, 327–36

*i 444–6

*ɨ 444–6

*L 235, 247, 251

*Labial 366

*Laryngeal 346, 348–53, 355–9, 361

*Low 320, 322–36

*Mid 219–20, 232, 314, 320, 322–36

*NC̥ 272–7, 279–84

*NV_Oral 89–90, 427–34

*p 294

*Pl/Cor 54–7, 61, 400

*Pl/Dors 400

*Pl/Lab 54–7, 61, 400–2

*Pl/Place 403

*Rising 237

*Spec 65, 549

*Struc 64

*T 233–42

*ü 444–5

*V_nas 427–34

*V_oral 429

Agree 347, 349–52, 354–61

AssocPA 470

Bound 253–4

Constraint(Class) 381

CV Link 442

Free-V 29–30

HavePlace 384–5, 388

Labial Attraction 545

License(Voice) 534

License(F) 534–41

NasVoi 535–41

No(a) 410

No-dd see NoVoicedGem

No-nt see NoNas Voiceless

No-p see NoVoicelessLab

other Markedness constraints (*cont'd*)
No-V-Place 408–9
NoNas⌒Voiceless 554, 556–64
NoV 410
NoVoicedGem 554–5, 557–64
NoVoicedObstruent 396
NoVoicelessLab 554, 556–64
Npa 383–9
OCP 85–6, 90, 246–64, 394–7, 399–400, 506–9
Palatalisation-i 443–7
PreNasal 399
Raising 410–12
Reduce 413
Rendaku 396
Share(high) 335
SonVoi 534
Specify(T) 253–5, 258–9, 263–4
Spread(Place) 315
Unique 335–6

Faithfulness constraints
Anchor-L 253–9
Anchoring 84
Contiguity 84
Corr(/a/) 410
Dep 82–5, 92, 276, 278–9, 281, 420, 559, 561
Dep(σ) 251
Dep(A) 252–5, 263–4
Dep-BR 82
Dep-C 503–5, 506–7
Dep(F) 84
Dep(T) 251–3
Dep-V 506
Fill 31–40, 44–5, 49–50, 54, 56, 60–1, 83–6, 452–9, 485–6, 515–16, 520–1
FillFeat 535
FillLink 535
Fill^{Nuc} 39–42, 51, 104, 106, 111–13, 116, 121, 123–4, 128–9, 131–3
Fill^{Ons} 38–40, 42, 49, 104, 106, 109, 111–13, 121, 123–4, 128–9, 131–4
Fill^{PL} 54–7, 60–1
Head(PCat)-Dep 232–3
Head(PCat)-Ident(F) 232–3
Head-Identity(F) 219–20
HeadDep, Head-Dependence 217, 219–24, 400
HeadFoot-Max(T) 238–42
HeadMax(F) 234

HeadMax(T) 234–7
HeadSyll-Max(T) 238–42
I-Contig 92
Ident 82–4, 92, 220, 278, 314–15, 321, 346, 420, 529–30, 559, 561–3
Ident(back) 423–4
Ident(continuant) 282–3, 525–8
Ident(coronal) 525–8
Ident(high) 314–15, 320–2, 324–5, 327–36
Ident(Laryngeal) 346, 348–61
Ident(low) 320, 322–5, 327–34
Ident(nasal) 278–9, 281, 315, 428–34
Ident(obs voice) 280–1, 284
Ident(Onset) 366
Ident(place) 315, 368, 401, 403
Ident(segment) 366
Ident(μ) 371–6
Ident-μ 562–3
Ident-σ_1 314–15
Ident-σ_1 (high) 314, 321–5, 327–32, 335–6
Ident-BR(F) 82–3
Ident-C$_{[+back]}$ 444–6
Ident-C$_{[-back]}$ 444–6
Ident-Head PWd(μ) 373–6
Ident-Position 321
Ident-V$_{[+back]}$ 444–6
IdentOnset(Laryngeal) 346, 348–57, 359–61
Integrity 93
Linearity 84, 93, 272, 274–5, 279, 281–4, 509
M-Parse 48
Match(V) 410
Max 82, 84, 92, 276–9, 281–3, 399, 420, 486, 489–91, 497, 502–8, 515–16, 559
Max(A) 256–64
Max(F) 84
Max(T) 234–8, 242, 249–51, 253–64
Max-BR 82, 497
Max$_{Root}$ 499–500, 503–6
NasMax 276
No-Flop 234
ObsMax 276
OO-Dep 420
OO-Ident(back) 423
OO-Ident(F) 420
OO-Ident(nas) 427–8, 432–4
OO-Max 420

PARSE 31–40, 44–5, 48–50, 54, 56, 60–1, 83–4, 86, 452–3, 455, 459, 485–6, 490–1, 515–16

PARSE$_{ATR}$ 411

PARSE$_F$, PARSE^{FEAT}, PARSEFEAT 54–7, 60–1, 277, 411, 413, 535

PARSE$_{HI}$ 408–9, 411

PARSELINK 535

PARSE$_{LOW}$ 408–9, 411–12

PARSE$_V$ 408–9

ROOTLINEARITY 275; *see also* LINEARITY

UNIFORMITY 93, 251–2, 260–4

WEIGHTIDENT 398–9

Index of Topics

a-kanje 218–20, 225
ablaut 160
absolute ill-formedness 47–9
accent 470–1; *see also* stress; tone
acquisition 273, 296, 305–6, 465; *see also*
    learnability
affixation 421
alignment 72–5, 167–75
    morphology/prosody *see* prosodic
        structure, alignment with morphology
    stress *see* stress, alignment
    tone 250–1
allomorphy 500–1, 513–21
allophony 147, 428–31; *see also* inventory
alternation with zero 153–4; *see also*
    deletion; epenthesis
apocope 196–7
aspiration 473–4
assimilation 80–1, 147, 152, 311, 368, 379–88
    direction *see* directionality
    nasal place 80, 152, 368–9, 379–88
    nasality *see* harmony
    partial nasal place 379–88
    voicing 344–61
augmentation 142
    unconditioned 152–3
autosegmental phonology
    and feature classes 380
    relation to correspondence theory 84
    see also assimilation; harmony; tone

bracket erasure 422

Cancellation/Domination Lemma 46
candidate *see* GEN

chain shift 407–14
    circular 148, 150, 152, 154–7, 159
    infinite 148, 150, 152
circumscription 73, 80
clitic 209, 465–6, 469–79
co-phonology 542–3, 545; *see also* lexicon,
    exceptions; stratal OT
coalescence 93, 155, 160, 453, 456; *see*
    also fusion
coarticulation 311; *see also* phonetics
coda devoicing 544–7
CON 120, 510; *see also* constraint
consistency of exponence *see* GEN
conspiracy 272, 281, 283–4
constraint *see* Index of Constraints
    active though dominated 189, 207; *see*
        also emergence of the unmarked;
        interaction, constraint; violability of
        constraints
    alignment *see* alignment
    binary 19–21, 28
    encapsulation 45
    faithfulness *see* faithfulness constraint
    as function 119
    functional basis 291–3; *see also*
        grounding; phonetics
    hierarchy *see* hierarchy, constraint
    interaction *see* interaction, constraint
    lexical domain 553, 557–8
    local conjunction 394–404, 527–30
    markedness *see* markedness constraint
    non-binary 21–3, 28, 173
    transderivational *see* faithfulness
        constraint, transderivational
constraint-hierarchy grammar 143–5

copying 93; *see also* reduplication
coronal unmarkedness *see* scales
correspondence *see* faithfulness constraint
counterfeeding *see* parallelism
counting, not in EVAL 19–20
cycle 422, 426–7, 452
  strict 523–5; *see also* derived
    environment effect
  see also faithfulness constraint,
    transderivational; parallelism; prosodic
    structure, alignment with morphology;
    stratal OT

debuccalization 556, 561–3
default-to-opposite *see* stress, unbounded
default-to-same *see* stress, unbounded
degemination 399
deletion 38–40, 48, 79, 81, 83, 85, 249–52,
    255, 257–9, 262–4, 275–7, 429, 452,
    507–8, 570
Dell–Elmedlaoui Algorithm 8
demotion, constraint 127–9, 305–6
  compared with promotion 133–4
  error-driven 135–6
denasalization 277–9, 284–5, 429
derivation *see* parallelism; rule,
    phonological
derived environment effect 523–30
devocalization 33
diphthongization 93, 155, 528, 547
directionality 172–5, 223–4, 285
  bidirectional assimilation 358–60
  of place assimilation 368–9
  of voicing assimilation 353–4, 360–1
  see also alignment; stress
dissimilation 147, 382, 397–404
  of complex segments 399
  labial 397, 400–3
  of length 397–9
  of marked structure 399
  root-initial exempt 314
  and strict layering 399–400
  of tone 247–67
domination 13, 27
  stratified hierarchy 129–31
  see also hierarchy, constraint
dynamic programming 102–3, 105–10

edge of constituent effects 458–60; *see also*
  alignment; faithfulness constraint,
  positional; initial syllable privilege

edge-based theory 467–8; *see also*
  alignment
Elsewhere Condition 29, 389
emergence of the unmarked 483–90,
    496–7, 503–4, 513; *see also*
    constraint, active though dominated;
    interaction, constraint; violability of
    constraints
epenthesis 34–5, 37–42, 46, 48, 64, 79, 81,
    85–6, 107, 110, 277, 452–8, 504–5,
    520, 555, 560
  interaction with stress 215–25
EVAL 4, 81
  comparison by a constraint hierarchy
    23–6; *see also* interaction, constraint
  comparison by a single constraint
    18–23
  with variation 576–7
exceptions *see* lexicon, exceptions
exchange rule 142, 153–5, 157
extrametricality 73, 182
  of consonants 454, 458–60
  final exceptionality 353
  see also alignment; stress; NONFINALITY
    in Index of Constraints

faithfulness constraint 4, 33–5, 145–6,
    515, 535, 545
  in allomorphy 515–19
  correspondence theory 77–93, 219, 225,
    274, 278, 320–1, 409, 419–22, 497,
    560, 563
  featural 82–4, 278, 281–3, 346
  indexed for lexical strata 560–4; *see also*
    lexicon
  PARSE/FILL model 34–5, 84–6,
    104–5, 120–1, 452, 516; *see also*
    syllabification
  positional 159, 219, 231, 234, 242–3,
    275, 310–42, 346–61, 366–9,
    499–500, 503; *see also* initial syllable
    privilege; markedness constraint,
    positional
  prosodic structure 83
  transderivational 419–34
  see also Index of Constraints
features *see* scales; underspecification
  color 380–1
  feature class theory 379–91
  feature geometry 382–5, 387–9
  floating 80, 84, 92

features *see* scales; underspecification (*cont'd*)
  markedness of *see* feature-driven
    markedness
  multiple linking 326, 335–6, 348
  place markedness 51–62
feature-driven markedness 326–8, 346–8
flapping 88, 474
flip-flop 154
floating segment 446–7; *see also* features,
    floating; tone, floating
foot, metrical *see* stress
  in tone sandhi 228–31
fronting 439–42, 445–7
function word 464–79
functionalism 290–3
fusion 259–62, 264, 273–5, 281–5; *see*
    also coalescence

gemination 555
GEN 4, 12, 80–1, 120, 145–6, 516, 521
  consistency of exponence 452, 455
  infinite candidate set 102
Generalized Template Theory 496, 510; *see*
    also emergence of the unmarked;
    reduplication
gradience 293, 381, 384
grounding 299
  inductive 297–305
  see also phonetics

H-EVAL *see* EVAL
harmonic bounding 46, 49–51
Harmonic Evaluation *see* EVAL
Harmonic Phonology 6
harmonic serialism 5; *see also* parallelism
harmony (phonological process) 380–1,
    388–90, 414, 425–34, 545
  color 381, 388–90
  nasal 87–9, 425–34
  vowel 197, 313–36, 380, 390, 545
harmony (relation in OT) 4
  harmonic bounding *see* harmonic
    bounding
  harmonic completeness 57–8
  harmonic ordering of forms 16–26, 121–2
  harmonic processing 11
  see also optimality
hierarchy, constraint 4, 23–6, 122–4,
    559–60, 573–5; *see also* demotion;
    typology, factorial
historical phonology 569–79

ineffability *see* absolute ill-formedness
infixation 73–4, 451
  interaction with phonology 426–8
initial dactyl effect 169–70, 174
initial ranking 134–5; *see also* demotion
initial syllable privilege 310–36, 365–9
  via alignment 455–6; *see also* faithfulness
    constraint, positional
input 12, 142, 146–7; *see also* lexicon,
    richness of the base
interaction, constraint 18–26; *see also*
    constraint, active though dominated;
    emergence of the unmarked; violability
    of constraints
intrusive *r see r ~ Ø* alternation
inventory 46–65, 351–2, 395–6, 484
  gaps 294
  positionally restricted 319–26; *see also*
    neutralization, positional
  root-initial syllable 312–15; *see also*
    faithfulness constraint, positional;
    initial syllable privilege
  universals *see* universals, of inventories
  see also allophony
iotation 439

labial attraction 544–5
labialization 59
learnability 118–38
lengthening 502
  compensatory 80
  vowel 373–6
lenition 524, 528
Lexical Phonology *see* stratal OT
lexicon
  allomorphy *see* allomorphy
  exceptions 542–9, 552–64
  learning 306
  lexicon optimization 63–5, 352, 539–40,
    548
  richness of the base 62, 536–40, 548
  strata 552–64
licensing 58–9, 292, 344–5, 371, 533–41
loan phonology *see* lexicon, exceptions
local conjunction *see* constraint, local
    conjunction
locality 26–7, 422
  importance in parsing 115
  see also constraint, local conjunction
lowering, vowel 414, 528
Lyman's Law 395–6

mark cancellation 122
markedness constraint 4, 145–6, 326–8,
    483
  positional 365–76; *see also* faithfulness
    constraint, positional
  see also emergence of the unmarked;
    Index of Constraints
maximal word effect 495–510
Meeussen's Rule 249–52, 257–9, 260, 264;
    see also dissimilation
metathesis 33, 79, 93, 142, 152–4, 314,
    508
  symmetrical 152–3
  see also LINEARITY, RootLinearity in
    Index of Constraints
minimal word effect 41, 49, 488–91, 495,
    508; *see also* maximal word effect;
    stress
morphology
  bound roots 457
  constraint domains *see* stratal OT
  correspondence relations 420–2
  effect on constraints 275
  imposes prosodic requirement 372
  prosodic alignment *see* prosodic
    structure, alignment with morphology
  root-initial syllables 311–15; *see also*
    initial syllable privilege
  see also allomorphy; infixation; lexicon;
    reduplication; truncation
mutation 160

nasal substitution 271–2, 283–5
neutralization 343–61, 367
  laryngeal 343–61
  low vowel 423–4
  place 367
  positional 312–36, 343–61
  syllable-final 81, 347–50, 366–9
  vowel height 312–36
  see also reduction
null parse 49; *see also* absolute ill-
    formedness; M-Parse in Index of
    Constraints

Obligatory Contour Principle (OCP)
    246–64, 394–7, 506–7
optimality 12–17
  universally optimal syllables 36–42
output 4, 125–6, 142, 146–7; *see also*
    GEN

output–output correspondence *see*
    faithfulness constraint,
    transderivational
overapplication 78, 86–91, 420, 423–34;
    see also faithfulness constraint,
    transderivational; reduplication;
    underapplication

palatalization 52, 88, 90, 438–47,
    524–30
Pāṇini's Theorem 29–30
paradigmatic replacement 153
parallelism
  of chain shifts 407, 413–14
  compared to serialism 27–8, 424–5,
    426–8
  rationale for in OT 438
  in reduplication 91
  transderivational 422–5
parameter 484, 491
parsing 101–16
  production-directed 125
  robust interpretive 125
perception 292, 298–9, 381; *see also*
    functionalism; grounding; phonetics
phonetics
  of duration 413
  of feature classes 385
  motivation for constraints 272–3,
    539–41; *see also* grounding
  phonetic map 297
  see also perception
phonotactics 292–305
polarity rule *see* exchange rule
positional faithfulness *see* faithfulness
    constraint, positional
positional markedness *see* markedness
    constraint, positional
prespecification 545–9; *see also*
    underspecification
priority of the base 424
processing, phonological 311–12
prominence alignment 17–18, 45, 192–3;
    see also scales
prosodic hierarchy 466–7, 488
prosodic structure
  alignment with morphology 451–61,
    476–8, 496–9, 505–6
  alignment with syntax 457–79
  see also stress; syllabification
push/pull parsing 44, 64

r~Ø alternation 476–7, 570–9
raising, vowel 410–14
ranking *see* hierarchy, constraint
reduction 155, 242, 369
  vowel 218–20, 225, 231–2, 238
reduplication 77–91, 92–3, 197, 484–92,
    509–10, 515–16, 521, 555
  fixed segment 79, 81
  interaction with phonology 86–91; *see*
    also overapplication; underapplication
  metathetic 79; *see also* metathesis
  partial 78
  prefixing 93
  suffixing 92
rendaku (sequential voicing) 395–6, 556
retraction 439–42, 445–7
retroflection 52
rhythm
  adjustment 6, 28
  alternation 178–82, 184
  see also stress
richness of the base *see* lexicon
root *see* initial syllable privilege;
    morphology
root-and-pattern morphology 80, 83
rule, phonological 4, 6, 75, 152, 344–5,
    389, 440–2, 514, 524–5
  mirror-image 358, 547
  ordering 215–16, 221–2, 234, 413, 438;
    see also parallelism; stratal OT
  see also exchange rule

scales 17–18, 192–3
  coronal unmarkedness 52–6, 400–3,
    407–8
  see also prominence alignment; sonority
sentence phonology 464–79
serialism *see* parallelism
shortening 155–7, 497
  cretic 497
sonority 8, 192–3
  in stress *see* stress, sonority-driven
  in syllabification 8–16, 43–6, 411, 520
spirantization 524–30
stratal OT 260–3, 424–5, 439, 445–7
Stray Erasure 34
stress 72, 74, 181–90, 191–200, 202–12,
    488–9, 498–500
  alignment 168–75, 179–81, 195–200,
    204–11, 223–4, 488–90, 497, 503,
    506–7

  clash and lapse 184–5, 228–9, 399–400,
    411, 497–8
  cyclic 421–2
  interaction with epenthesis 215–25
  maximal word 496–510
  minimal word 489–91
  sonority-driven 191–200
  syllable weight 206–7
  ternary 181–90
  unbounded 202–12
  window 193–5, 223
strict cycle *see* cycle, strict
strict layering 467; *see also* prosodic
    hierarchy
syllabification 8–28, 31–46, 62–4, 85,
    102–15, 120–9, 131–4, 168, 292, 321,
    453–61, 484–7, 557
  cyclic 456–7
  Jakobsonian Typology 31–3, 103–5,
    120–1
symmetry 294
syncope 408

tableau 13
  tableau des tableaux 539–40, 548
  templatic morphology 510
Theory of Constraints and Repair Strategies
    5–6, 389
tone
  floating 257–9
  loss 231–43
  reduction 236–43
  sandhi 150, 157–8, 160, 228–30,
    231–43, 252–5
  slip 255–7
  spread 229, 252–5, 264
  window 239
truncation 80, 207, 487, 497, 502–4, 509–10
  interaction with phonology 423–5
typology
  factorial 32–42, 124, 141, 173–5,
    347–60, 497, 529–30, 578–9
  justification for constraint 291
  of maximal word effects 509–10
  see also universals

umlaut 408
underapplication 78, 87–91, 420, 423–4,
    433; *see also* faithfulness constraint,
    transderivational; overapplication;
    reduplication

underspecification 533–41; *see also*
   prespecification
universals
   from basic structure of the theory 141–60
   implicational 57–62, 443
   of inventories 56–62
   of syllable structure 36–42, 43–6

variation 293, 569–79
violability of constraints 123, 173, 474,
   486–7, 506–9; *see also* constraint,
   active though dominated; emergence of
   the unmarked; interaction, constraint

vocalization 33
voicing
   aerodynamics 294
   difficulty 295
   post-nasal 279–81, 283–5, 293, 536–41,
     548, 556

weak local parsing 182
word *see* alignment; maximal word
   effect; minimal word effect;
   morphology; prosodic structure;
   stress
word level *see* stratal OT